Advance Praise

"*Somatic-Oriented Therapies* is a wonderful collection exploring the vital territory between mind, brain, body, and relationships. It is especially gratifying—years after I was both fascinated and moved by the writings of Wilhelm Reich and Ida Rolf—to see so many integrative ideas becoming part of the mainstream of psychotherapeutic thinking. This is a book that I will continue to read and reread in years to come. It will help all of us to deepen our understanding and appreciation of the indivisible unity of mind, brain, body, and relationships."

—**Louis Cozolino, PhD**, professor of psychology, Pepperdine University

"During the past few decades, the Polyvagal Theory has contributed to a framework for several somatically-based therapies. The readers of this volume will be enriched in their understanding by this inclusive theory. In this comprehensive volume, many of the contributors pay homage to Stephen Porges's breathtaking theory—a rare gift to a generation of practitioners and their clients."

—**Peter A. Levine, PhD**, author of *An Unspoken Voice, How the Body Releases Trauma and Restores Goodness*, and *An Autobiography of Trauma*

"Imagine an in-depth, compassionate, and science-packed compendium of practical, clinically focused chapters that provide both an introduction and deep dive into the application of body-based awareness in psychotherapy. This magnificent volume has been created with a clinician in mind, offering clear descriptions of physiological processes, accessible scientific discussions of research, and fascinating descriptions of real-life therapeutic examples applying these somatic principles in everyday practice. What an exciting offering for the waiting field of mental health!"

—**Daniel J. Siegel, MD**, founding editor of the Norton Series on Interpersonal Neurobiology, and *New York Times*–bestselling author of *Mind, IntraConnected*, and *Personality and Wholeness in Therapy*

"Since it is now widely understood that 'the body keeps the score' in traumatic stress, a deeper understanding of the underlying mental and neurobiological processes, and their therapeutic implications, is essential. *Somatic-Oriented Therapies* delivers precisely that: a brilliant, state-of-the-art compilation of therapeutic interventions for traumatic stress, as well as the underlying science. Read this book!"

—**Bessel van der Kolk, MD**, president of the Trauma Research Foundation, and author of *The Body Keeps the Score*

Somatic-Oriented Therapies

The Norton Series on Interpersonal Neurobiology
Louis Cozolino, PhD, Series Editor
Allan N. Schore, PhD, Series Editor, 2007–2014
Daniel J. Siegel, MD, Founding Editor

The field of mental health is in a tremendously exciting period of growth and conceptual reorganization. Independent findings from a variety of scientific endeavors are converging in an interdisciplinary view of the mind and mental well-being. An interpersonal neurobiology of human development enables us to understand that the structure and function of the mind and brain are shaped by experiences, especially those involving emotional relationships.

The Norton Series on Interpersonal Neurobiology provides cutting-edge, multidisciplinary views that further our understanding of the complex neurobiology of the human mind. By drawing on a wide range of traditionally independent fields of research—such as neurobiology, genetics, memory, attachment, complex systems, anthropology, and evolutionary psychology—these texts offer mental health professionals a review and synthesis of scientific findings often inaccessible to clinicians. The books advance our understanding of human experience by finding the unity of knowledge, or consilience, that emerges with the translation of findings from numerous domains of study into a common language and conceptual framework. The series integrates the best of modern science with the healing art of psychotherapy.

Somatic-Oriented Therapies

Embodiment, Trauma, and Polyvagal Perspectives

Edited by Herbert Grassmann,
Maurizio Stupiggia,
and Stephen W. Porges

Norton Professional Books
An Imprint of W. W. Norton & Company
WWNORTON.COM

Note to Readers: This book is intended as a general information resource for professionals practicing in the field of psychotherapy and mental health. It is not a substitute for appropriate training or clinical supervision. Standards of clinical practice and protocol vary in different practice settings and change over time. No technique or recommendation is guaranteed to be safe or effective in all circumstances, and neither the publisher nor the author(s) can guarantee the complete accuracy, efficacy, or appropriateness of any particular recommendation in every respect or in all settings or circumstances.

Any URLs displayed in this book link or refer to websites that existed as of press time. The publisher is not responsible for, and should not be deemed to endorse or recommend, any website other than its own or any content that it did not create. The author, also, is not responsible for any third-party material.

For information about permission to reproduce selections from this book, write to Permissions, W. W. Norton & Company, Inc., 500 Fifth Avenue, New York, NY 10110

For information about special discounts for bulk purchases, please contact W. W. Norton Special Sales at specialsales@wwnorton.com or 800-233-4830

Manufacturing by Versa Press
Production managers: Gwen Cullen and Ramona Wilkes

ISBN: 978-1-324-05272-2 (pbk)

W. W. Norton & Company, Inc., 500 Fifth Avenue, New York, NY 10110
www.wwnorton.com
W. W. Norton & Company Ltd., 15 Carlisle Street, London W1D 3BS

1 2 3 4 5 6 7 8 9 0

We dedicate this book to all those patients who taught us the profound importance of being fully present in therapeutic work, revealing that their transformation was always intertwined with our own as therapists.

We also dedicate it to the therapists who relentlessly seek new ways to reach the traumatic core, through the essential connection between mind and body, bringing peace to those who have endured unbearable experiences.

This book pays tribute to the pioneers, scientists, and therapists who have explored the complexities of human relationships. It is our hope that this work contributes to a future where healing is recognized as a deeply embodied and accessible journey for all.

Contents

Acknowledgments

We want to acknowledge the importance of those who have contributed to this project. During the last two years of editing work, it's been a pleasure for us to work with so many leading pioneers in the field of somatic and body psychotherapy.

The uniqueness of this book is, on one hand, the groundwork of those scientific researchers, reflecting the theoretical and clinical evidence of embodied experiences in the greater frame of psychology, and on the other hand, that we invited world leaders of somatic therapies to share their expertise and wisdom.

This book is prepared to send a key message from the community of body psychotherapists of the utility of somatic-oriented strategies to the broader community encompassing all clinical practitioners seeking embodied approaches.

We would therefore like to express our gratitude to all those who have supported and helped us to complete this work. Thank you very much.

We are also very grateful to all the clients who have come to us for care and treatment over the years. They have been the best teachers we have ever had. Despite sometimes tough challenges, each one of them has been willing to keep trying to change and grow. We express our gratitude for the confidence they have placed in us and the knowledge we have gained together. This allows us to disseminate this knowledge in ways that benefit more people.

In December 2021, we watched a video conversation with Steven C. Hayes, cofounder of ACT and a prominent leader in contextual behavioral science, and Stephen Porges, founder of Polyvagal Theory. They were discussing the role of embodiment, contrasting perspectives between those focused primarily on observable behavior with those emphasizing the mediating and moderating influences of the nervous system on observable behaviors, psychological processes, and health. As part of the scientific community, we recommended this video to our colleagues on the EABP Science and Research Committee. A huge discussion started among us with the idea of editing a book that would reflect this discussion and acknowledge the long history and tradition of body psychotherapy by catching up with the current state of the art in embodied research by emphasizing the ability to quantify intervening variables that were embedded in the body. This new understanding could hypothetically transform the prevalent cause-and-effect models (inferred from correlations) of both treatments and disorders to a more inclusive model incorporating bodily features as mediating variables.

Introducing the body into treatment requires changing aspects of the clinical treatment model, including diagnostic and prognostic criteria. This would lead to conceptualizing healing processes in a relational dimension that could include touch and other somatic interventions commonly used in somatically oriented therapies. A key message is that therapy can only be delivered effectively if the therapist is trained to recognize the cues of safety and threat being emitted by the client. Therapists gain this skill by learning to infer autonomic state from facial expressions, vocal intonation, muscle tension, and gestures, because these overt markers are linked to the neural regulation of our viscera, including our neural calming system involving vagal regulation of the heart. Moreover, therapists need to be trained to discern their own bodily reactions (i.e., interoception) to their clients and to appreciate that clients are responding to their physiological states.

We are now seeing long-established somatic psychotherapy approaches being woven into systems that until recently ignored the body. This challenge to our long-standing traditions requires a creative approach to preserve the integrity of our collective knowledge and an openness to change to drive therapeutic innovation and leadership. It invites authors not only to write about what we already know, but also to take the risk of writing about important developments that will have an impact in the future and for generations to come.

We have been lucky to have the best companion for this extensive work. Many thanks to Stephen W. Porges for developing Polyvagal Theory. Without your wisdom and constant availability to answer questions about the content of the book, it would not have been possible to bring such depth to this book.

It is our hope that this book will do justice to all the support we have had in its production, for which we are very grateful. Special thanks to Norton for completing this brilliant, cutting-edge compilation.

—Herbert Grassmann and Maurizio Stupiggia

About the Editors

Herbert Grassmann is a highly experienced clinician specializing in body psychotherapy and has chaired the Science and Research Committee of the European Association in this field. Author of several books and articles on somatic education and trauma therapy, he has developed the Somatic Memory method and introduced the concept of Polyvagal Embodiment Training. He is a professor of psychosocial studies and Bodymind Healing, fellow at Parkmore Institute, and associate professor at Matepe University, Istanbul for MA in clinical psychology with a certificate in body psychotherapy.

Stephen W. Porges, PhD, holds positions as a Distinguished University Scientist at Indiana University, professor of psychiatry at the University of North Carolina, and professor emeritus at the University of Illinois at Chicago and the University of Maryland. He has published more than 400 peer-reviewed scientific papers that have been cited in more than 55,000 peer-reviewed papers. He holds several patents involved in monitoring and regulating autonomic state. He is the creator of Polyvagal Theory and the Safe and Sound Protocol™, an innovative acoustic intervention. In collaboration with Anthony Gorry, he cocreated Sonocea® technology that is embedded in the Rest and Restore Protocol™. He has authored *The Polyvagal Theory, The Pocket Guide to the Polyvagal Theory, Polyvagal Safety,* and *Polyvagal Perspectives.* He has coauthored *Our Polyvagal World: How Safety and Trauma Change Us* with his son Seth and coedited *Clinical Applications of the Polyvagal Theory* with Deb Dana. He is a cofounder of the Polyvagal Institute.

Maurizio Stupiggia, PhD, is a body-psychotherapist professor in the department of clinical sciences faculty of medicine and surgery, University of Milano and is the founder, with Jerome Liss, of the International School of Biosystemics.

He has worked as a trainer in European countries, in Japan, and in Latin America. In Japan, he has worked with survivors of major earthquakes for over 20 years, and founded, with Rubens Kignel, the Bio-Integral Institute of Body Psychotherapy in Tokyo.

He also currently works as a supervisor in immigration centers in Italy for female victims of violence. In addition to several articles, he has published three books in Italian, which have since been translated into other languages: *La terapia biosistemica*, *Il corpo violato* and *Dalla sofferenza all'emozione*. In collaboration with other authors he has published *Il benessere nelle emozioni* (2009) and *Biosistemica, la scienza che unisce* (2015).

About the Contributors

Michael Allison is the developer of The Play Zone, a unique application of Polyvagal Theory to optimize performance. He writes a column for *Psychology Today*, The Pressure Paradox, exploring the physiological, psychological, and social paradoxes that underlie the challenges of living in a culture of competition, evaluation, and rapid, unpredictable change. Allison is an educational partner with Polyvagal Institute, a polyvagal performance consultant for high-profile organizations, executives, coaches, teams, athletes, and creatives, and provides a variety of courses and polyvagal-informed certificate programs accredited by the National Board for Health & Wellness Coaches and endorsed by Stephen W. Porges, PhD, developer of Polyvagal Theory. He has certified hundreds of professionals around the globe as Play Zone Pros©, applying his methodology to a wide variety of disciplines including sports, business, leadership, healthcare, and the performing arts.

Martina Ardizzi obtained her master's degree in neurosciences and neuropsychological rehabilitation at the University of Bologna, Italy in 2010. In 2014 she achieved a PhD in neuroscience at the University of Parma, Italy, under the supervision of professor Vittorio Gallese, studying the effect of childhood maltreatment on intersubjectivity development in Sierra Leone. At the moment, Martina Ardizzi is a fixed-term researcher at the department of medicine and surgery unit of neuroscience of the University of Parma where she coordinates national and international research projects examining the plasticity of multisensory integration processes, devoting particular attention to the role of early traumatic experiences and psychiatric diseases. To pursue her research interests, she has spent some time abroad. In particular, she has been a visiting researcher at Assam University in India, University of Essex in the UK, and Berlin School of Mind and Brain in Germany. She was invited to be a visiting professor by the Universidad Nacional de Cuyo in Argentina. Martina Ardizzi is the scientific director of FHM-Italy, a member of the Center for Bioethics at the University of Parma, and sits on the scientific committee of the Turin Biennial. Over the course of her scientific career, she has published several articles in international peer-reviewed journals, edited book chapters, and has been funded by national and international grants.

Ken Benau, PhD, is a clinical psychologist who maintains an independent practice in the San Francisco Bay Area, providing individual adult, couple, and family therapy; professional consultation; and national and international training. His expertise includes working with children and adults with various learning and developmental differences. Dr. Benau has written several peer-reviewed articles and a book (*Shame, Pride, and Relational Trauma* [Routledge, 2022]) about shame and pride-informed psychotherapy with survivors of relational trauma and attachment wounds.

David Berceli, PhD, is an international author, presenter, and trainer in the areas of trauma intervention, stress reduction, and resiliency training. He has lived and worked in war-torn countries and natural disaster zones around the world. He specializes in recovery with large populations. Dr. Berceli is also the creator of a revolutionary set of Tension and Trauma Releasing Exercises (TRE).

Sue Carter, PhD, is currently a Distinguished Research Scientist and director emerita of the Kinsey Institute at Indiana University. She also has held professorships at the University of Illinois and the University of Maryland. Her research with the socially monogamous, prairie vole and parallel studies in lactating women were the first to define the neuroendocrinology of social bonds. Dr. Carter's research has been integral to discovering the relationship between the oxytocin-vasopressin system and health and well-being in response to challenges.

Cristiano Crescentini, is an associate professor in clinical psychology, University of Udine, and a psychologist and psychotherapist. He holds a PhD in neuroscience and is an instructor of mindfulness-based interventions. He is director of the I-level master in meditation and neuroscience at the University of Udine, and the scientific referent of the university's psychological counseling service.

Francesca Ferroni is postdoctoral researcher at the University of Parma, Italy where she works in Vittorio Gallese's Lab of Social Cognitive Neuroscience. Francesca's research focuses on how the brain generates the experience of our body in space (i.e., peripersonal space) by integrating multisensory information and its alterations along the schizophrenic spectrum and the neurobiological bases of the bodily self.

Aaron Freedman is presently a supervisor in UCSF's department of psychiatry and behavioral sciences, where he works with individuals dealing with substance use disorders and severe mental illness. He earned a BA in dance from Wesleyan University and an MA in somatic psychology from the California Institute of Integral Studies. Aaron has collaborated with Dr. Wolf Mehling on the Multidimensional Assessment of Interoceptive Awareness (MAIA) and has studied under Don Hanlon Johnson.

Vittorio Gallese, MD, is a trained neurologist and professor of psychobiology at the University of Parma, Italy where he is director of the Lab of Social Cognitive Neuroscience. His research focuses on the relation between the sensorimotor system and social cognition by investigating the neurobiological grounding of intersubjectivity, psychopathology, language, and aesthetics. He is the author of more than 300 scientific publications and three books.

Jeltje Gordon-Lennox is a certified Swiss psychotherapist with expertise in the fields of psychotraumatology, addiction, and contemporary spirituality. Her professional publications in English and French center on the role of ritual as a psychosocial and somatic resource for healing trauma and restoring broken connections. Jeltje lives in Switzerland with her jazz musician husband and their two children. She enjoys music, theatre, modern art, hiking, and fiction writing.

Susan Harper, MSME/TA, Continuum Teacher since 1975, has contributed to the development of Continuum, originated by Emilie Conrad. Emilie and Susan cofounded the first Continuum Teacher Organization in 1999 and Susan is a founding member of Continuum Teacher Association. Working internationally with individuals and groups, Susan's work focuses on somatic awareness, perceptual inquiry, soulful movement, creative thinking, and skills of intimacy. Her life's work is the subject of the 2020 documentary *Heart of Continuum*.

Bach Ho is a writer and consultant for the Organic Intelligence organization, as well as an Organic Intelligence® Coach. Dr. Ho has a PhD in philosophy from the University of California at Riverside. One of his dissertation advisors was noted evolutionary biologist and philosopher Dr. Francisco Ayala. Dr. Ho taught philosophy, critical thinking, and ethics at universities for a decade, including specialized ethics courses for medical professionals, business professionals, and computer scientists. He has also worked as a computer programmer for classified programs relating to U.S. national security (and has a BS in computer science from the University of California at Irvine). In the field of philosophy, Dr. Ho specializes in ethics and is interested in a biological grounding for ethics, an interest which intersects with his interest in a biological grounding for therapeutics, such as found in OI™.

Steve Hoskinson is an internationally recognized teacher and mentor in post-trauma growth, and the founder of Organic Intelligence®, which trains coaches and other professionals in Trauma Safe™ OI therapeutics. Trained in somatics, mindfulness, research, and clinical psychology, Steve is former senior international instructor in SE®, and adjunct faculty for JFK University's Somatic Psychology program. He is also a founding member of the Northern California Society for Integrative Mental Health and the International Transformational Resilience Coalition. He created the online End of Trauma Course for personal resilience and hosts The End of Trauma Podcast. Hoskinson and the OI Team can be reached at Steven@OrganicIntelligence.org.

Hanneke Kalisvaart, PhD, is a Dutch psychomotor therapist, senior researcher, and teacher in sensorimotor psychotherapy. She specializes in somatic symptom disorders and the impact of serious illness. Hanneke earned her master's degree in human movement sciences from Vrije Universiteit in Amsterdam and her doctorate degree in social sciences from Utrecht University, the Netherlands. Her research concerns clients' relationship to their body with somatic symptoms, and nonverbal assessment methods such as own body drawings.

J. David Knottnerus is Emeritus Regents Professor of Sociology at Oklahoma State University, Stillwater, Oklahoma. He has published extensively in the areas of ritual dynamics, social theory, social psychology, group processes, social structure, and social inequality. Much of his work in recent years has focused on the development of structural ritualization theory and research, which analyzes the role rituals play in social life.

Jacek Kolacz, PhD, is a researcher at The Ohio State University Wexner Medical Center and is managing director of the Traumatic Stress Research Consortium (TSRC) at the Kinsey Institute at Indiana University. He uses neurophysiologically-informed assessments to track client progress, understand how treatments impact the nervous system, and explore ways to make existing therapies more effective.

Aline La Pierre, PhD, is the founder and director of The NeuroAffective Touch Institute and creator of NeuroAffective Touch® integrating psychotherapy and the therapeutic use of touch as a vital relational bridge for overcoming developmental trauma. She is a coauthor of *Healing Developmental Trauma: How Trauma Affects Self-Regulation, Self-Image, and the Capacity for Relationship*, published in twelve languages. Dr. LaPierre was faculty in the Somatic Doctoral Program at Santa Barbara Graduate Institute for ten years. Currently, she is president of the United States Association for Body Psychotherapy (USABP) and editor-in-chief of The *International Body Psychotherapy Journal* (IBPJ). For more information, visit her website at www.NeuroAffectiveTouch.com, or email her at aline@neuroaffectivetouch.com.

Rabih Lahoud is the singer of the successful jazz band Masaa, with whom he has already released five albums. In 2018 Rabih Lahoud was nominated for the ECHO Best Jazz Singer National. The 2021 winner of the German Jazz Award, Lahoud has been one of the most requested vocal coaches in Germany for several years. His passion is teaching diverse singing styles and the topic of Polyvagal Theory in vocal practice, which he has studied in depth, committing himself to the research.

As a neurologist for thirty years at the University Hospital of Caen in France, **Francois Le Doze** has always been interested in the relationship between the body and mind in sick individuals. His encounter with the Internal Family Systems (IFS) model deeply influenced his personal and professional life, leading him towards psychotherapeutic practice. His knowledge of neuroscience allows him to base his practice on recent neuroscience data in the field of psychotherapy. Since 2017, he has developed an original trauma-informed psychotherapy model addressing his challenges as a therapist, called Relational Intelligence. This method is based on IFS, Polyvagal Theory, and attachment theory.

Chiara Marazzi is a psychologist, counselor, and formator, specifically engaged in the field of psychosocial coping with perinatal bereavement that she teaches at Università Statale di Milano in a course on the obstetrics degree program. She carries out private clinical activities and supervises and trains counselors.

Alessio Matiz is a research fellow in clinical psychology at the University of Udine. He holds degrees in electronic engineering and professional education, and a PhD in emerging digital technologies. He is a mindfulness teacher for the Mindfulness-Oriented Meditation program for adults and for children, as well as an instructor of mindfulness teachers for these two programs.

Emily Newcomer, MEd, LPC, is a licensed psychotherapist in Durango, Colorado and curriculum design specialist and associate trainer for southwest trauma training (www.swtraumatraining.com). Specializing in posttraumatic growth somatic therapy, developed by Ruby Jo Walker, LCSW, SEP, CHT, she has provided therapy to adult clients in her private practice, Southwest Psychotherapy, since 2008. She attended graduate school at the University of Utah, where she earned a master's degree in educational psychology and was trained in Hakomi Somatic Mindfulness Therapy. Previously, she was the community education coordinator for Sexual Assault Services Organization in Durango for many years. Supporting others to live fully gives her great fulfillment.

Pat Ogden, PhD, is a pioneer in somatic psychology, the creator of the Sensorimotor Psychotherapy method, and the founder of the Sensorimotor Psychotherapy Institute (sensorimotor.org). Dr. Ogden is trained in a wide variety of somatic and psychotherapeutic approaches, and has nearly 50 years of experience working with individuals and groups. She is a clinician, consultant, international lecturer and author. Her current therapeutic interests include couples; children, adolescents, families; consciousness, and the philosophical and spiritual principles that underlie her work.

Antonia Pfeiffer, MD, PhD, has been researching the neuroscientific effect mechanisms of tapping techniques since her doctoral thesis. Another area of her research is the question of how memory reconsolidation can be translated into practical clinical work. Her favorite question is about how we can use science to make therapeutic work even more poetic. She has written a book the neuroscience of tapping and works as a body-oriented therapist in her own private practice.

An internationally recognized breathing/movement and somatic trauma work specialist, **Betsy Polatin, MFA, SEP, AmSAT,** was a professor at Boston University's College of Fine

Arts for 25 years. She is the author of the best seller *Humanual: A Manual for Being Human*, and her work has been presented at International Conferences in the U.S. and abroad. Betsy has cotaught with Peter A. Levine, PhD, and Dr. Gabor Maté. She offers trainings and private sessions at Humanual.com

Alessandra Pollazzon is a primary school teacher. She holds a degree in primary education sciences from the University of Udine with a thesis titled *The Effects of Mindfulness-Oriented Meditation on Self-Representation in Primary School Children*. She attended the Mindfulness-Oriented Meditation program for adults and for teachers. She practices MOM daily in class with her students and continues to study mindfulness meditation practices adapted for children.

Robert Schleip has a PhD in human biology and an MA in psychology. He is director of the Fascia Research Project (Technical Univversity, Munich and Ulm University, Germany), rResearch director of the European Rolfing Association, and founding director of the Fascia Research Society. His research on active fascial contractility was honored with the Vladimir Janda Award. Prior to becoming a fascia researcher he worked as a Rolfing practitioner and instructor as well as a Feldenkrais teacher for two decades. More at www. somatics.de and www.fasciaresearch.de.

Dr. Arielle Schwartz is a clinical psychologist and leading voice in the healing of trauma. She is an internationally sought-out teacher and author of eight books including *The Complex PTSD Workbook*, *The Post-Traumatic Growth Guidebook*, and *Applied Polyvagal Theory in Yoga*. As the founder of the Center for Resilience Informed Therapy, she provides a mind-body approach to trauma recovery. She believes the journey of trauma recovery is an awakening of the spiritual heart. Learn more at www.drarielleschwartz.com.

Dr. Raja Selvam, PhD, who has taught in over 25 countries on six continents, is a licensed clinical psychologist from the U.S., and the developer of Integral Somatic Psychology (ISP), a science-backed, body-based, emotion-focused complementary approach designed to reduce treatment times and improve outcomes in all therapy modalities including body psychotherapies. He is the author of the book *The Practice of Embodying Emotions: A Guide for Improving Cognitive, Emotional, and Behavioral Outcomes*, which has been translated into twelve languages.

Jane Shaw, MA, RCST, is a registered therapist and originator of the SIMPLE Listening program, marrying biodynamic craniosacral therapy, neurobiology, and Jungian psychology to support individuals to recover from adverse life experiences. As a writer and educator, Jane delivers training programs both online and in person, in Ireland and internationally. She holds an MA in economics from the University of Edinburgh and an MA in Jungian and archetypal psychology from Pacifica Graduate Institute.

Marlysa Sullivan, DPT, CIAYT, E-RYT, has over 20 years of experience working with people with chronic pain conditions. She has been an invited speaker at national and international conferences and faculty in yoga therapy and physical therapy programs. She is the physical therapy mindful movement coordinator for the Empower Veterans Program and serves as the yoga and meditation clinical champion at the Veterans Health Administration. She has authored articles, chapters, and books including *Understanding Yoga Therapy: Applied Philosophy and Science for Health and Well-Being* and *The Science for Well-Being*.

Jennifer Tantia, PhD, has been an author, educator, and practicing somatic psychotherapist in New York City for the past 18 years. She served on national boards and has taught psychotherapists how to conduct somatic psychotherapy in the U.S., Europe, and Asia. Her latest book, *The Art and Science of Embodied Research Design* (2021), received a distinguished Marion Chace Foundation grant. Dr. Tantia has recently become a certified meditation teacher through Tibet House.

Chantal Traub is a seasoned New York City doula, childbirth educator, and polyvagal-informed coach. In her 20-plus years of practice, she has become internationally well-known for her expertise on the pelvic floor and her Pushing Power technique. Through her classes, her one-on-one work, and her doula and coaching practice, Traub has helped thousands of women give birth without trauma. In recent years, Traub has expanded her training and practice to serve the health needs of women navigating motherhood, menopause, and beyond. Chantal's work has been published in Pathways to Family Wellness (2024). She coauthored *The Pelvic Floor: Everything You Needed to Know Sooner* (2022).

Donnalea Van Vleet Goelz, has a PhD in clinical somatic psychology and is executive director of Continuum Movement®, founded by Emilie Conrad Da'oud. She has taught and been on the faculty of several different educational institutions: University of Florida, University of North Florida, Esalen Institute, and Hollyhock Educational Institute. Currently she is involved in somatic research at the University of Florida Health and University of North Florida as well as presenting at important trauma conferences around the world.

Ruby Jo Walker, LCSW, SEP, CHT, is the founder of Southwest Trauma Training (www.swtraumatraining.com) located in Durango, Colorado. She has a private psychotherapy practice and is certified in Hakomi Somatic Mindfulness Therapy and Somatic Experiencing. She developed Post-Traumatic Growth Somatic Therapy, which includes applied Polyvagal Theory for trauma treatment and the development of resilience. She has provided training to psychotherapists, body work practitioners, pastoral care providers, medical personnel, educators, and agencies throughout the state, the Four Corners region, and the Navajo Nation. During the pandemic, she was a key member of Colorado's state-wide task force assisting in the development of a website to support health care workers (www.cohcwcovidsupport.org). She delights in how using the lens of Polyvagal Theory brings compassion and humanness to all of her work.

Jan Winhall, MSW, PIFOT, is an author, teacher, and seasoned trauma and addiction psychotherapist. She is an educational partner with the Polyvagal Institute where she offers a training program based on her book *Treating Trauma and Addiction with the Felt Sense Polyvagal Model* (Routledge, 2021). Her new book, *20 Embodied Practices for Healing Trauma and Addiction: Using the Felt Sense Polyvagal Model* (Norton), is due out March 2025. She is an adjunct lecturer at the University of Toronto and a certifying coordinator with the International Focusing Institute. Jan is also codirector of the Borden Street Clinic, where she supervises graduate students. She enjoys teaching all over the world. You can reach her at janwinhall.com.

Zabie Yamasaki is a sought-after trauma-informed yoga teacher, national trainer, consultant, and keynote speaker who has trained thousands of yoga instructors and mental health professionals in her trauma-informed yoga certification training. Her trauma-informed yoga curriculum is implemented widely at over 40 college campuses and trauma agencies across the country. Her work has been featured on CNN, NBC, KTLA 5, and in *The Huffington Post*. Learn about her work at zabieyamasaki.comor on Instagram, @transcending_trauma_with_yoga.

Silvia Zanotta, DPhil, psychologist and psychotherapist for children, adolescents, adults, and families in Zurich, Switzerland, is a certified trainer and supervisor in Ego State Therapy International and Resource Therapy International as well as in Somatic Ego State Therapy. She is a supervisor in hypnosis, founder and cochair of Ego State Therapy Switzerland, lecturer at the University of Applied Psychology in Zurich, and teaches in several European countries. Her book *Somatic Ego State Therapy for Trauma Healing: Whole Again* was published in August 2024.

Preface

Somatic-Oriented Therapies: My Personal Journey

Stephen W. Porges

Unlike my coeditors, I entered the world of body psychotherapy not as a therapist, but as a scientist informed by knowledge of the neural regulation of the autonomic nervous system. This perspective has freed me to be an unbiased observer of the profound impact that body-oriented psychotherapies have made in promoting mental and physical health. Although not an active participant, I was welcomed into the community, and have been in the shadows attending with curiosity and interacting with several founders as the field of body psychotherapy emerged.

As trauma-informed therapies become more body-focused there has been increasing interest in blending the principles of Polyvagal Theory into body psychotherapy. This emerging interest is documented in several of the chapters in this book. Initially I was surprised by the curiosity and interest in Polyvagal Theory that somatic therapists expressed. The impact of their interest in Polyvagal Theory shifted my role within body psychotherapy from the "shadows" to the "main stage" when in 2018 I was honored by the United States Association for Body Psychotherapy (USABP) with the Pioneer Award; unexpectedly changing my role from observer to influencer.

My role change also highlighted a shift in body psychotherapy from a focus on brand or school of treatment to a neurophysiological foundational perspective common to all successful therapeutic strategies. Thus, Polyvagal Theory has been helpful in focusing trainings on core underlying processes, while respecting the insights of several therapeutic models and methods.

My interest in trauma did not occur until my work on Polyvagal Theory was discovered by body-focused traumatologists. It is validating to see that several of the contributions to this book acknowledge Polyvagal Theory and expand the application of its principles into somatic practices. This interest in Polyvagal Theory within body psychotherapy was initiated and driven by my relationships with three body-oriented pioneers in traumatology: Peter Levine, Bessel van der Kolk, and Pat Ogden. Their work is well-cited

in our book. Each of these pioneers graciously welcomed me to join them on their journey to understand and rehabilitate the disruptive effects of trauma. It was through their
passion to help their clients, their commitment to learn, and their curiosity to understand
the processes involved in experiencing and recovering from trauma that they embraced
insights from Polyvagal Theory in their treatment models. Our interactions challenged
my understanding of human experiences and forced me to explore the role of autonomic
state regulation as mediating the consequences of traumatic experiences. But, perhaps
more importantly, it resulted in theory-driven options to rehabilitate and normalize mental and physical health that have led to more effective therapeutic strategies.

My personal story within the domain of body psychotherapy highlights the product of
learning and sharing with colleagues. In a way the story is very "polyvagal"—representing
a shared journey with trusted friends who share a passion to help, and curiosity to understand, the underlying mechanisms that resulted in the retuning of a nervous system from
supporting spontaneous sociality to a nervous system that was reluctant to relinquish its
defenses; a nervous system that thrived on coregulation and shared experiences to one
that withdrew and functionally interpreted accessibility as vulnerability.

My journey started in the late 1970s when I unexpectedly met Peter Levine. At the time,
I was a tenured associate professor in psychology at the University of Illinois–Urbana-
Champaign. Without an introduction, Peter's curiosity prompted him to call me and discuss the autonomic states of his clients, as he was exploring the links between autonomic
state and traumatic memories. During the early phase of my academic career, my work
was laboratory based and far from the world of trauma. I was developing time series statistical models to describe and quantify the vagal regulation of the heart from beat-to-beat
heart rate variability. Peter introduced me to the powerful impact of traumatic memories,
via top-down mechanisms, producing a dysregulated autonomic state. Our discussions
stimulated curiosity. Within a few months, in 1979, he invited me to participate in a conference that he was organizing at Esalen on the "Biology of the Affectional Bond." It was
quite an experience. I recall sitting on pillows mesmerized as I listened to John Lilly discussing his personal experiences with dolphins and his exploration with ketamine, which
he affectionately called Vitamin K. Peter and I co-organized a follow-up conference at
Esalen in 1981 entitled "The Perinatal Period: Interface of Biology and Behavior."

At the 1979 Esalen meeting, I met Jaak Panksepp. Being conventional academic scientists, Jaak and I were unusual participants at Esalen. At that time, we were two of the few
"young" scientists who had been awarded a prestigious Research Scientist Development
Award from the National Institutes of Mental Health. This award paid our salaries for
a decade, freeing us from mandatory university teaching responsibilities to focus our
time on our research. At Esalen we connected and remained in contact over succeed-
ing decades. Serendipitously, we played similar roles throughout our careers bridging
laboratory-based neuroscience with the clinical world. We were often on the same programs until he passed in 2017. He is missed.

Peter Levine and I have remained good friends. I give credit to Peter for introducing
me to the world of body-oriented therapy. His insights and curiosity stimulated my inter-

est in the dynamic interaction between "structure" and neural function. These meetings provided a forum to explore an innovative view of mental health that included an appreciation for the bidirectional communication via the autonomic nervous system of the brain and bodily organs. This interest in how physiological states influenced mental processes and how mental processes influence visceral organs became an embedded theme in future applications of Polyvagal Theory. Our discussions served as a forum to explore an innovative view of mental health that included an appreciation for the bidirectional communication via the autonomic nervous system of the brain and bodily organs. Over the years, I have seen Peter's insights crystalize and evolve into a powerful treatment model that became the basis of somatic experiencing. Through Peter, I unexpectedly was drawn into the community from which body psychotherapy would emerge.

He also introduced me to Rolfing, which triggered my interests in somatic-oriented therapies. Several pioneers in the eclectic and emerging domain of body psychotherapy have their roots in Rolfing. In the early 1980s, when I was a faculty member at the University of Illinois–Urbana-Champaign, I met John Cottingham. John was passionate about somatic-oriented therapies. He had dropped out of medical school to be trained as a Rolfer. We developed a strong friendship focused on identifying the neural mechanisms that were elicited by the structural manipulations defined by Rolfing procedures. He challenged me to explain how and why Rolfing could change functions and perspectives that did not seem related to the structural changes reliably observed. To be a good observer, we agreed that I would need to experience the entire Rolfing sequence. We had weekly Saturday meetings in which I was the recipient of a Rolfing session in his office. The session was followed by an hour or two at a coffee shop discussing my observations of each specific Rolfing manipulation on my autonomic nervous system. At about this time, I had developed a vagal tone monitor that was able to provide in real time online feedback indicating the dynamic shifts in heart rate and cardiac vagal tone (i.e., respiratory sinus arrhythmia). Based on our discussions, we decided to create a couple of experiments using the vagal tone monitor to test two manipulations that could be "deconstructed" from the Rolfing procedures. The research resulted in two publications that documented strong effects of pelvic tilt and soft tissue manipulation on autonomic state (Cottingham et al. 1988a, 1988b). These experiences stimulated John to complete a master's in biology and later to get a degree in physical therapy, in which he was able to incorporate his talents as a somatic therapist.

In the late 1990s I began to be invited to give talks in the more interdisciplinary and eclectic area of body psychotherapy. Soon I met and became good friends with Bessel van der Kolk as he ventured into the world of somatic therapy to expand his clinical resources. In 1999, I talked at his Boston trauma meeting, a meeting where I have frequently been a participant since. At that time Bessel was integrating the body into an understanding of trauma, and body-oriented therapies into his therapeutic strategy,

By the late 1990s I also had become a good friend with Pat Ogden. In the 1990s Pat was refining her work into a model that she labeled Sensorimotor Psychotherapy: a bridge between somatic therapies and psychotherapy. She, like Peter, emphasized the potent role of appropriately accessing, respecting, and managing implicit memories, which at times appeared to be metaphorically locked in the body. Through my friendship with Pat, I was also a frequent speaker at the annual meetings on attachment and trauma at UCLA organized by Marion Solomon and the Lifespan Learning Institute. These meetings formed the focal point for clinicians interested in interpersonal neurobiology, and especially the consequences of adversity history on biobehavioral systems. At these meetings an interesting hybrid group of therapists, researchers, and scholars was self-forming, and bonded through friendship and passion. It expanded beyond Pat, Bessel, and Peter to include Ed Tronick, Dan Siegel, Norman Doidge, Allan Schore, Diana Fosha, and Louis Cozolino. As the circle of colleagues expanded, the role of the body in trauma was further understood. Frequently, as our professional paths intersected, we had opportunities to mentor each other as we interacted at conferences and workshops.

Through these interactions, I became informed about the profound disruptive impact of trauma on a significant portion of the population. I became aware that survivors of trauma often go through life without an opportunity to understand their bodily reaction to the trauma or to recover the ability to regulate and to coregulate their physiological and behavioral state. Many of these individuals are revictimized when discussing their experiences and are often reprimanded for not fighting or fleeing. Others are chastised for not psychologically recovering when there is no apparent physical damage.

It is our hope that this volume fulfills the need for clinical examples of how somatic-oriented therapies can improve the quality of life of those who have experienced adversity. The chapters, by documenting how insightful clinicians have incorporated aspects of Polyvagal Theory into diverse clinical settings, include vivid examples of how a somatic perspective provides a language of the body that has enabled the authors to passionately express their desire to understand and to optimize the human experience.

When Herbert and Maurizio invited me to join them in coediting this book, I wanted to be supportive. Initially, I felt my role would be more advisory, and less relevant to content. However, as the list of authors and topics evolved, I realized that Polyvagal Theory had played an important role in this emerging discipline. Moreover, as we worked on editing the chapters, I realized that my long interest and involvement in somatic-oriented therapies had beneficially influenced my research, theory, and publications. Through the decades of interacting in the world of somatic therapies, my research questions expanded and were refined as I gained a deeper appreciation of the explicit bidirectional communication between the brain and body that is the core of somatic-oriented psychotherapies. As the book took shape, I began to appreciate the privilege of being involved in this amazing paradigm shift, bringing an awareness of the body into psychotherapy. This book celebrates the important transition within psychotherapy from the constraints of a top-down model to a more accurate view of an integrated nervous system dynamically managing the bidirectional communication between brain and body and between thoughts and feelings. The following chapters provide an exciting glimpse into the future as somatic-oriented therapies have come of age.

Introduction

Herbert Grassmann and Maurizio Stupiggia

This book is intended for a professional audience interested in the field of clinical somatic-oriented therapies (SOT) as an applied science of embodiment research and treatment. It is timely and consistent with contemporary neuroscience research (e.g., Porges, 2021) that has informed trauma treatment by illuminating the importance of bodily experience for self-regulation and interaction with others in a social context. Human behavior, especially in traumatic situations, is understood as a complex and fully embodied biobehavioral process expressed in thoughts, feelings, and behaviors that are controlled by neurophysiological sensors that detect features both in our body and in the external environment. This integrated sensorimotor system dynamically adjusts aspects of physiology, perception, behavior, and motivation to enhance our ability to cope with a full range of dynamic challenges, ranging from cues of safety to those of threat.

In addition to exploring embodied practices embedded in existing psychotherapeutic practices, there is a need to examine the scientific rationale for addressing embodiment in both quantitative and qualitative research paradigms in order to provide a platform for future research programs. Indeed, somatic psychotherapy has faced tremendous challenges—in particular, we have been challenged to develop our evidence base, which has resulted in our research being published in leading peer-reviewed journals.

This volume focuses on reframing psychotherapy to go beyond dialogue, memory retrieval, and behavior to include an objective assessment of both the client's and therapist's bodily states through reliable metrics that would include monitoring autonomic function (e.g., heart rate variability) and structured questionnaires assessing bodily feelings (e.g., the Body Perception Questionnaire [Porges, 1993]; the Neuroception of Psychological Safety Scale [Morton et al., 2022]).

During the past decade, there has been a dramatic shift in psychotherapy as the impact of the body and nervous system on mental health has been acknowledged. Many forms of psychotherapy, explicitly or implicitly, now integrate an understanding of the nervous system and bodily state in their treatment models. The body of research on psychotherapy, through both clinical trials and case reports, is increasingly documenting impressive evidence of the central role that the body, and in particular the client's nervous system, plays in the treatment of all psychological disorders, regardless of severity (Lanius et al., 2010, 2014; Cozolino, 2017; Payne et al., 2019). Complementing the empirical literature are several clinically relevant theoretical models (Nijenhuis et al., 1996; Martens et al., 2023; Rosendahl et al., 2021) linking mental processes to bodily states, including strong links that are frequently witnessed as comorbidities between mental and physical diagnoses.

Current theoretical concepts of mind-body and brain-body have led the psychotherapy community to rethink mental disorders and treatments. An increasing number of psychotherapists are recognizing the connection between mental processes and bodily function, and no longer treat them as separate entities. In fact, Allan Schore (2009) proposed that the inclusion of embodied experience in clinical practice, a process shared across several therapeutic approaches, represented a new paradigm.

The processes involved in regulating or disrupting the physiological states that underlie thoughts and behaviors are dynamically adjusting and adapting at every moment of life. Whether we focus our therapies on thoughts or behaviors, our physiological substrate is constantly adapting to optimize our survival. This is true not only from the perspective of the individual but also with respect to relationships. Thus, the coregulation that occurs between individuals reflects an embodied relationship, a crucial dimension for several psychological theories and for most forms of psychotherapy. We see this particularly in cases of trauma. From a neuroscientific perspective, trauma functionally permeates the survivor's nervous system, retuning it from a dynamic state that supports sociality and homeostatic functions (i.e., health, growth, and restoration) to a chronic state that supports defense (e.g., fight, flight, shutdown). Thus we see how trauma becomes physiologically embedded, altering the optimal trajectory of a flexible and resilient nervous system and profoundly disrupting the development of experience of self and others.

An innovative aspect of this book is the emphasis on the relational perspective of treatment. Prior to this publication, most strategies for either studying or treating trauma have focused on the client's range of functioning and identifiable features of dysfunction. Starting from the realm of body interaction and mutual coregulation, this volume emphasizes the importance of relational complexity in transforming the client's physiological and emotional regulation. In the treatment of trauma, and particularly complex trauma, the environmental and relational context is crucial and influences both the biobehavioral state of the client and therapist and the dynamic relational atmosphere created in the therapeutic setting.

For this reason, relational technical modalities that influence and normalize bodily functions are proliferating, including the following:

- Treating disorders of embodied self-awareness
- Using sensory processing as a layer of experience in human development
- Improving the capacity for embodied emotional attunement
- Integrating autonomic regulation into therapy
- Strengthening self-regulation through dyadic coregulation

The success of these technical modalities depends upon the theoretical basis on which SOTs are founded. The body-mind unity, which depends on bidirectional neural communication between brain and body, is the basic assumption upon which various forms of SOT have evolved. Thus, the current status of contemporary neuroscience provides a theoretical basis for treatments and investigations of SOT strategies within an integrated mind-body-brain theoretical model. Embodied methods could be useful in understanding difficult-to-treat conditions such as autism, chronic pain, and medically unexplained symptoms—or in the diagnosis and therapy of neurodiversity.

Reframing trauma from an event to a biological behavioral response transforms our understanding of the consequences of traumatic events. From this perspective, the traumatic event is viewed as being capable of overwhelming the survivor's neuroregulatory capacity to support underlying physiological homeostasis and observable resilient and flexible behavior and thinking. The result is a general breakdown in the client's physiological and emotional regulatory capacity, both within themselves and in relation to the world around them. Treatment becomes a gradual work of repairing these ruptures, involving both in a construction of a new form of functioning within a therapeutic framework that privileges and elevates a sense of safety as an essential condition for transformation and healing.

Complex trauma therapy can be challenging because attachment patterns, based on trust, develop within a neurobiological substrate occurring outside conscious awareness and expressed nonverbally via bodily reactions (van der Kolk et al., 2001). Mindfulness, somatic exercises, and touch-based interventions are powerful tools for revealing and studying unconscious patterns and facilitating healing. They provide an embodied experience of change within the context of a safe relationship without triggering an explanatory narrative, which would often recruit defensive memories and associations.

The Birth of the Book

This book was born out of an observation of a coincidence that two of us, Herbert and Maurizio, noticed in our own professional backgrounds. We both come from years of direct work on the body, from Rolfing and Postural Integration. Having collaborated for some time on issues related to trauma and intervention approaches to posttraumatic syndromes, we became aware of a compatible sensitivity watching the patient: an ability to pick up states and changes in the person's posture, muscle tone, and neurophysiological activation. In short, our basic approach was similar; although as body psychotherapists we came from different master teachers and different theoretical perspectives and lines of training, we found that we shared a common trust in the body.

This trust was not simply a blind reliance on the body's ability to soothe the person's pain and heal the pathological forms that the therapist might encounter; it was the understanding that we could question the body, thus finding unthought-of avenues of transformation. Often, while working together, we noticed a skill and ease in touching people. This attitude to question the body was also expressed in our use of touch, almost as if it were a kind of "knocking on the patient's front door."

At that moment, each of us revealed to the other the origin of this experience, with a certain modesty, as if it were less important compared to the unquestionable value of psychotherapy as such. The book was actually born in that moment, in our look of mutual complicity and the relief of being able to share totally our way of observing and acting with clients, as an obvious and preeminent way of approaching them. We realized that for us the body was not just a means to speed up the therapeutic process or to unhinge chronic defenses but that it was the working ground, the constant issue to work on.

That's why we were so dissatisfied with the traditional way of diagnosis and assessment, and we were looking for new tools for a different point of view. In short, we were looking for another form of approach and treatment. The origin and source had thus emerged. We had to figure out the direction of the journey we wanted to take together and assess whether the route and destination were really the same. This became evident as we observed one another in our respective ways of working with individual patients and with groups. Our formative history as body psychotherapists was different, but there was a remarkable similarity in our clinical gaze, in our choice of interventions, in our respect for the patient's time and experiences, and above all in the deeply phenomenological attitude that required us not to force the therapeutic process but to let it emerge from itself. To live this attitude fully, it was necessary to give up all ideology and prior knowledge, to have the possibility of reaching the subjectivity of the other. In each session, we tried to get to know the other person as if we were meeting him or her for the first time, rather than relearning him or her with preestablished concepts and categories. In a sense, every session was a constant beginner's workshop for us.

This way of working overshadowed the use of protocols, the exaltation of techniques, the rigidity of precoded procedures. Instead, it showed the importance of the body-to-body relationship between therapist and patient, the importance of building trust in the clinical setting as an essential condition for building a process of deep transformation.

Therefore, the meeting with Stephen Porges was inevitable: his theory, created over many years of research, was the ideal basis for our way of working and at the same time provided the explanation of what was happening in the delicate work of restoring the neurophysiological balance of traumatized people. The Polyvagal Theory is the necessary theoretical landing place for body practices that have worked for years in an intuitive and dispersed way, and that now have a home that contains them and gives them dignity and a clear scientific value.

The strong emphasis that Polyvagal Theory places on safety in therapy has thus begun to change the world of the clinic, prompting therapists to change their view, their attitude, and their way of intervening.

Overview of Concepts

Collectively, the volume supports a transformative view that somatic and psychological problems cannot be treated as separate domains. Rather, the premise of treating somatic and psychological problems with different therapeutic strategies is challenged by a perspective that integrates biological, behavioral, and neurobiological sciences and clinical observations. Thus, a central message of the book is that no therapy will be effective unless the individual's physiology welcomes and supports it. By accepting such a perspective, the therapist's knowledge, awareness of the physiological state of both self and client, and their capacity to self- and coregulate become essential tools for therapy. As therapists, we are engaged in a deep process whose effectiveness is related to our ability to engage with issues through a combination of participant experience and case presentation. Each section of the book is organized to open new directions in treatment. Identifying competencies is an essential part of defining the somatic psychotherapy profession, and increases its credibility among other psychotherapy modalities. By establishing clear parameters for therapists, the book also contributes to the development of a more robust framework for future research in the field. We aim to highlight a few qualitative and quantitative measures of interoceptive awareness and build on the conversation about when reactions can be adaptive and lead to further embodiment—especially in the realm of self-agency or autonomy, which are arguably most important in the clinical healing process. The book introduces a variety of different clinical approaches within somatic therapy, including chapters on touch work, the relationship between fascia and emotions, deep brain realignment, posttraumatic growth, the treatment of trauma and addiction, the effect of yoga in treating sexual trauma, the benefits of creating a sense of safety during birth, and much more. We will first look at the field of current science on embodiment before using the framework of scientific thinking for the concept of embodiment, and then finally look for examples of practice in clinical application.

Part I: Research

Jacek Kolacz, research assistant professor at the Ohio State University College of Medicine, presents tools that allow autonomic tracking in the course of therapy to monitor response to treatment or to be used as biofeedback tools by bringing measurements of autonomic function into the client's explicit awareness.

Aaron Freedman, University of California, who specializes in developing methods for measuring embodiment, highlights the current tools that we have to measure interoception as a necessary component of embodiment, to separate the adaptive or maladaptive outcomes of increased embodiment, and to briefly note the clinical implications and cultural considerations.

Alessandra Pollazzon, Alessio Matiz, and Cristiano Crescentini from the University of Udine focus their research on the effects of a program called Mindfulness-Oriented Meditation. They developed the MOM protocol, which appears to be a promising and significant intervention for children and adolescents with ADHD.

Vittorio Gallese, Francesca Ferroni, and Martina Ardizzi from the Department of Medicine and Surgery, Unit of Neuroscience, University of Parma, present an integrated approach to studying the nervous system in health and disease at multiple levels. The central thesis of their chapter is that early traumatic experiences influence the typical developmental course of multisensory integration processes, which can lead to damage to basic self-awareness, self-esteem, and intersubjective abilities.

Sue Carter, from the Kinsey Institute and the University of Virginia, Charlottesville, shares her lifetime achievement and expertise with love as embodied medicine. Throughout life, oxytocin influences sociality and helps to allow social experiences to influence behavior and physiology. Knowledge of the neurobiology of love helps explain the exceptional reproductive success of humans, and also our resilience in the face of fear and aggression.

Part II: The Science of Embodying

Jennifer Frank Tantia titles her chapter "Somatic Intelligence: Toward a New Competency for the Therapist." She describes how cultivating somatic awareness has the potential to become part of a new competency for psychotherapists who are interested in treating mental illness from a whole-person perspective. By using an embodied, present-moment, lived experience through somatic interventions in treatment, a therapist can offer a more complete healing process for clients.

Steven Hoskinson and Bach Ho, internationally recognized teachers and writers, propose guidelines for a safer framework of biologically informed therapeutics called Post-Trauma Growth (PTG). To promote PTG reliably and reduce harm to clients, treatments must increasingly align with the client's biology and self-organizing complexity.

Jan Winhall contributes a chapter called "The Felt Sense Polyvagal Model: Embodied Assessment and Treatment Tool." She points out that, with advances in neuroscience, somatic therapies are increasingly being recognized by potential clients as viable treatment options. However, as this field grows, assessment tools are needed that include embodied approaches that capture and honor the client's experiential process and somatic history, in addition to symptom-oriented diagnostic systems (e.g., *DSM*).

Antonia Pfeiffer takes us, in "Memory Reconsolidation in Body-Oriented Trauma Therapies," into a more profound understanding of emotional memories. Along with the history of memory research and what it can teach us, we understand better the process of memory reconsolidation.

For Raja Selvam in "The Practice of Embodying Emotions," the collective implication of this growing evidence base is that the role of the body in these primary psychological processes is so great that any psychotherapy modality that does not include the body in its treatment approach in some way is bound to have longer treatment times and less than optimal cognitive, emotional, and behavioral outcomes.

Arielle Schwartz introduces us, in "Neuroception Within Trauma Recovery: Sensing the Embodied, Social Self," to the concept of vagal regulation of the autonomic nervous system. She acknowledges that nervous system dysregulation is both an intrapersonal and interpersonal experience. Therefore, interventions focused on trauma recovery are best supported within a safe and respectful coregulating environment.

Ruby Jo Walker and Emily Newcomer, authors of "Applying the Neurobiology of Resilience," point out the limitations of a top-down approach. They emphasize that top-down interventions teach how to deal with psychological states, while bottom-up interventions aim to change physiological states. Embodiment offers an approach to resilient states without focusing excessively on cognition. Embodiment of resilient states and deactivation practices can train the nervous system to access the ventral vagal complex, leading to the utilization of neuroplasticity for profound change.

Aline LaPierre, president of the United States Association of Body Psychotherapy, in her chapter "The Therapeutic Use of Touch: A Bridge Between Body, Brain, and Mind," shares with us perspectives on the therapeutic use of touch. She explains why the benefits of therapeutic touch are often obscured by cultural overlays. This therapy awakens our sensory and emotional blueprint and embodies our cognition to directly access the hunger for connection that underlies neurological deficits, dissociation, dysregulation, and states of trauma and fragmentation.

Robert Schleip is a German biologist, university lecturer, and psychologist. He is considered one of the leading international fascia researchers. In his chapter, "Fascia as Sensory Organ and the Role of Interoceptive Techniques," he explains why the fascia is the richest sensory organ of the human body.

Herbert Grassmann is chairman of the scientific research committee of the EABP and provides a therapeutic change of perspective with his analysis and research theses. The focus of his trauma therapy work is on sensory analysis and techniques for the necessary sensorimotor integration of the senses. For him, a traumatic event is always an attack on our senses. The focus of his chapter is therefore on the interoceptive and proprioceptive processing possibilities of our senses, as can be seen in the example of the sensory processing of visual reaction patterns.

David Berceli has contributed "Body Tremors: The Natural Restorative Mechanism of the Human Body." He describes the tremor mechanism in the human body as the experience of energy and matter dialoguing with each other in this interplay of the human organism. It is this interplay that seems to help facilitate the intra/interpersonal dialogue. Body tremors help the individual to experience their own sense of self while engaging in relationship with another.

Ken Benau, in "'The Eyes (I's) Have It': Deep Brain Reorienting, Structural Dissociation, and Integration," describes a relatively new model called DBR as particularly well suited to processing somatic correlates of the deepest brain structures, including the Where Self and core self, and developmentally early nonverbal and preverbal sequelae of relational and physical trauma.

Silvia Zanotta examines, in her experiential chapter with case excerpts, the advantages of using Somatic Ego State Therapy with traumatized children.

François Le Doze contributes "The Relational Intelligence Model of Psychotherapy: A Neurobiological and Relational Approach to Treating Trauma." This model is a treatment approach for traumatic dissociation (TD) that has its origins in the internal family systems (IFS) model, Polyvagal Theory, and attachment theory.

Part III: Embodied Practice

Hanneke Kalisvaart and Pat Ogden, both pioneers in the field of trauma therapy, share their in-depth understanding of a scientifically based method of psychotherapy that addresses the body's experiences to stabilize, process, and integrate them in the here and now in "Sensorimotor Psychotherapy: Processing Trauma and Attachment Through the Body." Their therapy turns out to be a good way of addressing experienced realities through the body.

Maurizio Stupiggia contributes a chapter titled "Being Together to Face the Trauma: Intercorporeality as the Core of Treatment." He describes the attitude of the therapist: "The therapist receives the client's gaze rather than forcing it. He does not challenge. He does not push; he stands by." Such gradual and constant attunement can produce a sense of safety. This allows access to new memories enclosed in states of arousal that never emerged before. The therapeutic dyad can thus deal with compelling and dangerous neuro-emotional states, expanding the window of engagement of the therapist-client pair.

Betsy Polatin, with her chapter "Humanual Polyvagal Smile: Our Inherent Design and Connection to Wholeness," invites us to explore awareness, discovery, and movement. You begin with curiosity, by noting where you are with yourself, your thoughts, feelings, sensations, breathing, and movement.

Jane Shaw presents SIMPLE Listening, a unique approach derived from biodynamic craniosacral therapy and other fields, which promotes physiological safety and regulation.

Marlysa Sullivan in "Supporting Safety With Movement: Polyvagal Theory as a Framework for Mindful Movement Practitioners" describes four processes of mindful movement and how they can be understood through the framework of Polyvagal Theory. These synergistic processes provide a powerful method for insight and reinforcement of safety from a body-based, experiential perspective.

Chantal Traub, in "Creating a Sense of Safety in Birth: Fostering Connection and Coregulation to Minimize Trauma for Parents and Baby," shares specific exercises and how to choreograph the birthing process, while the mom relaxes and can recruit her ventral vagal complex to bring a sense of calm and safety.

Chiara Marazzi and Maurizio Stupiggia, both teachers at Milano University, write on perinatal mortality and grief: "There is a unique type of mourning that deals with more than one death: a biological one and a psychological one. The first is the actual loss of a child; the latter is the denial of the existence of a traumatic experience. This is equivalent to a retraumatization; the baby is no longer there, and the birth hasn't even happened: death therefore becomes a sort of disappearance."

Jeltje Gordon-Lennox and David Knottnerus, psychotherapist and Emeritus Regents Professor of Sociology respectively, contribute "Ritual Practice, Addiction, Obsessive-Compulsive Behavior, and Routine: Ritual Dynamics and Human Coping Strategies." Our profound human need for a sense of safety, connection, and well-being responds to a spectrum of ritualized behaviors, from typical ritual practice to addiction to obsessive-compulsive disorder (OCD) to routine. The tool set contributes to the examination of the processes of how and why some ritualized behaviors function as adaptive buffers against the feelings of emptiness, distress, and powerlessness associated with change, hardship, and trauma, as well as to determining criteria for reducing human distress and enhancing human flourishing.

Molly Boeder Harris and Zahabiyah Yamasaki are sought-after trauma-informed yoga teachers. In their chapter, "Transcending Sexual Trauma Through Yoga: Evidence-Based and Practical Applications for Integrating Trauma-Informed Yoga Into Your Scope of Work," they present a very gentle way of dealing with sexual trauma, because it is one of the most pervasive boundary violations that a human can endure. Survivors may experience that violation physically, psychologically, energetically, and/or spiritually.

Michael Allison, in "Turning Competition Into Coregulation: Competition Is Grounded in a State of Threat," explains how competition becomes an opportunity to elevate, a chance to challenge ourselves in ways we couldn't do on our own. It becomes an opportunity to play and coregulate. More than a mindset, our capacity to turn competition into coregulation, into play, resides in our physiology. Technically, to play we must have enough ventral vagal control of our bodily state, access to our social engagement system, and an efficient vagal brake. These are the neural mechanisms that enable a competitive environment to shift from a battlefield to a playground and make it possible to turn competition into coregulation.

Rabih Lahoud and Herbert Grassmann, in "The Free Voice: Awakening the Prosody," describe the voice as a complex instrument that allows us to connect with others, communicate, and express ourselves. Our voice is an expression of our personality and our feelings. But it is also a mirror of our nervous system. When the prosody (rhythm, intonation, etc.) of our voice conveys safety, others are drawn to connect with us and listen to us.

Donnalea Van Vleet Goelz presents her profound knowledge of somatic communication and the healing of trauma. Her chapter outlines the essential elements of Continuum Movement (CM)—breath, sound, movement, sensation, and innovation. Through these elements, we facilitate somatic communication within our bodies. This method intersects with contemporary research on trauma and the body in neuroscience, somatic psychotherapy, and other disciplines. CM's unique movement methodology helps practitioners cultivate interoception, self-regulate, and disrupt limiting bodily patterns through movement practice, thus offering a novel practice for working with trauma.

Susan Harper contributes a chapter titled "The Eros of Relational Aliveness and Continuum Inquiry." According to her, the way we perceive is a powerful force that shapes our lives and our version of reality. By actively engaging with new ways of perceiving, who we are changes through the way we behave. This affects our physical structure, our coordination, our psychological profile, the way we form relationships, and our capacity for intimacy. In the interrupted reciprocity of trauma, there is an inhibited exchange with the world and little trust in somatic intelligence and its inherent ability to heal. In the healing process, we encourage an exploratory engagement that promotes the basic goodness of the body and the goodness of the living world.

Somatic-Oriented Therapies

Part I

Research

1

Tools for Tracking Autonomic Activity in Treatment

Jacek Kolacz

SAFETY AND DEFENSE STATES ARE SUPPORTED BY THE AUTONOMIC NERVOUS SYSTEM (ANS), which manages functions throughout the body and operates chiefly outside conscious awareness. Autonomic reactions are sensitive to changes in momentary conditions, alter the activity of the body for anticipated needs, and are involved in emotional responses and regulation. Tracking autonomic activity over the course of treatment can provide insight into patterns of clients' physiological tendencies. This chapter reviews two types of autonomic monitoring that can be employed in clinic and research: wearable sensor-based measures and client reports of autonomic symptoms. First, the chapter describes wearable sensors and common validated metrics of autonomic activity that can be measured from them, including average heart period, breathing rate, respiratory sinus arrhythmia (high-frequency heart rate variability), and electrodermal activity. Second, the chapter describes the tracking of autonomic symptoms using the Body Perception Questionnaire Autonomic Symptom Scale (BPQ20-ANS), a validated self-report scale that measures day-to-day experiences of autonomic disruption to body functions. These tools enable autonomic tracking over the course of therapy to monitor treatment response or to use as biofeedback tools by bringing measures of autonomic function to the client's explicit awareness.

The brain and body are inseparably intertwined, coordinating responses to the needs of the moment and those that are anticipated in the near future. At the interface of the brain and body is the autonomic nervous system. This network of neurons branches from the brain stem and spinal cord to connect body organs with the central nervous system, forming a bidirectional arrangement that controls organ function and integrates signals arising from the body. This widespread coordination facilitates the processes that are needed to support life and respond to environmental conditions, coordinating organs to support physical needs and emotional states. These autonomic pathways are distinct from muscular-skeletal control, though the two can serve as complementary components of response to threats.

The ANS is a transdiagnostic component of mental and physical health, with disrupted autonomic function demonstrated in anxiety, depression, posttraumatic stress disorder (PTSD), and functional gastrointestinal conditions (Chalmers et al., 2014; Kemp et al., 2010; Koenig et al., 2016; Kolacz et al., 2021; Kolacz, Kovacic, et al., 2023; Pole, 2007; Schneider & Schwerdtfeger, 2020). Monitoring autonomic regulation over the course of treatment can provide information on a client's physiological state and emotional responses during therapy, or can be used as biofeedback modalities. Autonomic tracking modalities can utilize conscious or nonconscious data sources. Some autonomic changes can go unnoticed for clients and may not be visible to clinicians. These can be tracked using wearable sensors that provide information on physiological changes in real time or after monitoring is concluded. Some autonomic changes, such as sweating palms or difficulty catching breath, can be captured using measures that cue the client to notice body sensations. This chapter reviews the use of wearable sensors and self-reports of autonomic symptoms that can be used in research and clinical settings, with examples drawn from therapy sessions.

Wearable Sensors

Rapid advances in wearable technology have led to a proliferation of consumer-oriented devices for real-time monitoring and retrospective analysis of physiological states. This rapid evolution of hardware and techniques makes it impossible to conduct a comprehensive and up-to-date review. The methods described here are a selective overview of commonly used metrics. Each of these autonomic tracking metrics have an extensive literature to support their utility and are accessible for clinicians using a range of stand-alone commercially available equipment.

Heart Period

Heart period is the duration of time between cardiac contractions. The heart relies on pacemaker cells to trigger coordinated contractions that send blood through the circulatory system, without needing stimulation from the nervous system to beat. However, autonomic signals alter the timing of these contractions, shortening and elongating timing between beats in response to a range of physical and emotional needs. Shortened heart period intervals (in other words, faster heart rate) are well documented to result from mobilization for defensive responses (e.g., Kudielka et al., 2004). However, well-controlled animal models have also shown that increasing the pace of cardiac cell firing can promote anxiety behavior, demonstrating how changes in organ function can also influence defensive states (Hsueh et al., 2023). The ease of measurement, widespread availability of accurate equipment, and intuitive interpretation make heart period and heart rate among the most common physiological monitors in research, clinical settings, and in users' day-to-day lives. These metrics can be used to track clients' emotional arousal during therapy sessions (Figure 1.1) and can be used for biofeedback to help clients notice and determine opportunities for employing calming strategies.

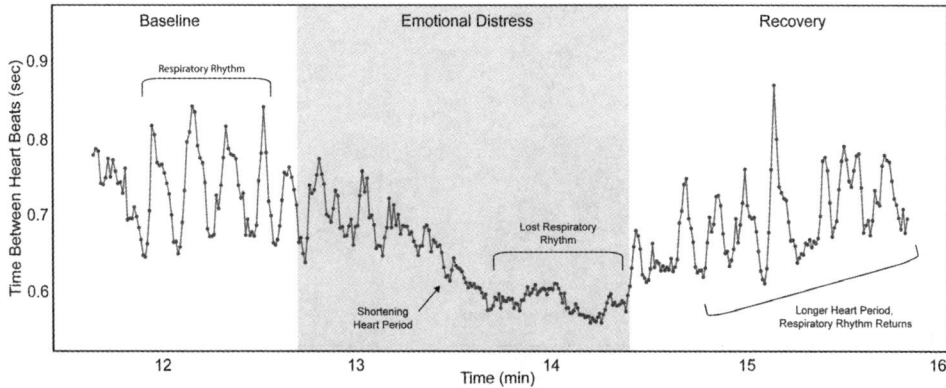

FIGURE 1.1 Electrocardiogram (ECG) heart period interbeat interval data from a therapy client during a period of emotional distress. The heart period pattern rapidly switches from a clear respiratory rhythm, followed by rapid decrease in timing between heartbeats and loss of interbeat interval variability.

Respiration and Breathing

Respiration is a process through which oxygen is brought into the bloodstream and carbon dioxide is expelled. Breathing, an aspect of respiration, is the mechanical process of lung expansion and contraction through which air in the chest cavity changes volume. Breathing serves multiple functions—to maintain adequate oxygen levels, remove carbon dioxide from circulation, protect airway and lung health, and coordinate with speech production. Breathing rate and depth change in coordination with emotional states, with shallow and rapid breathing indicative of physiological increase in demands for oxygen that are part of mobilization reactions (Figure 1.2). Breathing is also a powerful regulator of physiological state and emotions (Ashhad et al., 2022). Its application across a range of interventions for helping clients control their physiological arousal (e.g., Bryan & Rudd, 2018; Creswell, 2017) makes it a useful monitoring target to determine client engagement with breathing exercises or to provide physiological feedback for clients. Breathing rate and depth can be commonly measured using a pressure gauge sensor (e.g., a band or stretch measuring fabric) that wraps around the thorax, abdomen, or both.

Respiratory Sinus Arrhythmia

An emergent aspect of the heart's connection to the nervous system is respiratory sinus arrhythmia (RSA), the beat-to-beat variation in timing between heartbeats associated with respiratory rate. This metric is also commonly called high-frequency heart rate variability or vagally mediated heart rate variability. In general, inhaling is associated with shorter timing between heartbeats and exhalation associated with lengthening. These

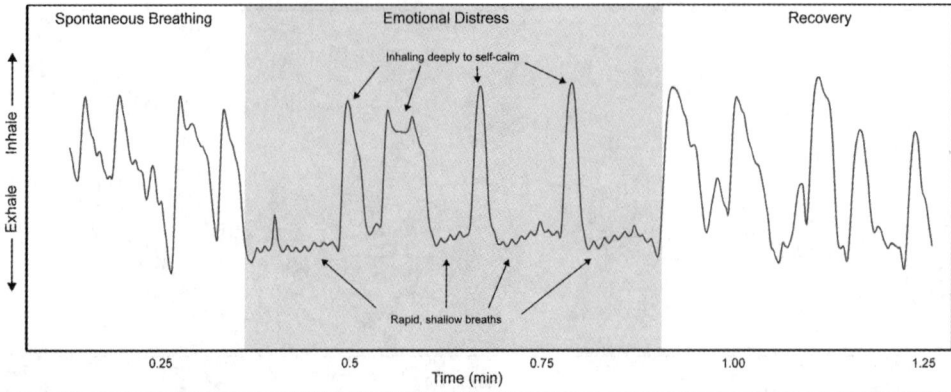

FIGURE 1.2 Breathing data from a therapy client during a period of emotional distress collected using a thoracic pressure band. Pattern rapidly switches from neutral spontaneous breathing, followed by bursts of rapid, shallow breaths. Client applied deep breathing techniques to normalize breathing.

heart period fluctuations are coordinated by brain regions that time respiratory rhythm (breathing) with the heart rate. This process is made possible by the myelinated branch of the vagus nerve (Berntson et al., 1997), which sends active signals that slow the heart's pace. These signals are more pronounced during exhalation and reduced during inhalation. In adults, this vagal outflow is the single strongest source of influence on resting heart rate (Mendelowitz, 1999).

RSA may be of particular interest for monitoring because of its index of the myelinated vagus, which several theoretical frameworks link to state regulation flexibility and emotion regulation capacity (Porges, 1995, 2011; Appelhans & Luecken, 2006; Thayer & Lane, 2000). However, RSA measurement during speaking may be influenced by speech-related alterations in respiratory rate, and so respiration must be closely monitored or controlled during measurements (Beda et al., 2007). During states that promote behavioral mobilization, RSA may decrease, indicating a withdrawal of parasympathetic vagal control of the heart (Figure 1.1). Research has shown that higher RSA at baseline is predictive of greater improvement in depressive symptoms in response to cognitive-behavioral therapy (Blanck et al., 2019) and improvement in patients with pain-predominant multisomatoform disorder (Angelovski et al., 2016). Vagal efficiency, the strength of coupling of heart period and RSA, may also be a useful marker of autonomic regulation (Porges et al., 1999; Kolacz et al., 2021; Kolacz, Kovacic, et al., 2023; Dale et al., 2022) and have utility for predicting or tracking autonomic treatment response (Kovacic et al., 2020; Porges et al., 2019).

The measurement of RSA can be sensitive to noise, artifacts, and interference from other sources of variability (Berntson et al., 1997). RSA also requires precise data on timing between heartbeats, thus requiring high-quality monitors. Before preparing to measure RSA, it is critical to ensure that data quality is adequate, quantification procedures will accurately extract the RSA signal from the raw signal, and that the conditions of the recording—including respiratory activity that can be impacted by speech—are considered (see Riniolo & Porges, 1997; Berntson & Stowell, 1998; Laborde et al., 2017; Lewis et al., 2012; Quintana & Heathers, 2014). The precise measurement of RSA requires either accurate estimation or direct measurement of respiration and the exclusion of heart period fluctuations slower than respiration and nonrhythmic trends in the data (Berntson et al., 1997). When the goal is meaningful interpretation of heart rate variability metrics, it is important to be aware of the evidence base for their validity and interpretation. In addition to RSA, many other heart rate variability indices can be calculated by commercial software packages, though the interpretation and neurophysiological mechanism of other metrics may be less well understood or may be situationally dependent (Berntson et al., 1997; Billman, 2013).

Electrodermal Activity

Sweating on the hands and fingers is regulated by the sympathetic nervous system (SNS), which is involved in triggering mobilization responses (such as fight/flight) and emotional reactions. As sympathetically innervated glands release moisture, they increase the electrical conductivity of the skin's surface, giving rise to skin conductance (Asahina et al., 2015; Dawson et al., 2007). These bursts of skin conductance can be used to measure client sympathetic activation (Figure 1.3). Electrodermal activity is most commonly measured using a pair of electrodes on the palms or fingers. However, if clients are completing other activities using both hands, these may interfere with the session. The soles of the feet can also be a location for sensors (Kasos et al., 2020), but this can be uncomfortable for some clients. Deploying electrodermal activity assessment in sessions may require some planning for client preferences and ensuring that all session-related activities can still be completed during monitoring. Alternatively, measurements may be taken at times when they will not interfere with treatment. Hardware for electrodermal activity measurement may be stand-alone or purchased as attachments to mobile devices.

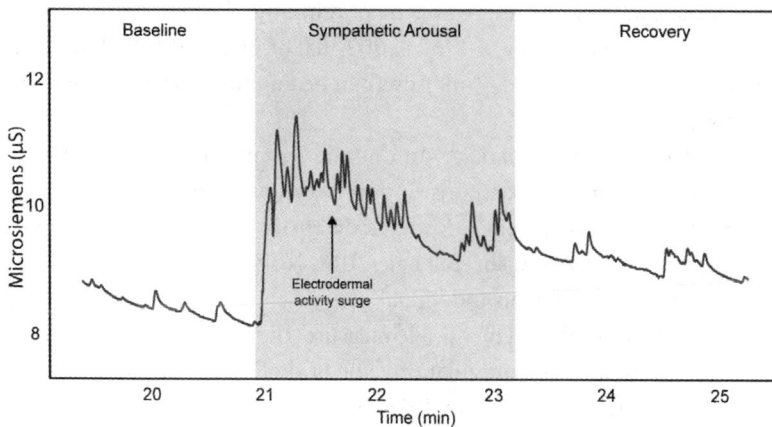

FIGURE 1.3 Electrodermal activity from therapy client, collected using a pair of electrodes on the index and middle finger.

Considerations for Wearable Sensors

To use wearable sensor data for making inferences about physiological state, it is important to ensure the device produces accurate data and to understand situations under which the sensors may provide inadequate quality. For optimal inferences, it is important to contextualize ratings. The ANS is sensitive to a range of conditions, including bodily demands. For example, transitions between lying down, sitting, and standing can cause marked changes in autonomic activity. These adaptations are important for maintaining body processes during changes in blood flow in response to gravity and muscle engagement (Wehrwein & Joyner, 2013). Other important considerations include use of medication, tobacco, alcohol, and other substances; physical fitness; age; and body mass (Alvares et al., 2016; Byrne et al., 1996; Hautala et al., 2009; Julian et al., 2020; Middlekauff et al., 2014; Parashar et al., 2016)—which can affect between-person comparisons (e.g., one client to another) as well as within-person comparisons (differences from one therapy session to another). Nonetheless, there can be substantial benefits of sensor-based approaches for a window into a client's physiological state regulation, particularly when changes may not be within the client's awareness. These methods can also be used for biofeedback or as a teaching tool about triggers and building awareness to help clients notice physiological state transitions and provide feedback on regulation strategies.

Self-Reported Autonomic Symptoms

Changes in autonomic state can rise to awareness particularly when they interfere with an individual's deliberate activities. Because organs often serve many simultaneous roles, alteration in their function for mobilization or threat responses can override their other uses. For example, the lungs coordinate gas exchange as part of the respiratory system but also control airflow through the vocal tract for producing speech. When respiration shifts to rapid ventilation that accelerates gas exchange (faster breathing), it can override the coordination of speech, leading to potentially choppy, strained speech with frequent pauses to inhale (Bailey & Hoit, 2002; Baker et al., 2008). The frequency of these types of disruptions on body functions can be an indicator of frequent autonomic threat responses.

The Body Perception Questionnaire Autonomic Symptoms Form (BPQ20-ANS) was developed to measure experiences of disruption in typical body functions that are likely to occur when the nervous system prioritizes defensive responding over social, safety-related function (Porges, 1993; Cabrera et al., 2018; Kolacz, Chen, et al., 2023). Though any single disruption can have an individual cause, when disruptions in multiple body functions over time are combined in a single measure, they can provide an overall impression of a person's autonomic state regulation. The Body Perception Questionnaire (BPQ) was first developed and introduced in 1993 (Porges, 1993), then refined to a 20-item autonomic symptoms version (BPQ20-ANS) over the course of subsequent psychometric studies (Cabrera et al., 2018; Kolacz, Chen, et al., 2023).

Factor Structure and Scoring

The results from factor analysis studies across several languages support a two-factor structure of autonomic symptoms above and below the diaphragm (Cabrera et al., 2018; Cerritelli et al., 2021; Wang et al., 2020; Kolacz, Chen, et al., 2023). This structure, which was developed using general population samples, holds consistently in mind-body practitioners whose training and practice includes close attention to body sensations, which indicates that it may be used with clients who are experienced or new to tracking body sensations (Jokić et al., 2023). Interestingly, correlations between subscales are lower among the mind-body practitioners than in the general population, suggesting that practitioners may be better at differentiating dimensions of body autonomic reactivity (Jokić et al., 2023). Though the distinction between sub- and supra-diaphragmatic symptoms is consistent, results across studies also show that the urge to vomit is associated with both types of symptom factors (Cabrera et al., 2018; Cerritelli et al., 2021; Kolacz, Chen, et al., 2023). This is likely due to both structures above and below the diaphragm being involved in vomiting (e.g., Babic & Browning, 2015). However, these factors repeatedly have been found to be strongly positively associated with one another (Cabrera et al., 2018; Kolacz, Chen, et al., 2023), have similar strength of association with prior trauma history, active PTSD symptoms, and depression symptoms (Kolacz, Dale, et al., 2020; Kolacz, Hu, et al., 2020), and have similar associations with sensor-based measures of autonomic activity (Kolacz, Chen, et al., 2023), highlighting that the functions that regulate the organs below and above the diaphragm are integrated, and autonomic states may impact both types of symptoms. However, additional research is needed to understand under which conditions the subscales converge or diverge.

Validity

A recent study on the associations of BPQ20-ANS with sensor-based measures has shown that autonomic symptom reports correspond with wearable sensor autonomic measures (Kolacz, Chen, et al., 2023; Figure 1.4). In this study, participants performed seated leg lifts while their heart period, RSA, and electrodermal activity were monitored. Participants who experienced few autonomic symptoms in daily life had well-organized physiological responses: changes in autonomic activity supported mobilization of metabolic resources during lifts, then returned to baseline levels when legs were back in the resting position. However, participants who experienced a moderate level of autonomic symptoms in daily life showed less flexible responses. Though they mobilized as needed, their sympathetic activation (electrodermal activity) did not return to baseline when their legs were returned to the floor, indicating that they may have a greater propensity to stay in mobilized states, which may interfere with daily bodily functions. Participants with the highest scores did not have consistently coordinated responses across either their parasympathetic or sympathetic branches. Overall, the results suggest that autonomic symptoms may exist on a gradient. Low levels of symptoms are associated with efficient and

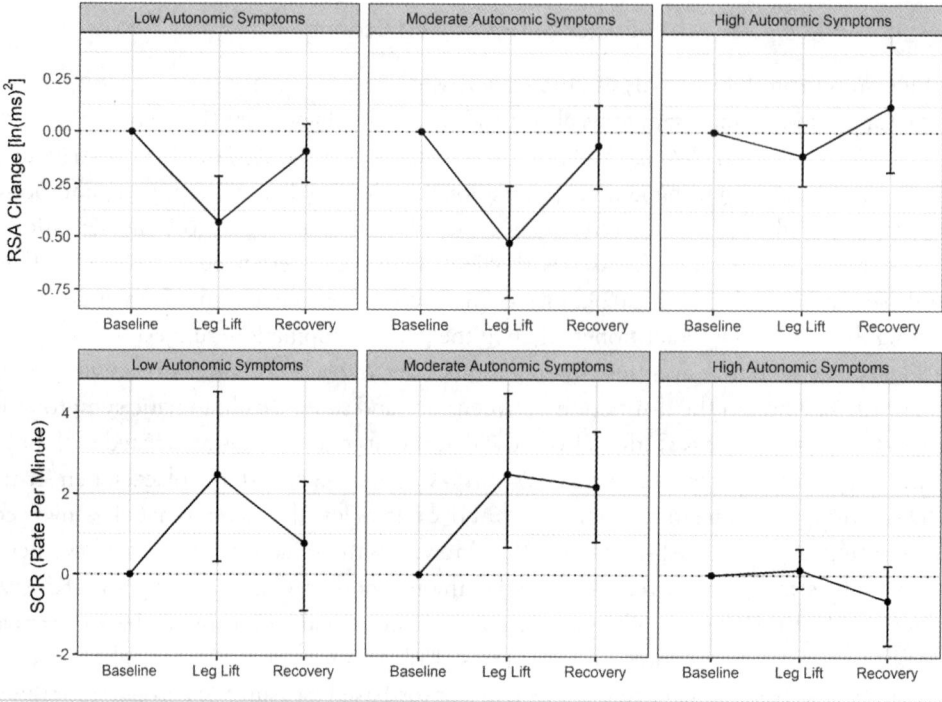

FIGURE 1.4 Parasympathetic vagal and sympathetic responses during leg lifts (respiratory sinus arrhythmia, RSA; and skin conductance response, SCR, respectively). Patterns stratified by autonomic symptoms on the Body Perception Questionnaire Autonomic Symptom Scale (BPQ20-ANS) scores. At low symptom levels (left column), parasympathetic withdrawal, sympathetic activation, and return to baseline show typical patterns. At moderate symptom levels (middle column), sympathetic activation is maintained during recovery. At the highest symptom levels (right column), there is no clear pattern of activation or withdrawal.

flexible autonomic adjustments to needs; moderate levels are associated with difficulty with calming the body after mobilization; and high levels may be indicative of impaired regulation.

Trauma History and Symptoms

Experiences of chronic threat or adversity may contribute to recalibration of the ANS so that it is better prepared for environmental risks (Porges, 2003; Del Giudice et al., 2011). Though these adaptations can help identify and quickly respond to danger, more easily triggered threat responses place a person at risk of experiencing more disruption in the activity of their organs in daily life. Across multiple studies, high levels of autonomic symptoms on the BPQ are more common among people who had maltreatment experiences in childhood, such as sexual and physical abuse, and other adverse experiences (Jokić et al., 2023; Kolacz, Dale, et al., 2020; Kolacz, Hu, et al., 2020). In addition, autonomic symptoms fluctuate in coordination with PTSD symptoms in those who have a history of adverse experience (Kolacz et al., under review). However, it is important for clinicians to note that although autonomic symptoms may indicate more sensitized autonomic threat reactions, they do not mean that a person has had a particular experience or that a trauma history should be inferred.

Tracking and Interpreting Autonomic Symptoms in Treatment

Tracking autonomic symptoms over the course of therapy provides an opportunity to monitor autonomic effects on the body. Clients may complete self-reports of autonomic symptoms during therapy sessions, while waiting for their appointment, or on their own time outside of session. To better track outcomes, the time window for symptoms can be specified (for example, symptoms within the past week or month). Longer windows allow for more opportunity to observe situations where autonomic disruptions occur if they may occur with low probability, but—on the other hand—longer windows may be less reliable due to limitations of memory. When tracking an individual client's symptoms over time, using a consistent time window of symptom reports is important to accurately compare measurements at different time points. For example, a clinician may consistently choose to have a client report on the past week's symptoms to track week-to-week changes.

While autonomic symptoms can provide useful information about client physiological states, scores can be influenced by factors beyond threat responses. It is common for people to experience some sensations of autonomic symptoms throughout their daily life. Scores higher than 0 are expected even if the person does not have chronic threat responses. Thus, clinicians have to be mindful about sources of individual influence. Physical symptoms may have many possible causes. While chronic threat responses may be a factor, it is also important to rule out other reasons that a person may be experiencing symptoms. Some diseases and medications may specifically affect organs that are controlled by the ANS or change autonomic function itself (e.g., Alvares et al., 2016). When interpreting results for a client who has a high score from a single measurement (for instance, an intake), it may be important to rule out causes due to medication or medical condition before concluding that the symptoms are related to chronic threat responses. However, even if clients take medication or have a disease that impacts the ANS, they may still benefit from interventions that help to manage chronic defense states, and repeated measures can be used to track improvements. For these clients, change over time can provide a meaningful metric of progress as long as confounding medication and disease factors are consistent over time (for example, no changes in medication).

Conclusion

Monitoring autonomic regulation can provide valuable insights into a client's physiological state. It can offer clinicians a window into their clients' emotional reactions during sessions and their daily life. These metrics can also provide tools for biofeedback, building clients' understanding of their physiological reactions or teaching regulation strategies. Wearable sensors have rapidly evolved to become accessible tools for real-time monitoring and retrospective analysis. These methods, in combination with self-reported autonomic symptoms measured by tools like the BPQ20-ANS, can offer a flexible and comprehensive approach to understanding and tracking autonomic activity. For clinicians using modalities that include education about body responses and improving awareness, the BPQ may be used alongside standard practice to support awareness of threat-related sensations. Importantly, for strong clinical interpretation of resulting data, clinicians need to take into account the various factors and potential confounds that can influence autonomic measures. A comprehensive approach that incorporates knowledge about various effects on the ANS can provide a more holistic understanding of autonomic function in the context of mental and physical health. As methods and hardware continue to advance, the integration of wearable sensors and self-reported symptoms holds promise for a personalized and autonomically informed approach to client treatment.

Acknowledgment

Work on this chapter was supported by the Chaja Foundation and the United States Association of Body Psychotherapy (USABP). I also wish to thank Olivia K. Roath for assistance with manuscript and figure formatting.

2

Defining, Measuring, and Exploring Interoception

The Scientific and Clinical Aspects of Interoception and Embodiment

Aaron Freedman

A ROUND WARM GLOW SETTLES INTO YOUR STOMACH, OR YOUR HEARTBEAT RACES, OR you feel an urgent twisting in your bowels, or you take a deep three-dimensional breath. All of these sensations are moments of interoception. Interoception is "the process by which the nervous system senses and integrates information about the inner state of the body" (Chen et al., 2021). This is in contrast to exteroception and proprioception. Throughout our lives, interoception is happening consciously and beneath our awareness, to keep us safe, alive, and functioning in homeostasis. It is also a door to the world of embodiment, where emotions are recognizable, self-regulation happens quickly, and goose bumps alert us to awe. This chapter highlights ways to measure interoception, the differentiation between adaptive and maladaptive types of interoception, cultural mediators of interoception, and clinical implications.

Underlying this work is the premise that interoception is a building block of embodiment. Control of our embodiment helps us integrate or separate from experience. Imagine someone who is dissociating during a traumatic experience, and you realize one way that our systems utilize the embodiment spectrum to maintain safety. Constant, maximal embodiment is not possible, nor the goal for health. Body-oriented or somatic psychotherapy presupposes that being able to titrate embodiment is a key skill for physiological, psychological, and spiritual health. An exciting systemic review of body psychotherapy showed that a main mechanism for change is the "reduction of arousal and an amelioration of interoception for bodily signals resulting in an enhanced self-awareness and self-efficacy" (Rosendahl et al., 2021, p. 2).

Given the stressors of daily living and traumatic events, we need the ability to self-regulate and process experience. There are numerous practices that people across the globe use to heal in this way: dance, yoga, mindfulness, drumming, bathing, shaking, and so on. Interoception and embodiment are baked into all of them. We focus this chapter on assessing people's interoception, bringing a cultural lens to the measures, and suggesting ways that relationships (with a therapist or others) can lead to healing.

As you read this chapter, I encourage you to connect to the experience of your interoceptive awareness. Notice your breath. Listen to your heartbeat. Sense your gut. Ask: How do I know if I'm hungry? What sensory information indicates my emotion right now? That conscious sensing foregrounds your embodiment and emotions. It can change your relationships and outlook.

Interoception

Interoception is a biological process that existed in animals well before human beings evolved. Our human ancestors inherently understood the benefits of cultivating and engaging the body, which we're now beginning to scientifically prove (Lock, 1993; Csordas, 1990). Sherrington first used the term *interoception* in Western written literature in 1906. It has grown rapidly since the early 2000s, led by Bud Craig (2002, 2003) and more recently Sahib Khalsa (Khalsa et al., 2018, Fig. 1A). While academia focuses on the written word, many other epistemologies were engaging with interoception well before Sherrington.

Interoception is quickly becoming popular and more frequently researched. Researchers and clinicians in the fields of psychology, philosophy, neuroscience, physiology, integrative medicine, and many others have brought their attention to this topic. The new attention that interoception has received is warranted. The director of the National Center for Complementary and Integrative Health (NCCIH), Helene Langevin, says it succinctly: "Dysfunctions in interoception may play important roles in many neurological, psychiatric, and behavioral disorders. Gaining a better understanding of how interoception works may help us develop better ways to treat these conditions" (NIH, 2021).

Much of our understanding of interoceptive pathways comes from very basic animal research. Interoception, exteroception, and proprioception are not as discrete as the abstraction of language makes them sound. Take our sense of taste, for example. Some researchers originally categorized taste as interoception, since it happens inside the body and uses similar afferent (ascending) nerve pathways, but it actually follows patterns similar to touch (Ceunen et al., 2016, p. 10; Craig, 2005). To understand something like taste, or our sense of our breath, it takes a combination of subjective and objective knowledge.

In some ways, the current state of understanding and applying interoception is similar to the early days of the somatic intervention of Eye Movement Desensitization and Reprocessing (EMDR; Shapiro, 2001). Shapiro was exploring some traumatic material while taking a walk and noticing the movement patterns of her eyes. She noticed a calming and distancing effect. This was a purely phenomenological exploration. There was initially no empirical basis. However, just 26 years later it is recommended by the World Health Organization as an advanced treatment for people with PTSD (WHO, 2013). As practitioners know, there are incredibly effective interventions that facilitate healing that are still waiting for scientific understanding of the mechanisms to catch up.

It is also important to note that interoception is an umbrella term that includes many separate subcategories of processes for perceiving conscious or unconscious signals from within the body. Examples include breath, heart rate, gastrointestinal sense, urge to urinate, and so on (Herbert et al., 2012). Farb et al. (2015, Box 1) provide a helpful taxonomy that includes interoceptive awareness, coherence, attention tendency, sensitivity, accuracy, sensibility, and regulation. To simplify, we focus on three dimensions of interoception for the remainder of this chapter: awareness, accuracy, and sensibility (Garfinkel et al., 2015; Forkmann et al., 2016; Murphy et al., 2020, p. 116). Interoceptive *awareness* is the conscious noticing of these sensations. Interoceptive *accuracy* is how accurate your perceptions of the actual sensations are. Interoceptive *sensibility* is your relationship with and beliefs about these internal sensations. After simply naming each term, it may seem that the field is coalescing on definitions. However, there are still significant variations in the definitions. Desmedt et al. point out that interoceptive sensibility and measures that assess it, often falsely, include "the trust given to internal sensations [confidence], tendency to focus on internal sensations [rumination], awareness of symptoms [awareness], capacity to predict disease from symptoms, emotional awareness" (2022, p. 2).

Take a deep breath and hold it longer than is comfortable. Your interoceptive awareness is your conscious tracking of your breath inside your body. Your accuracy is knowing whether you were engaging diaphragmatic breathing or costal breathing. Your sensibility is your relationship with the sensations of holding the breath longer than comfortable. Interoception accumulates and builds the mechanism for embodiment, where the afferent (ascending) and efferent (descending) nerve pathways from the central to peripheral nervous system of the body meet to create heightened experience of the physical self (Herbert & Pollatos, 2012).

Assessing Interoception

Now that the different dimensions of interoception have been named, we move to the ways that it can be assessed. It is important to be mindful of the wide range of experiences that people may have while paying attention to their bodies. Noticing your bodily experience is an ongoing developmental project to maintain homeostasis and support emotional regulation (Craig, 2013; Herbert & Pollatos, 2012; Seth, 2013). Babies, for example, have many interoceptive signals and processes to maintain homeostasis, but they have developed no conscious awareness, accuracy, or sensibility. While there is relatively little research with infants and children, that too is changing (Koch & Pollatos, 2014; Maister et al., 2017).

For the purposes of this chapter, there are three categories of ways to assess interoception: (1) physiological, objective tasks; (2) self-report surveys; and (3) clinical observation and assessment. Each of these approaches has its own strengths and weaknesses and should be matched to the desired area of understanding or outcome.

Physiological, Objective Tasks

There have been many different attempts to measure interoception using objective measures, such as inflating a balloon in the colon (Whitehead et al., 1990), measuring breath resistance (Harrison et al., 2021), and heartbeat-related tasks. Heartbeat tasks are one of the most easily researched types of interoception. They are fairly unobtrusive to measure and have relatively high variability that can provide statistical significance (Schandry, 1981). There are two major methods for relating heartbeat to interoception: the heartbeat counting task (HCT) and heartbeat detection task (HDT). HCT is done by counting heartbeats at rest with no external support and over a set time. HDT is usually matching the rhythm of the sensed heart to different sets of tones. While these can be helpful in assessing interoception, they also have major flaws and potential for poorly designed procedures.

People frequently underreport their heart rates, and reports can vary greatly depending on many confounding variables including the rate, strength, and knowledge of resting heart rate (Zamariola et al., 2018). Murphy et al. pointed out that HCT is problematic because there are "previous concerns over poor correlations with other measures of interoception (self-reported and objective, including other tests purporting to measure cardiac interoceptive sensitivity) and possible exteroceptive compensation strategies may be further exacerbated by the inconsistencies in administering the task" (2018, p. 194). Another significant flaw is the variation in interoceptive processes assessed (Ring & Brener, 2018; Desmedt et al., 2018; Dennis et al., 2021).

Some of the original tools that scientists used to study embodiment involved prosthetic devices. Researchers wanted to quantify the embodiment of a prosthetic device that had been integrated through neural pathways (Segil et al., 2022). To do that, they broke down embodiment into three categories, "ownership, body representation, and agency" (Segil et al., p. 2). Each of these are necessary for conscious embodiment. As you are reading, you might notice your hand that is holding the book or device and assess your embodiment in each of the three categories. Do you feel you own your hand? Does it represent yourself? Do you feel a strong sense of agency over it? Imagine that it is a prosthetic hand: How would you tell if you felt embodiment in that moment? As we assess embodiment, we are using cognitive and physiological measures, and rarely can an objective measure capture both at once. Weng et al.'s (2020, 2021) research with fMRIs is a good example of an exception to this rule, where they were able to track client self-report and brain patterns in tandem. Because interoception has a large self-awareness component, subjectively oriented measures play a large role.

Self-Report Surveys

Self-report surveys are effective research and clinical tools to help participants and clients assess and report their own body awareness. Giving a survey can inspire new understanding for clients or research subjects with little previous bodily awareness. The survey itself is an intervention to stimulate reflection as well as a research tool. Many such surveys are available, which have different strengths and weaknesses. A review of self-report measures conducted in 2009 found 12 measures that are developed enough for psychometric review (Mehling et al., 2009). A further review found the top most frequently used self-report measures (Desmedt et al., 2022, Figure 2).

One of the major surveys that we want to focus on is the Multidimensional Assessment of Interoceptive Awareness (MAIA; Mehling et al., 2012). The MAIA built on a review of previous self-report surveys, each with its own approach to body awareness (Mehling, 2009). The self-report surveys that came before the MAIA struggled with reliability and validity. This is for similar reasons that researchers of the topic struggled to coalesce on the definition and dimensions that make up interoception. Questions to assess these different dimensions frequently confuse readers, and they don't hold together as neatly as researchers would like.

The MAIA (now in version 2) is a 37-question survey that asks the respondent to rate themselves using a 0–5 Likert scale. The instructions include, "Indicate how often each statement applies to you generally in daily life." Many people may have not considered simple prompts such as Question 32, "I listen for information from my body about my emotional state." The 37 items are broken down into eight dimensions: Noticing, Not-Distracting, Not-Worrying, Attention Regulation, Emotional Awareness, Self-Regulation, Body Listening, Trusting (Mehling et al., 2018). Temptation is present to average and combine the eight dimensions, but the multidimensional nature of interoception makes this a false proxy for a nuanced phenomenon. For a thorough explanation and review of the MAIA, see Mehling et al. (2012, 2018) and Freedman and Mehling (2020).

Another frequently used survey in this area is the Body Perception Questionnaire (BPQ; Porges, 1993). This 122-item questionnaire was one of the first to attempt to support clients in reflecting on common everyday interoception tasks. With this many items on the survey, validation was difficult, and psychometric properties were weak. In 2018 a revision and validation was completed, creating the BPQ-SF (Cabrera et al., 2018). A 12-item very-short-form subscale was subsequently created. The survey instructions are to "rate your awareness on each of the characteristics" with a scale including "Never, Occasionally, Sometimes, Usually and Always." A sampling of items include, "How fast I am breathing"; "Stomach and gut pains"; "How hard my heart is beating."

If you have ever taken one of these questionnaires, you may be struck by the difficulty of matching direct experience with selecting a number on a page. You may further wonder how capricious your answers are during a particular moment and fluctuate between trying to measure your state or trait experience of the item. How subjective is the distance from *never* to *always*? Taking the test multiple times (e.g., pre- and postintervention) or measuring how similar one's answers are to similar questions is part of what gives the test internal consistency and leads to a statistical calculation of reliability (frequently measured by a Cronbach's alpha score). While multiple questionnaires attempt to measure interoceptive sensibility, for example, there remains significant discrepancy in the definition. A meta-analysis showed "weak to moderate positive associations" between different questionnaires (Vig et al., 2022).

And so, researchers continue to develop new questionnaires. The Body-Mind Connection Questionnaire is a recent example. It comprises three components,

"Interoceptive Attention, Sensation-Emotion Articulation, and Body-Mind Values" (Van Bael et al., 2023). It attempts to integrate different aspects of interoception and gain a more global score, which is difficult with other surveys that target individual dimensions of interoception. Similarly, Murphy et al. (2020) created the Interoceptive Accuracy Scale. It asks participants to rate statements based on how well they can perceive signals without using external cues, such as, "I can always accurately perceive when I am hungry" (Murphy et al., 2020). These questionnaires provide another lens to view interoception and can be combined with clinical observation. This is especially true for clients with very little experience with meta-awareness or for whom sensing into their body has frequently been unsafe. In these cases, it may be helpful for a clinician to observe and guide this process.

Clinical Observation and Assessment

Clinicians looking to get a baseline assessment of a client's interoceptive skills and embodiment might first use a self-report survey to stimulate discussion and awareness within the client. In addition to the survey, a clinician might follow a client's change over time. A recently created tool called the Somatic Post-Encounter Clinical Summary (SPECS) provides a means to engage in this type of tracking (Freedman et al., 2022). This one-page form is designed for clinicians to fill out after a session and will help them track their interventions, reflect on their embodied experience, and plan for the next session. This was engineered to be applicable for research and clinical purposes, particularly somatic psychotherapy sessions. It can also be aggregated across clinics or sessions to provide a larger picture of the trajectory of therapy and help clinicians continue to develop their tendencies and interventions.

Experienced clinicians will start to notice embodiment in many facets of the client's presentation. They can work to elicit awareness or maintain somatic engagement depending on the goal of the therapy. Factors such as gaze, tonicity, depth of breath, goose bumps, or other physiological markers may be indicators of embodiment taking place. Avoiding clinical complacency and repetitiveness is crucial for maintaining embodiment as a practitioner as well as assessing and helping clients maintain embodiment. Maybe a clinician is consistently coming out of sessions with a client feeling unbalanced or uneasy. When they start to track that phenomenon using the SPECS, they can begin to investigate the dynamics at play in the client's presentation and transference and how the therapist is responding nonverbally. As body-oriented practitioners, it is vital to be able to translate these felt sense experiences into verbal and written notation that can help clarify and solidify the nuances of embodied presence as well as build the evidence base for what is happening in sessions and what is the mechanism of change.

Cultural Aspects of Embodiment Tools

While the developers of these interoception and embodiment assessment measures may fantasize that there is universal applicability, it is clear that culture and environment have a significant impact on neurological processes. This is particularly noticeable in the meta-awareness aspects of interoceptive awareness and appraisal. Lux et al. (2021) describe a developmental framework for embodiment that incorporates environmental factors. We know culture impacts interoception based on the variability in studies across different populations. It therefore also impacts what types of measures may be best for collecting that interoception data.

Interoception that arises in an independent self-construal framework and highlights the agency approach of interoception and embodiment is the dominant mode in Euro-American contexts. It is easy to get lost in this Eurocentric perspective when evaluating these concepts. A contrasting example would be the West African Anlo-Ewe-speaking people, who have a word/concept called *seselelame*. It can be translated as "feeling in or through the body" or, more directly, "perceive-perceive-at-flesh-inside" (Geurts, 2002, p. 41). It encompasses cognitive awareness as well as sensation and even integrates the "embodied presence of others" (Geurts, 2002, p. 43, citing Csordas, 1993, p. 138). Many assessments of interoceptive awareness in the West are culturally bound.

The Singelis Self-Construal Scale helps further illuminate how unidimensional this Euro-American perspective can be (Singelis, 1994). Consider two of the 30 items, "I enjoy being unique and different from others in many respects," and "I will sacrifice my self-interest for the benefit of the group I am in." If measures of interoception and agency skew too far toward the worldview reflected in item 1, they will not capture the interoceptive capabilities of people who agree more with item 2. An example of a study that encountered this phenomenon was a small focus group of Japanese Americans. It explored the ways that acculturation impacted interoceptive awareness and highlighted some key problems with the translation and concepts of interoceptive awareness when viewed from an independent self-construal context (Freedman et al., 2020; Shoji et al., 2018). For other helpful examples of studies of cultural differences of interoception, see Maister and Tsakiris (2014).

In contrast to the focus on how interoception and embodiment contribute to individual agency, Lux et al. highlight the "environmental approach," in which "environmental (pre) conditions and events are incorporated into the body to become embodied experiences" (2021, p. 2). External factors, ocularcentrism (perceptual bias toward vision), and other culturally bound behaviors greatly influence individuals' relationship with interoception (Freedman et al., 2020).

A study done with 815 Malaysian Malay adults compared interoceptive sensibility and body image in a non-Western population and found "significant positive correlations between IS [interoceptive sensibility] and the positive body image indices for both women and men . . . [and overall that] relationships between IS and facets of positive and negative body image are present in a non-Western setting" (Todd et al., 2022, p. 53). Another study was done with 114 individuals, roughly half West African and half European American, and found results suggesting that "cultural scripts of attending to the body may affect coupling between actual and perceived physiological reactivity in the context of emotions" (Chentsova-Dutton & Dzokoto, 2014, p. 666). However, it is worth noting that this study used the Body Aware-ness Questionnaire, which had low internal consistency (Shields et al., 1989).

Another cultural comparison related to interoception and embodiment was done between European American and Asian (primarily Chinese, Korean, and Japanese) college students. It found that "Asian participants were less interoceptively accurate, they were sensitive to contextual cues regarding their visceral states. . . . Asians were more likely to infer their internal states as a function of the contextual cues" (Ma-Kellams et al., 2012, p. 725). Other researchers have pointed out the error of conflating multiple Asian cultures:

> Notably, previous studies testing for cultural differences in IAcc [interoceptive accuracy] involved East Asian individuals from several countries, including China, Taiwan, Hong Kong, South Korea, and Japan (Maister & Tsakiris, 2014; Ma-Kellams et al., 2012). In contrast, the current study focused only on Japanese participants. It is suggested that the degree of collectivism differs among East Asian countries. (Ubukata et al., 2023, p. 304)

A note of caution when analyzing culture and embodiment: It is easy to assume that language is a direct expression of experience. While the original creator of a body-based phrase may have drawn from interoception when creating a phrase, interoception is not necessarily involved when using the phrase. Take, for example, people who say they have a "heartache." They could use this word without actually having much conscious awareness of their heart. With that said, there is still much to be gained from exploring the connection between interoception, emotion, language, and culture (see Tsai et al., 2004; Ma-Kellams, 2014).

Clinical Application and Interventions

While scientists continue to hone the assessment of interoception, our knowledge can be brought into practice for supporting clients to safely build skills and mental health. Clinicians will find that interoception can be very valuable for helping clients become more in touch with their emotional states. Once the mind-body split has been explored experientially, the client may be able to associate sensations more directly with emotions. They will be able to discern and evaluate their metacognition about the meaning of those sensations. Critchley and Garfinkel (2017) provide a good overview of our emerging understanding of this connection between afferent signals and the appraisal that leads to emotional states.

Clinicians must stay keenly aware of both the adaptive and maladaptive potentials of increased interoceptive awareness in their clients. It is easy to make the false assumption that bright, consistent, max-aperture interoception and maximal, visceral embodiment leads to perfect health. However, it may be worth asking to what extent this assumption relates to ability, cisgender, and/or safety privilege.

Hyperawareness of interoception without a healthy metacognitive attitude can lead to rumination, perseveration, and hypochondriasis (Trevisan et al., 2021). Experiences and measures of interoception can be dangerously close to proxies for anxiety, rumination, and psychosomatization. There can even be a reduction in interoceptive accuracy for people who are typically high symptom reporters (Bogaerts et al., 2008).

Noticing your heartbeat when it's racing, sensing pressure in your chest, and being out of breath are frequently disconcerting. Therefore, dysfunction in interoception may be the cause of many maladies such as anxiety (Farb et al., 2015). People must "differentiate clearly an anxiety and hypervigilance-driven attention style (associated with emotional fragility) versus a more mindful attention style (potentially a virtue) towards interoceptive cues" (Mehling, 2016, p. 2). This mindful attention style can be developed with practice (specific interventions are discussed later in this chapter).

By combining awareness with agency, there is a new sense of embodiment that improves regulation and saturates you with the full spectrum of daily experience.

As we develop, we adapt to external cues, and our central nervous system responds using the stress response system (Price & Hooven, 2018). This is an adaptive way for our body to react to stress in acute situations, but can become maladaptive in chronic stressful environments (Schulz & Vögele, 2015). This is one of the main ways that stress can lead to malfunctioning interoception, which can lead to emotional dysregulation and mental illness. Nord and Garfinkel (2022) have a thorough review of how psychopharmacological and behavioral interventions affect interoceptive pathways and impact mental health.

An important starting place for the application of interoception and embodiment to clinical interventions is "Interoception and Mental Health: A Roadmap" (Khalsa et al., 2018), which came out of the 2016 Interoception Summit.

As researchers from different fields continue to see the utility of interoception, it will be used in many different ways and contexts. Occupational therapist Kelly Mahler has created the "Comprehensive Assessment of Interoceptive Awareness" (available for purchase online) as well as implementing an interoception curriculum in schools (Mahler et al., 2022). While these tools are not scientifically validated, we will continue to see similar options available, and it will be important for clinicians to continue to think critically about how they approach this topic with their clients.

While the majority of this book discusses trauma and its sequelae in the adult population, the application of clinical assessment and intervention on interoception and embodiment of children is the foundation upon which adult coping skills are built. It makes intuitive sense that interoception is something that can be developed across the life span, but not necessarily true that it is linear growth. Children may have much stronger and less mediated pathways between sensation and action, which may shift as awareness and the prefrontal cortex come online. New innovations for how to assess child interoception will be needed to identify indicators of atypical development potentially leading to maladaptive tendencies. Research is continuing to solidify our understanding of how interoception relates to emotional regulation in children (Schaan et al., 2019; Opdensteinen et al., 2021). Alexithymia as a proxy for atypical interoception could be a predictor of low social-emotional learning and can cause risky behavior in adolescents (Murphy et al., 2017).

People experiencing alexythymia and autism spectrum disorder have unique relationships with interoception that need further review. This is another place where clarity around the biomarkers and sensations of anxiety and an individual's interoceptive sensibility need to be clarified. As we noted before, with safe attention and regulation, increased interoceptive awareness can be harnessed for agency and health, but without autonomy, these signals may become overwhelming and dysregulating (Shah et al., 2016; DuBois et al., 2016). Clinicians will continue to tailor their interventions based on the assessments suggested above.

Interventions on Interoception

Many clinical interventions can be used to encourage clients to break free from daily schemas and sensory adaptation and instead engage in mindful awareness of internal or external stimuli. An example of this would be helping clients engage their default mode network, which is essentially the network that the brain engages when at idle rest without a specific task (Andrews-Hanna, 2012). The nuanced differences between focused meditation, idle mind wandering, dissociation, and social engagement are visible to the trained clinician and client and are starting to be studied through active fMRI studies (Weng et al., 2020).

Much of interoception happens below the surface of awareness, but contemplative practices can expand the reach of cognition to track these changes and ultimately have more agency (Weng et al., 2021).

Other methods to track and influence interoception are more physiologically targeted, such as vagus nerve stimulation (VNS). This is an FDA-approved method to treat depression, epilepsy, and chronic obesity, but requires invasive surgery and multiple hospital visits (Badran & Austelle, 2022). A more accessible intervention to target interoception is transcutaneous auricular vagus nerve stimulation (taVNS): "A non-invasive form of VNS which uses cutaneous or percutaneous electrodes to electrically stimulate the auricular branch of the vagus nerve at the ear" (Weng et al., 2021; Villani et al., 2019). Notably, the ear has been a target of healing interventions for millennia, well before being studied by Western medicine as a place for acupuncture, which may hold properties and pathways similar to taVNS (Hou et al., 2015).

Cynthia Price's mindful awareness in body-oriented therapy is a good example of a clinical method that specifically targets clients' interoception and ability to sustain sensory awareness. The core protocol includes verbal assessment of sensory and emotional baseline, massage with verbalization to stimulate body literacy, specific body awareness exercises such as sustained mindful attention without judgment, and increasing control and facility with breath variation and direction (Price et al., 2012, p. 456).

A clinical example: "The client is a 40-year-old woman with chronic low back pain and depressed mood. She naturally avoids and distracts herself from her pain as much as possible as a coping mechanism" (Price & Hooven, 2018, p. 6). This is not an uncommon start even for people who seek out body-oriented therapies. Chronic issues frequently dovetail with mood. And distraction is a valid and common way to deal with pain. After a 20-minute verbal check-in about how the pain is currently affecting her life, "the therapist asks the client to lie prone on the treatment table and places her hands around (one hand in back and one hand in front) the area of the client's low back, to provide the physical focus for the client's mindful attention" (p. 7). The goal here is to have the client bring her attention inside her torso. This is an important shift from surface-level proprioception to a deeper, internal sensing of the self: interoception. This is not easily done and requires the therapist's skills to track the client's presence using their visual attention to breath and hand sensitivity to warmth, blood flow, and movement in the area. The therapist keeps bringing the client back to the area of focus, assuming it's safe and the client is not in a retraumatization pattern. After minutes of staying present, the therapist asks what the client notices:

> The client is able to be present with her sensory experience in her back for many more minutes and as she does so, she feels her throat tighten and tears come to her eyes. The therapist asks what she is noticing, and she says "I just feel so sad." . . . The client explains that she is remembering her brother who died 2 years ago. "I've been trying my best to ignore my back pain and here I am remembering my brother and how much I miss him." (Price & Hooven, 2018, p. 7)

Key components of clinical usage of interoception in therapy in this instance include creating safety in the therapeutic relationship, training the client to maintain focus and attention inside their body, adding hands-on support for more feedback and therapist assessment of presence, staying with sensation, and soliciting verbalization with open-ended questions such as, "What are you noticing?" and then following and supporting the associations and emotions that arise. For more clinical examples, see Price and Hooven (2018), which explores the different stages of interoception that may describe where a client is starting.

Also consider the following example from a more talk-therapy-leaning somatic psychotherapy intervention: A client comes into a modern office, walking gingerly and holding tension in their gait, shoulders, and pelvis. After a few sessions, the therapist asks the client to describe their breath. "I don't know. It's shallow, I guess." The therapist continues to elicit more descriptors and encourages the client to stay present in the area where the sensations are centered that allow the client to make the assessment that it's shallow. At the next session, the client comes in breathing heavily from running to arrive, and after settling in, the therapist asks the client to lie down on the floor with their knees up. The therapist guides the client toward noticing how the different relationship with gravity affects their breath. The client notices and takes in this shift: "It feels more free and open." Then the therapist guides the client to experientially learn how to initiate the breath from the diaphragm, sense the three-dimensionality of the breath, and play around with deep and shallow breaths, eventually incorporating intercostal breathing as well. This psychoeducational process of interoception can help the client with agency and self-awareness and stimulate embodiment on a daily basis.

Conclusion

Interoception research is blossoming, and newfound understanding is transforming the way that we approach healing. Through physiological tracking, self-report measures, and clinical assessment, the state and trait aspects of interoception are becoming more clear. This helps clinicians address severe psychological distress as well as everyday experience. However, importantly, embodiment has to be adaptive to be healthy. With training and effective intervention, increased adaptive interoception can lead to positive changes in well-being. The increasing awareness of interoception provides hope that people will become more interconnected with each other and more present with themselves.

3

Clinical Application of Mindfulness-Oriented Meditation in Children and Adolescents With Attention-Deficit/Hyperactivity Disorder

Alessandra Pollazzon, Alessio Matiz, and Cristiano Crescentini

MINDFULNESS-ORIENTED MEDITATION (MOM) IS A SELF-REGULATORY TRAINING USED FOR attentional and behavioral problems. With its focus on attention and equanimity, MOM is a promising form of training that is gaining empirical support as a complementary intervention for attention-deficit/hyperactivity disorder (ADHD) in children and adolescents, eventually impacting positively also on family functioning. In this chapter, we provide a concise review of current state, future perspective, and limitations of applications of MOM interventions targeted at reducing ADHD core symptoms and possible ADHD-associated deficits or comorbidity (e.g., emotional dysregulation, anxiety, sleep problems, and possibly elevated spontaneous mind-wandering). The relationship between adverse childhood experiences and ADHD diagnosis and treatment is also discussed.

Mindfulness meditation (MM) is a practice that enables individuals to cultivate a heightened state of awareness by observing present-moment somatosensory and mental experiences. This may involve directing focus toward the breath, bodily sensations, or the ever-changing states of the mind (Fabbro & Muratori, 2012; Kabat-Zinn, 2003). Originating from Buddhist traditions, this practice has also been adopted in the West by Jon Kabat-Zinn, an American biologist who developed the Mindfulness-Based Stress Reduction (MBSR) protocol in the 1970s. This meditation training is specifically aimed at reducing stress and assisting patients in alleviating physical and/or mental suffering associated with different illnesses (Kabat-Zinn, 2003, 2019).

A team of researchers from the University of Udine has recently developed a program called mindfulness-oriented meditation training. The MOM protocol is based on the practices of meditation transmitted by the Buddha and on the teachings of the Chilean psychiatrist Claudio Naranjo Cohen. In particular, the final steps of the Buddha's Noble Eightfold Path emphasize mindfulness (and concentration) meditation techniques, which are incorporated into the MOM training. These practices are useful for nurturing self-awareness; staying rooted in the present moment, including grounding in the body; and reducing suffering (Fabbro, 2019; Fabbro et al., 2023; Mancuso, 2020).

This program is designed to be offered in a variety of settings, including hospitals, for both patients and health care staff, as well as nonclinical environments, like schools, for teachers and students (Fabbro & Crescentini, 2016, 2017; Fabbro & Muratori, 2012; Matiz et al., 2020). Similar to the structure of the MBSR protocol, MOM training typically involves a two-month course with weekly group sessions lasting about two hours. Each MOM session is typically organized in three phases, each lasting approximately 30–40 minutes: (1) a presentation of a theoretical topic related to meditation (e.g., what mindfulness is and is not, the ability to observe and stand in front of pain experiences, or what do concepts such as decentering, equanimity, and staying in the here-and-now mean); (2) a guided meditation, which includes 10 minutes of breath mindfulness practice, 10 minutes of body scan mindfulness meditation practice, and 10 minutes of observing-thought meditation practice; (3) a final sharing space for participants to discuss the experiences, thoughts, and feelings they have encountered during meditation practices in group and at home. Additionally, participants are encouraged to engage in daily meditation practice at home for about 30 minutes with an audio guide provided at the beginning of the course (Fabbro & Crescentini, 2016; Fabbro et al., 2023).

The meditation techniques taught in each session thus focus on cultivating mindfulness and attention toward the breath, bodily sensations, and the observation and monitoring of mental states (open-monitoring MM; Fabbro, 2019; Fabbro & Crescentini, 2016, 2017; Fabbro et al., 2023; Gunaratana, 1995). More specifically, in the breath mindfulness practice, participants are encouraged to focus their attention on the points in their nostrils where they feel the natural flow of air entering and leaving with each breath cycle. During the body scan practice, meditators are guided to shift their attention to individual body parts, starting from the lower extremities and moving upward to the top of the head, while observing the sensations that arise in the body with a nonjudgmental attitude. In the final part, which involves the observation and monitoring of mental states, meditators try to observe the flow of thoughts, emotions, and sensations that arise in the mind without reacting to these mental contents and without focusing on a specific meditation object. In all three meditative techniques, when distractions occur, practitioners are encouraged to recognize their distraction and refocus their attention on the task with a gentle and equanimous attitude (Fabbro et al., 2023).

The MOM protocol has been proposed for children with specific adjustments in duration and methods of meditation practice (Crescentini et al., 2016; Crescentini & Menghini, 2019; Fabbro & Muratori, 2012). Similar to the standard MOM protocol for adults, the program for children spans eight weeks; however, unlike the program for adults, the children's program includes three weekly sessions. Throughout the program, the duration of these sessions gradually increases, allowing for an increase in the time dedicated to formal meditation practice each week, starting from about 5 to 10 minutes in the initial sessions and reaching a total of approximately 30 minutes of practice in the final week of the course. Although the meditation techniques used in the children's program remain the same as those described earlier (e.g., awareness of breath, body, and mental states), they are presented in a more child-friendly manner. The aim is to make the meditative experience more tangible and relatable for children. For example, during the breathing cycle, a stuffed toy may be placed on the belly for children to observe its movement, or children may be encouraged to imagine the contents of their minds as soap bubbles, ocean waves, or passing clouds (Crescentini & Menghini, 2019; Matiz et al., 2023; Matiz & Paschetto, 2022). Furthermore, in recent MOM trainings for children, narrative support has also been incorporated to further engage children and facilitate their understanding and connection to the meditation practice (Crescentini & Menghini, 2019; Matiz et al., 2023; Matiz & Paschetto, 2022).

Since the emergence of various MM protocols, including the aforementioned MOM program, numerous scientific studies have been conducted to explore the positive effects of mindfulness meditation. These studies have particularly focused on attention regulation, body awareness, emotional regulation, and self-representation (Hölzel et al., 2011; Tang et al., 2015). These interconnected aspects are continually influenced by meditation practice, promoting improved self-regulation. Through increased attention regulation, individuals can enhance emotion regulation, resulting in a shift in self-perspective, reduced self-referential processing, and heightened body awareness.

Focusing specifically on the effects of meditation on the attentional system, attention regulation plays a central role in practice. It is indeed recommended for practitioners to develop attention regulation early on in order to fully engage in the practice itself (Hölzel et al., 2011). In general, during MM, practitioners engage the three attentional functions described by Michael Posner (alerting, orienting, and executive attention; Posner & Petersen, 1990): they cultivate the ability to focus and sustain attention on the object of focus, such as the breath, body sensations, or mental states; additionally, practitioners learn to gently redirect their attention back to the task when becoming aware of distraction (Malinowski, 2013; Posner & Petersen, 1990; Tang et al., 2015). According to the Liverpool Mindfulness Model (Malinowski, 2013), practicing this process of attentional self-regulation can lead to the development of greater cognitive and emotional flexibility. It also fosters a mental posture of equanimity toward the self. These cascading effects contribute to psychophysical and behavioral benefits.

Indeed, studies suggest that one mechanism through which MM can have a positive impact on individuals' cognitive and emotional functions is by reducing the negative influence of mind-wandering episodes, namely distracting thoughts unrelated to ongoing tasks or negative cognitions such as excessive worry and mental rumination (Feruglio et al., 2021).

Given the aforementioned framework, it is understandable why there is a growing interest in exploring the effects of MM on individuals diagnosed with ADHD. ADHD is a neurodevelopmental disorder characterized by symptoms of inattention and/or hyperactivity-impulsivity (American Psychiatric Association [APA], 2013). On the one hand, ADHD may entail significant deficits in focused and sustained attention, and heightened spontaneous mind wandering, as well as difficulties in impulse inhibition and in emotional and behavioral self-regulation (APA, 2013; see also Dekkers et al., 2023; Frick et al., 2020; Lanier et al., 2021). On the other hand, as shown above, MM may promote improved attentional regulation, nonreactivity, and nonjudgmental observation of present-moment experiences, and can yield positive effects on emotional regulation (Crescentini & Menghini, 2019; Hölzel et al., 2011; Smalley et al., 2009; Tang et al., 2015).

The prevalence of ADHD in the pediatric population is approximately 5%, while it is around 2.5% in adulthood, with a considerably higher incidence among males (APA, 2013). In order to diagnose this disorder, as per the *DSM-5*, at least six out of the nine symptoms concerning inattention and/or hyperactivity-impulsivity should be present for a minimum of six months, and these symptoms must manifest before the age of 12, significantly impairing functioning in at least two domains of life (APA, 2013). It has also been noted that ADHD significantly impacts the psychological well-being of children, increasing the risk of co-occurring psychiatric disorders such as depression, as well as affecting executive functions that can hinder academic progress (Crescentini & Menghini, 2019; Singh et al., 2015). Additionally, ADHD can impair the quality of social life, as relationships with peers are often limited and not always functional. Moreover, during adolescence and adulthood, ADHD is associated with an elevated risk of suicide, substance use disorders, mood disorders, conduct disorders, and challenges in academic and occupational domains (APA, 2013; Nigg, 2013).

Presently, pharmacological and psychoeducational therapies aimed at individuals with ADHD have demonstrated short-term benefits in symptom reduction. However, the evidence supporting their long-term efficacy is limited. Consequently, there is an increasing need for research focused on evidence-based interventions that can provide sustained advantages. In this regard, there has been a rise in studies investigating the relationship between mindfulness training and ADHD (e.g., Modesto-Lowe et al., 2015). In this chapter, we highlight recent and significant meta-analyses and literature reviews that explore the applications of mindfulness-based interventions in ADHD (Cairncross & Miller, 2020; Evans et al., 2018; Lee et al., 2022).

In the meta-analytic review by Cairncross and Miller (2020), involving analysis of self-report and observational data from 10 studies, MM trainings were determined to be effective in reducing ADHD symptoms associated with inattention and hyperactivity/impulsivity. More significant effects on inattention were observed in the adult population, while age did not significantly impact the outcomes concerning hyperactivity/impulsivity. However, the review also acknowledged limitations, including significant heterogeneity among the participants in the examined studies and a limited number of analyzed experiments.

In their systematic review, Evans et al. (2018) examined the effects of meditation-based interventions, such as MM and yoga, for children and adolescents with ADHD. Despite focusing on a relatively homogeneous participant group, the authors emphasized significant methodological limitations in the analyzed studies, which hindered drawing meaningful conclusions regarding the relationship between mindfulness and ADHD. Prominent limitations included the absence of control groups or nonrandom participant assignment. Nonetheless, the findings indicated that interventions incorporating yoga and/or mindfulness, particularly when involving both parents and children, yielded notable effects on children's ADHD symptoms, well-being, and internalizing/externalizing behavior. These results highlight the need for further research to investigate these types of interventions more extensively in the future.

In their systematic review and meta-analysis, Lee and colleagues (2022) sought to address the limitations identified in the previous reviews by exclusively including studies that incorporated control groups, participant randomization, and participants within the age range of 5–12 years (except two studies involving adolescents). The authors focused on MM and yoga training for children or for children and parents. They analyzed the effects of these trainings on ADHD symptoms, internalizing/externalizing behavioral problems, mindfulness levels, and parental stress levels. The findings revealed a reduction in ADHD symptomatology among children who underwent these trainings compared to the control groups. Moreover, the authors observed that the effects were more pronounced in older subjects. One possible explanation for this observation is that MM primarily enhances attention regulation, a component of ADHD that tends to become more compromised with age. It is also plausible that older children may better assimilate the practice or that the meditation techniques offered in the studies are more suitable for their developmental stage.

In summary, recent meta-analyses and literature reviews demonstrate the potential and significance of MM and/or yoga training as interventions for individuals with ADHD. However, further studies with more rigorous methodologies will contribute to a clearer understanding of the effectiveness and appropriate implementation of these interventions for individuals with ADHD.

Regarding the MOM protocol, a study focused on children and preadolescents aged 7–11 years with ADHD (Santonastaso et al., 2020), addressing some limitations of previous studies (see also Crescentini & Menghini, 2019). Participants were randomly assigned to either the MOM training group or an active control group, which received an Emotion Education Program (EEP) with the same duration and structure as the MOM training. Data collection involved neuropsychological measurements of attention and executive functions, as well as self-report questionnaires and parental evaluations. The study aimed to investigate the effects of MOM training on ADHD symptomatology, emotional and behavioral regulation, mindfulness levels, anxiety and depression symptoms, parental stress, and children's academic performance. The results indicated statistically significant changes in the neuropsychological measures only in the MOM group after the intervention. This suggests that the training may reduce ADHD-related deficits in attention and executive functions. Furthermore, the parental questionnaires also showed a reduction in behavioral symptoms after the intervention, indicating that MOM training positively influenced self-regulation, particularly in the attentional aspects.

A second study investigating the clinical application of MOM training aimed to explore the relationship between sleep disorders and ADHD (Zaccari et al., 2022). As previously mentioned, ADHD in children and adolescents often co-occurs with other conditions, such as sleep disorders, which can have an impact on their overall well-being (Singh et al., 2015). This study followed a structure similar to the previous one (Santonastaso et al., 2020), focusing on the same sample of children aged 7–11 years. The researchers specifically examined sleep quality and ADHD-related behavioral characteristics, including inattention, hyperactivity, and impulsivity. To gather data about sleep, both objective measures (actigraphy) and subjective measures (questionnaires completed by parents) were utilized. The results from the questionnaires revealed a significant improvement in sleep disturbances among participants in the MOM training group compared to the active control group. However, there was no significant variation in objective measurements of sleep from pre- to postintervention. The authors attributed this result to factors such as the young age and limited meditation experience of the participants, as well as the relatively short duration of the MOM training (eight weeks). On the other hand, the data reported on ADHD symptomatology and related behavioral disorders align with the findings of the meta-analyses described earlier. This suggests that MOM training can be beneficial for individuals with ADHD in terms of attentional regulation, for example. It is important to note that the latter study also had some limitations, including a limited number of subjects examined, unequal distribution between the MOM and active control groups, reliance on parent-completed questionnaires, and a limited number of nights measured using actigraphy.

However, we consider another reason regarding the possible usefulness of the applications of MM in ADHD. This concerns the relationship between ADHD and adverse childhood experiences (ACEs) on the one hand, and that between MM and ACEs on the other hand. In light of the potential bidirectional interaction between ADHD and ACEs, Lugo-Candelas et al. (2021) discussed literature proposing that ACEs can affect the development of ADHD. Furthermore, they presented data from their longitudinal study highlighting that ADHD, particularly the subtype characterized by a predominance of inattention, may increase the vulnerability to ACEs. The study observed that persistent attentional dysregulation over time, if not addressed, can lead to a cascade of negative consequences, including an increased likelihood of experiencing ACEs. Consequently, ACEs and ADHD appear to have a reciprocal influence, forming a vicious cycle that ultimately diminishes overall quality of life and socioemotional well-being (Lugo-Candelas et al., 2021). Indeed, both ADHD symptoms and adverse experiences in childhood negatively impact various aspects of a child's life, including relationships and academic performance (APA, 2013; Iacona & Johnson, 2018). From a related perspective, it is known that experiencing a trauma can cause chronic stress, resulting in neurobiological changes and negatively affecting overall health (Ortiz & Sibinga, 2017). Therefore, it is essential to consider prevention and regulation of exposure to ACEs in order to mitigate their negative effects. In this context, MM may be a valuable intervention to help children reduce their activation and reactive responses to traumatic stimuli, thus increasing their resilience to ACEs. Furthermore, introducing mindfulness-based interventions to parents (mindful parenting) of children with ADHD, as well as to the latter, could help them to alleviate their stress, improve their quality of care, and enhance their resilience in managing the disorder or the encountered ACEs (Evans et al., 2018; Ortiz & Sibinga, 2017).

In conclusion, mindfulness-oriented meditation appears to be a promising and significant intervention for children and adolescents with ADHD, promoting improved attentional and emotional regulation and fostering an attitude of nonreactivity and nonjudgmental observation of present-moment experience. Notably, mindfulness training may also benefit individuals who have encountered ACEs, as these experiences may correlate with the development of ADHD.

4

Bodily Self and Intersubjectivity Development After Childhood Trauma

Vittorio Gallese, Francesca Ferroni, and Martina Ardizzi

THE MATURATION OF THE HUMAN NERVOUS SYSTEM INTO ADULTHOOD NECESSITATES extended periods of exposure to environmental and social stimuli during early life. This gradual developmental trajectory facilitates the cultivation of sophisticated cognitive, social, and behavioral abilities in offspring. Nonetheless, the occurrence of adverse experiences also renders young individuals highly vulnerable to an array of far-reaching dysfunctions (Koss, 2019). Adverse experiences during early life can leave a profound and lasting imprint on the body's physiological systems. This phenomenon, often explored in the realms of psychology and neuroscience, underscores the intricate relationship between childhood trauma and physical health. This might manifest as heightened inflammation, alterations in immune function, disruptions in the autonomic nervous system, and even changes in the structure and functioning of the brain (Nemeroff, 2004; Maschi et al., 2013). Such physiological changes contribute to immediate distress and lead to a higher vulnerability to physical and mental health challenges later in life, including conditions like posttraumatic stress disorder (PTSD), anxiety, depression, cardiovascular issues, and autoimmune disorders (Lambert et al., 2017).

In recent years, altered multisensory integration mechanisms have been proposed among the neurophysiological mechanisms that might be responsible for some of the psychobiological consequences of early exposure to trauma. Multisensory integration is, indeed, the process by which the brain combines inputs from two or more senses to form a new holistic product that actually is the ongoing perception of ourselves and the outside world in interaction.

The central thesis of the present chapter is that early traumatic experiences can potentially derail the typical developmental course of multisensory integration processes resulting in damage of victims' basic sense of self and intersubjective abilities. In the following sections, we define and describe the process of multisensory integration and then review a series of research linking multisensory integration deficit and trauma in the attempt to provide a comprehensive neurobiological framework to account for altered sensory processing among traumatized individuals.

The Dynamic Nature of Multisensory Integration: Principles, Plasticity, and Developmental Implications

Multisensory integration is a captivating area of research that delves into the intricate mechanisms underlying the brain's ability to combine inputs from various sensory modalities, creating a cohesive perception of the world and scaffolding higher human capacities (Stein et al., 2020). In recent years, our understanding of multisensory processing has grown significantly, shedding light on the complex ways in which the brain seamlessly integrates information from different senses, shaping our perception, cognition, and interaction with others and the environment. The brain's capacity to merge inputs from sight, sound, touch, taste, and smell is far from a straightforward summation of individual sensory signals. Instead, it involves intricate neural pathways and processing mechanisms that allow the brain to enhance perception, improve accuracy, and even facilitate learning through cross-modal interactions (i.e., a facilitatory processing effect of one sensory modality on another). At the heart of multisensory integration lie several key principles that illuminate the brain's remarkable capacity to synthesize information from diverse sensory channels. First, the principle of temporal and spatial congruency highlights that inputs arriving simultaneously and from nearby sources are more likely to be combined into a unified percept. Second, the principle of inverse effectiveness suggests that multisensory integration is most potent when individual sensory signals are weak, emphasizing the brain's drive to enhance perception under challenging conditions. These principles collectively illuminate the complexity of multisensory integration, offering insights into how our perception of the world emerges from the harmonious interplay of our senses.

Although evidence supports the presence of multisensory integration processes as early as after birth (Ronga et al., 2021), today it is no less clear that these processes and their principles are extremely permeable to experience. The plasticity of multisensory integration processes stands as a testament to the remarkable adaptability of the human brain. This phenomenon highlights the brain's capacity to rewire and reconfigure its neural pathways in response to changing sensory inputs and environmental demands. Research has shown that multisensory integration is not a fixed, rigid process but rather a dynamic and malleable one that requires a long journey to achieve an adult-like form (Hillock-Dunn & Wallace, 2012; de Klerk et al., 2021). Furthermore, even after reaching maturity, specific training may result in short-term changes in integration processes. Whether through sensory deprivation, cross-modal training, or rehabilitation interventions, the brain can demonstrate remarkable plasticity in reshaping its multisensory integration mechanisms (Ferroni et al., 2020; Bassolino et al., 2015; Powers et al., 2009; Stevenson et al., 2013). This adaptability underscores the brain's innate ability to optimize behavior and perception by harnessing the synergy between different sensory modalities in the service of action, offering a deeper understanding of how our perceptions of the world are intricately shaped and refined over time to optimize our active openness to the world.

It is this extraordinary plasticity and long developmental window of multisensory integration processes that has attracted the attention of scholars interested in the psychobiological consequences of early trauma. Such plasticity, while adaptive under normal conditions, is at the same time susceptible to consistent deviations when life events and their consequent sensory stimuli are adverse or even traumatic. It is also worth noting that multisensory integration plasticity extends beyond sensory processing, potentially influencing the development of a cohesive sense of self and intersubjective skills. Indeed, multisensory integration acts as a cornerstone, shaping the intricate architecture of higher cognitive functions, such as memory, spatial navigation, empathy, language understanding, and contributing to the multifaceted nature of human behavior and cognition (e.g., Wallace & Stevenson, 2014; Blanke, 2012; Stein et al., 2020).

The Multifaceted Construct of Self: From Development to Trauma Effects on Multisensory Integration

Of the many relationships with the world that we exercise, the most important ones are those in which we relate to other human beings. We are not monads who later learn to live with and relate to others, but from the very beginning of our lives, starting with fetal development, we are programmed to be intersubjective (Castiello et al., 2010). Our neotenic nature, that is, our prolonged postnatal somatic and brain development, amplifies the effect of the social and cultural environment on central nervous system development. Neoteny amplifies and prolongs learning processes and enhances family relationships. Stronger family relationships enhance the ability to transfer knowledge between generations, helping to build traditions that, in turn, promote cultural practices (Gallese, 2017).

The sense of self represents a multifaceted construct that arises from the complex interactions between various brain regions and cognitive processes (Tsakiris, 2017). The concept of the sense of self encompasses a foundational aspect of human self-experience known as the basic sense of self or bodily self (Gallese, 2000; Gallese & Sinigaglia, 2010, 2011). This primary level, totally immediate and prereflective, involves the brain's ability to distinguish between oneself and the external world. It encompasses various dimensions, including the experience of owning a body (body ownership); the experience of being a body with a given location within our environment (self-location); and the experience of taking a first-person, body-centered perspective on that environment (perspective) (Gallese & Sinigaglia, 2010, 2011; Serino et al., 2013; Blanke, 2012). The basic self is rooted in the integration of internal and external body afferent signals, allowing individuals to perceive themselves as distinct from their environment and to engage in purposeful actions (Ferroni & Gallese, 2022).

Sensory and motor systems are multimodal and fully integrated, responding to and processing information associated with multiple modalities. The body's interactions with the external world, including interactions with other living bodies, are actually multimodal. Indeed, action performance contains motor components as well as various perceptual contents, like vision (what does the action look like, what are the visuospatial characteristics of the objects we interact with), sounds (what kind of sound accompanies a particular action), somatic sensations (body-object interaction, proprioception), and localization in space.

Starting from prenatal stages, infants begin to develop a basic sense of their own bodies through correlated multisensory experiences gained while they actively engage with and manipulate their bodies (de Klerk et al., 2021; Gallese, 2024). Whether it's interacting with the uterine wall, reaching for objects, crawling, or exploring their own face with their hands, these experiences create multisensory connections. Through the constant coupling between motor commands and the ensuing sensory signals, a predictive functional architecture is built. These sensory-motor connections, in turn, assist the infant in continually updating the demarcation between their own body and the external environment, thereby improving the precision of their body representations. Although a critical or sensitive window of development of this experience has not yet been identified, scholars seem to agree in pointing to a long process of maturation and maintenance of plastic porosity of multisensory integration mechanisms in favor of the construction of a bodily self (de Klerk et al., 2021). During this long-lasting developmental period, if the infant can gather adequate sensory experiences, the formation of the basic sense of self will be successful. This enables the child to establish distinct personal boundaries and remain adaptable in modifying them in response to various environmental demands or developmental shifts. However, being exposed to unexpected stimulation at a critical developmental stage may alter the proper achievement of that developmental milestone. Adverse or traumatic events can be described as a violation of the expected environment; that is, experiences that are expected do not occur (e.g., lack of caregiving; lack of nutrition) or are atypical in some way (e.g., physical abuse) (Nelson & Gabard-Durnam, 2020). A growing body of evidence supports the idea that early exposure to trauma can lead to modifications in the multisensory integration processes essential for the healthy development of a basic sense of self.

In one study, the spatial and temporal principles of multisensory integration for bodily self were tested in adolescents exposed to severe neglect in childhood (Ardizzi et al., 2024). The authors specifically measured the temporal and spatial ranges within which body-related multisensory signals were effectively integrated. The results demonstrated that, compared to controls, youths exposed to neglect showed a wider temporal window and a narrower spatial range for multisensory integration. Interestingly, the more the multisensory integration process was altered in its spatial and temporal principles, the more traumatic and obsessive symptomatology was present in the experimental population. These results are coherent with the findings of Rabellino and collaborators (2018), who investigated the sense of body ownership in adult patients suffering from PTSD through the manipulation of multisensory integration processes via the rubber hand illusion paradigm (Botvinick & Cohen, 1998). The authors demonstrated that people affected by PTSD were less susceptible to the illusion during synchronous stimulation, showing maintenance of a rigid body representation with respect to healthy controls. Differently, the patients who reported dissociative symptoms along with PTSD diagnosis had a more volatile response to the illusion, showing a deep perturbation of the processes devoted to the integration of sensory feedback for the maintenance of a coherent sense of bodily self.

Taken together, these results reinforce the hypothesis that the sequelae of traumatic experiences would largely extend below the psychological domain, reaching the sensory one with effects on the construction and maintenance of a coherent basic sense of self.

This perspective is further addressed by an elegant paper by Harricharan and colleagues (2021) describing a comprehensive neurobiological framework to account for the altered processing of sensory information from the internal and external world in the aftermath of trauma. The authors stressed that the bodily self, placed at the apex of the hierarchy of sensory processing, emerges from an effective integration of interoceptive and exteroceptive sensations, which collapse after trauma exposure. Indeed, extensive literature proves that people suffering from PTSD show specific functional and anatomical deficits in cortical (i.e., dorsolateral prefrontal cortex, insular cortex, posterior parietal lobe) and subcortical regions (i.e., vestibular nuclei, locus coeruleus, thalamus) feeding the inferential and predictive processes supporting multisensory integration for the development of the bodily self.

The Impact of Childhood Trauma on Multisensory Integration, Facial Expression Recognition, and Intersubjectivity

Multisensory integration is critical for understanding and interpreting incoming sensory information from multiple modalities and putting it to the service of action, and ultimately provides context to a sensory experience that shapes one's own embodied representation of the self but also of the self in relation to one's surroundings, including other people. Indeed, multisensory integration plays a pivotal role in the intricate process of intersubjectivity, which refers to our ability to understand and relate to others. Through the integration of sensory cues from various sources, we gain a richer and more nuanced understanding of the people around us. This sensory synergy enables us to decipher nonverbal cues, such as body language and facial expressions, facilitating empathy, social bonding, and effective communication. For example, when someone smiles while speaking in a cheerful tone, the combination of visual and auditory cues reinforces the perception of happiness. This multisensory synergy not only improves the accuracy of emotion recognition but also enables us to gauge emotional nuances that might be missed when relying on a single sensory modality (Lewkowicz & Ghazanfar, 2009). As a result, the harmonious syncing of auditory and visual cues in facial expressions plays a pivotal role in our ability to connect with others at the emotional level and navigate the intricate landscape of social interactions. The bulk of studies suggest that these human perceptual functions undergo developmental narrowing in early life and that this is crucial for the effective development of species-specific patterns of perceptual expertise in speech and face perception (Lewkowicz & Ghazanfar, 2009). For example, infants can discriminate and recognize speech sounds from a wide range of languages. However, as they grow and are exposed to their native language, their perceptual abilities become more finely tuned to the specific phonetic features of that language (Lewkowicz, 2014). This narrowing process enhances their proficiency in understanding their native language. In the context of perceptual narrowing in speech perception, studies involving the McGurk illusion have provided valuable insights. The McGurk illusion (McGurk & MacDonald, 1976) is a perceptual phenomenon where auditory speech information and visual lip movements conflict, leading to a fused perceptual experience that often aligns with the visual input. Research has shown that infants initially exhibit a broader capacity to integrate auditory and visual speech cues, which can result in susceptibility to the McGurk illusion. However, as they age and their language exposure becomes more focused on their native tongue, their susceptibility to the illusion diminishes (Lewkowicz, 2014). These findings underscore how perceptual narrowing in speech perception is not limited to auditory input alone but extends to the integration of auditory and visual cues, highlighting the brain's plasticity in shaping speech perception through multisensory integration during early development. Perceptual narrowing also applies to face perception, illustrating the brain's adaptability to early experiences. In infancy, toddlers are remarkably attuned to a wide range of facial features and expressions across different ethnicities and species. However, as they grow and their social environment becomes more culturally specific, their facial recognition abilities often become more tuned to the faces they encounter most frequently. This narrowing of perceptual sensitivity can sometimes result in reduced ability to distinguish and process facial characteristics that are less common in their immediate surroundings or belonging to different animal species (Lewkowicz & Ghazanfar, 2009). Being exposed in early life to threatening interpersonal stimulation might impact the typical development of multisensory integration processes for intersubjectivity.

Indeed, early adverse experiences can significantly affect an individual's ability to accurately perceive and interpret facial emotions. Children exposed to early adversity, such as neglect or abuse, often face challenges in recognizing and understanding facial expressions. Specifically, studies converge in describing a bias toward the recognition of angry faces, which indicates that individuals with a history of early adversity often exhibit a heightened sensitivity to and a bias for recognizing expressions of anger in others when they display different emotions. Research in this field has shown that children and adolescents who have experienced neglect or abuse during their early years tend to be more vigilant and attuned to potential threats in their social environment (Ardizzi et al., 2013, 2015, 2016, 2017; Masten et al., 2008; Scrimin et al., 2009). This heightened vigilance can manifest as a bias toward recognizing angry facial expressions more readily and relying less on sensory cues than on other emotions. These difficulties may persist into adulthood and can have implications for their social and emotional functioning, contributing to problems in forming relationships and regulating their own emotions.

Basic forms of intersubjectivity emerge also from the synchronization and tuning of visceromotor responses to social stimulation coming from the environment. In a series of studies conducted on children and adolescents exposed to severe forms of neglect, it has been demonstrated that such experiences suppress natural facial mimicry responses to emotions and alter the consistent vagal regulation of the victims (Ardizzi et al., 2013, 2016). On the one hand, facial mimicry is the automatic, unconscious, and congruent facial muscular activation in response to another person's facial expressions. Facial mimicry emerges from the integration of visual signal and motor outputs and facilitates emotion recognition, empathy, and social bonding. On the other hand, vagal regulation, often assessed through respiratory sinus arrhythmia (RSA), refers to the influence of the vagus nerve (the 10th cranial nerve) on heart rate variability during respiration. RSA is a natural fluctuation in heart rate that occurs with breathing, specifically a speeding up of the heart rate during inhalation and a slowing down during exhalation. This phenomenon is under the control of the parasympathetic nervous system, primarily the vagus nerve. Vagal regulation, as measured by RSA, provides a window into the body's ability to regulate and adapt its physiological responses to various situations (Porges, 2023). Higher RSA indicates greater parasympathetic activity and better autonomic nervous system flexibility, allowing for efficient responses to stress, emotional regulation, and overall cardiovascular health. Lower RSA, on the other hand, can be associated with reduced vagal regulation and may be linked to stress-related conditions and reduced emotional resilience.

In children and adolescents exposed to severe forms of neglect, besides a valuable deficit in explicit facial expression recognition, the authors showed flat facial mimicry responses to negative facial expressions and an ineffective suppression of RSA in response to nonthreatening emotions (Ardizzi et al., 2013, 2016). These studies reveal that childhood trauma penetrates under victims' skin and becomes physiologically embedded, altering the power that the body wields as the primary promoter of intersubjectivity. In a cohort study examining a youth population aged 4 to 18 years exposed to chronic forms of neglect, victims' natural patterns of resilience, deterioration, and chronicity have been revealed (Ardizzi et al., 2024). This diachronic look at the pathological consequences of neglect shows that: (1) the duration of maltreatment prevents the natural increase in emotion recognition skills; (2) anger recognition bias is not affected by the duration of maltreatment; and (3) the duration of maltreatment induces a progressive reduction in congruent facial expressions in response to negative emotions like anger and sadness. Chronic neglect affects more and more negatively victims' implicit empathic resonance ability, jeopardizing their ability to bodily simulate others' affective states. (4) Chronically living in contexts of neglect dissolves the activity of the myelinated vagal pathways, locking victims in a physiological state supporting defensive strategies and promoted by the sympathetic nervous system. Interestingly, the chronic neglect effect on RSA at rest follows a different trajectory. Indeed, the response to a constantly neglecting environment initially—during the first six years of exposure—involves an increasing physiological compensation that begins to decrease over time, turning into a progressive vagal withdrawal. Early therapeutic intervention is not only necessary but probably more effective (Ardizzi et al., 2024).

These findings highlight a long-term pattern of adaptation to chronic neglect in which the initial compensatory recruitment of the vagal system is, in the long term, suppressed to limit the social receptiveness typically conveyed by an active parasympathetic nervous system, as it could have potentially dangerous results in a permanently hostile environment (Holochwost et al., 2021).

Conclusion

Incorporating multisensory processing for bodily self and intersubjectivity into the lens through which we study childhood trauma would be critical to better understand some of the clinical sequelae frequently associated with such experiences (e.g., dissociative phenomena, interpersonal deficits, temporospatial distortions). The investigation of how sensations stemming from traumatized individuals' internal and external worlds are translated into the nervous system is paramount for understanding the neural pathways underlying embodiment, the agency to interact with others, and emotion regulation processes.

At the same time, the plasticity of multisensory integration processes following childhood trauma unveils the brain's astonishing ability to undergo adaptive changes even in the face of adversity.

While traumatic experiences during early life can disrupt the natural course of sensory development, research suggests that the brain retains a degree of plasticity that can be harnessed for healing and recovery. Studies indicate that therapeutic interventions and targeted sensory experiences can promote the rewiring of neural circuits involved in multisensory integration, offering potential pathways to mitigate the effects of trauma. By understanding and harnessing the brain's capacity for change, researchers and clinicians can work toward empowering individuals who have experienced childhood trauma to recalibrate their multisensory integration processes, thereby facilitating resilience and restoration in the aftermath of adversity.

Acknowledgment

This work was funded by the PRIN grant 2022NSWYK4 WOMBWISE and by the Ministry of University and Research (MUR), National Recovery and Resilience Plan (NRRP) Project MNESYS (PE00000006)—A Multiscale integrated approach to the study of the nervous system in health and disease (DN 1533 11.10. 2022) to V.G.

5

Love as Embodied Medicine

The Oxytocin Hypothesis

C. Sue Carter

THE FUNCTIONS AND PROPERTIES OF THE OXYTOCIN-VASOPRESSIN SYSTEM ALLOWED human evolution and play a major role in what humans experience as the healing power of love. Oxytocin is a peptide molecule with effects on both behavior and physiology. Historically, oxytocin was viewed as a reproductive hormone of major importance in birth, lactation, and maternal behavior. But it is now known that oxytocin is much more. Oxytocin also supports a sense of safety and helps to explain the capacity of social support and the experience of loving relationships to facilitate survival in response to both physical and emotional stressors, a process that we are calling *sociostasis*. Oxytocin can be released during acute stress but is of particular importance during chronic stress, and is part of a system that protects against threat and ameliorates trauma. In mammals, oxytocin functions in conjunction with a more primitive peptide, vasopressin. Vasopressin is a central component of the stress response, especially during repeated or chronic stress. Vasopressin and oxytocin have different, sometimes opposite consequences for behavior. In general, oxytocin facilitates sociality while vasopressin supports more individualistic survival strategies. These small molecules act on every cell and organelle in the body, interacting with the major chemistry necessary for health, and with complex consequences that are only now being discovered.

Healthy relationships can protect against disease and restore the body in the face of illness. Without positive relationships, especially in early life, humans fail to flourish, even if all of their basic biological needs are met. "Love lost" and betrayal of trust are among the most powerful forms of stress and trauma. Here I am using the word *love* as a metaphor for secure social bonds, social support, and trusting relationships. The combined effects of love and the biology that supports love allow social relationships to protect against disease, threat, and danger. The mechanisms through which love protects and heals are only now becoming apparent, but embedded in this biology of love are somatic secrets to healthy development and longevity (Carter et al., 2020; Horn & Carter, 2021).

The benefits of love and safety are most easily understood through the lens of our evolutionary past and in light of our contemporary ontogeny and physiology. I suggest here that at the epicenter of this story is a mammalian neuropeptide, oxytocin, and an even more ancient molecule, known as vasopressin (Carter, 2023). One molecule—oxytocin—sits at the center of a complex web of neural and biological systems that allowed social mammals, including humans, to have the capacity to form trusting and secure attachments. The biochemical building blocks of love are not unique to humans and are shared with other highly social species (Carter, 2022). Through the study of social behavior in other mammals, we are learning that the same physiology, including oxytocin, that lies behind the healing power of love reduces inflammation, modulates the autonomic nervous system and the immune system, and even influences the microbiome.

Furthermore, the oxytocin-vasopressin system is epigenetically regulated by experience across the life span, helping to explain the lasting physical consequences of early nurture for both love and adversity. By examining the biology of social bonds and early experience, we are uncovering pathways that allow humans to experience and embody love.

A Personal Journey and the Prairie Vole

For as long as I can recall, I have been mesmerized by this set of curious puzzles. What is love? How does "love cast out fear" and how does love heal? This gradually became my life's work as I trained to become a scientist (Carter, 2022, 2023). I was guided on this path by a series of events, the most relevant of which were probably the coincidence of living in that strange vessel known as the female body, with the capacity to fall in love, and eventually the experience of motherhood. Each of these experiences left me with more questions than answers, a few of which I share here.

Insight into the mechanisms through which love protects and restores requires awareness of mammalian evolution and neurobiology. The new science of love allows us to say that the causes and consequences of love—or its absence—are grounded in an ancient biology that operates largely below the level of human consciousness (Carter et al., 2020). To bring these questions into scientific focus required uncovering a kind of organic Rosetta Stone. We needed to find another creature that shared with humans the capacity for something that resembled love, grounded in the capacity to form lasting and secure relationships.

Remarkably, the origins of much of our current understanding of the science described here began in studies conducted in a small field mouse known as the prairie vole. Decades ago my colleagues and I uncovered evidence that both in nature and in the laboratory, prairie voles were capable of forming lifelong pair bonds—living together until one or both members of the pair died. Prairie voles lived together until "death them parted," and they shared with humans several other features of a human family (Carter et al., 1995).

In prairie voles, both parents care for the young, with fathers carrying out all aspects of infant care except nursing. Older siblings also babysat for younger siblings. Juvenile prairie voles moved out of the family to find mates and scrupulously avoided incest. Prairie voles exhibited the traits that humans associated with extended families, constructed around an apparently monogamous pair.

But we soon discovered that monogamy in voles, as in humans, can be a paradox (Carter & Perkeybile, 2018). In the 1980s, in the early days of our studies, DNA fingerprints became possible. Like a bad outcome on a TV reality show, DNA revealed that prairie voles were having sex outside of the pair bond. Monogamy, or at least the traits associated with monogamy, was real, and it was based in biology. However, monogamy was not simply about sexual exclusivity. In fact, sexual preferences were not the defining feature of monogamy. We did find that sexual interactions could facilitate pair bonding. But at the core of the prairie vole family were invisible social bonds, and what we were observing was more accurately called social monogamy. I came of age in a romantic era, and this part of the prairie vole story initially was a disappointment to me. But awareness that selective social behaviors were the central feature of social monogamy, and apparently more important than sexual monogamy, also opened avenues to understanding the physiological basis of social attachments or pair bonds.

The Biology of Love

Over the decades that followed, we, and then many others, conducted experiments showing that the capacity for pair bond formation was regulated by emotional states, which depended on physiology. Nature is conservative, and reuses neural and endocrine systems. We now know that the neurobiology of pair bonding in voles indeed had parallels with what humans call love (Carter, 2022). We also found that prairie voles, like humans, had high levels of oxytocin—as much as four times more than other laboratory rodents. Prairie voles also had heart rate patterns similar to those found in humans. The parasympathetic branch of the autonomic nervous system is regulated in part by oxytocin, and both are associated with the capacity to sustain safe relationships (Porges, 2021b). Prairie voles also were exquisitely sensitive to the effects of early nurture, another process that required oxytocin. The basic neurobiology of social bonding was centered around oxytocin and shared by humans and prairie voles (Carter & Porges, 2013; Grippo et al., 2007). Through good luck and with help from many brilliant collaborators, we had stumbled upon a rodent model that allowed us to examine the chemistry of love.

As these stories became public, oxytocin was termed by the media "the hormone of love." It certainly would be easier to understand the neurobiology of attachment if oxytocin acted alone. Of course, that is not the case. Many molecules and neural systems work behind the scenes to support the formation of social bonds (Carter, 2022). We were able to show that among the other factors essential for selective social attachments was a second ancient molecule known as vasopressin (Winslow et al., 1993). Neurotransmitters, including dopamine, GABA, and serotonin also support positive social experiences (Gobrogge & Wang, 2016).

Bonding in voles, as in humans, also occurred in the context of other physiological processes, including those associated with a sense of safety or fear. These are basic and very old emotions, and the story of love has biochemical origins long before the existence of humans or even primitive mammals (Carter, 2014).

The Evolution of Love Began Over 600 Million Years Ago

Oxytocin and its sibling hormone, vasopressin, began to appear over 600 million years ago, originating from an ancestral peptide that probably helped animals successfully move from the sea to life on dry land. Oxytocin and vasopressin are similar in structure and interact dynamically with each other's receptors (Theofanopoulou, 2021).

However, peptide molecules, like oxytocin and vasopressin, are particularly difficult to study. They have sticky sulfur chemical bonds that make them hard to accurately assay (MacLean et al., 2019). Furthermore, the actions of oxytocin and vasopressin are quickly changing, adaptive, and also strongly affected by emotional context and the history of the individual. Under conditions of safety, oxytocin promotes social engagement. For example, in a context of anxiety or fear, it is possible that oxytocin functions more like vasopressin, possibly by binding to and stimulating vasopressin receptors (Carter, 2017).

Although oxytocin and vasopressin were derived from a common ancestor, their general physiological functions are strikingly different. Vasopressin is at least 100 million years older than oxytocin and has more primitive functions (Grinevich & Ludwig, 2021; Theofanopoulou, 2021). Vasopressin is strongly associated with adaptive functions that protect against dehydration, regulate blood pressure, and increase reactivity to other threats. Vasopressin is associated with the neurobiology of anxiety, fear, and avoidance learning. Vasopressin and its receptors are foundational to aggression. Both males and females synthesize vasopressin. However, in areas of the brain implicated in defensiveness, vasopressin production is increased by androgens, which helps to explain sex differences in the expression of aggression. Vasopressin and its receptors are found in brain areas that regulate defense and aggression and may have especially important consequences in male behavior (Carter & Perkeybile, 2018).

The same novel properties that give oxytocin and vasopressin great power also create serious challenges for understanding their functions. The oxytocin-vasopressin system is constantly changing across the life cycle. Oxytocin can directly affect the development of the brain and cardiovascular system, and programs the immune system. Receiving love in early life can influence behavior and physiology across the life span, in part through changes in the receptors for oxytocin and vasopressin (Perkeybile et al., 2019; Perkeybile & Bales, 2017). As one example, my colleagues and I have demonstrated that the genes for the oxytocin receptor in voles are epigenetically tuned by early experience. In the presence of sensitive parenting, the genes in a baby vole that regulate the oxytocin receptor are more likely to be available for stimulation, and these changes can last a lifetime and possibly be transmitted to future generations (Perkeybile et al., 2019).

Parenthood: The Biological Prototype for Love

The evolutionary and biochemical prototype for love and social bonds is the mother-child interaction (Carter & Porges, 2011, 2013). Processes that help to define mammals, including lactation and parental care of their young, are facilitated by oxytocin. The same physiological pathways that permit social bonds are shared with parental behavior, birth, and lactation. Oxytocin is generally associated with positive social behaviors, including social engagement and bonding. Oxytocin also may induce a sense of safety, reduce reactivity to stressors, block fear, and increase trust. But even in maternal behavior, oxytocin does not work alone.

Vasopressin also is important to normal birth, parenting, and care of the young. Vasopressin can increase protective behaviors and aggression, which in some cases benefits the family. Although generally directed toward intruders, the emotional states that lead to aggression may escalate and spill over into violence within the family. Vasopressin is made primarily in the brain and is a classic stress hormone, with receptors in the cardiovascular system, in the kidneys, and throughout the body. Vasopressin, in conjunction with other major neurotransmitters and the autonomic nervous system, supports the capacity for flight/fight reactions (Porges, 2021a).

States of chronic arousal or stress are especially dangerous. Medical disorders such as preeclampsia, in which pregnant women retain water, have high blood pressure, and sometimes premature labor, have been linked to excessive emotional stress and to vasopressin. Furthermore, understanding fear- or stress-induced release of vasopressin or hypersensitivity of the vasopressin receptors may help to explain premature birth—among the world's most serious medical mysteries (Arrowsmith & Wray, 2014; Buckley et al., 2023).

Due to its primitive characteristics, vasopressin can be a double-edged sword. Generally, oxytocin tempers fear and increases both trust and social behavior. But in individuals who have a history of neglect, trauma, or extreme stress, oxytocin's actions may paradoxically trigger the vasopressin system, enhancing fear and protective responses (Carter, 2017). The unique properties of the oxytocin and vasopressin systems allow these two molecules to be highly adaptive and to dynamically support individual survival, as well as emotions that are associated with love. However, stimulating the vasopressin receptors may induce the dark side of love, including jealousy, territoriality, and aggression.

The Healing Power of Love and Trust

Good relationships are powerful medicine, with health benefits that are recognized throughout most cultures and across species (Horn & Carter, 2021). Epidemiological studies searching for secrets to longevity showed that individuals, especially men, living in psychological isolation were more likely to die after a heart attack than those with companions. After the death of a partner, especially in the elderly, the second member of the pair may become vulnerable to disease. Correlational studies such as these do not prove that oxytocin is the magic that explains social support. However, oxytocin does facilitate social engagement and under some conditions can increase a psychological sense of safety. Oxytocin contributes to the cardioprotective effects of the autonomic nervous system, especially via the regulation of vagal pathways within the parasympathetic nervous system. This integrated system allows a dynamic balance between growth and restoration, while enabling the body to respond quickly and adaptively to acute stress.

Experimental studies support the importance of oxytocin in the cardiovascular systems (Gutkowska & Jankowski, 2012). Mice that are genetically deficient in oxytocin develop abnormal hearts. Oxytocin is part of the mechanism guiding normal heart development. In tissue culture (and thus even in the absence of a central nervous system) oxytocin acts on undifferentiated stem cells, transforming these cells into clusters of miniature hearts beating in synchrony. Furthermore, in laboratory models of atherosclerotic plaques, oxytocin reduces inflammation (Carter & Kingsbury, 2022). Through processes such as these, oxytocin might be able to prevent or even reverse the effects of heart disease, with some of the benefits occurring locally at the site of damage.

Many other beneficial practices are associated with oxytocin. For example, exercise is one of the most reliable ways to both protect against disease and release oxytocin (de Jong et al., 2015). Oxytocin in turn helps to restore heart rate and blood pressure to normal, with potential benefits for the cardiovascular system. Heart disease is only one of many disorders that may benefit from the healing power of both exercise and oxytocin. It has been shown in animal models that exercise is beneficial in slowing the growth of breast cancer. Remarkably, animal studies suggest that this effect of exercise also is mediated by oxytocin and vasopressin (Kenkel & Carter, 2016). The growth of ovarian cancer also may be moderated by oxytocin, helping to explain the importance of psychological and social factors in the progression of this often deadly disease (Cuneo et al., 2021).

Oxytocin is a central component of the immune system (Carter & Kingsbury, 2022). The thymus is a source of oxytocin, and expressed in the thymus is an abundance of oxytocin receptors. Early experiences educate the immune system through functions that require the presence of oxytocin (Geenen et al., 1996). In a group of volunteers deliberately exposed to a treatment that causes inflammation, a concurrent exposure to oxytocin blocked symptoms such as fever. The capacity of oxytocin to reduce inflammation also is likely to be a factor in the beneficial effects of this molecule. But before we become excited about oxytocin as a wonder drug, the full picture that is emerging from this literature needs to be considered.

Biochemical Magic Beneath the Power of Love?

Oxytocin was essential to human evolution and the development of the massive human cortex (Carter, 2014). Even in modern humans, oxytocin continues to facilitate the birth, growth, and nurture of babies. Oxytocin helps, directly and indirectly, to promote healing and restoration (Gouin et al., 2010; Carter et al., 2020). For example, oxytocin has anti-inflammatory properties. Oxytocin also is involved in the regulation of the immune system and the generally protective vagal branch of the autonomic nervous system. Vagal pathways, modulated in part by oxytocin, are necessary for social communication and engagement through actions on the muscles of the face and head. Oxytocin is secreted in the presence of extreme stressors. Oxytocin receptors are especially abundant in the more ancient dorsal motor nucleus of the vagus and may protect against shutdown responses to trauma. Furthermore, the autonomic nervous system regulates all of our internal organs, as well as the distribution of blood and nutrients throughout the body. Through effects on the autonomic nervous system, oxytocin supports oxygenation of the brain, in turn facilitating human cognition, and eventually culture and civilization. The autonomic nervous system is one portal through which the peptide systems and a sense of safety may be accessed and influenced. Thus, it can be argued that oxytocin's actions on the autonomic nervous system are critical components of the healing power of love.

Does Oxytocin Have a Dark Side?

As explained in detail elsewhere, the complexity underlying the biology of oxytocin makes it difficult to use this hormone as a pharmaceutical agent or drug. Oxytocin is part of "Nature's medicine" (Carter et al., 2020), but it cannot substitute for trust, safety, or nurture in early life. Attempts to use oxytocin as a "love drug" have generally not been successful (De Dreu et al., 2021), possibly because of its ancient relationship with vasopressin. In fact, giving oxytocin as a drug to some people (possibly those with a history of adversity) may trigger anxiety or even defensive behaviors. One of the most perplexing unresolved mysteries associated with oxytocin is its role in cancer. A number of studies link social support and other methods for reducing stress to reductions in cancer. Studies of certain breast cancer cell lines and ovarian cancer suggest that oxytocin can inhibit tumor growth (Cuneo et al., 2021). However, under other conditions (at present not well identified), oxytocin appears to increase cellular proliferation and may stimulate the growth of cancers (Lerman et al., 2018). The strongest evidence for the capacity of oxytocin to increase the growth of malignant and nonmalignant tissue comes from studies of cells from the prostate. The conditions under which oxytocin is protective (or alternatively promoting the proliferation of cancers) may depend on its relationship to an individual's history of adversity. In addition, the type of subcellular processes that are stimulated have been implicated in oxytocin's capacity to increase malignancies.

The pathways for negative effects of oxytocin, especially on processes that might cause tumor growth, are not well identified. Furthermore, it is likely that large doses of oxytocin and chronic exposure to it have different consequences from effects seen when this molecule is produced internally or given in low doses, in a supportive context (Carter et al., 2020). Studies of individual and sex differences in endogenous oxytocin and the oxytocin receptor are largely missing from our current understanding of both the benefits and dangers associated with this molecule. Furthermore, as discussed above, the complex interactions between oxytocin and vasopressin and their receptors could be another important source of variation and sex differences in responses to oxytocin treatments, which at present remain largely unexplored.

Adding to the complexity of this emerging story is the capacity of reproductive steroids, including estrogen, progesterone, and testosterone to regulate sensitivity to the actions of oxytocin and vasopressin. Dynamic changes in these steroid hormones, especially around the time of birth, prepare the maternal brain for oxytocin and facilitate attachment to the baby. Actions of steroid hormones also lie behind sex differences in anatomy and behavior, including positive forms of infant care and defense of the young. Steroid-peptide interactions are at present not well understood, but probably differ between males and females. In some cases, the responses to oxytocin and vasopressin are in opposite directions in men and women. Why this happens remains poorly understood (Carter & Perkeybile, 2018). At present the value of exogenous oxytocin as a drug remains problematic (Carter et al., 2020).

Love Lost or Found

Love is one of nature's most rewarding experiences. But what happens when love is absent or lost? Behaviorally, the effects are well documented. The absence of a sense of trust, especially in early life, is associated in later life with patterns of self-defensive behavior and reactivity to perceived threats, in some cases even when the danger is not real (Porges, 2021b). If not repaired, this loss can inhibit the later capacity for love. With knowledge of the mechanisms underlying either the presence or absence of a sense of safety, there is an opportunity to inform both optimal parenting and responsible interventions. Because of the evolved and conserved nature of the need for safety, awareness of mechanisms through which negative or positive experiences across the life span affect this system will help us understand, predict, and possibly heal the consequences of neglect or trauma (Porges, 2021b).

Summary

Love is intrinsically beautiful, but also complex and mysterious. Although love can be difficult to define, the list of love's functions is long. Love influences all aspects of human existence. Love is powerful medicine. The mechanisms through which love protects and heals are only now being discovered. Throughout life, oxytocin influences sociality and helps allow social experiences to influence behavior and physiology. Knowledge of the neurobiology of love helps to explain the exceptional reproductive success of humans and also our resilience in the face of fear and aggression. The emotional and physical health and longevity of our species, and perhaps our planet, depends on our capacity to understand and apply our knowledge of the biology of the love. As we learn more about the way in which the mammalian body manages love, trust, and perceived safety—or their absence—we have opportunities to prevent trauma, reverse the damage induced by adverse experiences across the life span, and facilitate healing of both the body and spirit.

Acknowledgments

Portions of this essay were originally published in the *International Body Psychotherapy Journal*, *18*(1), 19–25. Research described here from the author's laboratory was funded by NIH, most recently by HD P01 07575 and HD R01 098117, as well as support from the Fetzer Institute. The editorial suggestions and other supportive inputs of Stephen Porges are gratefully acknowledged. Because of space limitations, I apologize to investigators whose primary work is not fully recognized and refer the reader to additional references in recent reviews cited here.

Part II

The Science of Embodying

6

Somatic Intelligence

Toward a New Competency for the Therapist

Jennifer Frank Tantia

THE BODY IS THE PLACE FROM WHICH WE FEEL, CONTAIN, AND DEFINE LIFE EXPERIENCES, and to be embodied is to engage the most dynamic and deepest encounters of living. Embodiment as a lived experience transcends and includes cognition and emotion. For instance, you can read about dancing, but you cannot grasp what it feels like to actually dance until you move your body or see it happening in front of you and feel how it affects you. Similarly, you can read or hear about a sense of wonder, or the depths of emotional pain, but until these states are experienced viscerally and energetically, they are only words and ideas.

This chapter expresses the need for therapists' somatic competence in psychotherapy treatment. I first describe the dichotomy between body and mind in traditional psychotherapy and briefly review extant literature on the increasing interest in somatic research across several fields, ending with the need to include embodied experience in psychotherapy in view of the current zeitgeist. Next, I suggest how the therapist's embodied somatic awareness can become a new competency for therapeutic practice and describe the unique ways in which to access embodied experience. Finally, somatic intelligence is introduced as the ability to use one's present-moment integration of somatic awareness to enhance presence and facilitate authentic communication with others, and I describe how it can help us collectively move forward during current global challenges.

Bodies Are Not the Problem

As far back as ancient Greece (785–481 BCE) the ideology of separating body and mind has prevailed in Western culture. The mind has been valued over the body, and some parts of the body have been valued over others (Gornicka, 2016). Even today, the body continues to be a scapegoat for unacceptable aspects of the human condition, dissected into parts or diminished as a weak, ugly, or incorrigible object to be tamed. However, bodies have never been the problem. It is the perspective on the body that is the problem.

In the current styles of therapy, the body-mind split is prevalent, as treatment often focuses on changing a client's thinking and behavior while overlooking the subjective experience of the client's condition. The *DSM-5* illustrates this oversight with descriptions of illnesses that have body-mind splits at the base (e.g., dissociative and somatoform disorders), while a cognitive and behavioral approach continues to be the gold standard of treatment (American Psychiatric Association, 2013). Even when a client's bodily experiences and perceptions are addressed in a cognitive-based therapy, they are often addressed by talking about or changing them, without considering the integration of the client's experience of those thoughts and behaviors.

Therapists who can support and integrate a client's somatic experience within the psychotherapeutic session may help the client access a sensory part of themselves that reveals their own considerable internal resources. It also builds the capability to access potential external support and connection. One key element in this process is the therapist's own somatic awareness for the purpose of understanding coregulation between themselves and the client. When the therapist is skilled in being embodied and present, and is aware of their own nonverbal communication, boundaries, autonomic nervous system (ANS) activation, and needs, they can provide a felt sense of safety for their client that is more deeply accessible than what arises from only talking about an issue. This body-to-body recognition is a two-way nervous system communication that can help cultivate positive change in a client in a way that no cognitive process can.

Era of the Soma

Somatic interventions in psychotherapy have been practiced on the outskirts of mainstream psychotherapy since the late 20th century (Chaiklin, 1975; Rogers et al., 1967; Lowen, 1958; Reich, 1945). In the 1970s, "somatics" (Hanna, 1970) and "focusing" (Gendlin, 1982) were introduced as models of self-inquiry for emotional healing. These somatic practices organically found their way into humanistic styles of psychotherapy treatment (Gendlin, 1996; Johnson & Grand, 1998; Kurtz, 1990), and since that time the idea that the body holds valuable information about human experience has periodically continued to surface.

It was during the Decade of the Brain (1990–1999) that thinking about embodiment in psychotherapeutic treatment became popular (Lakoff & Johnson, 1999; Varela et al., 1991), and somatic experience specifically for trauma therapy gained recognition (Herman, 1992; Levine, 1997; Ogden et al., 2006; Porges, 1995; Rothschild, 2000; Scaer, 2005; Schore, 2009, 2011; Terr, 1990; van der Kolk, 1994).

In the past 25 years, key individuals in a number of academic fields began to investigate the potential of somatic awareness for self-improvement. Sociologist G. Ignatow (2007, p. 116) suggested that we were in a "post cognitive revolution," and psychologist Allan Schore (2009, Slide 43) called the inclusion of nonverbal communication in the psychotherapeutic setting a "paradigm shift" in clinical research. Table 6.1 offers a sample of emerging literature on embodiment research from 2000 to 2023, which seems to begin the Era of the Soma that continues to evolve today.

Most recently, events in the United States have shed new light upon subjective experience. COVID-19 forced us into an existential disturbance that affected us on a bodily

TABLE 6.1 Era of the Soma

DISCIPLINE	SAMPLES OF RELEVANT LITERATURE
Philosophy	Arvidson, 2008; Fuchs, 2016; Gallagher, 2008; Koch & Fuchs, 2011; Sheets-Johnstone, 2010; Shusterman, 2008; Varela et al., 2012
Neuroscience	Cameron, 2002; Bechara et al., 2004; Gallese, 2009; Porges, 2004; Scaer, 2005; Schore, 2009
Sociology	Harrison, 2000; Ignatow, 2007; Shusterman, 2008; van Manen, 2015; West, 2011
Anthropology	Csordas, 2008
Education	Kiefer & Trumpp, 2014
Nursing	Gavin & Todres, 2009; Mason, 2014
Transpersonal Psychology	Anderson, 2002; Hartelius, 2007, 2020
Social Psychology	Meier et al., 2012; Louvel & Soulier, 2022
Health Psychology	Ellingson, 2006; MacLachlan, 2004; Mercarder-Rubio et al., 2023
Ecopsychology	Morrison, 2009; Rufo, 2023
Dance/Movement Therapy	Caldwell & Johnson, 2012; Cruz & Berroll, 2016; Hervey, 2000
Gender and Queer Theory in Research	Caldwell & Leighton, 2018; Ellingson, 2012, 2017; Johnson, 2018; Perry & Medina, 2015; Thanem & Knights, 2019
Artistic Inquiry	Leavy, 2009, 2017; Spatz, 2015
Research Methodology	Finlay, 2011; Tantia, 2020; Todres, 2004, 2007; Rennie & Fergus, 2006

level; mask-wearing, videoconferencing, and the serious illness of friends and family caused a significant shift in everyday life. The U.S. surgeon general wrote an advisory on the newly named epidemic of loneliness and isolation (Murthy, 2023) while the rates of drug and alcohol use and mental illness increased rapidly (National Institutes of Health, n.d.). Those affected by drugs and alcohol seemed to become dysregulated due to lack of human connection and social support, while access to their own natural internal, biological resources was weakened. When we separated from each other, we also seemed to separate from ourselves.

These unusual circumstances demanded attention to how our bodies, emotions, and environment interact, incidentally emphasizing our need for emotional coregulation through social engagement. Not surprisingly, there was simultaneously increased attention to embodied awareness in psychotherapy, namely in trauma therapy (e.g., Somatic Experiencing), during which a therapist helps a client to calibrate their ANS within the therapeutic relationship. Physiologically speaking, Porges (2023) identified these phenomena as activation of the ventral vagal system: the experience of feeling safe and connected with others. The integration of embodiment in the psychotherapeutic session for safe contact with oneself and others is the bedrock of somatic psychotherapy.

A New Competency for Therapists

Competencies are the necessary characteristics for effective performance of a particular profession and represent the requisite skills that collectively define successful job performance (von Truer & Reynolds, 2017). Somatic awareness has the potential to become part of a new competency for psychotherapists who are interested in treating mental illness from a whole-person perspective. By using an embodied, present-moment, lived experience through somatic interventions in treatment, a therapist can offer a more complete healing process for clients.

But what does it mean to be a somatically competent therapist? First, somatic psychotherapy is experiential by nature and therefore cannot be mastered by only reading or talking about it. A somatically competent therapist has participated as a client in their own somatic psychotherapy and has experienced their own embodied responses to their thoughts, emotions, actions, and interactions. Second, a somatically competent therapist must know how to self-regulate their nervous system and be comfortable navigating their present embodied states during sessions with clients. Finally, they can recognize and address how both their clients' and their own embodied experiences affect one another. Somatically competent therapists not only talk the talk—they walk the walk.

The Implicit Essential

To break down how talk therapy integrates into somatic psychotherapy, we can first think of explicit knowledge versus implicit knowing. In traditional psychotherapy, explicit knowledge is described as what is being said, while implicit knowing points to how one is speaking. Differentiating between conscious and unconscious material in psychodynamic psychotherapy, Stern (2004) identified the term "implicit" as a third branch of awareness that is neither conscious nor unconscious. He wrote, "The term 'unconscious' should be reserved for repressed material where there is a defensive barrier to entering consciousness. More precisely, implicit knowing is nonconscious" (p. 116). Stern defined how nonconscious material is different in that it has the potential to be brought to consciousness. Similarly, Gendlin (1982) named the emergent, nonverbal embodied experience the "felt sense" (p. 10) and created a six-step process to bring implicit material to consciousness through a dialogical process with the body called focusing (Gendlin, 1982, 1996). Focusing, like many styles of somatic psychotherapy, engages a top-down and bottom-up feedback loop of communication among thoughts, emotions, and somatic experience.

Cultivating Somatic Awareness

Somatic awareness is the process by which present-moment, nonverbal data emerge while bringing attention to one's body. Qualities of breath, posture, gesture, eye gaze, and prosody are some examples of these phenomena. To access this embodied data (Tantia, 2020), certain unconventional practices are required, with three main experiential facets.

First, cultivating somatic awareness requires one to be present. While the mind can travel into the past (e.g., with grief or regret) or to the future (with worry or anxiety), attending to one's body is an anchor for experiencing one's present moment. Second, one must slow down to be able to feel subtle nonverbal responses from the body. Slowing down is necessary to feel felt sense shifts in the body (Gendlin, 1982). Finally, one should be prepared to tolerate (or even welcome) surprises or intense feelings or sensations that might be difficult.

Once familiar with these three experiential practices, therapists can attend to more specific elements of a somatic approach. In addition to Gendlin's felt sense, Johnson (2005) outlines key elements such as interoception (sensations within the body); exteroception (perception through the five senses); neuroception (feelings of safety or danger); and proprioception (position of the body in space), as well as the concept of intercorporeality—the interactive exchange between self and other. To elaborate, interoception might involve shape, weight, location, pressure, or size of a sensation. Shrinking or expanding of the body (in fear or safety) may be indicative of neuroception. The posture or architecture of one's limbs may illustrate how proprioception is felt. Voluntary and involuntary movements are also significant. Qualities of gesture, balance, rhythm, and speed of movement can be portals to understand one's experience in the world (Tantia, 2020). Finally, prosody is of note (Levine, 1997), as a therapist's rhythm, pitch, and tone of voice may influence a client's experience. All of these elements plus more are active and available at any given time for use in treatment.

Sensing Ourselves

For the first three years of life, we navigate the world through senses and movement, but without narrative memory. You might experience this when recalling the smell of your childhood home or the texture and size of a beloved stuffed animal, yet with no autobiographical content. In trauma therapy, sensory memory is key to healing traumatic experiences, due to the ways in which sensory data are available for recall when narrative memory is inaccessible (Levine, 1997; Ogden et al., 2006).

In addition to sensory memory, during our earliest years we are developing preferences for kinetic expression according to how we are encouraged (or discouraged) to take up space in the world. Reich (1945) and Lowen (1958) created systems for identifying habitual postures and movements of the body. These character structures are the result of how one's body memories solidify and present over time. Preferences for personal rhythm and qualities of movement are also developing. Finally, other identifications such as gender, height, weight, physical ability, neurodiversity, temperament, illness, and mobility all play roles in how our sensory-emotional body develops in response to our environment.

Sensing With Others

Often a client walks into my office and asks "How are you?" while simultaneously taking off their coat and shoes. This common and acceptable greeting in the United States is often accompanied by my client's lack of eye contact and no pause to hear my response; incongruous actions to what seems like a sincere question. Since I am their therapist, I take their words seriously, and our embodied experience is a big part of our work together, so I wait until we are both seated and facing each other to answer. In silence, I check my posture, energy, gravity, tension and mood, and so on, and then respond. Sometimes I even respond with only a gesture or a larger movement. Most times the client laughs, and I then ask, "How are *you*?" New clients usually begin a story about what happened yesterday or last week. I then ask, "How are you *now*?"

Being present with oneself to check in and answer the simple question, "How are you?" from somatic awareness is difficult for most. An intentional moment of checking in without words makes one vulnerable and open to projections and to the cruelest self-judgment. Eye gaze is a courageous, intimate, and full-bodied act. Sharing a present moment with a client makes a therapist vulnerable as well. Attending to the space between us is even more difficult and energetically charged than navigating the space between words.

Eventually clients learn to tolerate the lack of small talk. They arrive at a session, sit down, and without my prompting check in with themselves before speaking. When they do this, they discover how they really are (possibly for the first time that day) and articulate honesty that only comes from being present with oneself. There is a gentle nature to this ritual that creates a safe and sacred space for the client to speak their truth within the moment.

The entire theory and practice of dance movement psychotherapy (DMP) is based on creating relationships through movement. In DMP treatment, the therapist uses movement to connect nonverbally with a client (Chaiklin, 1975). A primary intervention in DMP is "mirroring" (Berrol, 2016). In contrast to what one might think of as mimicking, mirroring is the practice of moving with a client to reflect the experience that, "I see you and I'm with you." While mirroring, the therapist gains a sense of a client; not to making presumptions about how they feel, but to gain access to feelings within the client that might be currently unconscious to them. It is easy for a client to say that they "feel fine" while being unaware that they are clenching their fists or stomach (a place that the therapist cannot see). Instead of pointing out their fists, a dance movement therapist can make a fist themselves, or mirror the client's torso to feel the effect of the posture. When the therapist mirrors the client's posture, the client can see and respond to it.

DMP practice is much more complex than what is written here, but the main point of including it is that moving with a client creates body-to-body communication that adds a layer of sensitivity for both the therapist and client. Nonverbal conversation in movement is genuine, vulnerable, and powerful in the psychotherapeutic process, and provides a strong and honest therapist-client relationship. A therapist who drops into their own somatic awareness and can work with nonverbal two-way intercorporeal communication with their client has begun to develop somatic intelligence.

Somatic Intelligence: Healing Beyond Trauma

Models of intelligence have been previously defined, such as Gardner's (2011) multiple intelligences, which suggests ways of learning, and Goleman's emotional intelligence (Goleman, 2006), which utilizes self-awareness skills for interacting in work environments. However, there has been little attention to the type of intelligence that underlies cognitive and emotional experience in everyday life. Somatic intelligence (SI) is the capacity not only to experience one's present-moment integration of embodiment, but to use that awareness for authentic communication with oneself and others. A therapist who regularly practices somatic awareness for themselves can use their own SI as part of the healing process for their clients. SI is the ability to recognize, analyze, and synthesize one's embodied experience for a greater sense of intrapersonal communication both verbally and nonverbally.

When one brings attention to one's embodied self, a potential arises for well-being beyond trauma healing. Embodiment may increase empathy (Schmidsberger & Löffler-Stastka, 2018), resilience (Fogel, 2021), agency (Tsakiris et al., 2010), boundary formation (Cariola, 2015), self-compassion (Khoury, 2019), self-responsibility (Køster, 2017), and potential recognition of implicit bias (Banakou et al., 2020). In the psychotherapeutic setting, embodiment supports work with somatic transference and countertransference experiences (Pallaro, 2007). These human qualities of conscious, realistic, and intentional interactions form SI.

We are not born with SI; our original somatic blueprint is wild and happens outside of cognitive awareness at an early age, stored as a disorganized nonverbal memory. These early impressions may recede in our conscious awareness over time but are not forgotten, as body memories from early years are often accessible in adulthood. Recall a favorite meal from your childhood: the smell of the food, how you sat at the table, the height of the table in relationship to your face. When working somatically in treatment, these experiences reveal an existential understanding of oneself that leads to SI.

Without processing and integrating somatic experiences, nonverbal memory links to and forms our narrative and emotional experience into patterns that can become automatic and inflexible. Our narrative then dictates who we are to ourselves, and we inadvertently teach others how to treat us based on that affected narrative. To rewire these patterns, somatic awareness is processed and integrated into a living experience of waking up to our adult reality. In short, SI encourages us to grow up.

When we become somatically intelligent, we become more than a person with a body; we live our body. Husserl's term, "Leib," which roughly translates to the innermost experience of our embodied experience, is more than possessing one's body as an object (Mensch, 2001). Just as having a body is neurologically different from moving one's body (Tsakiris et al., 2010), being or living through one's body changes one's perspective of living. Engaging with compassion and respect toward the somatic aliveness within, a whole-person resilience emerges that is both ancient and familiar to all of us. Our engagement with the somatic layer supports our ANS, which then has the potential to regulate, and our sense of self-worth begins to grow. When we become securely attached to ourselves, we can create secure attachments to others.

Borrowing from Buber's (1937/1970) philosophy of I/It and I/Thou, the "It" indicates that a body is a thing to be tamed, improved, worshipped, basically objectified. When you experience yourself as an It, everyone else is an It. However, once you start to sense yourself as a living, breathing, vulnerable being, you begin to relate to those precious parts in others. Sensing your own intrinsic value and worthiness of love, you may act toward others from that space with emotional generosity that holds integrity. SI provides a space of I/Thou in the psychotherapeutic setting by cultivating mutual and interpersonal vitality.

Somatic Cultural Sensitivity

Somatic psychotherapy literature offers a continued thoughtful and responsive exploration of oppression and the body (Caldwell & Leighton, 2018; Johnson, 2023). Just as it would be ethically unsound for a therapist to work with a client from another culture without having, at the very minimum, an appreciation and respect for that culture, SI adds a layer of awareness to cultural sensitivity. Gender, sexuality, race, romantic lifestyle, physical ableism, and neurodiversity are constantly expressed nonverbally in the treatment setting. Therapist and client affect each other through facial expressions, gestures, postures, and eye gaze (Caldwell & Leighton, 2018; Johnson, 2023), and it is the therapist's responsibility to understand, include, and query the ways in which these expressions are valued. To be sensitive and receptive to both subtle and overt nuances of culturally varied somatic experience is integral to being a somatically competent therapist.

Conclusion

This chapter has described the need for somatically competent therapists in psychotherapy practice by advocating for therapists' development of somatic awareness, not only for their client's sake, but for their own well-being. I discussed what it means to be a somatically competent therapist and provided examples of those responsibilities, such as developing presence, slowing down, and using nonverbal expressions from the body in a top-down and bottom-up process. I also defined what I call "Somatic Intelligence," an experiential interpersonal dynamic involving the ability to use one's present-moment integration of somatic awareness to communicate authentically with others. Some benefits of Somatic Intelligence include embodied agency, empathy, resilience, self-compassion, healthy boundaries, and self-responsibility. Finally, I suggested that Somatic Intelligence facilitates therapists' attunement to nonverbal subjective experiences of gender identity, sexuality, race, physical ableism, and neurodiversity. Beyond trauma and beyond therapeutic treatment, there is a potentially broader application for Somatic Intelligence to activate a new paradigm for human competency. How we attend to ourselves is ultimately how we affect and treat each other.

7

Post-Trauma Growth

Guidelines and Guardrails

Steven Hoskinson and Bach Ho

*It is necessary to help others, not only in our prayers, but in our daily lives. If we
find we cannot help others, the least we can do is to desist from harming them.*
—H. H. DALAI LAMA

GROWING RESEARCH FUNDAMENTALLY CHALLENGES THE RELIABILITY OF EMPIRICALLY SUP-
ported treatments (ESTs)—including common trauma therapy protocols—and their purported nonmaleficence. In view of these challenges, this chapter proposes guidelines for
a safer framework of biologically informed therapeutics. The post-trauma growth (PTG)
protocols of Organic Intelligence are ways to describe biologically based attunement, to
reduce the harm potential in treatments, and to improve client satisfaction and quality of
life. To promote PTG reliably and reduce harm to clients, treatments must increasingly
align with the client's biology and self-organizing complexity. This alignment centrally
involves reevaluating (1) negative intensity in session, and (2) directive control exerted
over the client's session content.

While in the West, psychotherapies are oft-touted supports for a variety of human ills,
the evidence for a generally safe passage through a course of therapy is faltering. Harm
caused in treatment is underrecognized (see Barlow, 2010; Bergin, 1966; Britton, 2019;
Farias et al., 2020; Healy & Mangin, 2019; Hirshberg et al., 2020; Klatte et al., 2023;
Lambert & Harmon, 2018; Parry et al., 2016; Wells et al., 2023), treatments advertised
as evidence-based are not (see Bryan et al., 2021; Farber et al., 2019; Moeller & Schmidt,
2023; Sakaluk et al., 2019; Williams et al., 2021), and there is a proliferation of unregulated
training programs offering work with serious mental health issues, such as posttraumatic
stress disorder (PTSD). People who are seeking help face a bewildering array of adver-
tisements from nonlicensed professionals without adequate background, while licensed
professionals have been shown to lack the awareness that their treatments are not having
the effect they think they are (Lambert & Harmon, 2018).

TABLE 7.1 Enhanced Post-Trauma Growth

Innate, cyclic modulation of positively valenced states, at specific intensity levels, emerging especially in the context of trait orientation, is what increases thresholds of innate processing capacity, or bandwidth.	
GUIDELINES	GUARDRAILS
1. The most potent clinical assessment is biological, in the moment, and related to allostatic functioning 2. Always track the client's degree of orientation (effortless sensory awareness of the environment) 3. Track intensity, both physiological and felt; the latter is a general proxy for the former 4. Track up and down cycles (intensification and de-intensification) 5. Track valence (positive, negative, neutral)	1. Relational attunement—empathy, congruence, positive regard—is more important than technical protocols 2. Orientation, of both practitioner and client, gauges successful attunement more reliably than social engagement or affective exchange 3. Practitioner's orientation must be stable, so that their attention is not dominated by attraction to intensity or what's wrong, in their client or themselves 4. Prefer shaping in free-association conversation over directing; if directing, get consent and aim for low demand on client and high probability of success 5. Err to the scenic route to post-trauma growth

It has been over 30 years since the APA's Society of Clinical Psychology (Division 12) published criteria for empirically supported treatments (Society of Clinical Psychology, 1993).[1] In 2006, an American Psychological Association task force elaborated these criteria in its adoption of a framework for evidence-based practice (EBP).[2] Robust dialogues documenting problems in the EST/EBP literature continue, with important suggestions for improvement (Korbmacher et al., 2023), notably the shift to an emphasis on effectiveness research over measures of symptom reduction (Tolin et al., 2015).

Somatic treatment methods are an increasingly utilized perspective that incorporates the awareness of bodily sensations. These somatic approaches are vulnerable to the established methodological shortcomings in outcome research. The aim in this chapter is to identify likely sources of harm in extant treatment and to offer reasonable alternatives that are likely to minimize adverse effects in therapy, especially in somatic approaches, and especially for trauma.

This chapter delineates the positive psychology framework of self-organizing systems of Organic Intelligence (OI) for post-trauma growth (PTG). PTG is the documented growth that some experience after trauma. People may not only recover from trauma but emerge more resilient after it than before: more resilient and with purpose (Hill et al., 2023). OI's therapeutic aim is somatic in the sense that it is directed primarily toward increased functionality of the physiology. It is not somatic in that it does not prioritize (but incorporates) client awareness of sensation. In fact, this therapeutic method arose from the primary author's attempt to create a more stable and effective treatment, with less potential for harm, than found in somatic protocols of directing the client's awareness to sensations associated with trauma. Instead, we focus on relational attunement and ease for the client and their biology, both inside and outside therapy sessions. Relational attunement, ease, and positivity are why these PTG protocols can be regarded as a mitigator of therapeutic harm, while we as a field await a coming wave of empirical research that will improve standards for ESTs.

This chapter has two main sections. In the first, we introduce the wider theoretical framework with which OI theory is aligned, the essentials of OI theory, and the implications of the theory for understanding and facilitating an enhanced PTG. The framework is allostasis (Barrett, 2022; Bassett & Gazzaniga, 2011; Koob & Le Moal, 2001; Lee, 2019; Sterling, 2004, 2012, 2014), a theory of organismic self-regulation according to which organisms self-regulate, not by preserving a constant internal milieu (cf. homeostasis), but by adapting their internal milieu in anticipation of future demands (Sterling, 2012). We posit a fundamental process of allostatic change: the process of growing the biological capacity for processing information and intensity, automatically and easily, for the purpose of predictive regulation. This growth process, which we call auto-organization (AO), underlies an enhanced PTG: not just resilience, but preparatory resilience.[3] In the second section, we introduce our clinical approach to facilitating AO (and thus PTG) and the measurement of PTG in terms of stated clinical assessment criteria, which center around life improvement, as opposed to just symptom reduction.

Auto-Organization and Post-Trauma Growth

Why does therapy, including purportedly evidence-based therapy, have high dropout rates and often not lead to positive outcomes (Strauss et al., 2021)? Part of the answer, according to brain researcher Sung Lee (2019), is that much therapy is shaped by a problematic view of organismic functioning: homeostasis.

According to the paradigm of homeostasis, there are biological set points—referring broadly to all measurable organismic activity—that are objectively normal. These include, for example, blood pressure, heart rate, sleep patterns, motor behaviors, sensory acuity, positive cognitive appraisals, and breathing cycles (Lee, 2019, p. 7). Deviations are (presumed) pathological. For example, if you suddenly get anxious at an ice cream social (where there's no sign of an oncoming tiger attack), some who accept the homeostatic paradigm (explicitly or implicitly) may assess your state as pathological. They may also tell you to do something (e.g., deep breathing, imagine running, reframing) to return to your correct set point, that is, being more relaxed. The homeostatic paradigm is expressed in the therapeutic practice of assessing a client's pathology or nonoptimal state and working to improve that condition.

The problem with the homeostatic paradigm is that it does not adequately account for the fact that set points are vastly interrelated within one's physiology; they can and regularly do change; and they change on the basis of evolved intelligence: The organism predicts future demands and environments and changes set points in order to navigate them more efficiently (Lee, 2019).

This predictive regulation is the essence of the paradigm of allostasis, which describes organismic dynamics, wherein the brain manages the energy budget of myriad systems interacting with myriad environments (Barrett, 2022).[4] Organisms are examples of complex systems: systems that consist of networks of interdependent interrelationships. The network is so complex that system behavior is difficult to predict. There are, however, characteristics that help describe system behavior, including feedback, nonlinearity, adaptation, spontaneous order, emergence, and unintended consequences. The allostatic framework of predictive regulation falls within complex adaptive systems: systems of many parts that undergo qualitative shifts that occur due to feedback loops within the system, and between a system and the environment. Allostasis is a necessary shift of perspective for understanding body, brain, and behavior that has already been established in areas such as addiction (Koob & Le Moal, 2001), human connectomics (Bassett & Gazzaniga, 2011), emotion (Barrett, 2022), brain function (Katsumi et al., 2022), and stress (McEwen, 1998), including childhood and developmental stress (Danese & McEwen, 2012; Tooley et al., 2021).

The homeostatic paradigm regularly mischaracterizes behaviors as disordered when they are actually manifestations of predictive regulation (Lee, 2019, pp. 15–17). For example, rather than considering a child's looking around the room as a regulatory attempt to map the environment, this might be described negatively as hypervigilance. Or therapists may notice clients' self-soothing behaviors and interpret them as a sign of anxiety, rather than of autonomic regulation. The primary mechanism of this mischaracterization is the negativity bias (what we call "What's wrong attention"). In homeostatic terms: something's off and the assumption is that we need to get it back to normal.

We work with a particular set point that defines allostatic efficiency: The capacity to process information and intensity automatically and easily. What is within an organism's capacity marks what is not stressful to begin with. Stress refers both to physiological stress (allostatic load) and to the subjective experience of stress (felt when load exceeds capacity). The selective advantage of increased capacity is the ability to adaptively engage in increasingly complex environments, such as human relationships. We work to increase capacity and to do so as a lasting trait.

It is increased capacity that underlies PTG. If a person suffers from symptoms—such as anxiety, depression, fight, flight, and freeze—that means their biology is not automatically processing the amount of input confronting them. Discomfort indicates that allostatic load exceeds capacity. As capacity increases, symptoms diminish, and a person's biology has more capacity not only to bounce back, but also to preempt challenge, proactively buffer from stress, and limit damaging effects of untoward experiences. Most importantly, we also find that capacity increase emerges alongside predictable, and prima facie innate, impulses toward healthy pleasure, sociality, bonding, expansion, exploration, following curiosity, and appreciating life: toward meaningful, purposeful, and joyful living.[5]

This impulse to increase capacity fundamentally differs from a focus on relief from negative experience and from the endless work of self-improvement. Negative intensity is a core feature of many therapies; psychological treatment has been driven by symptoms and diagnoses (including trauma). This negative intensity is a primary culprit in maintaining current levels of overall organismic disorder and adverse effects in treatment (Barlow, 2010). While negative intensity must be addressed in any attuned therapeutic interaction, it is unnecessary for—even counter to—organic healing. Instead, treatment can enhance capacity through a generally pleasant, if not joyful, experience for the client.

How does such organismic capacity increase? The fundamental characteristic of human functioning is oscillatory entrainment. From a single nerve cell to large-scale brain networks, circadian rhythms, clock cells, and respiratory sinus arrhythmia, the entirety of human functioning rests on the optimal person-to-environment adaptation in oscillatory patterns. PTG indicates a biology with more optimal rhythmic system interactions, such as waking and sleeping, breathing in and breathing out. While the particulars of such complex interactions are elusive in the literature, the aim of intervention is the aggregative, organismic coordination of up and down states, using, as the primary treatment focus, clinically visible representations of those positively valenced oscillations.

We suggest that capacity increases to the degree the biology generally reaches, without exceeding, specific biological set points of physiological intensity (arousal set points), and dearouses to a lower and corresponding biological set point (dearousal set points). In OI, these set points are called organic intensity thresholds (or learning thresholds, or simply organic thresholds). A *threshold*, however, usually refers to an arousal threshold; a dearousal threshold is usually reached by resting or completing a rest period after reaching the (arousal) threshold.

OI calls this process of reaching and resting at organic thresholds, and the system's reappropriation of this process overall, auto-organization (AO). The term is drawn from the concept of self-organization in complex adaptive systems, which holds that complex adaptive systems are capable of self-organizing, of reorganizing in ways that produce a fundamentally different and more resilient form.[6] Thus, *auto-organization* clarifies that the agent of organization is the physiology, not the self (as in the conscious doer or purported psychological self).

Facilitating Auto-Organization

To facilitate AO, we must (1) reinforce the trait of a very specific form of sensory awareness, called orientation (to be elucidated momentarily), and (2) increase tolerance of pleasurable arousal and dearousal (i.e., increase what we call the window of enjoyment). This model of easeful arousal and dearousal is illustrated by, for example, effortless inhaling and exhaling, and momentary excitement followed by easy and pleasant dearousal. Orientation and pleasure are the two initial conditions for AO.

The first author coined the usage of *orientation* to mean "connecting to the environment through the senses" (seeing, hearing, etc.). Orientation often begins as an effort on the client's part. But this effort primes the system for reappropriating this process as a natural, nonefforted trait. Thus, orientation falls under prepared learning (Seligman, 1970, 1971; Dunlap & Stephens, 2014). Orientation is the regulating bridge between inner and outer environments; it fundamentally shapes how our systems interrelate the two and is a prerequisite for predictive regulation (cf. neuroception; Porges, 2004). Orientation, for instance visually, involves the movement of the eyes, neck, and head—areas innervated by what Porges identifies as the ventral vagal complex (or social engagement system). During the course of treatment, orientation stands as a safe proxy for this complex, while capacity is grown for actual social engagement. The sensory system is a primary contributor to axes of interconnection and has been implicated in an fMRI study as a deficit in adults with PTSD (Leite et al., 2022). The centrality of this bridging is cited in a study where the sensorimotor-associative axis in the human connectome is described as "a core pillar of cortical organization" (Nenning et al., 2023). Orientation is thus likely a key aspect of a primary, perhaps the primary, organizing gradient for the brain.

Orientation facilitates a bottom-up neuroception of okayness.[7] Given the high prevalence of adverse childhood experiences and the general impoverishment of attachment status in the West in help-seeking individuals, orientation is a safer first step or proxy for social engagement. It reduces unwarranted intensity spikes, including fight, flight, and freeze. Care is taken to support continuity in the client's exterior focus, as opposed to the client's inner self-reflection. How easily can attention reside in the environment? How mobile are the eyes and face? Does attention keep getting drawn into interior intensity? The oriented client becomes biologically more present, naturally mindful, and in the moment. These orientation-supported conditions of downregulation (Weisbard & Graham, 1971) and modulation (cf. Dugué et al., 2018) are fundamental to AO.

Within the context of relational attunement and orientation, we work toward the awareness of pleasure. Prematurely evoking clients' experience of pleasure is contraindicated. Such arousal can quickly go over threshold, in part because it explicitly runs upstream to the negativity bias, and often the client's negative self-concept and disempowered identity. Instead, the first practices of positive affect might be through observing the client's experience of caring for others, because it is often at first more ego-syntonic (here meaning easy, or low load) and more likely to evoke a sustained positive state of arousal. Caring serves as the projective experience of self-valuing.[8]

The introduction of orientation in treatment had an unexpected and beneficent result: a correspondingly prolific production of spontaneous positive states in the client. Since these states arose autonomically, we believe they are expressions of allostasis. They arise as feedback from and to a complex auto-organizing system. The task then is to reinforce these states; an attunement challenge, because we are trying to reinforce behaviors that are almost entirely unconscious and therefore by definition cannot be self-initiated. We have incorporated an incremental, shaping paradigm of positive reinforcement of these often subtle and very brief signs of allostasis.

While clients cannot self-initiate the adaptive feedback, they can learn to sustain these states and their intensities by enjoying positive states, on both acceleration and deceleration, which we call riding the waves. Clients' aptitudes for pleasure, the second initial condition, vary widely, and develop in tandem with the skill of the practitioner for supportive attunement, the recognition of the emergence of such up and down cycles, and the ability to consistently reinforce these states.

The AO paradigm can be challenging to learn because negativity bias has both clients and practitioners looking at and for what's wrong, often with the idea of getting to the root cause. Getting to the root cause is unnecessary and improbable, and the phrase is often used vaguely. (We would suggest that the root cause is a disorganized biology.) Furthermore, the pattern of problem seeking is negative reinforcement at its most insidious. It is a key to understanding addiction (Hoskinson & Ho, 2022) and is one of the main dynamics that keeps the status quo of psychological treatment—and its clients—running in place. Despite the presumed advances in clinical psychology and the increased utilization of mental health care services (Cantor et al., 2023), mental health deterioration is increasing (APA, 2019).

Before explicitly facilitating AO, a practitioner must prioritize attunement. Harm from therapy arises significantly from misattunement (Parry et al., 2016; Strauss et al., 2021). Attunement is especially necessary in our approach: It enables a more native state to emerge in the client. We provide a relational container that reinforces spontaneous productions of autonomic support. Treatment must feel respectful and meaningful, and be nondirective: it must be improvised, by both client and practitioner. We train in nondirective free association conversations (FACs) with empathy, congruence, and unconditional positive regard (Rogers, 1957).[9] FACs are conversations in which the client is invited to talk, or not talk, about whatever is on their mind in the moment, to go in directions that feel natural to them (i.e., freely associate), and in which the practitioner follows the client, without any agenda by the practitioner to have the client confront a certain topic or memory, feel their body, or even the agenda of asking the client to set an agenda.

Clinicians who are trained in intersubjective, interactionist, systems, and interpersonal approaches recognize intrapsychic, relational, and other unconscious materials that emerge in FACs (cf. Bateson, 1972; Sullivan, 1970; Watzlawick et al., 1968). Our approach, by contrast, instead of postulating or illuminating unconscious dynamics, origins, or conflicts, preferences attention and reflection on states of initial conditions. Client content that arises from the FACs—which includes verbal content, emotion, sensation, images, and, especially, physical movements and positions—reveals vital information, not primarily about the client's history, but about their system's particular composition of AO-relevant patterns of interrelationships between prientation/the ventral vagal complex, intensity, amplitude, valence, inhibition, and excitation.

As FACs proceed, there is an associative trail that increases in intensity, in positive valence, step by gentle step. The explicit goal of FACs is to support what is important and meaningful, often in a freewheeling style of disinhibition-fueled oscillation. It can look like taking the scenic, sometimes comedic, route to nirvana.

One of the most characteristic and important aspects of AO is that the positive intensity cycles, and the growth of bandwidth, occur because at each step there is a slight increase in positive intensity. This scaffolding of states that naturally connect and sequence from one to the other rebuilds continuity of states. This defines integration: the return to continuity of states.

We work with five aspects (or channels) of states: image, sensation, orientation, meaning (cognition), and affect (emotion) (the acronym is ISOMA). For every client, attention trends toward particular channels, certain channels are more excitatory or inhibitory, and there are particular movement patterns between the channels that create a dynamic-state experience. Here is an example of a common fixated pattern: The client is aware of the emotion of anxiety (A), then notices a tightness in the throat (S), then sees in the mind's eye a scary image (I), then thinks, "Am I going to die?" (M), and then feels shaking in the jaw (S). While the specific content might change, that sequence is a likely pattern of

A → S → I → M for this person, one that might be a typical sequence that triggers, say, a panic attack.

In the above example, the client's attention tracked the "what's wrong" side of the ASIM experience. For each of those channels, there is a positive ASIM, a mirror reflection in intensity but positively valenced in the system, that has escaped detection. For instance, anxiety's other side (unique to each person and their pattern) might be empowered aggression (A); the other side of S might be a deeper breath; the other side of I might actually be orientation; and the other side of M might be, "I'm going to be okay." When initial conditions are stable, these allostatically supportive complementaries in ISOMA emerge and are recognized and apprehended more readily.

Using these organic complementaries to antidote uncomfortable intensities is a potent part of clinical practice, and actually only preparatory. Rather than limiting the experience to Pollyannaish positivity, capacity can increase to the point where a person can attend with equanimity to all manner of intensities, to everything life throws at them. Experiences that previously were judged as negative—pain, fear, loss, sickness—when they are available to attention in differentiated ISOMA channels and do not exceed threshold (even in one or two channels), can become topics of interest and exploration, vital aspects of life.

For those learning this approach, the recognition for themselves and their clients that this kind of help is already on its way is a bit like the Netflix series *Stranger Things* (Duffer & Duffer, 2016), where there is an alternate, dark parallel dimension called the Upside Down. In that series, young people were in the usual world, facing the dispiriting dread from the Upside Down. In this analogy, however, it is most of us in the Upside Down, unaware that an alternate, lighter dimension of compassion is just at our fingertips. This shocking awareness is most clear when we see session work around discontinuous or unintegrated memory experiences, such as what is called trauma.

Traumatic memory reconsolidation has received significant interest (Schiller et al., 2010). But the many interesting lines of research have yet to converge with much certainty around neural mechanisms or therapeutic viability (Bavassi et al., 2019; Elsey et al., 2018; Speer et al., 2021; Tambini et al., 2023; Tyukin et al., 2019). Until the research on adverse reactions and efficacy catches up to clinical implementation, we offer a safer, nonnegative intensity alternative.

Retrieval cues for memory recall—such as time (day, season, year), place, other people, and self-concept related to that time period—must include state-specific intensity. Here we have found something unexpected, and congruent with the initial conditions for AO: We consistently find that the biologically preferred valence of recall intensity is positive and that preferred content is not the traumatic memory, but rather corresponding states, associations, and memories, symbolically related and positively valenced. As FACs unfold, states analogous to trauma arise and are reexperienced symbolically, often with similar high intensity, and with tears, but of beauty, gratitude, or joy. Clients typically have no conscious recognition that the content and intensities might be related to previously unintegrated past experiences; nor do they need to recall or reassociate the troubling memory consciously. The point is biological integration, which happens in this positive-intensity, free-association framework.

In the appendix are two examples of OI sessions in which recall clearly offers a positively valenced reflection of high-intensity events. One is the Loma Prieta earthquake in California; the other is associated with wartime events. We believe these positive recountings are the system's own positive reinforcement analogue of, and organic opportunity for reconsolidating, the negatively intense (traumatic) recalls. The relevant cues are all in place—including emotional intensity—but in their redemptive, upside-down version.

While we do not expect the existing therapeutic infrastructure to change overnight, the theory we propose—the AO paradigm—is consistent with an established body of research. The successful clinical implementation of this paradigm by a wide swath of expert clinicians furthermore suggests that this novel—and conservative—paradigm warrants research attention.

Appendix: Two Clinical Examples

Below are excerpts from two OI sessions. The examples illustrate what is distinctive, and safer, about the approach: We enable recall of states—states that may be associated with an event, such as natural disaster or war—that is more positively valenced. Negatively valenced recall is generally a reflection of negativity bias. The safer, and biologically preferred, approach is to enable recall that encodes the relevant states in empowering and organizing ways. This recall is more positively valenced and arises organically when clients are sufficiently grounded in orientation and, consequently, not under the sway of negativity bias. The clients below were so grounded, in part due to prior experience with, and training in, the PTG protocols introduced in this chapter.

The examples below were edited and redacted, to clarify what is happening, to improve readability, and to disguise the identity of the clients. We present some of what clients shared during negatively valenced recall and then (in the same session) during more positively valenced recall. The latter arose organically from the client in the free-association context; clients were not primed or trained to try to manufacture it.

Example 1: Pleasanton

Negatively Valenced Recall

The client was sharing a number of natural disaster events they had experienced—hurricane, tornado, and earthquake. The earthquake was the 1989 Loma Prieta quake in Northern California. The client was living in Pleasanton at the time:

> I just remember the cement rolling and the Bay Bridge falling. Then the Berkeley Freeway collapsing. So, I have to honestly say that one was really . . . the feeling

of it gave me a lot of fear, because I felt not safe [shaking gesture]. Then, I think I told you, I was babysitting. I was a nanny for these two little boys. And the mom, and they all, lived in Berkeley, and the mom called me on the phone. . . .

More Positively Valenced Recall

I just had my son when we moved to Pleasanton, and it was probably, in my life, it was the start of really, really positive experience. It makes me feel emotional [teary]. I loved Pleasanton. . . . I played striker on a coed soccer team, Las Lobos, and we used to get together with the families. I mean, it was just this really great experience.

It was pretty. I felt like I was at home. They have the cutest little houses with all the flowers. California has so many flowers. The trees, all the beautiful trees. And at Christmastime, in the neighborhood, everybody decorates. It was just really cool [teary]. You live in California. I mean, they have Santa in his swim shorts, surfing. . . .

We lived near a creek, and we also lived near a train, so I always get fond memories when I hear a train. Because the train literally was from this far; it's like right in my bedroom. You could literally be on the phone and then you'd go, "Okay. Hang on a minute." Because we used to have wall phones. "Hold on a minute." Choo! [sound of train]. *The whole house would vibrate* [shaking gesture]. It was so fun. I mean, I just really liked living there. It was my hometown [Pleasanton, home]. It gives me a nice feeling of warmth in my heart. (Organic Intelligence, 2023)

Example 2: Protection

Negatively Valenced Recall

The client, in Israel, begins by sharing that they had been reading an account of the massacre at the music, dance, and nature festival in Israel that took the lives of over 250 people on October 7, 2023. "Horrifying. There are no words . . . and I keep forgetting that I've lost my voice" [physically hoarse]. A few days later, suddenly the client heard a "crazy zoom" overhead, and then "massive explosions":

There wasn't any warning siren before. We ran into my friend's house. And it was very scary because we just didn't know what it was, because there wasn't a siren before.

So he went upstairs to check on his partner. And I was just alone there and just a lot of things in my imagination. And then also just planning my escape routes in the place that I didn't really know. I was picturing a way that maybe I would climb up. Then I was like, "Okay, I could put my foot here and I could put my hands there, and I could maybe even just crawl up with my hands. . . . "

More Positively Valenced Recall

I was once camping by myself in nature, and no one knew where I was. And next thing [no warning], I just heard these really weird footsteps and this really weird noise. I was like, "Is that a human? Is that an animal?" So I just went into just, "Quiet, don't make a sound." And then next thing, this hyena showed up. So I grabbed a stick, and this hyena just started growling at me. But I just climbed up a tree. It wasn't even like something I could have preemptively thought of or planned. But next thing I knew, I was up in the tree.

The hyena continued growling at me.

So that day also happened to be Tu B'Av, which is the Jewish day of love [often celebrated with festivals of music and dancing]. It's after the destruction of the Temple, which is Tisha B'Av, the ninth day of Av, a day of Jewish sorrow where really terrible things have happened. [The October 7 terror attacks will come to be acknowledged on that day.] And then on Tu B'Av, it was a time when there was that relief, comforting, or renewal.

So I was just by myself up in the tree. And I was like, "This is not what I planned. No. It's not what I planned." The reality, versus what was actually happening—I was wanting to dance, and sing, and play my guitar, and look at the stars and the full moon, and be in nature.

No one knew where I was. So I sent my location to my cousin and I was like, "Stuck in tree with a wolf growling at me." So I called them and they were not really understanding the situation. So then they decided that they're going to call the police, and I wasn't really into that. But in that moment, it was hard stress, because I really didn't know what was going to happen.

So I put the phone down. I just started screaming [powerful voice] at the wolf like, "Go away!" Just screaming, "Go away!"

And then I could feel that it went away, even though I couldn't see because it was dark. Even though it was dark and I couldn't see, I could sense that it had gone.

It's so funny I'm talking about this story. I'm just seeing myself through the whole scene right now.

I got down from the tree.

And the calling out, because it was really the most primal place that I've been, where I really did not know what was going to happen, and it could go any way. And I was really vulnerable and by myself. There was a deep calling out to all of the resource, the deepest resource. The only thing that's going to help me is the One. I need protection, real spiritual reinforcement, protection.

And the thought, "I'm going to be okay."

So I was asking, "What should I do?" And this really clear, gentle voice [also powerful] came through, and it just said, "You can stay, my dear."

I was laughing a bit, because I heard that, but I was still scared. And, here I've called on, like, the big guns for protection [as many did on October 7]. And then it's like, "Okay, if I can trust that that deity protection is there, and also feel that in my body," is what I asked for next—the full integration of that.

Notes

1 ESTs are treatments that have been shown to be beneficial in scientific studies that are regarded as meeting stringent criteria (Society of Clinical Psychology, 2012).

2 EBP refers to clinical practice that is integrated with the best available research evidence.

3 Going forward, when we refer to PTG, we mean this enhanced PTG.

4 Barrett (2022, p. 903, footnote 14) writes, "The brain, for example, is thought to function like a complex adaptive system whose behavior emerges from the intricate interaction of neurons, glial cells, vascular, metabolic and chemical elements, their internal dynamics, and their interaction with elements of the environment (both the internal environment to which a brain is attached, i.e., the rest of the body, and the external environment outside the skin." See also Bassett and Gazzaniga (2011), Bressler and McIntosh (2007), Favela (2020), Kelso (2012), Krubitzer and Prescott (2018), Sporns (2011), Tononi and Edelman (1998).

5 This startling realization has implications well beyond trauma, psychopathology, and even positive psychology. Since we are proposing the possibility of fundamentally enhanced processing capacity, standard psychological notions such as IQ, crystallized intelligence, and other presumed inherited traits, to name but a few, must be reconsidered.

6 Capra and Luisi (2014) provide a good entry point into complexity science; see especially Chapter 8, which discusses the self-organization of a wide range of complex systems, including molecules, cells, individual living things, and social organization in various species.

7 Porges's neuroception is essentially an allostatic function. It is the assessment of the external environment—yes, for safety—but also for prediction and creating a model of the exterior world. Note that both interoception and exteroception are primarily unconscious.

8 OI recognizes the positive, nonpathological, function of projection: Once apprehended, it is a way clients can begin to relate to their inner experience at a level of positive intensity that is lower and thus more likely to be within threshold. The OI term for projection is *outsight*, capturing the implicit search for and gaining of insight through relating to the outer world, for example, "They're so generous" or "They have so much patience!" These are aspects of the unconscious impulse of AO that can be retrieved for threshold purposes. It is also the source of the OI saying, "Trauma means unintegrated resource."

9 The challenge of creating FACs in which the native system is speaking, without censorship or defensive maneuvers, has been articulated since Sullivan (1970). After Sullivan's reorientation of the psychodynamic milieu, the focus on this free association and the interpersonal and intersubjective developed rapidly.

8

The Felt Sense Polyvagal Model

Embodied Assessment and Treatment Tool

Jan Winhall

I BEGAN WORKING AS A TRAUMA AND ADDICTION THERAPIST IN THE EARLY 1980S. AT THAT time there was a small group of mostly feminist therapists advocating for embodied approaches to trauma treatment. Today with new advances in neuroscience, there is a growing recognition and development of somatic therapies. As our field grows, we need assessment tools that reflect the shift from a symptom-driven diagnostic system (i.e., *DSM*) to an embodied approach that captures the experiential process and somatic history of the client.

An Experiential Model of Assessment: The Primacy of Process

I created the Felt Sense Polyvagal Model (FSPM) and its accompanying Embodied Assessment and Treatment Tool (EATT) in response to the need for a paradigm-shifting modality that honors the wisdom of the body (Winhall, 2021). The traditional biopsychosocial model of assessment is content driven, focused on taking a history to develop a treatment plan. It is done in the first session or two when a sense of safety and collaboration are just forming. Sometimes it can result in clients feeling shamed and violated as they are asked to recount horrific experiences, all at once, to a stranger.

In sharp contrast, the EATT offers a unique experiential therapy assessment that prioritizes embodied process: the process of moment-by-moment experiencing in the context of a safe relationship. This process is developed in collaboration with the client over time. Attention is paid to whatever is present as therapist and client begin a mutual exploration. As coregulation evolves, the body leads in revealing the somatic history of wounded places.

Trauma survivors require somatic therapists who move slowly, cultivating their own sense of safety and embodied presence. In this context, the process of assessment and treatment merge as one informs the other in a flow of deep, nurturing coregulation.

Interoception and Neuroception: Two Embodied Processes

The EATT provides a structured diagnostic tool to evaluate clients' neurophysiological states and their capacity to coregulate by integrating Gendlin's (1981) embodied phenomenology of focusing/felt sensing (interoception) with Porges's (2011) Polyvagal Theory (neuroception). These two embodied processes are the foundation of the FSPM. Neural exercises are taught to target these two processes, including tracking neurophysiological states for neuroception and tracking the felt sense for interoception. While we can practice these processes separately, in an embodied sense they are interconnected. To reflect this interconnectedness, I created polyvagal-informed focusing.

The Conceptual Framework: A Bottom-Up/Top-Down Model

Resting on this embodied foundation are five theories that build the conceptual framework. I will briefly describe how each theory contributed to my understanding and formulation of the FSPM as an integrative process.

Feminist/Trauma-Informed Theory

My early teachers were feminist/trauma therapists such as Sandra Butler (1978) and Judith Herman (1992). They validated my appreciation for listening to the wisdom of the body and understanding the adaptive nature of self-harm. The feminist movement incorporated an antioppressive lens that emphasized the systemic nature of trauma and abuse. This broad understanding led me to a deep appreciation of the societal challenges in creating enough safety for healing to occur. Over decades, van der Kolk (2014), Maté (2018), Ogden (2006), and many others began to build a solid body of work in understanding how multigenerational trauma impacts brain development, memory, and learning. This knowledge led to a plethora of research and continues to have a huge impact.

Focusing and Focusing-Oriented Therapy

Gendlin's pioneering work in the field of philosophy and somatics gave me the experiential learning of felt sensing, and focusing-oriented therapy, a methodology for deeply somatic therapy (Gendlin, 1996). This was key in aiding my clients gently back to body wisdom.

Interpersonal Neurobiology

Siegel's contribution to the field of interpersonal neurobiology helped me to integrate somatics with new findings in neuroscience. His embodied assessment of the nine domains of integration (Siegel, 1999) is a significant contribution and is embedded in the EATT.

Learning Model of Addiction

Lewis's (2015) learning model was important in developing the FSPM because I needed a nonpathologizing understanding of addiction based on neuroscience. Lewis updated the medical model by appreciating the role of neuroplasticity in understanding how addiction develops as a learned response, not a disease.

Polyvagal Theory

Polyvagal Theory provided the container I was looking for. In 2012, I attended a conference where I first heard Stephen Porges speak. As I listened, I began to understand how trauma and addiction could best be understood through the lens of the autonomic nervous system (ANS). Porges's naming of the dorsal vagus as part of the ANS provided a neurophysiological explanation for something I knew instinctively: dissociation is an adaptive strategy for survival. It then became clear that addictions help clients to shift states back and forth from a sympathetic to a dorsal response to numb the pain. Finally, I had found a comprehensive nonpathologizing theory that honored the adaptive features of the body. As I incorporated Polyvagal Theory with the felt sense practice of deep embodied listening, it became apparent that neuroception and interoception are key processes in healing. Hence I formulated the Felt Sense Polyvagal Model.

Applying the EATT: Nine Components

The EATT has nine components that formulate assessment and treatment:

1. The Felt Sense Polyvagal Model (Winhall, 2021)
2. The Experiencing Scale (EXP; Gendlin, 1969)
3. The Felt Sense Polyvagal Dialogue (Winhall, 2021)
4. The Four Circle Harm Reduction Practice (Winhall, 2023)
5. The Trauma Egg (Murray, 2012)
6. The Nine Domains of Integration (Siegel, 2012)
7. The Privilege Wheel (Wheel of Privilege and Power, 2023)
8. The Neuroception of Psychological Safety Scale (Morton et al., 2022)
9. Specific concerns (ADD, autism spectrum, medication consultation, etc.)

The first two are done at the beginning of the assessment. We use the FSPM graphic model for tracking neuroception and Gendlin's Experiencing Scale (EXP; Gendlin, 1986) for tracking felt sensing/interoception. The other seven components can be used as needed based on what seems helpful and timely. The EATT is formulated on an ongoing basis and documented in a process recording summary. For the sake of brevity in this chapter, I will explain the first two components with more detail, and give a case example using components 1, 2, and 4. For elaboration of the components, see my book *Treating Trauma and Addiction with the Felt Sense Polyvagal Model* (Winhall, 2021).

THE FELT SENSE POLYVAGAL MODEL™ (FSPM)

7 F's

TRAUMA FEEDBACK LOOP

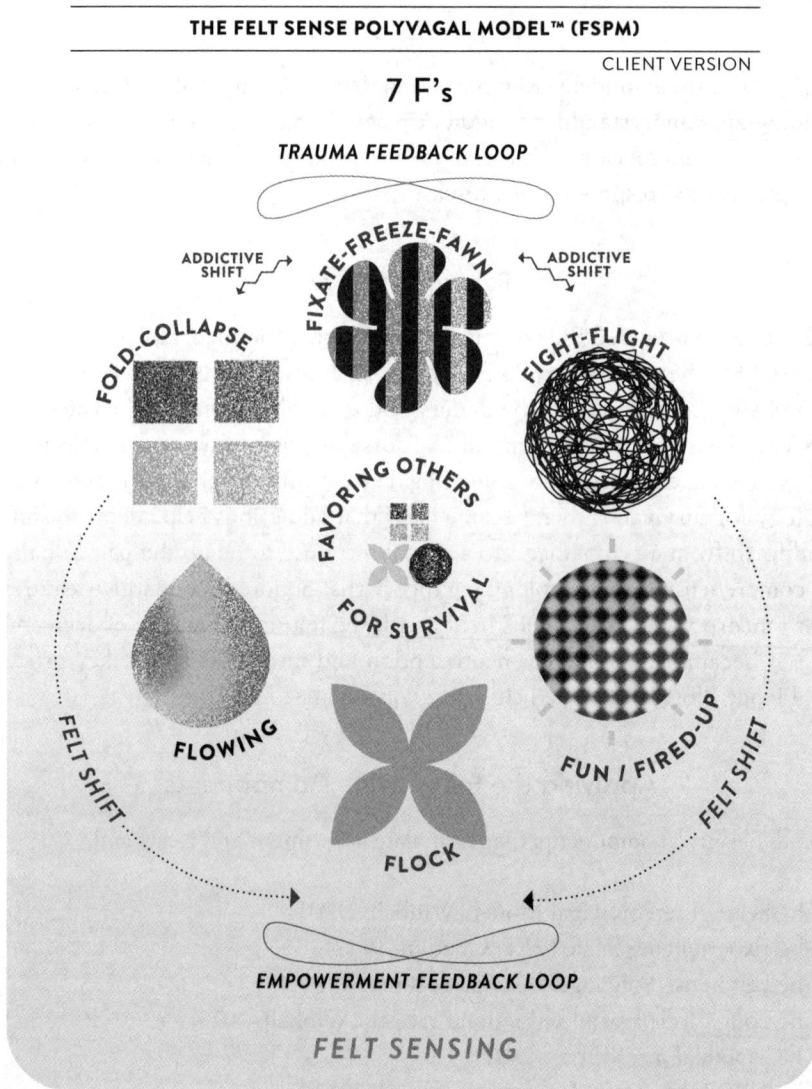

FIXATE-FREEZE-FAWN

FOLD-COLLAPSE

FIGHT-FLIGHT

ADDICTIVE SHIFT

ADDICTIVE SHIFT

FAVORING OTHERS

FOR SURVIVAL

FELT SHIFT

FLOWING

FLOCK

FUN / FIRED-UP

FELT SHIFT

EMPOWERMENT FEEDBACK LOOP

FELT SENSING

FIGURE 8.1 The 7 Fs: Three main pathways: Flock (ventral), Fight/Flight (sympathetic), Fold (dorsal).

1. The Felt Sense Polyvagal Model: Embodied Learning With Graphic Versions

Graphic images engage bottom-up processing by activating the right hemisphere. This is the area of the brain involved in the two key processes of interoception and neurocep-tion, as well as creative, nonlinear, big-picture thinking. I created two graphic models, a client and clinician version, that are designed to appeal to embodied processing with the use of playful imagery. I used circles to activate nonlinear thinking. The only place where boxes appear (linear, top-down processing) is in the dorsal state of disconnection. Color images (see my website, https://janwinhall.com) evoke emotional responses, activating interoceptive awareness.

The introduction of the model as a teaching tool early in treatment helps to create a safe and playful embodied container. It enables the clinician to teach complex top-down polyvagal concepts while simultaneously engaging bottom-up felt sensing. By targeting both, embodied learning is profoundly impactful. Figure 8.1 shows the client version.

1. Flock—ventral state of safety and social engagement. This state promotes health, growth, and restoration.
2. Fight/Flight—sympathetic response. Flight is a state of fear and anxiety. In this state, the body mobilizes to run and escape. Fight is a mobilizing state of anger. In this state, our immune system is compromised.
3. Fold—dorsal response. Fold is a collapse of the ANS into a dissociative state when the sympathetic response is ineffective.

Four blended states: Fixate/Freeze (sympathetic/dorsal), Flowing (dorsal, ventral), Fun/Fired Up (ventral/sympathetic).

4. Fixate (Fight/Flight and Fold) blended state. It is the blended freeze state of stopped processing. Addictions occur here as propellers that shift states between Flight/Fight and Fold. This is the trauma feedback loop in the top half of the model. Fawn is another blending of flight/fight and fold where people are caught in the trauma feedback loop and comply with perpetrators to ward against aggression. Notice that there is no ventral energy in the trauma feedback loop. The victim is dissociating, shutting down to hide and survive what is perceived by the body as a life threat.
5. Flowing (Flock and Fold) blended state. Flowing is a blended state between ventral and dorsal. It is a state of safety with stillness.
6. Fun/Fired Up (Flock and Fight/Flight) blended state. Fun is the blended state between ventral and sympathetic, a state of playfulness. Fired Up, an impassioned, activated state, is another blending of ventral and sympathetic.
7. Favoring others for survival (Flock, Flight/Fight, Fold). This is a blending of the three main states, ventral, sympathetic, and dorsal. It is the state described by Porges (2023) as appeasement. While fawning is similar in that the person is focused on meeting the perpetrator's needs, favoring others for survival includes some ventral energy that enables the person to stay more connected to self and awareness of the need to comply in order to survive. In this state, the victim is actively trying to please the perpetrator in order to avoid threat. There is conscious awareness of a purposeful intent, whereas with fawning, there is often no awareness of behavior. It remains dissociated.

Tracking Neuroception: The 7 Fs

A polyvagal-informed therapist teaches their clients how to understand their ANS and track their neurophysiological states. My clients helped me create a simple version where each state starts with the letter F. We call it the 7 Fs, making it easy to remember. As we describe and track states, I explain to them that the body engages in a process called neuroception, an unconscious system of shifting states when threat is detected. They keep track of their ANS by putting a download of the model on their phone and/or refrigerator. I have a large 3 × 5-foot image of the model in my office. Some clients like to stand up, placing their hands on their ANS pathway. We often do this at the end of a session so we can engage the body in tracking the healing journey.

In an EATT assessment, we always start with documenting the FSPM autonomic state. This is essential because the state that our client is in will determine our treatment. We explain to them that they need to have enough ventral energy available to begin to heal. Clients begin to understand this as they recognize how their body carries each state. Flight/Fight is held tightly, infused with fear and/or anger; Fold is collapsed and often limp or heavy, with sadness and numbing; Flock is relaxed and open, with happy/calm feelings. As clients become more familiar with each state, they begin to notice how blended states are held in different parts of the body. We slowly begin a process of connecting with a source of grounded, ventral energy. This process takes time, as trauma survivors slowly find their way into embodiment.

The Trauma Feedback Loop

While bodies possess inherent wisdom, they also become stuck in a rut of repeated trauma responses. The graphic images help clients see how their ANS is caught in a trauma feedback loop, the top half of the model. It becomes clear that they are missing out on the bottom half of the model that follows the ventral pathways, the states that support a fulfilling life. We explain how living in the top half of the model is adaptive when there isn't enough safety. However, this becomes problematic if we are triggered and our ANS continues to perceive threat when enough safety is present.

Tracking Interoception: Six Steps of Focusing

A somatic therapist embodies a deep connection with their own bodily knowing. This connection extends as an implicit invitation for clients to begin the journey into their own inner landscape, the place before words, where fresh awareness occurs. This is the language of the felt sense. How and when this somatic journey occurs is a delicate process, a dance between partners. Often it starts with an exploration of the four avenues into a felt sense: thoughts, feelings, physical sensations, and memories.

We guide our clients through the six steps of focusing (Gendlin, 1981) to help them slowly begin to come into the body. As their capacity for deep embodied listening develops, we track their felt sense. With the FSPM as our guide, they see how felt sensing occurs in the bottom half of the model where ventral energy is present. It becomes clear that they need to develop neural exercises such as felt sensing to activate the ventral branch of the ANS.

Felt Shift: A Shift in ANS State

> Feelings of safety are not equivalent to objective measurements of safety, which could pragmatically be defined as the removal of threat. Feeling safe is more akin to the felt sense described by Eugene Gendlin (2018). Although Gendlin, as a philosopher and psychologist, was not physiologically oriented, he described a "felt sense/shift" as not just a mental experience, but also a physical one. (Porges, 2022)

In the above quote, Porges points out a basic premise that Gendlin observed in his psychotherapy research. Feeling safe, a precursor for healing, occurs through the mental and physical process of felt sensing. When the body detects safety through the process of neuroception and interoception, a felt sense/shift occurs. The Felt Sense Polyvagal Model posits that the felt shift is accompanied by a shift in neurophysiological state. Clients learn to recognize the physical release that occurs with the felt shift. They can feel the relaxed, warm energy of ventral connection. They trust their bodies' knowing of the right next step toward integration. Gendlin called the felt shift the "motor of change" in the healing process.

Figure 8.2 is the clinician version of the FSPM that integrates the five theories and the felt sense. While I use this model for teaching clinicians, some clients are curious and feel excited to learn more about the complexity of the model.

The Experiencing Scale: Tracking Interoception

The Experiencing Scale (Klein et al., 1969) is an interoceptive tool developed by Gendlin and colleagues to aid in researching somatic awareness. Reliability and validity were developed for the scale. Judges were trained through standardized materials. It measures seven stages of experiencing involving emotional and cognitive awareness. During the first three stages, the client is focused on external events. During stage 4, there is a growing sense of inward connecting to feelings. Stages 5, 6, and 7 include the client's direct reference to the felt sense and the felt shift. The levels of experiencing are listed down the left side of the clinician model. The farther down the page, the deeper the client's level of embodiment. Several versions of the scale are available. Here is a simple one that we use:

1. The client simply talks about events, ideas, or others.
2. Refers to self but without expressing emotions.
3. Expresses emotions but only as they relate to external circumstances.

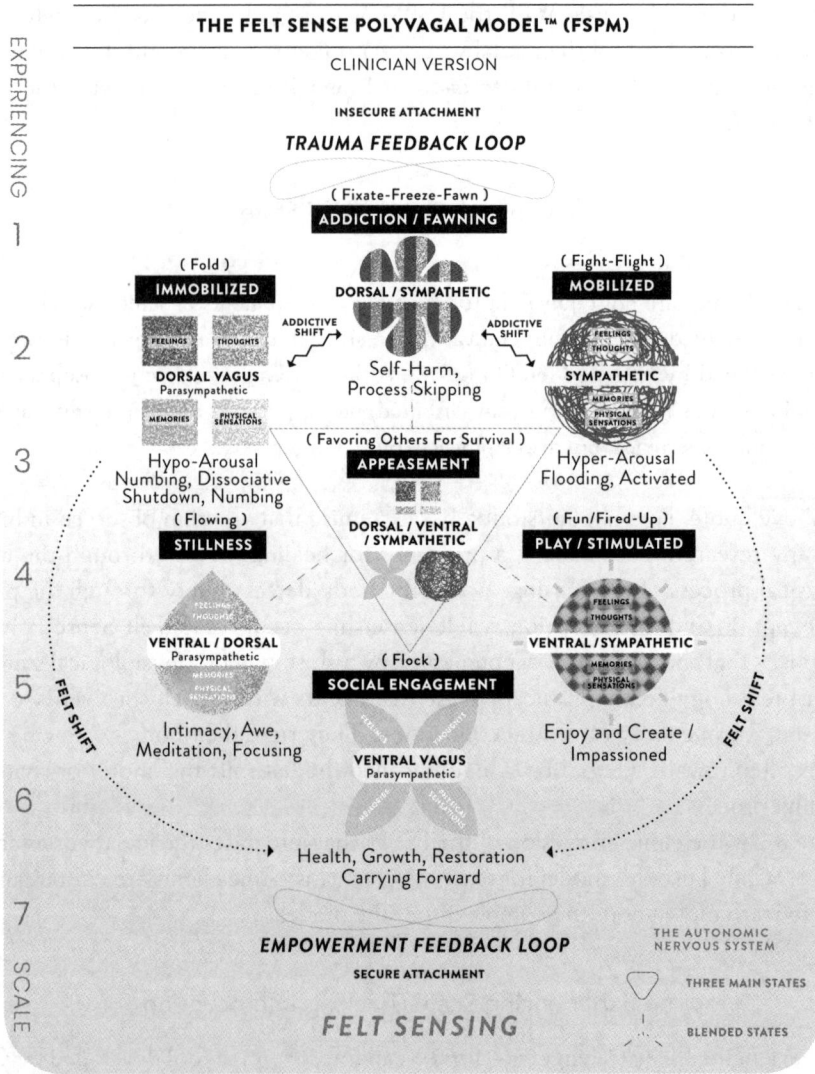

FIGURE 8.2 Clinican version of the Felt Sense Polyvagal Model.

4. Focuses directly on emotions and thoughts about self.
5. Engages in exploring their inner experience (felt sensing).
6. Gains awareness of previously implicit feelings and meanings (felt shift/ANS shift).
7. Ongoing process of in-depth self-reflection provides new perspectives to solve significant problems.

The Experiencing Scale provides a way of monitoring your client's progress over time by keeping track of EXP scores. We rate sessions as a way of discussing process and outcomes, noticing where low and high experiencing occurs, and where felt shifts happen. The Experiencing Scale can also be related to ANS states: What levels are present in different states?

Ventral States: Levels 1 Through 7 (Flowing, Flock, Fun, Fired Up)

If your client is presenting in a ventral state, you can expect to see a range of levels from 1 through 7 during a therapy session, depending on how deeply they are connecting with experiencing. For example, often at the beginning of a session when a client is retelling a story, they want to tell you the details of a situation and don't slow down to deeply connect. As the session progresses, we invite a deeper level of experiencing to develop, and we see them progress into levels 5, 6, and 7 as they connect with the felt sense/shift. The ventral state is reflected in a full range of experiencing.

Dorsal States: Levels 1 or 2 (Fold)

The dorsal shutdown state is disconnected from sympathetic and ventral energy. This dissociated state constricts affect, resulting in the very limited range of levels 1 and 2.

Sympathetic States: Levels 3 and 4 (Fight/Flight)

Your client can move beyond retelling and into connecting with feeling, but often spinning around in flight/fight, unable to pause and feel into a felt sense of the whole situation. This results in a chaotic, flooding state of hypervigilance. Felt sense is not available in this state. The range of experiencing is constricted, reflected in the absence of levels 5, 6, or 7.

The Process Recording: The Online EATT

CLIENT EXPERIENCE	THERAPIST RESPONSE	THERAPIST FELT SENSE/7 Fs	EATT COMPONENT	POLYVAGAL/ INFORMED FOT STRATEGIES	ADDITIONAL MODALITIES
			1. FSPM 7 Fs		
			2. EXP Scale		

The above table illustrates how the EATT can be completed online in an excel spreadsheet (https://janwinhall.com/fspm-chapter). It serves as an assessment tool, an ongoing treatment tool, and a clinical record. It can also be used as a supervision tool, where you watch a video of a session and share your screen with the EATT spreadsheet. You can complete an EATT for the whole session or choose an instance in the session that you want to explore and document. The process of completing an EATT aids the clinician in a deeper embodied understanding of the therapeutic process. This often occurs when therapists connect with their own felt sense of the session.

The online format facilitates an experiential therapy process by allowing you to document the process in a moment-by-moment way, filling in items as they occur. For the sake of this format, later in this chapter I describe an instance in the case example in paragraph form, describing the entries under each heading.

First, we describe the client's experience, how the therapist responds in the session, and the therapist's felt sense/7 Fs state to assess coregulation. Therapists engage in their own interoception/neuroception process as part of the EATT. This deepens their therapeutic presence by engaging somatic awareness, including any countertransference issues that may arise, thus improving coregulation in a unique way.

Next, we assess EATT Component 1, using the FSPM (7 Fs) to track the client's neurophysiological state. Then Component 2, using the EXP Scale to track clients' interoceptive state. We then document other components that we are working with in the session. In the case example I am working with, Component 4 is the Four Circle Harm Reduction Practice.

Under polyvagal-informed focusing-oriented therapy strategies (Winhall, 2021) we list the specific methods that we use in treatment. While working with the felt sense can be integrated into any treatment modality, focusing-oriented therapists have developed specific strategies that form the basis of the FSPM. Here are a few examples that I use in the case example:

1. Revolutionary pause: a mindfulness practice. Hendricks-Gendlin (2003), a major contributor to focusing, named the revolutionary pause. "Focusing is a force for peace because it frees people from being manipulated by external authority, cultural roles, ideologies, and the internal oppression of self-attacking and shame. This freeing has to do with the ability to pause the on-going situation and create a space in which a felt sense can form." Pausing in our culture is considered odd, or awkward at best. Yet it is through slowing down and welcoming silence that we are able to access a deeper bodily knowing. We teach our clients how to actively sense into their body. They learn how to regulate their attention through becoming skilled at pausing, a mindfulness practice that facilitates felt sensing.

2. The focusing attitude: cultivating presence and coregulation. Once we pause, we welcome everything that comes into the therapy room, as long as it is safe and respectful. We listen freshly, meaning that we try to clear our own preconceived interpretations and attitudes about the client experience. Gendlin would say that we must welcome the uncomfortable experiences because they give us the most information about how we are living our lives. Most of all, we honor the wisdom of the body.

3. Resourcing: We teach clients how to resource grounding felt sense practices that help them to find ventral energy when they are dysregulated.

4. Titrating: finding the right closeness and distance. This strategy teaches clients how to titrate the intensity of the felt sense experience by using the two main skills in the FSPM, recognizing and regulating the 7 Fs and using the six steps of focusing. In Step 5 the therapist may ask the client if the felt sense is too close or too distant to work with. Neural exercises including breath work, imagery, movement, clearing space (Step 1 in focusing) are used to help with autonomic regulation.

Additional modalities include other therapy modalities that you are working with. The EATT is compatible with any form of therapy. In the following case example, I include internal family systems parts work. This may also include other areas of referral, for example, medication or ADHD assessment.

Case Example: Meet Joe

Joe sits down across from me, slumping into his chair. His body sighs as he looks up and around my office, a place he knows well. I haven't seen him for six years. Joe grew up in the southern states, a young black man who learned to soothe the pain of poverty, the injustice of racism, and the absence of a father by masturbating and eating lots of sugar. As he got older, he discovered marijuana. Joe worked with me for several years developing his Four Circle Harm Reduction Practice (Figure 8.3).

The Inner Circle: Fixate

The inner circle represents addictive behaviors that clients are ready to change. Using interoception and neuroception as our guide, we collaborate with the body in placing the behaviors inside the circle. The behaviors must be quantifiable for clear accountability. Clients agree to check in with their therapist to build accountability on a daily or weekly basis. Clients are encouraged to form focusing accountability partnerships, where they take turns focusing and reflective listening. In deep connection with each other, they practice daily check-ins using the FSPM and the Four Circles.

The Second Circle: Fight/Flight, Fixate/Freeze, Fold

The second-circle experiences lead to the activation of addictive behaviors. Addictions function as state regulation strategies that shift from flight/fight to fold. Clients list stressors like job problems, conflicts in relationships, racism, misogyny, poverty, and early abuse histories. We help clients become aware of the trauma feedback loop and their need to assess triggers. This way they can anticipate and respond to stressors by using the Four Circles as a cue to practice third-circle activities. In Joe's case, loneliness would lead to smoking, eating, and watching porn, so he worked hard on third-circle behaviors such as spending time with friends to build more social engagement.

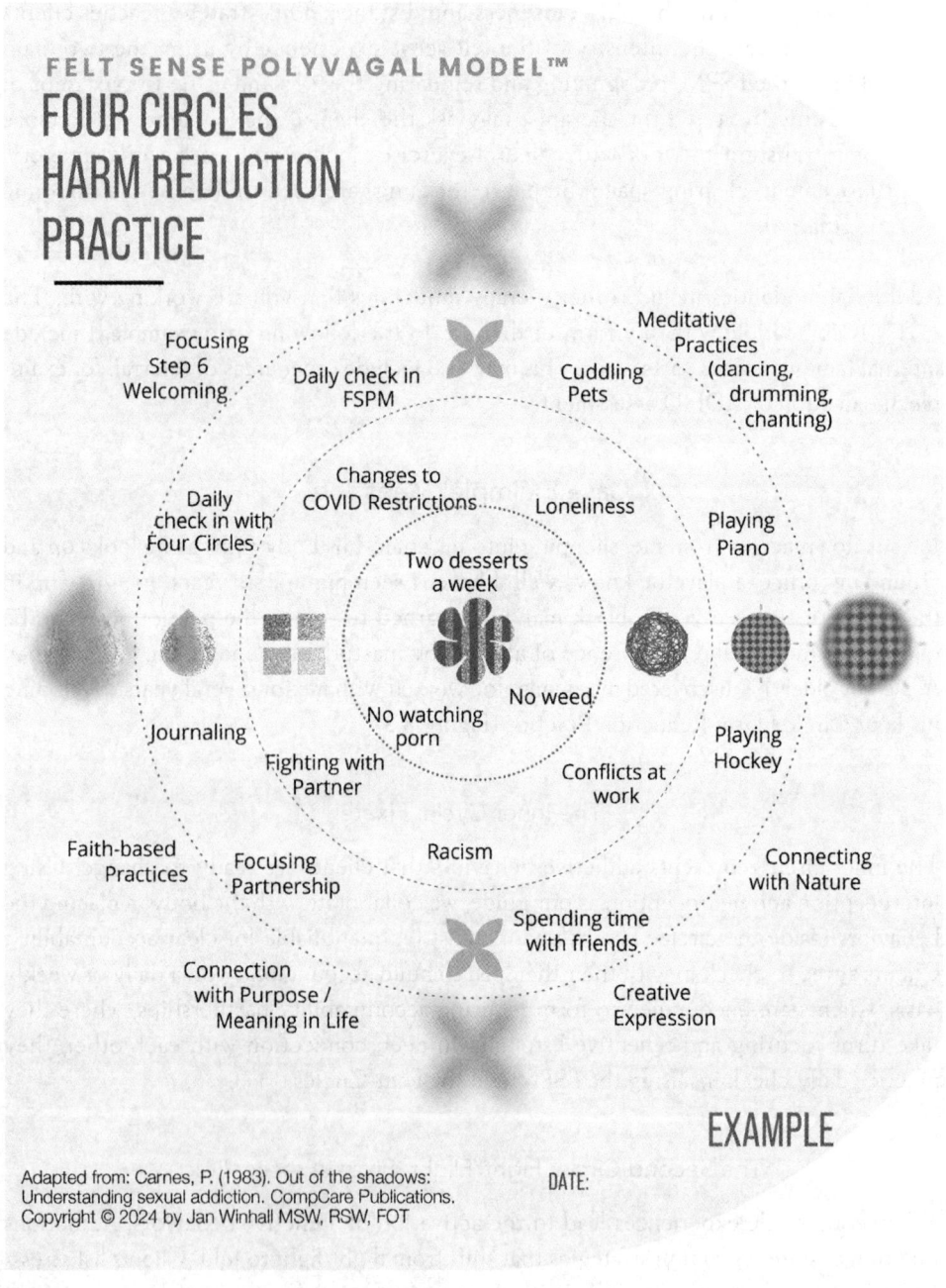

FELT SENSE POLYVAGAL MODEL™

FOUR CIRCLES
HARM REDUCTION
PRACTICE

Focusing
Step 6
Welcoming

Daily check in
FSPM

Meditative
Practices
(dancing,
drumming,
chanting)

Cuddling
Pets

Daily
check in with
Four Circles

Changes to
COVID Restrictions

Loneliness

Playing
Piano

Two desserts
a week

No weed

Journaling

No watching
porn

Fighting with
Partner

Conflicts at
work

Playing
Hockey

Faith-based
Practices

Focusing
Partnership

Racism

Connecting
with Nature

Connection
with Purpose /
Meaning in Life

Spending time
with friends

Creative
Expression

EXAMPLE

Adapted from: Carnes, P. (1983). Out of the shadows:
Understanding sexual addiction. CompCare Publications.
Copyright © 2024 by Jan Winhall MSW, RSW, FOT

DATE:

FIGURE 8.3 The Four Circle Harm Reduction Practice is a tool that I adapted from Patrick Carnes (1983). The circles provide a map for clients to document their management of addictive behaviors. I integrated the Felt Sense Polyvagal Model into the circles, introducing the ANS states and focusing practice.

The Third Circle: Flock, Fun/Fired Up, Flowing

The third circle is the place of health, growth, and restoration. The felt sense experience of life is engaged, and purpose and meaning carry us forward. Addictions are not active in this state of social engagement. Joe had established a regulated life for many years.

The Fourth Circle: Flock, Fun/Fired Up, Flowing

The fourth circle is an extension of the third, where deep spiritual practices occur. Here we cultivate intense connection with self, others, God, the natural world using practices such as dancing, chanting, singing, praying, or creating.

Joe's Process Recording

CLIENT EXPERIENCE: Joe starts the session saying that he cannot believe what he did. "I'm terrified, Jan. I haven't screwed up since I stopped seeing you six years ago. Then my mother dies, and I lose it. My brother lit up a joint after her funeral and I smoked with him. That was three days ago, and I have smoked twice since then." Our eyes meet, and Joe starts to cry. "I can't sleep, I can't work. I am losing it!"

THERAPIST RESPONSE: "I know it's a slippery slope, Joe. I feel how scared you are, but remember, we have neuroplasticity on our side. . . . You have done a lot of wonderful work on building new neuropathways, and that isn't lost. And you're here now, and we will find our way."

THERAPIST FELT SENSE/7 Fs: My chest tightens as a warm loving felt sense forms in the center of my body. Joe and I know each other so well. I am holding the grounded energy for both of us in Flock (ventral), with a tightening, sympathetic blended state in Fired Up. As I stay with the felt sense, I feel some fear for Joe. I slowly titrate the fear by resourcing my trust in Joe's embodied wisdom. It melts into a warm yellow glow. My interoceptive awareness helps to form a deep coregulation with Joe.

EATT Component

1. FSPM: Joe is in Fixate in his return to addictive behaviors, presenting in Flight (sympathetic). This shifts to ventral by the end of the session.
2. EXP Scale: Fixate levels oscillating between levels 1 and 4. This deepens to a level 6 by the end of the session.
3. Four Circle Harm Reduction Practice

Polyvagal-Informed Focusing-Oriented Strategies

A. Revolutionary pause: a neural exercise in autonomic regulation
   "Let's take some time to slow things down and pause. We need to find some

safe ventral energy. Is it okay to bring your attention to the room? Become aware of what is around you. . . . Notice your feet on the floor. Invite your body to slow down and begin to come into the present moment."

B. Focusing attitude: cultivating presence and coregulation
I take time to coregulate, finding my felt sense, remembering Joe's strength and my deep belief in body wisdom to guide us. I clear space so I can listen freshly, welcoming his uncomfortable feelings.

C. Titrating: finding the right closeness and distance (Winhall, 2021)
"We need to get the right distance from your feelings. Notice where you are in the 7 Fs." I help Joe work with titrating his sympathetic response. We put our feet firmly on the floor and extend the exhalation breath. Our bodies remember the felt sense of being grounded together in coregulation. I see him struggle to slow down, watch his breathing begin to tune into mine. "Would it be okay to close your eyes and bring your attention down into the center of your body?" Joe nods, settles into his body, placing his hand in the center of his chest. "My body remembers this safe place in my chest."

D. Resourcing
"Ask your body to find a time when it felt solid and safe." Joe breathes deeply and stays inside for quite a while.
   "I'm having trouble settling," he says.
   I say, "I remember a handle [Step 3] you had for feeling safe enough. It came from a part of you that you call Big Joe."
   The part of Joe that knows how to find grounding is forming. I see the felt shift in his body, from sympathetic constriction to ventral relaxation. The felt sense of Big Joe is a warm embrace. Joe puts his arms around himself, closing his eyes and welcoming this powerful part of himself.

Four Circle Harm Reduction Practice: Component Four

"Now that you are more regulated, we are ready to review your four circles. Let's look at the third circle and see how you can find more ventral energy."
   At the end of the session, we go back to the focusing attitude.
   I explain, "You got triggered, and your body took you back into the trauma feedback loop, back to smoking to numb your overwhelming feelings. That is understandable. It was adaptive when you didn't have enough safety. Now you do. As we rewire your ANS, you are shifting into a ventral state where you don't need addictions. You are safe enough now, Joe, right in this moment."
   Joe says, "Yes, I lost my grounding for a while, but I feel the strength of Big Joe. I know that if I stay with my Four Circle practice every day, I will not use. I'm not scared anymore. I feel safe when I am in my body."

Additional Modalities

The above example illustrates how any modality can be integrated into the FSPM. In this example, I used Richard Schwartz's internal family systems (IFS) to work with the part of Joe that he identifies as "self." This is Joe's ventrally regulated felt sense experience of being grounded and safe.

Conclusion

Current top-down models for treating trauma and addiction leave out the most important aspect of what it means to be a human being, the wisdom of our bodies. The traditional pathologizing paradigm views traumatic symptoms such as dissociation and addiction as maladaptive responses. This is a misunderstanding. Seen through the lens of our autonomic nervous system, these maladaptive responses are adaptive strategies that protect us, promoting survival when there is no perceived escape. This is body wisdom.

The Felt Sense Polyvagal Model sees the body as the focal point for healing by teaching clients how to harness two embodied processes, neuroception and interoception. In the case with Joe, we see how his body remembers the two basic skills of the FSPM, tracking his ANS state and finding the felt sense of safety through coregulating with me. His embodied memory helps him to efficiently get back on track with his Four Circle practice.

Top-down methodologies, such as cognitive therapies and 12-step programs, start with tasks that often require good executive functioning. We know that trauma and addiction compromise executive functioning, so the FSPM starts by inviting more embodied practices that activate ventral energy to improve Joe's capacity to think clearly. Once he is more grounded, we begin to work on his Four Circle practice, which involves more planning, organizing, and delaying gratification, all aspects of executive functioning.

The FSPM enhances the efficacy of any therapeutic method by integrating neuroception and interoception. In the case example using the IFS method, Joe's capacity to access the part he calls Big Joe is aided by his interoceptive skill in accessing the embodied felt sense of Big Joe. Engaging the somatic memory activates the ventral vagus, deepening the healing process.

The Embodied Assessment and Treatment Tool offers clinicians a new methodology for assessing clients' somatic functioning by tracking autonomic state and levels of experiencing. In completing the process recording of the EATT, clinicians experience a moment-by-moment accounting of the session. This pausing and documenting therapist felt sense and ANS state allows for deeper awareness and presence. In addition, the structure of the EATT aids in the therapist's intellectual journey by offering a variety of components to choose from in formulating a treatment plan. The therapist can review previous EATT assessments to track somatic functioning, document different treatment strategies, and track moment-by-moment processing.

I invite you now to pause, slowly bringing your attention inside. Invite your bodily felt sense of the concepts presented in the FSPM. In this way, mind and body lead in developing new intellectual frontiers.

9

Memory Reconsolidation in Body-Oriented Trauma Therapies

Antonia Pfeiffer

There is a voice that does not use words. Listen!
—RUMI

WHEN NEW CLIENTS ENTER OUR PRACTICE, WHAT ARE THEY TRYING TO OVERCOME? MANY clients suffer from strong, seemingly uncontrollable emotions, emotions that often feel irrational and trigger deep shame. Others experience unexplained pain, hyperarousal, and insomnia.

When clients leave our practice after successful therapy, what is the outcome? Some feel safe again in their bodies. They sleep better. Perhaps they can face their trauma triggers without being hijacked by their overwhelming emotions.

A lot of these results can be explained by a regulation of their nervous system. However, some of the results might also be explained by a transformational change in their implicit memory systems—the process of memory reconsolidation. This process leads to the permanent update of physiological and emotional reactions to the memory of the traumatic event. The stories and former triggers lose their emotional charge.

The process of memory reconsolidation is old and new. New because science is only starting to shed light on the underlying protocols that lead to transformational change: The process of memory reconsolidation was officially described in science in 2000. Yet it is old because it has always been there—there have been stories of deep emotional healing throughout history in ancient and modern therapeutic traditions.

One of the most fascinating facets of the protocols of reconsolidation is that they resemble the way body-oriented trauma therapies like Somatic Experiencing, tapping techniques, EMDR, or Integral Somatic Psychology confront triggers and strong emotions. This article is an attempt to translate 25 years of research on memory reconsolidation into the work of body-oriented trauma therapies.

Introduction

This is a small and perhaps complicated chapter on the neuroscience of emotional memory, included in a large book. First, I want to introduce myself and my history with the topic of this chapter and hope it entices you to read further. My name is Antonia. As a physician, I work with body-oriented trauma techniques in a small private practice. As a scientist, I study their underlying effect mechanisms.

I have studied the process of memory reconsolidation from the perspective of a scientist, a therapist, a patient, and an artist. After a series of medical errors, I was confined to a wheelchair for 10 years during medical school. Similar to a lab rat, I was subjected to one of the worst methods of fear conditioning—fear conditioning in a place where I couldn't move. As a passionate dancer, I tried every embodiment technique I could find. The beauty of continuum and my art helped me through. Yet, I developed very strange fear reactions, even to things I was definitely not afraid of. Why did these new fear reactions occur and how does one get rid of them?

I found answers to most of my questions in my doctoral dissertation on the neuroscience of tapping. And although it was not trauma therapy but the right medication that eventually got me out of the wheelchair, I am confident that I would not have healed without the following information.

Memory: A Difficult Word

When we talk about emotional memories, we usually mean the stories of important moments in our lives—such as a magical tango lesson in Buenos Aires or a horrific car accident. When we recall these moments, we are likely to experience a rush of pleasant or unpleasant bodily sensations—even years after the experience; a subtle change in posture when we think of the tango lesson, a cold shiver and a knot in the stomach when we think of the accident. Usually, we refer to the story as the memory, and the feeling is perceived as a spontaneous physiological or emotional reaction.

In reality, both are memory fragments that were encoded in different areas of the brain at the same time (Visser et al., 2018). One speaks through words, the other through bodily sensations. One was stored to later enable us to tell the story of the event, the other to automatically respond and ensure our safety when similar events occur in the future. They can be treated separately in therapy. Therefore, it is helpful to distinguish between them.

First, the memories we can verbally recall are explicit memories: our knowledge (semantic memory) and our biographical stories (episodic memory) combined. These memories are like books on a shelf for us. We can decide deliberately when we want to read them again. Sometimes it takes us a while to find them, but when we do, we can tell their stories in words. They have a beginning and an end (LeDoux, 2015).

In traumatic moments, a second form of biographical memory can emerge. The so-called flashbacks are sensory-perceptual imprints of the worst moments of a traumatic event that intrude involuntarily in everyday consciousness. They exhibit a sense

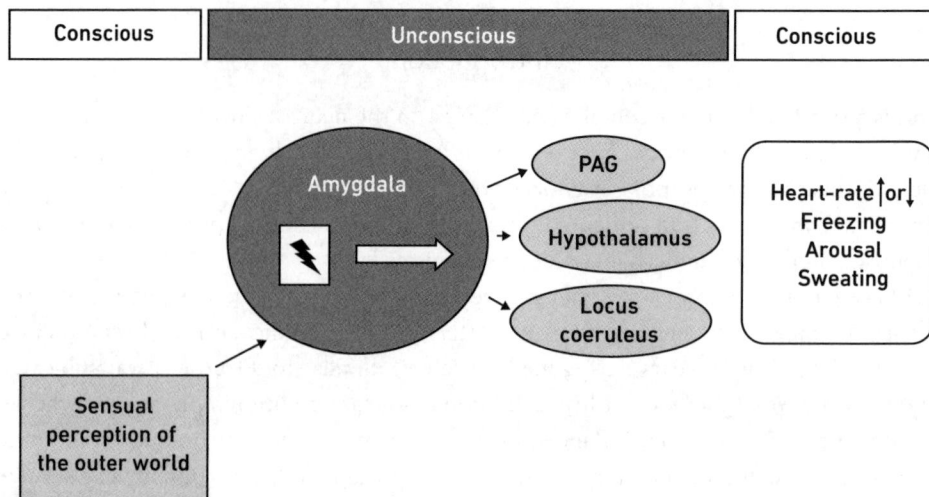

FIGURE 9.1 Conscious and unconscious processing of a trigger.

of nowness—we feel as if the trauma is happening right here, right now (Iyadurai et al., 2019; Visser et al., 2018).

Then there are our nonverbal implicit memories such as skills, habits, or implicit emotional memories. When they are activated, we experience them in our bodies. In the tango lesson example, the implicit memory would be the ability to tango. In the example with the car accident, the implicit memories are the conditioned responses to aspects of the traumatic incident. They manifest in physiology, behavior, and emotion: perhaps a fear of freeways combined with avoidance behavior, or physical reactions to the car such as sweating or a change in muscle tone (LeDoux, 2015). These implicit emotional memories are the main focus of this chapter.

Although the full range of our human emotions can be stored as conditioned responses in these memory traces, science has focused on fear memories in the amygdala. Most research on fear memories in the amygdala has been conducted using Ivan Pavlov's classical conditioning experimental paradigm. The experiment involves pairing an electrical shock with a neutral stimulus, such as a red square, until the stimulus itself elicits the same fear responses as the shock.

This associative learning is stored as a memory trace in the amygdala (Liu et al., 2022). Later, when something in the outside world resembles these traces, the physiological-emotional responses in the body are triggered. Since the amygdala is an unconscious area of the brain, these reactions are what reach consciousness from the implicit emotional memories (LeDoux, 2015).

The reactions can feel overwhelming, confusing, and frightening. Often, a situation in the outside world triggers old emotional learning that we are not aware of. It feels like the situation in the present is triggering the emotion. But the emotional response feels too big, inappropriate, or shameful in light of that situation. And somehow uncontrollable.

This is especially true for associative memories formed during trauma. In moments that are perceived as life-threatening, hopeless, or overwhelming, particularly strong and robust implicit emotional memories are formed under the influence of the stress hormones norepinephrine and epinephrine. Often, fear even generalizes to similar triggers (Kaczkurkin et al., 2017; Lis et al., 2020). Studies with subjects who have not experienced trauma show the role that the state of the nervous system plays in this memory formation. Only by increasing norepinephrine levels do these subjects develop robust fears that are difficult to unlearn and generalize to similar objects (Soeter & Kindt, 2011, 2012).

I would like to conclude this section about emotional memories with a particular feature of these memories that can't be learned from studies and plays an important role in attachment trauma. Even though implicit emotional memories do not contain biographical stories, they often tell a story. When they are activated, we revisit what we felt back then. We feel what we learned to be true about ourselves and the world at that time (Ecker, 2018). That is, unconscious emotional memories store not only emotional reactions, but also emotional truths.

I love the metaphor of frozen ice sculptures—because that's what it can really feel like for our patients. Sometimes it feels like a frozen posture; sometimes it feels like a frozen emotional response, like a frozen belief.

It may sound cheesy, but the experience of warmth, laughter, safety, and love is what—scientifically—invites these emotional truths to dissolve and change. But before we dive into the protocols for memory reconsolidation, we must understand why this process was not scientifically recognized until the year 2000. The historical view of science is almost as fascinating as the research itself.

The History of Memory Research and What It Can Teach Us

So why did scientists believe that emotional memories in the amygdala cannot be changed, or, as the German neuroscientist Gerhard Roth proclaimed in 2015, that the "amygdala does not forget"? The main reason for this lies in the research itself. Research focused on a scientific paradigm that actually quite rarely changes the original memory in the amygdala: the paradigm of extinction (Ecker, 2015).

Extinction is the classic paradigm Ivan Pavlov used to unlearn conditioned fear responses. It is the laboratory experiment for exposure-based therapies. In our example with the red square (that was previously paired with the shock), the red square is presented in a safe environment until the human or animal shows no (or less) physiological reaction to the stimulus. After a successful extinction there is a new memory trace that states that the feared object is neutral and, from now on, competes with the original fear memory (LeDoux, 2015).

However, the old and strong fear memory usually returns in stressful situations, after a certain amount of time, when the person or animal is confronted with the original context. From this, the researchers concluded that emotional memories are truly forever. But the researchers were unaware that they were only researching the process of extinction—not the memory itself (Ecker, 2015; LeDoux, 2015, 2022).

The Process of Memory Reconsolidation

In 2000, a researcher named Karim Nader challenged this paradigm of a change-resistant amygdala in a bold experiment. He had been digging into research that had long been swept under the rug by the scientific community; research that showed fear responses could be permanently altered.

He combined what he learned from these studies with basic research on the formation of a fear memory—in the first four hours, a memory goes through the process of consolidation. This process can be blocked with medication. After this was tested on experimental animals using the same red square method, the animals typically responded to the square without a fear reaction.

However, once a fear memory was consolidated, it was considered unchangeable. Nader now asked himself the following question: What if a fear memory is changeable even after a brief physiological activation? Research in the 1960s had provided evidence that this might be possible. Nevertheless, Nader's ideas were met with rejection. Even the renowned researcher Joseph LeDoux, who was also Nader's boss, considered the idea impossible and advised him against conducting his own research. Nader then took matters into his own hands and conducted research in private (LeDoux, 2022).

Nader reactivated a previously conditioned fear memory in experimental animals and injected a typical medication into the amygdala. As a result, his experimental animals permanently lost their fear reactions, and the bodily reactions could not be reactivated even by strong provocation. Nader was able to come to the following conclusion—fear memories become labile again after being reactivated. Before they reconsolidate, we can change them (Nader et al., 2000).

Some might ask: If it's this easy, then why are we not all reconsolidating all the time? Just like any kind of neuroplasticity, memory reconsolidation can only happen when certain boundary conditions are fulfilled.

The first condition is physiological activation through imagining or directly confronting the trigger, phobic object, or memory. In this process, it seems necessary to truly feel a part of what was felt back then. Preliminary studies with real trauma memories in humans show that those participants that could not access the felt sense associated with the event did not benefit from the reconsolidation protocol (Kindt & Van Emmerik, 2016). Also, reassuring the participants that a feared stimulus was now safe prior to a confrontation hindered a true activation and then, in turn, the process of reconsolidation (Sevenster et al., 2012).

However, violently activating the memory through the same condition that first caused the conditioning also impaired reconsolidation. This is because of the second boundary condition—the mismatch or prediction error. While thinking of the trigger and feeling whatever arises, we must experience something that believably assures us that this time the experience might have a positive ending, that the trigger is now safe (Sevenster et al., 2013).

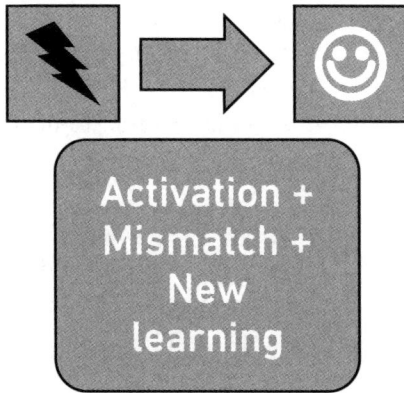

FIGURE 9.2 Sequence of the memory update process.

In human fear conditioning laboratory studies, this is achieved by using the red square without shock. However, the electrodes for the shock usually remain on the wrist. The possibility of shock is present, but it does not occur. Memory becomes labile again for four hours (Sevenster et al., 2012). In this time frame, the process of memory reconsolidation can be blocked with a medical agent. Then, physiological and emotional responses can remain permanently altered (Kindt, 2018).

In 2009, the researcher Marie Monfils was able to prove that it is also possible to update the memory without medication. If, in the time window of four hours after activation and mismatch, new information is incorporated into the memory trace, then the memory trace can be permanently altered. The bodily responses remain permanently changed (Monfils et al., 2009). This new learning or emotional counterexperience must surprisingly, credibly, and repeatedly convey that the trigger is now safe, that the stored emotional reaction is outdated, and that the emotional truth is not true anymore.

Therapist and reconsolidation expert Bruce Ecker describes the process of holding the old emotional learning and the new learning in consciousness until suddenly an "aha" moment occurs. In this, clients' embodiment changes. They understand on an embodied level that the past has passed (Ecker, 2018).

In the case of terrible emotional truths clients believe about themselves, they can now unravel them. This transformation can take place similarly to old fairy tales and fables. Like the beast in *Beauty and the Beast*, who transforms back into a prince when struck by an unexpected but hoped-for love (Belle's love), parts of us that secretly feel like a beast can transform and heal when they experience love and compassion. At least, that's how I experience working as a body-oriented trauma therapist.

Memory Reconsolidation in Body-Oriented Trauma Therapies

One of the central research questions that has preoccupied scientists since Nader's experiment is whether similar changes are possible in the domain of traumatic memories and intense fears. For a long time, researchers assumed that memory reconsolidation is impossible with particularly strong and old memories. However, after a series of successful studies, many scientists have shifted their perspective to the following premise: Old and robust memories are updated only when it truly makes sense from the memory's perspective to abandon the old assumption about the world (Filmer et al., 2022; Kindt, 2018). In the case of fear memories, this means that the client can experience a transformation when the memories are activated when cues of safety are present. This is the strength of body-oriented trauma therapies.

Many body-oriented trauma therapies have developed over the past 50 years in different regions of the world. They are united by a similar philosophy and, for all their differences, by a remarkably similar approach. Body-oriented trauma therapies understand the body in therapy not only as a stage for feelings but also as a gateway to feelings. During exposure to trauma memories and distressing emotions, the body is regulated through touch, movement, and vocalization. Likewise, the therapeutic relationship is designed to support coregulation. Through all of this, the physiological experience is altered while the emotional issue remains present.

The first way body-oriented trauma therapies resemble the protocols of memory reconsolidation experiments is that they also use structured protocols in their sessions. They both work on a single aspect of an emotional memory in an initial session while reviewing the protocol of the technique. The following paragraphs focus on typical protocols of exposure to unpleasant memories and feelings in some body-oriented trauma techniques. Each technique is briefly described below, with attention to the process of activation, adaptation, and new learning.

During the activation of an emotional memory, the focus in body-oriented trauma therapies is on the embodiment of this memory. This is activated in real time as clients recognize the typical emotions, thoughts, body sensations, and impulses they experience in everyday life. Often, activation initially leads to an increase in arousal (Wittfoth et al., 2022). The first condition of the memory reconsolidation protocol is thus fulfilled.

Now the felt sense, as first described by Eugene Gendlin, is explored. This is "the soft underbelly of thought . . . a kind of bodily awareness that . . . can be used as a tool . . . a bodily awareness that . . . encompasses everything you feel and know about a given subject at a given time. . . . It is felt in the body, yet it has meanings. It is body and mind before they are split apart" (Gendlin, 1978, p. 35). This exploration involves the patient's history with this particular felt sense.

For example, in the process and embodiment-focused psychology method, Michael Bohne (2021) asks, "How old do you feel right now?" The answer is often surprisingly clear. Exploring the history of the felt sense in this way can serve as the first mismatch. When it is sensed in the body that the emotional response has its roots in the past, curiosity arises, a sense of agency. An example would be the manager who inwardly, without realizing it, freezes and slips back to his childhood days with his violent father when criticized at work. With the question, "How old do you feel?" he realizes that as a manager with 30 years of professional experience, he can respond differently. He becomes curious.

In the step of the new learning experience, different methods have different emphases. In integral somatic psychology, for example, Raja Selvam (2022) guides clients to feel their emotions to the fullest throughout the body, until they subside on their own. In this way, clients learn that they have the ability to hold their emotions. This experience is described in studies of memory reconsolidation as a powerful mismatch and an emotional counterexperience alike. This is because clients often cite the fear of losing control when confronted with their trauma and thus their emotions as their greatest fear (Kindt & Van Emmerik, 2016).

In the Somatic Experiencing method, Peter Levine incorporates so-called pendulation. Clients slowly oscillate back and forth between feelings of safety or expansion and a trauma state, contraction. Through this action, the nervous system can learn to regulate. Then he allows his patients to renegotiate the trauma. Clients experience that during the activation of the old memory, they integrate new motor patterns into the experience and enact the inhibited response they could not do in the moment of trauma (Levine, 2010).

In trauma techniques that use a bifocal stimulation protocol, exposure is combined with physical stimulation. In tapping techniques, this is tapping on skin points used in classical acupuncture. In EMDR, exposure is combined with bilateral stimulation through eye movements or touch. Sinosomatics uses modalities from TCM such as acupuncture and moxibustion.

During bifocal exposure, clients are encouraged to feel emotions and unpleasant sensations in the body. While thinking of the trauma trigger that leads to arousal, somatosensory stimulation through movement and touch is incorporated until the arousal subsides. Often new aspects, images, or emotions emerge on their own while the same cycle of exposure and stimulation is run until at last the client can think of the event with little or no arousal (Wittfoth et al., 2022).

Movement and touch are included in so many body-oriented trauma therapies that it is useful to look at both in more detail. Movement is a general amplifier of neuroplasticity (Huberman, 2021). In the process of exposure, it can counteract dissociation and immobilization. David Berceli, Peter Levine, and Stephen Porges have long stated that animals use movement to dissolve the shock rigidity of immobilization (Porges & Dana, 2019). Touch can literally touch us through emotional mechanoreceptors of the skin. These so-called CT afferent were only discovered in humans in the 1990s (Nordin, 1990). They enable us to receive regulatory safety signals through the skin. These signals are processed primarily in the brain area of the posterior insula, which can directly regulate the amygdala (Eckstein et al., 2020). By touching the skin of the face, we can also activate the trigeminal nerve, which shares a nucleus with the vagus nerve (Baker & Lui, 2023). I know from my practical experience how often clients yawn when tapping on facial points.

Does a memory reconsolidation always occur in a protocol of such a session? Probably not. However, the process of exposure and bodily stimulation resembles another process that has been the subject of fascinating studies during the past decade: The combination of vagus nerve stimulation during exposure to fear memories in the laboratory. This seems to be very effective. For instance, in experiments involving rats, those that received vagus stimulation during exposure to a feared stimulus took only one fifth of the time to unlearn a conditioned fear compared to those without the stimulation. Furthermore, vagal stimulation resulted in the generalization of extinction to additional triggers. Rats that had developed PTSD-like symptoms due to life-threatening experiments were able to overcome them when exposed during vagal stimulation (Noble et al., 2017; Peña et al., 2013; Souza et al., 2021). Human participants with PTSD who were confronted with their trauma script while receiving electrical vagus stimulation had lower levels of inflammatory markers such as interleukin-6 and interferon-γ in their blood compared to a group that received sham stimulation (Bremner et al., 2020).

Even though finding and reading research articles can sometimes feel like hard work, this research is poetry to me—offering us hope in times when trauma, hyperarousal, and associated diseases feels like its own global pandemic.

Speaking of poetry, I would like to end this article with the words of Australian poet Erin Hanson. In her work, she captures, perhaps without knowing it, a profound moment of a mismatch. Hanson's poem "What If I Fly" delves into the fear of failure that comes with setting out into an alluring unknown—a frightening yet longed-for experience. She describes this fear, which is familiar to many, like the fear of a bird asking itself before its first flight into the wide-open sky: "What if I fall?" She responds to this moment of existential dread by asking, "Oh, but, my darling, what if you fly?" (Hanson, 2014).

In the face of our greatest fears and traumatic memories, faith, trust, and confidence in the eyes of another is perhaps the greatest mismatch of all.

10

The Practice of Embodying Emotions

Raja Selvam

THE PRACTICE OF EMBODYING EMOTIONS IS THE PRIMARY CLINICAL STRATEGY IN INTEGRAL Somatic Psychology (ISP), which is a science-backed, emotion-focused, and body-based complementary psychoneurophysiological approach. ISP has been developed for reducing treatment times and improving diverse outcomes (physical, energetic, cognitive, emotional, behavioral, relational, and spiritual) in all psychotherapy modalities, including other body psychotherapy systems. The chapter is organized in four sections. In Section 1, the clinical strategy of embodying emotions is introduced. In Section 2, the scientific basis of the practice of embodying emotions is presented. Section 3 presents a more detailed description of the practice of embodying emotions in four steps. Two treatment examples of embodying emotions with long-term outcomes can be found in Section 4.

Section 1: The Practice of Embodying Emotions

The practice of embodying emotions is simply the expansion of a person's conscious experience of emotion to as much of their body as possible. For example, if a client reported that their conscious experience of fear is limited to their chest, the practice of embodying emotions would attempt to expand their conscious experience of fear to other places in the body such as their abdomen, head, arms, and so on. When the conscious experience of an emotion is expanded to include more of the body, as we will see, it increases the likelihood that the person's experience of the emotion becomes more tolerable. When an emotional experience becomes more tolerable, a person can stay with it longer, giving the brain as much time as it needs to process it more fully. This in essence is what the practice of embodying emotions is and how it delivers its various benefits.

Valid questions might have arisen in the reader's mind already. Don't clients usually go to therapists to get relief from unpleasant emotions? Wouldn't expanding their emotional experience to more of their body increase their suffering, as opposed to alleviating it? How can expanding an emotional experience to more places in the body make it more tolerable? How can it improve diverse outcomes and shorten treatment times in all therapy modalities? Answers to these important questions that often arise in the minds of those who encounter the practice of embodying emotions can be found in the scientific understanding of both the role of the body and the neurology and physiology of cognition, emotion, and behavior that has been generated in the past 25 years in cognitive and affective neurosciences and cognitive psychology.

Section 2: The Scientific Basis of the Practice of Embodying Emotions

A therapeutic method can have two kinds of scientific validity. One is a priori scientific validity, where the outcomes of the application of the method can be predicted with a high degree of confidence from the science it is built from. Few psychotherapy methods have it. The practice of embodying emotions enjoys this hard-to-come-by scientific validity. The other is a posteriori scientific validity, which is usually gathered from outcomes research studies that show statistically significant differences in outcomes between randomized control and treatment groups from the application of the method. Most psychotherapy methods in use have neither.

The a priori scientific validity of the practice of embodying emotions that allows for the prediction of its outcomes with a high degree of confidence consists of a large number of empirically validated findings from a number of disciplines: cognitive and affective neurosciences, cognitive psychology, and somatic psychology.

How can embodying emotions increase affect tolerance and improve cognitive, emotional, and behavioral outcomes?

Emotion can be viewed as an assessment of the impact of a situation on the well-being of an organism, as registered by the entirety of its survival physiology, which in human beings is identical with the whole of the brain and body physiology. That is, the physiology of emotion in human beings is the brain and body physiology in its entirety. Pleasant emotions arise in response to favorable situations and unpleasant emotions in response to unfavorable situations. That the entire brain and body physiology is also the physiology of cognition and behavior, a dynamic systems perspective, has accumulated substantial neurological evidence in the past 25 years (Barrett, 2017).

We can use the understanding of emotion as the assessment of the impact of a situation on the entire organism to see how expanding the emotional experience to more of the body can lead to a greater capacity for tolerating the emotion. When one tries to limit the impact of a situation on one's brain and body physiology to a few places in the body, as opposed to allowing the impact to be shared by more places in the body, it tends to make the impact less tolerable. This happens in two ways.

One, the impact is prevented from spreading out to more of the physiology to dilute its intensity wherever it is felt. It is equivalent to reducing the strain involved in lifting a heavy bag with two arms as opposed to one. Two, as body psychotherapists know only too well, physiological defenses such as constriction in the muscular system and inhibition in the autonomic nervous system, such as the freeze response, often form to prevent emotional suffering (Marlock et al., 2015). These defenses disrupt essential physiological flows such as blood, oxygen, and lymph. Disruptions in basic regulatory physiological flows decrease the level of regulation and increase the level of stress throughout the body.

Such disruptions increase the levels of stress and dysregulation in the brain and the body and are a common cause of psychophysiological symptoms. These disruptions also make the experience of the body and of emotion in the body more difficult to bear when we try to access them and work with them in therapy (Selvam, 2022).

However, when such physiological defenses are undone, and emotional experiences are allowed to be present in more places in the body, the resulting increase in the level of regulation and decrease in the level of stress in the body makes it more possible to tolerate the experience of the body and of emotion in the body and be with them for a longer period. This gives the brain more time to process the situation cognitively, emotionally, and behaviorally in an optimal manner.

Next, we will look at additional scientific reasons why the approach focuses on emotion and why it is important to work with emotion to ensure its presence in the body.

Why is the focus on emotion?

The reason for the focus on emotion in ISP, rather than on cognition or behavior as the starting point, is due to the considerable evidence in cognitive and affective neurosciences that emotion determines every aspect of cognition (awareness, attention, focus, perception, memory, meaning, and language) and behavior in every moment of our lives (Dukes et al., 2021). These findings, in combination with earlier findings that behavior improves with the presence of emotion rather than its absence (Damasio, 1994) and the common-sense observation that the more regulated the emotions are, the more rational cognition and behavior are likely to be, provide a strong rationale for focusing on emotion as the starting point in this somatic psychology approach.

Why is the focus on the body?

The reason for involving the body in the treatment approach has to do with the virtual revolution in the scientific understanding of the role of the body in cognition, emotion, and behavior in the past 25 years, with very important treatment implications for all psychotherapy modalities. The involvement of the body in behavior is obvious in that it is through the body that all behavior, verbal and nonverbal, is enacted. The role of the body in emotion, the understanding of which has been present all along, has become increasingly established of late (Craig, 2015; Critchley & Nagai, 2012; Damasio, 2003; Laird & Lacasse, 2014). The role of the body in cognition, the least understood and the most surprising, has been the last to be established in affective and cognitive neurosciences in the research paradigm of embodied cognition (Fincher-Kiefer, 2019; Johnson, 2017). In effect, the collective implication of this growing evidence base is that the role of the body in these primary psychological processes is so great that any psychotherapy modality that does not include the body in its treatment approach in some way is bound to have longer treatment times and less than optimal cognitive, emotional, and behavioral outcomes.

Why is the focus on expanding emotional experience in the body?

Therapeutic approaches focused on cognition or behavior or both are evidence based. Their methods have been validated through outcomes research in which their methods have been found to be effective in terms of significant differences in outcomes in randomized treatment versus control groups. There are ways that these modalities can involve the body in their treatment approaches to improve their outcomes further without involving emotion. For example, cognitive approaches can simply incorporate the awareness of body sensations in their treatments. Behavioral approaches can explore whether adding actual physical body movements to their interventions is of additional advantage in resolving symptoms. They already use somatic techniques such as breathing strategies in any case.

Cognitive and behavioral approaches have also been found to be effective in regulating emotions. Practitioners of cognitive and behavioral approaches who do not usually focus on working with emotional experiences other than to change them through cognition and behavior might therefore have the following questions: What additional advantage can they gain from the practice of embodying emotions? Even if emotion determines cognition and behavior in every moment, can we not just regulate emotion through cognition and behavior as we usually do to ensure optimal cognition, emotion, and behavior without having to add emotion and its expansion in the body as extra interventions to ensure better outcomes? The answers can be found in the research on the paradigm of embodied emotions in affective and cognitive neurosciences. The evidence shows that ensuring as little of the body as possible is blocked from being involved in the emotional experience is essential for the brain to optimally process the situation cognitively, emotionally, and behaviorally.

For example, the psychologist Paula Niedenthal (2007) became interested in finding out whether increasing the embodiment of emotion improved cognition. Niedenthal and her colleagues set up an experiment in which subjects were exposed to emotionally charged stories. The subjects were divided into two groups: those whose facial muscles were prevented from participating in their emotional experiences while hearing the stories, and those whose facial muscles were allowed to function normally. The facial muscles are well known for their role in emotion (Ekman, 2016). To make the facial muscles unavailable for one group, the researchers had those participants bite hard on a pen while hearing the stories, to keep their facial muscles in a fixed position. The researchers recorded patterns of neurons firing in the brain during the experiment, immediately after the experiment, and one or two weeks after the experiment. In each instance, the participants were asked to recall the emotional experiences along with the details of the stories they had been exposed to.

The researchers found that during the experiment, the brain regions involved in processing emotions and those involved in processing the details of the situation were less active in people whose facial muscles were constrained than in those whose facial muscles functioned normally. The same patterns were observed in recall tasks about the emotions and the situational details, immediately after the experiment and one or two weeks after the experiment. That is, people who could allow their facial muscles to be involved in their emotional experiences were observed to process the emotions and situational details better in their brains during the experiment and during their noticeably better recall of the emotions and situational details during follow-up. These findings imply that the processing of emotions and their contexts, and the recall of both immediately afterward and one or two weeks later, are enhanced when emotion is more embodied than not.

Other studies (Peper et al., 2017) showed that preventing the embodiment of emotions of attraction and aversion by putting the body into postures that are contrary to the emotions they are associated with—leaning forward while processing emotions of aversion such as hate, and leaning backward while processing emotions of attraction such as love—interfered with the cognitive processing of the emotions and the situations involved. These studies strongly suggest that the expansion of the emotional experience to as much of the body as possible can improve the function of cognition because it ensures that as little of the body as possible is blocked from being involved in emotional experiences.

Section 3: The Method

The process of emotional embodiment has been conceptualized as involving four steps: (1) the situation; (2) the emotion; (3) the expansion; and (4) the integration (Selvam, 2022). Please note that the four steps need not always be implemented in the sequence they are presented. As is often the case, a clinical situation might warrant going back and forth between the steps or starting with a later step in the sequence. It is better to look at these four steps as ingredients for an emotional embodiment session that need to be added to the mix as and when needed to keep the process on track, rather than as a rigid sequential protocol. A brief description of the four steps is presented below, with one or two guidelines for their implementation. A detailed treatment of the four steps is beyond the scope of this chapter.

Step 1: The Situation

Emotions are reactions to situations. They express a specific understanding of a specific aspect of a situation and what we perceive as feasible in terms of behavior to cope with that aspect of the situation. Therefore, the more concrete clients are in terms of cognitive and behavioral details of the situation, the more likely we can help them to arrive at the specific emotional reaction to work with. For example, if a client is upset about not having good experiences in relationships and wants help to change this difficulty, we have to clarify whether we are talking about personal or professional relationships. If we are dealing with personal relationships, we have to ask about which specific personal relationship they are having difficulty with. We have to ask about details of that specific personal relationship: What is the other person's name? How long they have been in the relationship? What aspects of the relationship are troublesome? We have to ask about the details of a specific interaction or instance that was troublesome that serves as an example of the difficulty in that aspect of the relationship, in order to get to a concrete emotional reaction to work with.

At times, clients come in with troubling emotional experiences such as sadness and are unconscious of the situation they relate to. They are already in Step 2 (emotion). In such instances, one can go to Step 3 to expand the emotional experience to as much of the body as possible. Either the emotion will resolve or, as the expansion improves cognition, the person will become conscious of the situation the emotion relates to. The situation can then be used to support and keep the emotion alive during its expansion in the body.

Step 2: The Emotion

The support people receive from others for emotions is the most important factor in whether they will be able to access, stay with, expand, regulate, and express their emotions. In this important step, the therapist provides clients with different types of emotional support, sympathy, empathy, mirroring, validation, understanding, and so on. Some clients need education about what emotions are, the role they play, different types of emotions, language for emotional experiences, ways to express emotions, the role of the body in emotions, how they might be experienced in the body, differences between sensations and emotions in the body, and the benefits of expanding emotional experiences in the body.

Contrary to conventional wisdom, a person is never without emotion, when we expand the types of emotions to include sensorimotor emotions such as feeling bad or feeling good in a situation. The inclusion of such sensorimotor emotions, states of the body that make psychological sense, will help therapists to access emotions in their clients as quickly as possible. In order to access emotions, therapists also need to know how to work with various psychological defenses such as denial, projection, displacement, and so on.

At times, despite the therapist's best efforts, the client is not able to either access emotions or expand them in the body. Such instances might indicate the presence of strong physiological defenses such as constriction in the musculature or energetic defenses, in which case we might have to move to Step 3 (expansion) to undo the physiological and energetic defenses to access emotions or expand emotional experiences in the body.

Step 3: The Expansion

In this step, different tools such as awareness, intention, imagination, breath, movement, and client self-touch are used for undoing physiological and energetic defenses against emotions in the body to access emotional experiences blocked by the defenses, and to expand them to as much of the body as possible. There are specific physiological and energetic strategies for accessing and expanding emotional experiences in different parts of the body and for connecting emotional experiences in different parts of the body to each other. A simple example of the use of awareness in an intervention could be, "As you feel the sadness in your chest, please explore whether expanding your awareness to more of your chest or to the abdomen helps to expand the sadness to more of your chest or the abdomen." An example of the use of client self-touch could be, "As you feel the sadness in your chest, place one hand there and place the other hand on your abdomen to explore whether the sadness expands to your abdomen." The method uses a model of physiological regulation and a model of energetic regulation to make the step of expansion efficient. The discussion of these models of regulation is beyond the scope of this chapter.

Step 4: The Integration

In this step, improvements in physiological and energetic regulation, which can be expected to continuously improve as the emotional experience is expanded in the body, are used to stabilize the practice of embodying emotion, if needed, in different places in a session. These improvements are often in terms of ease of breathing, reducing muscular tension, and expansion and balancing of energy. These phenomena can be noticed locally in one place in the body or globally throughout the body. Noticing these easy-to-observe phenomena from time to time during a cycle of embodying emotion usually makes the experience of unpleasant emotional experiences more bearable and regulated. Switching to observing these experiences of integration can be a good way to end a cycle of embodying an emotion, especially when time is up in the session or the therapist assesses that the client has had enough. Integration can also be used at the end of a session to connect the individual to the collective in energy as the body is usually less defended and more open to the environment from the practice of embodying a difficult emotion.

Section 4: Treatment Examples

Example 1

Connie, a woman in her mid-40s, had suffered from migraines for as long as she could remember. They occurred once or even twice a week. Connie was a psychotherapist and a participant in a training I taught in Denmark. I heard from the team of assistant trainers that Connie found it difficult to stop crying during practice sessions with other training participants, leaving those who were trying to help her to feel helpless and puzzled, or she would come down with a migraine after the practice session.

When I chose Connie for a demonstration, even before we began, I knew that nothing would be accomplished if she just cried. Crying can be therapeutic, but in Connie's case, helpless crying appeared to have become a habitual response in therapy whenever any suffering was touched upon. It turned out that Connie had also done some therapy in which she had been encouraged to express her emotions strongly.

Getting Connie to contain her crying was indeed challenging. I introduced several interventions such as asking her to keep her eyes open and verbalize her inner experiences to help manage her crying and emotional overwhelm to some extent.

Between bouts of crying, with much guidance and reassurance, she was able to identify, tolerate, and express the suffering in her body in terms of the most basic sensorimotor emotions, such as feeling too bad, awful, or intolerable. While working with the basic sensorimotor emotions, such as feeling bad, awful, or unpleasant, Connie was able to distribute her energy downward away from her head and toward her feet. Migraines, if they are psychophysiological in origin, often have such a pattern of top-heavy concentration of energy.

As things slowed down and stabilized, and Connie was able to notice, expand, and tolerate the basic sensorimotor emotion of not feeling good in her body, it became more possible to work with the primary emotion of fear that was there right from the beginning of the session. It did not matter whether it was her fear of the suffering in her body or of something outside. Because it was there, stronger and more differentiated than before, it made sense to expand the fear to as much of the body as possible, from the upper body to the lower body, especially into the legs. Between bouts of crying that decreased in frequency as the session progressed, Connie was able to embody her deep fear of whatever it was she was afraid of.

I learned later that when Connie was a year and a half old, she put her fingers in an unprotected electrical outlet and was badly burned. She spent months in the burn unit of a hospital recovering from her wounds. As advised by the hospital staff, her parents did not visit her often. When they did, they often only saw her from behind a one-way mirror. To hear that history helped to make sense of many things: migraines, a symptom that often forms when the central nervous system is overwhelmed; the rush of energy toward the head; the overwhelming helplessness and crying; the lack of trust in any help from outside, especially during difficult times; and the repeated experience of people letting her down during practice sessions.

In the days that followed, I heard that Connie was having a better time during practice sessions and was working with a great deal of sadness about her childhood, more contained, without crying as often, and allowing others to support her more than in the past. I thought these were good signs. From what I had already been observing in my clients and myself, when people are able to embody emotions, they are often more able to work with other emotions in relation to the situation more fluidly. Their cognitions and behaviors often change for the better, in relation not only to the past but also the present. I also heard from an assistant trainer that she no longer had migraines after the session. And when I asked her years later how she was doing when I ran into her, she responded, "I am fine. And I am still without migraines. Thank you!"

Example 2

Sally suffered from asthma and wondered if we could work with it during a training in France. Asthma, like many diseases, can have multiple causes, from genetic predisposition to hormonal fluctuations to allergies. It can also be psychophysiological in origin, as a consequence of defenses against emotional suffering in the physiology of breathing, especially in the lungs.

Even though Sally had been prone to asthma attacks since her childhood, a more recent and intense outbreak had been triggered by a breakup with a man she said she had loved more than any other in her life. So it made sense to work with emotions surrounding the breakup.

It was not easy for Sally to track in her body how bad it felt and how sad it was that the relationship did not work out. Her physiological and psychological defenses appeared to be strong enough to keep the level and the intensity of emotion low and its presence in the body superficial and narrow, limited to the throat and the eyes. We managed to expand the low level of sadness in her throat and her eyes to the rest of the face and to the chest, but only superficially and for very short periods of time before it disappeared. It was, therefore, more than a pleasant surprise to hear from Sally many months later that she no longer suffered from asthma since the session. After the training, when she returned home, she was so overcome by sadness that she cried for a long time, she reported.

How can such an apparently uneventful piece of short-term embodiment work lead to the resolution of major long-term symptoms? The increasing tendency in the general population to form psychophysiological symptoms at rather low levels of emotional suffering—or, in other words, at low levels of emotion and intensity—offers one clue. Using emotional embodiment work to obtain even a small increase in the threshold of emotional suffering at which symptoms form could account for the outcomes observed in cases such as Sally's, in contrast to Connie's treatment that involved high levels of emotion and intensity, wider and deeper expansion of emotion in the body, and longer cycles.

When we go about the process of emotional embodiment, we might well find that experiences of emotional embodiment vary considerably, not only across individuals but also across time or situations for the same person. We have found that experiences of emotional embodiment can differ in terms of the level of the emotion, the intensity of the emotional experience, the width and the depth of the emotional experience in the body, and the duration of a cycle of processing the emotional experience. These variables, under the control of the therapist, can be adjusted to devise different strategies to accommodate the differing needs of individual clients with different levels of affect tolerance, different levels of dysregulation or dissociation, and different degrees of traumatic experience. For example, a seven-step protocol designed for clients who have low affect tolerance or high levels of dysregulation, often found in the treatment of complex traumas and psychophysiological symptoms, can be found in the blog section of Integral Somatic Psychology (Selvam, 2023).

Conclusion

The practice of embodying emotions can be used by all therapy modalities, including other body psychotherapy systems, as a complementary modality to improve treatment times and diverse outcomes under the following conditions: (1) when therapists find it difficult to regulate available emotions using methods from their primary modalities; (2) when therapists find it very difficult to access emotions in their clients using methods from their primary modalities; (3) when therapists run into emotions in any modality because of the higher likelihood of better outcomes when emotions are embodied for reasons discussed above; and (4) when therapists find client processes stuck in any modality, because embodying emotions has the ability to improve physical, energetic, cognitive, emotional, and behavioral processes in all clinical methods and situations. In each of these instances, therapists can switch to embodying emotions as long as necessary and then switch back to their preferred therapy modalities.

11

Neuroception Within Trauma Recovery

Sensing the Embodied, Social Self

Arielle Schwartz

EMBODIMENT IS NOT SOLELY AN INTERNAL PROCESS; RATHER, THE FELT SENSE PROVIDES us with feedback about our world. French phenomenological philosopher Maurice Merleau-Ponty (1962) described the felt self as a dynamic intersubjectivity between the individual, other people, and our environment. His concept of *intercorporeality* invited us to reconceptualize embodiment as neither static nor independent of our surroundings; rather, our existence reflects our relationships. This dyadic nature of embodiment is initially experienced in the parent-infant exchange through the nonverbal dance of playful exchanges along with regulation of physiological needs for food, proximity, and rest (Tronick, 2007). The countless coregulating interactions between caregivers and their infants require coordination of bodies, affect, and behaviors that honor the needs for both connection and separateness. The rhythmic synchrony that is fundamental to a secure attachment relationship is marked by a mutually regulated, harmonious, and reciprocal exchange, which not only forms the basis of self-regulation for the child but also supports the forming of the infant's bodily self-perception (Montirosso & McGlone, 2020). As we grow and develop, we emerge into ever-widening circles of influence within family, cultural, societal, and collective systems. Throughout our life span, somatic experiences continue to provide us with feedback and insight about relationships and the world around us (Tanaka, 2015). Just as embodiment is a reflection of our earliest attachment relationships, the felt sense must also be understood as a reflection of social and cultural dynamics of position, privilege, and power (Bennett & Castiglioni, 2004).

According to Dr. Stephen Porges (2022), the autonomic nervous system is integral in coordinating our relationships to our circumstances. He coined the term *neuroception* to describe how the nervous system is constantly assessing whether situations or people are safe, dangerous, or life-threatening. In other words, we are wired to be highly responsive to our environment, which promotes survival by allowing us to identify and respond to potential sources of danger. The vagus nerve plays a key role in this process as it relays feedback received from our five senses along with the interoceptive experience of bodily sensations. The autonomic nervous system utilizes this information to help us navigate the world by guiding us to move toward sources of safety and connection or retreat away and protect ourselves from sources of harm.

In order to best support a traumatized client's therapeutic process, we must first understand them within their developmental, social, and cultural contexts (Frey, 2013). Moreover, we must consider the social exchange that supports the recovery process (Herman, 2023). This chapter offers an understanding of neuroception and embodied self-awareness as reflections of our relational experiences of safety or threat. We begin with a discussion of the alternative vagal regulation models as compared to Polyvagal Theory. We then discuss the role of sensory integration in embodiment while exploring how predictive processing models and cognitive appraisals shape our perceptions of self and other. Several measures of neuroception are discussed as tools that assist clients to develop conscious perception of their nervous system states. From this ground of awareness, therapists can introduce neuromodulation interventions to support trauma recovery. This chapter concludes with a case example to help ground the material in a clinical setting.

Vagal Regulation of the Autonomic Nervous System

The Polyvagal Theory is not the only theory of vagal regulation of the autonomic nervous system. The neurovisceral integration model developed by Thayer and Lane (2000) proposes that autonomic regulation is the result of attentional capacities maintained by the prefrontal cortex that help to mediate the activation of emotional processing centers of the brain. Central to this model is an understanding of vagal tone, as measured by heart rate variability, which provides an inhibitory influence on the sympathetic nervous system. The parasympathetic system is viewed as a regulating system for sympathetic activation. When parasympathetic mechanisms are compromised, this can lead to emotional and physiological dysregulation, such as is seen with anxiety disorders (Smith et al., 2017). The biological behavioral model, developed by Grossman and Taylor (2007), highlights the role of vagal tone and regulation through the synchronization of cardiovascular and respiratory systems. Generally speaking, higher vagal tone as measured by resting heart rate variability or respiratory sinus arrhythmia can be understood as a measure of autonomic regulation; however, this is not always the case, and individual differences need to be accounted for. Moreover, the biological behavioral model challenges the evolutionary assumptions made by Polyvagal Theory. The resonance frequency model put forth by Lehrer and Gevirtz (2014) proposes that slow and paced breathing is an efficient manner of increasing vagal tone and improving affective, cognitive, and cardiovascular functioning. Likewise, the psychophysiological coherence model developed by McCraty and Childre (2010) proposes that paced breathing can promote a higher vagal tone when coupled with positive emotions, which leads to positive personal and social health outcomes. Last, vagal tank theory proposes three levels of cardiac vagal control analysis, which are resting, reactivity, and recovery, suggesting that the physiological tank of the vagus nerve can become both depleted and replenished (Hottenrott et al., 2019; Laborde et al., 2018). All of these theories of vagal regulation of the autonomic nervous system suggest a metaphorical closed circuit in which the primary sources of dysregulation or regulation exist solely within the individual.

Perhaps the most notable difference between Polyvagal Theory and these alternative models is the understanding that vagal tone is intricately connected to our relational, social, and cultural exchanges in the world. When seen through the lens of Polyvagal Theory, the nervous system can no longer be considered a closed circuit of autonomic regulation between heart, breath, and brain; instead, we are an open circuit that dynamically receives and responds to the world around us. Polyvagal Theory proposes that phylogenetic changes in neural structures have evolved to receive passive, nonconscious neuroception of cues of threat as well as cues of safety (Porges, 2022). We are in relationship to our surrounding environment that is at times a source of regulation through experiences of relational safety or a source of dysregulation when we have relational experiences of betrayal, maltreatment, abuse, or abandonment. In other words, we can draw upon the wise words of 17th-century theologian and poet John Donne (1987), who stated, "No man is an island."

Neuroception and Self-Regulation

The most recently evolved ventral vagal circuit of the vagus nerve, also termed the social engagement system, plays a key role in calming defensive reactivity, which allows us to seek proximity with others for the purpose of bonding, attachment, and intimacy (Porges, 2001). Neuroception plays a key role in this process. We are constantly registering cues of safety or threat from the world around us as well as from our internal sensations. Moreover, this process does not require conscious awareness (Porges, 2004). Neuroception relies heavily upon the automatic processing of the ventral vagal circuit, which receives sensory feedback from the world around us. It is through the sense organs of our eyes and ears along with our voice tone that we interact with the world around us. For example, the ventral vagus nerve helps to modulate the middle-ear muscle to help us better distinguish the human voice from background sounds and respond to perceived cues of safety from others. It is through our voice that we might call out in distress or offer compassionate care. When we feel safe, we tend to make more frequent eye contact, have more vocal prosody that expresses care, and offer warmer, more inviting facial expressions. Even without realizing it, we are constantly processing and responding to social cues. In response to cues of threat, the nervous system automatically adjusts our heart rate, breathing pattern, and level of muscle tone. For example, we might react defensively to the sound of someone's voice without fully understanding why we feel agitated. Moreover, when living as a person who is discriminated against because of race, class, sexual orientation, or gender identity, awareness of nonverbal cues of threat becomes a factor of daily living and survival.

As individuals, we have varying degrees of capacity to regulate our emotional and psychological reactions to perceived threats (Molden & Dweck, 2006). Perceptions of the world around us can differ substantially across individuals, even when faced with the same circumstances. For example, having a sense of agency and choice about our external circumstances can greatly improve our response, whereas a belief that we cannot handle the experience or that it will never end can worsen our degree of reactivity (Park et al., 2023). In general, our capacity to respond effectively to challenging situations is strengthened when we have adequate access to both external coregulating support systems (e.g., parent, caring friend, therapist) and internal self-regulation strategies (e.g., self-compassion, somatic awareness, mindfulness, conscious breathing).

Self-regulation is considered to be a learned capacity that is the result of having had nourishing coregulating relationships that help to myelinate the ventral vagal circuit. Ideally, we have at least one coregulating relationship with our caregivers and parents during the attachment phase of child development (Porges & Furman, 2011). Such coregulation has been described by Cozolino (2014) as the crossing of the "social synapse" and by Schore (2003) as a process of external psychobiological regulation. Importantly, even if we do not receive these regulating exchanges in infancy, we can seek coregulating relationships at later points in life, which helps us to build our internal capacity for self-regulation. Ultimately, self-regulation is dependent upon having an integrated and embodied felt sense of self (Cook-Cottone, 2015). Therefore, in order to better understand neuroception, we must look more closely at sensory processing as related to the internal system of the individual.

Sensory Processing, Posttraumatic Stress, and Faulty Neuroception

The external cues of safety or threat that we receive from our relationships and the world around us are housed within a complex internal world of cognitive, emotional, and physiological and sensory processing. Our bodily felt sense involves the integration of three key sensory systems: exteroception, interoception, and proprioception (Fogel, 2009). Exteroception is the integration of our five senses of sight, hearing, taste, touch, and smell. Interoception is the awareness of internal bodily sensations. Interoceptors are located in the heart, stomach, liver, intestines, and other organs, and they not only allow us to feel pain, thirst, or hunger but also help us recognize our emotions. Porges (2011) refers to interoception as our sixth sense because it forms the basis of our gut instinct, such as when you have a strong feeling about a person or place that feels unsafe. Proprioception refers to the sensory feedback that helps us to locate the body in space. This involves the integration of the vestibular system, which allows us to sense ourselves in relationship to gravity and helps us to coordinate our movements through the world. Neuroception integrates the information from these three sensory processing systems to assess for threats or cues of safety coming from the external world through the senses or from our internal felt sense of the body.

Posttraumatic stress, especially when rooted in developmental and complex traumatization, is associated with impaired self-regulation and alterations in sensory processing (Briere et al., 2010; Harricharan et al., 2021; van der Kolk et al., 1996). Traumatic life experiences tend to alter sensory processing in two different manners. Some individuals might experience heightened sensory sensitivity to sounds, bright lights, smells, or touch. This hypervigilance can also be directed toward internal bodily sensation, in that they are highly aware of interoceptive changes such as an increase in heart rate or physical tension. In contrast, chronic traumatization such as ongoing child abuse or domestic violence can overload an individual's sensory processing capacity. This can lead them to detach from the reality of the unsafe environment. In this case, the traumatized individual might present with predominantly dissociative symptoms such as depersonalization and derealization, meaning that they disconnect from the sensory reality of the body, other people, and the environment (Cramer et al., 2020; Lanius et al., 2012). These individuals tend to retreat into fantasy or intellectual defensiveness to avoid the terror they would feel by remaining present to sensory reality.

When relied upon over time, both the highly sensitive and dissociative responses can become conditioned into the nervous system and, as a result, shape how we perceive ourselves, other people, and the world (Ogden & Minton, 2014). Impaired sensory processing can lead to faulty neuroception. Such errors tend to occur in two primary patterns that mirror the hyper- or hyposensitivity to sensory input. An individual with heightened sensory sensitivity might be prone to excessively fearful reactions in response to situations that pose little to no threat. Individuals whose life circumstances led them to habitually dissociate from sensory cues of threat might not register legitimate sources of danger and, as a result, fail to protect themselves in situations that are unsafe. However, even if the individual is dissociated from their somatic experience, the nervous system might still be registering and reacting to nonconscious cues of threat.

There is a common comorbidity between PTSD, anxiety, dissociation, somatic symptoms, and chronic pain (Kratzer et al., 2022). Chronic stress and traumatic activation, especially when it originates in childhood, is associated with dysregulation of the autonomic nervous system, which can cause inflammation, digestive distress, and sleep disturbances (Kolacz & Porges, 2018). While most chronic health and pain conditions initially begin with an illness or injury, the symptoms of some of these conditions persist even though there is no longer any infection or current wound. Chronic pain is often maintained by patterns of physiological reactivity that occur below conscious awareness. Nociceptors are the sensory receptors specified to send pain signals to the brain, and they are prone to firing even in the absence of a current physical source of injury. When there is no current source of injury, pain is understood to occur as a result of maladaptive memory neural networks (Kuner & Kuner, 2020). Phantom limb pain is one of the classic examples demonstrating the presence of pain perception as a neural phenomenon (Flor et al., 2006). The level of intensity of pain is made worse by numerous factors, including our memories of historical injury, emotional response to the somatic experience, and accompanying negative appraisals. The somatic error hypothesis suggests that automatic appraisals of sensory experiences can lead us to anticipate a worsening of symptoms, which leads us to perceive the expected result even in the absence of any physical cause of pain (Khalsa & Feinstein, 2019). As a result, we might be more likely to generate faulty neuroception of threats in response to internal sensations that are innocuous and harmless. Moreover, some individuals might be highly sensitized to interpreting an increase in heart rate or respiration as signs of danger, which can lead to an enhanced anxiety response if not well understood (Critchley & Garfinkel, 2017). The internally sourced neuroception of threat can then lead to an increase in stress hormones, which underlies vicious cycles of pain and inflammation (Ashar et al., 2022).

Both PTSD and chronic pain can be thought of as stress-induced neuroplasticity in which reexperiencing symptoms reinforces the negative physical, mental, and emotional experience (Depperman et al., 2014; Wang et al., 2017). The predictive processing model suggests that our brain relies heavily upon past experiences to help us predict the future (Kiverstein et al., 2022). Furthermore, it is our predictions that tend to shape our current perceptions of ourselves, other people, and the world around us. Again, it is our memories of the past, affective responses, and cognitive appraisals that influence our perceptions of present experiences and can lead to faulty neuroception of threat. Ideally, we have opportunities to observe that our predictions are incorrect. For example, we might expect that going out with friends will be unpleasant, but we discover that we are unharmed and in fact had a good time. These mismatches between our expectations and actual experiences allow us to update our predictions about the future and facilitate our growth. However, having a history of trauma and chronic pain can lead an individual to avoid situations that might evoke distress. This limits the opportunities to confront inaccurate predictions and inhibits our growth.

Perception of Neuroception

Over time, our automatic and nonconscious processing of physiological, social, and environmental cues of threat can significantly impact our sense of self. When we are unaware of our reactions to threats, the related somatic and emotional reactivity tends to accumulate as physical tension, emotional irritability, restlessness, or anxiety. However, we can increase our ability to consciously perceive whether we are feeling defensive or relaxed. This requires that we bring conscious perception to our neuroceptive feedback, and we do so by mindfully paying attention to our somatic experience. Mindful body awareness is associated with an increase in blood flow to the prefrontal cortex, insula, and sensorimotor cortices (Larrivee & Echarte, 2018). When practiced over time, mindfulness of our embodied state can improve symptoms of PTSD and enhance affect regulation (Hopwood & Shutte, 2017). In contrast to the somatic error hypothesis, we build greater awareness of somatic markers that help to refine a more accurate perception of our felt sense of self, which helps to guide optimal decision making and empathic responses within our relationships (Damasio, 1999). The refinement process requires that we engage in a process of somatic reappraisal, in which we reflect upon our automatic interpretations about our sensory experience and integrate a more beneficial assessment of our experience (Price & Weng, 2021). Within psychotherapy, somatic reappraisal is facilitated by directing the client's attention toward their somatic experience while noticing their associated thoughts and emotional reactions. We might observe a client's tendency to fixate or ruminate about their somatic distress. Once they are aware of habitual beliefs, they can consciously develop a new relationship with their felt sense.

Clinicians can invite clients to develop greater self-awareness about whether they feel safe or if they are in a threat response through the use of assessment tools such as the

Body Perception Questionnaire (BPQ; Porges, 1993; Kolacz et al., 2023) or the Neuro-ception of Psychological Safety Scale (NPSS; Morton et al., 2022). These objective and empirically validated measures assist clinicians and clients to have a discussion about cues of threat and cues of safety within the body. The BPQ asks questions about the experience of body awareness of nervous system reactivity such as having a dry mouth, experiencing digestive distress, swallowing frequently, feeling muscle tension, or noticing how hard your heart is beating. These questions also alert the therapist as to whether a client might be hyper- or hyposensitive to these cues. The NPSS offers a complementary assessment of the client's capacity to recognize or identify cues of safety somatically, emotionally, and relationally. For example, questions assess whether the client notices times in which their breath felt effortless, heart rate felt steady, or their body felt relaxed. Socially and emotionally, the scale asks about times when they felt accepted, cared for, understood, comfortable expressing themselves, or capable of comforting and providing care for a loved one.

These measures of neuroception help us develop a shared language with our clients so that we can speak about symptoms of dysregulation in a nonpathologizing manner. The therapeutic relationship offers opportunities for coregulation in which the clinician's social engagement system offers cues of safety and connection. The nonjudgmental, compassionate presence of the therapist serves as the invitation for the client's own self-compassion.

Moreover, as clients learn to pay attention to their own nervous system state, they can better discern whether it is an accurate match to their circumstances. Fine-tuning this discerning awareness can take time and relies upon mindfulness of the embodied experience as well as accompanying thoughts and emotions. We respectfully explore with our clients how their defensive reactivity may be related to current or historical experiences of danger. This requires that we understand the social or cultural contexts of their lives to ensure that we understand how protective and defensive states might be necessary in certain circumstances. We can then explore pragmatic decisions that allow them to protect themselves, such as leaving unsafe situations or setting clear boundaries in relationships. Other times, it becomes clear that clients are unnecessarily defensive based upon historical traumatic events. For example, they may be pushing away people who are safe and loving, which inhibits reparative relational experiences. In this case, we can invite clients to explore letting go of their defensive stance within the safety of the psychotherapy and eventually in the outer world.

Neuromodulation and Embodiment in Trauma Recovery

Among the various theories of vagal regulation of the autonomic nervous system, the common factor across these models is an emphasis on enhancing vagal tone as measured by heart rate variability. Greater vagal tone is associated with reductions in anxiety, depression, symptoms of PTSD, and inflammation as well as improvements in decision making, emotion regulation, and stress recovery (Goggins et al., 2022; Kaniusas et al., 2019; Miller et al., 2017; Ruden, 2019). Neuromodulation interventions focused on vagus nerve stimulation send active or passive sensory input, which allows for a fine-tuned upregulation or downregulation of the nervous system. The goal is to create greater homeostatic balance between the sympathetic and parasympathetic branches of the autonomic nervous system. Electroceutical devices that are either surgically implanted or externally placed on the skin provide vagus nerve stimulation by sending barely perceptible electrical currents to the vagus nerve. Interventions focused on natural vagus nerve stimulation include conscious breathing, self-applied touch, tapping on acupressure points, eye movements, sound-based protocols (e.g., Safe and Sound Protocol, SSP), gratitude practices, loving-kindness meditation, self-compassion, and mindful movement such as yoga or tai chi (Schwartz, 2024).

Neuromodulation can be most beneficial when offered as psychosensory interventions that integrate psychological tools that invite the practitioner to suspend negative beliefs or cultivate positive mental states while simultaneously orienting their attention to nonnociceptive sensory input (Ruden, 2019). For example, the experience of touch, such as when receiving a massage, can help inhibit pain signals by activating positive sensations along with an experience of social connection (Meijer et al., 2022). Within psychotherapy, we can guide clients to engage in self-applied touch to their own arms or face within the coregulating environment of the therapeutic relationship to enhance the felt sense of connection. Likewise, conscious breathing is a prime example of facilitating autonomic integrity while creating a felt sense of calm in the body and a focused mental state. More specifically, slowing down the breath to approximately six breaths per minute is associated with regulation of the nervous system and associated improvements in decision making and mental concentration (Pagaduan et al., 2019; Sevoz-Couche & Laborde, 2022). Conscious breathing, yoga, and self-applied touch are enhanced when inviting the client to simultaneously engage in practices that evoke a state of appreciation, gratitude, or self-compassion (McCraty & Childre, 2004).

Neuromodulation practices invite an integration of sensory processing. Ideally, these interventions offer opportunities for the client to access a greater sense of inner calm and ease. However, for individuals with a history of trauma, the process of neuromodulation might temporarily increase sensory discomfort as they awaken to their felt sense. The increase in distress is often temporary and can be offset by orienting to cues of safety and connection within the current environment. When working with individuals who have little connection to their body, we often need to introduce interventions that facilitate embodied self-awareness slowly with respect to the pace that they can tolerate. Furthermore, when applying neuromodulation interventions in psychotherapy, it is valuable to recall that all psychotherapy takes place within the coregulating relationship. In time and with practice, you can help clients build an internally derived felt sense of well-being. Using the NPSS, we can invite our clients to notice signs of psychological safety as a way to objectively measure positive change. Once a foundation of safety has been achieved, we can then support clients to turn toward emotional and physical distress without overidentifying with or avoiding their discomfort. In other words, we help our clients to expand beyond the comfort zone into the growth zone (Russo-Netzer & Cohen, 2023).

Claudia's Story

Claudia initially came into therapy in her mid-20s, suffering from symptoms of anxiety, mild depression, and somatic symptoms of irritable bowel syndrome (IBS) and premenstrual dysphoric disorder that were collectively impairing her sense of well-being. As we developed a relationship with each other, I learned about Claudia's childhood, where she had experienced relational traumas in which she was emotionally abused by her mother and physically abused by her brother. All of this was compounded by her father's neglect; his lack of engagement left her unprotected from the abuse. I learned that Claudia would often direct her rage about her childhood toward herself through unrelenting self-criticism and self-sabotaging behaviors such as eating foods that worsened her IBS symptoms or avoiding movement, which increased her feeling of being disembodied and dissociated from her emotions. Claudia also had some key strengths that served as resources during our work together. She was in relationship with a caring partner, had good friends who supported her, had a great sense of humor, and was committed to coming to therapy weekly.

In sessions, Claudia would often start the session talking quickly while appearing restless and uncomfortable. However, as she began to sense and feel herself arrive more fully in the room, her affect would begin to change. She would then cast her gaze downward as she slumped in the chair. At this point, she would speak to a sense of helplessness. In our work together, I offered brief psychoeducation about how thoughts, body symptoms, emotions, and breath give us feedback about whether we feel safe or threatened. Together, we developed a shared language that helped her to recognize her own cues that let her know when she was feeling emotionally or physically dysregulated. For example, she described feeling bloated, having stomach pains and general digestive distress. She also noticed her tendency to attack herself when she was feeling distressed.

Initially, Claudia described feeling uncomfortable anytime I invited her to notice her somatic experience. Her lips would curl downward as she expressed feeling disgusted by her body. However, framing her symptoms as her body's way of communicating that she didn't feel safe allowed her to reflect upon her experience in a more compassionate manner. One day, when invited to place her hands over the heart and belly, soft tears fell from her eyes. She said, "I could never show anyone how scared I was when I was a little girl. I was either attacked or ignored. But this is my body telling me that I felt afraid, and I can love myself now."

Claudia's insight prompted us to explore what her body needed from her now. She shared that what her body needed from her was protection. Claudia described how she was still in contact with her mother, who continued to aggressively attack her when they spoke on the phone. She also realized that she felt compelled to call her mother and stay on the phone with her, even though she felt terrible inside. For the first time, she realized that she could choose to get off the phone when her mother was unkind. This process also brought forward grief, as she recognized how the little girl inside her was still waiting for her mother to finally love her. Claudia began to realize that while her mother hadn't changed, that she could change. I asked what that change might look like. She said she wanted to reach out to her friends and husband as sources of connection and support instead of habitually calling her mother. I asked her what she noticed in her body as she asserted her capacity to set a boundary or to reach for connection from people she trusted. This time she stated, "My stomach actually feels settled, like I can finally rest." Claudia had made significant steps on her journey of discovering what threat and safety felt like in her body. Now she had a new set of somatic markers that helped to guide her decisions in the world that allowed her to protect herself as needed and move toward true sources of safety. In time, she felt increasingly comfortable connecting to her embodied experience in sessions, which allowed her to benefit from gentle breath and movement practices, which further enhanced her felt sense of well-being.

Conclusion

The focus on neuroception within Polyvagal Theory provides a compassionate approach to understanding our clients' symptoms of both posttraumatic stress and related somatic concerns of chronic pain and illness. We acknowledge that nervous system dysregulation is both an intrapersonal and interpersonal experience. Therefore, interventions focused on trauma recovery are best supported within a safe and respectful coregulating environment. This process provides the necessary ground for us and our clients to explore interventions aimed to create a felt sense of well-being. In time and with practice, we help our clients cultivate an integrated sense of self as whole, resilient, and capable of growth.

12

Applying the Neurobiology of Resilience

Ruby Jo Walker and Emily Newcomer

THIS CHAPTER EXPLORES THE NEUROBIOLOGY OF RESILIENCE UTILIZING DR. STEPHEN Porges's (1995, 2011) Polyvagal Theory and applying resilience in therapeutic settings. Resilience is defined as being able to get through challenges with ease (Porges, 2022). It is dependent on the person's ability to hold a positive state in their body, as well as the ability to deactivate their autonomic nervous system (ANS) to recover quickly and become more regulated after trauma and stressful challenges. Because "trauma is a fact of life" (Levine, 1997, p. 2), supporting and cultivating resilience is necessary for anyone to live fully and flourish.

Resilience is inherent in many people. This is demonstrated in a mother who lost her teenage child unexpectedly in an accident and allowed her feelings of grief to be expressed while she was planning her child's funeral. The fluidity in her nervous system allowed for regulation to be accessed. She accepted support throughout her grief process and found activities that nourished her regularly such as hiking with others. This gave her body opportunities to enter positive states to support her. Eventually, she established boundaries in her work to increase simplicity in her life while also expanding into working with others who were dealing with grief. She experienced a horrific trauma, and the way she embodied resilience supported the integration of her trauma.

Not everyone has natural access to resilience, but because many human qualities can be learned (Roberts et al., 2017; Porges & Porges, 2023), we can develop this ability. Incorporating resilience into therapy settings supports strengthening clients' therapeutic work (Hanson, 2009). This chapter begins by discussing Polyvagal Theory (Porges, 1995, 2011) and resilience.

In addition, we will explore the conditions and processes needed to encourage and develop resilience in clients. This includes the regulated state of the practitioner, supporting embodiment of positive states in clients, and the deactivation process of the ANS, which leads to the integration of resilience.

Polyvagal Theory and Resilience

Using Polyvagal Theory as the foundation of resilience, the focus is on shifting underlying physiology to support resilience, rather than a psychological construct as was previously thought (Porges & Porges, 2023). Instead, resilience is seen as "an adaptive feature and physiological system that stretches throughout our entire bodies, allowing us to respond and recover from challenges" (p. 101). This changes the focus of resiliency work to go beyond management with top-down interventions, like cognitive-behavioral therapy, and instead offer interventions that shift the underpinnings of physiological states. This puts the focus on the nervous system's state of homeostasis, or "health, growth, and restoration" (p. 97). Porges and Porges (2023) also state, "While our resilience is innate, it is not fixed" (p. 101). It can be accessed by strengthening the portal of the ventral vagal complex (VVC).

The concept of resilience has previously used the model of the window of tolerance to describe the optimal state of the ANS as threading the center between hyperarousal (sympathetic nervous system, SNS) and hypoarousal (dorsal vagal complex, DVC; Ogden et al., 2006; Siegel, 1999). With new information from Porges (2022), we now know that

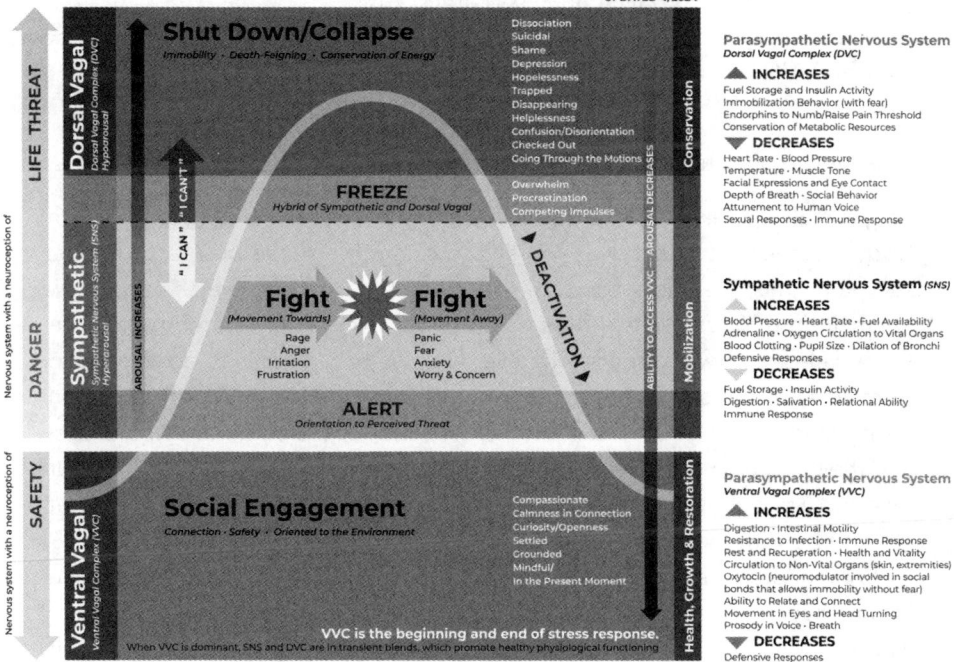

FIGURE 12.1 Polyvagal Theory chart of trauma response.

strengthening the VVC and growing the ability to tolerate all three primary states of the nervous system is true resilience.

These states are the DVC, SNS, and VVC. Therefore, all resilience training is about accessing, developing, or strengthening the VVC through both the embodiment of resilient states and the deactivation of the ANS. This leads to having the ability to move fluidly through all three states.

Practitioner Presence and State/Attunement

Supporting the growth of resiliency in others starts with the state of the practitioner and is critical into supporting the client process. The practitioner's task is to embody and hold the ventral state in the therapeutic relationship as the foundation of therapeutic work (Dana, 2018).

Foremost, the practitioner must be in a state of presence themselves (Geller, 2018; Geller & Porges, 2014). The state of presence includes holding the client's essential goodness and wholeness, being in loving-kindness, and having trust in the client's journey and organic unfolding (Kurtz, 1990). The synthesis of these qualities needs to be expressed in the face and voice for the practitioner to send a strong signal of safety to support clients in accessing their natural resilience and true essence (Porges, 2022). This sense of presence is inherently regulating for the practitioner and provides the neuroception of safety (Porges, 2003), accessing the VVC platform. The social engagement system of the VVC provides coregulation to support the client process (Porges, 2021).

The following script is an embodiment exercise for the practitioner to have more access to their own VVC state while working with clients.

Exercise for Practitioners to Guide Themselves Into Presence With Clients

Let yourself just take a moment to settle into yourself, connecting to your own body . . . making contact with yourself to bring in a sense of true presence. As you do this, feel the support of your body now that you are seated. Allow yourself time to just be with this . . . and now, bring your awareness to your heart. Feel your heart open in whatever way it is comfortable to do so . . . and from here, let yourself feel the person across from you. As you do this, bring in loving-kindness for this person and hold a sense of their inherent wholeness, and their essential goodness. Feel this in your body, particularly noticing your face and heart area, and noticing how it is now to have your attention here. Let yourself be with this in your own body.

Bring awareness to the idea that this person, like you, has had struggles in life and has done their best. Feel and honor this deep sense of shared humanity with them. As you notice this connection, feel the loving-kindness in yourself grow as you hold their essential goodness. Notice your body now, particularly your heart area and face. . . . Notice how it is to sit with this unique human being. . . . Feel all they have to offer the world . . . and your work is to help them be more in their true essence. . . . You are holding their wholeness for them, no matter what they are feeling about themselves at this moment. . . . You are resting in their essential goodness in your own body as you sit with them. Notice how this is to work from this place in yourself.

The relationship between practitioner and client is a significant part of supporting the client toward strengthening VVC and resilience (Geller, 2018; Porges, 2022). The relationship is fostered by the process of attunement, which starts with presence and then follows with tracking, perception, and response (Arvidson et al., 2011; Hatcher, 2015). This includes the practitioner tracking the client, perceiving what is needed, and responding in a way that signals being with the client in their process, thereby demonstrating resonance. Some examples of attunement could include tracking and responding to body movements, emotions, and themes. You might say, "It looks like something just relaxed in your body" or "There is a lot of sadness as you talk about this" or "It seems like it's hard for you to rely on others." Thus, attunement will cue a sense of safety to the client and their nervous system. Tending to the relationship on this level with presence and attunement increases access to VVC and is the foundation of the social engagement system and coregulation.

Attunement
Supports Deactivation and Embodiment, Develops Coregulation Capacity

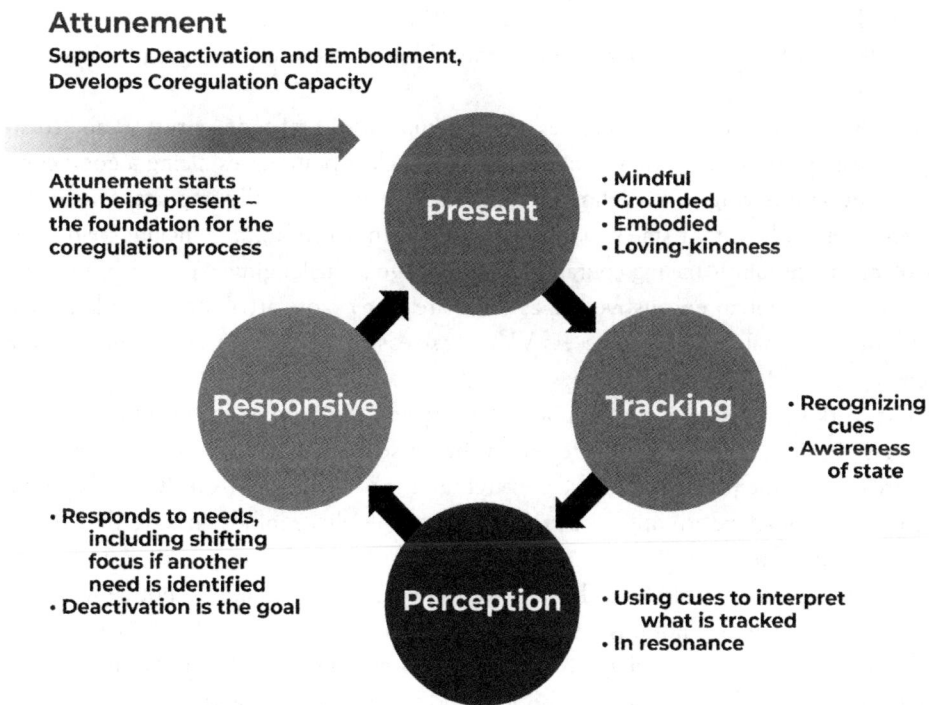

Attunement starts with being present – the foundation for the coregulation process

Present
• Mindful
• Grounded
• Embodied
• Loving-kindness

Tracking
• Recognizing cues
• Awareness of state

Perception
• Using cues to interpret what is tracked
• In resonance

Responsive
• Responds to needs, including shifting focus if another need is identified
• Deactivation is the goal

FIGURE 12.2 Attunement for developing coregulation capacity.

Supporting Embodiment of Positive States

Embodying positive states is being in the VVC and is necessary to change the physiology of the nervous system toward more access to the VVC and more fluidity in the ANS overall (Dana, 2018; Porges, 2022). Supporting this embodiment expands the ability of the ANS to access positive states and, as noted above, is foundational to resilience. Dana (2018) put forth the idea of looking for *glimmers*, defined as "cues of safety arising from a ventral vagal state" (p. 67). Hanson (2009) talks about "taking in the good" (p. 67) and installing positive sensations in the body. This is more than resourcing, as it is growing capacity for the ANS to hold positive states.

Because our nervous system moves easily into threat states, resiliency work is about supporting deactivation to the VVC. Accessing positive states primes the nervous system for this deactivation. Nervous system threat states hijack where attention goes, and this is deepened by the negativity bias of the brain. The negativity bias leads us to notice negative experiences, sensations, thoughts, and emotions (Vaish et al., 2008); the work is about shifting the focus to what is more positive or at least to what is neutral. The impact of negativity bias leads us to not recognize resilient states as they occur. These states do not become part of the narrative and integrated into the client's experience, as they are overlooked. The work then becomes to help the client both identify and install the resilient state in their body using their felt sense (Gendlin, 1996). This is very different from toxic positivity (Lukin, 2019) or unrealistic optimism (Shepperd et al., 2015), which are about denial. Instead, the focus is to change the physiological state of the ANS.

Positive states may include qualities of self-compassion, gratitude, curiosity, and trusting oneself. More broadly, they can include having clear boundaries, being a good communicator, and having grit. Feeling safe and present are especially important states for clients to embody. Other states that practitioners want to strengthen include being able to tolerate uncertainty, having courage, living through a challenging experience, and generosity. This is not an exhaustive list, as there are many more attributes, both large and small, that will enable clients to access VVC more easily and support the development of their capacity (Hanson, 2009).

The work then becomes for the practitioner to actively support the client in embodying these positive states. Clients are not in the present when they are in a trauma state and are either anticipating the future or caught in the past (van der Kolk, 2014). Teaching clients how to manage attention is a critical step, as this elicits mindfulness to the present (Ogden et al., 2006).

Mindfulness starts stretching the nervous system into being able to notice whatever is happening, such as emotions, sensations, thoughts, and images (Siegel, 2010b). The practitioner then becomes a detective, listening closely to hear and identify any positive and resilient states that are not being noticed and felt by the client and, as a result, remain unintegrated. It could be as simple and small as a client saying, "I feel cozy in this room" or "My boss listened to my idea." Noting positive and resilient states as they show up in sessions is assisted by the practitioner slowing the client down, inviting their attention to the state, and then claiming the state through embodiment.

Savoring supports deactivation (Dana, 2018), making it important to have the client take time to embody what feels good or even okay. This intention with attention means having the client embody what they are feeling. Because feeling a positive sensation can shift the trauma state, teaching clients to take those extra moments is very important. Examples of this include comments like, "Take a minute and notice that sense of the coziness. . . . Where do you feel that in your body? . . . How are you noticing that now? . . . Can we take a moment to just be with this?" It might be, "Notice how it feels to have your boss finally listen to you. . . . How do you notice that in your body?" Some will be significant positive states, and others may appear to be smaller, but when they are mindfully embodied, they often begin to settle the ANS and support more access to the VVC.

When clients have difficulty with positive affect tolerance and cannot fully embody positive states, then the focus of the work becomes titrating the embodiment (Hanson, 2009). These small and embodied practices signal safety to the body, making trauma integration with resilient states more accessible. With the right attention and repetition, positive affect tolerance can grow, and neurobiology can shift. The regular embodiment of a positive state can transform the state (more temporary) into a trait (more enduring; Hanson, 2018).

Developing Access to Ventral Vagal Complex State

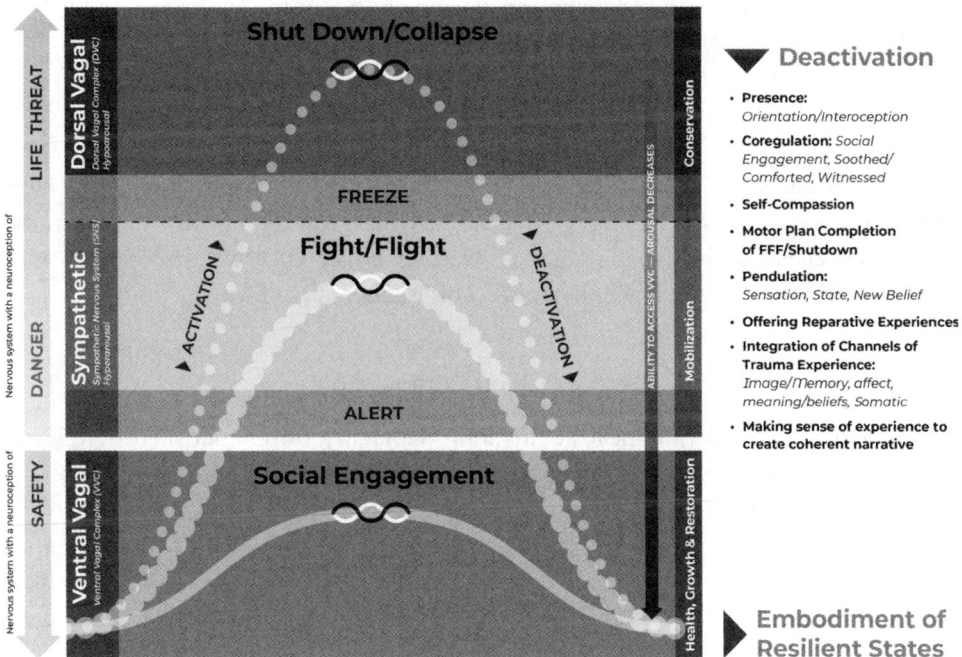

FIGURE 12.3 Deactivation pathways for downregulating the nervous system.

Because experience is what changes the brain (Hanson, 2009), managing attention to be focused on the environment, the senses, or an unintegrated positive experience can support more resilience; this shifts the state of the physiology. It also leads to being more present. The more dysregulation is present, the more directive the practitioner will need to be, as the nervous system in threat struggles with being in the here and now (van der Kolk, 2014). Mindfulness is both the antidote and the cure.

Deactivation

In addition to embodying positive sensations and experiences, deactivation of the nervous system is also part of resilience. The quicker our ANS downregulates to the VVC, the more resilience we can access (Porges, 2022). Habituated patterns of threat states, which are commonly seen in trauma presentations, will inhibit any kind of personal expansion. Therefore, it is critical that nervous system deactivation is part of developing resiliency. This downregulation from activation in the ANS supports the development of an underlying template of flexible nervous system functioning and resilience. The following therapeutic processes are pathways for downregulating the nervous system.

Mindful Awareness

Mindful awareness is the acknowledgment of what is occurring internally. The recognition of an emotion, a memory, a belief, or a sensation in the body can bring deactivation and relief to the ANS. Simply naming and allowing it softens the experience and helps it to integrate (Siegel, 2010b).

Self-Compassion

Self-compassion is also a way to deactivate the nervous system. It can bring in the kindness and connectedness of humanity, which are the main features of the VVC state. Self-compassion can be a way to parent oneself (Neff & Germer, 2018) as it becomes a way to hold one's experience with loving kindness. This is inherently downregulating.

Strengthening Coregulation

Strengthening coregulation means cultivating the ability to be nourished by the reciprocity of connection. Individuals with strong attachments can utilize the VVC to coregulate for deactivation (Porges, 2021). The relationship with the practitioner is a significant part of trauma work, as it provides the model and means for coregulation (Geller, 2018). Developing relational capacity for coregulation is part of the therapeutic relationship and can be worked live in a session. In practice, deactivation through coregulation means being witnessed, soothed, and comforted after a challenging experience. You might say something like, "Notice that right now I am happy to support you and let yourself feel this. . . . What is this like in your body?" This helps the client integrate support in the session and strengthens coregulation ability, accessing the VVC for deactivation.

Orientation

Using the orientation system of connecting to the environment through the senses will create deactivation in the ANS. Levine (1997) defines the orientation response as a biological process of responding to novelty in the environment to assess safety. When we recognize the absence of threat, this naturally deactivates the nervous system as we are exploratory orienting, or just noticing our surroundings (Ogden et al., 2006). This is different than defensive orienting or searching for threats, which is a place where humans can get stuck in trauma.

The orientation architecture in the body includes the heart, shoulders, neck, and head, which are connected to the VVC. Utilizing the orientation architecture to look around reinforces a sense of safety (Ogden et al., 2006). For example, the practitioner might say, "Let your eyes go where they want, taking in whatever might be pleasant or neutral." As we assimilate safety, the nervous system will naturally settle into exploratory orienting, creating more ease, relaxation, and downregulation. Other senses can also be used, such as orienting to sound, textures, smells, and taste.

Pendulation

Pendulation occurs both naturally and can be facilitated to support deactivation (Levine, 2010). It can assist in trauma metabolizing in the body. Pendulation is either holding two experiences at once or alternating between them. For example, "As you notice the fear of wanting to ask for what you want, notice that you are also feeling the importance of having your voice" or "As you notice the tension in your shoulders, notice what part of your body has less tension . . . and go back and forth between these two places." Pendulation is the natural state of the nervous system, and this process begins to restore that innate fluidity.

Completion of Motor Plans

Levine (1997, 2010) and Ogden et al. (2006) originated the concept of completing motor plans of fight, flight, and freeze/shutdown to create deactivation. These protective movements are often stuck in the body during trauma and therefore not completed. They stay live in the ANS, signaling the need for mobilization or immobilization/conservation physiology. Incomplete motor plans are permanently etched in procedural memory (Scaer, 2005), which is a type of long-term memory. This leads to creating dysregulated and frozen threat states. Completing motor plans is deactivating and brings the body back into ease.

To facilitate the completion of motor plans, the practitioner brings awareness to the protective movements that show up in sessions (Levine, 1997, 2010; Ogden et al., 2006). They then direct the client to complete the movements by following the biological impulse in the body. Following these impulses will lead to the needed completion. A common flight response is seeing a client's feet moving in a running motion and having the client just notice that movement. A possible fight response is observing fists tensing and having the client make the movement slowly. A freeze/shutdown motor plan could look like stillness, confusion, or quiet in the body. Practitioners could bring awareness to this state or encourage energy and movement as an opposite experience. This motor plan completion restores the biological impulses to have a regulated nervous system with full access to SNS and DVC when needed in life.

Reparative Experiences

Developmental trauma and the relational response to event trauma and current life situations can elicit threat responses, creating dysregulation in the nervous system. Reparative experiences can be effective in bringing the nervous system back into regulation. When a significant rupture has happened in a past relationship, the therapeutic relationship becomes key to healing (Murphy, 2015). The practitioner attunes to how the nervous system needs a different experience to support a new way of being.

For healthy development, some basic human needs to include safety, belonging, support, power, autonomy, and feeling valued. When these needs are not met, it creates developmental trauma and affects the ability to be downregulated by relationships. This rupture also leads to inaccurate core beliefs about oneself, others, and the world, which creates adaptations (Kurtz, 1990). These adaptations help one to survive the experiences but limit life options and will reduce the ability to integrate trauma. These circumstances can result in an internalized experience of a negative core belief, making resilience unreachable (Fischer, 2015). For example, someone who did not receive support during early life will not reach out for help, leading to dysregulation of the physiology as they repress a basic human need.

Past trauma event responses from others are very impactful. It might include someone getting assaulted and being told it was their fault, leading to activation in the nervous system (Wolf-Gramzow, 2023). Current life situations also can create ruptures and corresponding disruptions in the nervous system, such as having an unfair work situation (Kemeny, 2003).

Providing reparative experiences to the client includes the acknowledgment and normalization of their reactions and adaptations (Fischer, 2015; Kurtz, 1990). It could also include anything that needs to be integrated: reeducation around a core belief; an apology that something happened; or a fuller understanding of a more reality-based perception of the trauma that reduces self-blame. This supports the embodiment of a new experience, leading to a more accurate belief being integrated. An example might be having the client take in ideas such as, "Support is available now," "It is not your fault," or "That is not a fair way to be treated." Integrating the reparative experience supports the downregulation of the nervous system to the VVC.

Deactivation Summary

There are many pathways to deactivate the ANS that lead to resilience and regulation. They all require an active embodiment. The role of the practitioner is to determine which might be the optimal process to support deactivation. This may be one or a combination of several of these options.

Integration

Integration is the "linkage of differentiated parts" (Siegel, 2010a, p. 31). Strengthening VVC capacity and deactivation promote this differentiation and linkage, leading to a coherent narrative (Siegel, 2010b). This means that a person's story is part of their identity, and that it includes both resilience and trauma. This coherent narrative is linked to more ease and fluidity in the nervous system, which is the bedrock of resilience.

When a person overreacts to something occurring in the present, it is evident that there is a lack of internal integration (Siegel, 2010a). The practitioner takes the role of listening to what is not integrated and utilizes the pathways and processes described in the previous sections to move the system to more integration. This leads to responsiveness, rather than reactivity. This deeper integration is the foundation of accurate signaling, based on reality, not on the neuroception of threat.

Humans need a nervous system that signals the body in a way that can lead to necessary action, which brings the body back into safety. For example, if someone feels angry, they set boundaries, or when someone is anxious, it might mean they leave the situation that does not feel right. It is the job of the practitioner to look for these new and accurate signals and reinforce movement toward regulation of the nervous system. This can become the substructure that supports the new compass of the ANS. It is normal to become dysregulated as, we are a threat-sensitive species. It is also necessary to be able to find the way back to regulation. This includes having greater access to ventral vagal resources and finding the correct deactivation pathways that support coming into regulation again.

Summary

Resilience research has traditionally focused on utilizing top-down methods to support cognitive flexibility. These can include cognitive processing and appraisal, problem solving, meaning making, benefit finding, and self-reflection as the primary means of supporting resilience (Ord et al., 2020). These useful skills can improve general life functioning through the management of thoughts and emotions, and research demonstrates the effectiveness of these interventions (Ord et al., 2020). For this reason, these top-down methods should not be overlooked.

However, in primarily utilizing a top-down approach, integration can be limited (Ogden et al., 2006). Top-down interventions teach the management of states, whereas bottom-up interventions target changing physiological states to alleviate management.

Embodiment leads to having access to the resilient state without an additional focus on cognition (Hanson, 2009; Ogden et al., 2006). Embodiment of resilient states and deactivation practices can train the nervous system to access the VVC, leading to the use of neuroplasticity for deeper change (Siegel, 2017).

In summary, resilience is the ability to get through challenges with ease. Applying Polyvagal Theory and the neurobiology of resilience through the regulation of the nervous system and strengthening the VVC is critical. It is important that the practitioner always start with managing their own state. Then the practitioner can assist in strengthening positive states in the body as well as finding the right ways to deactivate the client's nervous system. Embodied resilience is essential for integration and to get through the stress and trauma of life. This resilience work can stand alone, or it can be an addition to any type of therapeutic practice.

13

The Therapeutic Use of Touch

A Bridge Between Body, Brain, and Mind

Aline LaPierre

Our bodies tell the story of our need to love and be loved.

Perspectives on the Therapeutic Use of Touch

I have yet to observe a single instance in which major psychic transformation
has been accomplished in an atmosphere of total abstinence of physical contact.
I cannot assert or assume that this work can be done without, at some point or
another, interpretation by way of human touch being necessary or optimal.
—LAWRENCE HEDGES

In *Touching*, his foundational work on touch, Ashley Montague (1971) noted that the psychological literature is in controversy around the issue of touch. Although touch has always been a valuable tool in somatic psychotherapy, Montague's statement stands today, much as it did five decades ago.

This chapter explores the therapeutic use of touch, based on the premise that splitting the causes of disease into physical and psychological origins leads to an impasse. Developments in psychobiology reveal the body as an energy transducer, with an uninterrupted chain of communication moving in reciprocal loops from bottom-up nonverbal physical microlevels to top-down cognitive awareness (Rossi, 1986). The therapeutic use of touch as a body-to-body nonverbal communication vital to trust and safety honors all levels and aspects of the body, brain, and mind as equal participants in an unfolding evolution.

Touch plays an important role in the emergence of the bodily self and the simultaneously developing psychological sense of identity. It supports the awareness of issues that lie encoded in nonverbal, state-dependent body memory and addresses breaches in the relational/emotional matrix that cannot be reached by verbal means alone.

Touch Illiteracy

The benefits of the therapeutic use of touch are often obscured by cultural overlays. Valuing mind over body reflects cultural beliefs that limit touch interactions and is responsible, in large part, for the slow progress of scientific research in this field.

The widespread injunction against the therapeutic use of touch is due to what I call touch illiteracy—a lack of education about touch as an implicit language. Its widespread professional rejection speaks to the pervasive touch dysfunctions that make us suspicious of the covert messages that may be embedded within it. They speak to the untold suffering that physical violence and sexual abuse—both touch dysfunctions—have visited upon so many, and to the deep yearnings and disappointments that the lack of loving touch leaves in our lives. Since it is known that parents who physically and sexually abuse their children were often themselves victims of touch violations, the question arises whether we can afford to remain touch illiterate. For individuals who require a reparative therapeutic experience to rework internalized attachment traumas, it can be argued that avoiding contact is a cruel recreation of the original physical neglect or abuse experienced as children.

The Neural Basis of Touch

Skin, nervous system, and brain are so closely related that one could describe the skin as the outer surface of the brain and the brain as the deepest layer of the skin.
—DEANE JUHAN

Touch cannot be explored without an understanding of its influence in shaping our capacity for embodiment and our sense of identity. There are direct connections between the skin's neural signaling, our interoceptive emotional responses, neuroceptive sense of safety, and mental states.

Touch defines our sense of reality—we are always touching something. Connected to the brain, our adult skin has some 300 to 600 million sensory receptors distributed over the whole body. In addition, our approximately 5 million body hairs have an additional 250 million receptors (Geuter, 2024). These figures indicate how the information our sense of touch gives us about the world around us is essential to our human experience. We can live without sight, smell, or hearing, but without our skin, we die.

- *Biologically*, as the body's main surveillance system, the skin provides immunological protection from invasion. In addition to sensation, the skin's permeable yet exquisitely selective barrier accepts nourishment from without, seals out toxins, and reacts to light, chemicals, moisture, and foreign and insulting elements.
- *Psychologically*, the skin is the line between me and not me. Metaphorically, it is a boundary containing all that is ourselves, sealing out all that is not. A sensory window through which our primary impressions of the world structure our experience, it sets the tone for our emotional patterns of acceptance, receptivity, avoidance, rejection, and retention.

Mother of the Senses

Touch is the first of the five senses to become functional. Skin sensors begin to come online in the sixth week of embryonic life, when we are less than one inch long. The skin, the central nervous system, and the brain develop from the same ectoderm layer and, throughout life, function as a single unit. Our surface and innermost core spring from the same mother tissue—the skin is the outer surface of the brain, and the brain is the deepest layer of the skin (Juhan, 1987).

We mistakenly have the impression that touch is limited to the surface of our bodies. In reality, long nerve fibers carry electrical impulses from the skin, joints, and organs to the somatosensory and pleasure centers of the brain. Sensory signals are processed through three separate but interacting systems:

1. An exteroceptive sensory system, which includes the sensory receptors of the skin, eyes, ears, nose, and mouth. Together, they form a surveillance system that signals the presence of external stimuli requiring attention.
2. A proprioceptive and kinesthetic system, which uses the information from specialized sensors in the joints, tendons, muscles, and organs of balance to monitor the position and movement of the body in space.
3. An interoceptive sensory system associated with the dorsal branch of the polyvagal system, which provides sensory information about internal body conditions such as temperature, pain, hunger, thirst, blood pressure, and visceral states, as well as its affective conditions: when asked to describe an emotion, most of us locate the experience in our internal body—we say we have a heavy heart, a lump in our throat, butterflies in our stomach. Damasio (1999) proposes that interoception—the perception of the internal sensory and affective condition of the body—lies at the core of selfhood.

Integrating exteroception (tactile sensations coming from the external environment) with proprioception (movement awareness) and interoception (visceral, vagal experience) gives rise to bodily representations in the brain that shape the core of our sense of self and contribute essential information for meaning making.

Sensory and Affective Pathways

Researchers have shown that exteroceptive, proprioceptive, and interoceptive systems each transmit their signals using two parallel neural pathways: one for sensory touch, with receptors that project to the thalamus and primary somatosensory cortex used for surveillance (Johnson & Hsiao, 1992), and one for affective touch, which projects to the insular cortex used for emotional and social appraisal (Olausson et al., 2002; Vallbo et al., 1999). This distinction is of key importance when working therapeutically with touch.

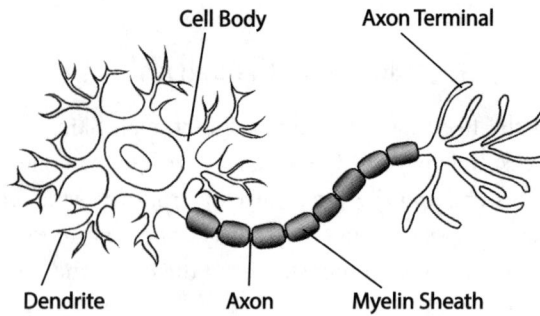

FIGURE 13.1 Myelin is a lipid-rich material surrounding a nerve cell's axon, insulating it and thus increasing the rate at which electrical impulses pass through. Afferent means from the body to the brain.

- *Sensory surveillance pathways*—referred to as Groups A and B—consist of large-diameter myelinated nerves that allow for the fast conduction of information from the skin to the brain. Appraising for pleasure, pain, or threat, they form an extensive surveillance system, immediately giving us the location of a stimulus on the skin. In touch therapy, they are instrumental for redefining the sensory deficits and chronic hypervigilance that are the outcome of neglect, misattunement, and violations.
- *Affective limbic pathways*—referred to as Group C or C-tactile (CT) afferents—are small-diameter unmyelinated nerves that respond to light touch. Found in hairy skin, CT afferents fire when the skin is touched lightly, stroked at a speed of about 1–10 centimeters per second—the feel of a light breeze, or the stimulation of a caress. CT afferents underly emotional, hormonal, and affiliative limbic responses to caress-like contact (McGlone et al., 2014). They signal relational intentions in interpersonal and social touch. CT affective touch has been reclassified as an interoceptive modality (Craig, 2003). In touch therapy, it is key to rescripting attachment issues and stabilizing the emotional dysregulation resulting from relational trauma.

Touch and the Relational Matrix

The emotional importance of touch in early development was clearly demonstrated in Harry Harlow's controversial studies with baby rhesus monkeys, who share 93% of our human genes (Harlow, 1958; Harlow & Zimmerman, 1959). Inspired by John Bowlby (1988), who conducted the first scientific study of how children respond to separation, Harlow and his team separated baby monkeys from their mothers and gave them access to two surrogate nonliving mothers—a soft terrycloth mother warmed by a lightbulb that provided positive tactile experience but no food, and a wire mother with a bottle attached to it. The baby monkeys clung to the terrycloth mother and cowered away from the wire mother. The soft tactile surrogate superseded the cold one who provided food. The babies feeding from wire mothers had trouble digesting their milk and eventually developed patterns of clasping their own bodies. As they matured, they did not develop typical grooming patterns and had reproductive difficulties.

If the findings of Harry Harlow on the innate need for touch in baby monkeys can be extended to human infants, it should be expected that the need to touch and be touched would arise in the lives and therapies of individuals who were deprived of caring touch. Since this experiment, converging data strongly indicate that touch is central to the development of attachment and bonding in humans. Additionally, a growing community of researchers have shown that mental abilities are embedded in the sensing, feeling body (Damasio, 1994; Panksepp, 1998; Schore, 2003). In other words, how the brain relates to reality emerges out of our early touch experiences.

Research conducted by Tiffany Field (1995) shows that it is through touch that we receive our first relational imprints. The power of touch to communicate emotional connection—or disconnection—affects an individual's life trajectory. When all is well, attachment and bonding happen within the matrix of the mother's body. From the internal environment of the womb within which we live the first months of our lives, to lying on our mother's belly while we transition away from the life-giving umbilical cord to find the agency of our own breath (assuming the cord was not cut before this process was complete), to latching onto the nipple to suckle the warm milk that opens our digestive system, the initial experiences of welcome into life are intensely tactile. The importance of the synchronized bioenergetic transmission (Schore, 2003) that happens through bodily connection cannot be minimized or ignored, particularly in individuals whose early memories evoke the distress of an emotionally or physically absent mother.

> *Here you are, looking at each other.*
> *At every moment, your massaging must be sensitive and responsive*
> *to the slightest flutter of this new being.*
> *You will be holding an unbroken dialogue. Not in words of course!*
> *True communication, true communion, is silent, as you know.*
> —FREDERICK LEBOYER

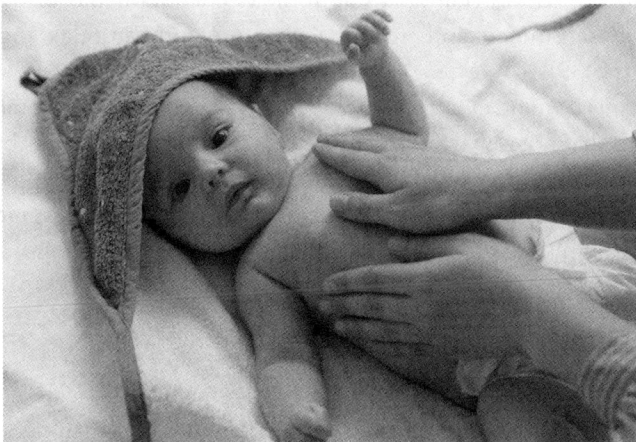

FIGURE 13.2 Photo 244934656 © Chernetskaya | Dreamstime.com

Nurturing Touch

The attuned gentle signaling of CT afferents plays an important emotional role in early bonding. This life-giving power is illustrated in the work of Eva Reich (Overly, 1994/2004). The roots of her technique lie in her experience observing her father, Wilhelm Reich, working with babies and children in the 1950s, and in her pediatric residency (1951–1952) at Harlem Hospital, a center for premature babies in New York. At the time, it was thought that babies did not feel or remember because their nervous systems were not fully developed. Suffering from sensory deprivation, infant mortality rates were extremely high. Using gentle touch, Eva found that these babies came out of shock, that their lungs expanded, allowing them to breathe down into their bodies (premature babies often die from pneumonia because their lungs do not fully expand), and that they opened their eyes and smiled at her. She continued to develop this light touch with adults in her rural medical practice, finding it equally successful with that population. She described the quality of her touch as so light that one could handle a butterfly without causing it harm. She called her work butterfly touch massage and taught it worldwide.

Life thrives in the presence of loving connection, pulls away from hostile encounters, and diminishes in the void of neglect. The effects of caring relational touch are mediated by hormonal mechanisms: attuned touch promotes the release of oxytocin—informally known as the cuddle hormone—in bonding behavior. It also decreases cortisol levels and stimulates growth hormones (Field, 2003).

As a therapeutic intervention with adults, nurturing touch addresses breaches in the development of the relational matrix that cannot be reached by verbal means. In the work of early repair, nurturing touch is particularly valuable to address neurological deficits, dissociation, states of chronic bracing, dread, fragmentation, and collapse. Attuned holding offers experiences of emotional connection essential for the development of trust and the capacity to feel safe, yield, and receive—building blocks for relational maturation. Osteopath Bevis Nathan (1999) describes how "holding and rocking allows unconscious, preverbal healing events to occur . . . as if, in the containing hands of the manual practitioner, the body-self understands itself a little more and can relax and grow in such understanding" (p. 139).

During moments of contact, attuned touch plays a pivotal role in communicating the positive emotions that not only strengthen attachment and social bonds but also support the body's physical development. Infants of mothers who use more stimulating touch during feeding develop better visual-motor skills, more advanced gross motor capacities, and better social cognition, such as empathy.

A Blueprint for Life

Lyons-Ruth (1999), a leading attachment theorist, concluded that developmental progression is based on unconscious, implicit representation rather than on verbal meaning. She argues that "*procedural systems of relational knowing develop in parallel with symbolic systems, as separate systems with separate governing principles* [emphasis added]" (p. 579). Lyons-Ruth points to the need to expand the therapeutic space to include implicit forms of experience that manifest through action—what Beatrice Beebe (2003) calls action dialogues. The therapeutic use of touch is such an action dialogue. Practitioners use highly developed palpation skills to connect with sensory and affective impulses as they arise from the body and interact with cognitive narratives, forming a reciprocal, interpenetrating exchange between soma and psyche.

TOUCH INTENTIONS

This chapter focuses on the nurturing aspects of touch that help set up implicit conditions for interoceptive safety and attachment. In addition, the intentions listed below synthesize a broad spectrum of approaches developed in body psychotherapy and somatic psychology that meet the contingencies of trauma healing and post-trauma growth at all stages of development.

Nurturing • Holding • Comforting • Caring

- Communicate safety and containment
- Support the neurological, emotional, and relational capacities to trust and yield
- Allow the receiver to rest in an experience of acceptance and support
- Cultivate heart-centered connection and invite attachment repair

Amplifying • Supporting Self-Awareness

- Heighten somatic awareness by focusing and magnifying attention on specific areas and systems of the body
- Clear emotional and relational shocks
- Support the capacity to mindfully witness the body-mind and emerging self

Working • Confronting • Challenging

- Release fear and bracing in the musculature, connective tissue, and viscera
- Use directed pressure to shift the state of the tissues, free blockages, highlight holding patterns, and support collapse
- Trigger release, shaking, movement, and other spontaneous reactions as the body reorganizes and opens to new possibilities

Teaching • Reflective

- Discover and integrate new somatic patterns
- Accompany the practice of new movements in body and mind
- Encourage active receptivity and interactive dialogue
- Support yielding, trust, and post-trauma growth

The Practice of Therapeutic Touch

When we reflect on the somatic experiences of the preverbal infant for whom language is yet unformed, or on the infra-verbal processes that underlie verbal thought throughout our lives, tending to the lifelong relationship between bodily experience and mental states is experiential territory only beginning to find its rightful place in our treatment approaches.

The therapeutic use of touch requires a specific focus of intention and attention, a body-to-body communication that opens a window into unconscious, unrecognized, and unarticulated adaptive behaviors—into the body's story, which often does not match the narrative held in the mind.

Touch brings vital contributions to the process of embodiment:

- *Present moment.* Touch therapists do not impose outcomes, but remain receptive to adaptive patterns as they emerge. They support compassionate acceptance of the body's adaptive efforts and use touch to offer moment-to-moment organizing options, respecting the body's rhythms and unfolding.
- *Novelty.* Tactile neurons, as the body's sensory surveillance system, excite or inhibit in response to novel sensations. Becoming familiar with the specificity of neuronal signaling is a first step to developing skillful touch. The novelty of varying thresholds of touch pressure, friction, temperature, and vibration keeps the neuronal pathways active and the brain interested and alert. As a resource for those who have difficulty connecting with their body, using an active touch that stimulates new sensory signaling brings body and mind into conscious connection.
- *Rhythm and pacing.* Somatic therapists use touch to support a collaborative dialogue between the body's systems—skeletal, ligamentous, muscular, visceral, endocrine, nervous, fluid, fascial, and into cellular microlevels—as they work to reestablish the soma-psyche dynamic balance. Thus, touch-trained therapists become a new kind of partner in the therapeutic endeavor, "speaking" directly with the physiological systems, exploring the connections—or lack thereof—between the body's adaptive states and the brain's meaning making.
- *Orientation.* Trauma states highjack the orienting reflex. Rather than orienting to time and place with open curiosity, traumatized individuals track for threat and danger. A present-moment touch connection can ground an individual in their orienting reflex, supporting a return to safety and curiosity.
- *Prediction.* The brain is a predictive organ—it predicts the future based on the past. Interrupting trauma-based predictive tendencies focused on threat and catastrophic futures is an important aspect of the present-moment orientation of touch.
- *Self-directed touch.* Affecting self-experiencing and body image, self-directed touch is a portal to help those who live primarily in their brains connect with their bodily self. Self-directed touch regulates autonomic bodily functions such as heart rate, blood pressure, and hormone secretion. It can support the capacity to handle strong

emotions and establish inner collaborative connections that strengthen the capacity for self-negotiation and growing integration.

- *Multisensory integration.* Touch fosters new body-mind connections. It often generates new information that emerges in awareness as an image, an inner voice or thought, an emotion, sensation, insight, or the reframe of an old belief.

Therapeutic Touch in Clinical Practice

The following session transcript illustrates the process of rescripting psychobiological levels of stress and hypervigilance that disrupt the capacity for relational receptivity. Using NeuroAffective Touch, the session integrates the use of touch with a relational psychodynamic approach to show how touch can be instrumental toward the resolution of attachment trauma. Integrating touch and psychotherapy typically goes through four phases: (1) orientation and connection, (2) finding a way in, (3) insight, and (4) integration.

Orientation and Connection

Maria is in her late 30s, and our work is in its beginning stages. She is troubled by her difficulty trusting others and consistently feels that she "does not belong." In this session, she explores why she cannot feel her heart—why she feels emotionally numb.

> Having previously talked about how breaks in relational connection are often felt as jolts or shocks to the heart, Maria and I develop an intention; she wishes for her mind to find her heart. I mention that the mind's narrative can be quite different from the body's story and suggest that we also extend an invitation to her heart—letting her heart know that her mind is open to the emergence of her heart's story. It is with an aligned intention and consent that we enter into a body-mind exploratory touch process.
>
> To open our nonverbal communication, I initiate contact by sitting at her head and lightly placing my hands on the side of her upper arms.

ALINE: We are going to take a little time for our rhythms to synchronize. . . . What do you experience as we establish our touch communication? . . .

MARIA: I feel light and calm.

A: Are there vulnerable areas you would not want me to touch?

M: Just my navel area.

> I am inviting her to set boundaries, thus establishing respect for her body's vulnerability. I then ask her to restate the intention we set for the session.

M: I don't know where my heart is, and my mind is curious about it.

A: Can your mind give us more details about this curiosity?

M: My mind is curious about how my heart is going to respond. It's also curious about where my heart is at the moment . . . about how disconnected it is from my heart.

A: Do you have any concerns along with your curiosity? Are there any other thoughts or feelings that come with the curiosity?

She ponders for a moment.

M: Fear. Fear that my mind won't let my heart open at all . . . or trust . . . ever.

A: It seems that your mind has learned to be in charge.

M: Yes.

A: And perhaps your mind has done such a good job of being in charge that it's hard now, inside yourself, to find your way to your heart.

M: Yes.

A: Do you have a sense of where your mind lives?

M: My head.

A: Perhaps giving your head some attention could help your mind. . . . I'm going to hold your neck and head for a bit. Remember when we talked about how the medulla in your brain stem regulates your heart rate and breath?

Particularly when the mind has taken charge, it is useful to accompany targeted touch with anatomical information. This helps the body feel acknowledged on the level of its own existence.

Finding a Way In

I cup my hands around her cranial base and notice how the muscles around the upper cervicals are tightly braced.

A: Even if you don't know where to find your heart, what does your mind know about it?

M: My mind knows that my heart is very open to giving . . . but it's the complete opposite when it comes to receiving.

A: Let's explore how your heart likes to give. Then we can pay attention to its difficulty receiving.

M: My heart likes to give care, protection, attention, presence, silence. I can feel my body trembling from inside.

A: I can feel it too. It started just now as you talked about the ways your heart likes to give.

M: I don't think my heart has ever been invited to share before.

I now want to give her heart support. To provide additional safety, I supplement my touch with small warm pillows of different shapes. I place a long warm pillow under her neck to continue supporting her brain stem and medulla while freeing my hands to move to her heart.

A

B

C

D

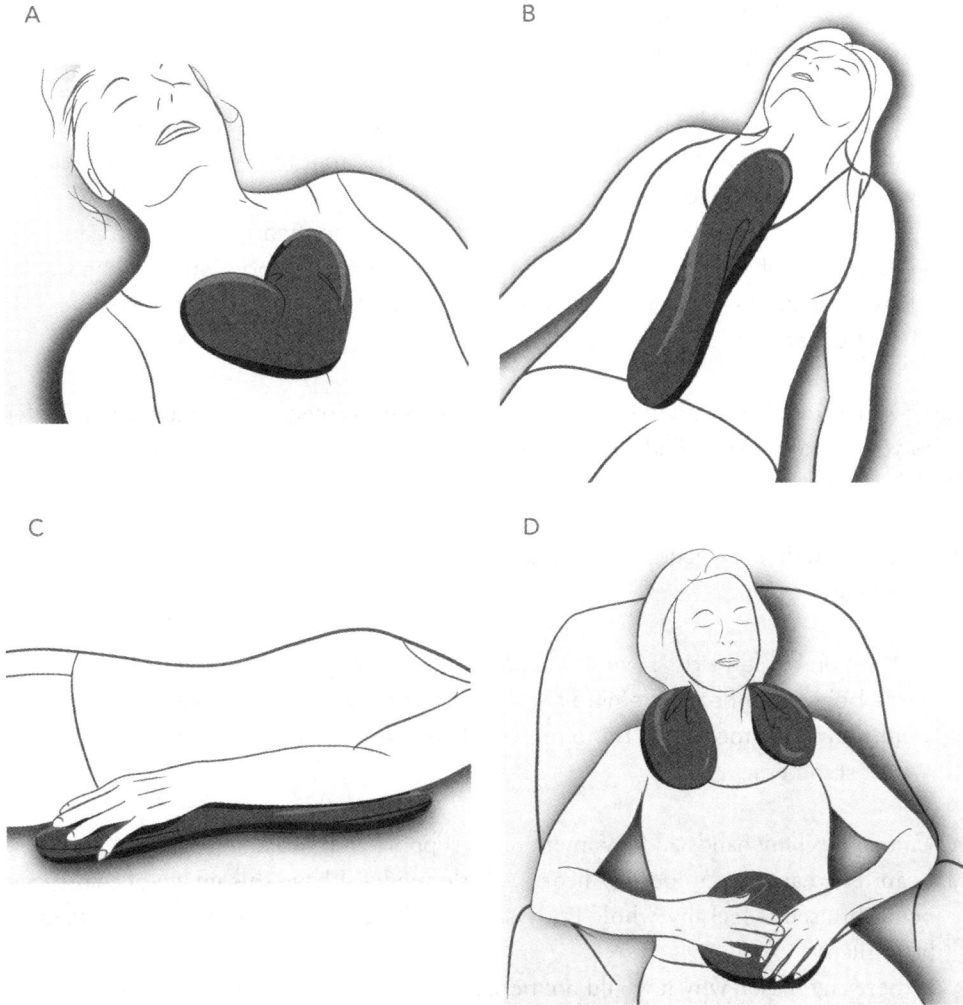

FIGURE 13.3 Nurture to Heal Pillows add a nurturing element that supplements my touch. Made of stretch velvet and filled with organic flaxseed that can be warmed or cooled, their shape adapts to various body areas. I can touch through the pillows' malleable seeds, giving my touch a warm and diffuse feel that is often easier to receive than direct touch. The pillows also serve as transitional objects that clients can take home to continue developing their body's receptivity.

Protecting the front of the body while supporting the back is an important NeuroAffective Touch principle. The experience of support to the back brings connection to the sympathetic nervous system, which branches from the spine to the organs. Supporting the spine "speaks" stability to the emotional vulnerability of the viscera and signals safety to the dorsal branch of the vagus, often

for the very first time. Most importantly, it invites the earliest relational movement of yielding. It is through yielding into secure holding that babies establish
their neurological trust baseline. Only as the body learns to yield at this most
fundamental level can it be open to receive. Secure holding teaches babies not
only that their vulnerable little body is secure, but that their emotional selves
will not be "dropped."

My intention, as I seek to help Maria's mind find her heart, is to set up a felt
experience where her mind experiences sympathetic support while her heart
feels protected—an experience of embodied safety. I place a warm pillow over
her chest and cover her with a blanket.

A: Let's give your heart and the front of your body some protection so that it can feel safer
   as your mind seeks to find the connection. . . . Take in the warmth and see if it feels
   right. Tell me if it's not quite right or feels too warm or too heavy.
M: It's perfect.
A: I'm going to slide my hands under your back. My intention is to support the area behind
   your heart.

Sitting on her left side, I use the flat of my hands to give broad support to the
area behind her heart. I remind her that she can give me directions: tell me to
withdraw if it's too much, bring more or less pressure, shift my hand position.
After some time, I ask:

A: Can you feel my hands and my intention to support your heart?
M: I can feel that space under my heart. A little tender. I have this image of that space
   being bruised. I feel my whole body saying, "What's going on here? Do I need to
   be vigilant?"
A: Is there any reason why it would not be safe right now to yield into my hands?
M: I must stay ready. My body needs to be ready to protect me. It tells me this care could
   be masked. That the love is not real.
A: It's true that there's a lot about me you don't know. Masked love must have happened to
   you. . . . People who presented as loving, but their love was a pretense. That must have
   been deeply hurtful.
M: My whole energy has gone into protection mode. I can't even think.
A: It seems that your protection mode is working really well.
M: Yes.
A: I'm going to remove my hands now. As you settle, we can explore what happened.

Insight

As Maria is settling, I suggest that when, and if, she feels ready, we can talk
about her body's response. When she lets me know she is ready, I review
our experience:

A: In the beginning, you said your heart knows how to give, but doesn't know how to receive. That's when your body started trembling. When I placed my hands under your back to offer support, your body braced even more, and your mind shut down. You talked about masked love—about how painful it is to open to what you think is loving, only to find out it's not.

M: I'm getting an image of my mother and how confusing it was for me as a baby. I didn't know she was suffering from schizophrenia until a little before she passed away 10 years ago.

A: It must have been very confusing.

M: I just got this image of a white cloud.

A: Your heart couldn't make sense of it, and it seems your mind couldn't either.

M: And then she passed away.

> I pause to let her body–mind process. . . .

A: What happened to your love for her and her love for you?

M: My heart doesn't know what love is. My mind is saying that the only way I know love is to be responsible. . . . I had to take care of her—otherwise she won't love me. I have to protect her. Otherwise, I won't survive.

> I have the impulse to support her back again, this time inviting her to let go of a little bit of responsibility, essentially continuing the emergent yielding process.

A: We can say to your back, "This is support so that you can let go just a little bit, and feel what it's like to not carry so much responsibility." Let's be curious about what happens. Are you on board to be curious? . . . We'll do this for just a few minutes, and you can tell me when it's enough.

M: If I let go, I'm not going to survive. And you are not going to survive either. . . .

A: Open your eyes and check in with me. Just a little peek. You know what? You *did* survive . . .

M: Yes.

A: Feel yourself breathe. You *are* surviving.

M: I'm surviving.

A: You are surviving . . . and I'm surviving too.

M: Yeah.

> Her breath deepens, and she is very quiet for about five minutes. Suddenly, a strong shaking takes over her body. I remove my hands from under her back and place one hand solidly on her shoulder. . . .

A: Does it feel okay to let the shaking happen? . . . [She nods yes.] This is your body learning to let go. You're surviving. This is part of knowing it's safe to let go.

M: My mind wants to check if you're okay.

A: I'm absolutely okay. You're pretty good at shaking! Is it okay if I put pressure on the pillow over your heart right here?

M: It feels good when you give me more pressure . . . I can feel my heart! It's so strange . . . I feel my mother's energy releasing . . . like she was holding me back.

Integration

The shaking subsides, and Maria rests in stillness; her face is relaxed, and her breathing slows down until it is barely visible—a shift into cellular breath. The shaking brought a lot of oxygen into her system, and her breath has shifted from diaphragmatic dominance to allowing the influx of oxygen to move into the cells, the newly released musculature and connective tissue. I sit quietly, letting my breath synchronize to hers. After a while, I say softly:

A: Can you feel your body breathing differently? That's your life force spreading through your body!

M: I'm not even trying. I don't even need to breathe.

A: That's cellular breath. It's a quiet breath. Deep healing happens here.

M: No need for words!

Ten minutes later, Maria sits up, and we move to my office armchairs to integrate the experience.

M: We survived! It was so helpful to have your solid presence. I always had to take care of my mother. Since I was a baby, I had to face the unexpected . . . always protecting her. I just realized that protecting her meant I would survive. And if I didn't protect her, then I didn't survive.

A: You needed a mother.

M: It was too much responsibility, and I left. A few years later, I found out she had schizophrenia. Soon after, she passed away. That was 10 years ago. It was really powerful to witness how enmeshed I was with that responsibility.

A: Yes.

M: To receive your support, I had to let go, which meant I had to let go of my mother. If I let go of my mother, she would fall, and I would die.

A: You did all you could to keep her alive so you could live.

M: Yeah. I just hated responsibility after that. Any responsibility, and my body would tighten.

A: That makes sense.

M: I've never experienced that kind of breathing—it was alive and empty at the same time inside my body. It was just so different from the meditative states I've experienced. There's a quietness to it, and an aliveness, and a stillness. Thank you.

Some weeks later, I received an email from Maria:

The session is still reverberating in my body. So many layers around survival and responsibility have been disintegrating, and many new ways of being, some still in gestation, are being birthed . . . and to have experienced cellular breathing was truly humbling—I bow to the life force!

A Paradigm Shift

Touch as an expression of care and connection belongs in families, within couples, with mothers, fathers, their babies and growing children, and with the elderly—in short, everyone at every stage of life. Given how much physical contact parents, caregivers, and extended family need to give their newborns and young children for emotional, cognitive, and social development, given the dissatisfaction and disappointment so many couples experience around touch and sexuality, taking into consideration the mental decline of the elderly in isolated or institutional settings, and the touch hunger expressed by individuals in therapy, there is a great deal of essential learning to be done in how we touch each other in life and for healing.

There is widespread evidence that the nonverbal mechanisms of the infant-parent relationship are activated in the transference–countertransference between adult client and therapist. From this perspective, the lack of knowledge about the depth and complexity of the therapeutic use of touch limits our psychotherapeutic horizons and robs us of effective forms of reparative intervention and embodied education.

Touch and the formation of identity are intimately related. When used therapeutically, the feeling, thinking, knowing, seeing hands of a touch-trained therapist seek to restore, or offer for the first time, an implicit experience of existential safety. Using direct body-to-body touch dialogues that include the right to be, the importance of one's needs, and the experience of true caring touch can provide experiences of yielding receptivity that help individuals connect to the value of their own life.

The therapeutic use of touch can awaken our sensory and emotional blueprint. It helps embody our cognition and directly access the hunger for connection that underlies neurological deficits, dissociation, dysregulation, and states of trauma and fragmentation. The therapeutic use of touch is a psychobiological approach that has the potential to create a paradigm shift for alleviating anxiety, stress, and depression. It also holds promise for individuals who find touch unbearable.

The strong evidence for the importance of touch, developmentally and in everyday life, begs the question of why it is not further explored and utilized in clinical contexts. Though it is the first sense to develop in utero, and is proven to be an essential need for healthy development, touch is the least studied of our senses. It is time to fully open to the vital exploration of the power of touch.

14

Fascia as Sensory Organ and the Role of Interoceptive Techniques

Robert Schleip

Fascia as a Body-Wide Interconnected Network

Traditional classical anatomy attributed a similar degree of importance to fascial connective tissues as we tend to attribute to the outside packaging of presents. The enveloping tissue keeps things nicely together, but in most cases one can respectfully remove it to understand the functions of the real organ below. While there were some brilliant pioneers in the field of complementary therapies who knew better—such as Andrew T. Still, the founder of osteopathy, or Ida Rolf, founder of the Rolfing method of structural integration—their related insights were mostly ignored in mainstream medicine.

This situation started to rapidly change when more accurate measurement technologies became available for the assessment of fascial properties, such as high-resolution ultrasound examination or refined immunohistochemistry. These permitted a more objective tissue examination complementing the more subjective palpatory and observational skills already practiced by many myofascial therapists. Inspired by that background, the first international Fascia Research Congress, hosted at the conference center of Harvard Medical School in Boston in 2007, elicited a drastic increase in subsequent scientific attention devoted to the former "Cinderella tissue" of musculoskeletal medicine (Grimm, 2007).

Emphasized by that congress, most contemporary concepts about the functional importance of fascia are inspired by the tensegrity concept in modern architecture, in which solid struts are seen as floating islands embedded in a continuous and interconnected network of tensional tissues. This fostered the proposition of a widened functional definition of the fascial system, as proposed by the Nomenclature Committee of the international Fascia Research Society:

The fascial system consists of the three-dimensional continuum of soft, collagen containing, loose and dense fibrous connective tissues that permeate the body. It incorporates elements such as adipose tissue, adventitiae and neurovascular sheaths, aponeuroses, deep and superficial fasciae, epineurium, joint capsules, ligaments, membranes, meninges, myofascial expansions, periostea, retinacula, septa, tendons, visceral fasciae, and all the intramuscular and intermuscular connective tissues including endo-/peri-/epimysium. The fascial system surrounds, interweaves between, and interpenetrates all organs, muscles, bones and nerve fibers, endowing the body with a functional structure, and providing an environment that enables all body systems to operate in an integrated manner. (Stecco et al., 2018, p. 354)

Fascia as the Richest Sensory Organ of the Human Body

For many decades, fascia was considered an inert wrapping organ, expressing mainly mechanical functions. Andrew Taylor Still in 1902 already recognized its sensorial function. He wrote, "No doubt nerves exist in the fascia," and he suggested that all fascial tissues are "the branch offices of the brain" (Still, 1902, p. 62). In 1988, Dutch researcher Jaap van der Wal reported the very rich presence and complex arrangement of sensory nerve endings in the muscular fascia of rats. But this was also largely ignored in mainstream medicine until the first international Fascia Research Congress in 2007, at which three teams from different universities independently reported their findings on the rich sensory nerves in fascial tissues (Findley & Schleip, 2007). After that event, many studies about fascial innervation were published, suggesting that fascia plays an important role in our bodies' perception and internal representation.

More recently, the quantity of sensory nerves terminating in the body-wide fascial system, based on histological examinations from different body regions, was estimated at 250 million (Schleip & Stecco, 2021). Compared with the sensory nerves in our eyes or in the skin, this new calculation suggests that the human fascial network is our richest sensory organ.

This brings up the question of which sensory functions are supported by this rich network (Figure 14.1). The largest proportion consists of interstitial receptors (including all neurons terminating in free nerve endings, encompassing type III fibers (aka C-fibers) and type IV fibers (aka A-delta fibers). These neurons are very thin and are usually sensitive to mechanical stimulation. If the extracellular matrix is chemically altered or if the mechanical stimulus is too strong, many of these receptors could become nociceptors (signaling potential tissue damage). Interestingly, the mechanical activation threshold of the fascial free nerve endings is two times lower than in skin and muscle (Taguchi et al., 2013). In addition, free nerve endings in the human thoracolumbar fascia are significantly more sensitive to chemical irritation than the underlying muscles, and they tend to maintain a long-lasting hypersensitivity (Schilder et al., 2014). Most of the interstitial (between fibrous tissue) neurons in fascial tissues are so-called polymodal receptors, meaning they are responsive to more than one kind of stimulation.

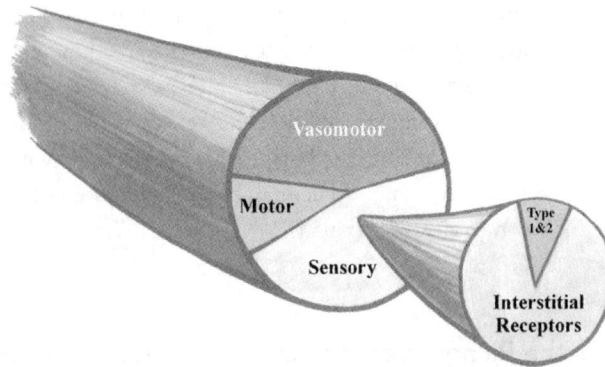

FIGURE 14.1 Composition of neurons in myofascial tissues: The diagram illustrates the proportions of distinct nerve types, derived from histological studies on a cat's lower leg. Although a fraction of interstitial neurons may terminate within the bone, the remaining neurons predominantly terminate within fascial tissues. Muscle spindles, sensory devices, are also housed within collagen-rich intramuscular tissues. Free nerve endings are the endpoints for interstitial neurons. Notably, some interstitial nerves serve interoceptive or nociceptive functions, but not all. An interesting observation is the abundance of nerves dedicated to refining nutrient distribution through the vascular system, regulated by the sympathetic nervous system. (Data sourced from Michell & Schmidt, 1977; with illustration credit to fascialnet.com)

Fascia and Proprioception

There are five types of specialized proprioceptive mechanoreceptors in fascia: muscle spindles, Golgi endings, Pacini corpuscles, Ruffini endings, and free nerve endings (Table 14.1).

The muscle spindle receptor is a fusiform specialized mechanoreceptor. It includes several intrafusal muscular fibers and is surrounded by a strong capsule of connective tissue (Stecco et al., 2018). Spindle capsules are usually embedded in the intramuscular fascial layer of the perimysium. Since muscle spindles can detect tensional differences of 3 grams, their sensitivity can be significantly impaired by increased stiffness of the surrounding perimysium (Stecco, 2014). Stiffness increases in the perimysium are frequently associated with chronic immobilization and with many fibrotic pathologies. Such tissue changes may therefore result in impairments of proprioceptive refinement.

Golgi endings are slowly adapting receptors that respond to tensional loading. Their presence is particularly enriched in the myotendinous junctions and close to the intermuscular septa. Stimulation of Golgi receptors tends to trigger a local relaxation response. Nevertheless, suppose tendinous extramuscular tissues are stretched in a series arrangement, in contrast to a parallel alignment, with muscle fibers in a relaxed condition. In that case, most of the respective elongation will be swallowed by the more compliant myofibers. In this way, the respective stretching impulse may not provide sufficient stimulation for eliciting any muscular tonus change (Jami, 1992). A practical implication is that a stretching impulse, aimed at reaching the tendinous tissues, may profit from including

TABLE 14.1 Fascia as Sensory Organ

RECEPTOR AND RELATED NEURONS	LOCATION	SENSITIVITY	RESPONSE
Muscle spindle Type I a	Perimysium	Rapid stretch stimulation	Proprioception Muscular tonus increase when rapidly stretched
Golgi ending Type I b	High density in musculo-tendinous and musculo-aponeurotic junctions	Not sufficiently stimulated, if tendon is stretched while the related muscle fibers are in a relaxed condition	Proprioception Decrease in muscular activation (of those muscle fibers which are mechanically connected with that tendon/aponeurosis)
Pacini corpuscle Type II	Aponeurotic fasciae Joint capsules	Insensitive to constant or slow stimulation High sensitivity to rapid stimulation	Proprioception
Ruffini ending Type II	Aponeurotic fasciae Apparently low density anywhere else	High sensitivity to directional specific stretch/ shear stimulation at slow speed	Proprioception ANS*
Free nerve ending Types III and IV	Most common receptor; found almost everywhere Very high density in periosteum	Approx. 50% require strong mechanical stimulation Other 50% are sensitive to even small stimulations	Intero- and/or proprioception ANS*

*ANS, autonomic nervous system

some moments in which the lengthened muscle fibers are actively contracting or temporarily resisting their overall elongation. In addition, a manual approach in which the fascial tissues are stretch-loaded in a direction orthogonal to the direction of closest myofibers, as is frequently practiced in manual cross-fiber techniques (based on the teaching of Tom Bowen), could mean that sufficient elongation can be achieved in the passively lengthened collagenous fibers, despite the more compliant myofibers in their vicinity.

The Pacinian corpuscles are rapidly adapting, as they are very sensitive to dynamic changes in mechanical stimulation. Gentle rocking, as well as more rapid vibratory stimulation, can be suitable stimulation methods. Such treatment could improve proprioception.

Ruffini receptors are slowly adapting and tend to remain sensitive in response to a continuous stimulus. As a result, they can monitor longer-lasting postural sensations as well as slowly melting myofascial techniques. In addition, they are also highly sensitive to differences in directional shear loading, which may correspond to the "local listening" approach used by many osteopaths when trying to detect with their hands in which specific direction a given tissue wants to move.

Fascia and Interoception

Body awareness can also be perceived by how we feel our body as a dynamic physiological organism from the inside. Current concepts describe interoception as a sense of the physiological condition of the body, a ubiquitous information network used to represent one's body from within. It is the ability to detect subtle changes in bodily systems, including muscles, skin, joints, and viscera (Dunn et al., 2010). It includes a range of physiological sensations, including:

- Warmth, coolness
- Muscular activity
- Pain, tickle, itch
- Hunger, thirst
- Air hunger
- Sexual arousal
- Wine tasting (in sommeliers)
- Heartbeat
- Vasomotor activity
- Distension of bladder
- Distension of stomach, rectum, or esophagus
- Sensual touch

These sensations are triggered by stimulating nerves that project to the insular cortex rather than to the primary somatosensory cortex, which is usually considered the main target of proprioceptive sensations (Berlucchi & Aglioti, 2010). Feelings from these sensations not only have a sensory, but also an affective, motivational aspect and are always

TABLE 14.2 Conditions That Tend to Be Affected by
Distressed Proprioception and Interoception

PROPRIOCEPTION	INTEROCEPTION
Low back pain	Irritable bowel syndrome
Attention-deficit/hyperactivity disorder	Eating disorders
Whiplash injury	Posttraumatic stress disorders
Adolescent idiopathic scoliosis	Anxiety, depression
Complex regional pain syndrome	Alexythymia (emotional blindness)
Other myofascial pain syndromes	Fibromyalgia

related to the homeostatic needs of the body. They are associated with behavioral motivations that are essential for the maintenance of physiological body integrity.

It has been proposed that the neural pathways associated with interoception may be considered a potential correlate for consciousness (Craig, 2009). The sensory receptors for interoception are free nerve endings, most of which are found in fascial tissues throughout the human body. It is helpful to understand that proprioception and interoception are organized differently in the human brain and that very different afferent pathways are involved in them. Table 14.2 shows some conditions that tend to be affected by distressed proprioception and interoception. If applied with an open-minded and careful attitude, it is an appealing thought that a more proprioceptive-oriented therapeutic stimulation may work better for some conditions and a more interoceptive-oriented approach for others.

Affective Touch

A recent and surprising addition to the list of interoceptive sensations is the sense of affective, sensual, or pleasant touch. This discovery was triggered by examinations of a unique patient lacking myelinated afferents. Slow stroking of the skin with a soft brush triggered a faint and obscure sensation of pleasant touch, although the patient was unable to recognize any stroking direction. Functional magnetic resonance imaging showed that this vague sensation was accompanied by a clear activation of the insular cortex, while no activation was seen in the primary somatosensory cortex (Olausson et al., 2010).

Based on the innervation of primate skin and on subsequent studies with other patients, it was concluded that there is dual tactile innervation of hairy human skin: in addition to fast-conducting myelinated afferent fibers, there is a system of slow-conducting unmyelinated type IV afferents (CT afferents) that respond to gentle touch (Figure 14.2). The CT afferents are a distinct type of unmyelinated, low-threshold mechanoreceptors that are connected with neural interoceptive pathways. Those afferents have a slow conduction velocity (half a second delay from stimulus to arrival in the brain). It is assumed that they are mostly present in hairy skin. The cells are stimulated by gentle pressure on the skin and respond preferentially to gentle caressing strokes. C-tactile afferents are connected to specific areas of the brain: the insular cortex, the posterior superior temporal sulcus, the medial prefrontal cortex, and the dorsoanterior cingulate cortex, which are known to be activated by affective touch (McGlone et al., 2014). It is concluded that primate skin contains touch receptors that form a system for social touch that may underlie emotional, hormonal (for example, oxytocin), and affiliative responses to caress-like, skin-to-skin contact between individuals. The profound importance of such a system for human health and well-being has long been indicated (Montague, 1971), at least since the classic study of Harlow (1958) with baby rhesus monkeys that express affection for a surrogate mother in response to tactile comfort. This is reiterated by McGlone et al. (2014), who suggested the "affective touch hypothesis": the essential role of the CT system is to provide a peripheral mechanism for signaling pleasant skin-to-skin contact in humans, thereby promoting interpersonal touch and affiliative behavior.

More recently, a related system for "pleasant deep touch" has been discovered (Case et al., 2021). By use of an oscillating compression sleeve, it was demonstrated not only that this touch was perceived as pleasant and calming, but that it also activated brain regions highly like those that respond to CT stroking. Further examinations revealed that the calming effect of this pleasant deep touch as well as in gentle skin stroking both involve myelinated type 1 fibers (most likely type 1a), in addition to the previously documented involvement of free nerve endings in gentle skin stroking (Case et al., 2023). No comparable studies have yet been conducted with manual therapies that use mechanical forces of a similar stronger magnitude, which are experienced as pleasant and calming.

FIGURE 14.2 Gentle touch as well as "deep pleasant touch" are capable of eliciting a calming effect, which is associated with an increased stimulation of the insular cortex. (Photo credit: Aleks Gudenko, Shutterstock, https://www.shutterstock.com/)

Posttraumatic Stress Disorder and Myofascial Pain

New research shows that chronic emotional stress can impact myofascial pain. In an experiment, rats were immobilized for one hour per day for 12 consecutive days. Consequently, these animals showed a significant increase in resting activity in the dorsal horn of the spinal cord, together with an increased nociceptive myofascial sensitivity (Hoheisel et al., 2015). A similar observation was reported from human back pain patients: those who had a history of childhood maltreatment expressed a lower-pressure pain threshold sensitivity compared with those who did not have that additional burden in their life history (Tesarz et al., 2016). These findings suggest that emotional stress may significantly influence the expression of myofascial pain.

Dynamic interactions between chronic sympathetic activation and immune system regulation could contribute significantly to several common health dysfunctions. For example, in many—but certainly not all—cases of fibromyalgia, there is an association between prior physically traumatic events and the first onset of this pathology (Yavne et al., 2018). While the precise neurophysiological dynamics of fibromyalgia remain a mystery, a study demonstrated that fibromyalgia patients have a diminished density of sympathetic nerve fibers surrounding tiny blood vessels in their skin. This suggests a possible relationship between altered sympathetic innervation and the impaired thermal tolerance commonly reported by fibromyalgia patients (Evdokimov et al., 2020). An investigation demonstrated that the injection of specific antibodies within blood serum from human fibromyalgia patients triggered fibromyalgia-like symptoms in mice. This response did not happen when the serum antibodies were deactivated before injection. It also did not occur when blood serum containing these antibodies was injected from healthy human patients (Onuora, 2021). While this is a novel and partly unexpected finding, it suggests that altered immune system activity—possibly coinfluenced by the sympathetic nervous system—could play a major role in many cases of this common complex pathology.

A publication by several German scientists revealed that patients with major depressive disorder had an increased myofascial stiffness of the posterior neck and thoracic erector spinae area compared to healthy controls (Michalak et al., 2022). In addition, they expressed a decreased elastic recoil capacity—or increased viscoelastic dampening quality—in the same tissues (Figure 14.3). This surprising finding, at least from a scientific perspective, stimulates new research questions: To what degree is the increased stiffness influenced by muscular fibers or fascial morphology? Is the change in viscosity related to an increased inflammatory milieu? How congruent or not is this finding with the "character armor" concept of Wilhelm Reich (1933)? How much does the common head-forward posture influence these tissue changes?

The same study investigated the question by administering a self-myofascial foam rolling program on the posterior neck and middle thoracic regions. The surprising finding is that patients that received self-myofascial release treatment recalled fewer negative words and tended to recall more positive words than the placebo group. In addition, the myofascial release group had a more positive mood than those in the placebo group. It seems

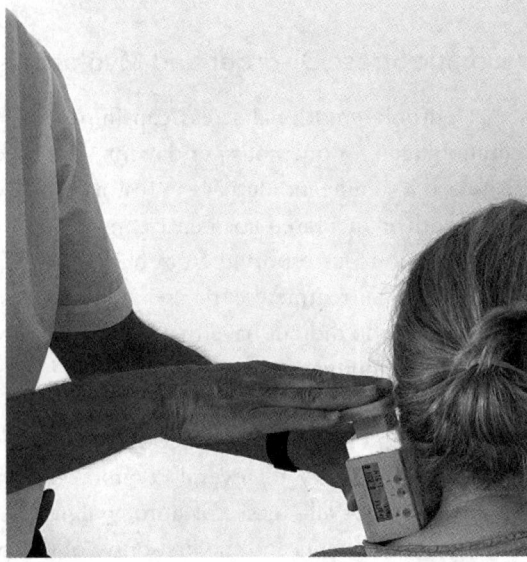

FIGURE 14.3 Measurement of biomechanical tissue properties with a newly developed mechanographic assessment tool (IndentoPro, developed by Chemnitz University; see www.indentopro.com) as used in the study by Michalak et al. (2022).

that changes in the myofascial tissue through self-myofascial release can causally affect critical pathopsychological processes involved in the maintenance of depressive disorder.

Another exciting study from Brazil investigated a local induced inflammation in the lumbar fascia of mice. A gentle myofascial massage was applied to some animals, while the others didn't receive the treatment. The study revealed that the myofascial stimulation elicited a clear anti-inflammatory effect on the local tissue, based on the altered expression of the cytokines IL-4 and TGF-β1 (França et al., 2020). If applicable to humans, this suggests that myofascial massage may influence the dynamic interplay between fascial biochemistry and immune system regulation. Further research is expected to explore to what extent similar profound effects may possibly be utilized in the treatment of mental disorders, which are frequently associated with a pro-inflammatory change in the biochemical milieu.

Complementary Therapy Interventions and Interoception

Complementary movement therapies, such as yoga, tai chi, qigong, Pilates, Feldenkrais, Body Mind Centering, or Continuum Movement, usually encourage a perceptual emphasis on finer sensations in one's own body. However, depending on the focus of the individual teacher or respective school, internal perception is sometimes directed almost entirely toward proprioceptive refinement. For example, a student of such training approaches may learn to feel minute movements of individual vertebrae or to control their lumbar lordosis

TABLE 14.3 Examples of Therapeutic Approaches Primarily Focused on Refinement of Proprioception and Interoception

PROPRIOCEPTIVE EMPHASIS	INTEROCEPTIVE EMPHASIS
Postural education training	Continuum Movement, Body-Mind Centering
Feldenkrais method of "awareness through movement"	Somatic Experiencing
Iyengar yoga (basic lessons)	Yoga styles with emphasis on physiological and energetic sensations (streaming, temperature changes, etc.)
Classical Pilates approaches (aka "controllogy")	Visceral osteopathy
F. M. Alexander work	Biodynamic bodywork (e.g., Reichian bodywork, Boyesen work, etc.)

within a multitude of loading situations. Nevertheless, they may remain an "interoceptive moron," for example, unable to differentiate visceral sensations from signs of an empty stomach, stage fright–oriented "butterflies," or empathy-driven gut feelings about another person's dilemma, which may simply be acute gastritis.

In contrast, some teachers of these practices also include a skilled fine-tuning of the student's perception of interoceptive sensations (Table 14.3). This may include emphasizing sensations such as a subtle tingling under the skin, a general or localized warming, a subjective sense of internal spaciousness, a feeling of aliveness, an inner silence, an emotional homecoming, or a meditation-like change in general self-awareness. For example, gravity-oriented changes in body position, such as some upside-down yoga postures, could easily trigger new and interesting (and hopefully unthreatening) sensations in visceral ligaments, which can foster interoceptive refinement. Given the recent research indications of a close correlation between disrupted interoception and many psycho-emotional disorders (Table 14.2), it is plausible that some of these movement practices may have strong therapeutic potential. Typically, these therapeutic practices foster an attitude of inner mindfulness, of refining internal listening skills, and they frequently alternate brief periods of active motor attention with subsequent periods of rest when the student pays attention to minor interoceptive sensations within the body. Not surprisingly, some studies already indicate a positive health-enhancing effect of such mindfulness-based therapies for many common clinical conditions (Astin et al., 2003).

In addition to mindfulness-based movement therapies, which often involve an increased interoceptive attention, manual therapies that involve human touch and aim to elicit a pleasant and calming effect via stimulation of the previously described mechanoreceptors for gentle touch and/or pleasant deep touch have shown promising effects in the treatment of posttraumatic stress disorder as well as other mental disorders (Reeve et al., 2020; Watt et al., 2021). Preliminary research indicates that this beneficial effect is significantly influenced by mindfulness-based interoceptive attention of the patient as well as nondistracted attention of the practitioner (Moseley et al., 2008; Cerritelli et al., 2017). It has been suggested that—due to the complex networking connections of the insular cortex—interoceptive perceptions are significantly shaped by predictive coding, often more than by the exact nature of the afferent stimulation (Barrett & Simmons, 2015). If applicable, this suggests that practitioners working with health conditions described in Table 14.2 might do particularly well to orchestrate the psychosocial context of their therapeutic interactions to encourage the expectation of healing among their patients.

15

Gates of Perception

Physiological Safety and Mental Strength

Herbert Grassmann

If the doors of perception were cleansed, every thing would appear to man as it is: Infinite.
For man has closed himself up, till he sees all things through narrow chinks of his cavern.
—WILLIAM BLAKE, "THE MARRIAGE OF HEAVEN AND HELL"

OUR NERVOUS SYSTEM IS NOT ONLY CAPABLE OF RECEIVING EXTERNAL STIMULI, IT ALSO responds to internal information—to messenger substances and nerve impulses from our organs, tissues, and joints. This interoceptive function is important for adapting our metabolism and behavior to our physical state. Interoceptive senses inform you of the internal state of your body. For example, sweaty palms can mean you're anxious and shivering can mean you're cold, and these cues often lead you to behave in ways that satisfy these needs to return your body to homeostasis, which is simply a stable internal biological state. A lack of interoceptive awareness is associated with a number of disorders, such as eating disorders or autism.

Scientists have shown that our sensitivity to interoceptive signals can determine our capacity to regulate our emotions, and our subsequent susceptibility to mental health problems such as anxiety and depression.

Interoception: The Awareness of Body Sensations

Phenomenology of Perception is Merleau-Ponty's (1945/1962) philosophical attempt to understand human experience through perceiving. Merleau-Ponty explores the complex relationship between the body, perception, and the world, challenging the traditional Cartesian dualism that separates mind and body. Merleau-Ponty emphasizes the embodied nature of perception. He argues that perception is not just a mental process but is deeply interwoven with the body. Our perceptions are shaped by our bodily experiences and movements in the world.

Another pioneer in this field, Antonio Damasio (1994), proposed the theory of somatic markers as part of his research into the neural basis of emotions and decision-making. His work has been influential in understanding how emotions are intertwined with bodily sensations and play a crucial role in decision-making processes.

The concept of somatic markers suggests that emotional responses are closely tied to changes in bodily states. When we encounter certain stimuli, such as seeing a wild animal, our bodies react involuntarily with physiological changes like increased heart rate, muscle tension, or sweating. These bodily changes occur before we are consciously aware of the emotion associated with the stimulus.

"Researchers and clinicians are recognising interoception as a key mechanism to mental and physical health, where understanding our body's signals helps us understand and regulate emotional and physical states," says Dr. Helen Weng at the University of California, San Francisco. Helene Langevin, says it succinctly: "Dysfunctions in interoception may play important roles in many neurological, psychiatric, and behavioral disorders. . . . Gaining a better understanding of how interoception works may help us develop better ways to treat these conditions" (Weng et al., 2021).

Camilla Nord and Sarah Garfinkel (2022), from the University of Sussex, explain in their research that we can all learn to tune in to how often our heart beats—and by doing so, become more in tune with our emotions. They demonstrated that a large subgroup of people with depression, for example, often show poorer interoceptive awareness on heartbeat detection tasks, and, for these patients, the reduced ability to feel their bodily signals may lie behind their sense of lethargy and emotional numbness—the sense that they can feel nothing at all. People with anxiety, in contrast, do report being attentive to their interoceptive signals—but they don't necessarily read them accurately. They may misinterpret a small change in heart rate as being much bigger than it really is, for example, which can lead them to catastrophize their feelings and amplify their sense of panic.

Hugo Critchley, at Brighton and Sussex Medical School, points out that poor interoceptive awareness can also lead to the sense of depersonalization and dissociation, which are early symptoms of psychosis and may be a precursor of delusions (Grimes et al., 2023). Interoception helps us to form our most basic sense of self, he says—and it seems to be askew in these patients.

Perhaps most intriguingly, the new awareness of interoception can help us to understand why certain physical exercises can be so good for our mental health. For one thing, regular workouts may change the nature of the signals that your brain receives. "If you're deconditioned from a lack of exercise, you're more likely to experience symptoms that you might associate with anxiety," says Critchley. "Your heart will race more when you experience challenges—be it physical or emotional" (Critchley et al., 2023). As you get more fit, however, and organs such as the heart become more adept at dealing with strain, your body will show a more resilient response to changing circumstances—changes that could spill over into your emotional well-being.

There is clinical evidence that if we train our interoception to be more accurate, we can help individuals who have lost their sense of self-perception. In research on autistic people and anxiety, Sarah Garfinkel showed that after clinical interoceptive training, individuals recovered from anxiety symptoms after they improved the accuracy of detecting their heart rate signals (Hogenboom, 2018). Lack of precision in reading the body may contribute to anxiety.

Autonomic control and greater accuracy of sensory perception are obviously early cues for self-regulation, such as deep breathing. There is also evidence that training one organ (the heart in this case) has a knock-on effect on the accuracy of perception of other bodily organs. If interoception does turn out to be a transdiagnostic risk factor, then the integration of interoceptive interventions into existing treatments could do a lot to improve a range of mental health outcomes.

In interoceptive discrimination disorder, a person has vague feelings, or difficulty recognizing what a feeling means. Signs of discrimination difficulty include having strong feelings but being confused by them, or not knowing whether one is hungry or not. A weak interoceptive system is associated with self-harm and suicidal behavior. Such people have difficulty knowing what they are feeling and communicating their feelings. Signs of hypersensitivity are associated with eating disorders, anxiety, and trauma.

Sense of Self and Other

Interoception gives us the sense that "this is me; this is my body; this is how I feel."
—KELLY MAHLER, *THE EIGHTH SENSORY SYSTEM*

According to a definition by Ceunen et al. (2016), the question of whether something is interoceptive depends on whether it contributes to subjective perception of the physical state:

- Interoception provides a large part of the information that forms the basis of the self-image, also in relation to other people. It is also a large part of self-communication, which is used to check whether one is safe or not and whether an experience or a person in the outside world is pleasant, exciting, or threatening (Ceunen et al., 2016).
- Interoception develops in context. That is, everything that is experienced daily, including on a social level, is incorporated into the perception and evaluation of internal sources of information: Interoceptive interpretation is calibrated, so to speak, by the considerable feedback from the social environment.
- Interoception is easy to influence. For example, when you are asked to indicate how strong the pain you feel is, and the assessment varies depending on your mood: A positive mood increases pain tolerance, and a negative mood lowers it. Physical sensations such as pain could be considered objectively measurable, but as interoception is also influenced by many nonphysical factors, there is no fixed standard state.
- The interoceptive system is there to provide people with information that they can use to make predictions about themselves and their environment. However, if the system has not developed congruently with the context and feedback, and the markers for perception and judgment are consequently oversensitive or set to unreliable signals, it can also mislead. In other words: We make judgments based on inaccurate cues and reach incorrect conclusions (Bechara et al., 2000).

- Information received via interoception is usually perceived as facts and not as judgments because it stems from so-called inner knowledge or gut feeling. Our task as practitioners is to support our clients in revising and changing their interoceptive self-talk.
- Interoception is flexible. The interoceptive vocabulary can be changed with professional help, leading to a more nuanced assessment of inner processes and more constructive self-communication.

Interoceptive perception also has existential dimensions. It generates an awareness of our self as a body and gives us an integrated sense of self. Poor interoceptive awareness also affects our ability to perceive and understand others. When our self-awareness (our feelings, thoughts, body, and desires) is solid, it forms a foundation on which we can understand the feelings, intentions, thoughts, and behaviors of others.

As we know from Polyvagal Theory, connectedness is a biological imperative. "We are designed from birth to connect, and we cannot survive without connection to another human being" (Porges, 2022). The fundamental and innate need to feel safe and connect with others is the force that drives people to build a trusting relationship, which is the cornerstone of effective therapy—be it individual, family, or couples therapy. Porges explored this concept in Polyvagal Theory with his colleague Deb Dana (2021). They provided guidelines for implementing a polyvagal lens for therapy and the process of interoception.

Accordingly, the principle of connectedness could serve as a guide for therapists to identify specific characteristics of a therapeutic presence, that is, neurophysiological conditions in which both develop a sense of security. People who have a more stable neurophysiological foundation tend to cope better with stress, have a lower risk of mental disorders, and can be more emotionally resilient. This shows how important a healthy autonomic nervous system is for psychological resilience.

The Polyvagal Theory explicitly points out that the human nervous system has several defense strategies, and that the decision whether to use a mobilizing fight/flight strategy or immobilization in a situation is not subject to our will. "Without us being aware of it, our nervous system is constantly assessing the safety of the environment and prioritizing adaptive behavior based on this assessment, which is not cognitive. Certain physical features of a challenge in the environment trigger fight-or-flight behavior in some people, while others react by freezing under exactly the same conditions" (Porges, 2022). According to Porges (2022) the difficulties therapists face in treating trauma stem from lack of knowledge of this adaptive biological response, more specifically, the lack of interoceptive awareness to engage with these defense systems. Therefore, understanding the specific response and not the traumatic event as such is crucial for the successful treatment of trauma.

Trauma Is an Assault on the Senses

Neuroception and interoception are two interconnected processes that play crucial roles in our ability to perceive and respond to both internal and external stimuli. While they operate in distinct domains, they can influence each other in various ways. Neuroception can modulate autonomic nervous system activity, which in turn affects interoceptive processing. For instance, perceived threats can activate the sympathetic nervous system, leading to physiological changes such as increased heart rate and respiration rate, which are monitored through interoceptive pathways.

The detection of safety or threat cues may influence interoceptive processes related to emotional regulation. For example, perceiving a safe environment may promote a sense of calmness and facilitate accurate internal bodily states associated with relaxation. Conversely, the neuroception of threat can trigger physiological responses associated with stress and activate interoceptive pathways associated with fight-or-flight responses.

Dysfunction in neuroception and interoception can contribute to various health conditions, including anxiety disorders, trauma-related disorders, and somatic symptom disorders. An altered neuroceptive response to environmental cues may disrupt interoceptive processes, leading to disturbances in emotional regulation, stress responses, and bodily awareness.

Kearney and Lanius (2022) describe the importance of somatic-sensory processing in trauma-related disorders. They view trauma as an assault on the senses. This is because any form of traumatic event is a highly arousing, multisensory experience that affects the lower levels of the brain. Sensorimotor dysfunction, or a full sensory memory, is experienced by the body as an inadequate response to an existential threat and corresponds to a disturbed sense of agency and disconnectedness.

While the organism contextualizes sensory impressions and receives them with emotional and cognitive information, sensory processing refers to the ability to register, organize, and modulate incoming sensory information. Sensorimotor disturbances are perceived by the body as an inappropriate response to an existential threat and correspond to a disturbed sense of agency. Lanius and her team (2022) believe that using sensory information to understand PTSD is important for its treatment.

Lanius explained that trauma is perceived through multiple sensory impressions and is a significant assault on the senses. While you see something terrible, at the same time you may also hear someone insulting you or smell alcohol. All these sensory impressions are transmitted to the reptilian brain. This part of the brain takes control and reacts without thinking. A typical trauma is characterized by an overreaction of the reptilian brain. It dominates the higher-order cognitive functions, which are too slow to respond effectively to the trauma.

The compulsion to repeat the past through traumatic reenactments or engaging in reckless behaviors is frequently one of the few ways that traumatized individuals can feel alive. It is well known that individuals with PTSD—particularly when associated with developmental trauma—often report a sense of self that does not exist entirely, illustrated eloquently through statements such as, "I do not know who I am," or "I feel like I have stopped existing."

More generally, the research field of multisensory integration is an intriguing area that looks at the complex mechanisms underlying the brain's ability to combine inputs from different sensory modalities to create a coherent perception of the world and promote higher human abilities:

- Enhancement of perception: Multisensory integration can enhance perceptual processing by combining information from different sensory modalities. For example, both seeing and hearing a moving object can provide more accurate information about its location and trajectory compared to using vision or hearing alone.
- Temporal and spatial binding: The brain synchronizes inputs from different sensory modalities in both time and space to create a unified perception. This temporal and spatial binding allows us to perceive multisensory events as occurring simultaneously and originating from the same source.
- Cross-modal plasticity: Multisensory integration is supported by the brain's ability to reorganize and adapt in response to sensory experience. In cases of sensory deprivation or loss, such as blindness or deafness, the brain may undergo cross-modal plasticity, where areas of the brain that would normally process one sensory modality become recruited to process inputs from other modalities.
- Functional significance: Multisensory integration is essential for various aspects of perception, cognition, and behavior, including spatial navigation, object recognition, social communication, and motor coordination. It allows us to interact effectively with our environment and adapt to changing sensory conditions.

Recently, altered multisensory integration mechanisms have been proposed as one of the neurophysiological mechanisms that may be responsible for some of the consequences of early trauma exposure. Clinicians should work toward empowering people who have experienced childhood trauma to recalibrate their multisensory integration processes to facilitate resilience (see Chapter 4, this volume). It involves the integration of three major sensory systems: exteroception, interoception, and proprioception (Fogel, 2018).

Based on these findings, Larissa and Herbert Grassmann (Grassmann & Grassmann, 2025) developed the Polyvagal Embodiment Training concept, which aims to achieve multisensory integration through a sensory training and the development of motor skills.

Accordingly, interoceptive training supports the body's sensorimotor needs for processing and integration. Sensory overload can be reduced by using the acquired motor skills to process sensory stimuli. In addition, improving the sensory performance of the eyes, ears, balance, and proprioception helps the body to orient itself quickly and make the right decisions in the event of danger.

Polyvagal Embodiment Training (PET)

For a long time, it was believed we have five primary sensory systems (touch, smell, taste, visual, and sound). Over the past several years, there has been increasing awareness of the three hidden sensory systems, including the vestibular, proprioception, and interoception systems.

Interoceptors are located in the heart, stomach, liver, intestines, and other organs and not only allow us to feel pain, thirst, or hunger but also help us to recognize our emotions. Porges (2017) refers to interoception as our sixth sense because it forms the basis of our gut feeling, such as when we have a strong feeling about a person or place that seems unsafe. Proprioception refers to the sensory feedback that helps us to locate the body in space. This includes the integration of the vestibular system, which enables us to orient ourselves in relation to gravity and coordinate our movements in the world.

Neuroception integrates the information from these three sensory processing systems to recognize threats or safety cues emanating from the outside world via the senses or from our inner body sensation. Posttraumatic stress, especially if it is based on developmental and complex traumatization, is associated with altered sensory processing in addition to impaired self-regulation.

By focusing on biologically based behaviors that are common to all people, we can imagine new intervention paradigms to help clients whose social behavior and attachment are impaired. We can change the environment so that it appears safer and less likely to trigger mobilization or immobilization responses.

Physical training to improve interoception promotes cognitive and motor skills on the way to strengthened neuroception. In daily therapy, for example, we assess the client's ability to perceive space. Attention to space requires integrated functioning of the vestibular, visual, and auditory systems, and sometimes the tactile and proprioceptive systems.

We can also intervene directly by training the neural regulation of brain stem structures, stimulating the neural regulation of the social attachment system and thereby promoting positive social behavior. While neuroception describes how neural circuits differentiate whether a situation is safe or dangerous, interoception allows us to answer the question, "How do I feel and sense?"

More generally, good orientation skills can help a person improve their neuroception by helping them to recognize and react to potential sources of danger more quickly. When a person feels safe and oriented, they are also better able to pay attention to and interpret their bodily responses. Improved neuroception, conversely, can help a person improve the ability to orient by helping him or her recognize and evaluate potential sources of danger more quickly.

PET Training: Reconstructing Visual Patterns
Through the Lens of Polyvagal Theory

We will focus on differences but also interconnectedness in working with the autonomic nervous system and the voluntary nervous system. We will look at what derails both systems, and how the repairs for each differ. We will address why to use one or the other, and how they complement but do not replace each other. We examine how the physiological states of fight/flight/freeze are reflected in the behavioral and emotional patterns of vision. The goal is to explore visual patterns through systematic and experimental eye exercises and to contribute to building more resilient visual patterns in the ventral vagal state.

In normal and healthy vision, the eyes automatically move smoothly, accurately, and quickly. Eye movements are an essential part of good vision. They support us by searching for information in the environment through fast and precise movements, whether tracking moving objects (eye tracking movements), focusing when jumping from one target to another (saccadic eye movements), or controlling hand movements (eye-hand coordination).

Eye Relaxation

Rub your palms together until they become warm. Then place your palms on your eyes to block out all light. Close your eyes and enjoy the warmth of your hands. Let the blackness behind your eyelids get blacker and blacker, and feel how you can let go a little inside. Repeat this two or three times. Then look around the room. Perhaps you can now see the world a little more clearly.

Generate Double Images

As children, we often did this without realizing what a great effect it had on our nervous system.

Double Images are created by moving the inner eye muscles. You do that by looking with both eyes at the tip of your nose. Hold your index finger in front of the tip of your nose and look at it. Then slowly move your finger away from the tip of your nose. If you now look at your index finger, you will see your index finger twice. Try it out with distance and close-up positions of your eyes. Sometimes you can see the finger clearly and then you can "blur" the eyes in such a way that it becomes double again. We unconsciously create the same lens setting of the double images during manual activities. That's why crocheting, knitting, and crafting are so relaxing.

Salamander Eye Exercise

Eye movement provides relaxation. The eyes are the sensory organ with which we are most familiar and on which we rely most. If we could not see, we would be in a lot of trouble. The brain eagerly gathers information about what is happening outside through the eyes. The better our eyes work, the clearer we can see, and the better the brain can analyze information about the nature of the threat. If I have poor eyesight, what my eyes see as a harmless stick can suddenly turn out to be a poisonous snake and my life is in danger. Everything we see goes straight to our brainstem and triggers a reaction. You can imagine that with the flood of visual information via social media, the nervous system can't keep up with the processing. This leads to a feeling of being full and empty at the same time. What's more, our eyeballs are actually designed to work with our neck muscles to turn our heads, orient ourselves in space and look around. The better the eyes can move in the head, the more secure the survival system feels.

The salamander eye exercise is an extremely effective instant exercise whenever you have the feeling that you have just been frightened by something, or when you are energetically knocked out and have lost the glimmer in your eyes. This exercise is also generally suitable for everyday office life to release strong neck tension and movement blockages. This exercise releases the first cervical vertebra from its blockage in a very gentle but immediate way.

This is how the exercise works: Sit upright on a chair or stand on both feet. Now interlock your fingers behind your head. Your elbows should point to the side. Look to the right with your eyes, without looking directly or fixating. Keep your eyes soft and relaxed. Stay in this position until one of the regulatory signs occurs: swallowing, sighing, or yawning.

The more stress you are under and the less practiced you are, the longer it may take for a sign to appear. Wait at least 60 seconds before giving up. This may feel like an eternity. Be patient—eventually the signs will come faster than you can count to one. Then look to your left and wait for a regulation sign. Don't force it. Be happy when they come, and trust that sooner or later, they will appear.

General Learning Outcomes

- Improved eye tracking movements
- Better cooperation between the two eyes
- Improved hand-eye coordination
- Focused attention
- Better balance, dexterity, and coordination
- Memory improvement
- Building more resilient visual patterns in the ventral vagal state
- Improved self-confidence, social behavior, and cooperation

In a recent peer-reviewed scientific study at Tel Aviv University in Israel (Dankner et al., 2017), researchers found strong evidence that involuntary eye movements are an indicator of attention-deficit/hyperactivity disorder, which is considered one of the most common neuropsychiatric disorders of childhood.

PET Training: Exercises to Help Train the Proprioception System

- Body scanning: Lie down or sit in a comfortable position and mentally scan your body from head to toe. Focus on each body part, try to sense its position in space, and notice any tension or imbalances.
- Single-leg balance: Stand on one leg with your knee slightly bent. Focus on keeping your balance and maintaining stability. Progress by closing your eyes or standing on an unstable surface like a foam pad.
- Joint position sense exercises: With your eyes closed, move a joint (e.g., elbow, knee) to a specific position and try to identify the angle without looking.
- Dynamic balance exercises: These activities involve slow and controlled movements that challenge your balance and body awareness.

- Catch and throw exercises: Toss and catch a ball with a partner while standing on one leg. This enhances proprioception and improves hand-eye coordination.
- Juggling or ball-handling drills: These activities require precise hand-eye coordination and body awareness.

Exercises to find your center involve cultivating a balanced and centered state of mind and body. Your center is considered the physical and energetic core of the body, located about two inches below the navel.

- Lower abdominal breathing: Practice breathing deeply into your lower abdomen (tanden/hara) rather than shallow chest breathing. This promotes relaxation and helps you connect with your center.
- Grounding: Imagine your body connecting with the ground beneath you. Feel a sense of stability and rootedness, allowing your energy to flow downward.
- Centering exercise: Stand with your feet shoulder-width apart, relax your shoulders, and drop your weight slightly to your center. Imagine your breath flowing into your abdomen, filling it with energy. Maintain this feeling of centeredness during movement and techniques.

Summary

Proprioception works with other sensory systems, such as the visual and vestibular systems (related to balance and spatial orientation), to provide a comprehensive understanding of body position and movement in space. Together, these sensory systems allow you to navigate the world smoothly and effectively. This information is crucial for coordinating movements and maintaining stability.

PET Training: The Vestibular System

The vestibular system is a complex sensory system responsible for maintaining balance and spatial orientation and coordinating eye movements. It is located within the inner ear and works with other sensory systems, such as the visual and proprioceptive systems, to provide a sense of equilibrium and help us navigate our surroundings.

When we experience head movements, such as turning, spinning, or tilting, the vestibular system detects these changes and sends signals to the brain, allowing us to maintain our balance and coordinate our movements. It also helps us to stabilize our gaze during head movements, ensuring that our vision remains clear and steady.

Trauma symptoms or issues with the vestibular system can result in conditions like vertigo, dizziness, and problems with balance and spatial orientation.

Training the vestibular system can be beneficial for improving balance, spatial orientation, and overall sensory integration. The following are some exercises to help stimulate and train the vestibular system.

Visual Tracking

- Eye exercises: Follow a small object or your finger with your eyes as you move it in different directions—up, down, left, right, and diagonally.
- Visual tracking: Focus on an object in the distance and turn your head from side to side while keeping your eyes fixed on the target.

Gaze Stability Exercises

- The stare game: Focus your gaze on a stationary object while your head moves side to side, up and down, or in circular motions.
- Head movement with numbers: Attach numbers to the wall and read them in order while moving your head around.

Spinning and Rotational Movements

- Slow spins: Stand with your feet shoulder-width apart, arms extended outward, and slowly spin in a circle. Stop if you feel dizzy and gradually increase the speed as you improve.
- Sit and spin: Sit on a swivel chair and have someone gently spin you around for a few rotations. Stop if you feel dizzy and gradually increase the number of spins.

Balancing Exercises

- One-leg stands: Stand on one leg and maintain your balance for as long as you can. Gradually increase the time and switch legs.
- Heel-to-toe walk: Walk in a straight line, placing the heel of one foot directly in front of the toes of the other foot with each step.
- Balance board: Use a balance board or wobble board to challenge your balance and stability. Start with a stable surface and progress to a more challenging one as you improve.

Especially with the balancing exercises, you can use also the Romberg test, which is used to investigate the cause of loss of motor coordination (ataxia). A positive Romberg test suggests that the ataxia is sensory in nature, that is, depending on loss of proprioception.

In general, polyvagal embodiment training (PET) is based on the principles of Stephen Porges's Polyvagal Theory. PET training offers a body-oriented approach to resolving stress-related disorders and their effects on psychosomatic behavior. Our interventions have the character of neuronal training. Through the interoceptive and proprioceptive practice of neuronal activation states, defensive tendencies are weakened, and resting states occur spontaneously as a reaction to a natural survival program. Through the application of polyvagal principles and resource development tools, participants begin to develop deeper body awareness and skills. They learn how to train their visual, vestibular, and proprioceptive senses to strengthen the neuroceptive performance of the nervous system. They utilize interoception for themselves and experience a sense of embodied safety for themselves and the people they work with.

Conclusion

Current neuroscientific research emphasizes the importance of one's own body experiences and interaction in a social context for self-regulation and neurophysiological changes. In every situation and interaction, we feel either safe or threatened. This reflexive mechanism, also known as neuroception, directly determines physiology and therefore the way we experience the world, how we interact with others, and how we feel internally.

A psychological trauma is a serious event that damages our mental health and is associated with a feeling of helplessness and insecurity. It overwhelms our coping strategies and causes considerable stress. The attack on the sensory system in particular takes the body from a safe home to a place of terror, where experience is split off to protect against overwhelming feelings. Dysfunction in neuroception and interoception can contribute to various health conditions, including anxiety disorders, trauma-related disorders, and somatic symptom disorders.

Polyvagal Theory provides a theoretical framework for understanding how the autonomic nervous system supports adaptive strategies. It also describes how these physiological states constrain the range of behavior and psychological experience.

Overall, multisensory integration plays a crucial role in shaping our perception of the world and is essential for adaptive behavior and cognitive functioning. While neuroception and interoception represent distinct processes, they interact dynamically to shape perception, emotional experiences, and autonomic responses to the environment. Understanding the interplay between these processes can provide insights into various psychological and physiological phenomena, including stress responses, emotional regulation, and somatic symptomatology. Polyvagal embodiment training influences the processing of sensory information by modulating the activity of neurons in the sensory pathways. It is about improving an organism's ability to modulate its sensory system depending on various factors such as attention, expectations, and previous experiences.

16

Body Tremors

The Natural Restorative Mechanism of the Human Body

David Berceli

The Human Body's Innate Survival Mechanisms

The 2011 conference of the National Institute for the Clinical Application of Behavioral Medicine included discussion of the need for strategies, so clients can unlearn the nervous system's response to trauma. Body tremors evoked by the human organism during stressful events are one of the mechanisms designed to help regulate the nervous system. They are the body's genetically encoded mechanism to unlearn or undo the high activation of the nervous system after stressful or traumatic events. This chapter discusses neurogenic activation, as it appears to be a direct activation of the body's natural nervous system's attempt to downregulate itself and restore internal equilibrium. It is quite simply the body's way of hacking the nervous system.

When I was living in Lebanon during a time of severe internecine conflict, I had the rare opportunity to watch the human organism's organic survival mechanisms in action. On one occasion, I was talking with a group of men in the streets. We were from several different countries. Without warning, a mortar rocket went streaming overhead, and the thunderous sound terrified all of us. In the blink of an eye (a second or two), all of us automatically crouched down into a fetal position for safety. Although I had seen and done this many times, this was the first time I really noticed this behavior and was fascinated. Since we were all from different countries, I knew that this protective posture was not culturally determined, so it must be a genetically encoded posture of survival in the human species. I wanted to know what part of the brain controlled this behavior. What myofascial patterns are involved in organizing this protective position? How is the human body able to engage this sequence of neurological processes while engaging its concomitant muscle patterns in a split second as a reflex reaction without conscious thought?

The second notable incident was a demonstration of the human organism's tremor response. Once, while I was in a bomb shelter with about 20 children, women, and men, I observed that all the young children's bodies were tremoring. I assumed this was because of the intensity of fear they were experiencing. However, although the adolescent children's bodies were tremoring, I could see they were trying to control or stop it. Finally, I realized that none of the adults, including myself, were tremoring at all. At that moment, I realized that it was in the children's freedom to tremor, and their untrained ability to stop it, that I was seeing the natural response of a living human organism in action. Their bodies were uninhibitedly discharging their fear and anxiety through the use of this self-regulating tremor mechanism. The adolescent children, on the other hand, were learning how to inhibit this mechanism, and finally, the adults had learned how to stop it completely. Essentially, it seems as though as human beings we have trained ourselves out of our innate ability to tremor. This led me to question if this tremor mechanism is the body's natural self-regulating mechanism to discharge chemicals of hyperarousal, downregulate nervous system arousal, and relax tightened myofascial patterns of protection. If this is so, then during our developmental process from childhood to adulthood, we learn how to control our natural pulsation of aliveness, so we are under control. With these two experiences, I began to research how the body can react instinctually and immediately to create the fetal response, and why an uninhibited body tremors when the nervous system is hyperaroused.

Neurogenic Tremors: Reframing the Narrative

Initially, it is necessary to reframe the contemporary paradigm of neurogenic tremors. The current medical narrative and research on body tremors primarily focuses on the dysfunction of the nervous system, which manifests itself as essential tremors, postural tremors, dystonic tremors, and so on (American Psychiatric Association, 2013). However, less research and publication has been done on the potential therapeutic benefits of another category of neurogenic tremors that most commonly occur before, during, and/or after traumatic or stressful experiences. These tremors have several names: fear tremors, emotional tremors, anxiety tremors, stress tremors (American Psychiatric Association, 2013). These tremors are not caused by dysfunctional neurological conditions, but rather are a very functional neural process to help the nervous system maintain equilibrium (Taylor et al., 2020).

Explanation of Body Tremors

Body tremors are a remnant of our mammalian evolution, or a genetic inheritance that helps to mitigate, dissipate, and possibly alleviate posttraumatic stress (Sapolsky, 2004). Their natural activation is most evident when people are experiencing what they interpret as a severely stressful event. We will often see individuals' hands shaking, legs tremoring, or voice quivering when they are feeling stressed, afraid, or excited. This comes from an overcharged nervous system. The tremor in this instance is not a pathological expression but rather a natural neurological activation of the nervous system to burn off the rapid surge of adrenaline that was pumped so quickly into the body's system (Hart, 1995).

Since this is an autonomic response of the nervous system for the purpose of assisting the body in the reduction of stress levels, it stands to reason that humans should be experiencing these body tremors much more frequently. This is actually possible; however, the contemporary narrative inhibits the freedom of individuals to accept this organic process. Body tremors are currently identified as signs of weakness, fear, vulnerability, and uncontrollable anxiety. Our current medical solution to these natural body tremors is medication to reduce or eliminate them. Additionally, our society accepts the use of substances to mitigate these body tremors.

After years of working and living in countries experiencing war, political violence, and natural disasters, I personally experienced and observed many people of diverse cultures tremoring before, during, or after highly stressful events. This was evidence that the activation of these tremors was not culturally determined and that these tremors were not derived from cortical activity but rather were elicited from subcortical (unconscious) parts of the brain. I realized that I was having the rare opportunity to see the human organism operating in its most primitive survival mode, and at this level it elicited one of its most natural protective bodily experiences as a mammalian species—tremoring. I then began to wonder: If the activation of this organic tremoring process originated from the subcortical regions of the brain, could it be producing a concomitant organic deactivation and downregulation of the nervous system elicited from the same region of the brain?

Through persistent exploration and study of the tremor mechanism, I discovered that this is true (Levine, 1997). After substantial reading and consultation with a neurosurgeon (Scaer, 2005), I was able to develop an easy and effective way to activate this tremor response and downregulate the nervous system. It was from the observation that the natural physical position of the body during stressful events is to pull the body forward into what is referred to as the fetal position. This is achieved by activating the primary flexor muscles that produce the adult fetal response. Since this is the protective position during stress, then it seemed to stand to reason that by activating a series of extensor muscles, we should be able to produce a release of the fetal position, thereby restoring physical relaxation of this muscle pattern with its concomitant downregulation of the nervous system. With this in mind, I had clients hold an inverted fetal position with the extension of the front muscles. This posture began to elicit a mild shaking, vibration, and/or tremoring that appeared to come from the subcortical regions of the brain because they were not under conscious control. I began teaching this posture to large populations as a self-help technique for stress reduction and physical reintegration after traumatic experiences. I called this process tension and trauma releasing exercises (TRE; Berceli, 2005, 2015, 2020). Over the course of several years, experiential evidence has demonstrated that the tremor mechanism in the human body appears to be an essential component of our self-regulatory system. This implies that all humans should know about this self-regulating mechanism as a means of supporting self-care, and that all people should be taught how to activate this "new/primitive" body mechanism safely and effectively in order to support self-care.

Therapeutic body tremors elicited in the TRE process also have a profound interpersonal relevance. They offer a unique opportunity for individuals to connect with their own bodies and emotions, which can then extend into their interpersonal relationships. Through the release of physical and emotional tension, individuals can develop a deeper sense of self-awareness, emotional regulation, and resilience. As a result, they are better equipped to engage in healthy and meaningful interactions with others. In the context of relationships, the ability to self-regulate and manage one's emotions is crucial. TRE can facilitate this by helping individuals release pent-up stress and trauma, reducing emotional reactivity, and promoting a more grounded and balanced state. This, in turn, fosters more empathetic and attuned interactions with others, improving the quality of relationships and communication.

Moreover, the coregulatory aspect of therapeutic body tremors is crucial in both individual and interpersonal contexts. TRE often involves a supportive and safe environment in which tremors can occur. This environment can be facilitated by a trained practitioner, spouse, partner, support community, or therapist. The presence of another person in a coregulatory role can help individuals feel secure and understood during the sometimes intense process of releasing tension.

A considerable amount of clinical literature speaks of the importance of interpersonal attachment and how this is compromised during childhood traumatic experiences. It is also relevant to note that the intrapersonal attachment of the child is also severely compromised. The interplay between the interpersonal and the intrapersonal sense of connection is important to be cognizant of as individuals struggle to reestablish relationships as adults. The tremor mechanism helps the individual to sense the places of safety or danger within their body schema, which can then be incorporated into the coregulatory process with other individuals. So it is equally important to assist the human body and psyche to experience its intraregulatory process in dialogue with the coregulation of extension to interpersonal relationships, where partners or loved ones may be involved in the process. Through shared understanding and support, partners can assist each other in regulating their emotional responses and coping with stress. This coregulatory approach strengthens the bond between individuals and fosters a deeper sense of trust, making therapeutic body tremors not only a personal healing tool but also a valuable resource for building and maintaining healthier and more connected relationships.

The Dynamic Duo: Fetal Contraction and Tremor Release

The human body functions as one, whole, integrated system. Although we have separated the parts of the body and their respective systems for the purpose of science and medical research, it still functions as one unit with many interacting systems and parts. Trying to understand and explain the way the body produces the systematic activation of the tremor mechanism is quite complex. It certainly needs considerable neurological and physiological research to understand and validate the role, purpose, and benefits of the tremor mechanism of a living human organism. However, attempting to give a thorough explanation and proper respect to this complex process is beyond the scope of this chapter.

In my years of experience, however, I have seen repeating patterns worthy of research. The human body has demonstrated that the amplitude and frequency of the tremors are clearly observable and vary in pattern distribution as they travel through the body structure. It appears as though the tremors follow the path of least myofascial resistance until they meet a place of severe chronic tension (Berceli et al., 2014). There are multiple ways to understand and appreciate the movement of this tremor mechanism. Muscle spindle fibers, central pattern generators, myofascial patterns, and subcortical regions of the brain all appear to work in tandem to facilitate this autonomic process of release and reintegration.

The Potential Effects of Neurogenic Tremors on the Nervous System

Although the research is ongoing, there have been numerous studies and trials on multiple populations globally. This was done for the purpose of exploring certain psychoemotional effects and/or physical limitations of the tremor mechanism's diverse applications on the human organism. In an Asian study, it was suggested that TRE could have an effect on various physical and psychological difficulties (Oh & Shin, 2021). In a German study, improvements in physical and mental well-being were reported (Nibel & Herold, 2019). A study led by Marcela Fiol, a neurologist at the Department of Neurology in Buenos Aires showed that TRE safely increased quality of life for people with multiple sclerosis (Fiol et al., 2022). These results were repeated in a Danish study by Lynning et al. (2021). Michael Morin Nissen (2015, 2019) has been working with more than 1,000 people with multiple sclerosis in the Danish MS Society. A study conducted by the Danish MS Society reported that there was a reduction in fatigue, pain, walking difficulty, poor bladder control, and so on (Lynning, 2019a, 2019b; Lynning et al., 2021). A more inclusive list of research studies, publications, reports and case studies can be found at TRE for All (https://traumaprevention.com/research/).

The Development of Intrapersonal to Interpersonal Relationships

Therapeutic body tremors elicited in the TRE process play a significant role in the construction and refinement of Alan Fogel's (2021) concept of the body schema. The body schema refers to an individual's internal representation and awareness of their body, including its size, shape, and potential for movement. Tremors, in this context, are rhythmic and involuntary movements that arise as a result of physical or emotional stressors being released from the body. They are believed to promote a profound reconnection with the body, helping individuals become more aware of their internal bodily sensations and boundaries.

Alan Fogel's work in somatic psychology and embodiment emphasizes the importance of experiencing and exploring one's own body through various practices, and therapeutic body tremors can be seen as one of these transformative practices. By inducing tremors, individuals are encouraged to become more attuned to their bodily sensations and to release stored tension and trauma. As tremors are allowed to flow and self-regulate, the body schema is continually refined and updated, fostering a more accurate and adaptable representation of the self. This process is thought to facilitate greater body awareness, improved emotional regulation, and a deeper connection between one's psychological and physical experiences. In this way, therapeutic body tremors contribute to the ongoing construction and reconstruction of an individual's body schema, promoting overall well-being and self-awareness.

Fogel postulates that the body deliberately evokes tremors for the reconstruction of the body schema following disorders of embodied self-awareness. This tremor response might be the same spontaneous prenatal and neonatal nervous discharges that were used to construct the body schema in the first place (Fogel, 2013). In neurophysiological terms, this means that the primitive responses of freezing, flooding, and dissociation during trauma may be produced by the interruption of the electrical charge from the brain stem and spinal cord to the muscle proprioceptors and motor neurons. The self-initiated neurogenic tremors through the TRE process might help to reactivate the electrical and chemical discharge of this primitive fetal twitching. This is considered a form of intrapersonal relationship, which helps to facilitate the necessary interpersonal relationships that were severed during the traumatic or stressful event. These adult-activated neurogenic tremors could be the same as the twitching, as Fogel explains, that "seems to be an essential mechanism to re-start the development of neuro-motor links that introduce one body part to another and serve to integrate the body schema" (2013, p. 85).

In a conversation with a professional colleague of mine, Richmond Heath (a physiotherapist), he explained how the first process of embodiment is led by the spontaneous movements of our body in utero. It has nothing to do with our conscious mind nor our cognition. For humans, reembodiment after trauma occurs through spontaneous movements generated below the level of our conscious awareness. It is neuroceptively determined by the body itself, which is well below the level of our cognitive awareness. It is these spontaneous movements that we deliberately invoke through TRE, not only to restore our body's capacity to move but to restore our mind's ability to sense our body as well. Ultimately the depth to which we are embodied is determined by the organic wisdom of our body—not our conscious mind. This is why the organic reawakening of spontaneous movement is such a simple yet profound process of reembodiment. This could help explain the process of self-regulation and coregulation as well as intrapersonal development in tandem with interpersonal relationships. Do the tremors help us neuroceptively to experience a deeper sense of self as subject in relationship to others as object?

This leads us to another trauma concern about the disruption of coregulation as a result of traumatic experiences. Because coregulation is another area of research that is most often explained through the social sciences, we often overlook that the biological sciences have a considerable influence in the form of autonomous innate coregulation. Another professional colleague, Dr. Andrew Cramb (a chiropractor) explained that in his professional view, the tremor mechanism seems to be a type of perturbation that helps to establish higher center rapport with impulses capable of evoking global ventral vagal shifts. With the activation of this tremor mechanism, the individual can continue to autonomously, innately coregulate. This concept appears isomorphic with Porges's concept of ventral and dorsal orientation (Porges, 2011). As both the innate and ventral intelligences are neither implicitly broken nor wrong, they are not in need of fixing or correcting.

The Tremor Mechanism's Contribution to Trauma's Evolutionary Potential

There is considerable research on posttraumatic growth (PTG) that demonstrates that the grief experience in some ways forces people to become different people and that the new person is sometimes better than the old one (Tedeschi et al., 2018). This process of dissociation and reassociation with one's body may be a natural human experience of the movement and/or interplay between our bodies as both subject and object. The organic nature of the tremor mechanism might help to reintegrate the traumatic experience in the body, thereby assisting the establishment of a new narrative of the event. We have all had the experience that when we calm down, we often have multiple perspectives about an event that we were only able to see through the more narrow vision of a trauma brain during our heightened arousal phase.

PTG causes a shift in perception, not only of the trauma but of life itself. This reintegration of trauma is often referred to as reframing the experience, a defining transformation point in one's life, the point of a new perspective on life, or moving from "dissolution to evolution" (Porges, 2011). People who have gone through the process of integrating their traumatic experiences into their lives often demonstrate deep human qualities of open-mindedness, patience, gentleness, joy, tolerance, and forgiveness. They speak about the transformation of time in that they now find it easier and more desirable to live more in the present moment. As stress and trauma are common experiences throughout all life, one must ask if this interplay is not only important and natural, but might be essential for the evolution of the human species.

Neurogenic Tremor's Contribution to the Transformative Experience

Body shaking has become more mainstream, but it presents itself under the category of exercises such as tai chi or qigong (Liao, 2014). This shaking is voluntarily elicited through prefrontal cortex activation. Body tremors seem to be elicited from subcortical regions of the brain. The activation of these tremors in different regions of the brain could affect the individual in substantially different ways.

Bradford Keeney studied body shaking among the Kalahari Bushman shamans. He recognized that this ancient tradition had tremendous contemporary value. He brought shaking from ancient wisdom to modern science. He explains how the shamans recognized that shaking not only loosens the physical body but, in the process, the tight grip of any totalizing ideology is loosened. It also helps to prevent the hardening of conceptual categories. In fact, during physical body shaking, "everything will shake—our understandings, actions, and experiences. You should shake in order to set free your mind, body, and soul" (Keeney, 2007).

Two good examples of the transformative experience of trauma come from Martin Luther King, Jr. (2010) when he said, "I have decided to stick with love. Hate is too great a burden to bear." He demonstrates in this sentence that he accessed a depth of traumatic experiences and went through a transformation whereby he came out with a new perspective. Nelson Mandela (2008) seems to have gone through the same deep and personal transformation: "As I walked out the door toward the gate that would lead to my freedom, I knew if I didn't leave my bitterness and hatred behind, I'd still be in prison."

As a human species continually undergoing stressful and traumatic events in life, it might be wise of us to consider the body's natural tremor mechanism not as a pathology-oriented behavior but rather a potentially resource-oriented behavior. We must ask ourselves if our bodies are genetically designed to know that we will experience trauma, be able to endure the trauma, survive the trauma, and potentially evolve as a result of the trauma. And is this tremor mechanism part of our nature as the human species moves through its own evolutionary process?

Rupert Sheldrake (2012) extends this concept further as he explains how consciousness (energy) manifesting as sentience (matter) is the human experience. He believes that the game, task, and joy of being human can only be found in the movement and/or interplay between these two experiences, rather than preferring one to the other. It is the interplay that is important. The tremor mechanism in the human body is the experience of energy and matter dialoguing with each other in this interplay of the human organism. It is this interplay that seems to help facilitate the intra/interpersonal dialogue. The body tremors help the individual to experience their own sense of self while engaging in relationship with another.

17

"The Eyes (I's) Have It"

Deep Brain Reorienting, Structural Dissociation, and Integration

Ken Benau

THIS CHAPTER DOCUMENTS THE PROGRESS OF MY PATIENT "SAMUEL," A SURVIVOR OF RELA-tional trauma (RT; Schore, 2001), using a new, body-based therapy, Deep Brain Reorient-ing (DBR). DBR treats "attachment disruptions and relational shock, chronic neglect, and other traumas occurring during critical periods of the brain's maturation" (Corrigan & Christie-Sands, 2020). Using verbatim transcripts of three DBR therapy sessions, readers witness Samuel's transformation from dissociation, as detachment and structural dissoci-ation (van der Hart, 2021), to integration, and newfound connection, calm, and joy.

Introduction to DBR

In DBR (Corrigan, 2020, 2021; Corrigan & Christie-Sands, 2020), patient and therapist mindfully attend to subtle somatic phenomena, including tensions, energy, and micro-movements, often in and around the neck and eyes, purportedly emanating from two structures in the midbrain of the brain stem. Within the midbrain, the superior colliculi (SC) orient toward or away from stimuli in order to rapidly assess safety versus threat, and the periaqueductal gray (PAG) responds to threat detection with active (e.g., going toward; lateral/dorsolateral PAG [l/dlPAG]) and/or passive (e.g., withdraw/collapse; ventro-lateral PAG [vlPAG]) defending. The locus coeruleus (LC) may also integrate information, first registered in the brain stem, with the limbic brain and neocortex, and hypothetically is involved in shock responses before defenses are deployed.

DBR therapists bring special attention to alarm, that is, the shock and horror of trau-matic abuse and neglect, followed by terror and other emotional responses, and active/passive defenses. DBR therapists understand generally RT's effects on the brain and body, and specifically midbrain functioning and its somatic/affective correlates, in order to facil-itate successful processing of archaic, deep brain trauma responses.

During traumatizing conditions, sensations associated with the orienting response in the SC occur rapidly, often within less than seconds, and typically remain outside awareness. Using mindful tracking of subtle physical sensations, especially but not exclusively in and around the neck and eyes, DBR therapists help patients discover their orienting-tension-affect-seeking (O-T-A-S) sequence. *Orienting* refers to SC activation and turning toward/away from incoming stimuli. *Tension* reflects muscle activation derived from deep layers of the SC when attention is grabbed. There may then be, via the LC and thalamus, a preaffec-tive, subliminal shock. *Affects* accompany PAG defensive reactions. *Seeking* indicates meso-limbic/dopamine activation associated with attachment behavior, drives, and motivations.

DBR pays special attention to basic affect systems (capitalized) identified as FEAR, RAGE, and GRIEF/PANIC (Panksepp & Biven, 2012); Corrigan and Christie-Sands (2020) add shame. With successful DBR processing, the patient's SEEKING finds CARE and PLAY, including safe, joyful relating with oneself and others.

What makes DBR different from other somatic, trauma-informed therapeutic modali-ties is that it is specially designed to transform the deepest layers of brain reactivity, that is, the midbrain of the brain stem, where traumatizing insults are first registered. DBR hypothesizes that neurophysiological changes within these deep brain structures clear higher-level, traumatic brain reactivity, including releasing no longer adaptive survival affects and reactions such as fight, flight, and freeze (limbic), and transforming implicit and explicit meanings associated with trauma (neocortical), in particular beliefs about self, abusing and/or neglecting other(s), and relationship. Following successful DBR processing, these beliefs are consistent with Pierre Janet's "realization," where the patient's experience of time (presentification) and self (personification) are updated to better fit present-day reality (van der Hart & Piedfort-Marin, 2023). Focusing on the somatic correlates of brain stem activation also allows patient and therapist to work with the somatic correlates of preverbal and nonverbal early developmental experience that might otherwise be inac-cessible to somatic therapy approaches associated with completing large motor, adaptive action tendencies originating in the amygdalae (limbic), such as sensorimotor psychother-apy (Ogden et al., 2006) and Somatic Experiencing (Levine, 2008).

Corrigan (2020) proposed three DBR change agents: reorienting toward threat, without fear and defensiveness; reprocessing, mindfully attending to sensations and affects until the brainstem settles; and memory reconsolidation (Ecker et al., 2012), when patients experience a physiological and postural mismatch between the old (traumatizing) and new (healing). Prelim-inary research showed DBR significantly reduced PTSD symptoms overall and as contrasted with waitlist controls, after eight sessions and three-month follow-up (Kearney et al., 2023).

Introduction: Samuel

Samuel was a bright, articulate, affable Caucasian man in his 50s, professionally successful working with teens, and happily married for 20 years, with a teenage child.

Samuel and I met individually, over 10 years, for five rounds of therapy. Each round, summarized, includes number of sessions, relational themes, and primary therapeutic approach.

Round 1, Year 1: 14 sessions. Father's profound emotional absence. Accelerated experiential dynamic psychotherapy (AEDP; Fosha, 2000).

Round 2, Year 3: 15 sessions. Disturbing relationship with mother and sibling. Psychodynamic, with parts work (Fisher, 2017).

Round 3, Year 7: 21 sessions. Overwhelming stress and depression. Parts work using the developmental needs meeting strategy (DNMS; Schmidt, 2009) and, primarily, the comprehensive resource model (CRM; Schwarz et al., 2017).

Round 4, Year 9: 14 sessions. Separation/individuation from mother. DBR.

Round 5, Years 10–11: 43 sessions, 30 DBR, 13 reviewing progress. Mother's psychological destructiveness and absence. DBR, with Samuel spontaneously initiating parts work. (Given the COVID pandemic, Sessions 1–34 and 36 used Zoom; the rest were in person.)

Samuel's Special Capacities and DBR Plus

Samuel was an especially good DBR candidate. As we worked together over 10 years, Samuel implicitly and explicitly trusted me and the therapy process. Samuel was gifted in tracking and describing his internal landscape. He spontaneously transduced somatic experience into a multisensory, affective, imagined narrative, interacting with younger self-parts. Samuel's use of story (cortical) and parts (limbic and cortical) were not strictly DBR. When this occurred, I typically returned his attention to body/midbrain activation.

At the same time, I have worked, and witnessed others work, quite successfully with patients using DBR that did not have the long history Samuel and I had, nor his psychological and creative gifts, including his facility engaging parts of self. While a trusting therapeutic relationship provides the necessary ground from which to perform DBR, I have met with patients for relatively brief periods of time before initiating successful DBR.

Round 5 of Samuel's therapy provided a window into deep transformations DBR achieved that other approaches could not. For example, while Samuel made regular use of parts work outside of and sometimes in session, during our last meeting (#43) he shared, unprompted, that DBR enabled him to achieve things in therapy he had never done before. DBR work with preverbal, brain stem–correlated somatic experience helped Samuel not only clear traumatizing effects of his mother's destructiveness and neglect, as never before, it opened him to an entirely new way of being with himself and his loved ones.

The Work

Passages from three DBR sessions, the first, last, and one in between, are presented. PT. refers to Samuel and TH. to me, therapist. Within brackets [ ], I clarify Samuel's remarks and highlight features of DBR process. An ellipse (. . .) demarcates words omitted. These transcripts do not convey often long pauses between somatic tracking and reporting.

DBR Sessions: An Overview

DBR patient and therapist first select a treatment focus and a prompt, activating the patient's shock and/or orienting response. The therapist instructs the patient to go inside (most close their eyes) and situate their body in space, for example, bringing awareness to their spine and sensations behind their eyes reflecting their Where Self. This neurophysiologically locates the patient inside and in relation to outside the room. Next, the therapist states the prompt, and the patient mindfully observes and intermittently reports physical sensations associated with their orienting tension (O-T) specific to that issue, defensive somatic reactions, and affect. Tension in the forehead, muscles around the eyes, and/or back of the neck opens an information file for processing. When patients dissociate or lose track of physical sensations, therapists gently bring their attention back to the O-T identified at the beginning of the session, to ground, reorient, and resume DBR processing. DBR therapists mostly listen, helping patients observe somatic sensations rather than engaging in cortical interpretations.

They occasionally reflect the patient's experience to facilitate processing, coregulate, and feel the therapist's safe presence.

Session 1: "I'm never enough" with mom, to "I'm enough" with myself and child

Samuel shared that work and "meditation" (CRM-modified parts work; Schwarz et al., 2017) were "great" until four months prior to Session 1, when his "ways of managing" work, particularly with one troubled teen, were "not working." "I can't handle this, can't be this vulnerable . . . PTSD . . . spinning thoughts and little sleep," feeling "alone [with] less agency."

Samuel noticed tension originating in his sternum, associated with "mother insert[ing] control": "Shooting up to my throat, tightness in my throat, constricting," something "solid, metal, pale, cold, but whole." Asked what this might mean, Samuel exclaimed, "This shit, oh fuck, again! Old, rattled, being alone . . . cut . . ." DBR processing began with Samuel's prompt, "Oh fuck!"

PT: Tension in both sides of my neck, and eyes. [SC. Tension around the eyes is orienting tension; tension in the eyes is part of shock.]
PT: [Right eye] Looking inward, where my neck was. [Left eye] Scary [Affect (A): FEAR], wants to help [right eye]. [Left eye] Looking out. Dungeon, high window, bars, wanting [to escape], giving up.

Right eye inward, left eye outward suggested Samuel's orienting conflict (SC). I speculated, privately, that this somatic split was a nascent brain stem marker preceding structural dissociation at higher brain levels.

Despite vivid imagery, Samuel resumed physical tracking without redirection.

PT: Dark, eyes, looking down, toward throat. Sensation of, big hole, eyes . . . looking down, bottomless pit . . . hard to judge, very dark.

TH: Track your body sensations.

PT: . . . Hear my heartbeat, doesn't feel constricted, calling out. Pool of liquid . . . oil, viscous. Shoulders.

TH: Physical sensation?

PT: Sturdy, propping everything up. Hands, very large, on a bed, from a base.

TH: Foundation?

PT: Yeah, breath.

TH: Sensation?

PT: As with heart. Decoding a rhythm. [With intensive scanning (SC), Samuel discovered a somatic connection, breath and heart in rhythm.] Still feel I'm in the dungeon. Floor solid, light streaming in. Standing up, eyes searching the walls. . . .

TH: Stay with the sensation in your eyes.

PT: Sadness, want to rest . . . nowhere, all hard and dark.

TH: Your body, searching for rest.

PT: Collapsing in on myself. Trying to curl up . . . cocoon. Provide warmth . . . curled around itself, very relaxed. . . .

Samuel's right eye tension scanning inward; left eye tension, outward, shifted to coordinated eyes (SC). Coordination, a noteworthy achievement, made scanning more effective and, perhaps, led to emergent GRIEF/PANIC (Affect, A). Alone, overwhelmed with GRIEF/PANIC activated passive defenses (vlPAG), a brain stem form of submission.

TH: Let the breath move through you. . . . Release. I'm here.

I thought "I'm here" offered Samuel a safe attachment figure (Fosha, 2000). I later learned the DBR therapist, a grounded and grounding presence, also makes contact statements so patients feel less alone. Hypothetically, this shifts the neurochemical balance in the vlPAG by bringing in oxytocin.

PT: I heard the door close. Jan [Samuel's teenage child] belongs to me. . . . That's . . . really more profound [than my isolation as a teen]. Really gratitude . . . 100% in my body.

TH: How so?

PT: . . . Boundaries of skin, very calm.

Samuel responded powerfully to hearing Jan. Moving from trapped, terrified (Affect, A: FEAR) and conflicted scanning; to coordinated scanning (SC) yet unbearably alone with GRIEF/PANIC, collapsed (vlPAG, passive defense); to reembodying his loving bond with Jan, creating a physiological and postural mismatch between traumatic (old) and healing (current) relating (Corrigan, 2020), auguring therapeutic memory reconsolidation (Ecker et al., 2012)].

Reorienting to his room, Samuel identified two transformational themes:

PT: Eyes stuck trying to extend out into the world and back . . . [to] unstuck [conflicted to coordinated scanning (SC). From] never enough . . . drowning in school [absent mother induced chronic shame and overwhelm to] I am enough [self with child, now].

TH: In your body?

PT: . . . Part of me doesn't believe it, bristly, top of neck, pinches in heart, chest open.

Samuel's conflicted to coordinated scanning (SC) was a significant achievement. While moving from "alone" to "connected," SEEKING and CARE affects (A) were not yet realized. Still, we were off to a good start.

Session 33: Two-year-old terror, "I'm all alone," to "I'm better off not bonding with her [mother]" (one year, three months into Round 5)

During Sessions 24–31, Samuel characterized being with his psychologically threatening, destructive, yet painfully absent mother as like living in "a war-torn, Cambodian-like," desolate "field." Samuel titrated the intensity of this work by alternating, at his pace, DBR (#24, 26, 30, 31) with review sessions, moving toward integration of several younger parts, ages 2 to 20. Session 33 prompt: "I'm [two-year-old] all alone."

PT: Feeling around my eyes.

TH: Good tracking.

PT: Looking out, through more of a tunnel. No peripheral vision.

TH: Sensations in your neck?

PT: Not neck, jaw—feels tighter, compressed.

TH: . . . Use your jaw tension to ground you. Track your eyes.

Samuel's tunnel vision indicated hyperfocus/hypervigilance (SC, orienting tension), a reaction to threatening aloneness. Jaw tension suggested his active defense (dlPAG). I wondered, privately, if this reflected preaffective RAGE.

PT: You're talking me into . . . my two-year-old self is with me, as I am now. A little nervous, beginning of roller coaster. Two-year-old's smaller head inside my head.

Head-within-head imagery indicated hypnotic, trance logic defending against heightened anticipatory anxiety.

TH: Stay with your sensations.

PT: Sunken-in [eyes], tightness in jaw, size of a two-year-old jaw inside my jaw now. Kinda feels dark. Clenched feeling in my heart, scary [Affect, A: FEAR]. Breathe in slowly through my nose. Hits two-year-old's head, remembers to breathe. . . . Breathe in sync. I'm breathing in, two-year-old breathing out.

Samuel's synchronized breathing served self-regulation. While DBR encourages patients to face threat directly rather than calm down, when needed it supports release breathing to modulate affect intensity.

TH: Track your sensations.

PT: As I breathe, feels [like] they're [adult and two-year-old] coming together as one. . . . Still looking in. Aware of my hands [two-year-old], reaching out for a hug. Nothing is coming back. Face is getting pushed in.

I viewed Samuel's SEEKING connection (Affect, A) failing, resulting in "face . . . pushed in" (passive defense, vlPAG). In contrast, I later learned in DBR consultation that reaching out into nothing, often with chest forward followed by head pulling back, is SC activated, that is, precedes PAG defenses.

PT: Adult taking words in, repeating to my two-year-old self.

TH: Letting him know you're there.

A DBR-informed response might have focused on Samuel's physical sensations or emerging affect associated with his deep-brain Where Self, rather than parts (Schwarz et al., 2017) or intrarelational attachment (Fosha, 2000), both upper-level constructs and brain activity.

PT: His eyes looking up, connected, then down [SC].

TH: Notice the physical sensations of "eyes connected."

Following CRM (Schwarz et al., 2017), Samuel's eye-to-eye gazing, adult with inner child, strengthened intrarelational attachment. I sought to integrate CRM with DBR.

PT: Hard to hold [connection]. Every time it holds a little, sensation of a . . . l-o-o-o-ng period of time.

TH: Doing great, keep tracking.

PT: Aware of feeling, cement in my throat, and my throat is down here [points to chest]. Not safe to talk about this.

Following Janet (1935/1994), trauma processing requires the patient realize the truth about their traumatizing other. Losing connection, Samuel's two-year-old could not bear this alone: "Not safe to talk."

TH: . . . Notice that sensation, in and around your eyes.

PT: [Two-year-old] . . . almost looking at me [adult], informing me this is serious. . . . I remember reading *Waiting for Godot*. Totally get it.

TH: [Mother] never shows up.

Samuel did parts work and intermittently DBR. DBR therapists must understand this distinction to process trauma held in the brain stem. My empathic response, "never shows up" was attachment-informed (Fosha, 2000). However, from a DBR perspective, I did provide Samuel receptive stimuli for his innate connection system (SC), where mother's absence first registered.

PT: Now, two-year-old doesn't feel the need to lock eyes. Comfortable moving his head [Samuel's head moved, side to side]. Yes, getting perspective. My adult self, "If you weren't getting what you need, locked on. If getting what you need, can move."

TH: Yes, when you get what you need, you can move around, see what's there.

While my response was informed by attachment research (i.e., with secure attachment, children explore), from a brain stem perspective, previously "locked" eyes, frozen in fear, "can move" with a safe adult present, in this instance Samuel.

PT: But that's as far I'm gonna get today.

TH: There's no hurry, as an infant, hang out, stay as long as you need.

DBR's processing very early, nonverbal trauma best proceeds slowly.

PT: Kind of a wave of sadness [Affect, A, GRIEF/PANIC]. Waterfall [sensation] from top of head to down here [chest]. Two-year-old wondering if it's okay [to feel this].

TH: And?

PT: It's fine. . . . Can't really describe this energy coming at me. Mother, like a train. . . . Two-year-old floated up away from me. Yippee! Exhilarating! I'm [two-year-old] being held, carried. I can look around. Walk some, every day, it's . . . familiar. . . . What it would be like if everything was okay.

Attending to Affect (A), GRIEF, and sensation (i.e., waterfall; energy), DBR processing resumed. Freed from passive and active defenses (vl and l/dlPAG), Samuel experienced hostile (e.g., "train") and absent mother (e.g., "Nothing . . . coming back"). SEEKING connection, two-year-old Samuel with adult Samuel felt freer to PLAY.

PT: . . . Seven-year-old getting glasses, feeling judged [shamed by mother]. Two-year-old telling [mother], "You don't get to do that!" . . . Same kind of energy. . . .

TH: You don't get to do that! [Validating Affect (A), RAGE.]

PT: Yeah.

PT: Different parts are lining up in myself, now.

TH: Physically?

PT: Yeah, like at one.

TH: Nice!

A better DBR response might have been, "Notice the physical sensations and feelings that go with 'at one.'" "[P]arts . . . lining up" displayed ongoing integration within Samuel's deeper Where Self.

PT: . . . "You don't get to do that! . . . Nope!" Two-year-old self, back to wave of sadness, grief. Touching the waterfall, curious about it. When in patch [desolate field], [I'm] caring for two-year-old and he's receiving it . . . kinda normal.

No longer affect phobic and alone, Samuel moved from FEAR and RAGE to GRIEF and CARE, all adaptive responses to mother's destructiveness and neglect.

PT: Feeling train [mother's attack], running at me, two-year-old. [Mother,] "I could run into you too!" [Affect (A), RAGE.]
TH: What are you feeling in your body?
PT: Joy. Throat open, shoulders set. . . . Two-year-old self, completely fading, blending into me now. Eyes back, super loose, aware of that . . . [two-year-old] can go and come back. Doesn't feel [like] a victim.

Somatic and affective integration of Samuel's two-year-old and adult selves achieved. Samuel's eyes no longer "sunken in" (vlPAG, passive defense). Samuel's RAGE released joy, with freedom to bond and explore (Affects [A], SEEK and PLAY).

TH: Your eyes are flickering.

Activation in Samuel's eyes suggested an orienting response (SC) with freer movement.

PT: Two-year-old running around, playing tag [Affect (A), PLAY].
TH: With?
PT: Me, maybe.
TH: Body sensations?
PT: Me tracking him, with my eyes.
TH: Your two-year-old's sensations [when tracked]?
PT: Being loved. Ah! . . . All energy, giggling [Affects (A), CARE and PLAY].
TH: Where is the energy?
PT: My head, torso.

Head and torso energetically connected indicated somatic integration.

TH: As you reflect upon where you started, "I am all alone," and now?
PT: Same feeling that I had, dealing with my dad [profound absence]. Oh, shit, I'm better off *not* bonding with mom. I'm aware . . . better as two-year-old, more secure.
TH: Grief, not having had parents?
PT: No, not having [GRIEF] at all. . . . Overall, a lack.

Samuel saw mother's "lack," not his own shame. This shift of locus of control is consistent with Janet's (1935/1994) "realization." Opening his eyes, Samuel reoriented to his room.

TH: How are you doing?
PT: Now, a little bit sad, not overwhelming [Affect (A), GRIEF]. My child going off to college. They're judgmental of my parenting . . . and then "Hey Dad!" back and forth.
TH: You're there for them, so they can push against you.

PT: Like seeing two-year-old, different strength there. . . .
TH: Fear versus fun? [Affects (A), past FEAR, present SEEKING and PLAY.]
PT: Not fun then.
TH: Safe now, can explore and play.

With some parts work, DBR successfully moved Samuel from structural dissociation to somatic integration: Two-year-old alone in war-torn fields, reaching out and being met by Samuel's loving, adult self. FEAR replaced by GRIEF, and SEEKING and PLAY accompanied Samuel's realization about the parents he never had.

Session 43: "If I let go, what will happen?!" to "If I let go, I'm free of it" (one year, 7½ months into Round 5)

During Session 38, three months prior to this last DBR session, Samuel's three-year-old self realized, for the first time, "My mother doesn't love me." In Session 39, Samuel's acceptance of this enabled him to stop "dreading her [upcoming] visit." During Session 41, Samuel recognized his three-year-old still held gut tension, explaining "[he] couldn't get mad, feeling suicidal, holding it together," feeling wordless rage toward his mother.

Beginning Session 43 (in person), Samuel shared that his two-year-old self felt terror when his needs to feel loved by his mother went repeatedly unmet. Reacting to this, his three-year-old self felt "stuck, holding his shit together . . . like jumping on hand grenades, holding it together in his gut." Samuel's prompt: "If I let go, what will happen?!"

PT: A jolt of energy, between my eyes, and sinking feeling in my gut.

I viewed Samuel's "jolt" as shock (SC), and "sinking feeling" as a passive defense (vlPAG). In DBR consultation, I later learned this likely reflected SC to LC, before defenses deployed. In either case, my focus would have been to help Samuel avoid collapse by remaining present with his shock-induced tension:

TH: What's happening in your neck? [orienting tension].
PT: My neck is opening, deliberately trying to make space for the [shock] energy, eyes, jaws tight.
TH: Your neck, let it happen, then turn your attention to your eyes.
PT: My left eye, vigilant, staring out, right eye not able to connect with [left eye]. Left eye not clear, kinda muddy. Left eye not moving, hawk eyes, not clear. Right eye, not reaching toward [left eye], trying to do the same thing [connect].

As in Session 1, I privately speculated Samuel's right/left eye scanning split (SC) indicated a brain stem–induced somatic marker preceding structural dissociation. Parentless, the three-year-old's terror of letting go was held in Samuel's right eye. Left eye "vigilant, staring" suggested overwhelmed scanning (SC) activated dissociation as detachment ("muddy") (passive defense, vlPAG).

PT: My right eye, feels silly at first, but doing it [trying to connect], my left eye noticing what the right eye is doing. . . . Picture of me, in my mother's bedroom, age three, terrified and shocked. My eyes getting in tune with that [aloneness]. If I breathe in, comes closer.

TH: What?

PT: The picture [three-year-old Samuel's photo, in mother's bedroom].

"Closer" suggested Samuel's breathing reduced detachment dissociation.

PT: Now, feel the picture not on the wall. That part . . . is inside of me . . . [the] picture me looking around behind my [adult] eyes. Looking at my kids, now. You [mom] did that to me?!

Previously trapped, lifeless three-year-old SEEKING (S) CARE (Affect, A) from adult Samuel.

PT: Looking at my kids, now, "You [mother] did that to me!" . . . Barb [Samuel's wife], Alice [troubled teen Samuel worked with], we, I . . . recognize we're the same.

TH: How?

PT: Everything I'm connected to. My kids, you, coworkers, friends. Very happy not to be up on that wall. Eyes merging into my eyes, not two sets of eyes. Pulsing energy in my head. Integrating into my being.

Moving from structural dissociation to somatic integration (two to one set of eyes), Samuel's pulsing, energetic aliveness was restored.

PT: My neck is reminding me, you said what happens if I let go. Now calling that up, from my gut. . . . "Anything I want I'd be freed up."

Samuel's SEEKING (Affect, A) reminded him of people he loved and who loved him, transforming alone, terrified, must not "let go," to "connected" to "everything."

PT: . . . The picture frame in [mother's] bedroom, can't see the picture there. Mother in my backyard, three-year-old seeing her as I see her now. [Three-year-old] not very interested [in mother]. My [adult] eyes turning toward three-year-old, where [does] three-year-old want to go? Three-year-old wants to be. Odd sensation, remembering my right eye looking out vigilantly . . . kind of remembering images when doing [DBR], all [parts] have different takes on this. Feel so grateful for [three-year-old] holding on. Not surprising three-year-old had to hold on. . . . Feels really peaceful.

TH: Body sensations?

PT: Kind of feel like, reintegrating, nerves, head, heart, legs. . . . It's filling things in. I can attune to that. Nothing else is happening. Sensation of being in my mother's bedroom, walking out with three-year-old self . . . and leaving that house. Now there's nothing left of me there.

TH: Body sensations?

PT: . . . Blood pulsing in my head, pulsing at the same pace with my heart and gut. All in same wavelength or vibe . . . [long pause]. Revelation, I don't know what to do with that. I could connect to whomever I want to, and I don't *have to* connect.

Somatic and affective integration of three-year-old brought peace with self, others, and the world. Samuel's three-year-old understandably sought connection with his mother, dangerously both present and absent. With full-bodied integration of his three-year-old and all other parts, Samuel could now choose connection, or not.

TH: As you reflect on where we started, "If I let go, what will happen to me?!" and now?

PT: If I let go, I'm free of it.

TH: In your body, now?

PT: Feel my skin, body is everything, feels in proportion.

Samuel left his trance state ("in proportion"), embodied and integrated. Opening his eyes, Samuel reoriented to my office:

TH: How are you feeling?

PT: Great! Super peaceful. My right eye [had] a sense of humor—"Oh shit, this again!" Parents doing this [to their kids], seems weird. Past, spirit animal [CRM (Schwarz et al., 2017)], not [able to achieve this]. . . . Sense of absurdity, saved me. Picture that haunted me, it's not there.

During our final Session 43, Samuel exclaimed, "I've never felt this calm before." Samuel's GRIEF/PANIC to SEEKING and PLAY, with embodied integration, completed DBR processing.

Conclusion

While there are many therapeutic approaches to early, relational trauma, DBR is particularly well suited to process somatic correlates of the deepest brain structures, including the Where Self and Core Self, and developmentally early, nonverbal and preverbal sequelae of relational and physical trauma. Samuel accessed and mindfully observed somatic sensations associated with what later organized as young, dissociated parts of self, frozen in terror, alone with a dangerously present mother and a profoundly emotionally/psychologically nonattuned, absent mother and father.

In most DBR sessions, not only those documented here, Samuel began with immobilizing tension in and around his neck and eyes, and soon thereafter painful energy radiating to his heart and gut. His eyes were typically not coordinated when scanning, the right frozen in terror or pulled back into his head, and the left oriented outward, searching for threat, and toward the right eye, trying to help (superior colliculi, SC).

These fixed, recurrent eye patterns, commonly observed during traumatic activation, may reflect developmentally early somatic precursors of dissociative detachment and structural dissociation Samuel experienced in adulthood. However, attending to the orienting tension in his neck enabled Samuel to remain mindfully present rather than dissociate in session. As a result, Samuel could track and process moment-to-moment somatic sensations, including subtle muscle tensions, in and around his neck and eyes, micromovements, and shifts in energy correlated with midbrain/brain stem activation associated with orienting tension and threat assessment (superior colliculi, SC), and active and passive defenses (periaqueductal, PAG), respectively lateral/dorsolateral PAG (l/dlPAG) and ventrolateral PAG (vlPAG).

Following DBR's model of therapeutic change, this therapy enabled Samuel to reorient toward threat (e.g., eyes coordinated, comfortably scanning outward); reprocess by mindfully attending to sensations and powerful affects until his brain stem settled; and achieve memory reconsolidation (Ecker et al., 2012), observed by contrasting the shock, freeze/terror, and sometimes collapse reactions at the start of DBR sessions to fluid movement and integration somatically (brain stem), emotionally (limbic), and with newly empowered beliefs about himself in relation to his mother and other family members (neocortical).

At the end of each DBR session, and by the end of therapy, Samuel and I observed several significant somatic changes, including fluid movement in his eyes and neck; coordinated, nondefensive scanning between his right and left eyes; and energy rhythmically flowing between Samuel's head, heart, and guts, consistent with somatic integration.

These somatic and affective changes in the session were accompanied, at the end of therapy, by welcomed emotional and behavioral changes in Samuel's world. Samuel initiated this round of therapy recognizing he needed to process the traumatizing effects of his mother's chronic destructiveness and profound emotional and psychological absence. During our last session, Samuel reported, "I don't want to be anyone else. I might be done with therapy [entirely]." This therapy was "thorough, really taking care of my young self." "I can separate this work from my mother's [current, physical and cognitive] decline." "My mother is not interested in me. I'm fine with that, only a little sad." That Samuel's teenage child "made clear connection [with his parents] matters," that is, their developmentally appropriate separation no longer felt threatening to Samuel. "My wife and I—really nice, quiet." As Samuel teared up some, I asked what he was feeling. "Feels really good. That was a lot of work!" "I went as deep as you can go. I totally trusted you the whole time." "I'm on top of my job. Getting in there every day," free of angst. "I feel clean. I don't need to ground myself emotionally. Feel really good." And finally, "I have never felt this calm, forever [in my life]." "I love myself."

Acknowledgment

Special thanks to Frank Corrigan, MD, developer of DBR, who generously provided feedback on this chapter.

18

Somatic Ego State Therapy With Traumatized Children

Silvia Zanotta

Key Factors for Trauma Healing in the Treatment of Children[1]

Safety and Connection

The Polyvagal Theory (Porges, 1995, 2009, 2022) explains what therapists have always known intuitively: The first step to healing trauma is to activate the ventral vagal complex and to offer safety, a reliable therapeutic relationship, compassion, and trust. With traumatized clients, especially kids who have repeatedly experienced violence, abuse, or rejection, this may be the biggest challenge in therapy. Their neuroception signals constant danger, and their environment and inner world are perceived as threatening. With the autonomic dysregulation syndrome (Levine, 2010) caused by complex or attachment trauma, calming attempts may be rejected. Trauma and abuse disrupt connection, distort social awareness, replace engagement behavior with defense (fight/flight/freeze) reactions, and interfere with healthy coregulation. Fortunately, there are opportunities for repair.

From Coregulation to Self-Regulation

It is essential when working with traumatized clients to start by providing a safe space for them to feel accepted and understood. This, in part, means their chaotic inner world has room to be clarified and mentalized, so that agonized, helpless, or aggressive personality parts can express themselves. A vital element in therapy is coregulation, which eventually leads to successful self-regulation and the ability to regulate and adjust emotional and behavioral responses. This is a key component of resilience and of social and emotional learning. When a person is threatened, overwhelmed, or overstimulated, a state of alarm is triggered. Over time, an organism chronically on high alert becomes exhausted and will begin to shut down and go numb for self-preservation and protection. It is more difficult to respond with a sense of competence and self-control in either a high-alert or depressed state. Self-regulation skills are therefore crucial for calming down or ramping up energy and returning to the just-right activation.

Resourcing Outside and Inside

Another important task as we accompany such clients is identifying outside resources—a caring adult (godmother, teacher), nature, pets, friends, sports—and inside resources—strength, competence, strong inner helpers or healers, the felt sense of being resourceful. The therapist must think systemically and collaborate with parents, and, if necessary, with school staff and other caregivers. Therapy with children is more demanding than with adults, but change tends to happen faster and more easily.

It is crucial to involve parents in therapy or ensure that they support the process. Parents or caregivers often have different goals than the client has. Therapists must clarify the differences and then make clear that the mission of the child will always be respected. If children are aggressive, we might wonder if it's their only defense. If this is the case, we should not be surprised when they aren't ready to change. The therapist could easily be trapped between the pressure for change that caregivers bring and the reluctance of the child to give up the only way they know how to prevail. It is important to understand this type of impasse before change can happen, to support both parties and to give time for small steps to be taken, so that no competition, ambivalence, or conflict of loyalties arises. The therapist should take the role of a caring grandparent rather than a better parent and in this sense nourish the parents too.

A Holistic Approach

Even if parents can't or won't give the necessary support, healing is possible. If children have the opportunity to act out their difficult feelings while contained by the therapist, and thus release body tension or energy captured in the body (bottom up), and connect with resources through conflict-free images, safe places, and resource states (top down), positive shifts can occur. Children's boundaries should be protected and their assertiveness strengthened in order to be engaged with others in safe, fun, and nurturing ways.

Psychoeducation

The Polyvagal Theory, developed by Stephen Porges (1995, 2009, 2022), teaches us that trauma is not in the event, it is in the nervous system. When there is no support and the surge of trauma energy gets frozen and trapped inside the nervous system, somatic symptoms—stomachaches or headaches, nightmares, muscle tension, outbursts, and so on—may ensue. And each time the implicit memory of the traumatic experience is triggered, neuroception signals danger and activates defense mechanisms automatically. One of the most difficult and distressing effects of trauma and freeze is the sense of disconnection: from oneself (dissociation, numbness), from others (feeling isolated), and from surroundings (feeling out of place or spacey). Children are especially vulnerable to freezing because they have fewer resources, and their coping skills are not yet fully developed.

Symptoms make sense as responses to trauma. Children and parents need to understand that these responses are autonomous strategies of their nervous system to ensure survival. It must be explained that their organisms react in this way to protect them, and so symptoms can be seen as creative attempts to protect the organism and to find a solution to trauma. An example of this is a child affected by domestic violence who hurts or bullies smaller children, thus reenacting what happens to him and feeling powerful and in control when in this bullying state. The therapist must understand these contexts before trying to change the child's behavior; otherwise, he will be confronted with resistance.

Even self-destructive symptoms provide an opportunity to learn more about traumatic reactions. It is important to speak the language of a child to impart information. Stories and metaphors can be used effectively when clients don't yet have fully developed cognitive capacities[2] (Herzog, 2018, 2022). Or drawings can be employed. For example, imagine a double-decker bus with all our states indicated on the top deck and the unconscious states represented on the lower deck. When triggered, the states on the lower deck hijack the wheel and endanger the whole bus because they are out of control. The therapist may invite clients and their parents to learn how to make sure that the right state has the steering wheel (Lynch, 2020).

Regulation and Development

Another vital factor in working with this vulnerable group is balance. Pleasure can be healing, but it should not last too long. Traumatized kids don't trust it. They need a lot of safety and structure. Therapists have the tendency to move too quickly to provide severely traumatized children with what they lack. Small steps are required, little experiences; otherwise they tend to become overwhelmed and anxious about what could happen next. It is important to pause, to give time to rest and integrate (Kline, 2012; Duarte, 2022). On the other hand, unpleasant experiences must not last too long either because there is a high risk of retraumatization. If the therapist notices signs of dysregulation, it is better to change the activity, for example, to stand up, sit on the floor, or focus on something outside. Trust, structure, and safety are the main ingredients for healing. As a general guideline, highlighting positive experiences is more important than focusing on problems.

The Importance of Resiliency

The opposite of powerlessness is strength—resilience. For resilience, self-regulation plays an essential role. The better self-regulation works in early childhood, the healthier, more successful, and more resilient we are. The pivotal place of self-regulation is made apparent in the results of the Perry Preschool Project, a long-term study over more than 40 years in Michigan, with high-risk children: The better self-regulation in childhood, the more there is success at school, a higher income, less unemployment, less addictive behavior, less obesity, better health, and less criminal behavior in later years. Key factors and strategies that help build resilience are social support (a sense of belonging), positive relationships, emotional regulation, education, coping skills, self-compassion, and self-care (Berrueta-Clement et al., 1984).

If children don't have resiliency, their symptoms will be more severe because they lack resources, self-regulation, and coping strategies. If children have a resilient nervous system, they heal themselves through play or games like tag. They move through the resiliency cycle: threat/terror—fight/flight/freeze/dissociation—deactivating and release—and then return to a relaxed state naturally. Every baby is born with more pleasure neurons than pain neurons. The abdomen has more pleasure receptors than pain receptors. But if there are more pain experiences than pleasure, the pleasure neurons diminish. The brain is pruned by sensations. This is why pleasure experiences are important (Kline, 2012).

Communicating Through the Body

Body Postures

Changing postures can easily be done in play and is a very powerful intervention. Body postures influence not only the emotional state but also the hormone balance. Conscious postures of strength or well-being even lead to an improvement in self-regulation, which is also perceived in the environment through mirror neurons (Cuddy, 2011). These interventions are especially helpful with anxious, bullied kids. They are practiced in games, role-play, dance, or art. Movement and somatic experiencing are the key factors. The therapist may take pictures of powerful postures or faces and add them to the child's therapy book, which is created as the therapy unfolds. Pivotal elements of the therapy process are represented in its pages. At the end of the therapy, the story of the therapy book is completed, the therapeutic process and achievements are honored, and the child can keep the book as a reminder.

Shifting from a weak to a strong body posture and shifting back and forth, imitating a powerful animal, fosters more body awareness, self-efficacy, and control. Further, it is playful, especially for younger children. Levine and Kline (2008) provide ideas for healing games in their book *Trauma-Proofing Your Kids*.

Healing Games

According to Maggie Kline (2012), who served with Alé Duarte after many environmental disasters worldwide, any ordinary game can become trauma healing, assuming the following ingredients are in place:

1. Time for establishing a sense of readiness, for developing strategies of defense (fight/flight), gaining safety, settling, and integrating. It is important to give time for every phase, for example, resting or drawing at the end (Duarte, 2022).
2. Freedom of choice and pleasant excitement.

3. The ability to develop defense skills.
4. The support of a protector-adult, such as a parent, teacher, or therapist.

Discharge of blocked body energy can happen during play or after playing when checking in. The less resiliency there is, the more checking in between phases is needed. With the release, the energy may shift, which may be frightening. In such a case, the therapist must offer comfort and validation: "That's great! If your energy system gets hot, that means that stress is released!" "This is so important! Feel the heat!" "These tears are yours! Your nervous system knows what to do and takes care of everything now!"

Anxious, Depressed Children, With Somatic Problems

When children have headaches, somatic problems, sleep disorders, or nightmares, or are clinging, anxious, withdrawn, or depressed, or they have low muscle tonus, they need some energy arousal. Playing with squishy pop balls is one way to allow a discharge. The focus is on the resource. They need to be oriented to the outside, because they are overfocused internally on spinning thoughts like, "I am not good enough!" or are fixated on past trauma. They need support, grounding, and containment in addition to empowering ego states, inner helpers, corrective experiences, and safe places. For instance, a child could be invited to draw or design anxiety on one sheet of paper, and then draw the opposite on another sheet. "Now, when you look at the picture [resource picture first], what is it like? Pleasant, unpleasant? Now look at the anxiety picture! How is that?" As the therapist and child move their focus back and forth, distance to the problem is created, and a resource opposed to the problem is introduced. Nightmares can be changed to adventure journeys in which the child triumphs.

Hyperactive Children

Hyperactive children tend to be more oriented toward the outside, so they need to focus on the inside. After active playing, they might be invited to draw a gingerbread person and color in their feelings. Often, they need touch to be in their body. The therapist could put a hand on the child's back or shoulder and ask them whether they feel it, or invite the child to tap their body, moving from the top down. It is important that therapists regulate their own energy, especially with aggressive children. The aggression can be paced appropriately, using approaches such as tugging on ropes or even fighting, but making sure to insert pauses and provide structure. Some fun and relaxing coregulation methods with children include yawning, making faces, humming, blowing soap bubbles, and laughing (Kline, 2012).

A child's language is play. Children do not have the capacity to discuss things. It is important to complete the natural cycles of play, from readiness to action, to interaction, to integration, and then to rest.

Impatient children want to be in action immediately and can hardly stand the energy of readiness. Anxious or shy children like to be in a state of readiness but have trouble getting into action. They need more time, smaller steps, freedom of choice, and options: "You don't have to do this; I'll help you." Or "You can choose how and what. . . . "

Hyperactive children tend to skip integration and rest, instead jumping from action to action. The therapist could try to keep them in readiness longer, predicting: "We do this now . . . and then we rest." Or "We make four attempts; the fifth is then the right one." Thus, the child can follow their impulse for movement, while experiencing an invitation for integration. The therapist facilitates by pacing and leading, helping the child to go through each phase and complete the cycle (Duarte, 2022).

The Three Levels of Expression

In order to differentiate and deepen processes, the therapist works on three levels, according to the maturity and development of the child:

1. **Inner experience, affect, emotion:** "Is it pleasant, unpleasant?"
   - Feeling the inner navigation system, orienting outward to explore sensations.
2. **Expression, movement (sensorimotor):** "Can you show me?"
   - Drawing, gestures, movement, and role-play.
3. Invitation to **cognitive expression, elaboration, imagination:** "Tell me more about it!"
   - Writing, explaining, thinking about, new ideas, interpretations (Duarte, 2022).

Many children (and adults) lack an inner schema, an inner imagination to describe sensations or images. In this case, the "show me" sensorimotor movement can be a great door opener to sensing. For children 12 years and under, it is best to start with expression because they have difficulty tracking sensations. If they focus on something, it changes. Expressing, pointing, and naming lead to differentiated perception. Children adapt very quickly to change. They often don't notice progress unless you point it out to them.

Therapists should not ask too many questions, so there is space for integration, but they should respond to their young clients' intentions, accompany them through the cycles, and provide time for reflection, integration, and digestion. Meanwhile, therapists should also be aware of their own cycles.

Case Example: Empowering Alan

At the age of four, Alan was attacked by the family's Rottweiler. He was badly injured and needed several operations. Alan has scars beside his left eye and around his mouth. When Alan returns to preschool, he is very aggressive, biting and scratching his classmates. He is jealous of his two younger sisters and seeks Mommy's attention all the time. Alan's mother has difficulty controlling her anger, and when Alan bullies his little sisters, she sometimes hits him. Mother and son must learn to control their impulses and self-regulate. In working with the mother and child, I utilize the fact that Alan is shy and won't stay without his mother during the first sessions. In the therapy room, Mother is an observer of the child and of our interactions; she is not in charge. Alan chooses puppets to act out his feelings in play; there is a lot of fighting and biting among the puppets. His resources include three protectors: two wolves and an octopus that successfully fight the aggressors. We install safe places for the wolves and octopuses, strong magic boundaries, indicated by ropes. By defending successfully, Alan experiences empowering competence, in contrast to his helplessness in the past. He understands physically that it is over, that he is safe now.

Toward the end of therapy, I see Alan with his parents. I tell Alan his trauma story, its protagonist being a little boy. The story starts when a boy was still safe, then continues with the dog attack and surgery. It ends with his sister's birthday party; he is out of hospital, back home, and safe again. First, he sits on father's lap and listens attentively. He says, "This is a true story." Then he wants to hear it again while sitting on his Mother's lap. Thus, he is supported, contained, and safe. At the end he says, "The scars have healed!" I offer Alan's mother separate sessions, as there are traumatized child-ego states that need to be nurtured. Finally, she can let go of her anger and better control her behavior. When Alan meets my therapy dog, he is a little timid. He doesn't like the dog to come too close, but he responds appropriately. Alan is better, but still having difficulty in preschool. I spoke to his teacher several times about how to deal with Alan's aggression. In a therapy session, Alan and I develop a story together. He calls it, "The Others Get on Black Dragon's Nerves." Together, we find ways for the black dragon to keep its distance if others get too close. Scratching and biting are fight responses, defense strategies. Like the black dragon, Alan wants distance. But we develop better solutions: the black dragon can withdraw or use his language or body postures to keep his boundaries. We role-play the story; we replay it with figures in the sand tray and put the story in Alan's therapy book. Like the black dragon, Alan manages to protect his space without hurting anyone. After one and a half years, we finish the therapy with a small party where we honor Alan's huge progress.

Adding Ego State Therapy

"Ego States are neurophysiological and psychological manifestations of the autonomic nervous system as response to positive and/or negative interoceptive as well as exteroceptive triggers" (Hartman, 2023). Ego state therapy as a relational therapy creates an important path to safety and empowerment. As this case illustrates, the past cannot be changed, but dissociated personality parts can be integrated so that the inner world can become more peaceful and safer through discovery and the utilization of resources, corrective emotional and developmental experiences, and internal secure attachment. Personality parts can learn, grow, and change. Weak ego states may be empowered and connected with strong states, and destructive states can be transformed into strong helpers. Working as a team, reliable inner alliances and parts support self-healing and resiliency.

Ideal parent parts subsequently nurture, provide security, and give unconditional love to formerly abandoned or rejected child states on the inner stage so that they can catch up on everything they have missed. Attachment ruptures are thus repaired through the safe

FIGURE 18.1 Benny's volcano, pretending to be a mountain.

therapeutic relationship and internally through nurturing figures. With children, there are many ways to create safe places, enhance safe activities, connect them to their resources, and strengthen their boundaries. Throughout, the therapist must consider the child's level of development and cognitive abilities.

Case Example: The Power of the Volcano

Ten-year-old Benny has started daydreaming at school. He is often sad and feels excluded by his peers. His parents, who separated amicably two years ago, are worried, as there seems to be no obvious reason for their son's problems. Benny has many resources, including music (drums) and sports (snowboarding, skateboarding, tennis). The symptoms started six months earlier, when his best friend told him that his parents were also separating. Benny draws a picture of a volcano, hidden in a mountain (Figure 18.1).

Benny says, "I am a volcano, but I have to pretend to be a mountain." I ask about the volcano. "He is sad, feels left alone." I ask about where the sadness is in his body. "In my belly." What's it like? "It is bubbling." He has tears in his eyes. I ask Benny for permission to talk to the sad volcano. I find out that the volcano is the eight-year-old Benny, who is shocked by the separation of his parents and frightened of losing his dad forever. I tell him, "I am sorry that this happened to you. You felt powerless, afraid of losing your father. I am going to share a surprise: It is over. You are no longer powerless. Even if you can't change anything on the outside, on the inside, you can always have your dad with you, night and day. From now on, you will never be alone. He is always with you." I give the eight-year-old "volcano" enough time to understand and integrate.

Then I ask, "What more do you need to feel completely safe?" He wants Spider-Man on his left side for reassurance, and Flash on his right. Now he feels completely safe. "How would you do the drawing now?" As "the volcano," he says, "I am a volcano that erupts once every 300 years." I ask what else he needs. He answers, "A theme park all around."

After this session, the symptoms are gone. Benny's grief and loss, and the shock of his parents' separation, were heard and understood, and his "volcano" ego state that was stuck in the past was saved, nurtured, and integrated!

The Advantages of Ego State Therapy

In ego-state therapy, the therapist works directly with the state responsible for the symptom, which makes thorough change possible. The personality parts are addressed in the context of (role) play, using puppets, figures, modeling, drawings, stories, and metaphors— all in the child's natural language. The ego state therapist helps these states express their sensations and emotions in a safe therapeutic relationship. Furthermore, ego states that are stuck in the past, continuing to feel hurt and anxious, can engage in corrective experiences that allow them to feel safe in the present and are no longer so easily triggered.

The therapist negotiates with conflicted states so that they start to cooperate and join to become a helpful team. The therapist builds alliances with all personality parts, including destructively acting or blocking states. The traumatized client's defenses are present for a good reason and therefore need to be respected. These states have often ensured survival, and the powerful energy of these states can be utilized to promote integration. As ego states are relational, they help expand access to the ventral vagal state (Phillips, 2019).

Somatic Ego State Therapy: A Holistic Approach[3]

CREATING BOTTOM-UP AND TOP-DOWN CORRECTIVE EXPERIENCES

The key factors are:

1. **Resourcing** through the body to shift traumatized relationships with body experiences.
2. **Reregulation** of nervous system responses to triggering; strategies to turn on ventral vagal rhythms to enhance self-regulation and coregulation.
3. **Repair and rewire** by exploring enduring self-integration and secure attachment with others; form alliances; and provide developmental repair to stabilize wholeness and enhance resilience (Phillips, 2019).

Through Somatic Ego State Therapy, secure attachment may be installed and embodied via inner alliances with protecting personality parts. Symptom-associated and traumatized ego states experience cooperation and wholeness through integration, and inner conflicts can be effectively resolved. The goal is to coordinate sensing (inner experiences) and acting (expressing through drawing, role-play, hand/body gestures, shifting positions, and moving around the space) and thinking (elaborate, put into words, images, metaphors, stories). Regulating the nervous system also means regulating the activation of the body and simultaneously developing sensing and thinking. With the guidance of the therapist, children can find their own answers in mind and body and move toward integration (Duarte, 2022). When combined with ego state therapy, our work with children can open up myriad opportunities for enduring holistic change, empowerment, and competency.

Notes

1 Here we are talking about children up to the age of 12. Adolescents have other requirements for therapy that are beyond the scope of this chapter.
2 Herzog: Lily, Ben, and Omid. Three children embark on a journey to find their safe place.
3 Somatic ego state therapy was created and taught by Maggie Phillips, a pioneer in the field of trauma therapy.

19

The Relational Intelligence Model of Psychotherapy

A Neurobiological and Relational Approach to Treating Trauma

François Le Doze

Genesis of the Model

The relational intelligence (RI) psychotherapy model is a treatment approach for traumatic dissociation (TD) that has its origins in the internal family systems (IFS) model (Schwartz, 1995), Polyvagal Theory (PVT; Porges, 2011), and attachment theory (Bowlby, 1969).[1] The development of the RI model was influenced by clinical challenges observed by IFS practitioners, in particular managing systems that resisted the interventions proposed by the IFS model,[2] which predominantly uses self-regulation and the paradigm of parts and the self. In such situations, applying coregulation based on the PVT paradigm proved quite effective. Thus, the initial phase of the RI model is proposed, using coregulation in situations where self-regulation has demonstrated its limitations and combining the parts and self paradigm with that of PVT to more comprehensively grasp the scope and complexity of the clinical manifestations of TD.

Further observations identified resistance from some patients to attempts at coregulation, especially when physical interventions were involved.[3] In these scenarios, metacognitive interventions were effective. Therefore, the second phase of the RI model proposes that coregulation encompasses not only a direct (physical) dimension but also an indirect (metacognitive) one. This combined type of coregulation is identified in the RI model as conscious therapeutic engagement (CTE).

The RI model holds that TD is clinically expressed as a continuum consisting of three levels, identifiable according to the system's response to the type of regulation:

1. If it responds positively to self-regulation, TD is manifesting in its most conscious form, which can be understood through the paradigm of parts and self.

2. If it responds negatively to self-regulation but positively to physical coregulation, the symptoms reflect a deeper TD that requires the PVT paradigm.
3. If it responds negatively to physical coregulation but positively to metacognition, TD corresponds to the deepest level, termed structural.[4]

Coregulation and self-regulation are two inseparable, noninterchangeable components of therapeutic action. In this regard, the RI view of the psychological system is consistent with attachment theory, which posits that coregulation with an attachment figure is a biological imperative that prepares and precedes the development of self-regulation mechanisms. Therefore, the RI therapist is encouraged to become a therapeutic attachment figure for their patient.

Preliminary Definitions and the Role of Attachment Theory

To clarify the terms used in this chapter, *traumatic dissociation* is described as the adaptive reaction initiated by a person's nervous system when exposed to danger and unable to experience a return to safety.[5] *Regulation* is understood as a mechanism employed by any biological system to return to its equilibrium state after adapting to environmental conditions. In the context of psychotherapy and the RI paradigm, the biological system consists of the nervous and psychological systems, and the regulatory agent is the self (that of the patient, in the context of self-regulation, and that of the therapist, in the context of coregulation).

Attachment theory and PVT intersect on a foundational concept in grasping trauma and its treatment: the biological imperative for the individual to access proximity to another—devoid of any danger or, in other words, secure. This encompasses not just the physical dimension, but also the emotional and psychological dimensions. It allows access to the ventral state described by PVT and thus to its inherent qualities: replenishment, rest, and healing. This constitutes the foundation of what is termed a secure attachment.

Conversely, psychological trauma can be characterized as an experience where secure proximity becomes inaccessible. Facilitating a patient's experience of secure proximity with the therapist is deemed pivotal in therapy. The patient's autonomic nervous system (ANS) regulates itself, thus creating an implicit memory on which they can rely to progress in the therapeutic process. In this sense, the RI therapist is indeed called on to become a therapeutic attachment figure.

However, closeness (especially physical) between the therapist and the patient has historically been discouraged or even prohibited. This cautious attitude, based on real risks generated by insufficiently addressed countertransference, should be reconsidered for the patient's utmost benefit. CTE provides a space for therapeutic coregulation where the therapist is encouraged to engage (approach) the patient, following strict criteria that ensure a high level of security. In my experience, these conditions allow for the treatment of very deep levels of TD.

The subsequent sections elaborate on the foundational principles of the RI model and the clinical tools derived from them, followed by an exploration of the principles guiding therapeutic interventions.

Foundations of the Model

This section highlights certain characteristic aspects of the model:

- The place of PVT
- The use of metacognition to regulate the ANS
- The therapist's commitment as a lever to address deep TD
- The importance of psychoeducation is to inform the ANS of both the patient and the therapist about neurobiological concepts in order to facilitate regulation processes

PVT in the RI Model: The Reference Neurobiological Model

While the RI model draws on two neurobiological models,[6] PVT holds a prominent place for the following reasons:

- It offers a representation of the anatomy and functioning of the ANS that the patient can easily grasp through psychoeducation.[7] This allows the patient to integrate the neurophysiological dimension of their trauma and, by providing a scientific validation to the therapist's intervention, enhances its effectiveness.
- It enables both the therapist and the patient to have a shared conceptual framework through which they can align their perspectives, thus forming one of the cornerstones of the metacognition protocol.
- It forms the basis of the physical coregulation protocol.
- It provides the analytical framework that allows the therapist to identify departures from TD.

Metacognition

Metacognition is defined as the ability to be aware of one's own and others' mental operations and mental states, and to apply this awareness to various mental operations (Brown & Elliott, 2016). When applied to the field of psychotherapy, it is defined as the ability to be aware of patterns and parts or states of the ANS in oneself and in others, and to apply this awareness to the practice of psychotherapeutic interventions.

This practice has proven highly effective in treating TD when physical coregulation does not facilitate the transition out of TD. Resistance to physical coregulation is interpreted in the RI model as a symptom of an underlying developmental trauma. This reluctance is a defense mechanism to avoid any risks associated with accepting coregulation, similar to what patients with insufficiently secure parental attachment figures experienced during childhood. In fact, it has been demonstrated that the quality of metacognition is linked to the quality of (secure) attachment (Brown & Elliott, 2016).

In the RI method, metacognition (or cognitive coregulation) essentially takes over from physical coregulation. The aim is to maintain relational engagement through an indirect modality rather than a direct (physical) one. This practice is also crucial from a neurobiological perspective, as it mobilizes the neocortical brain structures that support bodily awareness. Metacognition offers a way to regulate the brain from the cortex (top-down regulation), thereby functionally associating these structures with the ANS.

The section Therapeutic Intervention highlights that metacognition is essential for the safe practice of CTE. Additionally, the methods by which metacognition is implemented within the RI model are discussed.

CTE: Therapeutic Coregulation in Both Physical and Cognitive Dimensions

Conscious therapeutic engagement consists of a set of clinical practices that have proven effective in the treatment of deep TD—that is, TD that is ingrained in the ANS. These practices are largely inspired by proposals made by Deborah Dana (2018) to apply PVT to psychotherapy, based on the principles of coregulation. Coregulation is human beings' ability to regulate their physiological and emotional states by interacting with other individuals in a secure and adaptive way. It is based on the idea that the ANS communicates unconsciously through neuroception to detect clues of danger and safety in the environment and that the organism then responds accordingly with automatic behaviors to regain a state of safety.

PVT holds that coregulation primarily involves physical interventions: the distance between the patient and the therapist, physical contact, body posture, and the involvement of the social engagement system. In the RI model, coregulation also has a cognitive component: metacognition.

The main goal of CTE is to establish relational security between the therapist and the patient. In the RI model, this security is based on the patient's subjective experience of feeling safe or threatened in the presence of another. This perception stems from the nervous system's analysis of the information received from the environment via the ANS. The therapist's interventions within the CTE framework allow the patient to explore the notion of relational security for themselves and to provide the therapist with information regarding the dysregulation of their own ANS.

The TD Continuum

The TD continuum provides a representation that encompasses two key elements of TD expression: neuroanatomy and its influence on the patient's bodily awareness. These two aspects seem to be inextricably linked, each offering a different perspective of the same reality.[8]

As mentioned previously, it is suggested that the depth of TD be interpreted based on its mode of expression—from the most superficial, which only slightly affects awareness

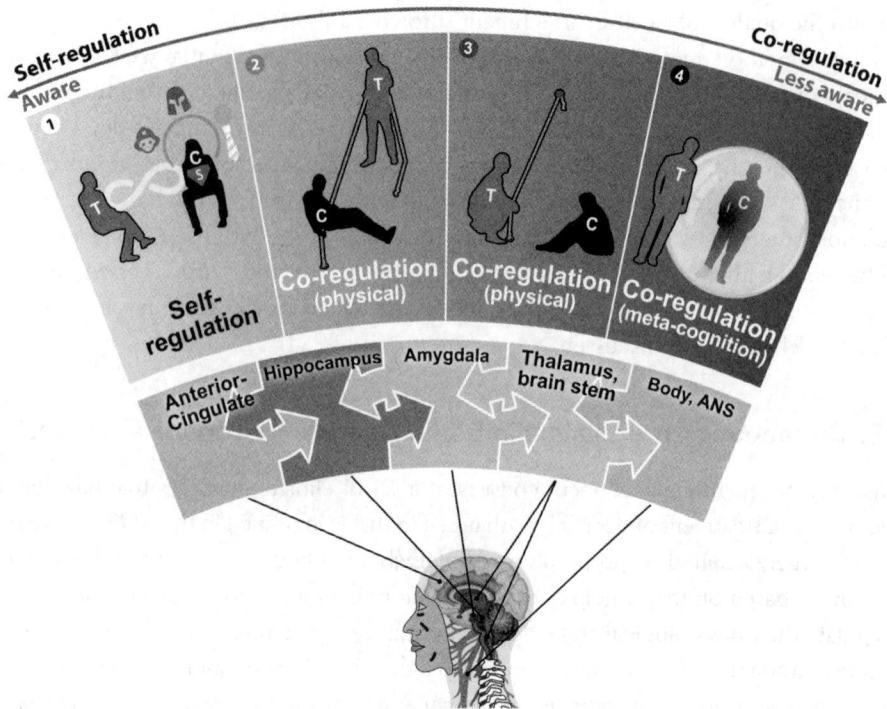

FIGURE 19.1 The continuum of traumatic dissociation. The indicated brain structures aim to provide, at a preliminary level, neuroanatomical references for the therapist.

(the experience of parts of oneself), to the level where bodily consciousness is deeply affected, corresponding to structural dissociation. An intermediate level has been further identified, corresponding to the experience of states (refer to the section below: Diagnose the TD Type). The TD continuum merges these two perspectives to present a model structured into four levels or quadrants (Figure 19.1).

The features of each quadrant are as follows:

1. The relational security between the client and the therapist is adequate; dissociation manifests in such a way that the client experiences parts as elements related to their problem.
2. The relational security between the client and the therapist is adequate; dissociation manifests in a way that the client feels, in their body, a state related to their problem.
3. The relational security between the client and the therapist is adequate; dissociation is expressed such that the client.
   - feels, in their body, a state related to their problem,
   - does not have the capacity to engage with the therapist, and
   - is biologically open to receiving coregulation.

4. The relational security between the patient and the therapist is no longer sufficient. The patient
   - is not biologically open to receiving coregulation, and
   - does not physically experience a state connected to this situation or experiences it only to a limited extent; this is the illusion of safety.

The modeling of Quadrant 4 accounts for paradoxical situations often encountered, in which the therapist's interventions do not lead to an exit from TD. It is suggested that this resistance be interpreted as an expression of relational insecurity. The term "bubble" used to describe this scenario implies that a deep level of TD prevents the therapist's interventions from accessing the patient's ANS, and the patient functionally remains in a bubble regarding CTE.

Healing the Brain by Addressing TD

In his seminal book *The Body Keeps the Score*, van der Kolk (2014) states, "Dissociation is the essence of trauma" (p. 66). In other words, PT is connected to a neurobiological reality rooted in TD. Therefore, enhancing brain function is considered vital to alleviate mental symptoms.

This means that the content of the issue presented by the patient does not guide the psychotherapy session. The therapist focuses on the physical manifestations of their patient when they discuss the issue, which leads them to the TD they will address. The initial issue can thus be revisited at the end of the session when the patient's nervous system is less dysregulated.

The Importance of the Patient Experiencing Secure Proximity

Polyvagal Theory (PVT) presents a model for the autonomic nervous system's (ANS) threat response, progressing from a ventral (safe) state to sympathetic (fight or flight) and possibly to a dorsal (freeze) state. Treatment focuses on safely guiding patients back to a ventral state through physical proximity.[9]

This approach to psychological trauma (PT) proved highly effective because it addressed the complexity that most often characterizes traumatic dissociation (TD).[10]

The "Two-Brain Model"

During the practice of physical coregulation, the therapist explicitly refers to the characteristics of the ANS,[11] thereby informing the patient about PVT. However, as mentioned above, some forms of TD resist physical coregulation, thus necessitating the use of metacognition.

From this perspective, referring only to the patient's ANS is deemed inadequate, as the ANS does not manage the cognitive functions upon which metacognition relies. Consequently, a representation that incorporates these brain areas has been chosen: this includes reference to the upper brain and the lower brain. In simple terms, the lower brain corresponds to the ANS, while the upper brain, managing cognitive functions, corresponds to the cerebral hemispheres.[12] This representation of brain organization has proved to be particularly operative with patients.

The two-brain model appears relevant in emphasizing the recommendation of poly-vagal theorists: to inform the nervous system about PVT before initiating interventions aimed at its regulation. It is postulated that this phase of informing the nervous system is primarily processed by the upper brain, which is equipped to handle cognitive learning. Given the constant communication between these two entities that takes place during the regulatory processes within the nervous system,[13] it seems logical to suggest that these two brains converse with each other. Introducing explicit information into the upper brain about the lower brain allows the latter to feel recognized and understood by the former.[14] Therefore, a nervous system informed about PVT is a system in which the interaction between the upper brain and lower brain is facilitated, contributing to an increase in their degree of association.

Therapeutic Intervention

The aim of any therapeutic intervention in the RI model is to create a relational space that allows TD to be exposed to a regulatory agency: the self (self-regulation) or the therapist's ventral state in the context of CTE (coregulation). Before discussing the various protocols of the method, it is important to emphasize that the key factor in their effectiveness lies in the therapist maintaining their ventral state throughout the session and therapy.[15]

The structure of this section reflects the cardinal principles stated in the introduction:

- Determine the type of TD.
- Intervene based on protocols developed for each type of TD.
- Identify the signs of exiting TD.

Diagnose the TD Type

What Is Happening in Your Body?

This question serves as a diagnostic tool to determine the type of TD. It invites the patient to

- tap into their bodily awareness,
- observe their physical manifestations, and
- make them explicit (linking the upper brain and lower brain).

One of three types of responses is obtained (Figure 19.2):

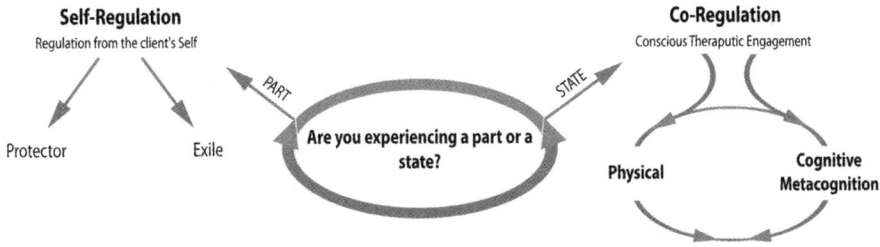

FIGURE 19.2 Basic structuring of therapeutic intervention in the relational intelligence model.

1. The patient indicates they experience one or several parts of themselves. For example, they might say, "It's just a part of me that's angry, not my entire self." The therapist suggests self-regulation.
2. The patient experiences a state. They might say, "I am in a state of anger. . . . It's my entire self that's angry," and reject the proposition that it is just a part of themselves. The therapist suggests coregulation.
3. The patient answers that they do not feel anything (neither a state nor a part). The therapist understands that a TD mechanism is preventing the patient's bodily awareness from accessing the information, and that this is related to insufficient relational security. The therapist proposes advanced coregulation.[16]

The question "What is happening in your body?" is open-ended. The therapist can facilitate the patient's expression with interventions such as, "Would you say that a part of you is angry or that it's your entire self that's angry?" They must be very careful not to guide or influence the patient's response.

The RI Therapist's Compass

Due to the complexity with which TD manifests during a session, I have developed a more sophisticated tool than the binary representation shown in Figure 19.3, which I have called the RI therapist's compass. This approach is based on the following observations:

- The type of TD varies during the session, often changing rapidly, unpredictably, and nonlinearly (e.g., moving from Quadrant 1 to Quadrant 4, from Quadrant 1 to Quadrant 3, or from Quadrant 4 to Quadrant 3).
- There are situations where two types of TD (Quadrants 1 and 4, for instance) present simultaneously: one in the foreground (Quadrant 1) and the other in the background (Quadrant 4).

The therapist's compass is an adaptation of the TD continuum. The changes made are

- the removal of neuroanatomical references,

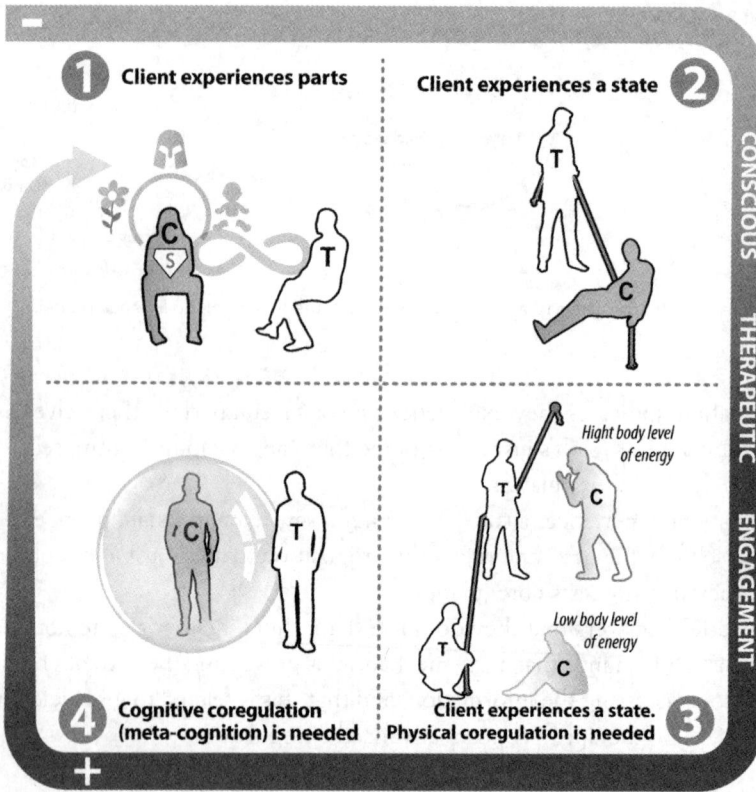

FIGURE 19.3 The RI therapist's compass. The deeper the alteration of bodily awareness demonstrated by the traumatic dissociation (from Quadrant 1 to Quadrant 4), the more the therapist is encouraged to implement conscious therapeutic engagement.

- a circular presentation mode (rather than linear), and
- reference to the impact of the TD on bodily awareness being replaced by an emphasis on the importance of coregulation compared to self-regulation and specifically the role of CTE based on the depth of the TD.

Intervention Based on Protocols Developed for Each TD Type

Self-Regulation: Quadrant 1

The purpose of self-regulation is to address TD located in the upper brain. The principles of self-regulation are inspired by the IFS model:[17]

- Identify the parts (*protectors* or *exiles*[18]) within the body.
- Establish the relationship between the parts and the *self*.

- Initiate a dialogue between the parts and the *self*.
- Unburden the *exile*.

However, there are significant differences between the two approaches. Working with a protector relies on an original protocol in the RI model. Note that the number of parts that manifest is reduced in the RI model for the following reasons: When the session takes place in Quadrant 1 and there are more than two protectors, this reflects relational insecurity with the therapist, and coregulation is therefore encouraged. Most patients exhibit states primarily at the beginning of therapy. Coregulation is therefore predominant at that stage. As the main psychological protective mechanisms are addressed by this modality, their manifestations in the form of protectors are significantly reduced.

Coregulation: Quadrants 2, 3, and 4

The aim of coregulation is to treat TDs located in the lower brain.[19] In the RI model, it is modeled in two dimensions: physical and cognitive, which should never be practiced independently of each other (see Figure 19.2).

- When initiating a physical engagement, the therapist should always pair it with the question, for example, "What do you feel in your body when I come closer to you?"
- When offering a cognitive proposition, the therapist should always ask, for example, "What do you feel in your body when you know that I know [understand] this about you?" This practice is the method recommended to ensuring sufficient safety in the application of CTE, as there is a risk of exposing the patient to potential abusive or compensatory acts by the therapist. The risk of actual malpractice exists with all psychotherapy methods. In the context of RI, it is acknowledged that CTE does entail a risk of therapeutic intervention being perceived as a transgression, especially in Quadrant 3 (physical coregulation). It is believed that this risk is present when interventions primarily rely on communication between the therapist's and patient's lower brains without involving (or without insufficient involvement of) the upper brains of both parties. Metacognition, which engages the upper brains of both the practitioner and the recipient, is the primary way in which the therapist safeguards against exposing their patient to the risk of feeling subjected to an unarticulated transgression that could leave the therapist unaware.

Physical Coregulation. This is the modality implemented in Quadrant 3, with elements taught by Deborah Dana (2018).[20] These are broken down into two phases. The first is diagnostic, with the therapist asking the question, "In which ANS state do you find yourself?" This question is complemented by "Do you feel a high or low bodily energy?

- If the answer is "high bodily energy," the therapist concludes there is a manifestation of dysregulated sympathetic state (according to PVT).

- If the answer is "low bodily energy," the therapist concludes there is a manifestation of a dysregulated dorsal state (likewise, as per PVT).

The second phase is interventional.

- In the case of a dysregulated sympathetic state, the therapist poses the following question: "What do you need from me to experience this state safely?" This question is followed by suggestions related to engaging the social engagement system—for example, "Would you like me to modify my facial expression, which may currently appear insufficiently reassuring to you?"; "Do you need to hear my voice more clearly?"; and "Would you like us to breathe together?"
- For a dysregulated dorsal state, the therapist asks, "What kind of movement do you need to exit this state?" If the patient provides guidance, the therapist follows it. If not (which is often the case), the therapist initiates a movement based on suggestions provided during their training. For instance, they might begin by moving closer.

Cognitive Coregulation. This is invoked when physical coregulation does not lead to an exit from TD.[21] If the patient's nervous system resists physically associating with the therapist's ventral state, the therapist, faced with a feeling of powerlessness, may be tempted to disengage, thereby giving the patient the impression that there is no way out of the situation. This frequently encountered situation can reaffirm patterns stemming from attachment disorders, manifesting as beliefs such as, "My problem is too severe; I can't be healed. I end up discouraging all my therapists."

The RI approach suggests that, at this point, the therapist should continue the association process using their own body and psychological space. They apply metacognition authentically to themselves and convey their observations to the patient. In my experience, this type of intervention has proven fruitful, in most cases allowing an exit from TD to occur.

This methodology demands extensive skill on the part of the therapist, who must acquire it in a training framework that includes supervisory follow-up. Here are some examples of interventions: "What is happening in your body when you know that I understand this about you?"[22] and "What is happening in your body when you are aware of what I'm feeling right now, as I'm connecting with you?"

Identifying the Exit From TD

Identifying the signs indicating the exit from TD is a crucial marker for the therapist. The reference framework to use for this purpose is PVT: the exit from TD (equated to the dysregulated dorsal state) is indicated by the expression of the sympathetic state—which, in the RI model, is understood in a broader sense than in PVT and refers to any change in the patient's state. While it is often an emotion, it can also be the emergence of a memory, tremors, physical sensations, awareness, the transition from one quadrant to another, or even the manifestation of a part.

The therapist then intervenes according to the procedure corresponding to the quadrant in which they believe their patient is located. They guide the work to allow the patient to access the self-state (Quadrant 1) or ventral state (other quadrants).

It is believed that the exit from TD is complete when the patient has been able to experience the dysregulated dorsal state (TD), then the sympathetic state, and finally, the ventral state. This ascending sequence, according to the hierarchical organization of the ANS, is indeed what PVT proposes as an indicator of the return to its homeostatic state.

Conclusion

Traumatic dissociation is at the heart of the psychopathology of psychological trauma. It is now possible to establish a map based on neuroscientific data, serving as a foundation for a clinical methodology to address TD. Within this approach, coregulation proves to be of crucial importance, although self-regulation remains appropriate when TD is not profound. Indeed, from the very beginning of life, coregulation is a neurobiological imperative at the center of the attachment experience. Psychological trauma fundamentally conflicts with this need. The challenge lies in developing a way for the therapist to establish a relationship with the patient while ensuring that the latter's nervous system can perceive and integrate the essential safety conditions for its reconfiguration.

The RI model emphasizes the importance of the therapist's ability to engage in a relationship with their patient—especially if the patient is stuck in deep, even structural, TD. Academic studies are needed (some of which are already underway) to confirm the effectiveness and safety of this model.

Acknowledgments

I would like to thank Quantum Way for their contribution to the publication of this chapter.

Appendix: The Two-Brain Model

The two-brain model is inspired by MacLean's (1990) triune brain model. This is based on an anatomical and phylogenetic foundation. It refers to three brains: a reptilian brain, a paleo-mammalian (limbic) brain, and a neo-mammalian (neocortex) brain. I propose a biune brain model that recognizes an upper brain and a lower brain (Figure 19.4).

The lower brain corresponds to the autonomic nervous system (Polyvagal Theory) and brain stem. The upper brain corresponds to the neocortex and the cerebral hemispheres. The limbic system is part of both the upper brain and lower brain. We attribute certain neuropsychological characteristics to each brain type, as summarized in Tables 19.1 and 19.2.

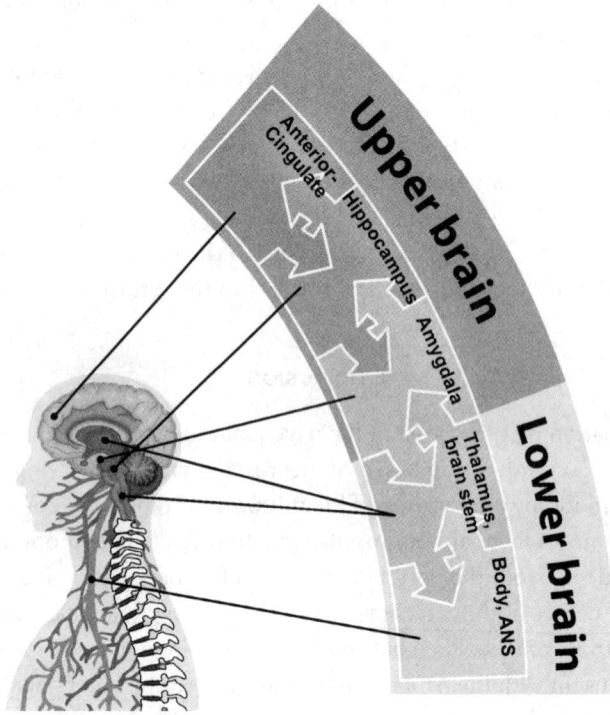

FIGURE 19.4 The two-brain model.

TABLE 19.1 Functional Characteristics of the Upper Brain and Lower Brain

UPPER BRAIN	LOWER BRAIN
Little information at birth; locus of cognitive learning	Wired at birth; locus of procedural learning
Explicit memory	Implicit memory
Conscious	Automatic
Social engagement	Relational security

TABLE 19.2 Correspondence Between Each Brain, the Mode of Expression of Traumatic Dissociation, and the Type of Regulation to Be Implemented

UPPER BRAIN	LOWER BRAIN
Experience of parts of the self	State experience
Self-regulation	Coregulation

Notes

1 Intelligence Relationnelle and Relational Intelligence are registered trademarks, exclusive property of Mr. François le Doze (European Union Trademarks No. 016435786 and No. 016485062).
2 In situations where the client is experiencing what the IFS model refers to as blending (a mingling between parts and self) and is unable to distinguish their inner parts from the Self.
3 Based on proposals put forward by Deborah Dana (2018).
4 Referring to the structural dissociation model in van der Hart et al. (2006).
5 Mostly in its autonomic part: the autonomic nervous system.
6 The defense cascade model (Kozlowska et al., 2015), and the two-brain model.
7 This is part of the metacognition skills.
8 This TD continuum serves as a foundation for the therapist in organizing the patient's care (see section The RI Therapist's Compass).
9 This issue of distance does not pertain to self-regulation.
10 I refer to the fact that the traumas encountered are most often complex, meaning they combine a developmental trauma dimension with manifestations of posttraumatic stress syndrome.
11 From the psychoeducation of PVT at the beginning of the therapy.
12 The appendix details the anatomical elements as well as the neuropsychological correspondences attributable to each of the two brains.
13 Top-down regulation and bottom-up regulation.
14 To use expressions that are not strictly neuroscientific, but which prove valuable in the service of the patient-therapist dialectic.
15 This fundamental aspect deserves extensive elaboration that cannot be provided within the scope of this chapter.
16 This cannot be elaborated upon here.
17 The reader is referred to the principles of IFS for further details.
18 In the IFS model, parts are categorized into two groups: protected parts (exiles) and protective parts (managers and firefighters).
19 Quadrant 2 represents a transitional situation between coregulation and self-regulation protocols. The methodology is not described in this chapter.
20 On the occasion of a workshop co-led by her in Paris in 2016, organized by Self Therapie Formation.
21 It is used with any physical coregulation intervention.
22 For example, related to a pattern, state, or element observed in the patient.

Part III
Embodied Practice

20

Sensorimotor Psychotherapy

Processing Trauma and Attachment Through the Body

Hanneke Kalisvaart and Pat Ogden

SENSORIMOTOR PSYCHOTHERAPY IS A BODY-ORIENTED PSYCHOTHERAPY METHOD DEVELoped by Pat Ogden in the United States. This bottom-up approach combines with top-down interventions with a focus on mindful study of bodily responses to traumatic events and relational issues for stabilization, processing memory, and integration (Ogden et al., 2006; Ogden & Fisher, 2015). This chapter gives an introduction to this method regarding therapeutic principles, treatment of trauma and attachment-related problems, and its scientific foundation. In closing, we include a client report about her experiences with this method.

The Body: Lifelong Learning Through Experience

As social beings, people grow and develop from attachment relationships that are originally physical (Maté & Maté, 2022; de Waal, 2019). The secure base of the womb, loving care, attunement to needs, physical contact, rhythmical rocking, mirroring expression and behavior, motor development, and play lay the neurological foundation for further development (Kearney & Lanius, 2022). Language and conscious memory are not yet involved. In those early years, children learn to relate to themselves and the world around them through significant others. With a safe base, children will learn to move freely and feel at ease in relation to others to express their needs and set boundaries. At the physical level, the child then has all the fundamental movements at their disposal: yield, push, reach, grasp, and pull (Ogden, 2021a; Frank & La Barre, 2010; Cohen, 1993). However, circumstances and attachment relationships vary, and these movements are modified according to the responses of others so that different skills and traits develop more and less. For example, if one child learns to face the world openly and expressively, another may learn that you are valued when you are quiet and move little.

Thus a physical neurobiological basis of procedural movement and interaction patterns forms in the early years. The child tends to interact with the world from a similar pattern unless circumstances require adjustments. Adaptations happen in normal development as the environment expands, for example, through school, media, relocation, travel, and contact with other cultures. Significant events, however, can alter familiar safe patterns (van der Kolk, 2015). Traumatic events require survival responses that override usual coping mechanisms: fight, flight, cry for help, freeze, shutdown, and feigned death accompanied by dysregulated arousal may be necessary in the face of threat (Kearney & Lanius, 2022). When such events are insufficiently processed, these survival impulses remain active. In the body, this can be evident in sympathetic hyperarousal in the form of tension, hyper-alertness, and agitation, and in hypoarousal in the form of numbness, low energy, and shutting down.

Sensorimotor Psychotherapy uses a bottom-up approach in which patterns and impulses of the body serve as the basis for processing and are integrated with emotional processing and cognitive meaning-making. The therapist tracks and deciphers the body through the lens of the nervous system and movement patterns, as well as trauma and attachment theory. Instead of focusing on conversation, Sensorimotor Psychotherapy focuses on the organization of experience. Each person organizes their experiences in a unique way, involving several core organizers: body sensation, muscle movement and posture, sensory perception, emotion, and cognition. Through mindful study of this organization of experience, and experiments with movement and posture, the client can (re)find their strength and sense of security and process old pain.

> M was born hearing impaired, but this was not discovered until she was six. As a result, in her early years, she received flawed attunement and much annoyance for "not listening." It wasn't until she learned to read that she was able to begin to understand the world around her. M experiences a lot of pain and fatigue in her body (sensation), and she has a stilted posture that is not very expressive (movement and posture). With her eyes, she is active (sensory perception), and thanks to her hearing aids, she can hold a conversation well. She hardly experiences any emotions but does experience stomachache when the tension gets too high. She tries to keep a grip on this by cognitively understanding situations. Her cognition is initially not connected to her feelings.
>
> M does not feel safe to connect with others, and she wants to feel less lonely. Together with the therapist, she does a boundary exercise in which M examines what distance feels comfortable and connected. At first she tells herself that the therapist should be safe (using cognition), but her stomachache tells her otherwise. Only when she dares to take her physical tension seriously does space arise to explore and challenge her boundaries, allowing for real contact. This is new for M, and by listening to her body, with her therapist's help, she also begins to listen to her feelings. This also brings sadness about many previous experiences in which she has felt alone.

Therapeutic Principles: A Safe Base

Sensorimotor Psychotherapy draws on several fundamental principles that guide the therapeutic attitude and embodied therapy process (Sensorimotor Psychotherapy Institute,

2023; Ogden, 2021a; Kurtz, 1990). First, mindfulness is an important means of studying with attention and without judgment the core organizers that determine each person's organization of experience in the present moment. In doing so, the engaged presence of the therapist is essential to coregulate through contact and to notice the client's experience. This is called embedded relational mindfulness, because mindfulness is not taught as a meditation technique but integrated within the therapeutic relationship as the client is asked to report on the core organizers experienced in the present moment. The relationship is based on unity: client and therapist are connected, equal, and unique at the same time. In addition, body-mind-spirit holism is assumed: body, mind, soul, and culture are inseparable. The therapeutic process relies on organicity: every living being has an inner wisdom and potential for growth that, given the right circumstances, naturally unfolds. The attitude of nonviolence reflects this intelligence: Both client and therapist respect boundaries and do not force anything, but instead create the space for organicity to emerge. Finally, the principle of relational alchemy assumes that each combination of therapist and client produces a unique relationship from which both can benefit, even when challenges and enactments occur. The totality of these principles provides a philosophical and spiritual ground for clinical practice, a foundation for studying embodied experience and healing traumatic and developmental wounds through safe connection.

Processing Trauma Through the Body

When an overwhelming experience is insufficiently processed, the body still has the survival reactions to the traumatic moment ready. It will thus react to traumatic reminders—triggers associated with the trauma—as if something threatening is about to happen again. The instinctive defensive responses of fight, flight, cry for help, freeze, shutdown, feigned death, or a combination of these reactions are then activated. This becomes apparent in muscle tension and movement impulses as well as dysregulated arousal.

Sensorimotor Psychotherapy assumes a phase-based trauma treatment approach in which the client must first cultivate sufficient stability to process trauma and then integrate the new experiences into their own life. Associated with these phases are various body-oriented techniques. Initially, in the first phase of treatment, the focus is on resources that help autonomic arousal to return to and then stay within the "window of tolerance" (Buckley et al., 2018). Since trauma-related dysregulation is physiological, the body is a natural and tangible starting point for strengthening the here-and-now sense of regulation and safety, for example, through breathing exercises, body awareness, alignment, containment, grounding, centering, the sense of one's own boundaries and the power to defend them, (self-)touch, support, rhythmic (bilateral) movement, sensory orientation, and walking.

> B is embarking on a journey of trauma treatment with a focus on feeling safe and regulated. To do so, she has started to become more aware of her body so she can explore what helps her feel safe enough. Together with her therapist, she builds a repertoire of resources: her feet firmly on a footrest so she is

grounded, a scarf she can pull tightly around her shoulders for containment, massaging her arm when she tends to dissociate, eye contact with the therapist for coregulation, holding a teddy bear as support, and getting up to walk when she feels stuck or trapped.

Survival reactions are designed to get us through drastic events. If they are successful and the experience can be integrated sufficiently on physical, emotional, and cognitive levels, posttraumatic stress disorder (PTSD) will generally not develop (Kearney & Lanius, 2022). However, if natural active defenses of cry for help, fight, or flight cannot be used, for example, due to overwhelm, violence, power differential, or being too young, the body will use hypoarousal, associated with shutdown and the feigned death response. Thereby, the natural feeling of being allowed to defend oneself, run away, or seek help becomes blocked. In general, because these defenses are instinctive, the reflex to active defense still exists, often in the form of tension or impulses in the body when the trauma is remembered or triggered. When processing traumatic memory, the second phase of treatment, Sensorimotor Psychotherapy uses the tension and impulses that emerge naturally to support reinstating active defenses. The client regains this ability instead of only drawing on the default defense of feigned death and hypoarousal that was used in the past.

> R was physically abused by his mother as a child. He reports that he did not try to protect himself from the switch because that would only make her angry. In his current life, R is compliant in his relationships and does not set boundaries. In Phase 2 treatment, R speaks about his mother's violence. His arms tense, and his fingers lift. His therapist notices the tension and says, "Just sense that tension in your arms. Is there an impulse, a movement they want to make?" R says he feels the impulse to push, and the therapist holds a pillow so R can follow the impulse by pushing against it. R feels his power, and the movement feels "really good."
>
> Through following the impulse of his body to push away, an action he could not do during the original abuse, an active defense is reinstated, replacing the immobility defense of freeze. Afterward, R slowly begins to be more able to protect himself and set boundaries.

In the second phase, processing memory, the physiological reactions to the trauma story are also addressed, following step by step the activation of the autonomic nervous system using the technique of sensorimotor sequencing. With this intervention, movement impulses and inner sensations such as trembling, tingling, and pain are not suppressed or gotten rid of. Their natural impulses are sensed in the body and encouraged to develop somatically until they are sequenced or processed.

> P has suffered from pelvic instability since the birth of her son. For her, there is a clear connection to sexual abuse as a teenager that prevents her from being in touch with her body sufficiently, which perpetuates the symptoms. At one

point in the processing phase, when she talks about the trauma, she feels a vibration in her upper body. The therapist invites her to feel and follow this, noticing what happens next in her body as she notices the sensation. P reports that the vibration slowly descends into her body, through her arms and torso to her legs and feet. When it has settled down, P notices that she can perceive her body as a whole from a greatly altered consciousness, and a connection to her body. From then on, she can respond with attention to her body's signals and thus recover from her pelvic pain.

Through sensorimotor sequencing, P is able to develop a trust in her body so that she can use the renewed contact with her body to recover, and she has started to use her body's signals again in her daily life. Sensorimotor Psychotherapy values such integration of new experiences and closes each session with ample attention to what is new, at the level of all core organizers: sensation, movement, sensory perception, emotion, and cognition. Somatic homework is often created: the body lends itself well to concrete practice of new skills through posture and movement and noticing sensation in everyday life. For instance, P rotated her hips regularly, reminding her of the safe firmness of her pelvis.

Processing Attachment-Related Problems

All family situations have their own dynamics in which children must adapt to maintain the best possible connection with their caretakers (Ogden, 2021b). At the physical level, the child will develop patterns involving the fundamental movements. Yield, push, reach, grasp, and pull (Cohen, 1993; Frank & La Barre, 2010; Ogden, 2018, 2021a) all develop in ways appropriate to one's position in the family system. The modifications of these actions to accommodate the reactions of others result in a unique, personal movement repertoire. In the case of an anxious-preoccupied attachment style, for instance, the child may easily reach out, grasp, and pull but have trouble with pushing. With an avoidant attachment style, pushing away may become more developed than reaching out or yielding. This has implications for nonverbal communication and thus for the quality of relationships, even in adulthood.

In therapy, all of these movements can be used as physical experiments with relational gestures. They can thus form the basis for exploring and learning new relational skills.

A group of therapists experiments with various relational gestures: Everyone shows their own way of reaching out to offer help. Then group members mindfully try out another person's gesture. M explores how it feels to extend her arm further forward while extending through her spine. She notices that this feels wrong for her because it makes her afraid of "being too much."

Fixed patterns also develop at the emotional level for the purpose of optimal connection. The emotions that are not met by an adult remain unconscious and are covered up with adaptive strategies: bodily and emotional patterns, and limiting beliefs that help avoid feeling the attachment wound (Ogden & Fisher, 2015). For instance, vulnerability can be concealed by inflating the upper body, needs can be suppressed by holding back the front of the body, and anger can seemingly disappear through excessive flexibility in the body. Such adaptive patterns also have implications for internal working models for the future: implicit predictions and expectations of ourselves, others, and the world around us are reflected in autonomic arousal, movement, and posture of the body (Sensorimotor Psychotherapy Institute, 2023; Ogden & Fisher, 2015; Ogden, 2021a).

Sensorimotor Psychotherapy uses these bodily adaptive strategies as an entry point to give space to the underlying pain. The core organizers (sensation, posture and movement, sensory perception, emotion, and cognition) serve as the basis for exploring the unique relational pattern. Then this here-and-now pattern can be connected to previous experiences that have necessitated the development of the adaptive strategy. Often this means that the client becomes aware of the adjustments they have made to adapt to their childhood relationships, and space for grief, compassion, and new relational patterns emerges. The body provides a wonderful entry point for this because it not only shows the protective strategy but often also reveals the patterns of the child that learned them. For example, the child part may be evident and can be framed in feet turning inward, pouting lips, feeling small, insecure eye gaze, or physical symptoms like abdominal pain. Such body signals of a child part can be helpful for the adult client to relate to the young experience that emerges. As adults, client and therapist can study what this child part needs and meet it, for example, by the client contacting or addressing the child part.

> J recognizes in his own way of sitting still and cautiously looking around (adaptive strategy) the feeling he had as a little boy who had to make himself invisible in an overwrought family situation. He has an image of the little boy playing quietly with his fire engine while his mother cooks and pays no attention to him. Together with the therapist, he looks at what this boy needs: to be seen and reassured. In his imagination, J sits next to the withdrawn child to let him know that he is seen and is no longer alone. There is some relaxation and movement in J's stomach, and gently the sadness of the boy that he was makes itself felt.

Scientific Foundation

Sensorimotor Psychotherapy draws on broad scientific knowledge such as attachment research (e.g., Bowlby, 1988; Main & Hesse, 1990), affective neuroscience (Schore, 2003), interpersonal neurobiology (Kearney & Lanius, 2022; Maté & Maté, 2022), mindfulness (e.g., Ardi et al., 2021; Farb et al., 2015), Polyvagal Theory (Porges, 2018), and body-oriented interventions (van de Kamp et al., 2019).

Although the method uses well-defined procedures and techniques, it is difficult to standardize it for research purposes since each client's process has a unique course. Therefore, single case studies and experience sampling methods would be the most appropriate research methods. These have not been executed so far. However, three studies have been published in which Sensorimotor Psychotherapy was offered in groups for clients with complex PTSD, with measurements pre- and posttreatment. In the first project, with 10 clients with complex PTSD, body awareness, dissociation, and self-soothing skills were found to improve (Langmuir et al., 2012). The second study was done with 16 clients with complex PTSD and yielded positive change in PTSD symptoms, depression, overall health, and work and social functioning (Gene-Cos et al., 2016). The third study was conducted with a waiting list control group and found improvement in body awareness, anxiety, and self-soothing skills in a group of fourteen clients with complex PTSD (Classen et al., 2020). Several new studies are currently being designed and conducted (Sensorimotor Psychotherapy Institute, 2023).

Clinical Case Example

To provide more insight into this treatment method, we present the case of S, who suffered from a disconnection from her emotions and a variety of somatic symptoms, suicidality, and more. S describes part of her complex story and the impact Sensorimotor Psychotherapy has had for her.

> I grew up in an Orthodox Christian family, and was raised with well-defined ideas about how God, my parents, the church, and the world are and should be; and how I fit in and how I was supposed to relate to it. This was mostly a solitary task: obeying God, parents, and church leaders unconditionally was the message. How I succeeded was secondary. Early on, I began to swallow emotions. Having feelings or anything that possibly resulted in a dissenting voice carried too many risks.

From her teenage years, S developed serious physical and psychological complaints, and the circumstances led to traumatic experiences.

> At age 12, psoriasis outbreaks, depressive episodes, and unstoppable crying fits started, and at age 14 I sometimes thought about wanting to die. I went out into the world, and began to rebel at home against my parents' strict restraints on the one hand, and their neglectful attitude toward their five children on the other. I fell into the hands of grown men who thought I was "so grown up already" and promised me the world. And in the meantime they sexually abused me. But I could only think in terms of my responsibility and where I fell short.

S learned how to suppress emotions and work hard, which were both adaptive strategies to cope with her circumstances.

> When I was 17, I brought myself back to a "responsible" attitude toward my parents and made a decision to approach everything intellectually from now on; emotions were way too troublesome and got me nowhere. I lived through

my young adult life in the same survival mode. The hard-work mode had always been my salvation and incantation from condemnation. That might still give me an opportunity to appeal to grace from God.

In the end, her body set the boundary to prevent her from overworking, and she started looking for help.

> After a failed marriage, I completely collapsed. That was the beginning of a reversal. Time after time, my body shut down, with extreme fatigue and exhaustion. This was accompanied by much panic, fighting, and despair.
> I ended up seeing a psychologist with whom I was able to slowly begin to connect with the inner me. From there on it has been a long journey, through admission to a clinic for personality disorders, an intensive trauma treatment program, and most recently a few years of Sensorimotor Psychotherapy.

Sensorimotor Psychotherapy was an important therapeutic next step for S after intensive top-down treatment trajectories.

> Especially in that last therapy trajectory, it started to sink in. The change in the clinic had mainly been to take care of myself, to take care of the girl in me, and to "mother." This sensorimotor sequel dealt with how I could feel and make space for myself, how I could do justice to what happened to me, and that I can choose at any time what I want. And I may protect myself, instead of serving others above all else and digest all the conflicts within myself, "having to let other people's sin pass through me." I learned that my body had not betrayed me but is my ally.
> What especially gave liberation was the release of deeply hidden emotions, which emerged when we went to the body: what showed itself, made itself felt, the wisdom that revealed itself, and the value that was given to all those stored signals. Precisely by going beyond cognition, which had become my highest coping mechanism, space was created for uncensored expression, which sometimes totally blew me over in intensity and accuracy of what I experienced as a young child.

S told about two therapy sessions that have been very meaningful to her.

The Wooden Man

As a start, S needed to create her own safe space physically. In Sensorimotor Pychotherapy, the therapist may guide the client to use pillows, ropes, or other objects to define "their space." A physical action such as this can induce a bodily felt sense of personal space in a way that verbal interventions do not.

We worked with a rope, which I had placed very broadly around me, as delin-
eating my space. I immediately experienced more breathing space. We dwelled
on that feeling; I described it as a break, to be ready again later. Recharging in
order to quickly meet the expectations again.

The therapist stated, "You can take a break every day." In my mind immediately the conviction came: "No, that is not possible." Also there was the wish
and despair: "How can I keep this around me, this space, breathing space,
pause, enlightenment, when I return to the outside world?" And even more:
"How do I keep this breathing space within me, between all the driving and
oppressive thoughts and beliefs?"

The experiments done in Sensorimotor Psychotherapy can be physical, as in using a
rope to define space, or verbal, as in the statement, "You can take a break." Because
experiments require the client's mindful awareness, their inner landscape is revealed. S
noticed an internal voice when she reported, "No, that is not possible." And the experiment also made clear her wish and despair, that she could no longer bear the constant
psychological and physical pressure. The simple verbal experiment also elicited a memory: a clear physical sense and an image from the time when she had to develop her
adaptive strategy.

Where I was actually always busy conjuring up disturbing issues and feelings,
now came to mind: "STOP SHUT UP!" A taunting exclamation against that ever-
lasting condemnation and heavy laws, which came up as an image of a huge
man made of wooden beams, pressing down on me from above and behind.

The therapist mentioned that such a statement is appropriate for the age
of that oppressed girl. That evoked an image that made me emotional: a little
powerless girl, weeping and defensive, who has got way too much to bear.

The therapist helped S to feel her anger and indignation by using the intervention of
"taking over" (Kurtz, 1990), in which the therapist does something for the client that
the client is doing for themselves. Taking over supports rather than challenges management or protective behaviors, which allows whatever is underneath such behaviors
to emerge. In this case, the therapist took over the pressure of the wooden man on S's
shoulder. She could then follow the bodily impulse of pushing that had never been
available before.

We continued. The therapist asked me what my body wanted to do; where it
wanted to move. I found it difficult to get to that. She stood behind me, and
in alignment with me she placed a cushion with gentle pressure on my shoulders, to emphasize the feeling of that burden and pressure from that wooden
man. Then I could name what my body was indicating: to stand up and throw
off the burden. But I couldn't do it yet, felt hugely inhibited and blocked. The

> therapist gave me time to move toward it, encouraging me to respond to my
> body's impulse.
>
>   Finally, daring to make the move, I stood up and threw the burden off
> my shoulders.
>
>   But I also immediately froze, and was overcome by a fear that tended to
> terror. Completely panicked, I didn't dare face what I had just done: to rebel
> and separate myself from the Law, the Judgment, the weighty conditions of
> existence.

It makes sense that S would feel frightened by the action of throwing off the burden, but
at the same time, S could experience that there were new possibilities in her current life,
even if she still had to get used to them. She could eventually recognize that this action
was okay and accepted currently, whereas it had not been in the past.

> We talked about it afterward; that I no longer live in that system, even though
> some of it still lives in me. It is hard to believe because in my consciousness
> those worlds intertwine. It takes time and is a tough mission. It makes sense
> that it confuses the little girl in me. And therefore it's important that I do it
> for the little girl, in order to protect her. It has really been enough; she's been
> through too much.

We can see that as new actions and new possibilities were evoked, S herself began to feel
compassion for and an impulse to help the internal child part.

Trampled in the Mud

At a later point in her therapy, S had a clear picture of painful emotions hiding in her
body. To be able to work with this, sufficient relational safety must first be created. In
Sensorimotor Psychotherapy, this is accomplished physically, not only verbally.

> The session was about a lid on deeply stored emotions, and how I had the
> sense of carrying them on my back, "under my shield." With the therapist, I
> zoomed in on sensing what's there and explored what I needed from her in
> order to work with these feelings: she sat diagonally behind me, as my backup
> circle. The dwelling on what was stirring within me made me aware of move-
> ment, as if there were mudslides lifting up within me. The feeling this evoked
> demanded action. That also immediately caused concern, because, "What
> will happen next?"

With her therapist as her "backup circle," S was able to challenge long-standing patterns of
suppressing her emotions. With her therapist's help, S experimented with a way to express
the feelings that had accumulated in her, but, as is common when patterns are challenged,

the new action elicited responses that had their origin in past traumatic experiences, in this case fear and shutting down.

> The therapist gave me beanbags, encouraging me to throw them against the wall at my own pace and in my own way. I put a bag on my stomach, to connect with what was stirring there, and then threw it away. A kind of rush arose in me, of everything that came up: fear, sense of danger, protest. Then I felt myself shutting down, and I became blank and flat. Together with the therapist, we looked back step by step: What did I feel, what did I do, what did that bring about?
>
> I felt that something came *out* of me and that I was speaking (instead of absorbing everything); I threw something back: mud, junk, pain. The therapist named it as giving back to whom it belongs. That touched me deeply; the realization that it is not mine, that I can put it away and lose it and clean it up; all the mess and filth that does not belong to me.

S began to experience the release that comes with giving these emotions back. She found a fitting way to express the emotions that had always been suppressed.

> Then I threw more beanbags. This evoked a lot of vehemence in me. At one point I saw and felt, like a flash, that I was lying on my stomach in the mud, underfoot. I could barely lift my head. The feeling of not being able to get up, of having to give up against that crushing weight of all the demands and laws and having to do well. And the burden of being subject to the needs of others (my parents). That broke me for a moment but also gave image and recognition of how I felt and what I experienced.
>
> I figured out how to throw the bags in a way that suited me in the moment: indignant and pained, but also scared. Throwing softer actually felt more appropriate than tossing as hard as possible. Then the emotions started to flow more.

Following her own organicity, her own internal wisdom, S was able to adjust her action so that it was right for her. The new physical and emotional experience transformed something essential in S, increasing her self-confidence from within her body.

> This image is still sharp in my experience. It unleashed a lot: a very primal fear reflex about rebelling, and a confusing mix of courage, anger, relief, fear, frustration, sadness, pain, and all the internal reactions to it. I felt more *new* space inside, once I was calm again.
>
> For me, the body-centered approach of Sensorimotor Psychotherapy has been very helpful. So much that was stored inside me could not be reached with just a cognitive perspective. It has strengthened my trust in my body and its wisdom, and helped me feel more in unity with myself.

Conclusion

Sensorimotor Psychotherapy is a methodical and scientifically sound psychotherapy method that addresses the experiences of the body for stabilization, processing, and integration in the here and now. For both traumatic events and attachment-related problems, it has specific interventions. And especially for complex problems, where attachment and trauma go hand in hand, Sensorimotor Psychotherapy proves to address the experienced reality well through the body. Based on an embodied therapeutic relationship, the body can safely tell its story, old patterns can be revealed, and new ways of being can be explored.

S gave permission to publish her testimony of her therapeutic process. The authors would like to express their gratitude for the personal story she shared for the purpose of this chapter.

21

Being Together to Face the Trauma

Intercorporeality as the Core of Treatment

Maurizio Stupiggia

The process of expanding a patient's self-experience is not based on the discovery of absolute truths, but on the reality of two human beings co-creating what they do together with an ever-increasing capacity for spontaneity.
—P. BROMBERG, *THE SHADOW OF THE TSUNAMI*

The Window of Engagement

The theory is clear by now: When therapists are fully present in the moment and attuned to their clients, their receptive and reassuring presence sends a neurophysiological message that clients are being heard and understood, which elicits a feeling of safety (Geller & Porges, 2014). According to Polyvagal Theory, when clients sense that they are being heard and understood by others, they not only feel aligned with that person, but it is likely that the nervous system establishes a neuroception of being safe.

Clinical practice, on the contrary, is not always that clear and straightforward, especially in cases of traumatic stress or deep and chronic distress that produce severe pathologies. In my experience as a therapist, people who are victims of trauma, for example, are only rarely responsive to the calm and secure presence of a therapist. They are used to enacting a whole series of sensory-motor-affective strategies that are related to the activation of past neurophysiological systems of defensive response, not allowing other more recent systems to come into play; thus, the therapeutic relationship itself is under threat.

The fundamental assumption of Polyvagal Theory that feeling of safe forms the foundation of therapy must be viewed within the countless clinical situations where there is evidence that the level of the complexity of the relationship forces the therapeutic pair to make different and creative adaptations to remain within what we call the window of engagement (Spinazzola, in Hopper et al., 2019).

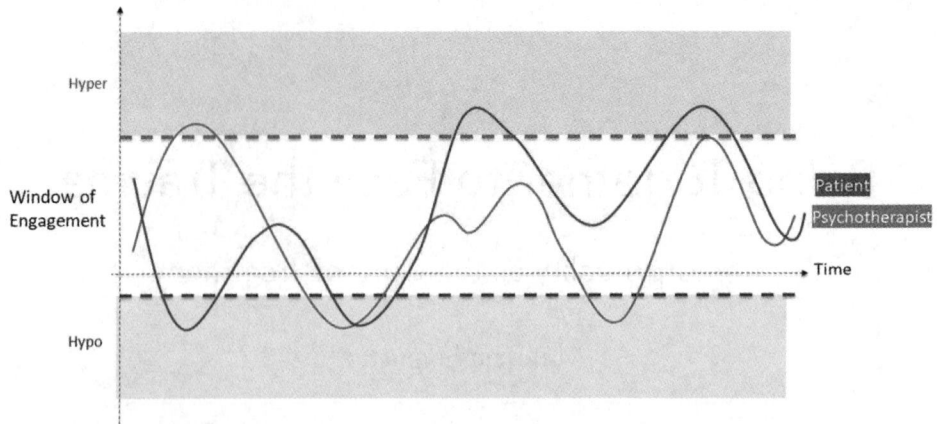

FIGURE 21.1 Window of engagement represents the ability of therapist and client to remain connected and attuned during the therapeutic interaction, even in moments of relational difficulty that may lead to states of hypo- and hyperarousal.

> By this term, we mean the range of arousal states within which there can be an authentic and present-moment connection between the therapist and the client. It is based on the windows of tolerance of the therapist and the client, and the match between the two. In particular, the window of engagement is dependent on the therapist's ability to meet the client where he or she is, and to sit with the client in his or her dark places (including hypo- and hyperaroused states), without becoming triggered himself. (Hopper et al., 2019, p. 135; Figure 21.1)

Put another way, with this concept, which is more qualitative than quantitative, we define those conditions that allow both participants to remain in a constructive and connected relationship. Furthermore, each individual fluctuation finds its balance in the adaptive ability of the other to keep the communication and the relationship constantly present in the moment. Thus, any disturbance or rupture will be repaired by reciprocal understanding and action.

It is a concept reminiscent, in another area, of Edward Tronick's dyadic system of development, regarding the early stages of the mother-child relationship. It proceeds similarly, by reciprocal movements of connection as well as those of differentiation, in a sort of relational pulsation that can be maintained through the typical match-mismatch-repair phases.

The treatment of people with past experiences of complex trauma has precisely to do with these relational aspects because it is within the old relationship that the conditions of that traumatic experience are constituted. This is always characterized by at least one of the two polarities, invasion and deprivation, or often by both, as in the case of sexual abuse. In fact, we have at least two types of traumatic experiences: overpowering and neglect. A dramatic lack in either produces a relational breakdown, as a result of the triggering of old and embedded defensive reactions that spill over and outside the window of engagement. I believe that one of the parameters that allow us to evaluate therapeutic work with trauma patients is the solidity and depth of the relationship, the sense of progressive trust that is built over time, even though mishaps are inevitable for people with highly sensitive and unstable structures.

Let us try to understand what can happen with such kinds of patients.

The Breakdown

The relational breakdown is always just around the corner, and sometimes it happens suddenly and for seemingly inconsequential causes. For example, I remember a client who, after a session that had seemed normal and even productive, returned to the following session in a somber mood and quite closed up. After a few attempts on my part to create a communicative opening, the client revealed to me, with much embarrassment, that she had come out of our previous meeting very upset because of something I had done. "Last time, you did something that disturbed me. . . . I was disgusted! You often touched yourself under your shirt . . . throughout the whole session. . . . I couldn't wait to leave."

I was dumbfounded, not understanding at all what she was referring to, and it seemed to me like a delusion on her part. I then realized that the intense summer heat, the air-conditioning failing, and my heavy shirt had forced me, now and then during the meeting, to open my collar, undo a button, and occasionally try to wipe off the sweat by reaching inside over my shoulder with my hand. I had actually touched myself under my shirt. Of course, with great delicacy, I started to point out to her the reason for my behavior (the great heat, the air conditioning not working, etc.), but I almost felt as if I were making the situation worse, as if I were trying to confuse her and manipulating her perceptions: "But, I don't know, I don't know if I should trust your explanations. . . . I was kind of grossed out last time," she replied, "and it stayed with me for a few days. . . . Then I didn't think about it anymore."

This situation can occur frequently with clients who had traumatic experiences of abuse, since manipulation and deception were at the basis of their traumas. It is not always possible to foresee these incidents, because, as in this case, they happen at an implicit level of communication, in that realm of gestural interaction that activates a nonconscious exchange. This is what Gallese (2017) called *intercorporeality*. We are within the sphere of body-to-body communication, where interactive exchanges occur very quickly, before and outside of consciousness, activating somatic memories that can deactivate cortical systems of control and modulation, and that instead turn on primary alarm reactions.

This confirms the fact that sometimes explanations and verbal interventions are not enough, or that they even complicate things. It is therefore necessary to work on the corporeal exchanges because it is precisely at that level that the relational breakdown occurred.

I did indeed stop arguing my interpretation of the facts and changed my approach. I said, "I understand that something may have bothered and upset you. . . . Indeed, I noticed that as you were telling me about the last time, you had a certain facial expression of annoyance, almost repulsion, and you moved your head a little to one side, then backward. . . . I then also saw that at the same time you made a brief hand gesture, in a forward motion, as if moving something . . . or someone away. Did you notice too?" She replied, "I don't know. I didn't pay attention to it . . . but it can be so, in fact, since I also feel it now, as we talk about it, a strange sense of discomfort." I then asked her, "Can I show you the gestures I noticed, to better understand together what was happening inside of you?" She nodded her head in consent, though somewhat hesitantly. I then began to make that retro-lateral movement with my head and, at the same time, a barely noticeable expression of annoyance with my mouth and eyes (I had to be very gentle, and careful about her reactions, because I realized how risky it was to show her such expressions). She suddenly reacted in a motion of spontaneous imitation, with similar expressions and gestures. Thus, we found ourselves, instantly, to be two mirroring parts of the same sculpture. We can speculate that this is point zero of a process of reconstruction (recoding) of the somatic memory system (Grassmann & Pohlenz-Michel, 2008).

In fact, after a few moments of mutual eye contact, I asked her to start amplifying those two gestures of the head and the hand to create a real movement with her hand, as if pushing something away, and to also intensify the energy she was levying at each repetition of the gestures.

This is where and how new work can begin, thus starting the transformation of the process, because at that point I reacted precisely according to her movements and, in a kind of mimicking dance, I moved away each time her hand pushed forward, as if to represent the effectiveness of her action. With my glance, moreover, I tried to show astonishment and a certain awe at her determination, as in a theater scene, where one person is subjected to the will of the other. This causes a sort of reversal of the power relationship, which can repair what the trauma had dramatically produced: the victim's almost total loss of power before the tormentor, or the overpowering force. This is precisely what I wanted to create and enact together with her, and which I hoped might constitute a brick toward building a different experience of her memory. The scene lasted a minute, but it seemed much longer, and at the end she had a new expression on her face, followed by a deep sigh of relief. Even her gaze had changed. It was solid and direct, seemingly admonishing and imposing a necessary distance. It was a look that controlled the other and kept him at bay.

Mirror Neurons

This way of working with mirroring is closely associated with the relational dimension, which becomes the clinical application of the mirror neurons theory (Gallese, 2005), in the interpersonal paradigm from a neurobiological basis.

Dance therapist Marian Chace first used the term *mirroring* to describe her clinical work (Chaiklin & Schmais, 1986). She developed her methods in the 1940s and 1950s, influencing dance and movement psychotherapy. Chace distinguished mirroring from simple imitation, which is a duplication of the external form of movement without the emotional content. She had the clear insight that by responding to movements in similar forms, we build a strong and deep relationship that can dispel feelings of estrangement or separation.

Regarding the session described above, mirroring was specifically applied to body psychotherapy, not only by the partial or almost total mirroring of the client's movements, but also with the additional participation of the therapist's involvement in the process. Such a session is an example of what we can call *following mirroring*, a concept that I am presently defining as a technique to be applied in this sort of work. When the client enters an impasse, the therapist, on the one hand, tries to tune into her microgestures, and at the same time produces a series of small corresponding or complementary movements that suggest someone is trying to get away from danger or from a hostile person. Viewed from the outside, this looks like an interactive dance, in which one person (the therapist) follows and adapts to the client's movement, thus producing an obvious effect for the client to be the one to lead the dance and manage the process.

It is important that the client be aware that she is the one leading this interactive dance, and, above all, it's crucial that she realizes that she has a noticeable effect on the therapist. In cases of traumatized patients, we work by focusing on reversing the client's past traumatic situation, when the person had to submit to someone else's oppressive power (or event), which was overwhelming for the individual. In this form of mirroring, the therapist intervenes and acts as a subordinate, partly mirroring the client's movements and partly adapting the movements in a complementary or subordinate manner. This variant in the technique allows the client to recover the power lost during the traumatic event, and to guide and take control of the process. For these reasons, I have decided to call this particular process, from the therapist's point of view, following mirroring.

Memories and Relationship

This brief clinical example shows one aspect of the outcome of traumatic experience, and a way of transforming its internalization in the archives of somatic memory.

What is interesting to note from this example, and many other similar ones, is the overall transformation of memory through different body interactions from the past, which reorganized the experience by adding new skills and possibilities to broaden the view of the past and shed new light on the future.

My client said, "Now I feel stronger, more solid, and you scare me less. . . . I realize that maybe I was overreacting the last time, but I'm also aware that I am sensitive to certain things. . . . Maybe I didn't tell you everything I have gone through. Now I see it's important to set myself free from so many things that have happened to me."

We summarize the considerations made above. The patient has begun to reprocess the memory of the past and propose a new way forward. In regard to the past, in fact, she seems to have come out of a feeling of total fear and helplessness that prevented her from sharing her story. About the future, she has already proposed that she wants to be free from so many accumulated issues.

I also want to point out that this example describes an aspect of clinical work that shifts the focus from the single person to the complexity of the relationship with the therapist. It enters into a dual paradigm that is not concentrated only on the functioning of the sole individual but looks at the therapeutic process as a development of a macrosystem, a dual organism, in which we cannot look at and interact with only one of the two participants.

We can imagine the therapeutic process (but also the experiences of everyday life) as a dynamic sculpture, always in transformation, and not separable or disassembled, which risks losing the meaning and effectiveness of the process itself if viewed otherwise.

Indeed, it is precisely traumatic experiences that profoundly alter a person's relationship with the self, with others, and with the environment. Repairing the damage due to trauma, requires acting on those sense-affective-motor patterns deformed or frozen by past experiences. One of the most difficult problems to treat is the loss of trust in oneself and the others and the environment (consequently experiencing fear and helplessness).

Attention to the body is necessary because the breakdown of trust results in the deformation of the capacity of interactive management from the bottom up and may also be due to the damage of certain neural functions, such as the mirror neurons (Stupiggia, 2013), which are necessary for the construction of empathy and mutual understanding. In short, we can say that trauma modifies and damages the dimension of intercorporeality.

Neuroception of the Therapist's Posture

I want to recall, in this regard, a bizarre situation that happened to me several years ago in a therapy session. One day, a client who had been coming to me for several months, but with whom I could not build a trusting relationship and work effectively, unexpectedly asked me to change my position from the usual face-to-face setting. He asked me to turn around and show my back to him, so that he could see me, but I was unable to see him, and I was facing the window. At first I did not agree, and I tried to understand together with him the significance of that request. The only thing that he managed to say was that he wanted to avoid feeling embarrassed, and that seeing my face was blocking him, and he would not consider having me behind him because this scared him.

Against my beliefs, but given my curiosity, I decided to do what he asked, and in the end the result rewarded our daring. The patient began to speak quite differently right away, without too many turns of phrase or confusing metaphors. After a while, he was able to recount what probably constituted the deepest core of his troubled condition.

He lived with his family in a small town in the mountains, and at the age of 14 he was sent to the city to attend high school. He was put in a boarding school for the full duration of his school years. He experienced profound loneliness, because he returned home only twice a year and was very rarely visited by family members. But what was truly traumatic began to happen after some time. He became the target of harassment from the older boys, to the point of being subjected to actual acts of molestation and abuse.

The therapy took off and was successful in producing good results, as it gradually rebuilt his self-esteem, and he regained trust in the world and in others.

Sometime later, he revealed to me that the session in which I had to turn my back to him had been essential. He was grateful to me for having gone along with a strange request, and he had realized that it had been perhaps the only way for him to be able to open up.

That client had asked me to look ahead rather than inside of him, and this had allowed him to get in touch with his own "room of fears" and then to come back up again toward a greater sense of himself that was closest to his own authenticity.

Again, we see here how the therapist needs to be able to change the way he acts with the client, and to change the game he plays, in a sense, but together with the client. Usually in analytic and explorative psychotherapy, there is an implicit agreement that the client is the subject to be examined, and the therapist is the one who interrogates, yet without actual questioning: the focus of this therapy is the inner life of the client.

The perspective in our case changed. The therapist cannot look inside the client when the deep core of his inner self is broken, and so the focus must shift and become a sort of external horizon. Therapy takes on the form of a process of initiation between the two, rather than that of a single inner journey, but with all its trials and obstacles, riddles, and traps.

When there is danger of death or psychic dissolution, our glance must become oblique, indirect, not inquisitive but comforting.

In the case of the abovementioned client and in other similar cases, what helped me was the memory of an old Andrei Tarkovsky film, *Stalker*. The protagonists of the story venture into the Zone, a desolate and rural area in ruins, where normal physical laws have been disrupted by unknown causes. It is said to contain a room in which the most intimate and secret wishes can come true.

The peculiarity of this place of desires is the fact that its extraordinary power of realization is directly connected to its condition of utter destruction. It is not, as in other tales, a kind of magical coffer as well as a dangerous one that can lead to death if the hero does not handle it carefully or follow the instructions correctly. It is the destruction itself that becomes an uncanny power in its pure state. The Zone is a metaphor for those areas that run across both boundaries of desire: that of folly or that of its marvelous potential. It is fundamentally a powerful metaphor for the most intimate core of traumatized individuals, who are desperately searching while at the same time avoiding the truth, fearing a self-destructive consequence.

Tarkovsky's *Stalker* is also a metaphor for the therapeutic attitude toward the client who is at risk of a psychic collapse. The therapist does not interrogate but points to the prospect of sense, or the horizon of meaning. He receives the glance of the client rather than forcing it. He does not challenge. He does not push; he stands by.

This is a clear example of the reciprocal adaptation between the therapist and the client, necessary to avoid a snag or imbalance in the process, to remain within the window of engagement. The therapist has sufficient clinical flexibility to allow a radical change of setting, enabling a new and more productive mutual coordination. It is also an example of how a different body-to-body interaction can change the individual's functioning and deactivate archaic neural systems, thus allowing other functions to be activated.

Niki: In and Out of the Window of Engagement

Let us move on to explore other more difficult clinical situations where this concept is at work. Niki is a 50-year-old man, good-looking, intelligent, and highly educated, with a successful professional life. He is married and has a relatively quiet life. He comes with a lifelong issue: He is bored. There is nothing he is passionate about, and despite all his efforts to spruce up his life, he eventually falls back into a sense of flatness, of resignation, and has little desire to live. Recently, this situation has become untenable.

In the first two sessions, he shares with me the events of his life as a boy. He had trouble fitting in at school and with peer groups. He experienced a sense of estrangement and felt he was radically different. Most important were the moments of anguish and humiliation due to constant teasing and ridiculing on the part of some of his peers. It was a situation close to bullying, but one that he tended to minimize, without seeing too many consequences in his adult life.

During the early period of therapy, my hypothesis was that Niki experienced for a long time a sense of fear and humiliation that unsettled him and forced him to retreat, lowering his level of vitality, and so became as if frozen. From this chronic reaction came his boredom, his lack of emotions, and his exile from vital impulses and desires.

When I shared this idea of mine with him, he nodded, but without much enthusiasm: "Yes, it could be. . . . There were guys who were all over me . . . but that was a long time ago, and then you saw what happened to them . . . junkies, losers. . . . I felt that I was very different from them, and I was right."

Indeed, Niki was right, he had managed to stay on his feet, to build a normal life for himself, but he had lost his energy. He had managed not to succumb to the constant "torture" of his peers, but he had paid a heavy price: "I feel good about my job. I have an important position in my company, but if I have to be honest . . . I'm not interested or passionate about it. . . . Many people envy me, but I don't enjoy it. . . . I know I'm privileged, but I am not happy. . . . I feel that I'm outside of life itself. I'm not interested in the company of others. I don't need the things that everyone else wants and seeks."

After this confession, I realized that explaining and sharing my hypothesis had not resulted in much. In the following sessions, this became clearer: Niki was even more disconsolate than before, and we were both becoming discouraged, slipping into a sea of apathy, without a sense of new horizons ahead.

We can say that our window of engagement was shrinking, and I distinctly felt that our connection was wearing thin, and that probably, if this continued, Niki would drop out of therapy.

What happened at the eighth session seemed even worse. He came into the office totally withdrawn, resigned, without energy, and with a look of despair. "Nothing changes," he began. "I thought therapy might do some good, but nothing happens. . . . Indeed, the more I go on, the more I lose confidence. . . . I don't see anything good coming out of this."

He was totally discouraged, as if he had fallen into a deep hole. He repeated the same things he used to say at the beginning of therapy, but this time he showed a more distressed tone and was hopelessly disappointed in the work done so far. I, too, was suddenly dismayed and sank low again. I had a sense of helplessness and guilt with respect to my inability to help him in his need. We were stuck and without direction.

A sense of worthlessness pervaded us, and we were close to a breakup. This sense activated in both of us a dorsal-vagal reaction of immobilization and fear. Niki was frightened

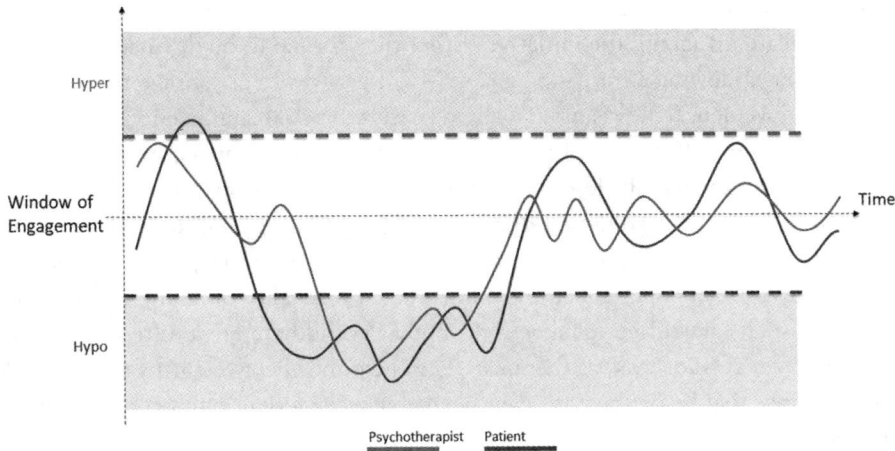

FIGURE 21.2 A phase of difficulty in the therapeutic relationship: both fall into a prolonged state of hypoarousal that keeps them out of their window of tolerance.

of never being able to have a full life again. I was concerned about my own impotence, connected to far more important experiences from my own past. Unlike the impasse described earlier, the situation now was more serious: this helplessness, and seemingly no solutions ahead, left us without a will to do something and react. On the contrary, the feeling that was spreading in me was one of mental dullness and muscular heaviness. In retrospect, I can say that at that moment I could understand very well what Niki had always expressed.

The time of this session seemed to run very slowly. Niki gradually closed up more and more, until he stopped in a sideways position in his chair, looking as if he were lost in a void or fixated at an imaginary point. I began to worry because I thought, "I am losing him."

In fact, the state of hypoarousal into which we had both fallen was pulling us out of our window of engagement, and our connection was at risk (Figure 21.2).

As I had done previously, I relied on my body as a last resort. As I looked at our stillness, I got an impulse to reach out to him with my hand, in a kind of attempt to rescue a person who is in danger of drowning. I said, "You always told me that there was nothing that attracts you, that draws you into this life. Try to take my hand. . . . Let me take your hand." Saying this, I extended my hand slowly and clearly toward him.

In retrospect, I ask myself whether I extended that hand for me, to be rescued and saved, or for him, to try to give him an anchor to life; and I answer myself that I did it for both reasons, in a kind of nonverbal enactment (Bromberg, 2011), where the therapist acts out his vulnerability as a bridge for the reconstruction of the relationship with the patient.

Niki looked at me, surprised, but at the same time his eyes began to sparkle. He took a deep breath and moved his face slightly, as if reviving after being under anesthesia.

He approached with his hand slowly and fearfully, until he touched mine. At that point, a quivering dance of approaching and touching our fingers began, with the intent, on my part, to stimulate his taking the initiative, rather than for me to be the main actor in this encounter, thus following a mirroring again. My intent was to encourage the emergence in Niki of a movement that was organically related to his state and need.

George Downing (1996) calls this a sense-affective-motor schema, a concept derived from Piaget's theory, which describes a series of complex repertoires that each child experiences from birth, throughout development, to build meaningful interactions with the other. In personal history, each of us has been in a position to develop these schemas positively, but also has experienced the unfortunate eventuality of failing to complete or even initiate such interactive sequences. In Body Psychotherapy we often have to deal with these schemas. Our task, as therapists, is to help the client reconstruct or complete contact schemas that he or she has never been able to experience and consolidate in his or her history.

I then left space for Niki to bring out his body intentionality. This means that I could not know what would happen in the encounter of our hands. In fact, Niki weakly clung to my fingertips with his own and seemed to anchor himself without doing anything else. It is a typical clinging pattern, something very ancient, that infants do before falling asleep, or when they sense a dangerous atmosphere.

I remained in this contact without doing anything else but waiting for something to happen to him. After a few moments, I perceived a slight pulling of my fingers, and at the same time he moved his head and jaw slightly forward. He gave me the idea of someone who wanted to pull out or go toward something. At this point, I tried to enter his motor process and facilitate his attempt by very gently pulling on his fingers, with a soft rhythm of pulling and letting go that allowed me to feel what motor response he was activating.

I noticed that Niki responded very well to my tugging, clinging to my fingers with his own and following this movement with the rest of his body as well, like an infant being lifted up by his mother after sleeping. A kind of elastic band was thus formed that created a tuning of breath and glances between the two of us: an intimacy without content, except for the fact that we were both doing something bizarre, unique, and without immediate meaning.

Five long minutes passed, during which the pace changed, the intensity rose and fell, and above all, we both entered an emotional atmosphere that transformed our state of consciousness. My muscular tension eased up, and the sense of worry I had before disappeared. Niki also seemed to enter another world, a world detached from the ordinary one. His usual apathetic expression dissolved, and his face relaxed into a light smile.

While we were in this mutual movement, an idea sprang forth in my head. Niki always complained about not being "attracted" to anything in life, yet now was blissfully being "attracted" to my hand, back and forth. I did not communicate my thoughts to him, not to interrupt his state, but I promised to talk about it later.

I did not have time to think further, however, because I saw Niki's expression gradually change: His eyes darkened, his movement became more abrupt, his breathing quickened and became shallower. Niki stopped and stared into nothingness again, or perhaps into an area of his life where something was deeply troubling.

"What's going on?" I asked him, holding his hand. "I see your expression has changed." He replied, "Yes, I felt nauseous . . . disturbed, and my throat became blocked." I quickly suggested, "Squeeze my hand. Squeeze it tightly with the other too, and try to breathe deeply, together with me . . . and feel what happens."

I observed something deeply disturbing that was shaking him. It appeared in the form of fear in his eyes; indeed, I would say almost terror.

The scene had suddenly changed. Niki was frightened, clinging to my hand, and speechless. The rapidity of the transition from a state of serenity to one of terror was striking. This is often the essence of trauma, a dramatic break from a state of tranquility, then a fall into an abyss.

After a while, Niki started to speak, launching words without stopping: "I wasn't think-ing about it. I didn't think about it anymore. . . . We went through a terrible time. I was little, but I remember some things. My mother became crazy. She would spend days in bed, and then . . . she was angry in the house, obsessed . . . cleaning all the time. . . . Her brother had hanged himself. . . . I had not seen him, but it was as if I always saw him in front of me. . . . The image was printed in my head, even though I had not seen it." Niki continued to narrate, and he was shaking, stiffening, breathing heavily. I tried to hold his hands firmly, breathing along with him and nodding with my head to his stories. Niki was afraid of what he was remembering; the idea of his uncle hanging himself exploded in his head. He had gone from a soft lulling to a feeling of terror and drama. This very intense experience lasted a few minutes, an experience that involved us both emotionally. Gradu-ally, keeping myself tuned in while at the same time tempering down his intensity, Niki's emotional wave calmed down, and then it dissolved into a very slow sobbing, with waves of crying that seemed to deposit him like a castaway on a beach.

But what had happened? How was this transition of a state possible: from great calm to a dramatic hurricane, and to an emotional meltdown?

Coregulation

If we look at the process described above, we notice meanwhile that the whole interac-tion takes place in an atmosphere of gradual and constant attunement that produces a sense of safety. This allows access to a new memory, which was enclosed in a state of arousal that had never emerged before. Finally, we can point out that the ability of the therapeutic dyad to deal with very powerful and dangerous neuro-emotional states had progressively increased, thus expanding the window of engagement of the therapist-client pair.

This is a process of coregulation that starts from a dysfunctional level of interaction, where connection is at risk, and which, through the gradual construction of microinterac-tions, allows the dyad to explore and share a psychobiological synchrony that forms the basis for navigating interpersonal relationships.

If a core component of well-being is the predictable opportunity for coregulating rela-tionships, then trauma might be described as the chronic disruption of connectedness

(Porges, 2014). Trauma creates ongoing adaptive survival responses that keep the auto-nomic nervous system from finding safety in connection.

When two people co-regulate and share a state of safety, their autonomic nervous systems create the possibility for health, growth, and restoration. Within a co-regulated relationship, your quest for safety is realized and you can create a story of well-being. (Dana, 2020)

With Niki, I began a precisely relational reconnection through gradual bodily interaction, following the methodology of following mirroring, which broke the icy cold wall this man was hiding and protecting himself behind.

22

Humanual Polyvagal Smile

Our Inherent Design and Connection to Wholeness

Betsy Polatin

THE HUMANUAL POLYVAGAL SMILE IS AN EXPERIENTIAL EXPLORATION THAT INVITES AWARE-
ness, discovery, and movement.[1] Humanual is an epic journey to your expanded self, a
book and a practice for accessing one's inherent function and true nature. It is a unique
and comprehensive approach to self-knowledge and self-improvement. Begin with curiosity, by noting where you are with yourself, your thoughts, feelings, sensations, breathing,
and movement. If you detect any discomfort or uneasiness in any of these realms, you may
want to explore the Humanual Polyvagal Smile. The sequence begins with a simple smile.
As you follow the next steps, the process integrates the muscular, respiratory, fascial, and
nervous systems, with the potential to unite body, mind, emotion, and spirit. Because this
exploration is organized from the ventral vagal social-engagement connection, wholeness
and coherence emerge, and the discomfort can be shifted. I start with a description of the
practice, presenting the steps in a simple and straightforward format. I then explain the
reasons for and possible results of the process, with greater detail about each step. Note
that not everyone will have the same experience as the one I am describing. As we know
from much research, the effects of trauma of any magnitude can linger and influence one's
present responses.

The Practice

Start with a small smile.

Feel the corners of your mouth extend to your outer ears. Like a band across your
lower face.

Smile again.

Take that energetic band inward toward the interior of your head, so that from the back
of your throat you feel a slight opening to your middle ears in the interior of your head.
It is a stretch from middle ear to middle ear.

You smile again.

This time, allow the smile to resonate up to your eyes. Often a slight opening can happen—a moment of excitement, a feeling of something elevated. The circular muscles around your eyes expand a bit.

With that there is often a breath. Stay with that for a moment or two.

Then again—slight smile.

This time drop your awareness down to your neck and notice how the smile feels in your throat, your voice, your larynx.

Another smile.

Bring your attention to your breath, lungs, and heart.

Spread out through your chest to your arms, to your fingertips, as you raise your arms up and out to the side.

And one more—slight smile.

This time, drop your attention down to see how the smile affects your belly. Then travel down mentally and energetically through your legs to the ground.

With practice, you can do all the steps quickly in succession, almost all at once, allowing yourself to experience the Humanual Polyvagal Smile—a full self/body event. Relish any and all small adjustments and discoveries each time you do it.

Reasons for Practicing This Smile Sequence

Amid life's challenges and traumas, we often lose our connection to the wholeness or unity of body, mind, and spirit. One of the most prevalent and impactful forms of physiological disconnection is between head and body—for many good reasons. Anytime life is difficult, overwhelming, or traumatic, stress responses kick in, which influence every aspect of our being, including but not limited to musculoskeletal, respiratory, and nervous systems (the systems addressed by this practice). The bodily feelings are uncomfortable, and often unbearable, especially to a small child. John Dewey (1928/1978), American psychologist and educational reformer, recognized this and called the emotional and resulting physiological disconnection of head and body "a disastrous division" (p. 105). An effective coping strategy in the short term that doesn't work as well over the long term is to live in your head, figuring out manipulations and solutions while ignoring painful bodily sensations. Living in your head often limits genuine meaningful social interaction in the present moment, and it reinforces superficiality and increases the possibility of danger, because you cannot perceive the body's warning signals.

To maintain this separation, there tends to be a holding or bracing pattern that keeps the head, neck, upper back, and body in place, with a reinforcement of the thoughts and beliefs that accompany the pattern. By introducing simple movements with awareness, attention can be drawn to these surface holding patterns, and new experiences may emerge that connect to a deeper, healthier organization of a coherent self. The Humanual Polyvagal Smile is a wonderful opportunity to intercept the habitual pattern and begin this transformation from traumatic bracing to easeful movement.

My observations come from 45 years of teaching individuals and working with groups. They form a kind of observational science. Nikolaas Tinbergen (1974), a Dutch biologist, praised observational science in his Nobel Prize acceptance speech in 1973. My work combines active studies of many tangible movement styles and trauma-resolution techniques with the more intangible practices of meditation and human intuition. I have observed an internal organization of physicality that allows for ease of movement and sociality. It can be seen, and it is part of every species of evolution with a head and a body. Rudolph Magnus (1926), the German physiologist who studied the automatic reflex actions by which a human body maintains posture, stated, "In animal movement the head leads and the body follows." For human movement, the head with its sensory apparatus (including neural detection) will pick up cues in the environment, and the body follows instantaneously and accordingly with ventral vagal, sympathetic, or dorsal activity. Excessive constriction can interfere with this integrative action of the nervous system. The physicality of what we call our body has a very specific inherent design. An obvious example would be that knees bend one way, forward. Yet many people stand with their knees locked, which is functionally trying to bend them backward. This pattern of standing, called hyperextension, often leads to pain and/or discomfort in the legs or lower back. But as we know, there is a somatic or traumatic good reason for standing this way. A child wanting to say *no* but who is being forced to be quiet or say *yes* will often lock his or her knees this way. The inherent design gives way to the emotional attachment of developmental trauma. We see many examples in popular culture of what we "should" do with our bodies, such as "hold your shoulders down." Sure, you don't want them up around your ears. But holding them rigidly down has many unwanted side effects, including but not limited to preventing the ribs from moving for breath, as they are functionally organized to do. The Humanual Polyvagal Smile aims to eliminate deviation from one's inherent design. This optimal internal organization facilitates the ventral vagal system, enabling "health, growth, and restoration" leading to homeostasis.[2] Of course, we all experience variations of sympathetic and dorsal states at many moments in the day, as life presents events, challenges, and surprises. The smile gives us an opportunity to return to ventral vagal. The aim is not to stay in ventral all the time but to perhaps shorten your time in defensive preparation, brooding, or shutdown; or to evaluate, "Is this a genuine threat in the present moment, or is this stimulating a thought, feeling, or sensory reminder of some past event or state?" A trigger.

As we look more closely at the components of this seemingly simple practice, a more extensive explanation will point out the inherent design of our physicality, related to integration and leading to wholeness. With the unfolding and enhancement of the potential integration and regulation of the social engagement system (starting with the smile), we see and experience many holding patterns shift in a return to inherent design and function. Thus, one has the availability of choice outside one's habitual realm of patterned behavior.

The Practice, in Greater Detail

Allow the corners of your mouth to extend to your outer ears, feeling somewhat like a band across your mouth and face. You will probably notice that the two sides of your mouth are different and do not have the same degree of ease or movement. You may want to pause here and explore this difference by expanding one side, then the other, and noticing the facial muscles that are involved or restricted. Be curious about the origins of the pattern: Is any emotion or image revealed? Living in an unhappy, fearful, or danger- ous environment will limit the probability of a smile, whereas living in a joyful, pleasant environment will invite the warmth of a smile. The idea of a smile has had many interpre- tations throughout history: the Mona Lisa, the Buddhist bodhisattva smile, seeing a friend or loved one, or just plain feeling good, to name a few. With the next smile, we move this band from the surface of the mouth and ears to the interior of your head, into the middle of your head. That band is now stretching slightly as it extends from middle ear to middle ear, whatever you picture that to be.

Take a moment to sense where your middle ear actually is. The middle ear includes three small bones—beautifully named and commonly known as the hammer (malleus), anvil (incus), and stirrup (stapes). This area is also called the tympanic cavity (imagine a hollow timpani drum). It is an air-filled, membrane-lined space located between the ear canal and the Eustachian tube, cochlea, and auditory nerve. The middle ear is separated from your external ear by the eardrum and is connected to the back of your nose and throat by a narrow passageway called the Eustachian tube, which helps equalize the air pressure in your ears. The middle ear transfers sound vibrations from your eardrum to your inner ear.

As you notice your own hearing, feel your middle ears very gently pulling apart from each other, a dynamic opposition. There is a widening inside your head. This can change the angle of your head, bringing your head slightly forward or actually just not pulling your head back.

The feeling is one of being more forward into your own face, as opposed to your head being collapsed back and down toward your back, often with shoulders pulled up. Especially after a traumatic incident, many people tend to collapse their head back and down and then jut the whole arrangement forward in a minor startle pattern, indicating danger is near, whether or not there is any danger in sight (Jones, 1976/1997, p. 131). Extreme examples of this pattern can be seen in some people who grew up in abusive homes and in some war veterans. The evolutionary directionality is useful to consider. From the research of Dr. Porges, we know that in the head, the migration of the dorsal vagal center was forward (Porges & Howard, 2023). The dorsal vagal fibers of the asocial reptile migrated forward into the striated muscles of the face and head (eyes, ears, etc.)

to become the ventral vagal complex for prosocial modern mammals. The ventral branch nucleus is slightly forward and up from the dorsal vagal branch nucleus, allowing more connection to others for safety or coregulation.

It is important that we recognize the forward potential of our heads for social interaction. Evolution moves and integrates this way. We do not want to be driven by a startle pattern that pulls the head back and down toward the spine for defense. Your head sits on top of your spine. How does yours stay there? Do you hold your neck tight to stabilize it? Or can you feel the slight stretching of your middle ears suspending it?

As far as I know, there is no recently published research on the relation of the angle of your head to your polyvagal nervous system state. But observation tells us that most people in a sympathetic or shutdown state have their head and body either constricted or somewhat collapsed, without a freely balanced head. And those in a more ventral vagal state are more perked up, engaged, and vibrant, with a freely moving head.

Before I go any further with the exploration, I want to mention the following: We are born with many biological expectations. Our systems are set up to respond and behave in certain ways. If there is a tiger, we perceive danger and respond to it with the sympathetic nervous system, engaging in fight or flight—or we respond with the dorsal vagal system for freeze and/or shutdown. If there is no tiger, we do not need these responses and may deem the environment safe. But with any sort of traumatic imprint, these biological expectations can get deprogrammed. Then when there is no tiger, one might have a sympathetic response, or the opposite: When there is a tiger, it will not be perceived as danger. The consequences of these disruptions and dysregulations in the autonomic nervous system are obvious.

In any treatise on human behavior, especially involving trauma, there are no hard and fast assumptions to be made about someone's experience. For instance, when we orient or look around for safety, and there is no immediate danger, we usually conclude, "Oh, I am safe. There is no danger now." But to someone with a trauma history, that lack of immediate danger might mean, "Soon there will be danger. I better be on the lookout and prepare."

As you engage the Humanual Polyvagal Smile exploration, do it in a way that is interesting, safe, and comfortable for you. You may not have the experiences and results I am describing, even if they are the biological expectation. My teaching experience has shown me that we all have an internal organization for well-being (a cut will heal), yet that might not be the lived experience. My exploration attempts to help you find your innate balancing and healing potential. You smile and feel the corners of your mouth extend to your ears, and then take the expansion inside your head so your middle ears are gently stretching apart. Allow the next smile to radiate to the upper part of your face, your eyes, so that the circular orbicularis muscle that surrounds each eye gets to expand, potentially producing social cues of interest, curiosity, or even exuberance. For your eyes, this is a different orientation from a trauma response. With trauma, there is a narrowing of vision as the eyes focus to see where the danger is, as noted by trauma expert Dr. Peter Levine (1997, 2010). With the smile, there is an expansion of peripheral vision. You may notice that each eye has a different capacity to expand and respond to your smile.

The recognition of the inclusion of the orbicularis helps to distinguish a true smile from a fake one. A fake smile, such as when someone is very uncomfortable and/or anxious but needs to put on a happy face to please those around them, often seen in developmental trauma with the child trying to please the adult, has only your mouth smiling. A genuine, true smile of delight and connection has the side corners of your mouth reaching up to your eyes by engaging the zygomatic major (cheek) muscles, so that your whole face is involved. We can see and feel the difference between these two smiles.

Look around the room or space with the expansion of your eyes, with the rest of you calibrating the change. All creatures oriented toward their surroundings, looking for danger or connection. Does the room look different? The colors? The shapes? Has your depth perception or connection to the environment changed? Again, for some this interaction may produce a fear response. We wonder about that: "How do I know I am afraid? What in my body tells me that? Is it something I am seeing or perceiving that might bring danger? Or is it the neuroception, my body reading cues of danger, the neural detection? Does my inner experience of fear match the outer environment?" Check the angle of your head. Are your middle ears still stretching apart, or has your head dropped down toward your back? If your middle ears are stretching apart, your head can rotate smoothly as you turn and look to orient.

Next, smile and feel the bottom of the smile touching your throat, jaw, and tongue. You might notice some restriction or holding patterns, as this area is instrumental in many emotions such as anger, fear, and sadness. Anger is often expressed in the lower part of the face, as tightness in the jaw. We can picture an animal showing its teeth to a predator, with a growl. Are you noticing any constriction in your jaw as you smile?

As you explore your smile here, might there be more space, especially at the back of your throat into your neck (Roberts, 1967)? Your neck is a passageway for (1) the trachea, the tube that moves air for breath; (2) the esophagus, the tube that moves food; (3) the spine, which houses the main part of the nervous system; (4) your larynx and voice; and (5) the vagus nerve. Any tightening or lack of space in your neck will restrict these functions, limiting or preventing continuous, unhindered, uninterrupted communication with self and other. This is especially evident in your voice. With freedom in your neck, your voice can be prosodic and fluctuate melodically, whereas a tight throat restricts your voice and communication ability. As I said earlier, one of the largest physiological disconnects is between head and body, making it imperative to take a moment to explore the possibility of more flow through your neck with your smile. The biological scientist George Coghill (1929), who did research to correlate the development of behavior with the development of anatomical structure, noted the importance of neck muscle freedom.

Allowing more freedom in your neck enables the head and heart to be congruent and will facilitate the next smile dropping into your lungs, heart, and breath, inviting the potential movement of the diaphragm and ribs. The ribs move on the sternum in front and the spine in back. From a biological perspective, lungs are thrilled to be moving and alive as they take in life-giving oxygen and release carbon dioxide, the poetic dance of life, enlivening the vagus nerve. From an emotional perspective, there may be a different story.

Emotions are often held down from expression by what we call holding or limiting breath. In reality, you are interfering with the breathing cycle. Breath comes in, breath goes out, and continues. The overall system of physicality has many cycles, pulsings, and rhythms. When we interfere with one, the breath, we interfere with all of them. If you detect any interference with your breath, if signals such as constriction show up, explore the story the constrictions are telling. Biologically, as breath comes in, the heart rate increases, and as breath goes out, the heart rate decreases. If there is residual trauma, this may not be the case.

As your ribs expand for respiration, your breath wants to extend out through your arms all the way to your fingertips. Extend your arms from your sides to be parallel to the floor. Feel the stretch across your chest from one hand to the other with a slight spiraling motion. It is vital to include your extremities, and the fingertips. Wiggle your fingers, feeling all the joints, including your wrist. Remember that your thumb has three bones like the other fingers. Your thumb moves from your wrist, where the third joint is. This is an important connection for your hand to your torso, neck, and head. There is potential for a very full arm extension, another dynamic opposition, supported from your breath, ribs, and torso, also inviting your head and heart to be congruent.

Become aware of the comfort or resistance to extending your full arm range. Does the arm movement bring pleasure or discomfort? The adaptive pattern of pulling in or protecting may have served you at some time in overwhelming circumstances. It may be left over from some past trauma. Recognize or sort out when the constriction and pulling in of your arms is serving you as needed protection, or when the pattern is harming your full life-force expression.

Another smile.

This time, see how your belly is affected. Many people cut off their gut feelings at a young age, because the feelings could not be expressed for one reason or another. The environment could not handle the child's emotions, so as a defense, the pattern developed to tighten and not feel belly information. In reality, you needed to recruit subdiaphragmatic vagal fibers for defense, so they were not available for homeostasis. As the belly has a brain of its own called the enteric brain, this adaptive pattern puts you at a disadvantage, because you are lacking vital information from the environment, which could be life-threatening. The tightening of your belly in front also has an impact on the back side of your body—on your lower back—and we know many people have discomfort in this area.

As you smile, you are not breathing into your belly per se, but you are allowing your belly to respond to the smile, breath, and movement. Much time can be spent exploring: "When do I hold my belly? In response to what thoughts, feelings, or ideas? When do I feel butterflies or knots or nothing at all?"

As your belly is able to respond to the smile, there is potential movement down through your legs and feet, meeting the ground. Just as we saw your chest spread spirals out to your arms, your belly spreads spirals down to your legs. This activates what is called the ground reaction force. A Wikipedia (2023) definition helps explain this: "An example in biomechanics may be: a person standing motionless on the ground exerts a contact force on it (the ground) equal to the person's weight, and at the same time an equal and opposite ground reaction force is exerted by the ground on the person."

As you get in touch with the ground, the ground will activate an upward force to support you. I like to explain it in terms of gravity and antigravity. Gravity is commonly perceived as a force coming down toward the Earth. The Earth is spinning, giving off a centrifugal force that we can call antigravity, an upward force on the planet. This can be another interpretation of the ground reaction force. When paying attention to the support from the ground, less effort is needed to hold yourself up, less pulling up in your upper torso. When your neck muscles lift your upper chest to be more upright, you are stimulating a sympathetic fear response of expecting and preparing for danger. That action takes you out of social engagement and out of the homeostasis of your inherent design of wholeness.

To embody the upward energy from the ground as you stand, let your foot and ankle move a little bit. Explore your range of motion with micromovements, tiny shifts, feeling the interior of your foot and ankle. Side to side, front to back, and spiraling and twisting are all available to one degree or another. Let the movement travel up to your knees so you can discover the different ranges of motion available in and around your knees. As you move up to your hips, you observe a still different pattern and direction of movement with ball and socket joints, potentially freely rotating. Now the major joints in your legs are moving you, over your support, your feet, connected to the ground as part of the inherent design of you on the planet.

Upward direction continues and fills your lower torso, middle torso, upper torso, arms, neck, and head. This allows your torso, arms, and head to sway slightly as this upward direction blazes throughout your being, allowing growth and repair, and supporting every cell with springiness and buoyancy. The fascial system of connective tissue is flowing. This is your life force. I find this experience similar to what Sir Charles Sherrington (1961), world-renowned physiologist, called tonic activity, which he defined as a continuous, low-level toning or enlivening in the muscles. This is different from more active contraction of muscles.

You now have the ground, yourself, and your environment, including the room and people in it. You now include what you see, hear, and sense in your field. It is an invitation to engage ventral vagal, without the pending danger of sympathetic. You now have more accessibility with less vulnerability. The wholeness of you and your surroundings brings a smile to your face, and we begin again.

Notes

1 Humanual is an epic journey to your expanded self, a book and a practice for accessing one's inherent function and true nature. It is a unique and comprehensive approach to self-knowledge and self-improvement.
2 This is a phrase Dr. Stephen Porges often uses when talking or lecturing.

23

SIMPLE Listening

A Program of Creating Safety and Connection in the Body

Jane Shaw

SIMPLE LISTENING IS A PROGRAM DERIVED FROM BIODYNAMIC CRANIOSACRAL THERAPY (BCST) and other fields that promotes physiological safety and regulation. This chapter explores how SIMPLE Listening supports a felt experience of safety, through the practitioner's intuitive sensorial listening to the subtle expressions of the body. The BCST-informed program teaches the practitioner to have a detailed perception of their own autonomic state and to develop sensitive skills to self-regulate in various situations. The practitioner is also taught to notice the rhythmic interchange between the practitioner and the environment—an inherent process of coregulation. Questions such as how we know when we are safe, why safety is important, and the spectrum of felt safety are examined here.

There is something wonderful about not needing to fear our environment and those around us, to be able to speak our truth when we desire. When we feel safe and connected, we embody a deep security that allows us to respond from a deeper place of knowing, of ease, and of understanding. We come back to our embodied self with safety and belonging. Furthermore, we do not need to try to control our environment when we feel safe, and we can allow others to express themselves more fully without fear of impact on ourselves. Creativity flows in safety states.

Nevertheless, so often we act from a place of defense, responding to a current situation using cues from our historical experiences (Porges, 2022). When we have suffered trauma, we often act as if those experiences are still happening. Because of early difficult experiences, a child might grow up to feel that the whole world is dangerous, meaning they are always in an angry, defensive state. Or they stay small and unseen for fear of attack. An accumulation of stressful experiences can equally cause dysregulation. However, when we know our own inner somatic landscape, we can better regulate our autonomic nervous system (ANS) consciously in relation to others and our environment, without falling into unnecessary protective states.

The SIMPLE Listening program promotes a felt experience of physiological safety and autonomic regulation through a series of practices informed by BCST, Jungian psychology, and creative and movement practices, and underpinned by Polyvagal Theory and the work of Porges (1995), Levine (2010), Maté (2003), van der Kolk (2014), Siegel (2012), Dana (2018), and other pioneers in the trauma recovery field. The SIMPLE practices foster the practitioner's intuitive, sensorial listening to the subtle expressions of the body, teaching the practitioner to have a detailed perception of their own autonomic state and to develop sensitive skills to self-regulate in various situations. The practitioner is also taught to notice the rhythmic interchange between practitioner and environment—an inherent process of coregulation. The program is shared with organizations and individuals to support them in finding regulation, safety, and connection.

The ANS is the instinctual or automatic part of the peripheral nervous system, comprising the sympathetic and parasympathetic systems, controlling involuntary functions such as heart rate, digestion, and breathing. The regulated practitioner can hold a safer therapeutic field for their client in a clinical setting (Dana, 2018), which, in a wider context, means we affect those around us. Regulation here refers to the ability of the person to maintain a balanced state in response to internal and external stimuli. When the ANS is regulated, individuals can experience a sense of calm, safety, and social engagement (Porges, 2011). On the other hand, dysregulation can lead to states of hyperarousal such as anxiety or anger, or hypoarousal such as dissociation or shutdown. However, we are afforded more behavioral choices by becoming conscious of these instinctive reactions. The SIMPLE Listening program is one of exercising our neurophysiology to build capacity for a biological safety state and thus a greater capacity for general affect.

The Biodynamic Craniosacral Therapy Foundations of the SIMPLE Program

SIMPLE Listening evolved from the practice of BCST and is informed by Jungian psychology and the pioneers of trauma recovery, particularly Porges's (1995) Polyvagal Theory.

Biodynamic craniosacral therapy was developed primarily by Franklyn Sills (2001) in the late 1970s, based on the early 20th-century writing and research of osteopath Dr. William G. Sutherland (1949/1990) and his student Dr. Rollin Becker (1965/1997a). The evolution of BCST has interwoven practices from many traditions whose origins are sometimes difficult to determine. It is useful therefore to view some concepts as metaphors. For example, metaphors used by Sutherland to describe his experience of the body organism were often reflective of his time, for example, describing the body in terms of mechanical tissue structures and as a fluid electrical system. Nevertheless, many of the original concepts remain relevant and are reflected in more recent research, such as that of Eugene Gendlin (1997) on the felt sense experience, Lisa Feldman Barrett (2020) on the brain as a fluid chemical milieu, Antonio Damasio (2000) on consciousness as internal feeling states, and Donald Kalsched (2013) on the importance of orienting to wholeness. Essentially, BCST practice relies on our inherent body wisdom and the organism's fundamental drive toward homeostasis.

In clinical practice, the BCST therapist first establishes a safe relational field before orienting to the client's body as a fluid electric system, witnessing its subtle rhythms and expressions (Sutherland, 1949/1990). By attuning to the rhythms and subtle body sensations, the practitioner and client move toward physiological safety and regulation. It is in essence an exercise in conscious, sensitive interoception—the process of sensing the internal body state. The result is coregulation, bringing attention to areas of ease and areas of dis-ease. Through gentle slow touch and compassionate, nonjudgmental presence, the BCST practitioner will often specifically attune to the body's craniosacral mechanism, the physiological system comprising the cranium, sacrum, spine, dura mater membranes, and cerebrospinal fluid. However, whole-body listening with "thinking, feeling, seeing, knowing, touch" (Sutherland, 1949/1990, p. 14) and with embodied presence was at the heart of Sutherland's work. The SIMPLE Listening program employs these BCST listening practices of attuning to the slow rhythms of the body, noticing the subtle sensations in constant change within, thus bringing awareness to how we relate to our environment.

Creating a safe relational field through embodied presence and nonjudging witness is fundamental to BCST, a notion seen in other therapeutic modalities. Jungian analyst Lionel Corbett (2014) spoke of the need to listen deeply without "interpreting or needing something to happen," and how, by doing so, "the relational field suddenly changes" (p. 20). BCST pioneer Rollin Becker (1986/1997b) claimed, "There is a basic primary rhythmic interchange taking place in all that is alive" (p. 16). He emphasized the importance of allowing this rhythmic interchange to do the therapeutic work. This relational reciprocity that can be felt in human interaction and in nature is at the heart of the SIMPLE Listening practices.

Corbett's (2014) reference to not "needing something to happen" speaks to the art of doing nondoing, another key principle in BCST (Sills, 2001). *Wei wu wei*, meaning "action without action" (Lau, 1963), is an important and central paradoxical theme in Taoist philosophy. In the Tao Te Ching, Laozi told us that the direction and intelligence of the Tao must be trusted. He said, "The way never acts yet nothing is left undone" (Lau, 1963, pp. xxxvii, 42, 81). In other words, it suggests that one should align oneself with the natural flow of the universe, letting things unfold naturally without unnecessary resistance or force (Watts, 2000). Through the progressive program of SIMPLE Listening, it is anticipated that the practitioner will move toward an increasingly deep experience of wu wei.

The key ingredients to be mined from BCST include establishing a safe relational field, a practice of detailed sensitive interoception, engaging the senses with intuitive awareness, embodied compassionate presence, and an ability to follow our natural subtle rhythms and attune to stillness. This combination supports an emergent order aligned in relationship with our environment.

The SIMPLE Listening Program

SIMPLE Listening is a program that educates the practitioner to listen to their environment using somatic intuitive awareness. Its objective is to gain ANS regulation and a conscious relationship to self, other, and the environment. Many practices bring a sense of deep physiological safety through stimulation of the social engagement cranial nerves, utilizing both the afferent and efferent aspects of the social engagement system.

SIMPLE Listening is an acronym for Somatic awareness, Intuitive inquiry, Mindful movement, Play and creative practice; Listening with the whole body, and Effortless action. It is constructed in a format that allows the participant to enter at a level appropriate to their experience and level of dysregulation. Each section has many practices to choose from to ensure a best fit for the participant. For example, a breathing exercise to promote vagal toning might be used first, or a play activity may be more appropriate for another group of participants. There are progressive steps to offer an increased depth of regulated experience.

First, the facilitator explains the basics of the Polyvagal Theory and the ANS states of safety, danger, and life threat, offering examples of the felt experience of each state. For example, in safety we can smile and look at each other; our heart feels open, throat feels soft, and voice is strong. I often use the physical expression of opening my arms wide and moving my hips and legs with ease to demonstrate a ventral vagal countenance. This contrasts with a sympathetically charged closed body, in danger, gripping with all flexor muscles on alert, ready to fight or run away, associated with emotions of anger, rage, anxiety, or irritation. A dry mouth and twitching eyes might be observed. I sometimes notice toes curling or legs swinging from a chair, getting ready to run away as signs of sympathetic mobilization.

The sympathetic response is differentiated from a dorsal vagal collapsed position, with shoulders rounded, legs turned in, and neck sunk into the shoulders, to demonstrate an immobilized, shutdown, dissociated expression. Additionally, an immobilized frozen body state can exhibit a held diaphragm, as if an inbreath had been frozen in time with other body parts also in a rigidly tense position. A deer in the headlights is an easy comparison for an immobilized, frozen state. It feels like the brakes and accelerator are simultaneously pressed.

When we are grounded in safety, we notice our sensory experience, we can be curious, we are mindful of our environment, and we have impulses to connect with others. I might notice the roses in my garden and want to hug my partner, in comparison to a state of coping and survival, when we are likely to put our curiosity on hold and employ techniques to stop anxious feelings, such as withdrawing from my partner and stomping around my garden mobilizing to ease my anxiety, rather than stopping to smell the roses. Curiosity only returns when we are safe again.

Although there is a marked difference between these three autonomic states, most people are not aware of their nervous system's expression.

The following sections go into the detail about each SIMPLE practice grouping, explaining the nature of each section with examples of specific practices.

Somatic Awareness

Develop an awareness of the somatic impact of internal and external resources to create a safer inner and outer landscape.

External resources are ways to create a nurturing environment for ourselves. For example, taking your adored dog for a walk each morning, playing your favorite music on a weekend drive, or just looking out the window at the ocean view. In this practice, the external experience is stitched together with the internal sensations created in each of these situations.

Internal resources support the physical body, such as breathing practices, body awareness scans, or a establishing a place of comfort within the body. Often, it is easier to start with external resources before moving toward developing internal resources.

Examples of Somatic Awareness Practices

1. Breathing practices with body scan
2. Establishing external resources; mapping to internal sensations

Clinical Note

Adaptability in our ANS is created step by step through continual observation, developing an awareness of our interoceptive process. Resilience and adaptability are built by increasing novelty in our experience—unfamiliar sensations can be good.

There are many somatic awareness practices to choose from that stimulate five cranial nerves, which innervate the actions of orienting, swallowing, chewing, and vocalizing: trigeminal (V), facial (VII), glossopharyngeal (XI), vagus (X), and accessory (XI). As we did in infancy, by stimulating these cranial nerves, we feed the pathways to tell us we are safe, therefore helping the whole ANS to regulate through heart, breath, and digestion regulation.

Intuitive Inquiry

Form reciprocal streams of connection through intuitive awareness, compassion, and empathy to engage and tend the field of personal and collective interactions.
Connection can be difficult for some people, but we live in a system of reciprocity where to see is to be seen, to hear is to be heard, and to sense is to be sensed. This practice supports us to become more conscious of our relationships with the animate and inanimate, at a pace that feels manageable. The reciprocity is felt through the system of sensory and motor vagal pathways.

Examples of Intuitive Inquiry Practices

1. Relating to an inanimate object through touch and interoception
2. Journaling exercise to explore embodied lines of inquiry

Mindful Movement

Equip oneself with the awareness to use movement as a self and coregulating tool promoting more conscious choices and behavior.
Simple movement practices shift the autonomic state.

Examples of Mindful Movement Practices

1. Make small movements with ankles, wrists, shoulders. Notice how breath changes.
2. Move from sitting to standing. Notice feet on the floor.

Clinical Note

Critically, the SIMPLE Listening program is paced to allow the immobilized individual to slowly emerge from shutdown. Mobilizing too quickly can often be overwhelming, with an "explosion" of emotion and sensation (Levine, 2010). Instead, offering exercises for gentle body awareness, establishing an interconnected relational field (Sills, 2001), and introducing gradual movement allows the individual to glimpse the ventral vagal state. I often use the analogy of a bird flying past a window. We start by glimpsing the bird, wondering if we saw something. The bird flies past again, and we recognize it as a bird. It flies past a few more times before coming to settle on our windowsill, where we can watch it carefully. In SIMPLE Listening, we invite glimpses of a safe experience, allowing them to accumulate until they are the ground upon which we walk. By offering safety cues to others, we allow them to slowly savor how it feels to be safe.

Play and Creative Practice

Develop physiological safety through play and foster creativity when experiencing a safety state.
Play occurs in a ventral vagal state, and equally, play can promote a safety state.

Examples of Play and Creative Practice

1. Exploring the body through images: drawing, painting, photography, dance
2. Engaging the senses in a group treasure hunt in nature (coregulating through play)

Listen With the Whole Body

Establish a witnessing, embodied presence that facilitates active attentiveness toward self and others through an auditory process.
This involves a series of auditory listening exercises, listening to how our internal body responds to sound. The vibration and expression of the voice can shift the ANS state.

Examples of Listening With the Whole Body

1. Active listening, speaking slowly with long phrases, and presence
2. Notice effect of voice on inner landscape through forming sounds such as *voo, eeh, aah*

Effortless Action

Align with the movement that comes from accommodating impermanence, change, and transformation.
In effortless action there is perfect balance between action and nonaction. It is sometimes compared to a nonstriving flow state. Studies have explored the psychological and physiological benefits of practices that emphasize the flow states of being present, nonstriving, and accepting the natural course of events (Slingerland, 2015), often influenced by Eastern philosophies like Taoism. In dialogue with a Zen master about the Chinese Taoist book *The Secret of the Golden Flower,* Carl Jung (1929/1967) also spoke about the practice of effortless states, observing that people seemed to "bring about development that set them free," but as far as he could see "they did nothing (*wu wei*) but let things happen" (p. 16). BCST experience suggests that achieving this neutral, grounded balance between action and rest indeed "sets us free," as Jung observed. A deep sense of inner stillness is often observed.

Examples of Effortless Action Practices

1. Orienting to stillness through guided meditation
2. Finding your embodied neutral state through meditation on expanding perceptual field

Clinical Note

Participants often ask how to know the difference between resting in stillness and an immobilized shutdown state. Feelings of disorientation, fragmentation, dissociation, disconnection, or distraction suggest a shutdown response. Stillness feels peaceful but present, resting but aware, calm and connected. Shutdown feels disconnected from the environment, a lack of responsiveness, collapsed, agitated but unable to move. A shutdown state often feels uncomfortable, but crucially, it can also feel floaty and pleasant due to a release of endorphins.

Case Studies

Because people become familiar with their default protective autonomic state, it can be difficult to recognize a ventral vagal state. For example, a highly sympathetic mobilized agitated state might be normal for some people and therefore feel more comfortable than sitting and quietly meditating. Equally, someone who has spent most of their life in a largely immobilized state might confuse being in a physiological endorphin-flooded shutdown with a healthy effortless-action state. With this in mind, it can be necessary to start gently with groups who have experienced trauma, and so we often choose some of the entry-level practices as a starting point. Creating safety is the priority.

Evaluation Methods Employed

This evaluation process is twofold, including both process measurements and outcome evaluation. The process measures real-time effectiveness of the SIMPLE skills program, measuring the quality of the learning experience and the uptake of action based on skills learned. The outcomes measure longer-term health outcomes, historically using various scorecard methods to measure psychological, behavioral, and physical symptoms. Currently we use a digital web-based application developed by Brough et al. (2021) called the Warwick Holistic Health Questionnaire (WHHQ). This is self-reported, taking a snapshot at the start of the program and again at the end. This evaluation can be an ongoing process.

Case Study: Bereavement

A group of 45 bereaved parents who had lost children to suicide came for two separate in-person days for the SIMPLE Listening program. There was a high level of anxiety in the group. Some had lost children to suicide many years earlier and others within 12 months, meaning there were many different levels of distress and grief. The group was so varied in experience and dysregulation that it was important to start gently, with an explanation of the ANS to locate their feelings within a neurophysiological framework—normalizing their response to their tragedies.

The practices employed over the two days were as follows. Somatic awareness: (1) simple 3:5 breathing practice, inhaling to a count of 3 and exhaling to 5, four times; (2) establishing external resources; (3) mapping external resources to internal sensations; and (4) body scan to become familiar with internal places of comfort and resource. Mindful movement: (1) moving shoulders, ankles, and wrists slowly and gently, and mapping the resulting sensations in the body. Play and creative practice: (1) nature walk to engage the senses.

The results after two days were significant. The main changes in the WHHQ were responses to questions: "I've been sleeping well"; "I've felt my inner strength"; "I've felt awareness of my body's needs." The responses that did not change significantly included: "I've felt connected to my family and friends," and "I've had lots of energy," which may be understandable considering the loss to suicide in the group. They reported that the exercises that they would take home were the 3:5 breathing practice, an awareness of resourcing for ongoing support, and the importance of coregulating through connecting with others who have experienced similar tragedies.

Case Study: Managing Burnout

A group of 12 health care workers engaged with an eight-week online program, consisting of weekly hour-long Zoom calls, followed by a one-day in-person workshop. This group was experienced and reasonably regulated but suffering from stress and burnout from working through the COVID-19 pandemic. The participants had experience with somatic awareness, so could deepen into these exercises well. The mindful movement exercises provided simple techniques to employ in professional settings during more stressful moments. For example, when their body responded by immobilizing, they learned to use some mindful movement exercises to allow easeful mobilization and prevent further freeze or collapse responses. Several reported the effortless action exercises to be "balm for the soul"; "my body wanted to drink the stillness"; "reminded me of my wholeness." The WHHQ results for this group were largely positive, particularly in the areas of "I've had lots of energy" and "I've felt my inner strength."

Conclusion

My 20 years of working as a therapist have shown me that some people are looking for ease and reasonably functional living, while others are seeking a more profound lived experience. The SIMPLE Listening program has been designed with all types in mind. It is a program of self- and coregulation, building capacity for biological safety. Small steps, pacing, and regular practice lead to positive cumulative results. This program supports pathways of self-understanding, strength, and resilience that lead to greater ease and confidence in engaging with the challenges, stresses, and opportunities of everyday life.

Future Direction

Biodynamic craniosacral therapy has developed over many years, with increasing evidence-based research to better understand its effect on health conditions (Sumner & Haines, 2010; Brough et al., 2015). While there is more research to be done in BCST, extracting some of its foundational principles into an easy polyvagal-informed SIMPLE Listening program has offered support to a greater and wider audience, including to legal, education, and health care professionals. SIMPLE Listening is a way of life, supporting a felt sense of the reciprocity of life, affording more choice in how to react in any given situation.

24

Supporting Safety With Movement

Polyvagal Theory as a Framework for Mindful Movement Practitioners

Marlysa Sullivan

THIS CHAPTER DESCRIBES FOUR PROCESSES OF MINDFUL MOVEMENT AND HOW THEY CAN be understood through the framework of Polyvagal Theory. These synergistic processes provide a powerful method for insight and reinforcement of safety from a body-based, experiential perspective. Body-based practitioners (e.g., physical therapists, yoga therapists/teachers, somatic therapists) can utilize this framework to deliver an embodied learning of safety for whole-person well-being.

Mindful movement involves four synergistic and interwoven processes: (1) attentional focus and intention, (2) breath regulation, (3) body awareness, and (4) posture and tone—including movement (Figure 24.1; Payne & Crane-Godreau, 2013; Russell & Arcuri, 2015; Schmalzl et al., 2015). While these processes can be understood separately, it is in their coming together that mindful movement provides a powerful embodied learning of safety, transforming the relationship with oneself, others, and one's life circumstances. When practiced together, their synergistic interactions become a vehicle for exploring the complex relationships between body, mind, and environment (BME) experience.

Safety and the Movement System: Understanding Pain and Neuroception

Before diving into these four processes of mindful movement for supporting safety, an understanding of the experience of pain is important. Chronic pain may start as a sole or combined physical, emotional, social, environmental, existential, or spiritual event, but it transcends these lines as each component influences the other. Regardless of how the experience of pain may start, each component of the whole person may become affected by the others. In terms of movement, the experience of pain can generate a feedback loop reinforcing a cycle of less movement, decreased mobility and strength, and increased fear or worry about future pain. For example, someone who has experienced something traumatic may present with patterns of guarding or holding in their body, which affects

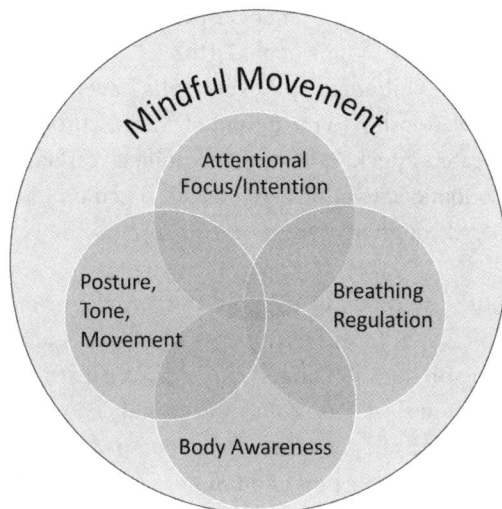

FIGURE 24.1 Four synergistic and interwoven processes of mindful movement.

their ease and facility with movement, while also affecting their emotions, mood, or feelings of social isolation as they may limit their activities, and even separation from their sense of self or spirituality. People begin to discover how their body holds tension, their disconnection from their body, how when their mood changes their body tension, posture, and movement change, or how movement affects their mood and sense of identity. People experiencing pain report a gamut of these interconnected changes and through mindful movement practice become aware of how each component of their experience is interconnected.

Rehabilitation specialists can utilize teachings from pain neuroscience education (PNE) to help break this cycle and to support the reconceptualization of pain. PNE includes learning opportunities to explore pain as a protective response and as an output based on various BME stimuli or input (Moseley & Butler, 2015; Robinson et al., 2016; Watson et al., 2019; Wood & Hendrick, 2019). Inputs that influence the experience of pain include nociceptive, interoceptive, and proprioceptive stimuli as well as thoughts, emotions, beliefs, exteroceptive stimuli, and social relationships or situations. As these inputs come into the system, they are integrated together, and then an assessment is made about potential safety or danger. If these inputs are consciously or unconsciously perceived as a threat, the experience of pain may increase (Moseley & Butler, 2015). An intention of pain education is to help the person become more aware of the complexity informing pain, and to shift the balance of processes away from prolonged threat appraisal and toward greater safety. Doing so may improve the pain experience and teach the person to become more aware of how inputs from the BME impact perceived safety or danger. The person learns to reassess stimuli to differentiate real versus perceived danger, as well as ways to modulate their experience and the output of pain. Ultimately the person learns the factors that increase safety and danger so that they can choose to engage factors that support safety and can then reframe beliefs and explore movement as perceived danger is decreased (King et al., 2016; Moseley & Butler, 2015; Wijma et al., 2018).

Neuroception adds an embodied and experiential layer to this learning of safety and danger input and the relationship to the output of pain. Neuroception describes how autonomic activations create a quick, efficient, and unified response of the body, mind, and behavior. These autonomic activations are created based on inputs gathered from inside and outside the body through a process of subconscious detection of safety or danger (Porges, 2021).

In my clinical work, methods to support this insight into neuroceptive processes include having people listen to different types of music as movement is introduced to notice how this input of sound changes patterns of breath, muscle tension, posture, and movement, and thoughts, emotions, and mood. People report finding out how the speed or type of music changes their breathing patterns; creates feelings of relaxation or calm, or energizes their body and mind; supports feelings of confidence with movement; or can create agitation with movement. Another way this understanding of subconscious neuroceptive processes is discussed is through the concept of muscle memory. The person considers how the body can learn repetitive activities to the point of no longer having to think about it (e.g., riding a bike, cooking a favorite dish). We then discuss the idea of the muscle memory of their experience of chronic pain to reflect on their own patterns of muscle tension, movement, posture, breath, thoughts, and emotions that arise when actual, remembered, or future pain are considered. People realize how their body is carrying the patterns of their pain during daily life, which can then lead to change.

The processes of mindful movement can thus help the person to become more aware through an enhanced attunement to interoceptive processes of one's body-mind reactions to inner and outer stimuli. What was previously subconscious processes influencing neural activations and subsequent physiological, emotional, and behavioral qualities are now brought to conscious awareness. This embodied approach to learning adds a vital component to PNE as the person discovers how inputs that contribute to the experience of pain show up as activations and changes in the body in breath patterns, muscle tensions, posture, and quality of movement. Over time the person learns through interoception to explore the neuroceptive processes that contribute to the activations of the body, mind, and behavior toward defensive neural platforms and greater output of pain. As they learn the neural platforms of safety or danger, they can trace these activations back to the various stimuli of the BME that influence them and ultimately contribute to the experience of pain.

This embodied and experiential approach empowers the person to learn how safety or danger inputs are processed and how they influence autonomic activations. Over time the person can engage the processes of mindful movement to engage and support safety inputs to change the experience of pain and to support whole-person well-being. The specific ways of utilizing these portals of attention/intention, breath regulation, body awareness, and posture/tone/movement will be described in reference to the framework of Polyvagal Theory.

Polyvagal Theory as a Framework for Engaging Safety in Mindful Movement

Polyvagal Theory describes how underlying neural platforms support a continuum of safety for the body, mind, and behavior (Porges, 2021). This continuum of safety includes safe mobilization, social engagement, and safe immobilization (stillness). When safe mobilization is present, there is an activation of body-mind-behavior that encourages creativity, inspiration, play, and improved coordination and dexterity in movement. From the activation of social engagement, the person has an improved capacity for social connection, with relaxed bodily states, vocal prosody, attunement to human sound, and capacity for compassion. Safe immobilization provides the foundation for experiences of stillness, quietude, and equanimity, such as are found in meditative states. Polyvagal Theory provides insight into how we can affect these underlying autonomic activations to support body-mind-behavior states of safety from more mobilized, to socially engaged to stillness. From the perspective of neuroception and pain education, mindful movement provides an opportunity to influence these neural platforms and to both develop insight into and engage the factors that activate safe neural platforms.

Mindful movement can shift these neural platforms through input into the preparatory set, defined as integrated action of subcortical systems preceding conscious appraisal and helping provide a quick, efficient response to stimuli (Payne & Crane-Godreau, 2015). The preparatory set in this context refers to the portals of mindful movement, including body awareness (proprioception and interoception), attention and intention (affective imagery, attentional control, modulation of expectation or appraisal), tone/posture/movement, and breath regulation (Payne & Crane-Godreau, 2015). From a polyvagal perspective, when safety is experienced or detected, a preparatory set is activated accordingly for body-mind-behavior aligned and appropriate to the situation. There are three safe preparatory sets aligning with the three safe neural platforms such that subconsciously detected safety provides the input for the preparatory set and neural platforms of mobilization (safe mobilization), connection with others (social engagement), and stillness (safe immobilization).

The framework of Polyvagal Theory supports the mindful movement practitioner to optimize input to the system for activations along the continuum of safe neural platforms. The person learns to self-regulate and widen the window of experience from safe mobilization, to social engagement, to safe immobilization. Each of these neural platforms provides different ways to explore safety: being more active, in relation with others, and with stillness.

Significance of Safety as a Continuum

This understanding of safety as a continuum is key for shared decision-making and client-centered, trauma-informed care. This more complex idea of safety is particularly vital when considering the difficulty of identifying what this might mean for someone who may have difficulty perceiving any kind of safety. The most accessible form of safety for one person might include some measure of mobilization (safe mobilization), whether that is movement, breath, imagery, or a creative endeavor. For another person it might be stillness (safe immobilization). And for another it might be in a relationship (social engagement). In my clinical work, we first identify what this safety might mean for the person. For some, the word *safety* does not resonate, and we then explore other words, such as *centered, calm, strong, vibrant,* or *confident.* After we have found this right word as an intention for our work together, we find the practices that might help them align with this experience. This can include movement, spanning from more restorative and still postures, to strengthening, to flowing movement; either staying away from a focus on the breath entirely or focusing on breath throughout the session; finding a focal point such as an image or word, or something outside of themselves, such as a kind of music, or a picture. When the very idea of body awareness or movement is particularly aversive to the person or they find it too painful, we explore visualization of movement, or placing intentions of safety (or whatever word they choose) in the body, first in easier places and then moving to more difficult places, or looking at videos of movement while noticing the reaction of the body-energy-mind and exploring the connection to this intention of safety (or whatever they choose) while watching others.

Starting where the person can access safety is important as foundational experiences that can be built upon for the development of a wider net and experience of safety along the continuum of mobilization, social engagement, and stillness. Any of the safety neural platforms builds experiential learning that can be carried into the others for greater body-mind-behavioral regulation for varied life experiences and circumstances.

The four portals of mindful movement provide a variety of ways to access and build safety that can be individualized to the person.

Four Processes of Mindful Movement Supporting the Continuum of Safe Neural Platforms

Attentional Focus and Intention—Setting the Stage for Safety

Attentional focus and intention shape the practice of mindful movement as it provides ways to orient and relate to the stimuli of the BME to support safe neural platforms. An accepting and kind attention to the body sets the stage for nonjudgmental noticing of patterns held in the body and the way the body-mind relates to and reacts to inner and outer stimuli. This attentional and intentional focus can be initiated in a variety of ways to support the continuum of safety with mobilization, engagement, and stillness.

Nonjudgmental awareness of the present moment can begin with the outer world, with practices such as curiously noticing the senses—what one sees, hears, feels, smells, tastes—and how they fluctuate with time. Adding intention to notice these stimuli with compassion can support a kind attention as a lens through which this noticing happens. This kind attention is then gradually encouraged as an option for how the person can relate to inner experiences of thoughts, emotions, beliefs, and physical sensations, including interoceptive processes. Ultimately this kind attention is brought into body awareness and movement practice. Whether it is using this kind attention, or using specific intentions such as compassion, confidence, or loving-kindness, the person is encouraged to notice this as a felt sensation and interoceptive experience of the body. This might include experiencing the intention as a feeling in a certain place in the body with terminology such as openness, spaciousness, lightness, or vitality. This realization of felt sensation is carried further into how these intentions change the breath (e.g., quality, depth, rate, rhythm), interoception, and experience of the body (e.g., muscle tensions or relaxations, posture, movement).

In considering the continuum of safety described above, the person might take this new experience of the body and notice if it can be maintained in relationship with others (social engagement); in times of activation (safe mobilization); and during stillness and quietude (safe immobilization). This intentional way of experiencing the body is particularly significant in defining a new way to approach movement. Oftentimes the goal in movement is to attain an external measure such as a number of repetitions, a duration, or a final position without consideration for how the body achieves this end. As an alternative, if the aim of movement is an internal one—to move in a way that strengthens this intention and felt sense of safety—the person is empowered to adjust speed, direction, and range of movement from an internal compass of greater balance of effort and ease. The experiential knowledge of safety in the body becomes the goal of movement itself such that the person learns to move in a way that is compassionate and kind, and supports greater safety. The person can use their own insight to gauge ways of moving that bring them toward or away from safety, including maladaptive habits that may increase stress or strain in the body. Over time, as the person learns to move with kindness and compassion, they create new ways of moving that optimize safety (safe mobilization).

When brought into body awareness, the processes of attentional focus and intention can help the person notice when they have moved into safe or defensive neural platforms (e.g., noticing body tensions or disconnections indicative of defense). From this insight, the person can utilize other processes of mindful movement such as breath regulation and shifting muscle tone, posture, or movement to shift the system to safety and to develop greater resilience along the continuum of safety from activation, to social engagement, to stillness.

Breath Regulation—Supporting Attentional Focus and Body Awareness for Safety

Breath regulation is a vital entryway to shift physiological and emotional activations. Supporting awareness of and altering breathing patterns can influence underlying autonomic activations, promoting neural platforms to support safety (Weng et al., 2021). Body awareness of breathing patterns and their relationships to emotions in the depth, rate, and pattern of breathing can foster insight into which neural platform is present. By shifting these breathing patterns, the person learns that they can move from one neural platform to another. By bringing awareness of how the breath shifts in interactions with others (social engagement), in movement or activation (safe mobilization), and in stillness (safe stillness), the breath becomes a cue for safety and a mechanism that can be utilized as

appropriate to the situation. Yoga, one mindful movement practice, teaches breath regulation as a bridge between the body and mind and as a mechanism to support steadiness and
tranquility of the mind (Patanjali, 1996; Svatmarama, 2012). Yoga offers breath techniques
that can assist the person in noticing their patterns as well as those that might activate
the system to move toward safe mobilization or to enhance quietude to move toward safe
stillness. In addition to breath techniques, breath-focused movement—such as is found
in yoga and other mindful movement practices—have demonstrated greater attentional
control than those solely focused on movement (Schmalzl et al., 2018).

Body Awareness—Intentional and Tangible Experiencing of Safety

Body awareness with attentional focus and intention can help the person develop healthy
and adaptive proprioceptive and interoceptive skills for greater self-regulation and ultimately to express fluidity along the continuum from safety to mobilization, to engagement,
to stillness. Interoceptive skills building can support homeostatic balance, self-regulation,
and whole-person well-being (Chen et al., 2021; Farb et al., 2015; Haase et al., 2016). The
person learns how to attend to bodily sensation, to notice where and how the body is
located in space and is moving, and to intentionally connect to the body through various
practices, including imagery, body scans, and purposeful movement. Practices to support
safety with body awareness might include bringing certain intentions such as kindness,
compassion, or other chosen or desired qualities and attitudes to each part of the body.
Guided imagery or visualization to form healthy relationships to various areas of the body
can also be incorporated to bring new attentional attitudes to the body.

   Other body awareness practices may focus on teaching the inseparability of the body
and mind. The person learns how emotions and bodily responses are related through
both interoceptive and proprioceptive skills building (Shafir, 2016). Insight is gained into
how emotions are reflected in the body through tensions, disconnections, postures, and
movement. Mindful movement is then utilized to provide new input to the motor system, and these proprioceptive and interoceptive practices help the person learn how the
body supports regulation of emotions (Shafir, 2016). These body awareness practices can
be further utilized in social situations as the person becomes aware of changes in their
breath, muscle tension, and posture in relationship to others. The body can become a
gauge for insight for the person as to when these safety neural platforms are present and
to engage in certain practices to shift the system as appropriate to the situation.

Posture, Tone, and Movement—Combining Intention, Breath, and Body Awareness for Dynamic Safety

As the person builds proficiency in body awareness and attentional focus and intention,
they can notice habitual ways of holding the body, including places of tensions, disconnections, overall posture, and quality of movement. How the body is held and how these
patterns relate to emotions, beliefs, social situations, or relationships can all be uncovered
through mindful movement practice. The person can learn to bring intentions such as

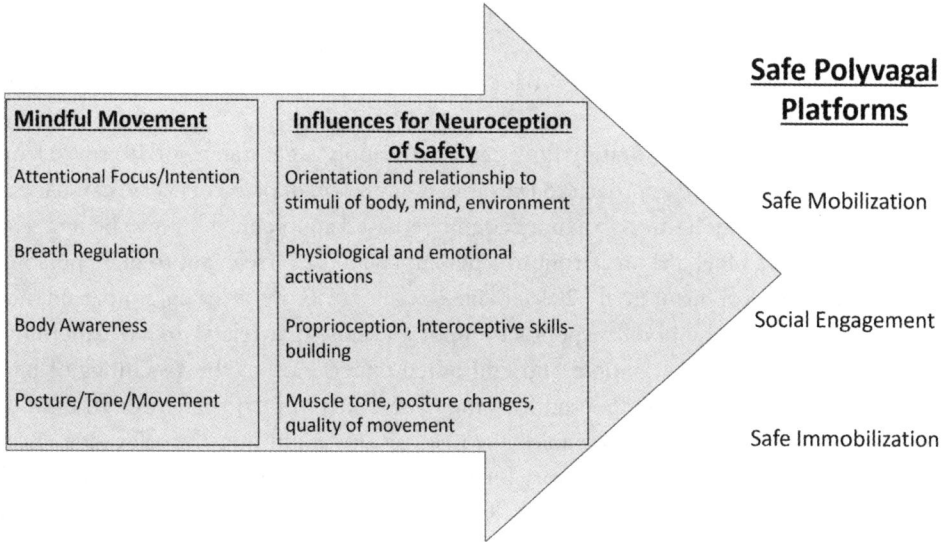

FIGURE 24.2 Polyvagal Theory as framework for mindful movement.

kindness, confidence, or vitality into the body in such a way that they find new ways to breathe, relax or engage the body, or hold their posture. These body postures and activations/relaxations become a template for the person to utilize to return to safe neural platforms that promote mobilization, social engagement, or stillness as appropriate to the situation. Specific postures have been found to enhance parasympathetic nervous system activation as well as emotions relating to movement or body positions (e.g., happiness relating to rising and expanding movement; Cottingham, Porges, & Lyon, 1988; Cottingham, Porges, & Richmond, 1988; Shafir, 2016; Shafir et al., 2015; Tsachor & Shafir, 2017). Using movement to provide a shift in physiological activations, emotions, and behavior provides a tangible method to shift one's experience that can bypass certain obstacles that may be put up by thoughts, emotions, or beliefs. These ways of holding the body or moving can then be translated into social situations (social engagement), during activations (safe mobilization), and for greater stillness and quietude (safe immobilization).

Examples of Two Kinds of Mindful Movement Practitioners Integrating the Framework of Polyvagal Theory

Mindful movement practitioners utilize these four processes to help the person bring attention to and transform the relationships between the body, thoughts, emotions, beliefs, and social relationships or situations for whole person well-being. The client is supported in noticing how stimuli from the inner or outer environment show up in the body and how the body forms a template for changing these reactions and relationships. The person learns to use these processes of mindful movement to enact change supportive of safety in the body, emotions, and behavior along a continuum of mobilization, social engagement, or stillness as appropriate to the situation. Physical therapists and Yoga therapists are examples of two types of mindful movement practitioner with different and complementary perspectives that can utilize this framework of Polyvagal Theory to support safety.

Physical therapists incorporating PNE can use this polyvagal framework to move from a didactic to an embodied approach to learning. A limitation of pain education can happen when it is communicated through a more cognitive-based approach. This may be met with reluctance, as it can feel like an affront to a person's beliefs or irrelevant to one's personal situation of pain (Robinson et al., 2016; Wijma et al., 2018). By offering a more implicit experiencing of how the body responds to input and how that relates to the experience of pain, the person has a tangible and embodied experience of the teachings of pain education. This shift to an embodied learning of safe neural platforms through mindful movement can provide the lived experience needed for insight into the relevance of the teachings to oneself as well as support for the curiosity and readiness to explore PNE for change (Eneberg-Boldon et al., 2020; King et al., 2016; Robinson et al., 2016; Wijma et al., 2018). These active strategies for learning have demonstrated an optimization of PNE with the added benefit of translating the skills learned into application to real-life situations and activities (Moseley & Butler, 2015; Siddall et al., 2022). Psychologically informed physical therapy practices that incorporate understandings of and attention to these body-mind relationships may also benefit from this polyvagal framework to explore safety through the lens of underlying neural platforms. The physical therapist using a polyvagal approach may focus on interoceptive learning to help the person realize how emotions, thoughts, beliefs, or situations in one's environment show up in the body (e.g., changes in heart rate, breath rate, muscle tone). The various practices of attention/intention, breath regulation, body awareness, and movement can then be utilized to support the shifting of neural platforms to an expression of safety, from engagement, to stillness, to mobilization. This model carries the potential for the person to become more empowered as they learn that they have the agency to shift their neural platforms and thereby the relationship to what arises in their body, mind, or environment.

Yoga teachers and therapists can also incorporate the polyvagal framework to support resilience along this continuum of safety for the practitioner. The wisdom tradition of yoga is founded on a philosophical path supporting insight to reduce suffering as the person finds a deep harmony within themselves and in relation to the world (Patanjali, 1996; Sullivan, Moonaz, et al., 2018; Sullivan & Hyland Robertson, 2020; Miller, 2004). This path of yoga provides a guide toward connecting to a deeper expression of oneself through the synergistic practices of cultivating ethical qualities (e.g., patience, compassion, nonharming) incorporated into mindful movement (including breath regulation, attentional focus, body awareness, movement) toward meaning and purpose for harmonious living.

Yoga research has supported the inclusion of these ethical components for greater well-being and physical and mental health benefits such as decreased depression and anxiety symptoms and improved mindfulness (Gaiswinkler & Unterrainer, 2016; Ivtzan & Jegatheeswaran, 2015; Ivtzan & Papantoniou, 2014; Smith et al., 2011). In yoga practice, these intentional qualities are interwoven into how one safely meets the breath, sensation in the body, movement, and relationships and outer circumstances (Sullivan, Moonaz, et al., 2018; Sullivan & Hyland Robertson, 2020). Yoga also supports safety by emphasizing connection, whether that is from a transcendental source, from inner resourcing, or between individuals. Additionally, in a synergistic perspective to the neural platforms, yoga offers a perspective of underlying qualities, the gunas, from which physiology, emotions, and behavior can be affected through yoga practices to enhance safety, connection, and ease (Sullivan, Erb, et al., 2018; Sullivan & Hyland Robertson, 2020). Through yoga practice there is an inherent embodied learning of how neural platforms are expressed in the qualities of the body, mind, and behavior as well as practices to explore shifting these neural platforms. The person learns to explore how qualities of the body, mind, and behavior emerge from these neural platforms with compassion as well as to shift the neural platforms through integrated intention, breath regulation, body awareness, and movement practices.

The yoga therapist using a polyvagal approach would explore how these neural platforms and guna qualities are expressing themselves in the body, mind, and behavior and support the person in a process of transforming their relationship to BME stimuli as they connect to their unique purposeful, harmonious way of living.

Conclusion

Rather than a process driven by cognition, mindful movement provides an opportunity to notice connections between the BME within bodily experience. The bodily experience becomes a personal laboratory for experiential learning to understand relationships between the BME and to create experiences along a continuum of safety, moving from mobilization, to social engagement, to stillness. The person learns to reconnect to the body in adaptive and healthy ways and to explore how the body relates to and responds to both inner and outer stimuli. The person learns what safety feels like in the body, including changes in breath, muscle relaxations or activations, and posture or movement. From that foundation of safety, the person can titrate their capacity to meet uncomfortable or even distressing sensations and to return to safe neural platforms. Over time, the person can more easily return to the experience of safety as it becomes a neural memory along a continuum inclusive of mobilization, social engagement, or stillness as appropriate to the situation. Ultimately this helps the person to widen their capacity to be with various stimuli without losing their connection to safety for greater resilience.

The new relationships to the body provided through mindful movement also provide an opportunity to support greater accessibility for meaningful ways to engage in life activities. Movement or exercise may create fear or anxiety around the potential harm that it can create based on current and past experience. Additionally, movement can lead to feelings of failure or not being good enough if it is tied to expectations of needing to reach a certain goal or vision of what it means to be an active person. However, this method of supporting safety with movement provides a different approach to what it means to create movement in the body. The shift to a more accepting and present-moment focus whereby the person acknowledges and appreciates what the body needs in the moment is encouraged through these processes. The person finds ways to move that align with this experience of safety in the body—the goal of movement becomes safety rather than an external goal or expectation.

In summary, mindful movement provides an opportunity to form a relationship with one's body as a path for supporting safety. The person learns to develop awareness of how stimuli from outer and inner worlds are reflected in the body and how to shift the activations to a continuum of safety appropriate to the situation. The four processes of mindful movement empower the person with strategies to change these inputs in mindful movement for healthy, adaptive responses to stimuli. Polyvagal Theory provides a framework for mindful movement practitioners to explore their practices for supporting a continuum of safety and, thus, whole-person well-being through their influence on neural platforms and neuroception. Practitioners such as physical therapists and yoga therapists can utilize the four processes of mindful movement in ways specific to their scopes of practice to support and empower the person for safety.

25

Creating a Sense of Safety in Birth

Fostering Connection and Coregulation to Minimize Trauma for Parents and Baby

Chantal Traub

MY WORLD IS THE BIRTH WORLD, AND MY APPRECIATION FOR THE VENTRAL VAGAL SYSTEM resides there. As a respected New York City birth educator and doula with more than 20 years in practice, I value Polyvagal Theory because it's what I do intuitively. When I'm facilitating a birth, I feel like I'm coregulating everyone in the room: the birthing person, the partner, and the medical team. It's a practice of reciprocity. I am perpetually sending and receiving signals of safety, calm, and connection.

But employing the ventral vagal system begins long before labor and delivery. When I meet with clients over the course of a pregnancy, I listen to their joys, acknowledge their fears, validate their concerns, and answer their questions. And when they inevitably ask me the Big Question—"How do I get this baby out?"—I reframe it in a way that helps recruit the mom's ventral vagal complex to calm and connect; this can shift the entire autonomic nervous system (ANS) into a state that is incompatible with fear reactions. How do I reframe? By conveying to the birther and partner that it's not so much "How do we get the baby out?" as it is "How do we *let* the baby out?"

In my mind, "getting the baby out," which is a common phrase in the United States, conjures mechanical extraction, rushing a natural process, or generally interfering with the physiology of childbirth. With that often comes episiotomy, tearing, or surgery. On the other hand, letting the baby out calls on the birther to relax as the baby makes its journey; it's a natural process of welcoming.

Reframing this huge, fear-based question is an essential step in creating a sense of safety for the birthing parent, throughout pregnancy and into labor. When the laboring parent feels safe and the nervous system calms down, the hormones of birth can function optimally. This is critical. Because when the opposite is true—when a birther's physiology is in a state of threat—the ANS goes into fear or stress mode, and the hormones of birth can be disturbed, which can lead to a slow or stalled labor.

But, as mentioned above, it's not just about the mom. Recruiting a sense of safety in the labor support team, from the partner to the medical professionals, also makes a difference. When all participants in the birthing process feel safe, supported, and authentically connected, we can optimize childbirth physiology and minimize the sense of overwhelm that can lead to a negative experience.

The Biology of Safety

The autonomic nervous system is the body's personal surveillance staff. Its job is to protect us by assessing risk. The ANS is constantly on duty, looking for cues of safety and cues of threat. It fields internal signals from the body while also tracking and responding to signals and sensations in our environment, including the interactions we have with others.

Safety is a felt sense that applies to the body, the mind, and the social environment. Social support helps reduce psychological and physical stress, so birthing with a team that feels safe, in a space that feels safe, can have a tremendous impact on the birther's experience.

In my work preparing clients for birth and facilitating births, what I am actually doing is providing a container of safety. When I'm in a state of calm, accessibility, and connection, I am helping the mom recruit her ventral vagal complex to bring a sense of calm and safety.

The Baby Choreographs the Birthing Process; the Mom Relaxes

As an experienced doula, I am the consistent trusted other. My work is a practice of paying attention and listening. I watch for clues and hints of the baby's journey through the pelvis, noting the mom's feelings of safety or threat. My job involves knowing when to step in and offer directions without disturbing the process. I am by the side of the mom every step of the way, gently guiding, making suggestions, following the mom—and, most importantly, following the baby.

The baby's role in birth is grossly underemphasized. Understanding and honoring it enables everyone involved to support the baby in its journey from uterus to pelvis to the outside world.

Let's take a look at part of the process: The baby has to navigate the pelvis, which is funnel-shaped and curved inside. The pelvic belt is made up of four bones, which are able to move slightly, allowing the pelvis to make small changes in shape. I think of the pelvis and the baby as shapeshifters working together to accommodate each other.

While there's generally not much movement in the joints of the pelvis during the life of a woman, due to hormones there is some during menstruation, more toward the end of pregnancy, and a lot of mobility during birth. The bony frame contains and protects the lower abdominal organs, with the perineum at its base. In a female pelvis, the lower abdominal organs are the bladder, uterus, and rectum. These organs are supported by the pelvic floor muscles. The pelvis partially ensures stability for the perineum and connects the spine to the legs. How a birther moves the spine and femur bones affects the shape and the space between the pelvic bones and the mobility of the pelvic floor.

When the baby is in the uterus, it has space to move. Usually by 32 weeks, the baby, due to gravity and the weight of its bony parts, turns its head down. While it generally stays in this position, it rotates from side to side. Ideally the baby enters the pelvis with its spine on mom's left, facing toward her right hip, following the natural shape of the uterus, which is more curved on the left side. This supports the baby's head. The bones of the baby's skull are not fixed; they slide over each other, molding to fit through the pelvis. If the baby were to come down on the right, where the angle is straighter, there's nothing supporting the head. This could bring the baby into what we call a sunny-side-up position, which can result in a much longer, harder labor.

Once the baby enters the pelvis, it needs to navigate a much narrower channel. It does this through a series of rotations. The rotations, which come just before the pushing stage, are very important.

When the team can work together and stay calm and connected, the baby has the time and support to do what it needs to do. The results can be wonderful. Here's one example:

> I was with a client in labor, and as she began to push, I noticed that her OB was getting uncomfortable. She turned to my client and said, "If this baby is not born in the next few pushes, I'm going to have to cut you. I know that you don't want an episiotomy, but this baby really needs to be born now." My client shot me a distressed look. We had been working for weeks preparing her pelvic floor, and I knew she didn't want an episiotomy. I asked the obstetrician, "May I make a suggestion for a position change?"
>
> Her doctor responded, "Yes, of course, how can I help? We don't have much time."
>
> When the doula and the OB or midwife are anchored in their ventral vagal, they are able to communicate cues of safety through their tone of voice, their facial expressions, and posture to everyone in the room, and the atmosphere becomes calm rather than panicked.
>
> I asked my client if she could turn over onto her side; I wanted to get her off her back to give her baby a break. She said, "I can't move." I told her, "I'm right here with you, and I'll help you." Her OB and I helped shift her onto her left side. This freed her sacrum. I said, "I'm going to lift your right leg up and over to provide space for your right sit bone." My hope was that this change would allow her baby to move. It did!
>
> On the next contraction, the baby rotated. Then, on the contraction after that, the baby rotated a bit more and began to crown. On the following contraction, the baby's head birthed, then the shoulders, and then the whole baby slipped out, without the mom needing a cut. An intact perineum!
>
> My client was relieved and thrilled. Her OB said, "Good call!"
>
> In the birthing room, relationships built on respect and trust foster connection and coregulation among everyone. When the doula is anchored in the

ventral vagal, she can become more curious and can make quick decisions based on intuition, creativity, and experience.

Safety as an Embodied Experience

While the baby has to navigate the pelvis, the mother's role is to relax and let the baby out. The safer she feels, the more she can let go on a deep level. We know that stress, tension, and fear are held in the body. So we need the strategies and the skills to become more aware of bodily stress. In my work, I've seen that imbalances show up; injuries show up; past adversity may show up in birth.

When I'm preparing my clients for birth, I am working with both parents. We explore together how they might respond in different stressful situations. The birth partner becomes protective of their loved one, and it's a beautiful thing to see. But seeing their loved one in pain and feeling helpless can be triggering. If they become reactive to what may feel like a threatening situation, they might get angry or defensive or dissociate. As a doula, I often find myself needing to coregulate the spouse, the nurse, or the obstetrician by offering cues of safety, using the tone of my voice, my facial expressions, and my body language. Here's an example:

> I was attending a long labor, and I became aware of my client's husband beginning to dissociate. He had been involved, confident, and protective during the prenatal sessions and during the earlier part of labor. As the labor continued, he began to look frustrated and tired. His wife was getting a lot of attention from me and the midwife as we assisted her through contractions. I noticed that the husband began to distance himself from us. Initially I thought he might need some personal space, but then I saw him sitting closed up and disconnected to the side, appearing upset or angry.
>
> I invited him to come over and join us, but he wouldn't move. I continued to encourage him. When my client got into the birth pool, I invited him to put on a swimsuit and get in with her. He timidly obliged. I supported him to get in close so she could lean her body against him. I then made sure he was physically close to his spouse throughout the rest of the labor, and when it became time to push, I suggested that he get behind her so that she could lean her back into him. This would ensure that he stayed in the inner circle and didn't feel excluded if things became dramatic during delivery. It was a calm and beautiful birth, and the husband was able to stay close and be an intimate part of welcoming his baby into the world.

Breath, Movement, and Ritual

As mentioned above, during the birthing process the baby must navigate the entire bony passage of the pelvis. It is not a straight path, but a curved tunnel. By incorporating breath work, practicing fluid movements ahead of time, and leaning into rituals, my clients often find they can shift to calm during labor and work with their baby as the baby makes its journey.

Breath is a portal to the calming mechanisms of the ventral vagus. Slow exhalations increase ventral vagal influence, slowing heart rate and softening the muscles of the pelvic floor. In labor, the mom wants to be able to harness the breath and ride those contraction waves, or be able to dive deep underneath the contraction surges and let them wash over her. This takes practice, to be able to thread the mind through the needle of the breath and to remain calm and centered. I'll remind clients that sometimes you may lose yourself, and that's okay: "Stop, catch your breath and then use your tools to coregulate and be present and grounded." I might suggest this exercise: Breathe gently, and on each inhalation, imagine that a refreshing breath washes over you. On each exhalation, imagine that just as a wave slides back out to the ocean, you are stepping into the present moment, trusting that you can relax, seeing clearly that you've got this. I also might try a very simple association technique, suggesting that my client try slow exhalations while adding a positive memory or thinking of a loved one. During exhalation, the vagal influence on the heart is greater than it is on inhalation; this inhibits the sympathetic nervous system's influence on the heart, producing a state of calm, openness, and trust.

Movement changes the shape of the pelvis. Integrating movement in pregnancy helps regulate the body and develop inner trust. Moving around and changing positions during labor helps the baby traverse the curved path of the pelvis. As a doula in the birthing room, when I want to move the baby, I move the mom.

Rhythm and ritual in labor can introduce some predictability to birth, which can help the mom feel safer and less anxious. Some rituals are specific to labor. Others can be started during pregnancy and pulled up as needed during labor. One example of a ritual specific to labor: As the contraction starts, the mom can stand up, lean over something, and allow someone to press on her back. When the contraction ends, she can sit down, catch her breath, and have a sip of water. (We keep this up until it doesn't work anymore, then we try something else.) Regarding rituals developed during pregnancy that can be useful in labor, I encourage my pregnant clients to integrate a self-care habit that can be part of their daily routine—for example, gargling in the morning when they brush their teeth; then in labor, if the client is getting dysregulated, I offer them a cup of water and a spit bowl and have them gargle and repeat. It helps ground them. I have also seen that rituals in labor can also elevate pain thresholds, increase confidence, and boost the ability to experience positive emotions.

All Women Need Safety and Support

The larger scope of my work is about supporting female needs across the life span. Pregnancy and labor are particularly intense periods. But through all stages, including adolescence, birthing, postpartum, perimenopause, menopause, and beyond, women need someone they can trust, who will listen to them and hear their concerns. Teaching women to recruit a sense of safety on their own—through self-knowledge, authentic connections, breath, movement, and more—is one of the most important things I can do as a health care professional. The ventral vagal complex is a crucial, if invisible, factor in the care I provide. My approach has always been to wrap my clients in resources so that they can build their resilience and, over time, become their own best resource.

By fostering a harmonious blend of physiological and emotional well-being, we enhance the overall birthing experience. Numerous exercises can be embraced to cultivate a sense of safety, incorporating rhythmic movement into your daily routine, whether it's walking, climbing stairs, swimming, or dancing, involving movements like rocking, swaying, hip circles, crawling, and marching. Additionally, the integration of breath work is paramount.

To optimize relaxation, consider the utilization of both bottom-up and top-down techniques. Implement bottom-up procedures, such as the deliberate practice of slow exhalation, effectively recruiting the ventral vagal circuit. This induces a state of calm, openness, and an overall sense of safety and trust. On the other hand, top-down approaches, such as revisiting positive memories or visualizing beloved individuals and joyful experiences, offer complementary avenues to relaxation.

Here are specific exercises tailored to your holistic approach:

- Positive visualizations: Envision cherished loved ones or trusted friends. Picture yourself in your favorite natural setting or recall a moment saturated with peace and love.
- Breathing exercises: Emphasize slow exhalations over short inhalations. The vagal influence during exhalation suppresses sympathetic nervous system activity, fostering states of calmness, openness, and trust.
- Vocalizations: Engage in vocal exercises such as singing, chanting, gargling, humming, or producing gentle sounds like *ah*, a low *oh*, *oooh*, *moo*, and *ha* on the exhale.
- Positive social interactions: Use video conferencing to exercise the social engagement system if face-to-face interactions are not feasible.

Coaching Session Approach and Objectives

In my coaching sessions, I adopt a client-centered, holistic, and polyvagal-informed approach. Each session begins with establishing a meaningful connection with the client. Understanding their background, vision, current challenges, and goals is crucial. Exploring their underlying nervous system profile becomes a foundation for developing strategies that instill feelings of safety, support, and connection. It may be hard to feel safety when one is feeling challenged or untethered, such as in labor or when one is feeling overwhelmed. The objective is to support clients in developing their intuition and interoception—cultivating an awareness of their embodied experiences. This capacity to focus inward, sensitively perceiving the inner world and interpreting bodily cues, is necessary for expectant mothers to connect with their baby during pregnancy.

Sessions are designed to raise awareness of neuroception, aiding clients in identifying cues reliably signaling a state of safety or threat. This exploration extends to comprehending their body's nuanced responses to challenges and uncertainties, such as those encountered in birth and early parenting, all while fostering flexibility in the nervous system. Integrating the nervous system into discussions aids clients in comprehending their biological responses, cultivating curiosity, and applying self-compassion during stressful situations.

Sessions typically encompass breath work exercises, appropriate movement, and visualizations to cultivate mindful awareness, guiding clients back to a calm, connected, and regulated state. Between sessions, clients incorporate learned techniques, practicing self-awareness through intermittent check-ins on bodily sensations and emotional states.

Encouraging clients to integrate breathing, movement, and sounding exercises during moments of stress, and infusing activities that bring micromoments of ventral vagal energy, such as marveling at a flock of birds in formation, appreciating a sunset, or spending time with loved ones, forms an integral part of building nervous system resilience. Ultimately, the aim is for clients to enhance their self-awareness and connection to the brain and body, enabling them to navigate the stresses of birth and parenting with increased efficacy.

26

Perinatal Mortality and Grief

Chiara Marazzi and Maurizio Stupiggia

I was born a year after my sister Clare died of fulminant leukemia. The pain of her loss deeply marked my life and permeated the life of our family. Nearly 10 years after I began treating perinatal bereaved parents, I realized that the older and deeper our bonds were, the more they struggled to emerge into consciousness, and that despite years of therapy and various life experiences, there was still much to unravel.
—CHIARA MARAZZI

Only after many years of this work, I remembered something I had always known: I came into the world after two stillborn siblings. I knew it, but it seemed of little concern to me. I always looked elsewhere, where things happened to others, and where I thought I could always do something.
—MAURIZIO STUPIGGIA

THERE IS A UNIQUE TYPE OF MOURNING THAT DEALS WITH MORE THAN ONE DEATH: A BIO-logical one and a psychological one. The first is the actual loss of a child; the latter is the denial of the existence of a traumatic experience. This is equivalent to a retraumatization; the baby is no longer there, and the birth hasn't even happened: death therefore becomes a sort of disappearance.

Studies and research regarding perinatal mortality highlight a real taboo, supported by a massive removal of this topic from public discourses and from narratives regarding mourning (Layne, 2003). We are convinced, however, after almost 20 years of treating parental couples, that the issue of mortality around birth causes a profound trauma on both personal and couple levels. Trauma also extends to the surrounding environment to a point that it can be defined as a widespread trauma. The work described here is not focused on the social aspects involved in perinatal bereavement. However, without addressing, at least in a synthetic way, some reflections on the broader context, it is impossible to account for the surplus of pain that parents face. This surplus originates precisely by virtue of the representations and discourses regarding death and grief, pregnancy, motherhood, and parental roles that are present at a social level.

The representation of death in modern media, even when it involves real human beings, is always reconstructed based on news strategies. These are extraneous to the event itself and refer to politics, entertainment, and media consumption. Death is depicted with traits of a crude and extraordinary nature: a portrayal that makes it unusable for a real understanding about how everyday death is experienced and how it may influence close relationships (Bauman, 2006; Sozzi, 2014).

There is an ambiguity in the cultural and social representation of the theme of death: on the one hand, a morbid sensationalism, and on the other, a tendency to cover up and deny its existence and experience.

In the case of perinatal mortality, cultural inconsistency is evident and marked by the lack of any regulated ritualization.

During funerals, a community shares a ritual farewell and celebrates the dead person. This allows the living to feel less alone in their grieving and marks a passage between a before and an after. A classic example of this ritual involves the colors of the clothes worn by those who are grieving. In the United States, the anthropological, pioneering work of Layne (2003) has already highlighted how much silence there is on pregnancy loss and how we are suffering from a lack of adequate social narratives. There is a need, regardless of the gestational phase in which the loss occurs, to legitimize grief. There are two aspects of grief, both of the woman as a mother and for the loss of the child as a son or daughter. Negative stereotypes related to this specific loss mainly affect the role of women, which would not be fully definable as such without motherhood. Layne talks about silences: social taboos regarding these losses. This is the broader framework in which to understand the issue of perinatal bereavement.

Defining Perinatal Mortality

The definition of perinatal mortality is not univocal. We will adopt the definition offered by the World Health Organization (WHO), which includes the following types of loss events:

1. Early stillbirths, from 22 + 0 weeks of gestation or weighing ≥500g
2. Late stillbirths, from 28 + 0 weeks of gestation or weighing ≥1,000 g
3. Early neonatal deaths, within 6 days, 23 hours, 59 minutes of birth starting at 22 + 0 weeks of gestation or weighing ≥500 g
4. Late neonatal deaths, within 27 days, 23 hours, 59 minutes of birth starting at 22 + 0 weeks gestation or weighing ≥500 g (Istituto Superiore della Sanità, 2020, p. 5)

In the case of perinatal mortality, beyond the categorizations, in contrast to incorrect common sense, the evidence for all operators and for research on the topic is that the loss of the baby during pregnancy, whatever the length of gestation, is comparable to the loss of a child. This is considered, in literature, to be the most difficult grief to overcome.

This said, it is important to recognize that there is a wide spectrum of loss events that can occur during pregnancy. As common perception understands, losing a child in the early stages when it is not fully formed is different from loss happening some days after birth.

From this evidence, we can deduce the intensity of grief during the mourning process. Parents have reported a different variety of devaluing attitudes and phrases expressed by doctors and health workers at birth centers regarding in utero losses. Sometimes these attitudes, often experienced by traumatized parents, are themselves driven by traumatic dynamics.

It is important, for the theme of loss in utero, to specify that a diversity of grief does not in any way establish its intensity. The intensity of what every human being feels in the face of painful events and how we respond to them depends not only on the formal typology of the event but also on other concurrent variables that give it its emotional connotation.

Confronting pain only by trying to overcome it and severing the bond with the lost child entails the risk of internalizing beliefs that may constrain, confine, and pathologize the experience of pain itself and cause the griever to avoid processing the trauma. Research shows that if perinatal grief is not processed in a positive way, up to a third of mothers involved risk developing clinical depression (Fenstermacher & Hupcey, 2013) or posttraumatic disorders (Krosch & Shakespeare-Finch, 2017). Results highlight how grief in perinatal loss is an ongoing experience for parents. It changes nature over time but involves a continuous relationship with those who have passed away, a sort of "walking backwards and living forward" (Moules et al., 2004). During the mourning, analyzing the nature of the attachment bond with the child, if and how it changes, is of fundamental importance to understand if the mourning process is healthy. Repositioning the child in the life and the memory of the family can prove to be positive from an emotional point of view and constructive in motivational terms. On the contrary, identification and dependence can be negative and may even lead to transferring unresolved grief onto subsequent children (Walter, 1999; Stroebe, 2001). The following clinical case is an example of change in the attachment bond with the lost child and of positive coping with the issue of loss with the living child.

Bianca

A couple lost their female baby at the end of pregnancy in February 2017. Both parents are in their 40s and live in Milan, near the Niguarda Hospital where Bianca was stillborn. Luciano runs a construction company and Antonella also works. Luciano cares deeply about his work and his family. They have a son, Mattia, who at the time of the loss of his younger sibling was 15 months old. In February 2017, the couple came to the hospital for the scheduled cesarean section. Antonella, who had not experienced problems during her pregnancy, suffered from high blood pressure toward the end of the pregnancy, and the doctor decided on a cesarean delivery.

Luciano left his wife at the reception desk of the ward and went to get a coffee from the automatic machine while they waited for a room. He was absent for about 15 minutes: the quarter of an hour that changed their lives. Antonella felt ill and was promptly assisted due to a massive detachment of the placenta. The infant girl died and Antonella was taken, dying, to intensive care. Returning from his coffee, Luciano was told that his daughter was dead and his wife's life was hanging in the balance. This was communicated by two doctors in the corridor without any perceived consideration, as a quick, offhand comment. Anyone with a minimum of familiarity with trauma can already identify with this communication method, in the tones and lack of empathy, the message that Luciano's neuroception will have decoded as: "I am in a hostile place."

On the psychological assistance side, our team, with which the hospital collaborates, was asked for help in managing the father's visible state of shock. Within an hour, a psychotherapist arrived at the hospital and offered the first comforting words to Luciano. Fortunately, Antonella's clinical situation evolved positively. However, unlike her husband, she didn't have time to see the little girl and hold her in her arms. Our contact person, the obstetrics manager, went to Luciano with the baby in her arms and passed her to him. At that moment, Luciano—he told us later—felt a strong impulse to escape. But he did not flee and instead froze. From a neurophysiological point of view, we can say that here Luciano reacted to this unexpected and intolerable situation with a defense defined as freeze-fright (Baldwin, 2013). In anticipation of an active response, simultaneous sympathetic activity with dorsal vagal parasympathetic activity engages the freeze-fright defense state (Baldwin, 2013; Zhang et al., 2004). Individuals in such a freeze state appear tonically still, tense, and ready to move. Dorsal vagal activity inhibits movement, including startle, and may elicit the sensation of being unable to move. As Davis and Astrachan (1978) noted, "at least two processes that have opposite effects on startle must operate when fear increases" (p. 102).

After a month, in March 2017, the couple, sent by the hospital, began to attend the self-help group operating in our association. The mourning process proceeded normally, and in September Luciano felt strong discomfort. After acknowledging the impossibility of further pregnancies without putting Antonella's life at risk, Luciano declared that he felt even angrier than before. He also declared that he felt unable to talk to his son Mattia about the death of his little sister, despite being aware that the child needed him as a father to give him answers.

Luciano reported feeling severe pain in his shoulder and right arm (with which he held the little girl) and the inability to express his anger. The couple was offered a bodywork intervention within a group setting. The work done in this group addresses the institutional, community, and social dimensions, which cannot be left out of the process given its disruptive entry into the scene at the very moment of the loss. The group reflects the social context, especially if it is a group, such as ours, that is open to different profiles.

Luciano accepted the offer of bodywork within the group without hesitation. He said that he was ready to do anything to free himself from the weight he bore inside. Antonella followed him, hoping that the intervention would be useful.

Therapeutic Theater

The group work practiced by our group has as its primary aim to experiment with a corporeal expressive modality. Within a group setting, this biosystemic methodology (Liss & Stupiggia, 2000) crosses and integrates body psychotherapy techniques with theatrical practices borrowed from social theater (Bernardi, 2004), improvisational theater, and more classical actor training.

The purpose of theatrical practices is not performative, but procedural. It is important to propose practices that liberate and enhance body awareness and expressiveness. Most of all, the practices must be acted out in groups, the ultimate social setting.

These theatrical practices mimic those of play. Playing is a device capable of achieving freedom and security, especially when traumatic experiences have flattened a subject's symbolic capacity and sense of security (Porges, 2014; van der Kolk, 2015). The testing of one's skills and competences occurs in mammalian pups within the safety of play: here, trying again and again is not only permissible but is a source of excitement and joy.

In our model, theatrical play is a liberating social game. It means feeling our own body and others' bodies, gentle eye contact, and touch meeting in total safety, all while respecting one's own and others' bodily and emotional experiences.

The group's work lasts approximately three hours. It is designed and conducted in comanagement from time to time and involves two phases: first, purely theatrical work, and second, clinical elaboration. The planning of the activities takes into account the personal background of the participants, their needs, the type of intervention, and what has already been experienced. These elements define the objectives to be pursued. The planning of the intervention carried out in the case of Luciano and Antonella had the following phases:

1. An explanation of the rules of the setting and the type of work.
2. Self-presentation of the participants, both verbally and through an initial use of sensory exploration.
3. A warm-up/socialization phase with theatrical exercises. It is customary to calibrate this phase to prepare for the topic that will be analyzed. In this case, taking into account that the parents had no previous clinical experience, we chose only activation and socialization exercises with a clear playful imprint and without in-depth emotional analysis. These parents carried a very strong emotional load, and therefore the dosage was to be as light and gradual as possible to avoid risking emotional overload. The proposed psycho-bodywork was intended to move emotions gradually, avoiding a catharsis that can retraumatize (Downing, 1995; Stupiggia, 2007).
4. The second phase of specific work focused on the father (Liss, 2004). For this phase, we decided to favor personal work with Luciano, as he was bearing a specific problem that emerged in the self-help group. Antonella was considered a privileged resource in her role as both wife and mother.
5. The third phase of symbolic-ritual work proposed to the couple aimed to relocate the experience of loss within their internal world.

The Beginning

The group work began with 11 people, including Luciano, Antonella, and two facilitators: a therapist and a theater worker.

After a brief presentation, the theater facilitator specified the rules aimed at structuring a safe environment. First, no one was obliged or forced to do anything; second, anyone might, at any time, stop or leave the activity. Working on safety is best achieved through giving the initiative to the participants while respecting their will. The therapist specified that it is completely normal in bodywork to feel uncomfortable and wonder what is happening and for what purpose. She stated that beyond the momentary perception, due to discomfort and embarrassment caused by the lack of familiarity with this kind of activity, everything proposed has meaning and purpose.

After these clarifications, the theatrical expression work began. In this phase, the atmosphere was playful, fun and full of energy. Participants socialized, with gradually decreasing embarrassment: the intention was precisely created to build a safe environment for play.

After this first phase, the setting changed. The participants sat in a circle, and the clinical work began, exploring the experiences that emerged from the previous exercises and games.

The therapist briefly introduced the sharing method for the participants, with no need for previous clinical skills: "Everyone can say how they feel, or how they felt in a certain exercise, trying to name the sensations of the body and to match the words with a gesture, a movement, a body position, and possibly even a sound. Sometimes I may ask the person to repeat and amplify their global expression, and I will ask the group to mirror the expression, for deeper sharing and identification."

People began sharing, until it was Luciano's turn to speak: "I feel a little contracted . . . that is, from here up." He indicated his belly as relaxed and then, referring to his chest and shoulders, said, "Everything is really tense here!"

T: Can you explain better what you mean by *tense*?
L: Stiffened, like a boulder that crushes me and imprisons me.

While he says this, he contracts his fists and arms, pushing them against his chest. He remains like this for a few moments, then gradually opens his fists, and his arms curl up on each other, apparently losing the previous tension. Now he simply has his arms folded.

T: Okay, is this a comfortable position for you and for your arms? [The trainer mirrors the position of Luciano's folded arms.]
L: Yes, I'm more comfortable.

Mirroring is fundamental with the whole group, and therefore the next request was for everyone.

T: Let's try to take this position. He says that this position is comfortable for him. . . . Is it like this?
L: Yes . . . but actually it's not very comfortable. . . .
T: It's not very comfortable. . . . Now let's see what the group tells you about this position.

The others mirror Luciano's position and his facial expression, and share their feelings: "I'm Luciano. I feel relaxed in one part and my heart beats in the other. . . . I'm not very comfortable—in fact I'm uncomfortable." "I'm Luciano, and actually my arms weigh me down and crush me." "I'm Luciano, and I feel like I'm standing at attention in a position that gives me the idea of control."

L: Yes, it's true. I control what happens. I'm like radar.

Other members of the group take inspiration from these last statements and continue with their identifications: "I'm Luciano, and this is how I defend myself." "I'm Luciano, and I'm afraid of what happens." "I'm Luciano, and I feel like I'd like to hide a bit." "I am Luciano, and I am hidden." "I'm Luciano, and I feel a little pissed off and weighed down."

Luciano, who listens carefully to all the identifications, summarizes: "Yes, I have to defend myself. I would like to disappear. I am very weighed down. I don't know if I'm pissed off, but I feel my arms . . . as if they had something to do with what happened."

The therapist then proposes a slight change:

T: Now I ask you if it is possible for you to do something with your arms, even something small.
L: I wouldn't know what to do. . . . Sometimes I'd tear them off.
T: You would take them off. . . .
L: Yes, because they weigh on me.
T: So let's try to explore a movement with the arms with which you can unload the weight. What would you do to push the weight away with your arms? You can try to make a gesture.

The Drama

The invitation to "make a gesture" connected to what he is talking about triggers a state-dependent memory process centered on the mood, which is directly dependent on the affective state. This process is structured around a mood-dependency effect: when the experienced situation is congruent in affective terms to the one experienced in the past, recovery of such memory is actualized. Therefore, there is access to the same emotional experience, the mood, and the meaning experienced in the past. At this point, this is the process taking place in Luciano. Let's look at this crucial step.

L: I wouldn't push them away because this would mean letting my daughter fall. . . . [As soon as he says this, he starts to cry softly. From this moment he alternates crying and deep sighs.] I can't do it because then I would let her go.
T: I understand . . . and it would be painful! What if someone helped you hold your arms up? Can I have people step in to support your arms—two on one arm and two on the other—and you just let your arms go?

Four people stand beside him and support his arms.

L: Yes . . . if I close my eyes I have her in my arms.

T: Hold her in your arms. Make the gesture. . . .

L: No, because she isn't there. [Crying continues and becomes more intense.] I don't feel like letting her go. . . . I don't know how to explain it. . . . I don't want to let her go down. . . . I can't explain.

T: [In an attempt to encourage Luciano to trust his arms to whoever was supporting them] No, don't let them go . . . but you can get help holding this weight. You don't have to lose the baby, but you don't have to be alone . . . just because you were so alone in the worst moments. . . . You were alone when she [turning to Antonella] couldn't give you a hand. Is it good for you if Antonella comes close?

L: Yes . . . [Cries, sighing, while tension on his face starts to release. As Antonella approaches, Luciano suddenly blurts out] I miss Bianca so much.

T: You can tell her . . . "Bianca, I miss you." You have never felt supported, but now you can let yourself go. You are among people who can support you, and Bianca is in no danger now.

L: I can't do it. . . . [It's impossible to let go of his arms.]

T: So try to hold her tightly against you. Tight! Hold her tight! [Referring to Antonella, who is nearby.] Do you regret that she wasn't able to hold her?

L: Yes, I'm sorry. I asked but it just wasn't possible.

T: You can try to give the baby to her now. You can do it. You can try to hand her to your wife.

L: [One person gives him contact on the shoulders while two people support his arms, with two hands on each of his arms.] I'm like . . . the same moment they gave her to me, I had a feeling of total block. . . . For a fraction of a second my brain told me "go and run," but I couldn't do it.

In this passage the chain of reactions to the traumatic situation is evident: first, the fight and flight response, then the dorsal vagal block.

T: Here you can share whatever your deep reactions are, even wanting to escape.

L: I would like to . . . but it's absurd, because my feet are still. . . .

T: Try to move your feet. . . . We'll help you. . . . We'll help you with our feet. . . .

A couple of people place their hands on Luciano's feet and ankles, gently stimulating a movement: "Push with your feet against our hands. . . . You'll feel your feet activate with this contact. . . . Push as hard as you want."

L: I can't, I can't. . . . If I run away, I'll lose her!

He doesn't feel like pushing, because he feels like he couldn't hold her. All the energy is blocked in supporting the little girl, and nothing is in the legs.

T: You keep her and also run away from there. You can hold her and go to your
   wife. . . . You can give her the baby.

At that point, Luciano suddenly explodes into desperate tears: "No, no . . . no, I didn't do
anything." In this sentence lies all the helplessness he has experienced. He was unable to
keep his daughter alive; he was unable to escape; and he found himself totally alone.

    Antonella gets as close as possible. The two stand facing each other at a short distance.

    Luciano, with his arms still in the same position, looks at her and says, "Come
here. . . . I'm sorry. . . . I never managed to bring her to you."

T: You can look at her [prompting Luciano to look at Antonella].
L: Well, I can't . . . because when I look at her I reexperience everything all over again. . . .
T: Do you feel guilty?
L: I feel guilty, and I live in terror. . . . She was dying. It's mind-boggling. . . . It's tough.
A: [Moves a little closer.] Give her to me. . . . Now try giving her to me.

Antonella is so close now that there is no chance for the little girl to fall. He makes a
gesture of giving the baby to her with a titanic effort and incredible slowness. Then they
hug and cry for many minutes. The strong emotion overwhelms all the members of the
group, who start crying.

T: You may find a space in the room where you can stay close, especially with your
   arms. . . . [A few minutes pass.]
A: It's the first time he expressed what he had inside. I'm happy because I've never managed
   to do anything.
T: Now we'll ask you something which, having reached this point, won't be difficult to
   do at all. You have brought the objects. So choose a place and try to represent your
   couple's space with these objects. You may take them and place them inside that space
   as you want. You must obviously take into account each other's object because it is the
   couple's common space. If you need other items in the room, pillows and so on, take
   them. Also, please consider other people as objects and put them inside. We won't look
   at you. We are here, but we're doing something else. You may furnish a part of the room
   as if you had to represent your relationship.

In the context of dealing with perinatal bereavement, the national recommendations (Fondazione Gonfalonieri Ragonese, 2023) follow international guidelines that recommend
the collecting of memories such as photos, clothes, and the weight and physical measurements of the child, to trace the passage of the "real child." This helps the mourning
process, which needs to take place around something tangible, in order to be carried out
in a positive way. A physical child came into the world, a child that, at full-term gestation,
corresponded in its individuality to some traits similar to her parents. Reality is therefore
no longer just internal, but objective, measurable, and as such recognizable to oneself and
to the world.

As the parents arrange all the objects brought from home, they smile.

L: Well, I'm a bit ashamed . . . but this bear is from when I was little, and I'm very attached to it. . . .

T: Good! . . . And I see that you have supported your teddy bear well on his back [the toy is placed leaning on a pillow]. You both need support right now.

L: Then I placed Mattia's first pacifier, then my cell phone because it has photos of Bianca. It's the only way to be close to her without being judged by others.

A: I brought the photo album from when I was little because it contains some of the expectations, the happy and carefree moments of my life. I too brought Mattia's pacifier and also Bianca's shoes that were a gift for me. The shoes were one of the few things I kept, because a photograph and the footprints are all we have left. Ever since they gave them to me, I've imagined her wearing them as if I could accompany her in her first steps. . . .

T: And the candle?

A: I often light one at home too.

The group stands up, and all the members approach and some hug each other. The work ends in a highly emotional atmosphere.

The proposal to give shape to the couple's space by placing objects of their choice in it made it possible to put Luciano's teddy bear, Antonella's objects, and Bianca's photos together. They are placed in a visible and physical space and recognized at a group level. It facilitated the tracing of a permeable boundary between internal and external dimensions and facilitated the reappropriation of a living space, the home, finally permeated by the explicit positive presence of Bianca. As an outcome, this phase produced a process of embodied integration, made visible and shareable due to the physical shaping.

Two Months Later

Two months later, we met Luciano and Antonella for a verification interview. During that period, intentionally, there was no contact with the therapeutic team. The meeting, aimed at verifying the postintervention outcomes, was held in an informal atmosphere at the couple's home. Only a few significant excerpts are reported here.

A: When we got home, we put Bianca's photo on the cabinet. He previously didn't want to, but instead it seemed such a natural thing now, and I'm sure it's due to the work.

L: Now I see her [Antonella] differently. Now I realize if she's pissed because I came home late from work or for something else. Before, she just looked pissed off, but now I understand the reason, if it's for Bianca or if for something else that happened. I also ask about it in a different way. . . .

A: We talk about it more easily. . . .

L: Everything we did helped me. It allowed me to get closer to her and to get closer to Mattia, because, with that act of sharing, the sharing of my mourning began. I feel calmer since we had that meeting, and I recommend it to everyone in the group. I see her [Antonella] in a completely different way.

A: I really felt everything he just said because . . . as soon as we returned home, I saw him more serene. He spoke to me about Bianca like he had never done before and shared with me what he felt. . . . It was something he had kept more to himself. . . . He also started talking about it with Mattia and going to the cemetery with him. So, for me it was something that helped the two of us as a couple. In that moment, it was as if I had found the piece that was missing . . . that is, that piece of experience that I had missed. It was as if I was there in front of him, and there she was in his arms, and he passed her to me. . . . In that moment it was as if I had reconciled with myself because I had never held Bianca in my arms, and this thing made me feel so angry. At that moment, I had actually picked her up. . . . For me it's been a strong experience, very strong and beautiful. I still get goose bumps now.

The outcome of integration at the different levels mentioned—individual internal space, couple space, physical life space—is well explained by her statement. Here we see how a cycle has been completed, the cycle of the couple who welcomes the child and also shares this complex and still largely unknown traumatic experience.

27

Ritual Practice, Addiction, Obsessive-Compulsive Behavior, and Routine

Ritual Dynamics and Human Coping Strategies

Jeltje Gordon-Lennox and J. David Knottnerus

OUR FUNDAMENTAL NEED FOR A SENSE OF SECURITY, SOCIAL TIES, AND WELL-BEING IS challenged by change, disorder, extreme difficulties, and trauma. Resulting feelings of stress, anxiety, and ineffectiveness can lead to severe illness, mental and emotional problems, and possibly death. Successful treatment of addiction and obsessive-compulsive disorders relies on approaches that recognize the human need for body-mind unity. Strategies for coping and healing guided by this requirement often involve a wide array of ritualized practices, both individual and collective in nature.

This chapter challenges the mind-body divide underpinning much of current medicine and psychotherapy with a unique transdisciplinary tool set composed of innovative diagrams and two theories—structural ritualization theory (SRT) and Polyvagal Theory (PVT). The tool set contributes to understanding the dynamics and function of ritualized behaviors such as ritual practices, addiction, obsessive-compulsive actions, and strict routines.

Following the trail left by the material traces of prehistoric human activity reveals that ritualized behaviors are an ancient human strategy for coping with change and challenges such as death, adversity, and catastrophic events (Nilsson Stutz & Stutz, 2022). In times of uncertainty, such behaviors may serve to reassure people or be weaponized to increase fear or power. They have long functioned to underpin social structures and values. For good or for ill, they are singularly effective in imposing order and controlling chaos.

After a brief look at the mind-body problem, this chapter focuses on a spectrum of ritualized behaviors that function as adaptive buffers to take the edge off suffering. A transdisciplinary tool set—tools to work with rather than tools that work for us—is applied to explore how we humans use certain ritualized behaviors with varying degrees of effectiveness to meet our deepest needs. The tool set includes innovative illustrations and two theories that contribute to awareness of why a person acts to give some activities a privileged status vis-à-vis others. It is also valuable for identifying strategies most likely to reduce human distress and enhance human flourishing.

The Mind–Body Problem

The gap between body and mind is not new, but current scientific approaches, particularly in education and medicine, are accelerating the harm caused. The dangers of severing body from mind were already recognized by Avicenna, a medieval philosopher and medical doctor known as a pioneer in psychosomatic medicine, notably neurology (McGinnis, 2010). He challenged his contemporaries with a thought experiment to show him how a healthy person, suspended in midair, might be aware of herself without using sensations to do so. The relevance of Avicenna's work to this chapter goes beyond his accent on body-mind unity. He tested drugs like opium for pain relief and anesthesia, treated various psychiatric disorders including obsessive-compulsive behaviors, and encouraged ritual and routine practices that promote well-being (ablutions, diet, and exercises involving sight, hearing, and voice modulation).

The mind-body divide remains problematic today as it has become the norm for human functioning. Humankind has become a renewable socioeconomic resource—with women, racial minorities, exiles, and migrants at the lower end of the scale. The individual is an assemblage of spare parts: an unsolvable case gets passed from doctor to doctor, becomes an experimental opportunity, or is simply abandoned.

Ritualizing Meets Human Needs

Modern values of individualism, competition, self-reliance, and self-examination make modern humans lonely in an unprecedented way, observes ethologist Ellen Dissanayake. She argues that ritualized behaviors satisfy evolving human needs: It is better to have something to do—preferably with others—in times of uncertainty than to try to cope by oneself or do nothing at all (Dissanayake, 2017).

Take handwashing: a common ritual activity found in numerous spiritual traditions and a sign of routine hygiene in most cultures and health care settings. During the recent COVID-19 pandemic, handwashing represented a strategy that helped many people cope with hardship: first as a sanitary and safety measure (body), then as an activity that reinforced a sense of connection and social integration (mind). Yet some people compulsively wash their hands even when it seriously damages their skin, even when they feel that the practice isolates them. How do useful, ordinary ritualized activities become harmful? Why do some ritualized behaviors attain a privileged status vis-à-vis other actions?

Structural Ritualization Theory

Questions like these led J. David Knottnerus to develop SRT. The theory has relevance for individual and collective behaviors because rituals can have profound consequences for people's cognitions, feelings, and overall character. SRT provides plausible explana-

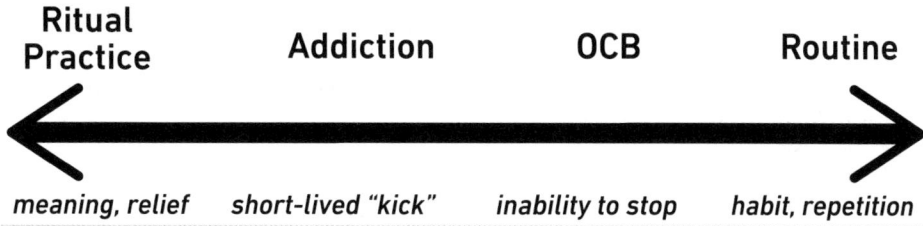

FIGURE 27.1 A spectrum of ritualized actions (SRT). Visually aligning ritualized actions gives a dynamic overview of the spectrum. © Jeltje Gordon-Lennox

tions for how everyday and exceptional ritualized behaviors impact the well-being of individuals and groups in a wide variety of settings, from placement in nursing homes, to prisons or refugee camps, to the aftermath of earthquakes, to polar expeditions, and the artificial environments driven by virtual reality (Knottnerus, 2016, 2023a). Simply stated, "ritual is like an engine that drives much of social life, sometimes quite intensely" (Knottnerus, 2016, p. 11).

SRT is particularly useful for shedding light on how and why personal, social, and global disruptions affect individuals or groups the way they do. It also contributes to understanding how a spectrum of ritualized behaviors respond to disruption (see Figure 27.1).

SRT ranks ritualized actions or ritualized symbolic practices (RSP) according to four observable factors: repetitiveness (frequency), salience (perceived prominence or centrality), homologousness (perceived similarity), and resources (e.g., materials and human traits; Knottnerus, 1997, 2023b). These four factors offer clues about the nature and effectiveness of the RSPs and how they may serve as social buffers against disruptive events, particularly in contexts that involve de-ritualization and re-ritualization (Knottnerus, 1997, 2016, 2023a, 2023b). Disruption, de-ritualization, and re-ritualization refer to the breakdown of social and personal rituals, their consequences, and the ways people may cope with such experiences by reconstituting old or new ritualized activities (Knottnerus, 2022).

In addition, SRT presents an analytical scheme that provides a framework for understanding how social rituals operate at different levels of society. The model depicts the influence of ritual dynamics over six structural levels of social order that consider the relationships between macro (global) and micro (interaction) systems as well as how rituals may be transmitted throughout society and have different consequences.

When SRT is applied to the four ritualized behaviors on the spectrum, we see that ritual practices have a high RSP ranking: they are fundamentally social, perceived as having a positive impact on well-being, and carry significant symbolic meanings or themes (high salience). Social (macro) and individual (micro) perspectives may differ. While society ranks cultural funerary practices high in repetitiveness, individuals who may rarely attend funerals rank them high only in salience. At the other end of the spectrum, routine has low RSP ranking; habits are consistently high in repetitiveness and contribute to well-being but are ill-suited to carrying symbolic meanings and so are perceived as having low centrality to social life. Addiction and OCB (obsessive-compulsive behavior) appear between these poles: like routine, they are associated with highly repetitive actions; like ritual, they can carry symbolic meanings; yet their perceived negative impact on the well-being of individuals and groups makes for low salience.

Polyvagal Theory

Polyvagal Theory, a complex neurophysiological "science of safety" developed by Stephen W. Porges, is described, applied, and referenced in many works, including this book (Porges, 2011, 2022b; Porges & Porges, 2023). Most relevant to this chapter are PVT's plausible neurophysiological explanations for shifts in inner and outer states that occur during ritualized behaviors. A sense of safety during ritualizing is less about being safe than about feeling safe—a state that goes far beyond the removal of objective threat.

The transitions (vagal, sympathetic, or dorsal) one makes when ritualizing in safe versus threat states are illustrated in Figure 27.2. Keeping this schema in mind helps us understand why people choose to practice certain behaviors over others as well as how these behaviors work for or against their well-being. The curly arrow (center left) suggests a certain fluidity of movement up and down between the three states: connected/serene (ventral vagal), flow/fear (sympathetic), and still/immobile (dorsal vagal). A sense of safety while in a dorsal vagal state contributes to rest, intimacy, or meditation (cf. Figure 27.2, left panel). Stretching and yawning luxuriously when awakening from sleep moves us smoothly from dorsal states through sympathetic states and finally to easeful ventral vagal states. In contrast, the thicker arrows show how moving from dorsal vagal upward toward a ventral vagal state requires passing through the sympathetic state (cf. Figure 27.2, right panel). A sense of threat while in a dorsal state (bottom right) may (re) produce feelings of embodied terror. To relieve these feelings, we must pass through a sympathetic state (middle right) to reach a more comfortable ventral vagal state (top left/right). This shift is not without risk. Many people resort to unsafe fight/flight behaviors such as addiction, OCB, or even suicide to relieve the sense of desperation (see situations in Gordon-Lennox, 2022).

A Spectrum of Ritualized Behaviors

In this section, the transdisciplinary tool set is brought to bear on a spectrum of ritualized actions as well as on their origins, function, and efficacy. Three illustrations compare the cyclic processes of ritual, addiction, and OCB (see Figures 27.3, 27.4, 27.5).

Ritual Practice

Typical ritual practice is stimulated by a conscious, compelling need to respond to perceived disruption (threat or stress) by marking a situation or life event with symbolic gestures and words. Whether the rituals are derived from our own sociocultural traditions or crafted anew, the resources used—metaphors, symbols, language, setting, and

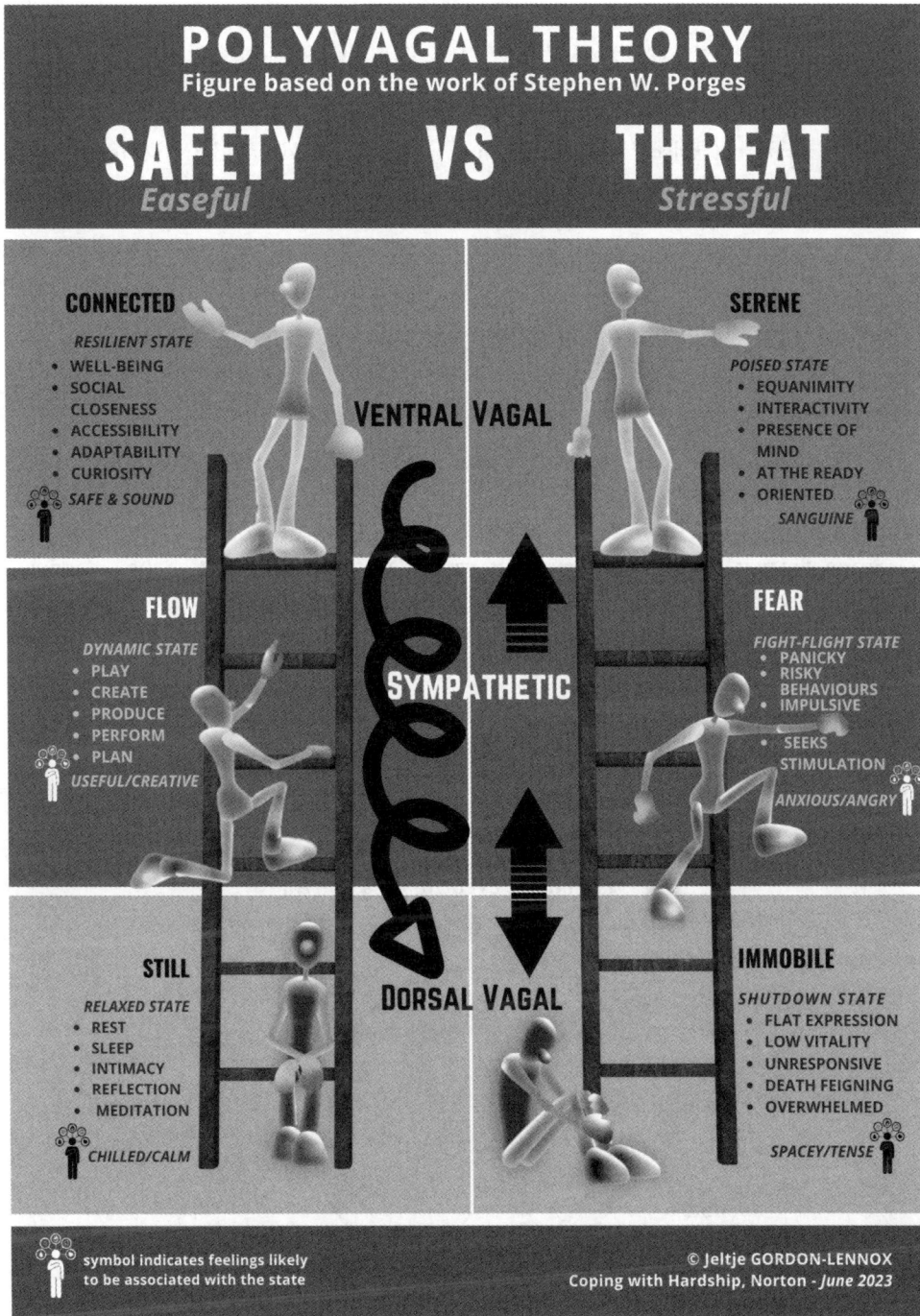

FIGURE 27.2 Applying Polyvagal Theory to ritualized action. A sense of safety or threat influences the dynamics and efficacy of ritualized activities. © *Jeltje Gordon-Lennox*

objects—must feel right to be right. During ritualizing that feels right, the practitioner feels safe, fully present (body), and aware (perception, cognizance). This state fosters curiosity, creativity, and social engagement, which may lead to a sense of freedom and restoration. Examples of ritual contexts conducive to feelings of joy or of moving forward include funerals that reflect the life and values of the deceased, weddings centered on the couple's shared values, hopes, and dreams, or even a cup of coffee consciously enjoyed (Gordon-Lennox, 2016, 2017, 2019, 2020).

PVT suggests that intentional ritual practices "create an inner space (time) between the interoceptive reflexive response associated with neuroception and the outer behavioral response" (Porges, personal communication). Accordingly, the O in the cycle—portrayed here as stimulus-organism-response (S-O-R)—accounts for an open time/space where inner/outer states and our surroundings can influence how we react to stimuli with a rit-ualized response (see Figure 27.3).

Applying SRT to concrete situations shows how everyday rituals play, and have always played, an important role in regulating human society to impact the well-being of indi-viduals and groups in a wide variety of settings. Disruptions experienced as extreme (e.g., hurricane, financial crash, internment) can cause de-ritualization, that is, the breakdown of social and personal rituals. Re-ritualization is about how people cope with disruption and de-ritualization by reconstituting old or creating new ritualized activities. A Soviet labor camp survivor recalls:

> Despite my fatigue and the cold, I kept the exercise routine I had followed at home and
> in the Red Army, washing my face and hands at the hand pump. I wanted to retain as

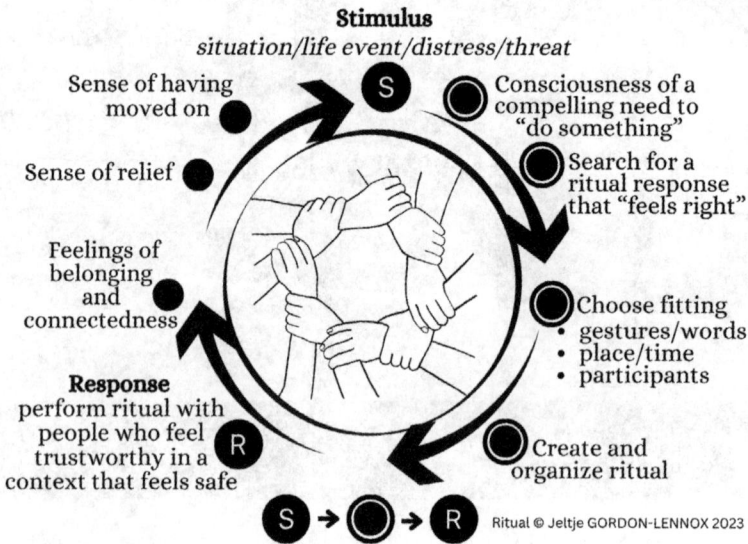

FIGURE 27.3 Cycle of typical ritual practice. The cycle of ritual practice typically contributes to containing strong feelings such as fear, sadness, and joy to promote a sense of relief and moving on.

much pride in myself as I could, separate myself from the many prisoners [who] stop caring. . . . If I had control over nothing else, I had control over this ritual which I believed would keep me from degradation and certain death. (Bardach, cited in Knottnerus, 2016, p. 125)

Ritual dynamics and meaning that are difficult to grasp or lack predictability appear to contribute to unsuccessful outcomes. Another SRT study, this time of polar expeditions, demonstrates the vital role of ritual practice for dealing with the disruption and de-ritualization caused by the monotony and extreme isolation of daily life; re-ritualization provided participants with meaningful focus, order, stability, and enhanced social relationships. Remarkably, successful expeditions ranked high in RSPs whereas unsuccessful ones ranked low (Knottnerus, 2023a).

Predictability, often associated with traditional religious rituals, is enhanced by dynamic interaction and connection with other people that feels safe. Thus, chants, prayers, meditation, dance, and posture can function as neural exercises of the vagal pathways to provide a behavioral platform for moving a person from a dorsal vagal immobilized state (see Figure 27.2, bottom right) to a sympathetic state that feels safe (middle left). Moreover, "the processing of this [ritual] space (time) preserves the nervous system from falling into addiction or psychopathologies such as OCB" (Porges, personal communication).

Ritual behaviors that feel (practitioner), look (observer), and function (efficacy) in a way that gives them privileged status vis-à-vis other acts involve embodied intentionality. Such intentionality may produce a sense of slipping into a time-out-of-time space where sensations (feelings) are richer, slower, and more intense than usual, paving the way for a sense of resolution. Embodied intentionality may well be what distinguishes ritual practice from other ritualized behaviors such as ordinary habits, routines, obsessive-compulsive actions, and addiction (Gordon-Lennox, 2022).

Addiction Behaviors

The addiction cycle represents another way of dealing with fear, disruption, and deritualization. Addiction behaviors—including substance abuse and compulsive behaviors such as gambling, overeating, the pursuit of power, and excessive use of technology—follow a cycle in which there is usually a kick or some form of satisfaction that activates the reward centers of the brain to provide temporary feelings of relief that facilitate relapse during the next bout of distress (see Figure 27.4).

Early studies on stress and psychosocial trauma give us further clues about the function and efficacy of addiction as a ritualized behaviour: "Overeating, increased and excessive consumption of alcohol and drugs are common manifestations of stressors beyond our natural endurance. . . . We are actually dealing with flight reactions. . . . They help us forget the cause of our distress and tend to temporarily replace it by the eustress of psychic elation, or at least tranquillization" (Selye 1956/1984, p. 177). Stressful events and anxiety are not necessarily traumatic. Trauma is less about what happens to us than about what it does to us (Scaer 2001/2014).

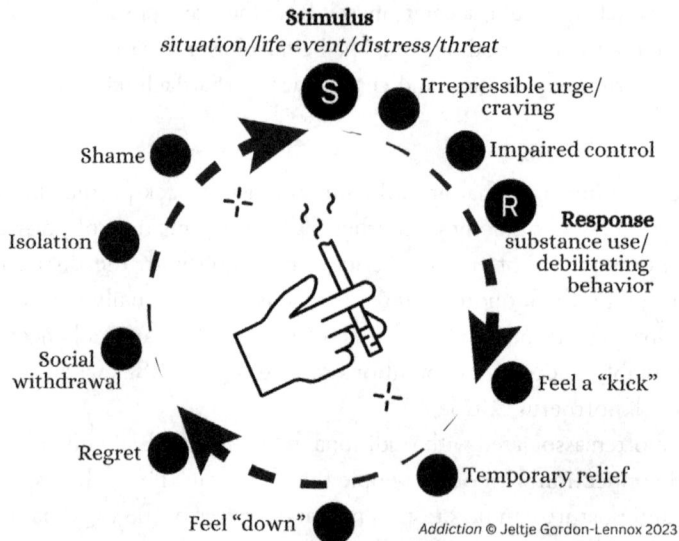

Stimulus
situation/life event/distress/threat

S

Irrepressible urge/ craving

Shame

Impaired control

R **Response**
substance use/ debilitating behavior

Isolation

Social withdrawal

Feel a "kick"

Regret

Temporary relief

Feel "down"

Addiction © Jeltje Gordon-Lennox 2023

FIGURE 27.4 Cycle of addiction behavior. Distress, craving, impaired control, and irrepressible urges lead to addiction behaviors that give short-lived feelings of relief that are inevitably followed by feelings of regret, social isolation, and shame.

SRT associates addiction behaviors with highly repetitive actions that may carry symbolic meanings for the practitioner; salience, however, is low on account of the harmful impact on well-being. Unlike ritual practice, which is designed to enhance predictability, addiction behaviors foster "biological rudeness" (Porges, 2017, pp. 8, 232–234; Porges & Porges, 2023, p. 83). It is less the behavior that is rude than a sense the addicted person has gone missing that violates our unconscious neural expectancies. This absence may consist of just a few seconds of unintentional disconnection—as when an internet addict glances away from us to check their phone. Such discourteous behavior is not due to faulty upbringing. Rather, it occurs on a neurological level with a shift in the autonomic in reaction to a sense of fear. Such behaviors oscillate between the fight/flight of sympathetic activity and dorsal vagal immobilization (see Figure 27.2, middle and bottom right). The O of stimulus-organism-response (S-O-R), which accounts for time/space in ritual practice, is absent in addiction behaviors.

Thus, addiction functions as an incomplete neural exercise; the lack of a sense of resolution feeds the need to return for another kick. Addiction thus generates a closed cycle that moves essentially from dorsal vagal to sympathetic and back again. Neither moralizing, nor prevention, nor the criminalization of addiction have proven successful. Nonetheless, about three-quarters of the people who become addicted to a drug as young adults recover—usually without receiving any treatment (Alexander & Smyth, 2022, p. 157). One of the first to formulate a clear understanding of epidemic addiction, Plato insisted that the root cause of addictive behaviors lies not with individuals who become addicted, nor with the addictive property of particular drugs or habits, but in the structure of unjust societies. Even the most harmful addictions serve a vital adaptive function for dislocated individuals in a fragmented world (Alexander & Smyth, 2022, p. 153). Although nothing can replace the kick, the most effective treatment options aim at restoring a sense of safety and connection, often in collaboration with other dislocated people, though self-help groups or local community groups.

> This [effort to form community] is often referred to as the recovery movement; it provides community-oriented support, acceptance, and treatment to prevent and overcome addictions through small-scale social change. Rather than focus directly on addiction, it deals more broadly with dislocation—with or without the support of professional social workers or therapists—to help people to find and retain a place in their community. (Bruce K. Alexander, cited in Alexander & Smyth, 2022, p. 158)

Obsessive-Compulsive Behavior

OCB cycles begin with a sense of foreboding and distress that mutates into obsessive thoughts before spawning irrelevant repetitive, compulsive behaviors. Ritualized actions such as counting, checking, or handwashing follow a rigid set of rules designed to prevent an unrelated imagined catastrophe (see Figure 27.5). There is little or no logical relationship between the thoughts, actions, and superstitious beliefs of impending disaster. Failure to perform the actions will trigger unrelated dreadful outcomes. For example, an adult man may check his locks repeatedly to keep his (healthy) mother who lives in another town from dying of a heart attack. Although the exact origin of the obsessive thoughts and compulsive actions is not fully understood, OCB clearly functions as an ineffective defensive reaction to a sense of threat or looming catastrophe. The obsessive-compulsive cycles may occur several times a day or months apart.

Using our tool set, we see that OCB ranks low as an RSP. Like addiction behaviors, OCBs are high in repetitiveness but low in salience. The irruption of unwelcome thoughts and compulsive ritualized behaviors causes de-ritualization by disrupting ordinary routines and rituals. Unlike addiction, OCB delivers no kicks. Unlike re-ritualization, relief is brief; the symbolically meaningless repetitive actions leave the sufferer no sense of resolution. The neurobiological explanation of "biological rudeness" applied to addiction also fits OCB—as when the sufferer must count until the right feeling is achieved. OCB patients with handwashing compulsions self-reported feeling unsatisfied about having washed enough. In both OCB and addiction, bidirectional influence of the behaviors operates on physical and emotional states; a sense of powerlessness, shame, or social isolation can relaunch a cycle.

Researchers who view the repeated performance of security-related behaviors "as a pathology of stopping, versus starting" recommend therapeutic options such as exposure with response prevention, cognitive-behavioral therapy, hypnosis, biofeedback, and pharmacology (Hinds et al., 2012).

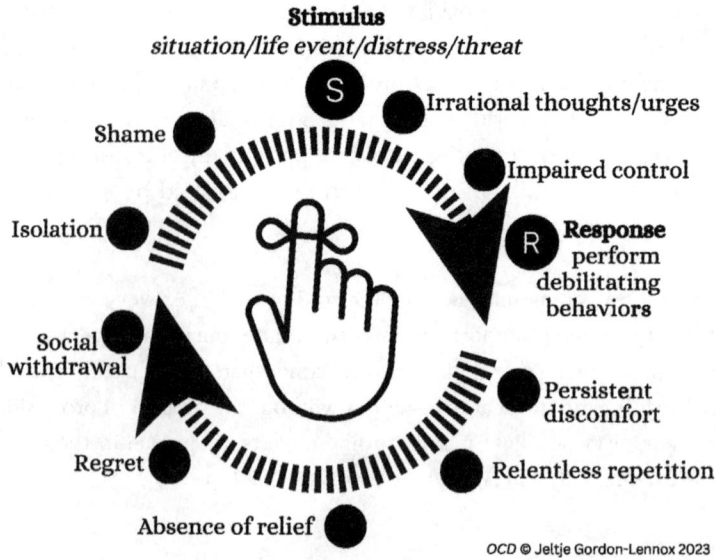

FIGURE 27.5 Cycle of obsessive-compulsive behavior. In OCB, a sense of threat engenders obsessive thoughts, which lead to unrelated repetitive behaviors aimed at preventing perceived danger. The stress of embarrassment, social isolation, and shame may be enough to relaunch the cycle.

An alternative hypothesis views the persistent feelings of danger in OCB as a normal autonomic nervous system (ANS) reaction to threat rather than a stop-signal deficiency. This points to a new understanding of the pathology and thus different approaches to treatment. The same bidirectional influences that enhance efficacy in ritual practice make OCB particularly inefficient for dealing with stressful circumstances and strong emotion. As with addiction behavior, such defensive reactions to a sense of threat may point to feelings of alienation or injustice linked to past trauma. Addressing an underlying sense of threat, isolation, and shame through conscious re-ritualization may be a challenge for OCB sufferers who have little experience with effective RSPs to draw upon. Yet, as for sufferers of addiction behaviors, those with OCB may benefit from a sense of safety in community and experiencing ritual space/time in the present.

Conclusion

We have seen that today, as in times past, humankind draws upon a spectrum of ritualized actions to cope with distress. Ritual practice, performed with embodied intentionality, can provide the practitioner with a sense of safety, social connection, and resolution. Routines contribute to individual and collective well-being but support neither symbolic meaning nor a sense of closure. Addiction and obsessive-compulsive behaviors are problematical coping mechanisms that interfere with relationships, well-being, and daily functioning.

Moreover, the behaviors provide only temporary escape from the disruption of emotional pain, stress, perceived threats, anxiety, and shame.

Human flourishing depends on our creativity to discover new ways of calming the body-mind in safe ways. A unique transdisciplinary tool set contributes to grasping the crucial role ritual dynamics play in human responses to distress. This chapter succinctly illustrates the social and neurophysiological bases for understanding how and why a person acts to give some activities a privileged status vis-à-vis others. Disruption, de-ritualization, and re-ritualization represent normal phases in the course of life (SRT). Ritualized actions that meet the criteria of the science of safety (PVT) and increase our capacity to feel safe and socially engaged have high potential for improving well-being. This chapter represents a starting point for new research and treatment, as well as for the formulation of principles and policies, designed to reduce human suffering and enhance healing.

28

Transcending Sexual Trauma Through Yoga

Evidence-Based and Practical Applications for Integrating Trauma-Informed Yoga Into Your Scope of Work

Molly Boeder Harris and Zahabiyah Yamasaki

Be Gentle With Yourself

Before you make your way through this chapter, I want to acknowledge that so often we come to this work because of our own experiences of trauma. This requires us to be so gentle as we tend to our unique lived experiences. We can honor our embodied stories with care and acknowledge all the ways that doing this work can also bring up our own wounds.

At the level of our psychobiology, our nervous system is constantly absorbing information as we move through our days, which can add to our depletion. We are not having uniform experiences. I invite you to honor the way the information lands for you in your body, as some of the material may feel triggering at times. Please rest, take breaks, and take care of yourself. Please know that the choices you make with your body are absolutely celebrated in this space.

I would love to begin with a practice to support you with nourishing your nervous system. You can listen to an audio version of this practice at https://www.zabieyamasaki.com. Please take as much time as you need to set up your space in a way that feels supportive, accessible, and nourishing for your body.

As it feels right for you, I invite you to find a unique shape of rest. Today, the invitation is to take all of the time you need and take up all of the space you deserve. You might take a few moments to set up your space in a way that feels kind and compassionate. You might even visualize that you are creating a space for someone you cherish. When you think about setting up a space for someone you cherish, what do you notice in regard to the amount of care and intention you are providing? You are worthy of the same compassion and care you pour into others. Perhaps reach for a pillow or bolster, an extra blanket, soft socks, or an eye pillow if that feels comfortable. Anything that would allow you to tend to your needs with extra gentleness. This is your soft place to land. You are deserving.

Know that the choices that you make with your body are absolutely celebrated in this space. I always say that showing up is the hardest part. If you wanted to find one shape and stay there for the entire practice, that would be amazing and supported. This is your body, your practice, and always your choice. Send yourself a moment of gratitude just for carving out this time for you today. For choosing you.

Today's practice offers a supportive space for refuge and time to intentionally nurture yourself and tend to your nervous system. As you start to settle in, I want to invite you to gently orient in your space. Maybe take a moment to notice the support beneath you. You might be sitting in a chair, resting on a mat, or feeling the soles of your feet on the ground. Can you take some time to embody what it feels like to be held, amid all the holding that you do? Know that you are strong and supported. You are never alone in your experience. Perhaps take a scan around your space and take note of anything that brings you a sense of resource or ease. It might be gazing out the window and seeing nature, cuddling with a pet, or taking a sip of water. You are welcome to keep your eyes open or closed or find a soft gaze. You may always choose what feels best for you.

Can you trust the strength of your body to hold you here today? Can you intentionally prioritize your nervous system? Can you let peace make its way? What does that look like for you?

Take all the time you need to settle in, rest and restore, and find beauty in being held and supported. There's no rush. Stay here for as long as feels comfortable for you.

When you feel ready, I invite you to slowly invite movement back into your body at your pace and in any way that feels accessible to you. You might bring some circles to your ankles and your wrists. Perhaps wiggle out your toes and your fingers. Compassionately and gently invite the awareness back in. Take all the time you need. There is no rush.

Contextualizing the Complexity of Sexual Trauma Recovery

I would like to contextualize the complexity of sexual trauma recovery within the current societal landscape. This context demonstrates the necessity for innovative approaches to transform how we respond to the trauma of sexual violence, so that in doing so, we may transform survivors' lives. While my personal experiences led to my professional focus on increasing sexual trauma survivors' access to trauma-informed, holistic health care and healing support, I believe that all trauma survivors deserve access for the very same reasons: trauma impacts all aspects of the human person, and healing is nonlinear.

I invite you to consider the scaffold of community-based rape crisis centers spread across our country and identifiable through an online search. I also invite you to think of the hotlines survivors contact in emergencies—whether to find the nearest rape crisis center, to make informed medical and legal choices, or to seek support during acute distress. These are tremendous resources in times of need.

Still, as trauma impacts various aspects of our brain and body, survivors often require the support of multiple professionals who can attend to specific, often interconnected, facets of their recovery over a lifetime. This team may include psychotherapists, bodyworkers, movement instructors, medical doctors, birth workers, and more. The long-term effects of sexual trauma on a survivor's life deserve long-term support. Survivors experiencing a combination of physical, psychological, spiritual, and relational changes and challenges are worthy of resources that address all of those aspects of the human person.

The acute crisis of sexual trauma is just a slice within the larger arc of a survivor's experience, yet resources are often limited to short-term and cognitive-oriented solutions. Many survivors are recently coming out of shock states when their access to support is terminated, or for the majority, support was never available in the first place. Other survivors have intellectually integrated pieces of their traumatic experiences through talk therapy; however, the echoes of trauma live on in body memories and physiological disruptions that haunt them.

There remains a gap between crisis resources and the nonlinear journey that awaits survivors after they exit those systems and spaces. We have the collective knowledge and ability to offer resources that reach beyond a single moment in a survivor's life. Rather than designing resources solely to help someone survive a trigger, we can empower survivors with the skills to transform the imprints of trauma. In doing so, their triggers may become less frequent and/or less debilitating. The resources we provide should reflect a belief that survivors deserve care whether or not they go to the emergency department, report, or publicly disclose. Survivors need resources that are accessible whether it's been five hours or five decades. This isn't simply a stance I bring as a survivor and an advocate who has navigated these systems and supported others in navigating them—this is a best practice in trauma-informed care. When we consider the countless barriers that prevent survivors from being able to fully face, understand, and express the horrors that they have endured, combined with the time, energy, and resources that have to come together to enable them to feel safe enough to bring their experience forward for healing, it is clear that resources need to be available across the life span.

There is a canyon between trauma survivors who are living most of their days in survival physiology and survivors who have been able to access and cultivate embodied healing practices. Many survivors fall into the canyon debilitated by a range of physiological, psychological, and relational challenges that go unmet by a health care and healing system that continues to separate physical and mental health care and that compartmentalizes psychological trauma from physical trauma. Still, even in the absence of readily available holistic healing resources, survivors continue to identify ways to heal, and their tenacious efforts deserve our acknowledgment and awe.

I would like to highlight the complexity of what survivors are handling, and what practitioners are encountering, as drawn from traffic on the Breathe Network's website. The Breathe Network is a national organization that I founded in 2012 to support survivors with trauma-informed, holistic health care and healing support. I created the Breathe Network for myriad reasons, including to address the gaps in sustainable healing care, the limitations on the forms of care being offered, and the lack of trauma-informed practice in many health care and healing spaces that prevented survivors from accessing support and/or retraumatized them in the process. I analyzed the search terms that led people to our work and found that the terms reflect the nuance, preciousness, and need for holistic, trauma-informed healing resources. I invite you to consider these intimate inquiries:

Learning to breathe after trauma
Massage triggered forgotten rape
Can an adult heal from childhood trauma
Why students ignore the breath in yoga
Regaining your body from sexual abuse through swimming
Finding safety inside and outside
Healing sexual blockages from trauma
Yoga sequence for trauma
Body modalities for trauma healing
How to create a safe space for a client
Embodiment and complex trauma
Sexual trauma hip healing
Shame and freeze responses

Brené Brown (2010) once said, "stories are data with a soul," and for me, the story of these data should embolden our collective efforts to increase access to resources that address the physical, psychological, relational, and social wounds of trauma. When survivors are connected with somatic practices, including yoga, they have direct access to personalized resources that can empower them as they navigate the vast and nonlinear landscape of healing. These practices invite a new conversation with the body, a new relationship with the body, and a more compassionate way of both listening and responding to the body. By fortifying survivors with greater embodied capacity, tools, and relationships upon which they can draw for support, these practices help to mitigate the intensity of the inevitable acute states that arise in the recovery process and increase the states of being affiliated with resilience.

The Breathe Network's Yoga Research

In 2016, under the umbrella of the Breathe Network, I codesigned a research study exploring the use of alternative healing therapies for survivors of sexual assault. There was minimal available research on the impacts, benefits, and barriers to accessing holistic forms of healing for this specific population, and yet I knew both anecdotally and through my own direct experience that practices like yoga, acupuncture, bodywork, Somatic Experiencing, and EMDR were profoundly impactful. Approximately 250 survivors participated in the online survey, and 40 participated in an hour-long interview. Our quantitative and qualitative research on survivors' use of alternative healing practices centered survivors as the experts who can deepen our understanding of how it is we heal in the wake of trauma (Breathe Network, 2023). As one survivor shared with us:

It's important for people to understand that a survivor's healing is nonlinear and may vary greatly from another. Survivors do not exist in a monolith. We deserve to be validated in the healing ways that resonate with us—even if these practices don't work for someone else. Survivors have the key to their own healing. They may need a guide, but they are the ones who know the most. (Einolf & Boeder Harris, 2015)

Initially, we collected and reviewed existing research about alternative and complementary healing methods for survivors of various forms of trauma. We identified an immediate dearth of research specifically attending to sexual trauma survivors' use of holistic and somatic therapies. Determining what we still need to learn about survivors' experiences navigating healing could influence and improve the way services are organized across a range of advocacy, health care, and academic spaces. One of our respondents affirmed the value of this research with their statement:

The way society and social structures are set up often re-traumatize us. Going outside the "conventional" methods (usually punitive measures) can be the most healing option because they offer you more control. In holistic healing spaces, often all of you is considered and accepted since these are the spaces created to help you heal, not just to carry out "justice."

I would like to highlight the portion of the study dedicated to yoga.

As sexual trauma involves being forced to leave the body, whether physiologically, psychologically, or otherwise, healing must incorporate a range of accessible pathways for survivors to come back to their body. Of the 250 survivors we surveyed, 63% of them had utilized yoga in their recovery after sexual assault. When we asked why they chose yoga, 70% responded that they wanted to address the impact of sexual violence on their body, 62% wanted to address the impact of sexual violence on their spirit, and 56% wanted to address the impact of sexual violence on their mind. Clearly, survivors are seeking a resource that addresses the embodied impacts of sexual trauma, and yet the majority of mainstream resources do not provide such support. Related, when we asked survivors what were the primary symptoms and/or responses that yoga helped to resolve, the highest ranking among them were anxiety, fear, depression, grief, guilt, panic attacks, sleep problems, alcohol and drug abuse, chronic pain, and eating disorders. Survivors are telling us with their bodies, behaviors, moods, and physical, psychological, and physiological symptoms how they have been impacted, and they require resources that can fully address the scale and scope of those impacts.

Among the many uniquely beneficial aspects of yoga for trauma healing is that it is relatively ubiquitous in the culture and that it offers more than just a platform for tending to trauma. It is also a place where survivors can experience the joy, comfort, and vitality that comes with inhabiting their body as well as the social resource of being in community with other yoga practitioners. When we asked survivors how long they used yoga as a healing practice, 81% of them said they were still using yoga in their regular life at the time of our study, and 74% said they had practiced yoga for more than a year. These percentages were significantly higher than other modalities surveyed.

With the rise of research on the benefits of yoga for addressing the impacts of trauma, survivors are being encouraged or feeling compelled to explore yoga as a healing modality. Unfortunately, most yoga schools rarely incorporate education on trauma-informed practice or the impacts of sexual trauma within their curriculum. This can result in practitioners unintentionally causing harm to their clients and patients. Due to social stigma and victim blaming, it takes tremendous effort for survivors to initially seek help. We know from survivors that negative experiences seeking out healing can exacerbate the somatic shame already associated with surviving sexual trauma, while reinforcing a belief that the survivor is simply not capable of recovering. Related to practitioner preparedness, one of the many key findings of our study came from asking survivors to prioritize the elements that increased their capacity to seek out care. Of our 250 participants, 89% shared that the provider holding specialized training on the topic of sexual violence was most essential.

The Risks and Rewards of Turning Toward the Body With Yoga

With the increase of research on the impacts of yoga on the brain and body, I have noticed trauma-informed yoga being promoted to survivors with an emphasis that yoga is the way for survivors who struggle to feel their bodies in ways that are resourcing to develop interoceptive skills or the capacity to sense inner-body experiences. As a survivor, a yoga practitioner, and a teacher, I believe this is a diluted understanding of interoception that fails to recognize trauma survivors' diverse experiences of embodiment. I have worked with survivors everywhere along the spectrum of feeling numb most of their waking hours to feeling far too much from the inside, and often alternating between those extremes. When I combine this with my years studying with somatic trauma healers (namely Joshua Sylvae and Kathy Kain) who, recognizing that each of us has our own somatic experience, not only center the body's voice, yet specifically center the unique voice of the body in front of them—I am reminded of the importance of resisting universalizing trauma responses. As found in the Breathe Network's study on yoga, what some survivors reported as most supportive in the yoga practice were experienced by other survivors as uncomfortable and even harmful. There was no one way or style of practicing yoga that was described as most therapeutic; rather, the practice, the teacher, the environment, and the community aligned in ways that uniquely served the survivor's physiology, identity, needs, and intentions in engaging the practice.

One of the most fundamental pieces of learning I have encountered in my study of the nervous system and somatic trauma healing is that interoception is both created and developed in a context. I owe this more comprehensive appreciation of interoception to Kathy Kain and my studies with her through Online Somatic Skills and Touch Skills for Trauma Therapists. The interoceptive context begins in utero and continues to be shaped and reinforced throughout the child's primary developmental years, which are considered as zero to three or zero to five. That said, the Adverse Childhood Experiences (ACE) Study tracked children's experiences between the ages of zero and 18 and found correlations between the impacts of trauma and the onset of physical and psychological health challenges within a wider age span (Centers for Disease Control and Prevention, n.d.). This allows us to make meaningful assumptions that while there are periods of more acute structural building in the brain and body, the shaping of the brain-body relationship does not complete at ages three or five, yet rather may be a continuous process.

If the context within which a person learns to sense their body is laden with threat or lacks consistent physical and emotional safety, their internal signaling systems may become tuned toward tracking for danger, since that feels more critical to survival. These somatic shifts in how we notice ourselves are not limited to children who grow up in traumatic or overwhelming circumstances. Adults who survive (sexual) trauma, and those who are also surviving other forms of systemic oppression, may develop survival strategies that include tracking for danger with their various attention-paying systems.

Given this, it's obvious why simply inviting survivors in yoga to engage in more internal noticing or focusing primarily on interoception is not necessarily going to be resourcing. The generalization that survivors struggle to feel their bodies and that yoga will be beneficial to them because it can awaken those internal feeling channels is well-intended, yet insufficient. As I mentioned earlier, survivors may oscillate from acute sensitivity to absence of sensation. It's not just about their ability to feel, it's about the accuracy of what they feel. There is research available that demonstrates how people with high levels of anxiety, which is common though not universal among trauma survivors, feel a lot inside their bodies. They might even report that they feel "too much" and that this abundance of feeling contributes to states of anxiety. The relationship between trauma and interoception is not universal; therefore it is essential that we attune to the embodiment of trauma and how survivors heal in a person-specific manner.

The shock of (sexual) trauma and the physiology required to survive it places a high demand on the whole body. There is an enormous amount of energy to process, and naturally, we cannot fully metabolize nor integrate it at once. Dr. Peter Levine (2012) introduced the concept of titration to the trauma healing field as a method for renegotiating trauma by working with one small dose of activation at a time and then taking time to land the experience of settling. As healing professionals, we may allocate months or longer to supporting a survivor in learning how to notice when there is safety. Survivors may be encouraged to track: What are the signals in the body? What happens to the muscles, facial expression, pace of thinking, their way of orienting, or how they take up space in their body and in their environment when they feel safe? How does their body move when safety is on board? How does their body feel when safety is on board? How does their body breathe when safety is on board? Building a "safety map" is crucial to healing (Kain & Terrell, 2018). Part of building the safety map is learning how to notice where there is safety and to be able to rest into it when it is present.

One example of how yoga teachers can infuse a sense of safety mapping in their teaching is the way they hold space during savasana (corpse pose) as their students are resting. The teacher can give them options for how they might organize their body and encourage them to choose a shape that feels most supportive. Teachers can remind them that changing their shape or moving during rest is okay, let them know what the duration of the resting pose will be, periodically check in with their voice to orient students in the room and in their body, and so forth. In some ways, there may be no more important moment of coregulation a yoga teacher offers than how they create a steady and supportive container for students during resting poses. Any of these ways of demonstrating that the survivor is in charge of their own embodied experience can be easily applied throughout a yoga class.

When safety is on board, yoga can be one of the places where survivors start developing greater capacity to discern among their body's interoceptive cues. This allows them to realize the rumbling in their belly may not mean that something bad is about to happen—it may mean they need something to eat. Their racing heart may not indicate that they need to run for cover—it may mean they are, in fact, having a wonderful experience. The floaty feeling they observe during a resting pose may not mean they are dissociating—it may mean they are settling into deep relaxation. The physiology of these experiences can feel the same, so it is being able to attend to the context of their internal and external environment, in combination with past experiences, that influences how they interpret those bodily cues.

Over time, the somatic practice of yoga can support survivors in being able to parse out the present context from their historical context or from their trauma-oriented referencing systems. Importantly, for survivors navigating ongoing oppressive and traumatic systems, yoga can offer pockets of letting down the vigilance that is too often required of their system. Somatic trauma healer and antiracist educator Danielle Murphy presents the possibilities these pockets create: "When the collective nervous system of our world is really disorganized, I'm looking for pockets of coherence. I'm tending to them and supporting their growth. That's protective for me" (Ndefo, Murphy, & Kelly et al., n.d.). Those moments of refuge are essential for survivors' personal healing and ongoing sustainability when societal conditions don't do a good job of supporting safety or are actively hostile toward individuals and groups. Meanwhile, knowing that advocates for social justice are striving every day to transform the societal conditions within which trauma is organized and enacted can be a resource while tending to one's own personal healing. For some survivors, the first pocket of coherence may be recognizing that there is a healing practice and healing space, like a trauma-informed yoga class, that has been adapted and expanded to include them.

While survivors are practicing yoga and building an intimate relationship with their body, they have the opportunity to cultivate a new inner map that includes both the imprints of trauma as well as those of their resilience. With practice, their interoceptive cues may begin to highlight experiences of neutrality, safety, or perhaps pleasure. Still, this takes time, and yoga is one of many pathways to developing this more accurate self-awareness. It's important for yoga teachers who are excited about trauma-informed yoga to understand and communicate that amplifying interoception is not initially the goal when the survivor's internal map is laden with trauma markers. For many of our students, our primary intention may be to support them in building the internal architecture for a new "somatic vocabulary" by noticing what they notice, discerning among those experiences, and then tracking where inside of them things feel more quiet, more comfortable, more easeful, less painful, or perhaps neutral (Kain & Terrell, 2018). Over time, survivors can embed those newer sensations and cues as valuable markers within their being.

Yoga can offer an environment to develop more interoceptive capacities and a sense of the body as a resource, and still, for many survivors, this also requires working with other practices. As one survivor in our research study reported:

> Many of us thought there were just a few ways to recover from sexual trauma: talk therapy, group therapy, and medication. This is often not enough. The trauma we experience impacts us throughout our being. We hold memories throughout our bodies, including our muscles, neuropathways, and areas of our brain. There are healing methods which are gentle and effective for this kind of healing.

Accessing complementary healing modalities that are explicitly focused on helping our body understand how the current signaling systems have long been associated with danger and how to bring those systems up to date, beginning to explore the body for signals of safety, comfort, belonging, or connection, and moving toward a place in our body where the survivor has access to the wide range of internal cues will serve to deepen their enjoyment of the experience of yoga as not only a practice where they heal but also a practice where they thrive.

Laying the Foundation: Overview of Trauma-Informed Yoga and Evidence-Based Benefits

Trauma-informed yoga in many ways is applying the broader frameworks of trauma-informed care (safety, trust, choice, control, empowerment, and cultural competence) to the practice of yoga. The ultimate goal of trauma-informed care is to support the healing and growth of survivors and, at all costs, to avoid retraumatization. Its underlying philosophy is actually grounded in grassroots and survivor-centered models that stem from early rape crisis center and anti–domestic violence movements. The framework was built from the powerful work of Black and Brown feminists who were doing direct service work to center the nuanced and culturally specific needs of survivors.

Trauma-informed yoga is an evidence-based modality and an empowering yoga practice that prioritizes the lived experience and healing of each and every student. Safety, trust, choice, and control are some of the core components of the practice.

Since safety is a critical foundation of trauma-informed yoga, I would like to highlight it here. Sometimes safety can feel like exhaustion because our bodies finally have permission to rest. This is an anchor for me in the scope of my work because oftentimes I am holding space for collective rest, for folks to slowly unpack their own unique and nuanced relationship to rest after navigating years of survival mode, hypervigilance, increased physical sensations, and the relentless moments that can accompany the journey of healing from trauma. As we move through these moments in life, it can become incredibly challenging to switch off the sympathetic nervous system.

So often the various symptoms we experience are somatic reenactments of past trauma. For example, we may dissociate as a way to help us create a safe container because what we are currently managing in our life is too much and has completely flooded our nervous system. We may be overtaxed, and our body is simply doing its best with the resources available. Survivors are worthy of honoring all the ways their body has supported their survival without shame or stigma.

When we feel safe, the parasympathetic nervous system helps us access ease, calm, and safety. Trauma-informed yoga can support this daily downregulation as survivors navigate the ebbs and flows of their healing journey. The practice can support them with tending to their physiological symptoms with care, building neuroplasticity and vagal tone, and enhancing their overall health, well-being, and resilience. Trauma-informed yoga often helps survivors build incremental shifts over time to widen their window of tolerance, strengthen their coping skills, and, most importantly, feel empowered in their choices and grounded in their worth.

I still remember the very first trauma-informed yoga series that I taught, nearly 10 years ago. I remember the butterflies. I remember the passion. I remember the pathways for healing that suddenly became possible. I began teaching trauma-informed yoga classes in the community for many reasons: To support survivors in what is oftentimes a lifelong process of healing. To create spaces in which to love ourselves throughout the journey and be reminded that our pain is not invisible. To affirm that we are not broken and that we can return to our bodies on our own terms. To support empowerment and empathy and space in which to be seen. To foster compassion when we tap into the deep knowing that there may be no sense of finality to this thing called healing. To hold on fiercely to our worthiness amid the many storms we will navigate in this life. To let ourselves be present with moments of relief and of joy. To consciously practice self-love with the many paradoxes of healing and hurt, courage and fear, joy and grief. To know that there are many entry points to healing.

I take into account all of the ways trauma impacts a student's mind, body, and spirit and offer intentionality and sensitivity in the way that I teach. I honor each student's pace, remind them that their choices are celebrated, offer many variations of each posture, integrate invitational language and trauma-sensitive breath practices, and cocreate with them. Every student has a unique and nuanced journey, and I remind them often that their lived experience is their greatest teacher.

Trauma-informed yoga supports students in activating their parasympathetic nervous system and creates more space for safety, rest, growth, and abundant joy. When given these tools, students can also access greater depths of inner capacity and resilience in navigating not only chronic stress, trauma, and crisis but also the everyday challenges that life presents.

Some of the frameworks of teaching from a trauma-informed lens include the following.

Empowerment-Based Language

Empowerment-based language is one of the foundational elements of teaching from a trauma-informed lens. Integrating empowering, compassionate, supportive, and invitational language into your classes offers survivors of trauma a sense of control over their own lives.

Supportive Presence and the Embodied Practice of Holding Space

The framework of supportive presence centers the way we authentically show up every time we teach and/or hold space. In the context of trauma recovery, until the stress-response system within our bodies is functioning well and has flow and space, it can be challenging to access safety. Having a supportive presence empowers survivors to experience a safe connection and attunement to another human being and creates opportunities for coregulation.

Self- and Community Care for the Teacher

Engaging in regular practices and rituals to support your own mental health is one of the most important ways to do this work in ongoing and sustainable ways. This might take the form of colleague support and supervision from a mentor, boundaries, personal nervous system practices, a manageable workload, time off, and self- and community care.

Consent and Physical Assists in Yoga Spaces

We must be mindful of creating consent frameworks and structures of safety in yoga studios and spaces when it comes to offering physical assists. It is hard to reconcile that in so many movement spaces, the assumption is that it is okay to touch people. Students are often asked to opt out of being touched. Yet the burden should never be placed on students to communicate this.

Creating Safety in Physical Yoga Space

There are so many mindful shifts we can explore to help make the space more nourishing, comfortable, and accessible and support folks with accessing what Deb Dana calls "a ventral space." Students who live with ongoing trauma symptoms and PTSD can be sensitive to sounds, temperature, and physical proximity, among many other elements. Changes in language and empowering agency throughout class can support survivors in working toward an internal and external sense of safety in the room.

A Trauma-Sensitive Approach to Breath Work and Mindfulness

In her book *Trauma and the Body*, Pat Ogden shares how those who have experienced trauma "often experience inner-body sensations as overwhelming or distressing" (Ogden et al., 2006). As a result, breath work and mindfulness meditation practices can trigger traumatic experiences and memories for survivors in many different ways. Teaching with a trauma-sensitive approach involves watching for dysregulated arousal, offering a variety of cues and choices to engage with the breath, encouraging and empowering survivors to integrate movement into a meditation practice if stillness is too triggering, and more.

Supporting Students Who Are Triggered

I invite you to take some time to develop a tool kit of exercises that you can draw from to assist students with managing triggers, as it may not be the best time to introduce something new. This might involve self-regulating asana poses, inviting students to reorient by engaging their senses, providing additional resources, and more.

Cultural Considerations and Accessibility

It is critical that, as folks sharing this practice with trauma survivors, we root ourselves in the framework of ahimsa. Being an ally is committing to showing up and helping people feel seen, welcomed, cared for, and enough. The power of trauma-informed and culturally affirming collective movement is that oftentimes there are just no words—the connection is felt. Communities who have been historically marginalized deserve supportive tools for nervous system regulation as they navigate daily experiences of systemic oppression and ongoing trauma resulting in embodied inequality.

Evidence-Based Benefits of Trauma-Informed Yoga

This modality can help survivors safely reconnect to their bodies, allowing them to access resources when they are ready. Below is an overview of our research at the University of California.

A study conducted with survivors participating in an eight-week trauma-informed yoga program across eight campuses in California measured the following (Davidson, 2019):

- Psychological symptoms: depression, anxiety, PTSD
- Self-compassion: mindfulness, self-kindness, self-judgment
- Common humanity, isolation
- Body awareness and dissociation
- Safety

The assessment process as outlined by the researcher involved a pretest, a posttest, and an eight-week follow-up. The sexual assault response offices provided an informed-consent process and online questionnaire during the survivor-intake process, as well as attendance sheets and checklists to confirm the facilitation of the curriculum (to ensure some sense of consistency across each campus). And last, students were invited to fill out the same online questionnaire at the end of the last session of the eight-week series, and again eight weeks later.

The outcomes of this study demonstrated significant decreases in depression, anxiety, PTSD symptoms, self-judgment, dissociation, and isolation. There were significant increases in self-compassion, body awareness, and mindfulness (Davidson, 2019).

Additional benefits of the practice that survivors of trauma have shared include:

- The recognition of choices in one's life
- Feelings of safety and strength
- Ability to be more expressive in therapy
- Positive coping skills, including strengthening inner resources
- Self-care strategies
- Understanding of how to ask for help
- Improved trust in self and others
- Development of a strong sense of community
- The establishment of boundaries and understanding how to be assertive
- The ability to be intimate again
- Decreased feelings of depression, stress, and anxiety
- Decreased symptoms of PTSD
- Empowerment to seek other resources such as counseling and medical support
- Increased confidence and courage
- Increased feelings of self-compassion
- Increased awareness of needs, mindfulness skills, and resiliency
- Strengthened self-esteem
- Strengthened emotional, physical, mental, spiritual, and interpersonal skills
- Increased feelings of being seen, valued, and affirmed

Healing the Embodiment Conflict With Yoga

Sexual trauma is one of the most pervasive boundary violations that a human can endure. Survivors may experience that violation physically, psychologically, energetically, and/or spiritually. The threat cycle that initiates a cascade of physiological responses, actions, and changes within a person's body is experienced systemically. As feminist philosopher Ann Cahill (2001) describes in her book *Rethinking Rape*, "It cannot be assumed that there is one aspect of that person's being that is untouched by the experience of rape. There is no pristine, untouched corner to which to retreat. . . . The extent of the rapist's influence is broad, but not infinite." In my experience, bodily breaches require bodily repair.

On top of the acute injury of trauma, there are the long-term impacts of the boundary breach. Survivors may develop management strategies to protect against intrusion into their inner world, including creating physical or emotional distance from others. They may also discard parts of their own body that they no longer feel safe inhabiting. Some survivors will live with a sense of absolute permeability, where there is no differentiation between themselves and everything in their surrounding environment. This could be because they never existed in a body where their sovereignty was recognized and honored, because incidents of trauma were repeatedly committed against them, or simply because the intensity of how sexual trauma impacted them shattered their capacity to consciously and joyfully inhabit their body.

In the wake of sexual trauma, many survivors face an embodiment conflict. They may have a desire to access a felt sense of being in their body, a longing to find or come home to themselves, while simultaneously there is an understandable aversion to sensing inside because so much trauma residue is there. Even the absence of feeling the body, for example identifying an emptiness inside, can be a reminder of the heartbreaking loss of one's body, so they stop paying attention. Yoga offers a practice for tending to this embodiment conflict. Particularly meaningful for survivors is the way in which yoga allows for and can facilitate the radical transformation of one's relationship to one's body. In the throes of a traumatic event, and often for years or decades after, the body can feel like an enemy. The survivor may feel like they are being held hostage within their own shape. It no longer feels like their own, or perhaps it never felt like it was theirs to begin with. Through yoga, they can recover and reclaim a sense of ownership and belonging within their body. They can become fluent in the language of their own physiology. They can recognize how various systems and structures of their brain and body collaborated in service of their survival. In time, the body may no longer be solely a container housing fear, grief, or tension, yet rather may be recognized as a powerful, adaptive, and highly sensitive tool to move them both through and beyond the deepest manifestations of pain.

Within the Breathe Network's study, survivors reported how yoga assisted them in coming back to their body:

Yoga helped me reclaim my body. I dissociate a lot, and yoga keeps me grounded with my body and my mind connected, in a way I can feel. It lowers my anxiety levels and gives me a sense of control. It also reminds me to be kind to my body and allow myself to feel good.

Feeling comforted by using body movement and exertion in a soothing way. Simply knowing that yoga has been used by some for mental healing caused me to expect that effect on myself.

I had to learn not to push myself too much.

I learned how to live in my body. To feel body sensation. I learned to breathe through difficult experiences. These simple skills have been the most helpful in helping me cope with depression, confront anxiety and fear, and live more mindfully so I don't participate in compulsions like binge eating, drinking, or self-harming.

Survivors also shared ways in which the yoga practice was challenging. This had to do with not only the practice but also how the teacher led the practice:

Yoga brought up flashbacks for me.

In yoga classes, there was a "positive thinking" bias that felt dismissive and negating.

Yoga can be very triggering and there isn't always a convenient place to get triggered, with nowhere to go and nothing to do about it. Many yoga teachers are not trauma-informed and can say and do fairly invasive things. For me, yoga caused panic.

Given the social, emotional, psychic, relational, and personal challenges that individuals must brave after surviving sexual assault, it is clear that a comprehensive yoga practice involving a personalized combination of organic movement, exploring sensation, conscious breathing, mindfulness, meditation, and deep rest can naturally bolster healing. A survivor can benefit from connecting to their own rhythm within a vinyasa yoga class as well as by tapping into the comfort that accompanies a yin yoga sequence. Since there is no such thing as a one-size-fits-all approach to practicing yoga, survivors are able to explore and identify a style, a setting, and a teacher that resonates with them. Depending on their needs, abilities, and preferences, at any given point, the yoga practice can be tailored to a survivor's sense of what will best support their unfolding process. How this looks may be dramatically different from one survivor to another and from one day to the next.

As a physical, psychological, and spiritual practice, yoga creates a unique environment where survivors can explore their internal environment—sensation, patterns, emotion, meaning, and so on—with inquisitiveness. It is here they can cultivate compassionate responses to all that they might discover inside. This unfolds in tangible ways in the body, such as making a conscious choice to adjust one's position in a pose to make it more tolerable or pleasurable, or backing out of a pose completely and trying something different that offers greater comfort. Survivors can translate yoga insights into how they approach their changing states throughout their recovery—valuing sensitivity, curiosity, and flexibility. The feedback of the body becomes a map that guides and informs both the yoga practice and the larger arc of the healing journey.

Importantly, yoga creates a space where survivors can build intimacy with their innermost selves. Counter to the feeling of brokenness or fragmentation that trauma can create, yoga recognizes and offers survivors a practice to affirm their innate wholeness. Identifying a practice that uniquely serves the survivor is a worthy investment of their resources. In that search, they come into contact with a somatic exploration of what for them is healing, what is resourcing, what liberates them from a trauma narrative, and what exists beyond the trauma they have survived. The yoga practice and the inquiries that it opens up not only nourish healing during the most difficult times but also sustain and magnify the gift of somatic empowerment that the survivor may continually cultivate through a dedicated practice. As yoga teachers, somatic practitioners, and healers, we have the enormous privilege and responsibility to create a wide container for our students and clients to discover not only the healing possibility of the practice we offer yet, importantly, to tap into the healing wisdom they already embody within their own shape. One of the teachers who has most inspired me in yoga and far beyond, Kristin Laak, once said that prior to starting her class she "set(s) the intention to get out of the students' way." For me, this is one of the most simple and profound reflections on the shape of a trauma-informed yoga class. Ideally, in the way they hold space, the teacher is actively creating a steady and spacious container that allows the student to discover their own inner teacher.

29

Turning Competition Into Coregulation

Competition Is Grounded in a State of Threat

Michael Allison

MERRIAM-WEBSTER'S DICTIONARY DEFINES COMPETING AS STRIVING TO GAIN OR WIN something by defeating or establishing superiority over others who are trying to do the same. In this definition itself, we see the underlying physiology of how most of us compete in this world. We look to defeat the other. We try to establish ourselves as superior to them. We approach our competition as the enemy standing in the way of getting what we want. This approach to competition, two rivals striving to obtain something that only one of them can possess, is grounded in a threat-oriented physiology, a body that doesn't feel safe enough, resourced enough, or good enough to belong.

It is only when we don't feel safe enough, resourced enough, or good enough, that we approach competition as a fight or a battle over something. In contrast, when we actually feel safe enough, resourced enough, and that we are good enough to belong here, in this moment, on this stage, against this opponent, competition changes into something else. Competition becomes an opportunity to elevate, a chance to challenge ourselves in ways we couldn't do on our own. It becomes an opportunity to play and coregulate. More than a mindset, our capacity to turn competition into coregulation, into play, resides in our physiology. Technically, to play we must have enough ventral vagal control of our bodily state, access to our social engagement system, and an efficient vagal brake. These are the neural mechanisms that enable a competitive environment to shift from a battlefield to a playground and make it possible to turn competition into coregulation.

Our capacity to engage and disengage our vagal brake provides the physiological substrate for playing (i.e., coregulating) in competitive environments against opponents that might normally trigger attacking, defending, or protecting. This is functionally how we play. The neural mechanisms that enable us to coregulate and play are the same neural mechanisms that support optimal and efficient energy production, metabolic output, biomechanics, coordination, problem solving, recovery, resilience, sociality, and creativity.

To play is to see, hear, and feel the opponent as a partner versus an enemy. To play is to explore and possibly elevate our game and the expression of our skill set through the interaction we are having with the other, the person on the other side of the net, or the team on the other side of the field. Technically, our capacity to play resides in, and emerges from, a physiology that feels safe, that is regulated and resourced, and that has efficient and effective access to the social engagement system.

Our World View of Competition

We live in a world that is continually bombarding us with cues of risk, uncertainty, unexpected change, constant evaluation, and relentless competition. In addition, we have a foundational belief that permeates our culture and the institutions we live, learn, work, and play in, that to survive we must compete. We must be faster, stronger, smarter, fitter than everyone else. We must win, take what's ours, and grab the resources we need to survive and thrive—otherwise someone else will. Otherwise we will be left behind.

As humans, we also crave competition. We celebrate it in sport and in life as a battle between rivals, as warriors, looking to dominate, take control over, and at times even destroy the other. We celebrate ourselves as competitors for doing whatever it takes to win, at any cost, letting nothing stand in the way as we fight for power, fame, fortune, and status. We continually compete for these valuable resources we need to survive in our combative, competitive culture.

As spectators to competition, we are intrigued by the uncertainty of the outcome. We are fascinated by the unexpected, the unpredictable actions and reactions, sudden outbursts of emotion, and the seemingly uncontrollable temper tantrums, meltdowns, and displays of giving up or full collapse. We are captivated by the random, unanticipated momentum shifts that come out of nowhere and turn everything around in the blink of an eye. We marvel at the meteoric rise of an unknown rookie, and when the underdog miraculously overcomes the greatest of all champions.

As competitors ourselves, we enjoy the surge of energy, the exhilarating excitement, and the challenge of what might unfold as we compete against an opponent. We love the adrenaline rush of taking the field and the nervous tension of stepping out of our comfort zone into the unknown. We dream of winning big in front of our peers on the grandest of stages. We fear that others are closing in on us and realize that our time is now or we might never win again. We yearn for that flow state where we effortlessly move with fluidity, creativity, and freedom, playing as if nobody's watching. Once we taste this, once we tap into this amazing bodily feeling of being fully present, entirely connected to who we are and completely dropped into what we are doing, we long to experience it again and again and again.

What Prize Are We Seeking?

But what are we really competing for? For what prize are we willing to do whatever it takes to win? What are we compromising in our quest to fight for what's ours at any cost? And could there be a different way, a better and more sustainable approach to competition? Or better yet, a way of living, a cultural belief system, and institutions to support our learning, working, playing, and ultimately healing that are more accurately and appropriately aligned with our biological imperative and our evolutionary heritage?

To find out, we need to look beneath the surface. We need to dive beneath the motivation, the drive, the hunger, the enduring quest to be the best. Beneath all of it, inside the bodies of everyone involved, is our shared biological need to belong, our enduring need to be seen, included, valued, liked, and even loved. We can see, hear, and feel a sense of safety or threat in ourselves in the face of competition, whether we are watching two rivals battling it out or whether we are on the field ourselves.

More than a belief, psychological construct, learned behavior, or emotional response, being good enough to belong is necessary for our survival in a dangerous world. From our very first breath until our last, we need others to gather and share resources, to cooperate in solving problems, to come together to reproduce and help raise, protect, and provide for our offspring. To feel unworthy of belonging, dismissed, defeated, alone, and left out would be adaptively and reflexively interpreted by our very primitive survival networks as extremely dangerous and even life threatening.

I belong here. I don't belong here. I am good enough. I am not good enough. I feel safe. I don't feel safe. Safe enough, good enough, I belong here—we know it when we see it in others. We know it when we feel it in ourselves.

It's this feeling in our body that attracts us, holds us there, and keeps us coming back for more. It's what unites us together and at the same time separates us into opposing sides. Us versus them. Me versus you. It lies beneath the fear and the motivation to keep going, and it's truly at the heart of competition on any stage. It's what it really means to be human.

Competition is an attempt to win resources to fulfill our enduring quest to feel safe, connected with others, and that we are good enough to belong.

We want to prove to ourselves, the people who care for us, and the world around us, that we are good enough. Good enough to belong. Good enough for this stage. Good enough to be on the team. Good enough to be here, right here, and right now, in this moment. When we understand this lifelong journey, embrace this biological need in our own body, and connect to this shared core of humanity, we can look at our opponents not as enemies but as reflections of ourselves. We can see another body searching for safety, connection, and belonging. We can hear another human wanting to be heard and needing to be good enough to belong. We can sense and feel another soul on the same journey to be who they really are. Another being, just like us, longing to trust that who they really are is good enough to belong.

A Field of Play

For many of us, especially those of us who have been deeply hurt by those we trusted the most, we are living in bodies that don't trust that it's safe to feel safe. We might prefer competition over play because competition matches our bodily state of threat and fear. To play might feel dangerous. To relax might feel risky. To treat the enemy as a partner in play might feel like extreme vulnerability.

However, when we look at competing through a biological lens, the battleground may become an opportunity to strengthen our resilience, measure our progress, and elevate our game. Competition may become a chance to reach our highest potential and access levels of expression, performance, and creativity that we could never reach alone. This is the physiology of the true champions, artists, deep thinkers, leaders, and performers. This is the physiology of what it really means to be human. This is the physiology of what I call the Play Zone.

From a polyvagal perspective, play is a neural exercise whereby we build the physiological capacity to flexibly navigate a wide variety of bodily states while maintaining access to our social engagement system. Play is not done alone or in isolation but involves others and is a reciprocal, synchronous, and spontaneous act. Play also involves violations of expectancy, interruptions in the exchange of safety and connection that might trigger reflexive reactions of defense. However, these disruptions are quickly repaired through an exchange of cues of safety via tone of voice, facial expressions, postures, and body language.

Play builds physiological resilience, which is the capacity to flexibly navigate a range of bodily states with awareness, intention, and skill, to maintain access to our social engagement system in the face of challenge, and to recover efficiently into a state supporting homeostasis when disrupted by a challenge. Simply put, we must feel safe enough and connected enough in order to play. At the same time, we can meet a body that is mobilized in a defensive, threat-oriented state, and add some safety, some comfort, and some interaction with others, to turn this mobilized threat response into play. And through this process we can help a body begin to trust that it's safe to feel safe, even in the face of competition. We can play our way into healing and trusting that it's safe to coregulate with others.

Our Adaptive, Reflexive Reactions

- What if competition didn't have to feel like a battleground?
- What if our fear of failure could morph into the thrill of seeing what plays out?
- What if we could find a way to play when we might otherwise be triggered to attack, defend, or protect?
- What if we could turn competition into coregulation?

All of this is possible when we understand how our bodies adaptively, reflexively respond to risk versus safety, challenge versus connection, and feeling alone versus feeling like we are part of a team. All of this is possible when we feel safe enough, connected enough, and good enough to let down our guard, drop our defenses, and free ourselves up to be who we really are.

We can realign our body in the face of competition to support our intentions, values, and performance only when we:

- meet our body where it is, without shame, blame, guilt or criticism;
- recognize where we are in the predictable pattern of adaptive reactions to pressure, uncertainty, and challenge; and

- relate to what's happening inside of ourselves, and care for our reflexive bodily responses, in ways that cultivate a felt sense of safety, connection, and belonging.

In essence, we don't try to stop our bodily reactions from occurring. We don't try to ignore, repress, or numb what's going on inside our bodies. Instead, we meet ourselves where we are, and we relate to what's happening on the inside in ways that help to realign our physiology to support our intentions, values, goals, the expression of our skills, and ultimately our highest potential.

When we appreciate the neural mechanisms beneath our conscious control that govern our bodily reactions to features of safety, danger, and life threat, we have an opportunity to step out of our stories of shame, blame, guilt, and criticism, for ourselves and for others. Instead, we can see things for what they are and differentiate behaviors, emotions, thoughts, and beliefs from intentions, character flaws, lack of discipline, or mental weakness.

Putting Our Feelings Into Play

As he stepped up to the line to serve out the match and claim his first ATP title, the tennis player described to me that he felt "a bit tight." When I asked him what he did with that feeling, he didn't know how to respond. "What do you mean, what did I do with that feeling? I just served the ball, did what I always do, just served it into the box." This was a player ranked in the top 100 in the world of professional tennis, and he didn't have any idea of what to do or not to do with this bodily information. I said, "I am a 50-year-old amateur player, and I don't even serve the ball when I feel tight." He didn't understand at first. I repeated this again, and again for a third time. We suddenly burst out in laughter together as we both realized the absurdity of what we were really talking about here. To pretend that we don't feel tense under pressure, or to repress and ignore how we feel in the biggest moments is not the way of the professional. Instead, we feel the tension, the heart pounding, the breath quickening, and we see it for what it is. We then find what our body welcomes as reassuring, grounding, and within our control such as slowing our exhales, widening our shoulders, relaxing our jaw, or focusing our attention on the feel of the grip. We speak the language of safety to the body without criticism because we respect our body's attempt to keep us safe in the onslaught of risk, uncertainty, and evaluation we face on the court of challenge. In the three years since our conversation, this professional tennis player has learned how to relate to his feelings and the adaptive bodily reactions we experience in high-stakes situations in ways that have helped him not only win several tournaments but firmly establish himself within the top 20 in the world, and climb as high as number eight in the rankings.

Finding Our Play Zone

As social mammals, from our very first breath to our last, we are seeking, and longing for, a felt sense of safety, connection, and belonging. When we find it, feel it, and absorb it, we

Safety

The Play Zone

Connection

Belonging

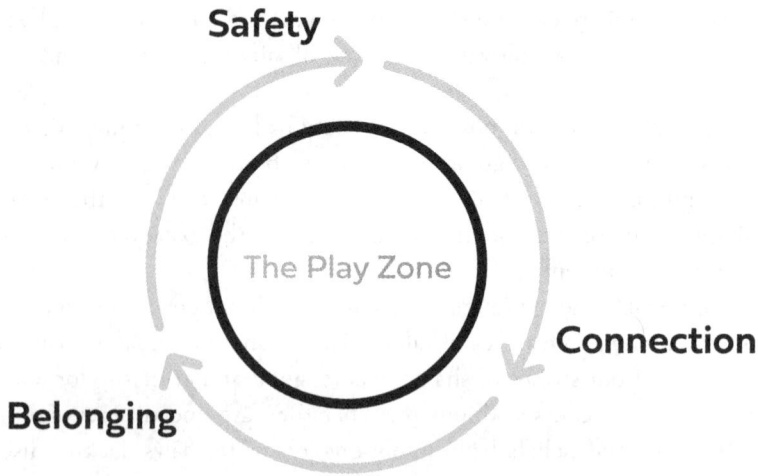

FIGURE 29.1 The safety, connection, and belonging loop.

aren't done; rather, we've just begun. This biological quest is a lifelong cycle of needing to feel safe and at ease in our body, connected to ourselves, others, and the world, and a felt knowing that we belong here, in this place, at this time, with our people, doing what we are doing. This is a dynamic process that is continually being challenged or supported by features in our internal, external, and relational environments. These environmental cues are being subconsciously detected and evaluated, and trigger very primitive regulatory centers in the brain stem that shift our physiology to optimize survival. This not only changes metabolic output and the autonomic regulation of all our internal organs and bodily systems, but it also influences every aspect of how we experience the world, relate to ourselves, and act, react, and interact with others.

These bodily feelings of safety, connection, and belonging are interconnected, while at the same time they may also be independent and dependent experiences, emerging in isolation or in combination with one another.

More than a subjective feeling, a felt sense of ease and safety reflects a body being autonomically regulated to support our health, wellness, and even our performance. Neurophysiologically, when we feel safe and in control, our autonomic nervous system is optimizing the neural regulation of our internal organs, bodily systems, facial expressions, tone of voice, movements, postures, and overall body language to promote our wellness, resilience, and our ability to relate with others. Functionally, when we feel safe and at ease in our body, we have a physiological opportunity, a neural platform available to us, for connecting with our own bodily feelings, as well as with the bodily feelings of others.

When we feel safe enough physiologically, and connected enough to our own bodily feelings and the bodily feelings of others, we have the opportunity to tap into an authentic felt sense of inclusion, being an integral part of a collective whole, and a deep knowing that we belong in our body, in this moment, with everyone and everything else around us, on this planet.

In contrast, when we don't feel safe, when we are in a body on guard, adaptively triggered into a physiology to protect and defend, we may spontaneously have an experience of connection to a trusted other, which might instantaneously drop our defenses and reflexively spawn a feeling of safety in our body. This might enable a felt sense of connection and belonging with the other, as we "get each other" in this moment, despite the presence of other features of risk, uncertainty, and danger.

This loop of safety promoting connection and belonging, or connection promoting safety and belonging, or belonging promoting safety and connection becomes an experiential autonomic feedback loop supporting the physiological state of health, healing, recovery, well-being, and the Play Zone (see Figure 29.1). The internal, external, and relational features supporting this feedback loop may be spontaneously present and available, or they may need to be deliberately cultivated through strategies, inner resources, and ways of relating to others.

Theoretically, when the Play Zone is interrupted, acutely or chronically, a reliable pathway back into a physiological state supporting the Play Zone could be through skillfully and deliberately cultivating internal experiences of safety, connection, and belonging, independently, in any sequence or combination, or through a dynamic, interactive social feedback loop comprising all three components through reciprocal and synchronous communication, touch, movement, engagement, and play with trusted others.

How We Feel Is More Than a Feeling

When we strip away its complexity, Polyvagal Theory is a science of feelings. More than a subjective experience, how we feel reflects our physiological state. How we feel is our conscious brain telling us how our autonomic nervous system is regulating our internal organs and bodily systems to either support or interrupt homeostasis. When we feel safe, we engage the neural feedback loops that optimize the homeostatic processes promoting our health, growth, and restoration, whereas when we don't feel safe, our metabolic resources and the neural regulation of our bodily systems are being diverted toward attacking, defending, protecting, or conserving what's left in an effort to survive.

More than the removal of threat, safety is a feeling. When we feel safe, we are primed to detect more of who and what is safe in the environment around us, even when there is danger. When we feel unsafe, we see the world as more dangerous and are biased to see, hear, and recognize who and what else might be threatening around us, even when there is safety. How we feel influences how we experience the world, how we act, react, and interact with others, how we think, the emotions we experience, and what we see, hear, and feel.

How we feel becomes an opportunity to meet ourselves where we are. When we relate to how we feel in ways that our body welcomes, we have an opportunity to realign our physiology to support our heartfelt intentions, goals, and values. At the same time, we also have an efficient portal into optimizing our health, resilience, well-being, and performance. Most of all, we have an opportunity to turn competition into coregulation.

When we feel comfortable, at ease, relaxed, present, and basically content, our internal organs and bodily systems are being neurally regulated to support our health, recovery, growth, and wellness.

When performing or engaging in activities that require some additional metabolic output beyond the demands of resting in homeostasis, we begin to divert resources toward mobilizing. This physiological shift will feel different in the body depending on how the mobilization of resources occurs.

When we feel a sense of comfort and control while engaging—being confidently challenged or having a calm energy or a relaxed focus that can be turned on and off rapidly and efficiently—this reflects a physiology whereby the ventral vagal brake on the heart's pacemaker is managing metabolic output through efficient neurally regulated changes in heart rate and breathing patterns. This way of effectively raising and lowering energy, focus, and engagement while feeling comfortable and connected to what we are doing reflects a physiology that has a sufficient baseline of ventral vagal tone, adequate metabolic resources available, and the necessary levels of vagal efficiency to appropriately manage metabolic output for the context, situation, or challenge.

When we feel overly amped up, aggressive, angry, and attacking while engaged in a competitive environment (e.g., sport, conflict), from a neurophysiological perspective, we have lost ventral vagal control and coordination of our sympathetic nervous system, and exhibit higher levels of muscle tension and metabolic output, while compromising our capacity for finite motor control, problem solving, or creativity. We are essentially locked into a sympathetically driven physiological state of threat with limited access to our social engagement system and vagal brake, which is metabolically costly and sustainable for only short periods of time, and puts us on a trajectory of implosion, collapse, or behavioral shutdown. When we are primed to attack, defend, or protect, we are also primed to detect more of what's dangerous in the environment around us, and see others as threats to our safety, winning, and success.

We see this play out in competitive sports all the time—a player that attacks with reckless abandon, is aggressive, or screams in anger, and when that doesn't overwhelm their opponent, we see them reflexively shift, begin to make excuses, lose energy, and eventually give up. These aren't conscious choices, deliberate decisions, or a reflection of intentions, mental weakness, or flaws in character. More accurately, these are bodies following a predictable pattern of response to the pressures of competing, to the challenges of fighting a relentless battle against an army of enemies standing in their way of the resources they crave. This is the inevitable path we follow when we compete in bodies that don't feel safe.

When We Stop Feeling

More than a feeling, when we dismiss, numb out, repress, detach from, and override our feelings, we are interrupting the neural feedback loops that optimize the function of our internal organs and bodily systems. Over time, this puts us on a trajectory toward illness, disease, disconnection, loneliness, burnout, and compromised wellness and well-being. When we don't feel, we put ourselves on a path toward illness, injury, disease, systemic inflammation, and multisystem shutdown.

In the world of performance and resilience, when we think that we can make ourselves perform, we are putting ourselves on a trajectory toward suboptimal performance at best, and eventual implosion, burnout, exhaustion, and disconnection from our passion, purpose, and joy.

We Must Feel Our Way Back Home to Ourselves

We must feel to be human. We must feel to be optimal. We must feel to be healthy, to be happy, to heal, and to be connected. We must feel so that we can listen to what our body is telling us. We must feel so that we can support the neural feedback loops that regulate our health, growth, and restoration. We must feel so that we can feel the sometimes subtle, and other times dramatic, shifts in our bodily reactions to threat and to safety. We must feel to give ourselves a chance to realign our body to support our intentions, values, and relationships. We must feel so that we can feel when we are safe, and when we are not safe.

We must feel so that we can begin to trust that it's okay to feel again. We must feel so that we can understand one another and build trusting, supportive relationships. We must feel so that we can cooperate, collaborate, and coregulate in this highly competitive world we live in. This is our enduring quest, embedded in our DNA, and our opportunity to change the trajectory of what we see playing out in the world today. We must feel to heal, to witness, to grow, to understand, to play, to love, to coregulate.

When we feel safe enough, connected enough, and a sense of belonging, we can be who we really are. We can be the generous, kind, patient, caring, cooperative, compassionate, creative, and loving humans we are at our core. We can play with each other, accept one another, collaborate together, and elevate our human potential beyond what we could ever reach alone. We can compete on level playing fields, not in an attempt to humiliate, destroy, take something from, or prove something to anyone else. Rather, we compete against one another for the joy, excitement, and curiosity of exploring our game, measuring our progress, fueling our motivation, and seeing what plays out. We can play and coregulate together in ever-expanding circles, when we might otherwise resort to attacking, defending, protecting, or hiding. When we are able to help ourselves and others to feel safe, and to trust that it's safe to feel safe together, we have an opportunity to turn competition into coregulation and play our way back into who we really are.

Coming Full Circle

I am a father of two wonderful daughters, now 22 and 18 years of age. As I reflect back, particularly on my oldest daughter's teenage years, I realize that I was hyperfocused on keeping them, and particularly her, safe. And when my oldest began doing things that I thought were dangerous to her own health and longevity, I lost sight of what was even more important than keeping her safe—helping her to feel safe with me, no matter what. I didn't see beneath the behaviors that were playing out, and I didn't meet her body where it was. I failed to recognize and respect her biological quest for finding safety, connection, and belonging in her peer group. Instead, I zeroed in on those behaviors as threats to her life.

In my attempts to stop her from "harming herself," I violated her trust in me. I stopped being a safe witness. She no longer felt safe with me. Instead, she felt judged, criticized, and evaluated for what she was doing and who she was choosing to surround herself with. In a subconscious way, I was sending her signals of threat and danger and a powerful message that she didn't share our family values, and therefore she didn't belong. Now, many years later, we are in the process of repairing my violation of her trust, and I am grateful for the opportunity and that her body is welcoming my heartfelt intentions.

I share this personal story for two reasons. First, my hope is that you keep this in mind when it comes to the most important relationships you have in your life. More than keeping someone safe, it's about doing what we can to let them know, in their body, that they are truly safe with us, no matter what.

Second, it's to acknowledge a bigger reason why beginning to feel again, and feeling our own bodily feelings, and relating to these bodily feelings with awareness, self-care, and compassion is so vital. We may get a second chance, or we may not. We may have a moment of clarity whereby we can see how the world around us and the culture we live in tends to disconnect us from who we really are, and who we really can become when we feel safe, in connection, together. We can't do this alone. In fact, we aren't meant to. It's time to turn competition into coregulation and replace attacking, defending, and protecting with playing, cooperating, and loving.

Playing With the Faces of Competition

As the 2023 US Open Finals came to a conclusion, Novak Djokovic, the champion, and arguably the greatest player in the history of the game of tennis, fell to the ground in a bodily mixture of joy, relief, celebration, and gratitude. As he gathered himself up off the court and shook hands with his opponent, he immediately walked toward the stands, but not in the direction of his team box. Over the railing separating the court from the fans, he was handed his six-year-old daughter, who was too young to sit in the players' box but watched from another area of the stadium.

> Actually, that was the first thing I wanted to do, once I dropped the racket on the side after I shook hands with my opponent, just to hug her. She was facing me when I was sitting on the bench. And she smiled at me. Every single time I needed that kind of innocent child energy, I got it from her. When I was going through very stressful moments, when I needed a little bit of a push of strength, of just lightness, she gave me a smile, a fist pump! (Eichenholz, 2023)

In the face of competition, even at the highest level and on the grandest of stages, it is the faces of the people who care about us the most, who we trust will support us, hold us, and stay with us whether we win or we lose, that have the biggest impact and influence on our capacity to play and coregulate when we might otherwise attack, defend, or protect. The neural mechanisms that enable us to exchange facial expressions, voice, and body language to communicate, cooperate, and signal that we are aligned together on the same team are the same neural mechanisms that promote our performance and resilience, whether we are competing on the pitch or on the court of life.

30

The Free Voice

Awakening the Prosody

Rabih Lahoud and Herbert Grassmann

THE ACOUSTIC ENVIRONMENT CAN AFFECT THE NEURONAL REGULATION OF OUR MIDDLE ear muscles and change our physiological state. When we hear the human voice, because it sounds so melodious or warm, the middle ear muscles are involuntarily engaged. The human voice tends to have its frequency components in the middle and higher tone ranges. By tensing the middle ear muscles and the eardrum, these middle and high tones are increasingly transmitted to the inner ear. Our body and brain say *yes* to the other person's voice and get our middle ear muscles to work properly. For both authors, Awakening the Prosody is a new collaborative project. Two different worlds come together, that of the singing artist and teacher who performs nationally and internationally, and that of the researcher and therapist—both of whom study and apply Polyvagal Theory in their practice.

The Voice and the Nervous System

The voice is a complex instrument that allows us to connect with others, communicate, and express ourselves. Our voice is an expression of our personality and our feelings. But it is also a mirror of our nervous system. When we are stressed or tense, our voice often sounds raspy, uncertain, or quiet. Conversely, a healthy voice can help us to feel better and cope better with stress.

The voice is susceptible to moods; it reacts when we are not in tune with ourselves or reveals when something is not right. But the voice is not just an instrument of communicating with others. It is also an important gateway to ourselves.

The voice plays an important role in regulating the auditory system. It helps to modulate the volume and sound quality of perceived sounds. Voice and prosody are closely linked. The voice is the medium through which prosody is expressed. Prosody gives the voice expression and meaning.

Stephen Porges (2021) explicitly places the function of the middle ear muscles in this context. Together with the ventral vagus, their tension is always present when our brain believes that we are in a state of safety and well-being. In terms of child development, this means that the tension of the middle ear muscles is very likely to be associated with an experience of secure attachment. We develop an expressive and free voice as a result of the inner interplay between the need for connection and the joy of communication. The skills of the voice therefore grow on the fertile ground of inner safety.

The central and peripheral nervous systems could be described as the hardware of the nervous system. The hardware has two basic programs: somatic and autonomic software. The somatic software is responsible for conscious muscle movements. Whenever we consciously decide to move our index finger, for example, we use somatic software to tense or relax the muscles of the finger as we wish. We can make a conscious movement because we have this somatic software. The autonomic software, or autonomous nervous system, on the other hand, operates underground. It tends to operate in the dark web of the nervous system.

This software is responsible for involuntary muscle movements and ensures that we do not have to deliberately activate vital muscles and organs to stay alive. From a neurological point of view, our voice is a child of interpersonal connection. As soon as we are in a state in which we want to communicate and connect with others in an atmosphere of safety, our voice is ready to unfold freely.

On the other hand, this also means that as soon as we sing, we activate the voice's capacity for communication and interpersonal connection based on neuronal safety and create an atmosphere of communication and connection. Porges's work is centered on feeling safe. His main message is that feeling safe is emphatically not just about the absence of threat; it is about being able to engage socially. Our sense of safety therefore depends on the cues we get from our environment and relationships—mainly facial and bodily expressions and tone of voice. When the prosody (rhythm, intonation, etc.) of our voice conveys safety, others are drawn to connect with us and listen to us.

When our inner safety fluctuates, we immediately feel it in our body. The body, as an instrument of the voice, will feel tight, and the ability to nuance and change the voice will be limited. This shift between safety and uncertainty happens often and in a very subtle way.

It is important to feel this change, recognize it, and guide it toward safety to achieve a ventral vagal state in singing. In the dorsal vagal state, the nervous system is no longer or only very slightly connected to the vocal function. Here we experience a kind of inner helplessness and feel the lack of access to control the body. The neuronal state of rigidity creeps into the vocal system and renders it mute. It feels rigid and inflexible. For safety reasons, so to speak, it can no longer sound.

It is as if the neuronal instruction from the dorsal vagus is as follows: It's best to stay quiet. The danger is overwhelming, and the only protection is not to be heard. A group of cranial nerves works together with the ventral vagus in the state of interpersonal connection and inner security. Porges calls this nerve team the social engagement system.

These nerves innervate the bronchi, the heart, the head, the throat, the larynx, the facial muscles, the muscles of mastication, and the middle ear muscles:

- The ventral vagus (larynx, pharynx, respiration, and heart)
- The trigeminal nerve (facial muscles, muscles of mastication, and middle ear muscles)

- The facial nerve (facial expressions)
- The glossopharyngeal nerve (pharyngeal cavity and tongue)
- The accessory nerve (head turner)

A Vocal Ensemble of Cranial Nerves

When one nerve sings, the others sing along, or at least listen attentively. To summarize, the social engagement system is responsible for following vocal-relevant elements that influence each other: the prosodic voice, the alert face, attentive listening, and deepened breathing—the neural pathways of human vocal connection. In a state of connection, the ventral vagus allows these nerves to be utilized in a nuanced way, depending on the type of connection. Therefore, everything remains flexible and ready to resonate. The same goes the other way around: The key to the flow state in singing is practicing the self-controlled change in more or less activity of these vocal nerves.

Singing Is a Ventral Vagal State Activity by Human Nature

However, the inner critic in singing is so powerful in today's society that its dominance often prevents us from getting into a flow state when singing. This is why most people's nervous systems have stored negative experiences with their own voice in their subconscious. A secure feeling while singing is no longer a matter of course for most people. If a secure inner feeling cannot be actively and consciously initiated, at some point the dorsal vagus takes over the inner guidance of the vocal function out of habit, and the voice cannot develop freely. The protective function of our musculature has developed into a sphincter system in which the trachea is protected from threatening substances by much more complex closure mechanisms, but at the same time additional functions such as phonation and double-valve function are also impaired (Jacoby, 1991; Feuerstein, 2000).

Singing in front of others is a very stimulating experience. In this situation, the nervous system becomes alert, and the focus jumps—a perfect opportunity to initiate the flow state. However, the overwhelming power of inner criticism often causes us to miss this opportunity, and negative feedback often leads us out of wakefulness and into a complete shutdown. Instead of concentrating the focus, the nervous system decides to switch off the focus completely. Based on stored autonomic evaluation, the nervous system tries to warn us of danger and brings negative concepts and actions back into consciousness.

If we listen to these concepts and carry out the automated actions, we live in the past and miss the present moment of wakefulness. However, this moment has the potential to accompany us into the flow state. Everything in life is subject to constant change, the dynamic of becoming. As Heraclitus said: "No man ever steps in the same river twice, for it's not the same river and he's not the same man."

This is all the more true for the voice. It is created and can be experienced as it unfolds and changes, that is, while it is in process.

The ability to focus on the vocal process in order to always experience it in the present moment is of great importance.

Connection ♪

♪ Presence

Volume ♪

♪ Restraint

Timbre ♪

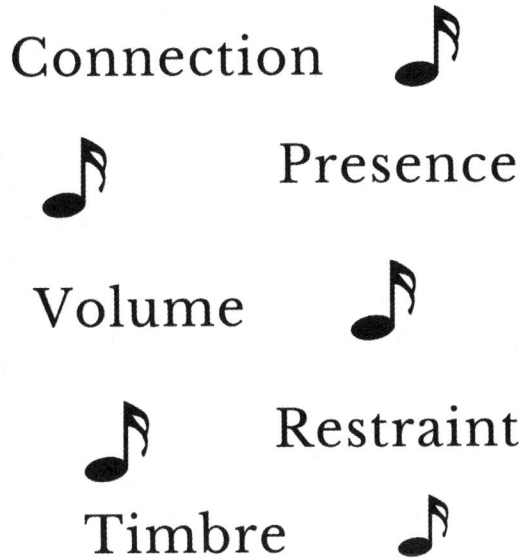

FIGURE 30.1 Five parameters for awakening prosody.

Awakening Prosody: Five Parameters

Prosody refers to the rhythm and melody of the voice, including intonation, emphasis, and pauses. The voice, in turn, is a function of inner safety. It helps us connect with others in order to tell our own story. Prosody, or diversity of vocal expression, is the characteristic of a secure and confident voice. This expression is regulated by five parameters (see Figure 30.1). They are comparable to five adjusting knobs on a mixing board. They can be controlled separately, and each parameter can be activated more or less intensively with regard to a specific vocal expression. The elemental condition of vocal sound production (connection), adaptive hearing, and making oneself heard in certain overtone ranges (presence), the conscious control of air pressure changes through the vocal function (volume), and the conscious control of overtones for a restrained, free, dark, or bright vocal sound (restraint and vocal timbre).

Connection

The diaphragm is the most important breathing muscle. It is innervated by motor nerve fibers (the diaphragmatic nerve) and can therefore, like other skeletal muscles, be moved consciously. Its movement is also under the influence of the ventral vagus and is therefore connected to the autonomic nervous system. This means that it is also influenced by our own subconscious state of safety. Work with the diaphragm thus connects the conscious and subconscious in the nervous system.

The position of the diaphragm when breathing and singing regulates air pressure in the lungs and below the vocal folds (subglottic pressure). This fine adjustment of pressure between the lungs and the subglottic space produces the primary vocal sound at the level of the vocal folds when singing. In prosodic singing, a balance is created between the movement of the respiratory muscles. The muscles of exhalation include the internal intercostal muscles and the abdominal muscles. The internal intercostal muscles work opposite to the external intercostal muscles. They also run in between the ribs but, when they contract, they pull the rib cage down and in and cause exhalation.

Practicing ventral vagal state in singing during exhalation and the internal muscular resistance slows down this movement and thus adapts the air release to the desired vocal sound. In an inner state, this fine-tuning between moving and resisting becomes possible. Questions need to be explored such as, "What do I need today? More movement or more resistance?" The play between movement and resistance is the regulator in this parameter.

Presence

In a safe environment, human hearing focuses on high frequencies and can block out low frequencies in a noisy environment. Two small muscles in the middle ear, the tensor tympani and the stapedius, tense and relax the eardrum in such a way that we can hear certain high frequencies without having to hear low frequencies. The trigeminal nerve (the fifth cranial nerve) innervates the tensor tympani. The mimic facial nerve (the seventh cranial nerve) innervates the stapedius.

The trigeminal nerve also innervates the tensor veli palatini, a muscle that stretches and lifts the soft palate. This means that there is a direct neuronal connection between the middle ear (state of tension of the tympanic membrane), the face, and the soft palate. This connection ensures that we can hear higher frequencies (between 2,000 and 5,000 Hz) and produce them vocally.

The motor influence of these nerves in the soft palate and middle ear can amplify the sound of the voice in the upper frequency range, making it audible and easier to understand. It is as if one's own intention to be heard manifests itself in a more present and focused voice. What do I need now? More or less presence? That is the regulator in this parameter.

Volume

The higher the subglottic pressure under the vocal folds, the greater the change in air pressure generated when the vocal folds vibrate. We perceive this as loud, for example, when we shout spontaneously. By contrast, subglottic pressure is low when we whisper or sing a lullaby to a baby.

The ventral vagus innervates the inner muscles of the larynx and also ensures the adjustment of exhalation and thus influences the regulation of air pressure in the lungs. This coordination of the muscular conditions of the inner laryngeal muscles with the pressure conditions in the lungs makes it possible for us to sing louder or softer—another regulator that can be adjusted.

Restraint

The ventral vagus innervates the following muscles in the pharynx: the levator veli pala-tini, a muscle in the soft palate that sits behind the abovementioned tensor veli palatini; the posterior palatine arch (the palatopharyngeus); and the second constrictor (or swal-lowing muscle).

The more "tendinous" a vocal sound is, the more active this muscular area in the pos-terior soft palate and pharynx becomes. This change in the vocal tract alters the strength ratios of the overtones in such a way that the vocal sound appears to be restrained. Do I need more or less restraint right now? That is the factor in this parameter.

Timbre

A large room amplifies the low frequencies of a sound, whereas a smaller room amplifies the high frequencies. The size of a room determines the darkness or brightness of the sound produced.

The ventral vagus innervates the muscles of the pharynx, soft palate, and tongue, so it has a major influence on the shape of the vocal tract. How do I want to sound? With more space in the vocal tract, that is, with a darker vocal sound? Or with less space in the vocal tract, with a brighter vocal sound? That is the factor in this parameter.

Conclusion

The voice is more than just the perfect interplay of different muscles. We use our voice to make contact with other people. It is a mirror of our nervous system. When we are stressed or tense, our voice often sounds raspy, uncertain, or quiet. Conversely, a healthy voice can help us to feel better and cope better with stress.

The voice plays an important role in regulating the auditory system. It helps to mod-ulate the volume and sound quality of perceived sounds. Voice and prosody are closely linked. The voice is the medium through which prosody is expressed. Prosody gives the voice expression and meaning.

31

Continuum Movement

Somatic Communication and the Healing of Trauma

Donnalea Van Vleet Goelz

SOMATIC PRACTICES THAT COMBINE AWARENESS, BREATH, AND MOVEMENT HAVE BEEN shown to be effective in working therapeutically with trauma. This chapter outlines the essential elements of Continuum Movement (CM)—breath, sound, movement, sensation, and innovation. Through these elements, we facilitate somatic communication within our bodies. This method intersects with contemporary research on trauma and the body in neuroscience, somatic psychotherapy, and other disciplines. CM's unique movement methodology helps practitioners to cultivate interoception, to self-regulate, and to disrupt limiting bodily patterns through movement practice, thus offering a novel practice for working with trauma.

Continuum Movement (CM) was founded in 1967 by somatics pioneer Emilie Conrad Da'oud. Rather than seeing the human body as a fixed, mechanical object, Conrad Da'oud understood the body as innately "bio-intelligent"—having the capacity to understand what it needs to flourish and heal. CM methodology uses breath, sound, and movement practices to connect practitioners to this bio-intelligent state, honoring the intrinsic wisdom of the body. From this bio-intelligent state, practitioners can access bodily sensations from a self-directed, gentle, and nurturing place, which allows for the safe exploration of difficult emotions and limiting patterns. In CM, we trace bio-intelligence to the process theory of Alfred North Whitehead (1929) and the theoretical physics of David Bohm (1980). Inspired by these theories, Conrad Da'oud saw the human body as fundamentally interconnected with all life forms, as part of a larger planetary intelligence. Thus, bio-intelligence happens on multiple registers—from the macro level of evolutionary process (University of Southampton, 2015) to the micro level of how individual immune systems learn, through exposure, to protect the body from disease (Chaplin, 2010; Marshall et al., 2018) and throughout interconnectedness of the plant kingdom (Simard et al., 2012; Simard, 2022).

In CM, we learn to listen to bio-intelligence by cultivating bodily awareness (or interoception) to sharpen the communication within and beyond our bodies. For example, a student shared their experience of bio-intelligence during a CM sequence or dive:

I start to feel a sweeping sensation in my ankle and begin initiating movement from that place. I start to notice that the movement in my ankle changes the flexion at my knee joint, which creates a palpable hydrating sensation in my inner thigh/adductor area. I think of this as bio-intelligence because the body knows where to initiate movement to increase fluidity and facilitate release elsewhere in the body.

In CM, we learn how to facilitate this kind of somatic communication within the body through specific breath and movement practices.

Unsurprisingly, such CM techniques are increasingly akin to best practices in somatic psychotherapy. CM stresses the development of an environment of contextual safety, trust, and social engagement; the use of gentle, experiential, and agentive practices for increasing body awareness (or interoception) and thus somatic communication; and the teaching of self-directed breathing and movement techniques that support self-regulation of the nervous system. In this chapter, I connect the five essential elements of CM—breath, sound, movement, sensation, and innovation—with advances in somatic psychotherapy and neuroscience, showing how CM's methods of facilitating somatic communication offer a novel approach to working therapeutically with individuals who are impacted by their prior trauma.

Trauma and the Body

Research by Porges (2001, 2011), van der Kolk (2002, 2014), and Ogden et al. (2006) has transformed our understanding of how traumatic experience affects the body. For example, van der Kolk (2002, 2014) demonstrated a trend of autonomic dysregulation—elevated autonomic nervous system activity—in study participants diagnosed with PTSD. This elevation could be seen symptomatically through physical changes, such as elevated heart rate and blood pressure. Further, research by Doussard-Roosevelt and Porges (1999) showed that extended episodes of traumatic stress can result in chronic stress responses that become neurologically habitual. Such work influenced Conrad Da'oud, who claimed, "Trauma . . . becomes patterned into the system. Much like a scar added to a fingerprint, the trauma continues as an inevitable imprint. These can be softened or erased, particularly through the work of Continuum, once it's recognized it's there" (Conrad, 2007, p. 265).

Therapeutic approaches that use breath and movement techniques, such as CM, offer a practical method to work with the dysregulation that occurs after trauma imprinting. Van der Kolk (2014) found that 52% of survivors diagnosed with treatment-resistant chronic PTSD no longer met the diagnostic criteria for PTSD after completing a weekly trauma-informed yoga class over a 10-week period. From his work, van der Kolk (2014, p. 277) asserts

effective treatment needs to involve the following three factors: (1) learning to tolerate feelings and sensations by raising the capacity for interoception; (2) learning to modulate or control arousal; and (3) learning that it is critical to engage in effective action after confrontation with physical helplessness.

In what follows, I dive into CM's essential elements, showing how the method helps support these goals in trauma therapy.

Essential Element 1: Breath—Vagal Tone and Self-Regulation

In Continuum, we often say that movement originates with breath. We can experience this by physically tuning in to our body, noticing how the rise and fall of our diaphragm from each inhalation and exhalation allows movement throughout the body. All movement in Continuum is first preceded by breath and/or a breath sounding; the very activity of breathing is actually movement itself. We start by attuning to inner sensations, feeling the movement of the lungs, the ribs, the muscles as we inhale and exhale. CM plays with variations in audible breath, using methods that are based on decades of inquiry by Emilie Conrad Da'oud and her students. Different types of breath are connected to different bodily systems and motifs, which can be combined to improve specific physical, psychological, and emotional difficulties. By beginning with breath, we start with the foundation of human life to find movement specific to individual bodies, conditions, and physical/psychological material. As Conrad Da'oud wrote, "Healing, growth and all mobility, whether physical, emotional, or spiritual, are enhanced by the dexterity of breath" (Continuum Movement, 2023).

Over the past 20 years, research in physiology and neuroscience has shown a connection between breathing practices and vagal tone (Brown & Gerbarg, 2005). The work of Dr. Stephen Porges (2004, 2005, 2011) and his Polyvagal Theory have revolutionized the way we understand the importance of the vagus nerve in self-regulation, trauma response, and social engagement. CM uses Porges's Polyvagal Theory (PVT) as a foundation for understanding the body, its nervous system, and our responses to the world we live in. Earlier chapters of this book have gone into PVT in depth; therefore, I will only bring in the specific relevant research pertaining directly to CM's somatic approach. Porges and colleagues (Porges, 2021; Denver et al., 2007; Lewis et al., 2012) have shown a relationship between breathing patterns and cardiac vagal tone, demonstrating the importance of breath in bodily self-regulation, moving us out of sympathetic response back into the ventral vagal system. Conrad Da'oud also argued that breath is central to regulation, and that adaptive breathing patterns can change the physical structure of the body:

> All adaptive patterns are maintained in our breathing styles. Our tissue structure will accommodate whatever our historical-emotional climate is and will shape breath accordingly. If I have learned to hold my breath due to hypervigilance or other threatening circumstance, my shoulders will likely be cemented upward cutting off breath to the upper chest. Tissue structure will adhere to defensive postures as a form of protection. . . . When one is . . . in a trauma of any kind, one pulls the breath up into the throat. This strategy inhibits movement. (Conrad, 2007, p. 302)

Richard Brown and Patricia Gerbarg (2005, 2009) have also investigated breath and its use in treatment of stress, anxiety, and depression. By looking at vagal tone and its association with emotional disorders, their research indicated that body-mind interventions are beneficial in stress-related mental and physical disorders. The Brown-Gerbarg (2005) project involved teaching different breathing patterns to participants from several different groups, such as an addiction group, a prison program group, and juvenile offenders. Brown and Gerbarg (2005, p. 715) concluded that, while more controlled clinical trials are needed, there is now sufficient evidence to consider yogic breathing as a "potentially beneficial, low risk adjunct for the treatment of stress, anxiety, PTSD, depression, stress-related illness and substance abuse."

In CM, we use dozens of different breaths or breathing techniques similar to ones that have been previously studied. As Conrad Da'oud (Conrad, 2007) argued, over time our breathing creates patterns in our body; we become used to breathing in a certain way. Often our breathing is a compensatory pattern that can relate to trauma, a physical illness, or even our family history. In CM training, we often see that trauma and emotional stress are maintained in the movement or inhibition of breath. The more we work with our breath consciously, the more we release patterns and create more possibilities. The first step is that we start to feel the patterns that we are holding without conscious awareness. From this perspective, we can create many other possibilities for how to breathe. When in fear, the body usually takes a large inhalation, and the lungs may go into a static freeze. This occurs before one can even think about it. By consciously connecting to our breath and consciously taking control of its pace by making a conscious effort to work with the timing of the inhalation and exhalation, we can evoke a great deal of change in a very short time (Zaccaro et al., 2018).

In CM, we use a sequence of exercises that we call dives. During a dive, we become conscious of our breath and breathing, while also learning to activate the different branches of our nervous system. An example would be that we may play with slowing down and relaxing our system in the parasympathetic state; or we may play with how to activate and get more energy running through our bodies in the sympathetic state. By learning and playing with this in the safe context of a CM class, we have found that one's capability to regulate the breath and nervous system can be consciously expanded in everyday life. This offers the opportunity to not be at the mercy of external situations, including states of fear, but to be able to take control, be present, and be more conscious.

Essential Element 2: Sound—Healing Vibrations and Social Connection

"Sound emerges as audible breath, suggesting new forms, dissolving density, refining movement and perception," wrote Conrad Da'oud (Conrad, 2007, pp. 141–142). In CM, we see sound as a vehicle to penetrate the density of locked tissue in the body. Sound waves are physical manifestations that produce vibrations of particles—or vibrational movement—as the sound moves through them. The relationship between sound, healing, and altered states of consciousness has been known for centuries, across many different cultural traditions, and we are still in the process of understanding the effect that sound has on the body (Kerna et al., 2022; Beaulieu & Perez-Martinez, 2018). In CM, we note that sound can operate in two important ways: to produce vibrational frequencies that affect specific body systems; and as a form of social engagement through collective sounding.

Specific sound frequencies engage various systems of the body. We combine sound and breath with movement to increase the potency of possibilities. As Dr. Valerie Hunt (1996, p. 241), a close collaborator of Conrad Da'oud, observed,

> The density of tissue helps determine the frequency and pattern of energy released. Dense tissues, like bone and cartilage, present a slower-moving, lower frequency, with more sluggish energy, while lighter tissues such as nerves and glands produce a faster, higher, more dynamic frequency.

While the physical benefits of sounding/chanting have been known for centuries, scientists have begun to study the effect of body-generated sound—like humming, bee sound, and om chanting—on heart rate variability, a global measure of vagal tone (Inbaraj et al., 2022; Damerla et al., 2018; Selvaraj et al., 2008). Similarly, researchers have continued to study "sound healing" (Beaulieu & Perez-Martinez, 2018) and therapeutic applications for sound-based vibrational frequencies on the body (Kerna et al., 2022). In CM, we use sound to wake up various body systems through these vibrational frequencies, which opens new avenues for body awareness and movement pathways, while also regulating vagal tone, keeping practitioners in the ventral vagal state of safety and social engagement.

In CM, we know that sounding, including singing and chanting, can connect us with each other. Through sound, a resonance with each other is created. When you feel in resonance with another, you feel connected. If you look around the world with its many cultures and religious traditions, singing and chanting (a form of breath and sound) are almost universal. This is especially true when spiritual communion and/or rituals are being performed. Thus, sound, breath, and singing are used worldwide as a form of communication but are also an ancient method for exercising what Porges (2011) has called the social engagement system. During CM dives, individuals come together into shared resonance. There is a shift of personal expressions and change in the emotional tone of a group after they have engaged in singing or chanting together. These practices, which are essential components of CM, directly relate to the human need for safety and social engagement. In CM, we see sound as having a profound effect on individual body physiology while also creating a sonic field that connects and engages practitioners using their voices.

Essential Element 3: Movement—Breaking Patterns Through Fluidity

The human body is approximately 70% water. In CM, we see the body as a fluid system, which is very different from other modalities that view the human body as a mechanical, bone-muscle lever system. As the body began to be seen as a mechanical organism after the Industrial Revolution, we forgot about this fluid nature and its possibilities. In CM, we believe that tapping back into the fluid nature of the body provides us with access to the bio-intelligent wisdom within. By using breath and sound intentionally, we can tap into this fluidity, which frees us from the mechanistic patterns we have come to believe are our body. So, the question is, how does water move? It flows in waves and spirals; it undulates and gushes—and it stagnates if it does not move. CM's movements are specifically designed to enhance and amplify the spirals, flows, and waves of our body and its fluid system. It is from this fluid place that we can break out of limiting patterns and find new pathways in the body. As Conrad Da'oud wrote,

> Patterns are not only familiar, they represent all we know. It's difficult to imagine how the grooving of patterned tissue structure forces all other tissues to accommodate a habitual shape. As my throat released I felt streams of movement in places that had never previously moved. (Conrad, 2007, p. 151)

Such ideas share deep resonance with principles of body psychotherapy, particularly the work of Wilhelm Reich (1973, p. 269), who famously wrote, "Once we open up the flow of energy within our body, we can also open up the flow of energy in the universe." While CM differs in important respects from some of Reich's philosophy, learning to feel and enhance the fluid flow of our bodies is what practitioners learn to do during a Continuum dive. As Professor of Somatics Don Hanlon Johnson said,

> Reich developed what we called bioenergetics, which was focusing . . . on two regions of body experience: sexual excitement and breathing. Although we got this notion of really being in touch with our organic being, our flowing being and rhythms, he was so male and so patriarchal in his being, he couldn't quite transcend that, so much of it was focused on a male approach to orgasm. When I first met Emilie [Conrad Da'oud], I thought, "Oh, Emilie is the one who really understands Reich!" . . . She had that focus on excitatory, creative juices in us, that are flowing and mobile . . . but was doing it in a way that wasn't contaminated by that patriarchal [perspective]. . . . She had this understanding that helps us recover our animal, plant, fish-like nature that had been so cut off from the Industrial Revolution. (Continuum Movement, 2020)

In this way, CM is different from many other movement methods that are used for healing. Because we are interested in nonhabituated, fluid movements, CM is not directed or guided, as are other modalities, such as yoga (asana) and tai chi. While the latter methods offer powerful practices of bodily awareness through the linking of breath and movement, they may not help practitioners cultivate intuitive, free, fluid movement. CM offers a gentle way to help practitioners and clients regain a sense of agency by allowing any form of movement that follows the breaths/sounds used during dives. We use a wide range of movements, from dynamic full-bodied movements to the subtle micromovements. Micromovements are tiny movements of the body that are very subtle from the outside but create a large activation within. When doing micromovements, you can feel the neurological vibrancy and aliveness. Conversely, by doing undulating wave motion, tissues may soften, and sensation amplifies. For Conrad Da'oud, wave motion is the primary way to access our bio-intelligence, which is not bound by time, space, or condition—allowing us to open up new pathways in the body.

Essential Element 4: Sensation—the Healing Power of Interoception

Every dive begins with a baseline, which is a tool for exploring interoception, or the awareness of bodily sensations. As in any experiment, it is important to take a baseline, as you must know where you begin to know and recognize the change that has occurred at the end. We learn to begin our movement explorations by becoming aware of our bodily experience, without judging or attempting to change. During a baseline, we ask: Do we notice any immediate sensations, areas of difficulty, or regions of neutrality? Temperature? Heaviness or lightness? Constriction or openness? What is the rhythm of the breath? How large or small is the inhale/exhale? What parts of the body move when we become aware of the breath? Can we feel the blood flowing or the heart pumping? Or activity and movement in the gut area?

We do a baseline at the beginning and end of every dive. The body speaks to us through sensation, which is a first-order experience. First-order experience is the most fundamental level of awareness, before meaning making, stories, and narratives about the sensations in our body. Staying with first-order experience is important because it allows us to break free of mind-body habits that are entrenched by the stories we tell about them. Some first-order sensation words include: hot, cold, shaky, pounding, tremble, relaxed, calm, releasing, gushing, creaky, frozen, burning, flowing, weak, scratchy, itchy, throbbing, dense, bubbling, rippling, dense, crepitus, silent, slow.

As van der Kolk (2014) has written of trauma survivors, "Sensing, naming, and identifying what is going on inside is the first step to recovery." Further, he saw that

> trauma victims cannot recover until they become familiar with and befriend sensations in their bodies. . . . To change, people need to become aware of their sensations and the way that their bodies interact with the world around them. Physical self-awareness is the first step in releasing the tyranny of the past. (van der Kolk, 2014, p. 125)

Research has shown how such interoceptive capacity is connected to our ability to regulate emotions (Price & Hooven, 2018), as self-regulatory difficulty has been found at the core of many mental health challenges (Heatherton & Wagner, 2011). Recent research has shown great success in using practices that cultivate interoception for trauma therapy (Payne et al., 2015; Reinhart et al., 2020; Neukirch et al., 2019), which draw on the work of Levine (2012), Siegel (2003), and van der Kolk (2014). Such research shows the power in helping clients begin to feel sensations in their bodies after years of dissociation, allowing a connection to the present moment.

In CM, we learn to listen to sensations slowly and gently. As we begin to listen, sensations help guide us toward movement from a place of bio-intelligence, where new pathways can be learned, and healing can begin.

Essential Element 5: Innovation—Creativity, Neuroplasticity, and Bioplasticity

To innovate is to change, to make new; it is a creative process. Life on Earth has always been in the state of innovation. Consider that four and half billion years ago, life began on earth. We evolved and developed from single-cell (prokaryotes) to multicell (eukaryotes) creatures to the multiplicity of the many forms of life that have developed on this planet. It is deeply inspiring to consider the changes. In CM, our idea of innovation is connected to systems theory, particularly the work of Ludwig Bertalanffy (1968), who described an open system as a complex of interacting elements that are open to, and interact with, their environments. He also brought forth the idea that open systems can acquire qualitatively new properties through emergence, and therefore could be seen as in continual evolution. On the other hand, closed systems are isolated from their environments and eventually dissipate, break down, and die. In CM, we aspire toward innovation in our movement dives with the support of the first four essential elements. The hope is that with breath, sound, and movement guided by sensation, we are able to innovate in our bodies—to make new connections, to discover insight, to create new pathways, and break through limiting patterns.

Current academic and clinical literature is focused on neuroplasticity, or the brain's ability to rewire itself, to change in relationship to its circumstances. What is being missed, however, is that the entire body can change, not just the brain. We also have "bio-plasticity." We are beginning to recognize our body's ability to change, heal, and evolve, particularly when supported by somatic practices based in movement (Fontanesi & DeSouza, 2021; Fontanesi, 2020; Kshtriya et al., 2015; Barnstaple et al., 2021).

Further research has shown how creativity and plasticity are supported by fluid movement in particular. Slepian and Ambady (2012) tested whether fluid movement had an effect on participants in three domains: creative generation, cognitive flexibility, and connecting remote associations. Experiment 1 examined whether fluid relative to nonfluid movement would enhance creative generation. They found that "participants who made fluid movement demonstrated fluency and originality more than did those who made non-fluid movement" (Slepian & Ambady, 2012, p. 2). In Experiment 2, their hypothesis was that flexibility embodied by fluid movement could lead to a more flexible thought process. The results were that fluid movement enhanced flexible thinking relative to non-fluid movement. In Experiment 3, they hypothesized that fluid movement would enhance creativity but not mental performance in analytical tasks. The results of the testing supported this hypothesis. In their final discussion they reported, "Bodily movement can influence cognitive processing, with fluid movement leading to fluid thinking" (Slepian & Ambady, 2012, p. 4).

Conclusion

Continuum Movement offers a novel approach for working therapeutically with trauma. Through its unique combination of breath, sound, movement, sensation, and innovation, the method puts together a series of practices that are increasingly shown to support physical and emotional well-being. In CM, as we practice somatic communication by tuning into our bodies' intrinsic bio-intelligence through these practices, the body responds with a deeper state of balance and wholeness. In working with our fluid system, we release tensions, patterns, and constraints. We thrive on openness and curiosity about what is possible. CM is a process of refining our ability to sense, feel, experience, and consciously respond with more versatility to various of circumstances. As we develop the ability to return to a sense of safety, our homeostasis, we create an environment to process the effects of trauma on our bodies and minds.

32

The Eros of Relational Aliveness and Continuum Inquiry

Susan Harper

IN 1993, I BROUGHT A GROUP OF CONTINUUM STUDENTS TO DANCE WITH ORANGUTANS IN Tanjung Puting National Park in Borneo. Some of the orangutans were wild; some were used to interacting with humans and had returned to live in the wild. To my surprise, the following experience unfolded.

> I am walking on a remote dirt path deep in the jungle. A female orangutan slides up and takes my hand. She is walking on her curled back feet, so her center of gravity is way forward. Her weight is strong, pulling me down. I have a few moments of mild panic and try to wriggle my hand from her firm grip. No action I take to release my hand from her hand works.
>
> I pause, breathe, and listen. I see/feel our larger shared context, the path, the surrounding trees, and the sky. My attention flows into the soft tender flesh of my hand meeting the rough leathery textures of her large strong hand. Inside this haptic embrace, I sense how we are listening to one another in a felt sense way. A mutual desire to meet each other is happening. We drop into a rhythm of walking together. Reciprocal pleasure in our communion grows. I stroke her upper arm, feeling the texture of her wiry fur. Palpating her strong supple muscles, I meet her eye gaze. I see that she appreciates this quality of sensuous contact and respectful acknowledgment. Looking at me intently, she smiles and lets go.

In this experience, both of us were changed by a quality of mutual participatory consciousness. Stephen Harrod Buhner describes how the ancient Athenians referred to this as *aesthesis*. It is the moment of exchange in which a flow of life force, imbued with communication, moves from one living organism to another. We have an innate capacity for engaging in *aesthesis*, for feeling the touch of the living world upon us, for understanding what that touch means, and offering a response in turn (Buhner, 2004).

To experience the touch of the living world upon us, and to understand what that touch means, we need to develop our felt sense (Gendlin, 1978) and sensuous haptic perception. Eugene Gendlin described felt sense as a deep bodily knowing, a bodily awareness of a situation or person or event. Haptic touch involves simultaneously touching and sensing—allowing the skin and flesh to touch and be touched. For example, with the orangutan, I was consciously, actively touching and simultaneously I was allowing the roughness of her skin and the warmth of her hand to touch my hand. I was experiencing the interactive sensations of our contact. At an affective level, I was offering a curious attention while simultaneously wondering if this interaction with this wild animal was safe. Relationally attuning, I intuitively felt that we were resonating in mutual listening.

Through relational engagement, we grow in unexpected ways. With felt sense listening and haptic contact, confidence in attuning and participating in the human and more-than-human world deepens. When we live with an *ecocentric* sense of identity, we identify with the relational dynamism in all life, and we recognize that all beings are sacred and deserving of respect.

Eros of Belonging

> To allow oneself to be fully enlivened is to love oneself—and at the same
> time, to love the creative world, which is principally and profoundly
> alive. This is the fundamental thesis of erotic ecology.
> —A. WEBER, *MATTER AND DESIRE*

Belonging is an active verb that occurs through perceiving and participating. Eros is a natural drive to relate with the appetite of sensory experience: to open the eyes, to listen, to touch and be touched, to meet and be met. The experience of being touched by moonlight, the wind, a loving hand, an act of courage, and music evokes the emotion of awe. We feel awe in our bodies; our hearts open, and our minds expand. In the research, Dacher Keltner (2023) speaks of the experience of awe as the "vanishing of the self." The more defined egoic sense of self softens, and there is the sense of being related to something larger—an immensity of being. Awe brings about a sense of connection and belonging.

In trauma, in stark contrast, the desire to exchange and the desire to relate wither as the primal need for safety and self-protection grows. Shame arises when the natural impulses of physical expression and the emotional impulses to connect are thwarted, belittled, or punished. A primal loss of trust in one's aliveness and capacity to relate ensues. Bodies tighten, perception narrows, and thinking contracts. The loss of felt sense of aliveness, of the ability to think fluidly, and of the capacity to connect meaningfully, along with the overwhelming unpleasant sensations of despair, creates painful suffering. No longer trusting relational impulses, one is left feeling isolated in a perpetual state of disconnection.

"The trauma that many experience early in childhood is a catastrophe of broken reciprocity. It is ecological because it impairs our capacity for connection. . . . The tragedy begins when we pay no attention to our own aliveness" (Weber, 2014). Instead of trusting the life intelligence innate in ourselves, we look to others for what to believe and how to act.

Continuum Inquiry for Accessing Aliveness, Opening Creativity, and Healing Trauma

Founded by Emilie Conrad in 1967, Continuum is a unique inquiry into our capacity to innovate and participate with the essential, generative, and biological movement processes of life. Having taught thousands of Continuum events since 1975, I have personally witnessed and been moved by what happens when participants cultivate a refined sensuous attention to feel intrinsic movements and an internal sense of aliveness. Subtle, wise sensations and movement impulses in our bodies are a key for metabolizing the experience of trauma and for the emergence of new expression.

In Continuum workshops, rather than teaching protocols and procedures, we teach a creative process of evocative inquiry. We explore movement in the language of life with micromovements, subtle wave motion, primordial breathing, and sound streams. This contributes to a heartful, listening, responsive organism. The explorations are guided by a philosophy of respect for innate organismic intelligence, which guides healing and creativity.

In Continuum, we resonate with the movement capacities of living water. We play in arching, waving, curling, forming, dissolving, spiraling movement explorations. Connective tissue becomes more fluid with these movements. Fluid dynamics are creative shaping forces that formed the first biological organisms in the sea and each of our bodies in utero. These continue throughout our life. When we consciously participate with the fluid dynamics inside our organism, we engage a system that has, as its essential nature, flexibility, fluidity, and wholeness.

The adult body is composed of approximately 70% water that expresses as blood, lymph, tears, cerebrospinal fluid, and interstitial fluids moving between cells, just to name a few. Schwenk (1965) observed that all fluids, whether in the body or flowing in the planet, function as a resonant intelligent whole in one unbroken circulatory system. When we sensuously experience fluid presence and resonance, we actuate a primal connectedness and well-being that can be profoundly healing to the painful psychological states of isolation and disconnection.

In a Continuum workshop, after some initial instructions, we enter what we call a dive, where each student explores specific themes and inquiries. We call it a dive as each person is entering the "ocean" of their body, "swimming" through their inner living waters. We are in a collective field of sounding and moving, each in a self-paced process. Each participant is self-regulating and simultaneously coregulating with others in the field. As one person deepens, there is often a creative emergence that moves through the whole group. For the length of the dive, participants are collectively in a nonworded communion together. This creates a profound sense of belonging while each participant is simultaneously in their own process. This form of coregulating is quite different from our usual social engagements.

In Continuum explorations, we might soften our tissues with the play of breath and diverse sounding. We may invoke small rippling waves into our torso, pelvis, limbs, hands, and feet. Through these soft oceanic undulations, habitual defenses that are no longer needed can gently melt. We become resonant and more capable of communion with all life. Psychotherapist and Continuum teacher Don St John (2022) says,

> As we engage this work, we gradually enhance our capacity for fluid resonance. Resonance is how we can tune in to another in a very deep, whole-body way. Resonance allows two people to vibrate in each other's presence. As bodies become more fluid and more resonant, they can transmit and receive, simultaneously, a force that is delicious to experience. . . . We can call this love.

In modern times, there has been a profound loss of humans relating with the more-than-human world. Many eco-psychologists say that the severance of humans from the living world of nature is the original trauma. When we feel separate from the living earth, it changes how we treat plants, animals, and the wild. "We are meant to be cosmos streaming, cosmos singing, cosmos weeping, cosmos dreaming" (Weller, 2023). As human beings, we are as much an extension and expression of the planetary process as a tree is, or a deer, or a river or a mountain. There is a tendency to be so embedded in modern civilized thinking that we forget that our deeper nature *is* nature.

Throughout her life, Emilie Conrad, founder of Continuum, was passionately engaged with meeting the mystery through movement, breath, and sound. She was a visionary mover, a radical thinker, and an innovative teacher. Earlier in her life, Emilie had been in profound grief, living in a modern culture that had lost touch with soul and had no conscious initiatory path. Rather than trying to fix the existential pain, she allowed this ache to be a communicator of the need to live from a deeper reality. Her response was to listen deeply inside to the movements of the underlying creative flux. From insights arising from this deep listening, a multidimensional inquiry process called Continuum was born. I, along with others, am grateful to have contributed to its development, which is carried by Continuum teachers worldwide as it continues to unfold. As teachers of Continuum, we function as creators of contexts where people can explore, heal, and discover creative gifts.

Continuum views the body and self not as an object, but rather as a fluid unfolding process. One of Emilie's early evocative statements was, "The human dilemma is that we are an ordinary human living a cultural life, and we are part primordial soup, and we are part star" (E. Conrad, personal communication, 1978). She observed that, in primordial attunement, we come into "species inclusiveness" and a potent trust of bio-intelligence. In cosmic attunement, we enter the all-inclusive field of consciousness and a sense of timelessness (Conrad, 2007). In both the primordial and cosmic attunements, we experience prelinguistic knowing and expression, and expansive awareness.

Somatic listening to inner experience and allowing intrinsic impulses to move us accesses pre-egoic states of consciousness prior to the formation of psychological beliefs and self-identity. This dissolution of the egoic self softens the fixity of self-image and personal identity. A greater range of possibilities emerges. A subtle inner feeling of awe awakens. Continuum offers a pathway to discover one's uniqueness within a greater sense of wholeness. Physical, imaginal, and soulful impressions flow forth into revelatory expression.

Our uniqueness is echoed by John O'Donohue, who sees that each person is an astonishing sacred frontier of experience that has never appeared before in the whole of time and will never appear again. Each of us occupies a corner of creation in the way we taste, see, and experience (O'Donohue, 2004).

Portals of Perceiving

The way we perceive is a powerful force shaping our lives and our version of reality. We have ingrained habits in how we see, listen, move, touch, and breathe. Habits are styles of perceiving, feeling, or acting that have become second nature to us. By actively participating in new ways to perceive, who we are transforms through how we are relating. This affects our physical structure, coordination, psychological profile, how we relate, and our capacity for intimacy.

As therapists and teachers, we are in relational inquiry: How can I be with you and simultaneously be with me? In haptic attunement, we are listening to our clients and listening inwardly to the inner flow of impressions and felt sense experiencing. It is important to be with our own haptic relationship to gravity and to the larger context that contains us both.

In the broken reciprocity of trauma, there grows an inhibited exchange with the world, with little trust of somatic intelligence and of the inherent ability to heal. In the healing process, we encourage exploratory engagement that fosters the basic goodness of the body and the goodness of the living world.

Hubert Godard, a distinguished French movement researcher and teacher, sees that the haptic system has two functions, exploratory or defensive (personal communication, 2023). We build discernment through these haptic functions to know when to open and experience, and when to stiffen, withdraw, or brace. These movements are responsive to the immediacy of the context. Based on our early relational contexts and how we interacted and participated, we may have developed a habit of stiffening, bracing, defending.

Exploratory haptic sensory perceiving is simultaneously active and receptive. With the ability to receive information, we can somatically discern responsive wise action. If one cannot haptically receive, one is stuck in past tendencies to defend and protect regardless of the current context. This results in haptic dissociation (H. Godard, personal communication, 2023). We can touch the world, but we are not touched by the world. We are not getting new information. In the narrowed trance of trauma, we cannot refresh.

The first step in working with haptic defense is to help the client settle with gravity to receive support. Then with small steps, we introduce sounds, smells, visuals, or attuned touch. As the habit to stiffen or withdraw arises, it is first necessary to be with it as it is. We open a space to fully perceive what is and to hold what is with the creative tension of what is possible. We honor the wisdom of the original inhibition in the earlier relational context. Gently and slowly, we introduce curiosity to explore relationally what was forbidden. What else might be possible to feel? This invites a new range of sensations. Through this process, one recovers the appetite to explore, to feel, and to experience wonder.

Similarly, in depression there is a diminishment of receiving. Somatic activity is encouraged. While it is helpful to get outside and move, it is crucial that the client also explores through the senses and begins to allow themselves to be touched by what they see, hear, smell, or touch (H. Godard, personal communication, 2023).

Increasing intimate contact allows us to know more. This applies to another person, creature, stone, or a plant. We zoom in with focal gaze to know detail and color. We zoom out with peripheral gaze to perceive the whole of the current context. We include awareness of connection to ground and space. Experiencing takes full awareness, as we use all our senses and attend to the inner field of physical sensations, impressions, and intuitions. Connecting to all of the elements, we are actively perceiving the flow of the world and being touched by that flow in our living flesh. This process is the elemental body of relating that can heal an existential sense of separation, as we experientially feel our interwoven connectedness.

Five Elemental Resources for Presence and Resonance

Somatic/Psyche Tools for Well-Being for Therapists and Clients

Direct sensory experience with the air, water, light, gravity, and space—that which surrounds us and moves within—provides a fundamental connection to life. Attuning to the intelligent dynamics of each element builds natural presence.

Here are some experiential suggestions and inquiries to foster sensuous experience. As you attune to each element, be curious about whatever you experience, including preference and new possibilities.

Attune to the Element of Earth

The earth is a teacher of contact. Through the eros of gravity, each body has a direct connection to the core of the Earth. Gravity can be recognized as a physical force of belonging. In zero gravity, weight disappears. Weight is therefore a relational conversation with gravity. Aligning well with gravity brings stability, flow, and adaptability. Our resonance with the earth can help in coregulating when we sit with someone in a highly dysregulated state. Directly perceiving our connection to the earth fosters a sense of belonging and support.

The following activities can help you attune to the earth.

- Bring inquiry to the process of perceiving and receiving support.
- Can you simultaneously be held by the support of the ground as you hold something heavy? This practice of holding and being held is a resource for parents and caregivers.
- With aware self-touch, palpate and gently squeeze your earthy, fleshy, bony body to sense substance. Feeling substantial can be especially helpful when we are nervous or lost in thought.

- Invite a variety of movements to explore contact, ground, and a dynamic relationship with gravity.
- Attend to sounding as a vibrational form of touch.

Attune to the Element of Air

The process of respiration includes all living organisms. Our breath is in a continuous loop with the larger breath that loops into and out of the animate kingdom of plants and other animals. The breathing planetary body breathes our organism while we are asleep and awake. Issues of existence, of feeling alive or not feeling alive, can be addressed in meeting our patterns of breathing. Every emotion expresses through the breath. By bringing mindfulness/awareness to the sensations, movements, and inner touch of our breathing, we meet ourselves where we are. We honor where we may have needed to hold our breath for safety. We explore slowly and with respect as we explore new possibilities. Our health and happiness depend on breathing freely.

- Sense the myriad sensations of air on the inner skin of your nostrils, mouth, throat, lungs, diaphragm, and belly in the movement of breathing.
- Sense the tide turn in breathing, inhaling becoming exhaling and exhaling turning to inhaling.
- Feel the way your body changes shape with each inhale and exhale.
- Play with shape-changing textures of sounding and breathing.
- Bring awareness to the dynamic relationship of breathing with the green plants with whom you exchange breath.

Attune to the Element of Fire

Fire carries the heat, energy, and light of primordial creation in the combustion of the big bang. It still radiates in the stars, in the sun, in the core of the earth, and in living bodies. Fire is a source of nourishment. Fire devours and transforms the outworn. Light allows us to see. Developing the warmth of compassion for ourselves and others is essential for meeting suffering.

- Relate to basic aliveness, vitality, warmth, subtle energy, and the inner sense of light and radiance.
- Nervous system regulation: How do you handle activating charge and discharge?
- Light allows sight. Explore the joy of seeing—inner vision and outer seeing.
- See if you can feel the subtle energies and inner sense of light and radiance.
- Sense your heart fire, mind fire, sexual fire, belly fire to metabolize and digest.
- Fire is generative, and it consumes. How might you bring inquiry to your patterns of generating and consuming?

338 SOMATIC-ORIENTED THERAPIES

Attune to the Element of Water

All over the world, water is used for blessing, cleansing, benediction, and baptism—all expressions of love and devotion. The capacity to flow is a resource inherent in the fluid systems of biological, cellular beings. Water is a teacher of rhythmic variations, shape changing, and state changing. Each phase of the water cycle is vital to the cycle of life. Continuum offers movement explorations to attune to water's capacity to freeze, melt, flow, or evaporate, to fall as rain and snow, to rest in stillness and reflect.

- Play with the movement capacities of water in movement explorations.
- Explore the rhythms of water—sometimes quick and sometimes slow.
- What happens when you engage somatically in the state-changing movement qualities of water?
- Explore gently meeting where you are frozen and where you flow.
- Rest in stillness as water does in a still pool.
- What is it like to mirror your surrounding context—to reflect without preference?

Attune to Space

Space is enveloping and suffuses everything. In some Buddhist teachings, it is said that everything arises from space, exists in space, and dissolves in space. In the space of your childhood homes, there may have been a sense of too much space, or not enough space for your expression. You may have rightfully formed a conclusion about space being dangerous. With fresh perceiving, it is possible to attune directly to the element of space and recover the goodness of space.

- Reach, suspend, expand, sound, emote, and feel how space receives your expression.
- Attune to the space, behind you, in front, to the right, to the left, above and below. Spatially, are you in the center of your field?
- Offer tiny micromovements in the intimacy of inner space as you dwell in the surrounding vast space.
- Attend to your capacity for silence and the joy of listening to and being with what is.

Integration for Embodied Relational Well-Being

With embodied relational well-being, we deepen the capacity to experience life. We actively participate in perceiving, attuning to elemental intelligence, resonating with the primordial life expressions of the natural world and the vastness of the ever-expanding cosmos. We refine our capacity to listen to the animate voices of the world. We experience this vast array through somatic listening and with attunement to all manner of bodily experiences, sensations, and sense discoveries in worded and nonworded knowing.

In Continuum explorations and anytime we sensuously experience life-giving movements, we open a large repertoire of sensations. An immense variety of sensation provides more choices in our responsiveness. The body knows how to attune relationally, through sensuous haptic perception, to the living world, and how to make sense intuitively of experiences. Courage grows to feel the difficult sensations and wondrous feelings. We dare to love, weep, laugh, and meet the splendor and heart-wrenching terrible beauty that the river of life delivers.

We see the vivid colors of the green earth, listen to the songs of birds in the ever-changing sky, and flow with the movements of living waters. We open in conjunctive resonance (Schrei, 2023). As we are actively perceiving, our cells are rippling with the flow of the world in the eros of belonging. The process of marveling at the world heals and unfolds the self.

David Spangler (2009) says, "The impulse to incarnate in the soul is a profound, deep, primal, creative, spiritual impulse; it is an impulse to participate in creation, to serve, to bless, to grow. It is most certainly an impulse of love and an impulse to love."

A heart that is awakened has a huge capacity for genuine love. We need the heart's capacity for wholeness, both in healing trauma and in times of increased polarization when we have forgotten the innate beauty of differences. Our hearts are capable of being with paradox—of weeping at the destruction we see in the world and dancing with wild joy. Not knowing the way, we enter the generative mysteries, to discover ancient yet fresh, innovative ways to meet the enormity of our current personal and ecological challenges.

We contribute vital energy to the healing and renewal of the world when we each sing the unique song that lives deep within us. For the healing of trauma, our gifts need to be relationally received and reflected in accurate mirroring as we receive the gifts of others. This is the nature of healthy relational ecology. We expand our capacity for healing wounds, building community, and embracing wholeness, which deepens the process of incarnating in our shared world.

References

Preface

Cottingham, J. T., Porges, S. W., & Lyon, T. (1988a). Effects of soft tissue mobilization (Rolfing pelvic lift) on parasympathetic tone in two age groups. *Physical Therapy, 68*(3), 352–356.

Cottingham, J. T., Porges, S. W., & Richmond, K. (1988b). Shifts in pelvic inclination angle and parasympathetic tone produced by Rolfing soft tissue manipulation. *Physical Therapy, 68*(9), 1364–1370.

Introduction

Cooper, R. (2018). *Diagnosing the Diagnostic and Statistical Manual of Mental Disorders: Fifth Edition.* Routledge.

Cozolino, L. (2017). *The neuroscience of psychotherapy: Healing the social brain* (3rd ed.). Norton.

Lanius, R. A., Vermetten, E., & Pain, C. (2010). *The impact of early life trauma on health and disease: The hidden epidemic.* Cambridge University Press.

Lanius, U. F., Paulsen, S. L., & Corrigan, F. M. (2014). *Neurobiology and treatment of traumatic dissociation: Towards an embodied self.* Springer.

Mahler, K. (2016) *Interoception: The eighth sensory system.* AAPC Publishing.

Martens, U., Schweitzer, D., & Herholz, I. (2023). Körperpsychotherapie. *Psychotherapie, 68,* 172–178. https://doi.org/10.1007/s00278-023-00643-z

Morton, L., Cogan, N., Kolacz, J., Calderwood, C., Nikolic, M., Bacon, T., Pathe, E., Williams, D. J., & Porges, S. W. (2022). A new measure of feeling safe: Developing psychometric properties of the Neuroception of Psychological Safety Scale (NPSS). *Psychological Trauma: Theory, Research, Practice, and Policy.* https://doi.org/10.1037/tra0001313

Nijenhuis, E. R. S., Spinhoven, P., Van Dyck, R., Van Dee Hart, O., & Vanderlinden, J. (1996). The development and psychometric characteristics of the Somatoform Dissociation Questionnaire (SDQ-20). *Journal of Nervous and Mental Disease, 184*(11), 688–694. https://doi.org/10.1097/00005053-199611000-00006

Payne, H., Koch, S., & Tantia, J. (2019). *The Routledge international handbook of embodied perspectives in psychotherapy: Approaches from dance movement and body psychotherapies.* Routledge.

Porges, S. (1993). Body perception questionnaire. Laboratory of Developmental Assessment, University of Maryland.

Porges, S. W. (2021). *Polyvagal safety: Attachment, communication, self-regulation*. Norton.

Porges, S. W. (2022). Polyvagal theory: A science of safety. *Frontiers in Integrative Neuroscience, 16*, 27.

Rosendahl, S., Sattel, H., & Lahmann, C. (2021). Effectiveness of body psychotherapy: A systematic review and meta-analysis. *Frontiers in Psychiatry, 12*. https://doi.org/10.3389/fpsyt.2021.709798

Saint Arnault, D. (2022). The Somatic Post-Encounter Clinical Summary (SPECS): A new instrument for practitioners and researchers to measure the wisdom of somatic intelligence. *International Body Psychotherapy Journal, 21*(1), 66–75.

Schore, A. N. (2009). Right-brain affect regulation: An essential mechanism of development, trauma, dissociation, and psychotherapy. In D. Fosha, D. J. Siegel, & M. F. Solomon (Eds.), *The healing power of emotion: Affective neuroscience, development and clinical practice* (pp. 112–144). Norton.

van der Kolk, B., Fischer, J., Korn, D., Van der Hart, O., Ogden, P., Spinazzola J., & Levine, P. (2001). The assessment and treatment of complex PTSD. In R. Yehuda (Ed.), *Traumatic stress*. American Psychiatric Press.

1. Tools for Tracking Autonomic Activity in Treatment

Alvares, G. A., Quintana, D. S., Hickie, I. B., & Guastella, A. J. (2016). Autonomic nervous system dysfunction in psychiatric disorders and the impact of psychotropic medications: A systematic review and meta-analysis. *Journal of Psychiatry and Neuroscience, 41*(2), 89–104.

Angelovski, A., Sattel, H., Henningsen, P., & Sack, M. (2016). Heart rate variability predicts therapy outcome in pain-predominant multisomatoform disorder. *Journal of Psychosomatic Research, 83*, 16–21.

Appelhans, B. M., & Luecken, L. J. (2006). Heart rate variability as an index of regulated emotional responding. *Review of General Psychology, 10*(3), 229–240.

Asahina, M., Poudel, A., & Hirano, S. (2015). Sweating on the palm and sole: Physiological and clinical relevance. *Clinical Autonomic Research, 25*, 153–159.

Ashhad, S., Kam, K., Del Negro, C. A., & Feldman, J. L. (2022). Breathing rhythm and pattern and their influence on emotion. *Annual Review of Neuroscience, 45*, 223–247.

Babic, T., & Browning, K. N. (2014). The role of vagal neurocircuits in the regulation of nausea and vomiting. *European Journal of Pharmacology, 722*, 38–47.

Bailey, E. F., & Hoit, J. D. (2002). Speaking and breathing in high respiratory drive. *Journal of Speech, Language, and Hearing Research, 45*(1), 89–99.

Baker, S. E., Hipp, J., & Alessio, H. (2008). Ventilation and speech characteristics during submaximal aerobic exercise. *Journal of Speech, Language, and Hearing Research, 51*(5), 1203–1214.

Beda, A., Jandre, F. C., Phillips, D. I., Giannella-Neto, A., & Simpson, D. M. (2007). Heart-rate and blood-pressure variability during psychophysiological tasks involving speech: Influence of respiration. *Psychophysiology, 44*(5), 767–778.

Berntson, G. G., Bigger, J. T., Eckberg, D. L., Grossman, P., Kaufmann, P. G., Malik, M., Nagaraja, H. N., Porges, S. W., Saul, J. P., Stone, P. H., & Van Der Molen, M. W. (1997). Heart rate variability: Origins, methods, and interpretive caveats. *Psychophysiology, 34*(6), 623–648.

Berntson, G. G., & Stowell, J. R. (1998). ECG artifacts and heart period variability: Don't miss a beat! *Psychophysiology, 35*(1), 127–132.

Billman, G. E. (2013). The LF/HF ratio does not accurately measure cardiac sympatho-vagal balance. *Frontiers in Physiology, 4*, 26.

Blanck, P., Stoffel, M., Bents, H., Ditzen, B., & Mander, J. (2019). Heart rate variability in individual psychotherapy: Associations with alliance and outcome. *Journal of Nervous and Mental Disease, 207*(6), 451–458.

Bryan, C. J., & Rudd, M. D. (2018). *Brief cognitive-behavioral therapy for suicide prevention.* Guilford.

Byrne, E. A., Fleg, J. L., Vaitkevicius, P. V., Wright, J., & Porges, S. W. (1996). Role of aerobic capacity and body mass index in the age-associated decline in heart rate variability. *Journal of Applied Physiology, 81*(2), 743–750.

Cabrera, A., Kolacz, J., Pailhez, G., Bulbena-Cabre, A., Bulbena, A., & Porges, S. W. (2018). Assessing body awareness and autonomic reactivity: Factor structure and psychometric properties of the Body Perception Questionnaire–Short Form (BPQ-SF). *International Journal of Methods in Psychiatric Research, 27*(2), e1596.

Cerritelli, F., Galli, M., Consorti, G., D'Alessandro, G., Kolacz, J., & Porges, S. W. (2021). Cross-cultural adaptation and psychometric properties of the Italian version of the Body Perception Questionnaire. *Plos One, 16*(5), e0251838.

Chalmers, J. A., Quintana, D. S., Abbott, M. J. A., & Kemp, A. H. (2014). Anxiety disorders are associated with reduced heart rate variability: A meta-analysis. *Frontiers in Psychiatry, 5*, 80.

Creswell, J. D. (2017). Mindfulness interventions. *Annual Review of Psychology, 68*, 491–516.

Dale, L. P., Kolacz, J., Mazmanyan, J., Leon, K. G., Johonnot, K., Bossemeyer Biernacki, N., & Porges, S. W. (2022). Childhood maltreatment influences autonomic regulation and mental health in college students. *Frontiers in Psychiatry, 13*, 841749.

Dawson, M. E., Schell, A. M., & Filion, D. L. (2007). The electrodermal system. In J. T. Cacioppo, L. G. Tassinary, & G. Berntson (Eds.), *Handbook of psychophysiology* (3rd ed., pp. 159–181). Cambridge University Press.

Del Giudice, M., Ellis, B. J., & Shirtcliff, E. A. (2011). The adaptive calibration model of stress responsivity. *Neuroscience and Biobehavioral Reviews, 35*(7), 1562–1592.

Hautala, A. J., Kiviniemi, A. M., & Tulppo, M. P. (2009). Individual responses to aerobic exercise: The role of the autonomic nervous system. *Neuroscience and Biobehavioral Reviews, 33*(2), 107–115.

Hsueh, B., Chen, R., Jo, Y., Tang, D., Raffiee, M., Kim, Y. S., Inoue, M., Randles, S., Ramakrishnan, C., Patel, S., Kim, D. K., Liu, T. X., Kim, S. H., Tan, L., Mortazavi, L., Cordero, A., Shi, J., Zhao, M., Ho, … & Deisseroth, K. (2023). Cardiogenic control of affective behavioural state. *Nature, 615*(7951), 292–299.

Jokić, B., Purić, D., Grassmann, H., Walling, C. G., Nix, E. J., Porges, S. W., & Kolacz, J. (2023). Association of childhood maltreatment with adult body awareness and autonomic reactivity: The moderating effect of practicing body psychotherapy. *Psychotherapy, 60*(2), 159.

Julian, T. H., Syeed, R., Glascow, N., & Zis, P. (2020). Alcohol-induced autonomic dysfunction: A systematic review. *Clinical Autonomic Research, 30*, 29–41.

Kasos, K., Kekecs, Z., Csirmaz, L., Zimonyi, S., Vikor, F., Kasos, E., Veres, A., Kotyuk, E., & Szekely, A. (2020). Bilateral comparison of traditional and alternate electrodermal measurement sites. *Psychophysiology, 57*(11), e13645.

Kemp, A. H., Quintana, D. S., Gray, M. A., Felmingham, K. L., Brown, K., & Gatt, J. M. (2010). Impact of depression and antidepressant treatment on heart rate variability: A review and meta-analysis. *Biological Psychiatry, 67*(11), 1067–1074.

Koenig, J., Kemp, A. H., Beauchaine, T. P., Thayer, J. F., & Kaess, M. (2016). Depression and resting state heart rate variability in children and adolescents—a systematic review and meta-analysis. *Clinical Psychology Review, 46*, 136–150.

Kolacz, J., Chen, X., Nix, E. J., Roath, O. K., Holmes, L. G., Tokash, C., Porges, S. W., & Lewis,

G. F. (2023). Association of self-reported autonomic symptoms with sensor-based physiological measures. *Psychosomatic Medicine, 85*(9), 785–794.

Kolacz, J., Dale, L. P., Nix, E. J., Roath, O. K., Lewis, G. F., & Porges, S. W. (2020). Adversity history predicts self-reported autonomic reactivity and mental health in US residents during the COVID-19 pandemic. *Frontiers in Psychiatry,* October 27.

Kolacz, J., Hu, Y., Gesselman, A. N., Garcia, J. R., Lewis, G. F., & Porges, S. W. (2020). Sexual function in adults with a history of childhood maltreatment: Mediating effects of self-reported autonomic reactivity. *Psychological Trauma: Theory, Research, Practice, and Policy, 12*(3), 281.

Kolacz, J., Kovacic, K., Dang, L., Li, B. U. K., Lewis, G. F., & Porges, S. W. (2023). Cardiac vagal regulation is impeded in children with cyclic vomiting syndrome. *American Journal of Gastroenterology, 118*(7), 1268–1275.

Kolacz, J., Kovacic, K., Lewis, G. F., Sood, M. R., Aziz, Q., Roath, O. R., & Porges, S. W. (2021). Cardiac autonomic regulation and joint hypermobility in adolescents with functional abdominal pain disorders. *Neurogastroenterology and Motility, 33*(12), e14165.

Kolacz, J., Tabares, J., Rooney, E., Secor, A., Tomlinson, C., Roath, O. K., & Bryan, C. J. (under review). Longitudinal fluctuations in PTSD and autonomic symptoms in a population-based U.S. sample.

Kovacic, K., Kolacz, J., Lewis, G. F., & Porges, S. W. (2020). Impaired vagal efficiency predicts auricular neurostimulation response in adolescent functional abdominal pain disorders. *American Journal of Gastroenterology, 115*(9), 1534–1538.

Kudielka, B. M., Schommer, N. C., Hellhammer, D. H., & Kirschbaum, C. (2004). Acute HPA axis responses, heart rate, and mood changes to psychosocial stress (TSST) in humans at different times of day. *Psychoneuroendocrinology, 29*(8), 983–992.

Laborde, S., Mosley, E., & Thayer, J. F. (2017). Heart rate variability and cardiac vagal tone in psychophysiological research—recommendations for experiment planning, data analysis, and data reporting. *Frontiers in Psychology, 8,* 213.

Lewis, G. F., Furman, S. A., McCool, M. F., & Porges, S. W. (2012). Statistical strategies to quantify respiratory sinus arrhythmia: Are commonly used metrics equivalent? *Biological Psychology, 89*(2), 349–364.

Mendelowitz, D. (1999). Advances in parasympathetic control of heart rate and cardiac function. *Physiology, 14*(4), 155–161.

Middlekauff, H. R., Park, J., & Moheimani, R. S. (2014). Adverse effects of cigarette and noncigarette smoke exposure on the autonomic nervous system: Mechanisms and implications for cardiovascular risk. *Journal of the American College of Cardiology, 64*(16), 1740–1750.

Parashar, R., Amir, M., Pakhare, A., Rathi, P., & Chaudhary, L. (2016). Age related changes in autonomic functions. *Journal of Clinical and Diagnostic Research, 10*(3), CC11.

Pole, N. (2007). The psychophysiology of posttraumatic stress disorder: A meta-analysis. *Psychological Bulletin, 133*(5), 725.

Porges, S. (1993). Body perception questionnaire. Laboratory of Developmental Assessment, University of Maryland.

Porges, S. W. (1995). Orienting in a defensive world: Mammalian modifications of our evolutionary heritage. A polyvagal theory. *Psychophysiology, 32*(4), 301–318.

Porges, S. W. (2003). The polyvagal theory: Phylogenetic contributions to social behavior. *Physiology and Behavior, 79*(3), 503–513.

Porges, S. W. (2011). *The polyvagal theory: Neurophysiological foundations of emotions, attachment, communication, and self-regulation.* Norton.

Porges, S. W., Davila, M. I., Lewis, G. F., Kolacz, J., Okonmah-Obazee, S., Hane, A. A., Kwon, K. Y., Ludwig, R. J., Myers, M. M., & Welch, M. G. (2019). Autonomic regulation of preterm infants is enhanced by Family Nurture Intervention. *Developmental Psychobiology, 61*(6), 942–952.

Porges, S. W., Doussard-Roosevelt, J. A., Stifter, C. A., McClenny, B. D., & Riniolo, T. C. (1999). Sleep state and vagal regulation of heart period patterns in the human newborn: An extension of the polyvagal theory. *Psychophysiology, 36*(1), 14–21.

Quintana, D. S., & Heathers, J. A. (2014). Considerations in the assessment of heart rate variability in biobehavioral research. *Frontiers in Psychology, 5*, 805.

Riniolo, T., & Porges, S. W. (1997). Inferential and descriptive influences on measures of respiratory sinus arrhythmia: Sampling rate, R-wave trigger accuracy, and variance estimates. *Psychophysiology, 34*(5), 613–621.

Schneider, M., & Schwerdtfeger, A. (2020). Autonomic dysfunction in posttraumatic stress disorder indexed by heart rate variability: A meta-analysis. *Psychological Medicine, 50*(12), 1937–1948.

Thayer, J. F., Hansen, A. L., Saus-Rose, E., & Johnsen, B. H. (2009). Heart rate variability, prefrontal neural function, and cognitive performance: The neurovisceral integration perspective on self-regulation, adaptation, and health. *Annals of Behavioral Medicine, 37*(2), 141–153.

Thayer, J. F., & Lane, R. D. (2000). A model of neurovisceral integration in emotion regulation and dysregulation. *Journal of Affective Disorders, 61*(3), 201–216.

Wang, N., Ren, F., & Zhou, X. (2020). Factor structure and psychometric properties of the Body Perception Questionnaire–Short Form (BPQ-SF) among Chinese college students. *Frontiers in Psychology, 11*, 530340.

Wehrwein, E. A., & Joyner, M. J. (2013). Regulation of blood pressure by the arterial baroreflex and autonomic nervous system. *Handbook of Clinical Neurology, 117*, 89–102.

2. Defining, Measuring, and Exploring Interoception

Andrews-Hanna, J. R. (2012). The brain's default network and its adaptive role in internal mentation. *Neuroscientist: A Review Journal Bringing Neurobiology, Neurology and Psychiatry, 18*(3), 251–270. https://doi.org/10.1177/1073858411403316

Badran, B. W., & Austelle, C. W. (2022). The future is noninvasive: A brief review of the evolution and clinical utility of vagus nerve stimulation. *Focus, 20*(1), 3–7. https://doi.org/10.1176/appi.focus.20210023

Bogaerts, K., Millen, A., Li, W., De Peuter, S., Van Diest, I., Vlemincx, E., ... Van den Bergh, O. (2008). High symptom reporters are less interoceptively accurate in a symptom-related context. *Journal of Psychosomatic Research, 65*(5), 417–424. https://doi.org/10.1016/j.jpsychores.2008.03.019

Cabrera, A., Kolacz, J., Pailhez, G., Bulbena-Cabre, A., Bulbena, A., & Porges, S. W. (2018). Assessing body awareness and autonomic reactivity: Factor structure and psychometric properties of the Body Perception Questionnaire Short Form (BPQ-SF). *International Journal of Methods in Psychiatric Research, 27*(2), e1596. https://doi.org/10.1002/mpr.1596

Ceunen, E., Vlaeyen, J. W. S., & Van Diest, I. (2016). On the origin of interoception. *Frontiers in Psychology, 7*, 743. https://doi.org/10.3389/fpsyg.2016.00743

Chen, W. G., Schloesser, D., Arensdorf, A. M., Simmons, J. M., Cui, C., Valentino, R., ... & Langevin, H. M. (2021). The emerging science of interoception: Sensing, integrating, interpreting, and regulating signals within the self. *Trends in Neurosciences, 44*(1), 3–16. https://doi.org/10.1016/j.tins.2020.10.007

Chentsova-Dutton, Y., & Dzokoto, V. (2014). Listen to your heart: The cultural shaping of interoceptive awareness and accuracy. *Emotion*, *14*(4), 666–678. https://doi.org/10.1037/a0036193

Craig, A. D. (2002). How do you feel? Interoception: The sense of the physiological condition of
the body. *Nature Reviews Neuroscience*, *3*(8), 655–666. https://doi.org/10.1038/nrn894

Craig, A. D. (2003). Interoception: The sense of the physiological condition of the body. *Current
Opinion in Neurobiology*, *13*(4), 500–505. https://doi.org/10.1016/s0959-4388(03)00090-4

Craig, A. D. (2005). Forebrain emotional asymmetry: A neuroanatomical basis? *Trends in Cognitive
Sciences*, *9*(12), 566–571. https://doi.org/10.1016/j.tics.2005.10.005

Craig, A. D. (2013). An interoceptive neuroanatomical perspective on feelings, energy, and effort.
Behavioral and Brain Sciences, *36*(6), 685–626. https://doi.org/10.1017/S0140525X13001489

Critchley, H. D., & Garfinkel, S. N. (2017). Interoception and emotion. *Current Opinion in Psychology*,
17, 7–14. https://doi.org/10.1016/j.copsyc.2017.04.020

Csordas, T. J. (1990). Embodiment as a paradigm for anthropology. *Ethos*, *18*(1), 5–47. https://
doi.org/10.1525/eth.1990.18.1.02a00010

Csordas, T. J. (1993). Somatic modes of attention. *Cultural Anthropology*, *8*(2), 135–156. https://
doi.org/10.1525/can.1993.8.2.02a00010

Dennis, E. O. L., Esposito, G., Critchley, H. D., Dienes, Z., & Garfinkel, S. N. (2021). Sensitivity
to changes in rate of heartbeats as a measure of interoceptive ability. *Journal of Neurophysiology*,
126(5), 1799–1813. https://doi.org/10.1152/jn.00059.2021

Desmedt, O., Heeren, A., Corneille, O., & Luminet, O. (2022). What do measures of self-report
interoception measure? Insights from a systematic review, latent factor analysis, and network
approach. *Biological Psychology*, *169*, 108289. https://doi.org/10.1016/j.biopsycho.2022.108289

Desmedt, O., Luminet, O., & Corneille, O. (2018). The heartbeat counting task largely involves
non-interoceptive processes: Evidence from both the original and an adapted counting task.
Biological Psychology, *138*, 185–188. https://doi.org/10.1016/j.biopsycho.2018.09.004

DuBois, D., Ameis, S. H., Lai, M., Casanova, M. F., & Desarkar, P. (2016). Interoception in autism
spectrum disorder: A review. *International Journal of Developmental Neuroscience*, *52*, 104–111. https://
doi.org/10.1016/j.ijdevneu.2016.05.001

Farb, N., Daubenmier, J., Price, C. J., Gard, T., Kerr, C., Dunn, B. D., … & Mehling, W. E. (2015).
Interoception, contemplative practice, and health. *Frontiers in Psychology*, *6*, 763. https://doi.org/
10.3389/fpsyg.2015.00763

Forkmann, T., Scherer, A., Meessen, J., Michal, M., Schächinger, H., Vögele, C., & Schulz, A.
(2016). Making sense of what you sense: Disentangling interoceptive awareness, sensibility and
accuracy. *International Journal of Psychophysiology*, *109*, 71–80. https://doi.org/10.1016/j.ijpsycho
.2016.09.019

Freedman, A., Hu, H., Liu, I. T. H. C., Stewart, A. L., Adler, S., & Mehling, W. E. (2020). Simi-
larities and differences in interoceptive bodily awareness between US-American and Japanese
cultures: A focus-group study in bicultural Japanese-Americans. *Culture, Medicine and Psychiatry*,
45, 234–267. https://doi.org/10.1007/s11013-020-09684-4

Freedman, A., & Mehling, W. (2020). Methods for measuring embodiment, an instrument. In J. Tantia
(Ed.), *The art and science of embodied research design: Concepts, methods and cases* (pp. 63–74). Routledge.

Freedman, A., Silow, T., Gold, S., Pope, T., & Saint Arnault, D. (2022). The somatic post-encounter
clinical summary (SPECS). *International Body Psychotherapy Journal*, *21*(1), 66–75.

Garfinkel, S. N., Seth, A. K., Barrett, A. B., Suzuki, K., & Critchley, H. D. (2015). Knowing your
own heart: Distinguishing interoceptive accuracy from interoceptive awareness. *Biological Psychology*, *104*, 65–74. https://doi.org/10.1016/j.biopsycho.2014.11.004

Geurts, K. L. (2002). *Culture and the senses: Bodily ways of knowing in an African community.* University of California Press.

Harrison, O. K., Köchli, L., Marino, S., Luechinger, R., Hennel, F., Brand, K., ... & Stephan, K. E. (2021). Interoception of breathing and its relationship with anxiety. *Neuron, 109*(24), 4080–4093. https://doi.org/10.1016/j.neuron.2021.09.045

Herbert, B. M., Muth, E. R., Pollatos, O., & Herbert, C. (2012). Interoception across modalities: On the relationship between cardiac awareness and the sensitivity for gastric functions. *PloS One, 7*(5), e36646. https://doi.org/10.1371/journal.pone.0036646

Herbert, B. M., & Pollatos, O. (2012). The body in the mind: On the relationship between interoception and embodiment. *Topics in Cognitive Science, 4*(4), 692–704. https://doi.org/10.1111/j.1756-8765.2012.01189.x

Hou, P., Hsu, H., Lin, Y., Tang, N., Cheng, C., & Hsieh, C. (2015). The history, mechanism, and clinical application of auricular therapy in traditional Chinese medicine. *Evidence-Based Complementary and Alternative Medicine: eCAM, 2015,* 495684. https://doi.org/10.1155/2015/495684

Khalsa, S. S., Adolphs, R., Cameron, O. G., Critchley, H. D., Davenport, P. W., Feinstein, J. S., ... & Interoception Summit 2016 participants. (2018). Interoception and mental health: A roadmap. *Biological Psychiatry: Cognitive Neuroscience and Neuroimaging, 3*(6), 501–513. https://doi.org/10.1016/j.bpsc.2017.12.004

Koch, A., & Pollatos, O. (2014). Cardiac sensitivity in children: Sex differences and its relationship to parameters of emotional processing. *Psychophysiology, 51*(9), 932–941. https://doi.org/10.1111/psyp.12233

Langevin H. M. (2021). Moving the complementary and integrative health research field toward whole person health. *Journal of Alternative and Complementary Medicine, 27*(8), 623–626. https://doi.org/10.1089/acm.2021.0255

Lock, M. (1993). Cultivating the body: Anthropology and epistemologies of bodily practice and knowledge. *Annual Review of Anthropology, 22*(1), 133–155. https://doi.org/10.1146/annurev.an.22.100193.001025

Lux, V., Non, A. L., Pexman, P. M., Stadler, W., Weber, L. A. E., & Krüger, M. (2021). A developmental framework for embodiment research: The next step toward integrating concepts and methods. *Frontiers in Systems Neuroscience, 15,* 672740. https://doi.org/10.3389/fnsys.2021.672740

Mahler, K., Hample, K., Jones, C., Sensenig, J., Thomasco, P., & Hilton, C. (2022). Impact of an interoception-based program on emotion regulation in autistic children. *Occupational Therapy International, 2022,* 1–7. https://doi.org/10.1155/2022/9328967

Maister, L., Tang, T., & Tsakiris, M. (2017). Neurobehavioral evidence of interoceptive sensitivity in early infancy. *eLife, 6,* August 8. https://doi.org/10.7554/eLife.25318

Maister, L., & Tsakiris, M. (2014). My face, my heart: Cultural differences in integrated bodily self-awareness. *Cognitive Neuroscience, 5*(1), 10–16. https://doi.org/10.1080/17588928.2013.808613

Ma-Kellams, C. (2014). Cross-cultural differences in somatic awareness and interoceptive accuracy: A review of the literature and directions for future research. *Frontiers in Psychology, 5,* 1370. https://doi.org/10.3389/fpsyg.2014.01379

Ma-Kellams, C., Blascovich, J., & McCall, C. (2012). Culture and the body: East-West differences in visceral perception. *Journal of Personality and Social Psychology, 102*(4), 718–728. https://doi.org/10.1037/a0027010

Mehling, W. (2016). Differentiating attention styles and regulatory aspects of self-reported interoceptive sensibility. *Philosophical Transactions of the Royal Society of London. Series B, Biological Sciences, 371*(1708), 20160013. https://doi.org/10.1098/rstb.2016.0013

Mehling, W. E., Acree, M., Stewart, A., Silas, J., & Jones, A. (2018). The multidimensional assessment of interoceptive awareness, version 2 (MAIA-2). *Plos One, 13*(12), e0208034. https://doi.org/10.1371/journal.pone.0208034

Mehling, W. E., Gopisetty, V., Daubenmier, J., Price, C. J., Hecht, F. M., & Stewart, A. (2009). Body awareness: Construct and self-report measures. *PloS One, 4*(5), e5614. https://doi.org/10.1371/journal.pone.0005614

Mehling, W. E., Price, C., Daubenmier, J. J., Acree, M., Bartmess, E., & Stewart, A. (2012). The multidimensional assessment of interoceptive awareness (MAIA). *Plos One, 7*(11), e48230. https://doi.org/10.1371/journal.pone.0048230

Murphy, J., Brewer, R., Catmur, C., & Bird, G. (2017). Interoception and psychopathology: A developmental neuroscience perspective. *Developmental Cognitive Neuroscience, 23*, 45–56. https://doi.org/10.1016/j.dcn.2016.12.006

Murphy, J., Brewer, R., Hobson, H., Catmur, C., & Bird, G. (2018). Is alexithymia characterised by impaired interoception? Further evidence, the importance of control variables, and the problems with the heartbeat counting task. *Biological Psychology, 136*, 189–197. https://doi.org/10.1016/j.biopsycho.2018.05.010

Murphy, J., Brewer, R., Plans, D., Sahib, S. K., Catmur, C., & Bird, G. (2020). Testing the independence of self-reported interoceptive accuracy and attention. *Quarterly Journal of Experimental Psychology, 73*(1), 115–133. https://doi.org/10.1177/1747021819879826

Nord, C. L., & Garfinkel, S. N. (2022). Interoceptive pathways to understand and treat mental health conditions. *Trends in Cognitive Sciences, 26*(6), 499–513. https://doi.org/10.1016/j.tics.2022.03.004

Opdensteinen, K. D., Schaan, L., Pohl, A., Schulz, A., Domes, G., & Hechler, T. (2021). Interoception in preschoolers: New insights into its assessment and relations to emotion regulation and stress. *Biological Psychology, 165*, 108166. https://doi.org/10.1016/j.biopsycho.2021.108166

Porges, S. (1993). Body perception questionnaire. Laboratory of Developmental Assessment, University of Maryland.

Price, C. J., & Hooven, C. (2018). Interoceptive awareness skills for emotion regulation: Theory and approach of mindful awareness in body-oriented therapy (MABT). *Frontiers in Psychology, 9*. https://www.frontiersin.org/articles/10.3389/fpsyg.2018.00798

Price, C. J., Wells, E. A., Donovan, D. M., & Brooks, M. (2012). Implementation and acceptability of mindful awareness in body-oriented therapy in women's substance use disorder treatment. *Journal of Alternative and Complementary Medicine, 18*(5), 454–462. https://doi.org/10.1089/acm.2011.0126

Ring, C., & Brener, J. (2018). Heartbeat counting is unrelated to heartbeat detection: A comparison of methods to quantify interoception. *Psychophysiology, 55*(9), e13084. https://doi.org/10.1111/psyp.13084

Rosendahl, S., Sattel, H., & Lahmann, C. (2021). Effectiveness of body psychotherapy: A systematic review and meta-analysis. *Frontiers in Psychiatry, 12*. https://www.frontiersin.org/articles/10.3389/fpsyt.2021.709798

Schaan, L., Schulz, A., Nuraydin, S., Bergert, C., Hilger, A., Rach, H., & Hechler, T. (2019). Interoceptive accuracy, emotion recognition, and emotion regulation in preschool children. *International Journal of Psychophysiology, 138*, 47–56. https://doi.org/10.1016/j.ijpsycho.2019.02.001

Schandry, R. (1981). Heart beat perception and emotional experience. *Psychophysiology, 18*(4), 483–488. https://doi.org/10.1111/j.1469-8986.1981.tb02486.x

Schulz, A., & Vögele, C. (2015). Interoception and stress. *Frontiers in Psychology, 6*. https://www.frontiersin.org/articles/10.3389/fpsyg.2015.00993

Segil, J. L., Roldan, L. M., & Graczyk, E. L. (2022). Measuring embodiment: A review of methods for prosthetic devices. *Frontiers in Neurorobotics, 16,* 902162. https://doi.org/10.3389/fnbot.2022.902162

Seth A. K. (2013). Interoceptive inference, emotion, and the embodied self. *Trends in Cognitive Sciences, 17*(11), 565–573. https://doi.org/10.1016/j.tics.2013.09.007

Shah, P., Hall, R., Catmur, C., & Bird, G. (2016). Alexithymia, not autism, is associated with impaired interoception. *Cortex, 81,* 215–220. https://doi.org/10.1016/j.cortex.2016.03.021

Shapiro, F. (2001). *Eye movement desensitization and reprocessing (EMDR): Basic principles, protocols, and procedures* (2nd ed.). Guilford.

Sherrington, C. (1906). *The integrative action of the nervous system.* Yale University Press.

Shields, S. A., Mallory, M. E., & Simon, A. (1989). The body awareness questionnaire: Reliability and validity. *Journal of Personality Assessment, 53*(4), 802–815. https://doi.org/10.1207/s15327752jpa5304_16

Shoji, M., Mehling, W. E., Hautzinger, M., & Herbert, B. M. (2018). Investigating multidimensional interoceptive awareness in a Japanese population: Validation of the Japanese MAIA-J. *Frontiers in Psychology, 9,* 1855. https://doi.org/10.3389/fpsyg.2018.01855

Singelis, T. M. (1994). The measurement of independent and interdependent self-construals. *Personality and Social Psychology Bulletin, 20*(5), 580–591. https://doi.org/10.1177/0146167294205014

Todd, J., Barron, D., Aspell, J. E., Lin Toh, E. K., Zahari, H. S., Khatib, N. A. M., & Swami, V. (2022). Examining relationships between interoceptive sensibility and body image in a non-Western context: A study with Malaysian adults. *International Perspectives in Psychology: Research, Practice, Consultation, 11*(1), 53–63. https://doi.org/10.1027/2157-3891/a000022

Trevisan, D. A., Tsheringla, S., & McPartland, J. C. (2023). On the relation between interoceptive attention and health anxiety: Distinguishing adaptive and maladaptive bodily awareness. *Cogent Psychology, 10*(1), 2262855. https://doi.org/10.1080/23311908.2023.2262855

Tsai, J. L., Simeonova, D. I., & Watanabe, J. T. (2004). Somatic and social: Chinese Americans talk about emotion. *Personality and Social Psychology Bulletin, 30*(9), 1226–1238. https://doi.org/10.1177/0146167204264014

Van Bael, K., Ball, M., Scarfo, J., & Suleyman, E. (2023). Assessment of the mind-body connection: Preliminary psychometric evidence for a new self-report questionnaire. *BMC Psychology, 11*(1), 309. https://doi.org/10.1186/s40359-023-01302-3

Vig, L., Köteles, F., & Ferentzi, E. (2022). Questionnaires of interoception do not assess the same construct. *PloS One, 17*(8), e0273299. https://doi.org/10.1371/journal.pone.0273299

Villani, V., Tsakiris, M., & Azevedo, R. T. (2019). Transcutaneous vagus nerve stimulation improves interoceptive accuracy. *Neuropsychologia, 134,* 107201. https://doi.org/10.1016/j.neuropsychologia.2019.107201

Weng, H., Feldman, J., Leggio, L., Napadow, V., Park, J., & Price, C. (2021). Interventions and manipulations of interoception. *Trends in Neurosciences, 44,* 52–62. https://doi.org/doi:10.1016/j.tins.2020.09.010

Weng, H., Lewis-Peacock, J., Hecht, F., Uncapher, M., Ziegler, D., Farb, N., … & Gazzaley, A. (2020). Focus on the breath: Brain decoding reveals internal states of attention during meditation. *Frontiers in Human Neuroscience, 14.* https://doi.org/10.3389/fnhum.2020.00336

Whitehead, W. E., Holtkotter, B., Enck, P., Hoelzl, R., Holmes, K. D., Anthony, J., … Schuster, M. M. (1990). Tolerance for rectosigmoid distention in irritable bowel syndrome. *Gastroenterology, 98*(5, Part 1), 1187–1192. https://doi.org/10.1016/0016-5085(90)90332-U

WHO. (2013, August 6). WHO releases guidance on mental health care after trauma. https://www
    .who.int/news/item/06-08-2013-who-releases-guidance-on-mental-health-care-after-trauma

Zamariola, G., Maurage, P., Luminet, O., & Corneille, O. (2018). Interoceptive accuracy scores
    from the heartbeat counting task are problematic: Evidence from simple bivariate correlations.
    Biological Psychology, 137, 12–17. https://doi.org/10.1016/j.biopsycho.2018.06.006

3. Clinical Application of Mindfulness-Oriented Meditation in Children and Adolescents With Attention-Deficit/Hyperactivity Disorder

American Psychiatric Association. (2013). *Diagnostic and statistical manual of mental disorders* (5th ed.).
    American Psychiatric Association.

Cairncross, M., & Miller, C. J. (2020). The effectiveness of mindfulness-based therapies for ADHD:
    A meta-analytic review. *Journal of Attention Disorders, 24*(5), 627–643.

Crescentini, C., Capurso, V., Furlan, S., & Fabbro, F. (2016). Mindfulness-oriented meditation for
    primary school children: Effects on attention and psychological well-being. *Frontiers in Psychol-
    ogy, 7*(805).

Crescentini, C., & Menghini, D. (2019). *La mindfulness per l'ADHD e i disturbi del neurosviluppo* [Mindful-
    ness for ADHD and neurodevelopmental disorders].Erickson.

Dekkers, T. J., Flisar, A., Karami Motaghi, A., Karl, A., Frick, M. A., & Boyer, B. E. (2023, June 29).
    Does mind-wandering explain ADHD-related impairment in adolescents? *Child Psychiatry and
    Human Development.* 10.

Evans, S., Ling, M., Hil, B., Rinehart, N., Austin, D., & Sciberras, E. (2018). Systematic review of medita-
    tion-based interventions for children with ADHD. *European Child and Adolescent Psychiatry, 27*(1), 9–27.

Fabbro, F. (2019). *La meditazione mindfulness: Neuroscienze, filosofia e spiritualità* [Mindfulness meditation:
    Neuroscience, philosophy and spirituality]. Il Mulino.

Fabbro, F., & Crescentini, C. (2016). La meditazione orientata alla mindfulness (MOM) nella ricerca
    psicologica [Mindfulness-oriented meditation (MOM) in psychological research]. *Ricerche di
    psicologia, 4*, 457–460.

Fabbro, F., & Crescentini, C. (2017). Metodo ed efficacia della meditazione orientata alla mindful-
    ness [Method and effectiveness of mindfulness-oriented meditation]. *Giornale Italiano di Psicologia
    44*, 2, 293–296.

Fabbro, F., Crescentini, C., & Matiz, A. (2023). Parte pratica: La Meditazione Orientata alla Mind-
    fulness (MOM) [Practical part: Mindfulness-oriented meditation (MOM)]. In A. Chiesa & C.
    Crescentini (Eds.), *Gli interventi basati sulla mindfulness: Quali sono, come agiscono, quando utilizzarli*
    [Mindfulness-based interventions: What they are, how they work, when to use them], (pp.
    457–470). Giovanni Fioriti Editore.

Fabbro, F., & Muratori, F. (2012). La Mindfulness: Un nuovo approccio psicoterapeutico in età
    evolutiva [Mindfulness: A new psychotherapeutic approach in the developmental age]. *Neuro-
    psichiatria dell'età evolutiva*, 1–12.

Feruglio, S., Matiz, A., Pagnoni, G., Fabbro, F., & Crescentini, C. (2021). The impact of mindfulness
    meditation on the wandering mind: A systematic review. *Neuroscience and Biobehavioral Reviews,
    131*, 313–330.

Frick, M. A., Asherson, P., & Brocki, K. C. (2020). Mind-wandering in children with and without
    ADHD. *British Journal of Clinical Psychology, 59*(2), 208–223.

Gunaratana, H. (1995). *La pratica della consapevolezza in parole semplici* [Mindfulness in plain English].
    Ubaldini.

Hölzel, B. K., Lazar, S. W., Gard, T., Schuman-Olivier, Z., Vago, D. R., & Otto, U. (2011). How does mindfulness meditation work? Proposing mechanisms of action from a conceptual and neural perspective. *Perspectives on Psychological Science, 6*(6), 537–559.

Iacona, J., & Johnson, S. (2018). Neurobiology of trauma and mindfulness for children. *Journal of Trauma Nursing, 25*(3), 187–191.

Kabat-Zinn, J. (2003). Mindfulness-based interventions in context: Past, present, and future. *Clinical Psychology: Science and Practice, 10*(2), 144–156.

Kabat-Zinn, J. (2019). *Vivere momento per momento: Sconfiggere lo stress, il dolore, l'ansia e la malattia con la mindfulness* [Full catastrophe living]. TEA.

Lanier, J., Noyes, E., & Biederman, J. (2021). Mind wandering (internal distractibility) in ADHD: A literature review. *Journal of Attention Disorders, 25*(6), 885–890.

Lee, Y. C., Chen, C. R., & Lin, K. C. (2022). Effects of mindfulness-based interventions in children and adolescents with ADHD: A systematic review and meta-analysis of randomized controlled trials. *International Journal of Environmental Research and Public Health, 19*(22), 15198.

Lugo-Candelas, C., Corbeil, T., Wall, M., Posner, J., Bird, H., Canino, G., Fisher, P. W., Suglia, S. F., & Duarte, C. S. (2021). ADHD and risk for subsequent adverse childhood experiences: Understanding the cycle of adversity. *Journal of Child Psychology and Psychiatry, and Allied Disciplines, 62*(8), 971–978.

Malinowski, P. (2013). Neural mechanisms of attentional control in mindfulness meditation. *Frontiers in Neuroscience, 7*(8).

Mancuso, V. (2020). *I quattro maestri* [The four masters]. Garzanti. (Ed.). *Mediterranean Journal of Clinical Psychology, 9.*

Matiz, A., Cimenti, M., & Crescentini, C. (2023). Promoting primary school children's mental health through a 24-session mindfulness-based program: Qualitative analysis of children subjective experience and their association with personality traits. *Mediterranean Journal of Clinical Psychology, 11*(2), 361.

Matiz, A., Fabbro, F., Paschetto, A., Cantone, D., Paolone, A. R., & Crescentini, C. (2020). Positive impact of mindfulness meditation on mental health of female teachers during the COVID-19 outbreak in Italy. *International Journal of Environmental Research and Public Health, 17*(18), 6450.

Matiz, A., & Paschetto, A. (2022). *Sid e le otto sfere di luce: Come insegnare la meditazione mindfulness ai bambini* [Sid and the eight balls of light: How to teach mindfulness meditation to children] Mimesis.

Modesto-Lowe, V., Farahmand, P., Chaplin, M., & Sarro, L. (2015). Does mindfulness meditation improve attention in attention deficit hyperactivity disorder? *World Journal of psychiatry, 5*(4), 397–403.

Nigg, J. T. (2013). Attention-deficit/hyperactivity disorder and adverse health outcomes. *Clinical Psychology Review, 33*(2), 215–228.

Ortiz, R., & Sibinga, E. M. (2017). The role of mindfulness in reducing the adverse effects of childhood stress and trauma. *Children, 4*(3), 16.

Posner, M. I., & Petersen, S. E. (1990). The attention system of the human brain. *Annual Review of Neuroscience, 13,* 25–42.

Santonastaso, O., Zaccari, V., Crescentini, C., Fabbro, F., Capurso, V., Vicari, S., & Menghini, D. (2020). Clinical application of mindfulness-oriented meditation: A preliminary study in children with ADHD. *International Journal of Environmental Research and Public Health, 17*(18), 6916.

Singh, A., Yeh, C. J., Verma, N., & Das, A. K. (2015). Overview of attention deficit hyperactivity disorder in young children. *Health Psychology Research, 3*(2), 2115.

Smalley, S. L., Loo, S. K., Hale, T. S., Shrestha, A., McGough, J., Flook, L., & Reise, S. (2009). Mindfulness and attention deficit hyperactivity disorder. *Journal of Clinical Psychology, 65*(10), 1087–1098.

Tang, Y. Y., Hölzel, B. K., & Posner, M. I. (2015). The neuroscience of mindfulness meditation. *Nature Reviews Neuroscience, 16*(4), 213–225.

Zaccari, V., Santonastaso, O., Mandolesi, L., De Crescenzo, F., Foti, F., Crescentini, C., Fabbro, F., Vicari, S., Curcio, G., & Menghini, D. (2022). Clinical application of mindfulness-oriented meditation in children with ADHD: A preliminary study on sleep and behavioral problems. *Psychology and Health, 37*(5), 563–579.

4. Bodily Self and Intersubjectivity Development After Childhood Trauma

Ardizzi, M., Evangelista, V., Ferroni, F., Umiltà, M. A., Ravera, R., & Gallese, V. (2017). Evidence for anger saliency during the recognition of chimeric facial expressions of emotions in underage Ebola survivors. *Frontiers in Psychology, 8*, 1026.

Ardizzi, M., Ferroni F., Ravera V., Ravera R., Caroti V., & Gallese V. (2024). Early traumatic experiences alter both spatial and temporal principles of multisensory integration. [Manuscript in preparation.]

Ardizzi, M., Martini, F., Umiltà, M. A., Evangelista, V., Ravera, R., & Gallese, V. (2015). Impact of childhood maltreatment on the recognition of facial expressions of emotions. *PLoS One, 10*(10), e0141732.

Ardizzi, M., Martini, F., Umiltà, M. A., Sestito, M., Ravera, R., & Gallese, V. (2013). When early experiences build a wall to others' emotions: An electrophysiological and autonomic study. *PLoS One, 8*(4), e61004.

Ardizzi, M., Umiltà, M. A., Evangelista, V., Di Liscia, A., Ravera, R., & Gallese, V. (2016). Less empathic and more reactive: The different impact of childhood maltreatment on facial mimicry and vagal regulation. *PLoS One, 11*(9), e0163853.

Bassolino, M., Finisguerra, A., Canzoneri, E., Serino, A., & Pozzo, T. (2015). Dissociating effect of upper limb non-use and overuse on space and body representations. *Neuropsychologia, 70*, 385–392.

Blanke, O. (2012). Multisensory brain mechanisms of bodily self-consciousness. *Nature Reviews Neuroscience, 13*(8), 556–571.

Botvinick, M., & Cohen, J. (1998). Rubber hands "feel" touch that eyes see. *Nature, 391*(6669), 756.

Castiello, U., Becchio, C., Zoia, S., Nelini, C., Sartori, L., Blason, L., D'Ottavio, G., Bulgheroni, M., & Gallese, V. (2010). Wired to be social: The ontogeny of human interaction. *PLoS One, 5*(10), e13199.

de Klerk, C. C., Filippetti, M. L., & Rigato, S. (2021). The development of body representations: An associative learning account. *Proceedings of the Royal Society B, 288*(1949), 20210070.

Ferroni, F., Ardizzi, M., Ferri, F., Tesanovic, A., Langiulli, N., Tonna, M., ... & Gallese, V. (2020). Schizotypy and individual differences in peripersonal space plasticity. *Neuropsychologia, 147*, 107579.

Ferroni, F., & Gallese, V. (2022). Social bodily self: Conceptual and psychopathological considerations. In A. J. T. Alsmith & M. R. Longo (Eds.), *The Routledge handbook of bodily awareness* (pp. 522–541). Routledge.

Gallese, V. (2000). The inner sense of action: Agency and motor representations. *Journal of Consciousness Studies, 7*, 23–40.

Gallese, V. (2017). Neoteny and social cognition: A neuroscientific perspective on embodiment. In C. Durt, T. Fuchs, & C. Tewes (Eds.), *Embodiment, enaction and culture: Investigating the constitution of the shared world* (pp. 309–332). MIT Press.

Gallese, V. (2024). From pre-natal relations to self-constitution: A neuro-behavioral perspective on primary narcissism [Manuscript in preparation].

Gallese, V., & Sinigaglia, C. (2010). The bodily self as power for action. *Neuropsychologia, 48*, 746–755.

Gallese, V., & Sinigaglia, C. (2011). How the body in action shapes the self. *Journal of Consciousness Studies, 18*, 117–143.

Harricharan, S., McKinnon, M. C., & Lanius, R. A. (2021). How processing of sensory information from the internal and external worlds shape the perception and engagement with the world in the aftermath of trauma: Implications for PTSD. *Frontiers in Neuroscience, 15*, 625490.

Hillock-Dunn, A., & Wallace, M. T. (2012). Developmental changes in the multisensory temporal binding window persist into adolescence. *Developmental Science, 15*(5), 688–696.

Holochwost, S. J., Wang, G., Kolacz, J., Mills-Koonce, W. R., Klika, J. B., & Jaffee, S. R. (2021). The neurophysiological embedding of child maltreatment. *Development and Psychopathology, 33*(3), 1107–1137.

Koss, K. J. (2019). Understanding the neurobiological implications of maltreatment: A commentary on the special issue. *Child Maltreatment, 24*(4), 452–457.

Lambert, H. K., Meza, R., Martin, P., Fearey, E., & McLaughlin, K. A. (2017). Childhood trauma as a public health issue. In M. A. Landolt, M. Cloitre, & U. Schnyder (Eds.), *Evidence-based treatments for trauma related disorders in children and adolescents* (pp. 49–66). Springer.

Lewkowicz, D. J. (2014). Early experience and multisensory perceptual narrowing. *Developmental Psychobiology, 56*(2), 292–315.

Lewkowicz, D. J., & Ghazanfar, A. A. (2009). The emergence of multisensory systems through perceptual narrowing. *Trends in Cognitive Sciences, 13*(11), 470–478.

Maravita, A., Husain, M., Clarke, K., & Driver, J. (2001). Reaching with a tool extends visual-tactile interactions into far space: Evidence from cross-modal extinction. *Neuropsychologia, 39*(6), 580–585.

Maschi, T., Baer, J., Morrissey, M. B., & Moreno, C. (2013). The aftermath of childhood trauma on late life mental and physical health: A review of the literature. *Traumatology, 19*(1), 49–64.

Masten, C. L., Guyer, A. E., Hodgdon, H. B., McClure, E. B., Charney, D. S., Ernst, M., … & Monk, C. S. (2008). Recognition of facial emotions among maltreated children with high rates of post-traumatic stress disorder. *Child Abuse and Neglect, 32*(1), 139–153.

McGurk, H., & MacDonald, J. (1976). Hearing lips and seeing voices. *Nature, 264*(5588), 746–748.

Nelson, C. A., & Gabard-Durnam, L. J. (2020). Early adversity and critical periods: Neurodevelopmental consequences of violating the expectable environment. *Trends in Neurosciences, 43*(3), 133–143.

Nemeroff, C. B. (2004). Neurobiological consequences of childhood trauma. *Journal of Clinical Psychiatry, 65*, 18–28.

Porges, S. W. (2023). The vagal paradox: A polyvagal solution. *Comprehensive Psychoneuroendocrinology, 16*, 100200.

Powers, A. R., Hillock, A. R., & Wallace, M. T. (2009). Perceptual training narrows the temporal window of multisensory binding. *Journal of Neuroscience, 29*(39), 12265–12274.

Rabellino, D., Burin, D., Harricharan, S., Lloyd, C., Frewen, P. A., McKinnon, M. C., & Lanius, R. A. (2018). Altered sense of body ownership and agency in posttraumatic stress disorder and its dissociative subtype: A rubber hand illusion study. *Frontiers in Human Neuroscience, 12*, 163.

Ronga, I., Galigani, M., Bruno, V., Noel, J. P., Gazzin, A., Perathoner, C., … & Garbarini, F. (2021). Spatial tuning of electrophysiological responses to multisensory stimuli reveals a primitive coding of the body boundaries in newborns. *Proceedings of the National Academy of Sciences, 118*(12), e2024548118.

Scrimin, S., Moscardino, U., Capello, F., Altoè, G., & Axia, G. (2009). Recognition of facial expressions of mixed emotions in school-age children exposed to terrorism. *Developmental Psychology, 45*(5), 1341.

Serino, A., Alsmith, A., Costantini, M., Mandrigin, A., Tajadura-Jimenez, A., & Lopez, C. (2013). Bodily ownership and self-location: Components of bodily self-consciousness. *Consciousness and Cognition, 22*(4), 1239–1252.

Stein, B. E., Stanford, T. R., & Rowland, B. A. (2020). Multisensory integration and the society for neuroscience: Then and now. *Journal of Neuroscience, 40*(1), 3–11.

Stevenson, R. A., Wilson, M. M., Powers, A. R., & Wallace, M. T. (2013). The effects of visual training on multisensory temporal processing. *Experimental Brain Research, 225*, 479–489.

Tsakiris, M. (2017). The multisensory basis of the self: From body to identity to others. *Quarterly Journal of Experimental Psychology, 70*(4), 597–609.

Wallace, M. T., & Stevenson, R. A. (2014). The construct of the multisensory temporal binding window and its dysregulation in developmental disabilities. *Neuropsychologia, 64*, 105–123.

5. Love as Embodied Medicine

Arrowsmith, S., & Wray, S. (2014). Oxytocin: Its mechanism of action and receptor signalling in the myometrium. *Journal of Neuroendocrinology, 26*(6), 356–369. https://doi.org/10.1111/jne.12154

Buckley, S., Uvnäs-Moberg, K., Pajalic, Z., Luegmair, K., Ekström-Bergström, A., Dencker, A., Massarotti, C., Kotlowska, A., Callaway, L., Morano, S., Olza, I., & Magistretti, C. M. (2023). Maternal and newborn plasma oxytocin levels in response to maternal synthetic oxytocin administration during labour, birth and postpartum—a systematic review with implications for the function of the oxytocinergic system. *BMC Pregnancy and Childbirth, 23*(1), 137. https://doi.org/10.1186/s12884-022-05221-w

Carter, C. S. (2014). Oxytocin pathways and the evolution of human behavior. *Annual Review of Psychology, 65*, 17–39. https://doi.org/10.1146/annurev-psych-010213-115110

Carter, C. S. (2017). The oxytocin-vasopressin pathway in the context of love and fear. *Frontiers in Endocrinology, 8*, 356. https://doi.org/10.3389/fendo.2017.00356

Carter, C. S. (2022). Sex, love and oxytocin: Two metaphors and a molecule. *Neuroscience and Biobehavioral Reviews, 143*, 104948. https://doi.org/10.1016/j.neubiorev.2022.104948

Carter, C. S. (2023). Close encounters with oxytocin. *Comprehensive Psychoneuroendocrinology, 15*, 100189. https://doi.org/10.1016/j.cpnec.2023.100189

Carter, C. S., DeVries, A. C., & Getz, L. L. (1995). Physiological substrates of mammalian monogamy: The prairie vole model. *Neuroscience and Biobehavioral Reviews, 19*(2), 303–314.

Carter, C. S., Kenkel, W. M., MacLean, E. L., Wilson, S. R., Perkeybile, A. M., Yee, J. R., Ferris, C. F., Nazarloo, H. P., Porges, S. W., Davis, J. M., Connelly, J. J., & Kingsbury, M. A. (2020). Is oxytocin "nature's medicine"? *Pharmacological Reviews, 72*(4), 829–861. https://doi.org/10.1124/pr.120.019398

Carter, C. S., & Kingsbury, M. A. (2022). Oxytocin and oxygen: The evolution of a solution to the "stress of life." *Philosophical Transactions of the Royal Society of London. Series B, Biological Sciences, 377*(1858), 20210054. https://doi.org/10.1098/rstb.2021.0054

Carter, C. S., & Perkeybile, A. M. (2018). The monogamy paradox: What do love and sex have to do with it? *Frontiers in Ecology and Evolution, 6*(202). https://doi.org/10.3389/fevo.2018.00202

Carter, C. S., & Porges, E. C. (2011). Parenthood, stress, and the brain. *Biological Psychiatry, 70*(9), 804–805. https://doi.org/10.1016/j.biopsych.2011.09.003

Carter, C. S., & Porges, S. W. (2013). The biochemistry of love: An oxytocin hypothesis. *EMBO Reports, 14*(1), 12–16. https://doi.org/10.1038/embor.2012.191

Cuneo, M. G., Szeto, A., Schrepf, A., Thaker, P. H., Goodheart, M., Cole, S. W., Sood, A. K., McCabe, P. M., Mendez, A. J., & Lutgendorf, S. K. (2021). Positive psychosocial factors and oxytocin in the ovarian tumor microenvironment. *Psychosomatic Medicine, 83*(5), 417–422. https://doi.org/10.1097/PSY.0000000000000935

De Dreu, C. K. W., Fariña, A., Gross, J., & Romano, A. (2021). Prosociality as a foundation for intergroup conflict. *Current Opinion in Psychology, 44*, 112–116. https://doi.org/10.1016/j.copsyc.2021.09.002

de Jong, T. R., Menon, R., Bludau, A., Grund, T., Biermeier, V., Klampfl, S. M., Jurek, B., Bosch, O. J., Hellhammer, J., & Neumann, I. D. (2015). Salivary oxytocin concentrations in response to running, sexual self-stimulation, breastfeeding and the TSST: The Regensburg Oxytocin Challenge (ROC) study. *Psychoneuroendocrinology, 62*, 381–388. https://doi.org/10.1016/j.psyneuen.2015.08.027

Geenen, V., Benhida, A., Kecha, O., Achour, I., Vandermissen, E., Vanneste, Y., Goxe, B., & Martens, H. (1996). Development and evolutionary aspects of thymic T cell education to neuroendocrine self. *Acta Haematologica, 95*(3–4), 263–267.

Gobrogge, K., & Wang, Z. (2016). The ties that bond: Neurochemistry of attachment in voles. *Current Opinion in Neurobiology, 38*, 80–88. https://doi.org/10.1016/j.conb.2016.04.011

Gouin, J.-P., Carter, C. S., Pournajafi-Nazarloo, H., Glaser, R., Malarkey, W. B., Loving, T. J., Stowell, J., & Kiecolt-Glaser, J. K. (2010). Marital behavior, oxytocin, vasopressin, and wound healing. *Psychoneuroendocrinology, 35*(7), 1082–1090. https://doi.org/10.1016/j.psyneuen.2010.01.009

Grinevich, V., & Ludwig, M. (2021). The multiple faces of the oxytocin and vasopressin systems in the brain. *Journal of Neuroendocrinology, 33*(11), e13004. https://doi.org/10.1111/jne.13004

Grippo, A. J., Lamb, D. G., Carter, C. S., & Porges, S. W. (2007). Cardiac regulation in the socially monogamous prairie vole. *Physiology and Behavior, 90*(2–3), 386–393.

Gutkowska, J., & Jankowski, M. (2012). Oxytocin revisited: Its role in cardiovascular regulation. *Journal of Neuroendocrinology, 24*(4), 599–608. https://doi.org/10.1111/j.1365-2826.2011.02235.x

Horn, A. J., & Carter, C. S. (2021). Love and longevity: A social dependency hypothesis. *Comprehensive Psychoneuroendocrinology, 8*, 100088. https://doi.org/10.1016/j.cpnec.2021.100088

Kenkel, W. M., & Carter, C. S. (2016). Voluntary exercise facilitates pair-bonding in male prairie voles. *Behavioural Brain Research, 296*, 326–330. https://doi.org/10.1016/j.bbr.2015.09.028

Lerman, B., Harricharran, T., & Ogunwobi, O. O. (2018). Oxytocin and cancer: An emerging link. *World Journal of Clinical Oncology, 9*(5), 74–82. https://doi.org/10.5306/wjco.v9.i5.74

MacLean, E. L., Wilson, S. R., Martin, W. L., Davis, J. M., Nazarloo, H. P., & Carter, C. S. (2019). Challenges for measuring oxytocin: The blind men and the elephant? *Psychoneuroendocrinology, 107*, 225–231. https://doi.org/10.1016/j.psyneuen.2019.05.018

Perkeybile, A. M., & Bales, K. L. (2017). Intergenerational transmission of sociality: The role of parents in shaping social behavior in monogamous and non-monogamous species. *Journal of Experimental Biology, 220*(Pt. 1), 114–123. https://doi.org/10.1242/jeb.142182

Perkeybile, A. M., Carter, C. S., Wroblewski, K. L., Puglia, M. H., Kenkel, W. M., Lillard, T. S., Karaoli, T., Gregory, S. G., Mohammadi, N., Epstein, L., Bales, K. L., & Connelly, J. J. (2019).

Early nurture epigenetically tunes the oxytocin receptor. *Psychoneuroendocrinology*, *99*, 128–136. https://doi.org/10.1016/j.psyneuen.2018.08.037

Porges, S. W. (2021a). Cardiac vagal tone: A neurophysiological mechanism that evolved in mammals to dampen threat reactions and promote sociality. *World Psychiatry*, *20*(2), 296–298. https://doi.org/10.1002/wps.20871

Porges, S. W. (2021b). Polyvagal Theory: A biobehavioral journey to sociality. *Comprehensive Psychoneuroendocrinology*, *7*, 100069. https://doi.org/10.1016/j.cpnec.2021.100069

Theofanopoulou, C. (2021). Reconstructing the evolutionary history of the oxytocin and vasotocin receptor gene family: Insights on whole genome duplication scenarios. *Developmental Biology*, *479*, 99–106. https://doi.org/10.1016/j.ydbio.2021.07.012

Winslow, J. T., Hastings, N., Carter, C. S., Harbaugh, C. R., & Insel, T. R. (1993). A role for central vasopressin in pair bonding in monogamous prairie voles. *Nature*, *365*(6446), 545–548.

6. Somatic Intelligence

American Psychiatric Association. (2013). *Diagnostic and statistical manual of mental disorders* (5th ed.). American Psychiatric Association.

Anderson, R. (2002, Autumn/Winter). Embodied writing: Presencing the body in somatic research, Part I. *Somatics*, 40–44.

Arvidson, S. (2008). Attentional capture and attentional character. *Phenomenological Cognitive Science*, *7*, 539–562.

Banakou, D., Beacco, A., Neyret, S., Blasco-Oliver, M., Seinfeld, S., & Slater, M. (2020). Virtual body ownership and its consequences for implicit racial bias are dependent on social context. *Royal Society Open Science*, *7*(12), 201848. https://pubmed.ncbi.nlm.nih.gov/33489296/

Bechara, A., Damasio, A. R., Damasio, H., & Anderson, S. W. (2004). Insensitivity to future consequences following damage to human prefrontal cortex. *Cognition*, *50*(1–3), 7–15.

Berrol, C. (2016). Reflections on dance/movement therapy and interpersonal neurobiology: The first 50 years. *American Journal of Dance Therapy*, *38*, 303–310.

Buber, M. (1970). *I and thou*. Charles Scribner's Sons. (Original work published 1937)

Caldwell, C., & Johnson, R. (2012). Cultivating a somatically-informed research mind. In C. Young (Ed.) *About the science of body psychotherapy* (pp. 27–35). Body Psychotherapy Publications.

Caldwell, C., & Leighton, L. B. (2018). *Oppression and the body*. North Atlantic.

Cameron, O. G. (2002). *Visceral sensory neuroscience*. Oxford.

Cariola, L. (2015). Semantic expressions of the body boundary personality in person-centered psychotherapy. *International Body Psychotherapy Journal*, *14*(1), 48–64.

Chaiklin, S. (1975). Dance therapy. In S. Arieti (Ed.), *American handbook of psychiatry*. Basic Books. https://www.freepsychotherapybooks.org/ebook/dance-therapy/

Cruz, R., & Berroll, C. (2016). *Dance/movement therapists in action: A working guide to research options* (3rd ed.). Charles C. Thomas.

Csordas, T. J. (2008). Intersubjectivity and intercorporeality. *Subjectivity*, *22*(1), 110–121.

Ellingson, L. (2006). Embodied knowledge: Writing researchers' bodies into qualitative health research. *Qualitative Health Research*, *16*(2), 298–310. https://doi.org/10.1177/1049732305281944

Ellingson, L. (2012). Interview as embodied communication. In J. F. Gubrium, J. A. Holstein, A. B. Marvasti, & K. D. McKinney (Eds.), *The Sage handbook of interview research: The complexity of the craft* (2nd ed., pp. 525–540). Sage.

Ellingson, L. (2017). *Embodiment in qualitative research*. Routledge.

Finlay, L. (2011). *Phenomenology for therapists: Researching the lived world.* Wiley-Blackwell.

Fogel, A. (2021). *Restorative embodiment and resilience: A guide to disrupt habits, create inner peace, deepen relationships, and feel greater presence.* North Atlantic.

Fuchs, T. (2016). Interocorporeality and interaffectivity. In C. Meyer, J. Streeck, & S. Jordan (Eds.), *Intercorporeality: Emerging socialities in interaction.* Oxford.

Gallagher, S. (2008). *How the body shapes the mind.* Oxford.

Gallese, V. (2009). Mirror neurons, embodied simulation, and the neural basis of social identification. *Psychoanalytic Dialogues, 19*(5), 519–536.

Gardner, H. (2011). *Frames of mind: The theory of multiple intelligences.* Basic Books.

Gavin, K., & Todres, L. (2009). Embodying nursing openheartedness: An existential perspective. *Holistic Nursing, 27*(20), 141–149.

Gendlin, E. T. (1982). *Focusing.* Bantam.

Gendlin, E. T. (1996). *Focusing-oriented psychotherapy.* Guilford.

Goleman, D. (2006). *Emotional intelligence.* Bantam.

Gornicka, B. (2016). *Nakedness, shame, and embarrassment: A long-term sociological perspective.* Springer.

Hanna, T. (1970). *Bodies in revolt: A primer in somatic thinking.* Holt, Reinhart and Winston.

Harrison, P. (2000). Making sense: Embodiment and the sensibilities of the everyday. *Environment and Planning: Society and Space, 18*(5), 497–517.

Hartelius, G. (2007). Quantitative somatic phenomenology: Toward an epistemology of subjective experience. *Journal of Consciousness Studies, 14*(12), 24–56.

Hartelius, G. (2020). Somatic phenomenology: Maps of bodily experience. In J. F. Tantia (Ed.), *The art and practice of embodied research design* (pp. 87–99). Routledge.

Herman, J. (1992). *Trauma and recovery.* Basic Books.

Hervey, L. W. (2000). *Artistic inquiry in dance/movement therapy: Creative research alternatives.* Charles C. Thomas.

Ignatow, G. (2007). Theories of embodied knowledge: New directions for cultural and cognitive sociology. *Journal for the Theory of Social Behavior, 37*(2), 115–135.

Johnson, D., & Grand, I. (1998). *The body in psychotherapy: Inquiries in somatic psychology.* North Atlantic.

Johnson, R. (2005). *Some components of a somatic approach* [Unpublished manuscript]. Dept. of Somatic Psychology, California Institute of Integral Studies.

Johnson, R. (2018). Queering/querying the body: Sensation and curiosity in disrupting body norms. In C. Caldwell & L. B. Leighton (Eds.), *Oppression and the body* (pp. 97–112). North Atlantic.

Johnson, R. (2023). *Embodied activism: Engaging the body to cultivate liberation, justice, and authentic connection—A practical guide for transformative social change.* [Audiobook]. North Atlantic.

Khoury, B. (2019). Compassion: Embodied and embedded. *Mindfulness, 10,* 2363–2374. https://doi.org/10.1007/s12671-019-01211-w

Kiefer, M., & Trumpp, N. M. (2014). Embodiment theory and education: The foundations of cognition in perception and action. *Trends in Neuroscience and Education, 1*(1), 15–20.

Koch, S., & Fuchs, T. (2011). Embodied arts therapies. *Arts in Psychotherapy, 38,* 276–280.

Køster, A. (2017). Narrative self-appropriation: Embodiment, alienness, and personal responsibility in the context of borderline personality disorder. *Theoretical Medicine and Bioethics, 38,* 465–482. https://doi.org/10.1007/s11017-017-9422-z

Kurtz, R. (1990). *Body-centered psychotherapy.* LifeRhythm.

Lakoff, G., & Johnson, M. (1999). *Philosophy in the flesh: The embodied mind and its challenges in Western thought.* Basic Books.

Leavy, P. (2009). *Method meets art: Arts-based research practice.* Guilford.

Leavy, P. (2017). *Research design: Quantitative, qualitative, mixed-methods, arts-based, and community-based participatory research approaches.* Guilford.

Levine, P. (1997). *Waking the tiger: Healing trauma.* North Atlantic.

Louvel, S., & Soulier, A. (2022). Biological embedding vs. embodiment of social experiences: How these two concepts form distinct thought styles around the social production of health inequalities. *Social Science and Medicine, 314,* 115470. https://doi.org/10.1016/j.socscimed.2022.115470

Lowen, A. (1958). *Language of the body: Physical dynamics of character structure.* Alexander Lowen Foundation.

MacLachlan, M. (2004). *Embodiment: Clinical, critical and cultural perspectives on health and illness.* Open University Press.

Mason, D. M. (2014). Holism and embodiment in nursing: Using Goethean science to join 2 perspectives on patient care. *Holistic Nursing Practices, 28*(1), 55–64.

Meier, B., Schnall, S., Schwarz, N., & Bargh, J. A. (2012). Embodiment in social psychology. *Frontiers in Cognitive Science, 4*(4), 705-716. https://doi.org/10.1111/j.1756-8765.2012.01212.x

Mensch, J. R. (2001). *Postfoundational phenomenology: Husserlian reflections on presence and embodiment.* University Park, PA: The Pennsylvania State University Press.

Mercarder-Rubio, I., Angel, N., Sila, S., & Moisao, A. (2023). Relationships between somatic anxiety, cognitive anxiety, self-efficacy, and emotional intelligence levels in university physical education students. *Frontiers in Psychology, 13.* https://www.frontiersin.org/articles/10.3389/fpsyg.2022.1059432/full

Morrison, A. L. (2009). Embodying sentience. In L. Buzzell & C. Chalquist (Eds.), *Ecotherapy: Healing with nature in mind* (pp. 104–110). Counterpoint.

Murthy, V. (2023). *Our epidemic of loneliness and isolation: The U.S. Surgeon General's advisory on the healing effects of social connection and community.* https://www.hhs.gov/sites/default/files/surgeon-general-social-connection-advisory.pdf

National Institutes of Health. (n.d.). Mental health during the COVID-19 pandemic. Retrieved March 29, 2024, from https://covid19.nih.gov/covid-19-topics/mental-health

Ogden, P., Minton, K., & Pain, C. (2006). *Trauma and the body: A sensorimotor approach to psychotherapy.* Norton.

Pallaro, P. (2007). Somatic countertransference: The therapist in relationship. in P. Pallaro (Ed.) Authentic Movement: Moving the body, moving the self, being moved, Vol. 2. London: Jessica Kingsley.

Perry, M., & Medina, C. L. (2015). *Methodologies of embodiment: Inscribing bodies in qualitative research.* Routledge.

Porges, S. (1995). Orienting in a defensive world: Mammalian modifications of our evolutionary heritage. A Polyvagal Theory. *Psychophysiology, 32*(4), 301–318. https://pubmed.ncbi.nlm.nih.gov/7652107/

Porges, S. W. (2004). Neuroception: A subconscious system for detecting threats and safety. *Zero to Three, 24*(5), 19–24.

Porges, S. W. (2023). The vagal paradox: A polyvagal solution. *Comprehensive Psychoneuroendocrinology, 16,* 100200. https://doi.org/10.1016/j.cpnec.2023.100200

Reich, W. (1945). *Character analysis.* Farrar, Straus and Giroux.

Rennie, D. L., & Fergus, K. D. (2006). Embodied categorizing in the grounded theory method: Methodical hermeneutics in action. *Theory & Psychology, 16*(4), 483–503.

Rogers, C., Gendlin, E., Keisler, E. T., & Truax, C. B. (Eds.). (1967). *The therapeutic relationship and its impact: A study of psychotherapy with schizophrenics.* University of Wisconsin Press.

Rothschild, B. (2000). *The body remembers: The psychophysiology of trauma and trauma treatment*. Norton.

Rufo, R. (2023). Humans, trees, and the intimacy of movement: An encounter with Ecosomatic practice. *European Journal of Ecopsychology, 8*, 88–113.

Scaer, R. (2005). *The trauma spectrum*. Norton.

Schmidsberger, F., & Löffler-Stastka, H. (2018). Empathy is proprioceptive: The bodily fundament of empathy—a philosophical contribution to medical education. *BMC Medical Education, 18*, 69. https://doi.org/10.1186/s12909-018-1161-y

Schore, A. (2009). *Paradigm shift: The right brain and the relational unconscious* [Plenary address]. American Psychological Association Annual Convention, Toronto, Canada.

Schore, A.N. (2011). The right brain implicit self lies at the core of psychoanalysis. *Psychoanalytic Dialogues, 21*(1), 75–100. DOI: 10.1080/10481885.2011.545329

Sheets-Johnstone, M. (2010). Why is movement therapeutic? Keynote Address, 44th American Dance Therapy Association Conference, October 9, 2009. *American Journal of Dance Therapy 32*(1), 2–15. https://doi.org/10.1007/s10465-009-9082-2

Shusterman, R. (2008). *Body consciousness: A philosophy of mindfulness and somaesthetics*. Cambridge University Press.

Spatz, B. (2015). *What a body can do: Technique as knowledge, practice as research*. Routledge.

Stern, D. (2004). *The present moment in psychotherapy and everyday life*. Norton.

Tantia, J. F. (2020). Embodied data. In J. F. Tantia (Ed.), *The art and science of embodied research design: Concepts, methods and cases* (pp. 40–51). Routledge.

Terr, L. (1990). *Too scared to cry*. Basic Books.

Thanem, T., & Knights, D. (2019). *Embodied research methods*. Sage.

Todres, L. (2004). The meaning of understanding and the open body: Some implications for qualitative research. *Existential Analysis, 15*(1), 38–54.

Todres, L. (2007). *Embodied enquiry: Phenomenological touchstones for research, psychotherapy and spirituality* (2nd ed.). Palgrave Macmillan.

Tsakiris, M., Longo, M., & Haggard, P. (2010). Having a body versus moving your body: Neural signatures of agency and body-ownership. *Neuropsychologia, 48*, 2740–2749.

van der Kolk, B. A. (1994). The body keeps the score: Memory and the evolving psychobiology of posttraumatic stress. *Harvard Review of Psychiatry, 1*(5), 253–265. https://doi.org/10.3109/1067322940901708

van Manen, M. (2015). *Researching lived experience: Human science for an action sensitive pedagogy*. Routledge.

Varela, F., Thompson, E., & Rosch, E. (1991). *The embodied mind: Cognitive science and human experience*. MIT Press.

von Truer, M., & Reynolds, N. (2017). A competency model of psychology practice: Articulating complex skills and practices. *Frontiers in Education, 17*(2). https://doi.org/10.3389/feduc.2017.00054

West, W. (2011). Using the tacit dimension in qualitative research in counseling psychology. *Counseling Psychology Review, 26*(4), 41–46.

7. Post-Trauma Growth

American Psychological Association. (2006). Evidence-based practice in psychology. *American Psychologist, 61*(4), 271–285. https://doi.org/10.1037/0003-066x.61.4.271

American Psychological Association. (2019, March 13). Mental health issues increased significantly in young adults over last decade. https://www.apa.org/news/press/releases/2019/03/mental-health-adults

Barlow, D. H. (2010). Negative effects from psychological treatments: A perspective. *American Psychologist, 65*(1), 13–20. https://doi.org/10.1037/a0015643

Barrett, L. F. (2022). Context reconsidered: Complex signal ensembles, relational meaning, and population thinking in psychological science. *American Psychologist, 77*(8), 894–920. https://doi.org/10.1037/amp0001054

Bassett, D. S., & Gazzaniga, M. S. (2011). Understanding complexity in the human brain. *Trends in Cognitive Sciences, 15*(5), 200–209. https://doi.org/10.1016/j.tics.2011.03.006

Bateson, G. (1972). *Steps to an ecology of mind: Collected essays in anthropology, psychiatry, evolution, and epistemology.* Aronson.

Bavassi, L., Forcato, C., Fernández, R. S., De Pino, G., Pedreira, M. E., & Villarreal, M. F. (2019). Retrieval of retrained and reconsolidated memories are associated with a distinct neural network. *Scientific Reports, 9*(1), 784.

Bergin, A. E. (1966). Some implications of psychotherapy research for therapeutic practice. *Journal of Abnormal Psychology, 71*(4), 235–246. https://doi.org/10.1037/h0023577

Bolt, T., Nomi, J. S., Bzdok, D., Salas, J. A., Chang, C., Thomas Yeo, B. T., Uddin, L. Q., & Keilholz, S. D. (2022). A parsimonious description of global functional brain organization in three spatiotemporal patterns. *Nature Neuroscience, 25*(8), 1093–1103. https://doi.org/10.1038/s41593-022-01118-1

Bressler, S., & McIntosh, A. (2007). The role of neural context in large-scale neurocognitive network operations. In V. K. Jirsa & A. McIntosh (Eds.), *Handbook of brain connectivity* (pp. 403–419). Springer. https://doi.org/10.1007/978-3-540-71512-2_14

Britton, W. B. (2019). Can mindfulness be too much of a good thing? The value of a middle way. *Current Opinion in Psychology, 28*, 159–165. https://doi.org/10.1016/j.copsyc.2018.12.011

Bryan, C. J., Tipton, E., & Yeager, D. S. (2021). Behavioural science is unlikely to change the world without a heterogeneity revolution. *Nature Human Behaviour, 5*(8), 980–989. https://doi.org/10.1038/s41562-021-01143-3

Cantor, J. H., McBain, R. K., Ho, P.-C., Bravata, D. M., & Whaley, C. (2023). Telehealth and in-person mental health service utilization and spending, 2019 to 2022. *JAMA Health Forum, 4*(8), e232645. https://doi.org/10.1001/jamahealthforum.2023.2645

Capra, F., & Luisi, P. L. (2014). *The systems view of life: A unifying vision.* Cambridge University Press.

Dalai Lama [Tenzin, G.]. (1990). *The Dalai Lama, a policy of kindness: An anthology of writings by and about the Dalai Lama.* Snow Lion.

Danese, A., & McEwen, B. S. (2012). Adverse childhood experiences, allostasis, allostatic load, and age-related disease. *Physiology and Behavior, 106*(1), 29–39. https://doi.org/10.1016/j.physbeh.2011.08.019

Duffer, M., & Duffer, R. (Executive Producers). (2016). *Stranger things* [TV series]. Netflix.

Dugué, L., Merriam, E. P., Heeger, D. J., & Carrasco, M. (2018). Differential impact of endogenous and exogenous attention on activity in human visual cortex. In *bioRxiv*, 414508. https://doi.org/10.1101/414508

Dunlap, A. S., & Stephens, D. W. (2014). Experimental evolution of prepared learning. *Proceedings of the National Academy of Sciences, 111*(32), 11750–11755. https://doi.org/10.1073/pnas.1404176111

Elsey, J. W., Van Ast, V. A., & Kindt, M. (2018). Human memory reconsolidation: A guiding framework and critical review of the evidence. *Psychological Bulletin, 144*(8), 797.

Farber, B. A., Blanchard, M., & Love, M. (2019). The Columbia project on lying in psychotherapy: What did 1,345 psychotherapy clients tell us? In B. A. Farber, M. Blanchard, & M. Love,

Secrets and lies in psychotherapy (pp. 113–143). American Psychological Association. https://doi.org/10.1037/0000128-007

Farias, M., Maraldi, E., Wallenkampf, K. C., & Lucchetti, G. (2020). Adverse events in meditation practices and meditation-based therapies: A systematic review. *Acta Psychiatrica Scandinavica, 142*(5), 374–393. https://doi.org/10.1111/acps.13225

Favela, L. H. (2020). Cognitive science as complexity science. *Wiley Interdisciplinary Reviews: Cognitive Science, 11*(4), article e1525. https://doi.org/10.1002/wcs.1525

Healy, D., & Mangin, D. (2019). Clinical judgments, not algorithms, are key to patient safety—an essay by David Healy and Dee Mangin. *BMJ (Clinical Research Ed.), 367*, l5777. https://doi.org/10.1136/bmj.l5777

Hill, P. L., Olaru, G., & Allemand, M. (2023). Do associations between sense of purpose, social support, and loneliness differ across the adult lifespan? *Psychology and Aging, 38*(4), 345–355. https://doi.org/10.1037/pag0000733

Hirshberg, M. J., Goldberg, S. B., Rosenkranz, M., & Davidson, R. J. (2020). Prevalence of harm in mindfulness-based stress reduction. *Psychological Medicine, 52*(6), 1080–1088. https://doi.org/10.1017/s0033291720002834

Hoskinson, S., & Ho, B. (2022) A non-directive positive reinforcement framework for trauma and addiction treatment. *International Body Psychotherapy Journal, 21*(1), 53–65.

Katsumi, Y., Theriault, J. E., Quigley, K. S., & Barrett, L. F. (2022). Allostasis as a core feature of hierarchical gradients in the human brain. *Network Neuroscience, 6*(4), 1010–1031. https://doi.org/10.1162/netn_a_00240

Kelso, J. A. S. (2012). Multistability and metastability: Understanding dynamic coordination in the brain. *Philosophical Transactions of the Royal Society B: Biological Sciences, 367*(1591), 906–918. https://doi.org/10.1098/rstb.2011.0351

Klatte, R., Strauss, B., Flückiger, C., Färber, F., & Rosendahl, J. (2023). Defining and assessing adverse events and harmful effects in psychotherapy study protocols: A systematic review. *Psychotherapy, 60*(1), 130–148. https://doi.org/10.1037/pst0000359

Koob, G., & Le Moal, M. (2001). Drug addiction, dysregulation of reward, and allostasis. *Neuropsychopharmacology, 24*(2), 97–129. https://doi.org/10.1016/s0893-133x(00)00195-0

Korbmacher, M., Azevedo, F., Pennington, C. R., Hartmann, H., Pownall, M., Schmidt, K., Elsherif, M., Breznau, N., Robertson, O., Kalandadze, T., & Yu, S. (2023). The replication crisis has led to positive structural, procedural, and community changes. *Communications Psychology, 1*(1), 3.

Krubitzer, L. A., & Prescott, T. J. (2018). The combinatorial creature: Cortical phenotypes within and across lifetimes. *Trends in Neurosciences, 41*(10), 744–762. https://doi.org/10.1016/j.tins.2018.08.002

Lambert, M. J., & Harmon, K. L. (2018). The merits of implementing routine outcome monitoring in clinical practice. *Clinical Psychology: Science and Practice, 25*(4), e12268. https://doi.org/10.1111/cpsp.12268

Lee, S. W. (2019). A Copernican approach to brain advancement: The paradigm of allostatic orchestration. *Frontiers in Human Neuroscience, 13*. https://doi.org/10.3389/fnhum.2019.00129

Leite, L., Esper, N. B., Junior, J. R. M. L., Lara, D. R., & Buchweitz, A. (2022). An exploratory study of resting-state functional connectivity of amygdala subregions in posttraumatic stress disorder following trauma in adulthood. *Scientific Reports, 12*(1), 9558.

McEwen, B. S. (1998). Stress, adaptation, and disease: Allostasis and allostatic load. *Annals of the New York Academy of Sciences, 840*(1), 33–44. https://doi.org/10.1111/j.1749-6632.1998.tb09546.x

Moeller, J., & Schmidt, D. (2023, July 11). Inference in the data science era—do we need a new epistemological debate in the Social Sciences? *PsyArXiv Preprints*. https://doi.org/10.31234/osf.io/hj3rw

Nenning, K.-H., Xu, T., Franco, A. R., Swallow, K. M., Tambini, A., Margulies, D. S., Smallwood, J., Colcombe, S. J., & Milham, M. P. (2023). Omnipresence of the sensorimotor-association axis topography in the human connectome. *NeuroImage, 272*, 120059. https://doi.org/10.1016/j.neuroimage.2023.120059

Organic Intelligence. (2023). *OI Demo: Pleasanton*. https://organicintelligence.org/

Parry, G. D., Crawford, M. J., & Duggan, C. (2016). Iatrogenic harm from psychological therapies—time to move on. *British Journal of Psychiatry, 208*(3), 210–212. https://doi.org/10.1192/bjp.bp.115.163618

Porges, S. W. (2001). The polyvagal theory: Phylogenetic substrates of a social nervous system. *International Journal of Psychophysiology, 42*(2), 123–146. https://doi.org/10.1016/s0167-8760(01)00162-3

Porges, S. W. (2004). Neuroception: A subconscious system for detecting threats and safety. *Zero to Three, 24*(5), 19–24.

Porges, S. W. (2007). The polyvagal perspective. *Biological Psychology, 74*(2), 116–143. https://doi.org/10.1016/j.biopsycho.2006.06.009

Rogers, C. R. (1957). The necessary and sufficient conditions of therapeutic personality change. *Journal of Consulting Psychology, 21*(2), 95.

Sakaluk, J. K., Williams, A. J., Kilshaw, R. E., & Rhyner, K. T. (2019). Evaluating the evidential value of empirically supported psychological treatments (ESTs): A meta-scientific review. *Journal of Abnormal Psychology, 128*(6), 500–509. https://doi.org/10.1037/abn0000421

Schiller, D., Monfils, M. H., Raio, C. M., Johnson, D. C., LeDoux, J. E., & Phelps, E. A. (2010). Preventing the return of fear in humans using reconsolidation update mechanisms. *Nature, 463*(7277), 49–53.

Seligman, M. E. (1970). On the generality of the laws of learning. *Psychological Review, 77*(5), 406–418. https://doi.org/10.1037/h0029790

Seligman, M. E. (1971). Phobias and preparedness. *Behavior Therapy, 2*(3), 307–320. https://doi.org/10.1016/s0005-7894(71)80064-3

Society of Clinical Psychology. (1993, October). *Task force on promotion and dissemination of psychological procedures*. Div12.org. http://www.div12.org/sites/default/files/InitialReportOfTheChamblessTaskForce.pdf

Society of Clinical Psychology. (2012, July). *Empirically supported treatments*. Div12.org. https://div12.org/empirically-supported-treatments/

Speer, M. E., Ibrahim, S., Schiller, D., & Delgado, M. R. (2021). Finding positive meaning in memories of negative events adaptively updates memory. *Nature Communications, 12*(1), 6601.

Sporns, O. (2011). *Networks of the brain*. MIT Press.

Sterling, P. (2004). Principles of allostasis: Optimal design, predictive regulation, pathophysiology, and rational therapeutics. In J. Schulkin (Ed.), *Allostasis, homeostasis, and the costs of physiological adaptation* (Vol. 372, pp. 17–64). Cambridge University Press.

Sterling, P. (2012). Allostasis: A model of predictive regulation. *Physiology and Behavior, 106*(1), 5–15. https://doi.org/10.1016/j.physbeh.2011.06.004

Sterling, P. (2014). Homeostasis vs allostasis: Implications for brain function and mental disorders. *JAMA Psychiatry, 71*(10). https://doi.org/10.1001/jamapsychiatry.2014.1043

Strauss, B., Gawlytta, R., Schleu, A., & Frenzl, D. (2021). Negative effects of psychotherapy: Estimating the prevalence in a random national sample. *BJPsych Open, 7*(6), e186.

Sullivan, H. S. (1970). *The psychiatric interview.* Norton.

Tambini, A., Miller, J., Ehlert, L., Kiyonaga, A., & D'Esposito, M. (2023). Structured memory representations develop at multiple time scales in hippocampal-cortical networks. *bioRxiv,* 2023-04.

Tolin, D. F., McKay, D., Forman, E. M., Klonsky, E. D., & Thombs, B. D. (2015). Empirically supported treatment: Recommendations for a new model. *Clinical Psychology: Science and Practice,* 22(4), 317–338. https://doi.org/10.1037/h0101729

Tononi, G., & Edelman, G. M. (1998). Consciousness and complexity. *Science,* 282(5395), 1846–1851. https://doi.org/10.1126/science.282.5395.1846

Tooley, U. A., Bassett, D. S., & Mackey, A. P. (2021). Environmental influences on the pace of brain development. *Nature Reviews Neuroscience,* 22(6), 372–384.

Tyukin, I., Gorban, A. N., Calvo, C., Makarova, J., & Makarov, V. A. (2019). High-dimensional brain: A tool for encoding and rapid learning of memories by single neurons. *Bulletin of Mathematical Biology,* 81, 4856–4888.

Watzlawick, P., Bavelas, J. B., & Jackson, D. D. (1968). *Pragmatics of human communication: A study of interactional patterns, pathologies and paradoxes.* Faber.

Weisbard, C., & Graham, F. K. (1971). Heart-rate change as a component of the orienting response in monkeys. *Journal of Comparative and Physiological Psychology,* 76(1), 74–83. https://doi.org/10.1037/h0031048

Wells, S. Y., Morland, L. A., Hurst, S., Jackson, G. L., Kehle-Forbes, S. M., Jaime, K., & Aarons, G. A. (2023). Veterans' reasons for dropping out of prolonged exposure therapy across three delivery modalities: A qualitative examination. *Psychological Services,* 20(3), 483–495. https://doi.org/10.1037/ser0000714

Williams, A. J., Botanov, Y., Kilshaw, R. E., Wong, R. E., & Sakaluk, J. K. (2021). Potentially harmful therapies: A meta-scientific review of evidential value. *Clinical Psychology: Science and Practice,* 28(1), 5–18. https://doi.org/10.1111/cpsp.12331

8. The Felt Sense Polyvagal Model

Butler, S. (1978). *The conspiracy of silence: The trauma of incest.* Volcano Press.

Carnes, P. (1983). *Out of the shadows: Understanding sexual addiction.* Hazelden.

Gendlin, E. T. (1981). *Focusing.* Bantam Dell.

Gendlin, E. T. (1986). *Let Your Body Interpret Your Dreams.* Chiron Publications.

Gendlin, E. T. (1996). *Focusing-oriented psychotherapy.* Guilford.

Hendricks-Gendlin, M. (2003). Focusing as a force for peace. [Keynote address]. The 15th Focusing International Conference, Pforzheim, Germany.

Herman, J. (1992). *Trauma and recovery.* Basic Books.

Klein, M. H., Mathieu, P. L., Gendlin, E. T., & Kiesler, D. J. (1969). The experiencing scale: A research and training manual. University of Wisconsin Extension Bureau of Audiovisual Instruction.

Lewis, M. (2015). *The biology of desire: Why addiction is not a disease.* Public Affairs.

Maté, G. (2018). *In the realm of hungry ghosts: Close encounters with addiction.* Vintage Canada.

Morton, L., Cogan, N., Kolacz, J., Calderwood, C., Nikolic, M., Bacon, T., Pathe, E., Williams, D. J., & Porges, S. W. (2022). A new measure of feeling safe: Developing psychometric properties of the Neuroception of Psychological Safety Scale (NPSS). *Psychological Trauma: Theory, Research, Practice, and Policy.* https://doi.org/10.1037/tra0001313

Murray, M. (2012). *The Murray Method: Creating a wholeness beyond trauma, abuse, neglect, and addiction.* Vivo.

Ogden, P. (2006). *Trauma and the body.* Norton Series on Interpersonal Neurobiology. Norton.

Porges, S. (2011). *The polyvagal theory.* Norton.

Porges, S. (2017). *The pocket guide to the Polyvagal Theory: The transformative power of feeling safe.* Norton.

Porges, S. W., & Porges, S. (2023). *Our polyvagal world: How safety and trauma change us.* Norton.

Siegel, D. J. (1999). *The developing mind: Toward a neurobiology of interpersonal experience.* Guilford.

Siegel, D. J. (2012). *The developing mind: How relationships and the brain interact to shape who we are.* (2nd ed.). Guilford.

van der Kolk, B. (2014). *The body keeps the score.* Penguin.

Winhall, J. (2014). Understanding and treating addiction with the felt sense experience model. In G. Madison (Ed.), *Emerging practice in focusing-oriented psychotherapy: Innovative theory and applications* (pp. 178–193). Jessica Kingsley.

Winhall, J. (2021). *Treating trauma and addiction with the felt sense polyvagal model.* Routledge.

Winhall, J. (2025). *20 embodied practices for healing trauma and addiction: Using the felt sense polyvagal model.* Norton. [Manuscript in preparation.]

Winhall, J., & Porges, S. W. (2022). Revolutionizing addiction treatment with the felt sense polyvagal model. *The International Body Psychotherapy Journal, 21*(1), 13–21.

Wheel of privilege and power. (2023, January 13). Just 1 Voice. Retrieved from https://just 1 voice./com/advocacy/wheel-of-privilege/

9. Memory Reconsolidation in Body-Oriented Trauma Therapies

Baker, E., & Lui, F. (2023, July 24). Neuroanatomy, vagal nerve nuclei. *StatPearls.* http://www.ncbi.nlm.nih.gov/books/NBK545209/

Bohne, M. (2021). *Psychotherapie und Coaching mit PEP: Prozess- und embodimentfokussierte Psychologie in der Praxis.* Carl-Auer-Systeme Verlag and Verlagsbuchhandlung GmbH.

Bremner, J. D., Gurel, N. Z., Jiao, Y., Wittbrodt, M. T., Levantsevych, O. M., Huang, M., Jung, H., Shandhi, M. H., Beckwith, J., Herring, I., Rapaport, M. H., Murrah, N., Driggers, E., Ko, Y.-A., Alkhalaf, M. L., Soudan, M., Song, J., Ku, B. S., Shallenberger, L., ... & Pearce, B. D. (2020). Transcutaneous vagal nerve stimulation blocks stress-induced activation of interleukin-6 and interferon-Y in posttraumatic stress disorder: A double-blind, randomized, sham-controlled trial. *Brain, Behavior, and Immunity—Health, 9*, 100138. https://doi.org/10.1016/j.bbih.2020.100138

Ecker, B. (2015). Memory reconsolidation understood and misunderstood. *International Journal of Neuropsychotherapy, 3*(1), 2–46. https://doi.org/10.12744/ijnpt.2015.0002-0046

Ecker, B. (2018). Clinical translation of memory reconsolidation research: Therapeutic methodology for transformational change by erasing implicit emotional learnings driving symptom production. *International Journal of Neuropsychotherapy, 6*(1), 1–92. https://doi.org/10.12744/ijnpt.2018.0001-0092

Eckstein, M., Mamaev, I., Ditzen, B., & Sailer, U. (2020). Calming effects of touch in human, animal, and robotic interaction—scientific state-of-the-art and technical advances. *Frontiers in Psychiatry, 11*, 555058. https://doi.org/10.3389/fpsyt.2020.555058

Filmer, A. I., Peters, J., Bridge, L. A., Visser, R. M., & Kindt, M. (2022). Over the edge: Extending the duration of a reconsolidation intervention for spider fear. *Translational Psychiatry, 12*(1), 261. https://doi.org/10.1038/s41398-022-02020-x

Gendlin, E. T. (1978). *Focusing.* Everest House.

Hanson, E. (2014). *The poetic underground.* [Self-published.]

Huberman, A. (2021, February 21). *Optimize your learning and creativity with science-based tools* [Video]. Huberman Lab. https://www.hubermanlab.com/episode/optimize-your-learning-and-creativity -with-science-based-tools

Iyadurai, L., Visser, R. M., Lau-Zhu, A., Porcheret, K., Horsch, A., Holmes, E. A., & James, E. L. (2019). Intrusive memories of trauma: A target for research bridging cognitive science and its clinical application. *Clinical Psychology Review, 69*, 67–82. https://doi.org/10.1016/j.cpr .2018.08.005

Kaczkurkin, A. N., Burton, P. C., Chazin, S. M., Manbeck, A. B., Espensen-Sturges, T., Cooper, S. E., Sponheim, S. R., & Lissek, S. (2017). Neural substrates of overgeneralized conditioned fear in PTSD. *American Journal of Psychiatry, 174*(2), 125–134. https://doi.org/10.1176/ appi.ajp.2016.15121549

Kindt, M. (2018). The surprising subtleties of changing fear memory: A challenge for translational science. *Philosophical Transactions of the Royal Society B: Biological Sciences, 373*(1742), 20170033. https://doi.org/10.1098/rstb.2017.0033

Kindt, M., & Van Emmerik, A. (2016). New avenues for treating emotional memory disorders: Towards a reconsolidation intervention for posttraumatic stress disorder. *Therapeutic Advances in Psychopharmacology, 6*(4), 283–295. https://doi.org/10.1177/2045125316644541

LeDoux, J. E. (2015). *Anxious: Using the brain to understand and treat fear and anxiety.* Viking.

LeDoux, J. E. (2022). The day I told Karim Nader, "Don't do the study." *Brain Research Bulletin, 189*, 1–3. https://doi.org/10.1016/j.brainresbull.2022.08.012

Levine, P. A. (2010). *In an unspoken voice: How the body releases trauma and restores goodness.* North Atlantic.

Lis, S., Thome, J., Kleindienst, N., Mueller-Engelmann, M., Steil, R., Priebe, K., Schmahl, C., Hermans, D., & Bohus, M. (2020). Generalization of fear in post-traumatic stress disorder. *Psychophysiology, 57*(1), e13422. https://doi.org/10.1111/psyp.13422

Liu, J., Totty, M. S., Melissari, L., Bayer, H., & Maren, S. (2022). Convergent coding of recent and remote fear memory in the basolateral amygdala. *Biological Psychiatry, 91*(9), 832–840. https:// doi.org/10.1016/j.biopsych.2021.12.018

Monfils, M.-H., Cowansage, K. K., Klann, E., & LeDoux, J. E. (2009). Extinction-reconsolidation boundaries: Key to persistent attenuation of fear memories. *Science, 324*(5929), 951–955. https:// doi.org/10.1126/science.1167975

Nader, K., Schafe, G. E., & Le Doux, J. E. (2000). Fear memories require protein synthesis in the amygdala for reconsolidation after retrieval. *Nature, 406*(6797), 722–726. https:// doi.org/10.1038/35021052

Noble, L. J., Gonzalez, I. J., Meruva, V. B., Callahan, K. A., Belfort, B. D., Ramanathan, K. R., Meyers, E., Kilgard, M. P., Rennaker, R. L., & McIntyre, C. K. (2017). Effects of vagus nerve stimulation on extinction of conditioned fear and post-traumatic stress disorder symptoms in rats. *Translational Psychiatry, 7*(8), e1217. https://doi.org/10.1038/tp.2017.191

Nordin, M. (1990). Low-threshold mechanoreceptive and nociceptive units with unmyelinated (C) fibres in the human supraorbital nerve. *Journal of Physiology, 426*, 229–240. https://doi.org/10.1113/ jphysiol.1990.sp018135

Peña, D. F., Engineer, N. D., & McIntyre, C. K. (2013). Rapid remission of conditioned fear expression with extinction training paired with vagus nerve stimulation. *Biological Psychiatry, 73*(11), 1071–1077. https://doi.org/10.1016/j.biopsych.2012.10.021

Porges, S. W., & Dana, D. (Eds.). (2019). *Klinische Anwendungen der Polyvagal-Theorie: Ein neues Verständnis des Autonomen Nervensystems und seiner Anwendung in der therapeutischen Praxis* (T. Kierdorf & H. Höhr, Trans.). G. P. Probst Verlag.

Roth, G. (2015, July 14). *Wie das Gehirn die Seele macht: Erklärt von Gerhard Roth* [Video]. Hertiestiftung, YouTube. https://www.youtube.com/watch?v=wqMIC2QSN10

Selvam, R. (2022). *The practice of embodying emotions: A guide for improving cognitive, emotional, and behavioral outcomes*. North Atlantic.

Sevenster, D., Beckers, T., & Kindt, M. (2012). Retrieval per se is not sufficient to trigger reconsolidation of human fear memory. *Neurobiology of Learning and Memory, 97*(3), 338–345. https://doi.org/10.1016/j.nlm.2012.01.009

Sevenster, D., Beckers, T., & Kindt, M. (2013). Prediction error governs pharmacologically induced amnesia for learned fear. *Science, 339*(6121), 830–833. https://doi.org/10.1126/science.1231357

Soeter, M., & Kindt, M. (2011). Noradrenergic enhancement of associative fear memory in humans. *Neurobiology of Learning and Memory, 96*(2), 263–271. https://doi.org/10.1016/j.nlm.2011.05.003

Soeter, M., & Kindt, M. (2012). Stimulation of the noradrenergic system during memory formation impairs extinction learning but not the disruption of reconsolidation. *Neuropsychopharmacology, 37*(5), 1204–1215. https://doi.org/10.1038/npp.2011.307

Souza, R. R., Oleksiak, C. R., Tabet, M. N., Rennaker, R. L., Hays, S. A., Kilgard, M. P., & McIntyre, C. K. (2021). Vagus nerve stimulation promotes extinction generalization across sensory modalities. *Neurobiology of Learning and Memory, 181*, 107425. https://doi.org/10.1016/j.nlm.2021.107425

Visser, R. M., Lau-Zhu, A., Henson, R. N., & Holmes, E. A. (2018). Multiple memory systems, multiple time points: How science can inform treatment to control the expression of unwanted emotional memories. *Philosophical Transactions of the Royal Society of London. Series B, Biological Sciences, 373*(1742), 20170209. https://doi.org/10.1098/rstb.2017.0209

Wittfoth, D., Beise, J., Manuel, J., Bohne, M., & Wittfoth, M. (2022). Bifocal emotion regulation through acupoint tapping in fear of flying. *NeuroImage: Clinical, 34*, 102996. https://doi.org/10.1016/j.nicl.2022.102996

10. The Practice of Embodying Emotions

Barrett, L. F. (2017). *How emotions are made: The secret life of the brain*. Houghton Mifflin Harcourt.

Craig, A. D. (2015). *How do you feel? An interoceptive moment with your neurobiological self*. Princeton University Press.

Critchley, H. D., & Nagai, Y. (2012). How emotions are shaped by bodily states. *Emotion Review, 4*(2), 163–168. https://doi.org/10.1177/1754073911430132

Damasio, A. (1994). *Descartes' error: Emotion, reason, and the human brain*. Penguin.

Damasio, A. (2003). *Looking for Spinoza: Joy, sorrow, and the feeling brain*. Houghton Mifflin Harcourt.

Dukes, D., Abrams, K., Adolphs, R., Ahmed, M. E., Beatty, A., Berridge, K. C., Broomhall, S., Brosch, T., Campos, J. J., Clay, Z., Clément, F., Cunningham, W. A., Damasio, A., Damasio, H., D'Arms, J., Davidson, J. W., de Gelder, B., Deonna, J., de Sousa, R., ... & Sander, D. (2021). The rise of affectivism. *Nature Human Behavior, 5*(July), 816–820.

Ekman, P. (2016). What scientists who study emotion agree about. *Perspectives on Psychological Science, 11*(1), 31–34.

Fincher-Kiefer, R. (2019). *How the body shapes knowledge: Empirical support for embodied cognition*. American Psychological Association.

Johnson, M. (2017). *Embodied mind, meaning, and reason: How our bodies give rise to understanding*. University of Chicago Press.

Laird, J., & Lacasse, K. (2014). Bodily influences on emotional feelings: Accumulating evidence and extensions of William James' theory of emotions. *Emotion Review, 6*, 24–37.

Marlock, G., Weiss, H., Young, C., & Soth, M. (Eds.). (2015). *The handbook of body psychotherapy and somatic psychology*. North Atlantic.

Niedenthal, P. (2007). Embodying emotion. *Science, 316*(5827), 1002–1005.

Peper, E., Lin, I., Harvey, R., & Perez, J. (2017). How posture affects memory recall and mood. *Biofeedback, 45*(2), 36–41. https://doi.org/10.5298/1081-5937-45.2.01

Selvam, R. (2022). *The practice of embodying emotions: A guide for improving cognitive, emotional, and behavioral outcomes*. North Atlantic.

Selvam, R. (2023, April 19). The 7-Step protocol for embodying emotion. Integral Somatic Psychology. https://integralsomaticpsychology.com/protocol-embodying-emotion

11. Neuroception Within Trauma Recovery

Ashar, Y. K., Gordon, A., Schubiner, H., Uipi, C., Knight, K., Anderson, Z., ... & Wager, T. D. (2022). Effect of pain reprocessing therapy vs placebo and usual care for patients with chronic back pain: a randomized clinical trial. *JAMA Psychiatry, 79*(1), 13–23.

Bennett, M. J., & Castiglioni, I. (2004). Embodied ethnocentrism and the feeling of culture: A key to training for intercultural competence. In D. Landis, J. Bennett, & M. Bennett (Eds.), *Handbook of intercultural training* (3rd ed., pp. 249–265). Sage.

Briere, J., Hodges, M., & Godbout, N. (2010). Traumatic stress, affect dysregulation, and dysfunctional avoidance: A structural equation model. *Journal of Traumatic Stress, 23*(6), 767–774.

Cook-Cottone, C. P. (2015). *Mindfulness and yoga for self-regulation: A primer for mental health professionals*. Springer.

Cozolino, L. (2014). *The neuroscience of human relationships: Attachment and the developing social brain* (2nd ed.). Norton.

Cramer, A. O., Leertouwer, I., Lanius, R., & Frewen, P. (2020). A network approach to studying the associations between posttraumatic stress disorder symptoms and dissociative experiences. *Journal of Traumatic Stress, 33*(1), 19–28.

Critchley, H. D., & Garfinkel, S. N. (2017). Interoception and emotion. *Current Opinion in Psychology, 17*, 7–14.

Damasio, A. R. (1999). *The feeling of what happens: Body and emotion in the making of consciousness*. Harvest.

Deppermann, S., Storchak, H., Fallgatter, A. J., & Ehlis, A. C. (2014). Stress-induced neuroplasticity: (Mal)adaptation to adverse life events in patients with PTSD—A critical overview. *Neuroscience, 283*, 166–177.

Donne, J. (1987). *Devotions upon emergent occasions*. Oxford.

Flor, H., Nikolajsen, L., & Staehelin Jensen, T. (2006). Phantom limb pain: A case of maladaptive CNS plasticity? *Nature Reviews Neuroscience, 7*(11), 873–881.

Fogel, A. (2009). *Body sense: The science and practice of embodied self-awareness*. Norton.

Frey, L. L. (2013). Relational-cultural therapy: Theory, research, and application to counseling competencies. *Professional Psychology: Research and Practice, 44*(3), 177–185

Goggins, E., Mitani, S., & Tanaka, S. (2022). Clinical perspectives on vagus nerve stimulation: Present and future. *Clinical Science, 136*(9), 695–709.

Grossman, P., & Taylor, E. W. (2007). Toward understanding respiratory sinus arrhythmia: Relations to cardiac vagal tone, evolution and biobehavioral functions. *Biological Psychology, 74*(2), 263–285.

Harricharan, S., McKinnon, M. C., & Lanius, R. A. (2021). How processing of sensory information from the internal and external worlds shape the perception and engagement with the world in the aftermath of trauma: Implications for PTSD. *Frontiers in Neuroscience, 15,* 625490.

Herman, J. L. (2023). *Truth and repair: How trauma survivors envision justice.* Hachette UK.

Hopwood, T. L., & Schutte, N. S. (2017). A meta-analytic investigation of the impact of mindfulness-based interventions on post-traumatic stress. *Clinical Psychology Review, 57,* 12–20.

Hottenrott, L., Ketelhut, S., & Hottenrott, K. (2019). Commentary: Vagal tank theory: The three Rs of cardiac vagal control functioning—resting, reactivity, and recovery. *Frontiers in Neuroscience, 13,* 1300.

Kaniusas, E., Kampusch, S., Tittgemeyer, M., Panetsos, F., Gines, R. F., Papa, M., ... & Széles, J. C. (2019). Current directions in the auricular vagus nerve stimulation I—a physiological perspective. *Frontiers in Neuroscience, 13,* 854.

Khalsa, S. S., & Feinstein, J. S. (2018). The somatic error hypothesis of anxiety. In H. De Preester & M. Tsakiris (Eds.), *The interoceptive mind: From homeostasis to awareness* (pp. 144–164). Oxford.

Kimmel, M. (2013). The arc from the body to culture: How affect, proprioception, kinesthesia, and perceptual imagery shape cultural knowledge (and vice versa). *Integral Review, 9*(2), 300–348.

Kiverstein, J., Kirchhoff, M. D., & Thacker, M. (2022). An embodied predictive processing theory of pain experience. *Review of Philosophy and Psychology, 13*(4), 973–998.

Kolacz, J., Chen, X., Nix, E. J., Roath, O. K., Holmes, L. G., Tokash, C., ... & Lewis, G. F. (2023). Association of self-reported autonomic symptoms with sensor-based physiological measures. *Psychosomatic Medicine, 85*(9), 785–794.

Kolacz, J., & Porges, S. W. (2018). Chronic diffuse pain and functional gastrointestinal disorders after traumatic stress: Pathophysiology through a polyvagal perspective. *Frontiers in Medicine, 5,* 145.

Kratzer, L., Knefel, M., Haselgruber, A., Heinz, P., Schennach, R., & Karatzias, T. (2022). Co-occurrence of severe PTSD, somatic symptoms and dissociation in a large sample of childhood trauma inpatients: A network analysis. *European Archives of Psychiatry and Clinical Neuroscience, 272*(5), 897–908.

Kuner, R., & Kuner, T. (2020). Cellular circuits in the brain and their modulation in acute and chronic pain. *Physiological Reviews, 101*(1), 213–258.

Laborde, S., Mosley, E., & Mertgen, A. (2018). Vagal tank theory: The three Rs of cardiac vagal control functioning—resting, reactivity, and recovery. *Frontiers in Neuroscience, 12,* 458.

Lanius, R. A., Brand, B., Vermetten, E., Frewen, P. A., & Spiegel, D. (2012). The dissociative subtype of posttraumatic stress disorder: Rationale, clinical and neurobiological evidence, and implications. *Depression and Anxiety, 29,* 701–708.

Larrivee, D., & Echarte, L. (2018). Contemplative meditation and neuroscience: Prospects for mental health. *Journal of Religion and Health, 57*(3), 960–978.

Lehrer, P. M., & Gevirtz, R. (2014). Heart rate variability biofeedback: How and why does it work? *Frontiers in Psychology, 5,* 756.

McCraty, R., & Childre, D. (2004). The grateful heart: The psychophysiology of appreciation. In R. A. Emmons & M. E. McCullough (Eds.), *The psychology of gratitude* (pp. 230–255). Oxford.

McCraty, R., & Childre, D. (2010). Coherence: Bridging personal, social, and global health. *Alternative Therapies in Health and Medicine, 16*(4), 10–24.

Meijer, L. L., Ruis, C., van der Smagt, M. J., Scherder, E. J., & Dijkerman, H. C. (2022). Neural basis of affective touch and pain: A novel model suggests possible targets for pain amelioration. *Journal of Neuropsychology, 16*(1), 38–53.

Merleau-Ponty, M. (1962). *Phenomenology of perception.* Routledge and Kegan Paul.

Miller, E., Miller, L., Turner, R. P., & Evans, J. R. (2017). The use of music for neuromodulation. In J. R. Evans & R. Turner (Eds.), *Rhythmic stimulation procedures in neuromodulation* (pp. 159–192). Academic Press.

Molden, D. C., & Dweck, C. S. (2006). Finding "meaning" in psychology: A lay theories approach to self-regulation, social perception, and social development. *American Psychologist, 61*(3), 192.

Montirosso, R., & McGlone, F. (2020). The body comes first: Embodied reparation and the co-creation of infant bodily-self. *Neuroscience and Biobehavioral Reviews, 113*, 77–87.

Morton, L., Cogan, N., Kolacz, J., Calderwood, C., Nikolic, M., Bacon, T., Pathe, E., Williams, D. J., & Porges, S. W. (2022). A new measure of feeling safe: Developing psychometric properties of the Neuroception of Psychological Safety Scale (NPSS). *Psychological Trauma: Theory, Research, Practice, and Policy.* https://doi.org/10.1037/tra0001313

Ogden, P., & Minton, K. (2014). Integrating body and mind: Sensorimotor psychotherapy and treatment of dissociation, defense, and dysregulation. In U. F. Lanius, S. L. Paulsen, & F. M. Corrigan (Eds.), *Neurobiology and the treatment of traumatic dissociation: Towards an embodied self.* Springer.

Pagaduan, J., Wu, S. S., Kameneva, T., & Lambert, E. (2019). Acute effects of resonance frequency breathing on cardiovascular regulation. *Physiological Reports, 7*(22), e14295.

Park, L. E., Naidu, E., Lemay, E. P., Canning, E. A., Ward, D. E., Panlilio, Z. A., & Vessels, V. (2023). Social evaluative threat across individual, relational, and collective selves. *Advances in Experimental Social Psychology, 68*, 139–222.

Porges, S. (1993). Body perception questionnaire. Laboratory of Developmental Assessment, University of Maryland.

Porges, S. W. (2001). The polyvagal theory: Phylogenetic substrates of a social nervous system. *International Journal of Psychophysiology, 42*(2), 123–146. https://doi.org/10.1016/s0167-8760(01)00162-3

Porges, S. W. (2004). Neuroception: A subconscious system for detecting threats and safety. *Zero to Three (J), 24*(5), 19–24.

Porges, S. W. (2011). *The polyvagal theory: Neurophysiological foundations of emotions, attachment, communication, and self-regulation.* Norton.

Porges, S. W. (2022). Polyvagal theory: A science of safety. *Frontiers in Integrative Neuroscience, 16*, 27.

Porges, S. W., & Furman, S. A. (2011). The early development of the autonomic nervous system provides a neural platform for social behaviour: A polyvagal perspective. *Infant and Child Development, 20*(1), 106–118.

Price, C. J., & Weng, H. Y. (2021). Facilitating adaptive emotion processing and somatic reappraisal via sustained mindful interoceptive attention. *Frontiers in Psychology, 12*, 3543.

Ruden, R. A. (2019). Harnessing electroceuticals to treat disorders arising from traumatic stress: Theoretical considerations using a psychosensory model. *Explore, 15*(3), 222–229.

Russo-Netzer, P., & Cohen, G. L. (2023). "If you're uncomfortable, go outside your comfort zone": A novel behavioral "stretch" intervention supports the well-being of unhappy people. *Journal of Positive Psychology, 18*(3), 394–410.

Schore, A. (2003). *Affect regulation and the repair of the self.* Norton.

Schwartz, A. (2024). *Applied polyvagal theory in yoga: Therapeutic practices for emotional health.* Norton.

Sevoz-Couche, C., & Laborde, S. (2022). Heart rate variability and slow-paced breathing: When coherence meets resonance. *Neuroscience and Biobehavioral Reviews, 135*, 104576.

Smith, R., Thayer, J. F., Khalsa, S. S., & Lane, R. D. (2017). The hierarchical basis of neurovisceral integration. *Neuroscience and Biobehavioral Reviews, 75*, 274–296.

Tanaka, S. (2015). Intercorporeality as a theory of social cognition. *Theory and Psychology, 25*(4), 455–472.

Thayer, J. F., & Lane, R. D. (2000). A model of neurovisceral integration in emotion regulation and dysregulation. *Journal of Affective Disorders, 61*(3), 201–216.

Tronick, E. (2007). *The neurobehavioral and social-emotional development of infants and children.* Norton.

van der Kolk, B. A., Pelcovitz, D., Roth, S., Mandel, F. S., McFarlane, A., & Herman, J. L. (1996). Dissociation, somatization, and affect dysregulation: The complexity of adaptation of trauma. *American Journal of Psychiatry, 153*(7 Suppl), 83–93.

Wang, F., Pan, F., Shapiro, L. A., & Huang, J. H. (2017). Stress induced neuroplasticity and mental disorders. *Neural Plasticity, 2017,* 9634501.

12. Applying the Neurobiology of Resilience

Arvidson, J., Kinniburgh, K., Howard, K., Spinazzola, J., Strothers, H., Evans, M., Andres, B., Cohen, C., & Blaustein, M. E. (2011). Treatment of complex trauma in young children: Developmental and cultural considerations in application of the ARC intervention model. *Journal of Child and Adolescent Trauma, 4*(1), 34–51. https://doi.org/10.1080/19361521.2011.545046

Dana, D. (2018). *The polyvagal theory in therapy: Engaging the rhythm of regulation.* Norton.

Fischer, A. (2015). The role of core organizing beliefs in Hakomi Therapy. In H. Weiss, G. Johanson, & L. Monda (Eds.), *Hakomi mindfulness-centered somatic psychotherapy: A comprehensive guide to theory and practice* (pp. 66–75). Norton.

Geller, S. M. (2018). Therapeutic presence and polyvagal theory: Principles and practices for cultivating effective therapeutic relationships. In S. W. Porges & D. Dana (Eds.), *Clinical applications of the polyvagal theory: The emergence of polyvagal-informed therapies* (pp. 106–126). Norton.

Geller, S. M., & Porges, S. W. (2014). Therapeutic presence: Neurophysiological mechanisms mediating feeling safe in therapeutic relationships. *Journal of Psychotherapy Integration, 24*(3), 178–192. https://doi.org/10.1037/a0037511

Gendlin, E. T. (1996). *Focusing-oriented psychotherapy: A manual of the experiential method.* Guilford.

Hanson, R. (2009). *Buddha's brain: The practical neuroscience of happiness, love and wisdom.* New Harbinger.

Hanson, R. (2018, September 11). *Positive neuroplasticity: The mindful cultivation of resilient well-being* [PowerPoint slides]. http://media.rickhanson.net/slides/9.11.18Google_Pos_NP_Hanson.pdf

Hatcher, R. L. (2015). Interpersonal competencies: Responsiveness, technique, and training in psychotherapy. *American Psychologist, 70*(8), 747–757. https://doi.org/10.1037/a0039803

Kemeny, M. E. (2003). The psychobiology of stress. *Current Directions in Psychological Science, 12*(4), 124–129. https://doi.org/10.1111/1467-8721.01246

Kurtz, R. (1990). *Body-centered psychotherapy: The Hakomi method.* LifeRhythm.

Levine, P. A. (1997). *Waking the tiger: Healing trauma.* North Atlantic.

Levine, P. A. (2010). *In an unspoken voice: How the body releases trauma and restores goodness.* North Atlantic.

Lukin, K. (2019, August 1). Toxic positivity: Don't always look on the bright side. *Psychology Today.* https://www.psychologytoday.com/us/blog/the-man-cave/201908/toxic-positivity-dont-always-look-the-bright-side

Murphy, J. (2015). The therapeutic relationship in Hakomi therapy. In H. Weiss, G. Johanson, & L. Monda (Eds.), *Hakomi mindfulness-centered somatic psychotherapy: A comprehensive guide to theory and practice* (pp. 93–107). Norton.

Neff, K., & Germer, C. (2018). *The mindful self-compassion workbook: A proven way to accept yourself, build inner strength, and thrive.* Guilford.

Ogden, P., Minton, K., & Pain, C. (2006). *Trauma and the body: A sensorimotor approach to psychotherapy.* Norton .

Ord, A. S., Stranahan, K. R., Hurley, R. A., & Taber, K. H. (2020). Stress-related growth: Building a more resilient brain. *Journal of Neuropsychiatry and Clinical Neurosciences, 32*(3), A4–A212. https://doi.org/10.1176/appi.neuropsych.20050111

Porges, S. W. (1995). Orienting in a defensive world: Mammalian modifications of our evolutionary heritage. A polyvagal theory. *Psychophysiology, 32,* 301–318. https://doi.org/10.1111/j.1469-8986.1995.tb01213.x

Porges, S. W. (2003). Social engagement and attachment: A phylogenetic perspective. *Annals of the New York Academy of Sciences, 1008*(1), 31–47. https://doi.org/10.1196/annals.1301.004

Porges, S. W. (2011). *The polyvagal theory: Neurophysiological foundations of emotions, attachment, communication, and self-regulation.* Norton.

Porges, S. W. (2021). Polyvagal theory: A biobehavioral journey to sociality. *Comprehensive Psychoneuroendocrinology, 7,* 100069. https://doi.org/10.1016/j.cpnec.2021.100069

Porges, S. W. (2022). Polyvagal theory: A science of safety. *Frontiers in Integrative Neuroscience, 16,* 871227. https://doi.org/10.3389/fnint.2022.871227

Porges, S. W., & Porges, S. (2023). *Our polyvagal world: How safety and trauma change us.* Norton.

Roberts, B. W., Luo, J., Briley, D. A., Chow, P. I., Su, R. & Hill, P. L. (2017). A systematic review of personality trait change through intervention. *Psychological Bulletin, 143*(2), 117–141. https://doi.org/10.1037/bul0000088

Scaer, R. (2005). *The trauma spectrum: Hidden wounds and human resiliency.* Norton.

Shepperd, J. A., Waters, E. A., Weinstein, N. D., & Klein, W. M. P. (2015). A primer on unrealistic optimism. *Current Directions in Psychological Science, 24*(3), 232–237. https://doi.org/10.1177/0963721414568341

Siegel, D. J. (1999). *The developing mind: How relationships and the brain interact to shape who we are.* Guilford.

Siegel, D. J. (2010a). *The mindful therapist: A clinician's guide to mindsight and neural integration.* Norton.

Siegel, D. J. (2010b). *Mindsight: The new science of personal transformation.* Bantam.

Siegel, D. J. (2017). *Mind: A journey to the heart of being human.* Norton.

Vaish, A., Grossmann, T., & Woodward, A. (2008). Not all emotions are created equal: The negativity bias in social-emotional development. *Psychological Bulletin, 134*(3), 383–403. https://doi.org/10.1037/0033-2909.134.3.383

van der Kolk, B. (2014). *The body keeps the score: Brain, mind, and body in the healing of trauma.* Penguin.

Wolf-Gramzow, S. D. (2023). *Traumatization resulting from interpersonal disclosure: Developing a measure of disclosure-induced neo-trauma.* Syracuse University ProQuest Dissertations.

13. The Therapeutic Use of Touch

Bainbridge Cohen, B. (1993). *Sensing, feeling, and action.* Contact Editions.

Beebe, B. (2003). Faces-in-relation: Forms of intersubjectivity in adult treatment of early trauma. *Psychoanalytic Dialogue, 14*(1), 1–51.

Bowlby, J. (1988). *A secure base: Clinical applications of attachment theory.* Routledge.

Craig, A. D. (2003). The sense of the physiological condition of the body. *Current Opinion in Neurobiology, 13,* 500–505.

Damasio, A. R. (1994). *Descartes' error: Emotion, reason and the human brain.* Vintage.

Damasio, A. R. (1999). *The feeling of what happens: Body and emotion in the making of consciousness.* Harvest.

Field, T. (1995). *Touch in early development.* Lawrence Erlbaum.

Field, T. (2003). *Touch therapy.* Churchill Livingstone.

Geuter, U. (2024). *Body psychotherapy: A theoretical foundation for clinical practice.* Routledge.

Harlow, H. F. (1958). The nature of love. *American Psychologist, 13*(12), 673–685. https://doi.org/10.1037/h0047884

Harlow, H. F., & Zimmerman, R. R. (1959). Affectional responses in the infant monkey: Orphaned baby monkeys develop a strong and persistent attachment to inanimate surrogate mothers. *Science, 130*(3373), 421–432.

Johnson, K. O., & Hsiao, S. S. (1992). Neural mechanisms of tactual form and texture perception. *Annual Review of Neuroscience, 15*, 227–250.

Juhan, D. (1987). *Job's body*. Station Hill Press.

Leboyer, F. (1987). *Loving hands: The traditional art of baby massage*. Collins.

Lyons-Ruth, K. (1999). Two-person unconscious: Intersubjective dialogue, inactive relational representation, and the emergence of new forms of relational organization. *Psychoanalytic Inquiry, 19*, 576–617.

McGlone, F., Wessberg, J., & Olausson, H. (2014). Discriminative and affective touch: Sensing and feeling. *Neuron, 82*(4), 737–755.

Montague, A. (1971). *Touching: The human significance of the skin*. Columbia University Press.

Nathan, B. (1999). *Touch and emotion in manual therapy*. Churchill Livingstone.

Olausson, H., Lamarre, Y., Backlund, H., Morin, C., Wallin, B. G., Starck, G., Ekholm, S., Strigo, I., Worsley, K., Vallbo, Å. B., & Bushnell, M. C. (2002). Unmyelinated tactile afferents signal touch and project to insular cortex. *Nature Neuroscience, 5*(9), 900–904.

Overly, R. (2004). *Dr. Eva Reich's butterfly touch massage*. Gentle Bio-Energetics Institute. (Original work published 1994)

Panksepp, J. (1998). *Affective neuroscience: The foundation of human and animal emotions*. Oxford.

Rossi, E. L. (1986). *The psychobiology of mind-body healing*. Norton.

Schore, A. (2003). *Affect regulation and the repair of the self*. Norton.

Vallbo, Å., Löken, L., & Wessberg, J. (2016). Sensual touch: A slow touch system revealed with microneurography. In H. Olausson, J. Wessberg, I. Morrison, & F. McGlone (Eds.), *Affective touch and the neurophysiology of CT afferents* (Kindle ed.). Springer.

Vallbo A. B., Olausson H., & Wessberg J. (1999). Unmyelinated afferents constitute a second system coding tactile stimuli of the human hairy skin. *J Neurophysiology, 81*(6), 2753–63. doi: 10.1152/jn.1999.81.6.2753

14. Fascia as Sensory Organ and the Role of Interoceptive Techniques

Astin, J. A., Shapiro, S. L., Eisenberg, D. M., & Forys, K. L. (2003). Mind-body medicine: state of the science, implications for practice. *J Am Board Fam Pract, 16*(2), 131–147.

Barrett, L. F., & Simmons, W. K. (2015). Interoceptive predictions in the brain. *Nature Reviews Neuroscience, 16*(7), 419–429.

Berlucchi, G., & Aglioti, S. M. (2010). The body in the brain revisited. *Exp Brain Res, 200*(1), 25–35.

Case, L. K., Liljencrantz, J., McCall, M. V., Bradson, M., Necaise, A., Tubbs, J., Olausson, H., Wang, B., & Bushnell, M. C. (2021). Pleasant deep pressure: Expanding the social touch hypothesis. *Neuroscience, 464*, 3–11.

Case, L. K., Madian, N., McCall, M. V., Bradson, M. L., Liljencrantz, J., Goldstein, B., Alasha, V. J., & Zimmerman, M. S. (2023). Aβ-CT affective touch: Touch pleasantness ratings for gentle stroking and deep pressure exhibit dependence on A-fibers. *eNeuro, 10*(5), ENEURO.0504-22.2023.

Cerritelli, F., Chiacchiaretta, P., Gambi, F., & Ferretti, A. (2017). Effect of continuous touch on brain functional connectivity is modified by the operator's tactile attention. *Frontiers in Human Neuroscience, 11*, 368.

Craig, A. D. (2009). How do you feel—now? The anterior insula and human awareness. *Nature Reviews Neuroscience, 10*, 59–70

Dunn, B. D., Galton, H. C., Morgan, R., Evans, D., Oliver, C., Meyer, M., Cusack, R., Lawrence, A. D., Dalgleish, T. (2010). Listening to your heart. How interoception shapes emotion experience and intuitive decision making. *Psychol Sci, 21*(12), 1835–1844.

Evdokimov, D., Dinkel, P., Frank, J., Sommer, C., & Üçeyler, N. (2020). Characterization of dermal skin innervation in fibromyalgia syndrome. *PloS One, 15*(1), e0227674.

Findley, T., & Schleip, R. (Eds.). (2007). *Fascia research: Basic science and implications for conventional and complementary health care.* Elsevier Urban and Fischer.

França, M. E. D., Sinhorim, L., Martins, D. F., Schleip, R., Machado-Pereira, N. A. M. M., de Souza, G. M., Horewicz, V. V., & Santos, G. M. (2020). Manipulation of the fascial system applied during acute inflammation of the connective tissue of the thoracolumbar region affects transforming growth factor-β1 and interleukin-4 levels: Experimental study in mice. *Frontiers in Physiology, 11*, 587373.

Grimm, D. (2007). Biomedical research: Cell biology meets rolfing. *Science, 318*(5854): 1234–1235.

Harlow, H. F. (1958). The nature of love. *American Psychologist, 13*(12), 673–689.

Hoheisel, U., Vogt, M. A., Palme, R., Gass, P., & Mense, S. (2015). Immobilization stress sensitizes rat dorsal horn neurons having input from the low back. *European Journal of Pain, 19*(6), 861–870.

Jami, A. (1992). Golgi tendon organs in mammalian skeletal muscles: Functional properties and central actions. *Physiology Review, 72*(3), 623–666.

McGlone F., Wessberg J., & Olausson H. (2014). Discriminative and affective touch: sensing and feeling. *Neuron, 82*(4), 737–755.

Michalak, J., Aranmolate, L., Bonn, A., Grandin, K., Schleip, R., Schmiedtke, J., Quassowsky, S., & Teismann, T. (2022). Myofascial tissue and depression. *Cognitive Therapy and Research, 46*(3), 560–572.

Mitchell, J. H., Schmidt, R. F. (1977.) Cardiovascular reflex control by afferent fibers from skeletal muscle receptors. In Shepherd J. T. et al. (Eds). Handbook of Physiology, Sect. 2, Vol. III, Part 2. American Physiological Society, 623–658.

Montague, A. (1971). *Touch: The human significance of the skin.* Harper and Row.

Moseley, L. G., Zalucki, N. M., & Wiech, K. (2008). Tactile discrimination, but not tactile stimulation alone, reduces chronic limb pain. *Pain, 137*(3), 600–608.

Olausson, H., Wessberg, J., Morrison, I., McGlone, F., & Vallbo, A. (2010). The neurophysiology of unmyelinated tactile afferents. *Neurosci Biobehav Rev., 34*(2), 185–191.

Onuora, S. (2021). Antibodies induce fibromyalgia symptoms. *Nature Reviews Rheumatology, 17*(9), 507.

Reeve, K., Black, P. A., & Huang, J. (2020). Examining the impact of a healing touch intervention to reduce posttraumatic stress disorder symptoms in combat veterans. *Psychological Trauma, 12*(8), 897–903.

Reich, W. (1933). *Character analysis.* Farrar, Straus and Giroux.

Schilder, A. Hoheisel, U., Magerl, W., Benrath, J., Klein, T., & Treede, R-D. (2014). Sensory findings after stimulation of the thoracolumbar fascia with hypertonic saline suggest its contribution to low back pain. *Pain, 155*(2), 222–231.

Schleip, R., & Stecco, C. (2021). Fascia as a sensory organ. In: R. Schleip, J. Wilke, & A. Baker (Eds.), *Fascia in sport and movement* (2nd ed., pp. 169–179). Handspring.

Stecco, C. (2014). *Functional atlas of the human fascial system.* Elsevier Health Sciences.

Stecco, C., Adstrum, S., Hedley, G., Schleip, R., & Yucesoy, C. A. (2018). Update on fascial nomenclature. *Journal of Bodywork and Movement Therapies, 22*(2), 354.

Stecco, A., Stecco, C., & Raghavan, P. (2014). Peripheral mechanisms contributing to spasticity and
implications for treatment. *Current Physical Medicine and Rehabilitation Reports, 2,* 121–127.

Still, A. T. (1902). *The philosophy and mechanical principles of osteopathy.* Hudson-Kimberly.

Taguchi, T., Yasui, M., Kubo, A., Abe, M., Kiyama, H., Yamanaka, A., & Mizumura, K. (2013).
Nociception originating from the crural fascia in rats. *Pain, 154*(7), 1103–1114.

Tesarz, J., Eich, W., Treede, R. D., & Gerhardt, A. (2016). Altered pressure pain thresholds and
increased wind-up in adult patients with chronic back pain with a history of childhood maltreatment: A quantitative sensory testing study. *Pain, 157*(8), 1799–1809.

van der Wal, J. C. (1988). The organisation of the substrate of proprioception in the elbow region
of the rat [Doctoral dissertation]. Maastricht University, Faculty of Medicine.

Watt, J. A., Goodarzi, Z., Veroniki, A. A., Nincic, V., Khan, P. A., Ghassemi, M., Lai, Y., Treister,
V., Thompson, Y., Schneider, R., Tricco, A. C., & Straus, S. E. (2021). Comparative efficacy of
interventions for reducing symptoms of depression in people with dementia: Systematic review
and network meta-analysis. *BMJ (Clinical Research Ed.), 372,* n532.

Yavne, Y., Amital, D., Watad, A., Tiosano, S., & Amital, H. (2018). A systematic review of precipi-
tating physical and psychological traumatic events in the development of fibromyalgia. *Seminars
in Arthritis and Rheumatism, 48*(1), 121–133.

15. Gates of Perception

Bechara, A., Damasio, H., & Damasio, A. R. (2000). Emotion, decision making and the orbitofrontal
cortex. *Cerebral Cortex, 10*(3), 295–307. https://doi.org/10.1093/cercor/10.3.295

Ceunen, E., Vlaeyen, J. W., & Van Diest, I. (2016). On the origin of interoception. *Frontiers in Psychology, 7,* 743. https://doi.org/10.3389/fpsyg.2016.00743

Damasio, H. (1994). *Descartes' error: Emotion, reason and the human brain.* Penguin.

Dana, D. (2021). *The polyvagal theory in therapy: Using the rhythm of regulation.* Norton.

Dankner, Y., Shalev, L., Carrasco, M., & Yuval-Greenberg, S. (2017). Prestimulus inhibition of sac-
cades in adults with and without attention-deficit/hyperactivity disorder as an index of temporal
expectations. *Psychological Science, 28*(7), 835–850. https://doi.org/10.1177/0956797617694863

Fogel, A. (2018). *Self-perception and embodiment in body psychotherapy: From body awareness to cognition.*
Schattauer.

Grassmann, L. & H. (2025) *The polyvagal first aid remedy at home: From an unconscious to conscious orientation
physiology.* https://www.carl-auer.de/magazin/sich-sicher-sein

Grimes, P. Z., Kampoureli, C. N., Rae, C. L., Harrison, N. A., Garfinkel, S. N., Critchley,
H. D., & Eccles, J. A. (2023, October 9). The neural correlates of autonomic interoception in a
clinical sample: Implications for anxiety. *MedRxiv.* https://doi.org/10.1101/2023.05.25.23290230

Hogenboom, M. (2018, April 4). How our heartbeat shapes our thinking. BBC. https://
www.bbc.com/future/article/20180423-how-a-s

Kearney, B. E., & Lanius, R. A. (2022). The brain-body disconnect: A somatic sensory basis for
trauma-related disorders. *Frontiers in Neuroscience, 16.* https://doi.org/10.3389/fnins.2022.1015749

Mahler, K. (2016). *Interoception: The eighth sensory system.* AAPC Publishing.

Merleau-Ponty, M. (1962). *Phenomenology of perception* (C. Smith, Trans.). (Original work published 1945)

NCCIH. (2021, September 3). NIH research projects on interoception to improve understanding of brain-body function. National Institutes of Health. https://www.nih.gov/news-events/news-releases/nih-research-projects-interoception-improve-understanding-brain-body-function

Nord, C. L, & Garfinkel, S. N. (2022). Interoceptive pathways to understand and treat mental health conditions. *Trends in Cognitive Science, 26*(6), 499–513. https://doi.org/10.1016/j.tics.2022.03.004

Porges, S. W. (2022). Polyvagal theory: A science of safety. *Frontiers in Integrative Neuroscience, 16*(27).

Weng, H., Feldman, J., Leggio, L., Napadow, V., Park, J., & Price, C. (2021). Interventions and manipulations of interoception. *Trends in Neurosciences, 44*, 52–62. https://doi.org/10.1016/j.tins.2020.09.010

16. Body Tremors

American Psychiatric Association. (2013). *Diagnostic and statistical manual of mental disorders* (5th ed.).

Berceli, D. (2005). *Trauma releasing exercises (TRE): A revolutionary new method for stress/trauma recovery.* Booksurge.

Berceli, D. (2015). *Shake it off naturally: Reduce stress, anxiety, and tension with TRE.* CreateSpace.

Berceli, D. (2020). *The revolutionary trauma release process: Transcend your toughest times.* Namaste.

Berceli, D., Salmon, M., Bonifas, R., & Ndefo, N. (2014). Effects of self-induced unclassified tremors on quality of life among non-professional caregivers: A pilot study. *Global Advances in Health and Medicine, 3*(5), 45–48.

Fiol, M., Meni Bataglia, F., Belaustegui, F., Martinez Canyazo, C. A., Ysrraelit, M. C., Morin Nissen, M., . . . Correale, J. (2022, October 26–28). Body-mind therapy intervention improves quality of life in people with relapsing remitting multiple sclerosis: A pivotal study. ECTRIMS 2022, 38th Congress of the European Committee for Treatment and Research in Multiple Sclerosis and the 27th Annual RIMS Conference, Amsterdam.

Fogel, A. (2013). *Body sense: The science and practice of embodied self-awareness.* Norton Series on Interpersonal Neurobiology. Norton.

Fogel, A. (2021). *Restorative embodiment and resilience: A guide to disrupt habits, create inner peace, deepen relationships, and feel greater presence.* North Atlantic.

Hart, A. D. (1995). *Adrenaline and stress: The exciting new breakthrough that helps you overcome stress damage.* Thomas Nelson.

Keeney, B. (2007). *Shaking medicine: The healing power of ecstatic movement.* Simon and Schuster.

King, M. L., Jr. (2010). *Where do we go from here: Chaos or community?* National Geographic Books.

Levine, P. (1997). *Waking the tiger: Healing trauma.* North Atlantic.

Liao, X. (2014). *Chi energy: Harness your chi through meditation techniques.* Speedy.

Lynning, M. (2019a, June). Exploring outcomes of tension and trauma releasing exercises (TRE) on people with multiple sclerosis: A pilot study. European Conference for Rehabilitation in Multiple Sclerosis (RIMS), Ljubljana.

Lynning, M. (2019b, June). Perceived benefits of tension and trauma releasing exercises (TRE) among people with multiple sclerosis: Qualitative results from a pilot study. European Conference for Rehabilitation in Multiple Sclerosis (RIMS), Ljubljana.

Lynning, M., Svaneb, C., Westergaard, K., Bergien, S., Gunnersen, S., & Skovgaard, L. (2021). Tension and trauma releasing exercises for people with multiple sclerosis: An exploratory pilot study. *Journal of Traditional and Complementary Medicine, 11*(5), 383–389.

Mandela, N. (2008). *Long walk to freedom: The autobiography of Nelson Mandela.* Hachette.

Nibel, H., & Herold, A. (2019). Körperorientiertes Coaching für ressourcenschonendes Auflösen chronischer Stressreaktionen. In J. Heller (Ed.), *Resilienz für die VUCAWelt: Individuelle und organi-satorische Resilienz entwickeln*. Springer.

Nissen, M. (2015). Using TRE with people with multiple sclerosis (MS) in the Danish Multiple Sclerosis Society. In D. Berceli (Ed.), *Shake it off naturally: Reduce your stress, anxiety and tension with TRE* (pp. 102–120). CreateSpace.

Nissen, M. (2019). TRE as a body-mind therapy working with traumatic consequences of phys-ical and mental illness: Using TRE (tension and trauma releasing exercises) with people with multiple sclerosis (MS) in The Danish Multiple Sclerosis Society. Symposium on the 7. Biennal ESTD (European Society for Trauma & Dissociation) Conference: The Legacy of Trauma and Dissociation: Body and Mind in a New Perspective. October 2019, Rome. Symposium ID SM-0.

Oh, J., & Shin, C. S. (2021). A pilot study on the anxiety reduction effect of tension, stress, and trauma releasing exercises (TRE). *Asia-Pacific Journal of Convergent Research Interchange, 7*, 379–388.

Porges, S. (2011). *The Polyvagal Theory: Neurophysiological foundations of emotions, attachment, communica-tion, and self-regulation*. Norton.

Sapolsky, R. (2004). *Why zebras don't get ulcers: The acclaimed guide to stress, stress-related diseases, and coping*. Holt Paperbacks.

Scaer, R. (2005). *Trauma spectrum: Hidden wounds and human resiliency*. Norton.

Sheldrake, R. (2012). *The physics of consciousness: In the quantum field, minerals, plants, animals and human souls*. Deepak Chopra Books.

Taylor, N., Müller, E., & Shine, M. (2020). Shaking with fear: The role of noradrenaline in modulat-ing resting tremor. *Brain, 143*(5), 1288–1291. https://doi.org/10.1093/brain/awaa109

Tedeschi, R., Shakespeare-Finch, J., Taku, K., & Calhoun, L. (2018). *Posttraumatic growth: Theory, research, and applications*. Routledge.

17. "The Eyes (I's) Have It"

Corrigan, F. M. (2020, May). *Deep brain reorienting: Healing trauma and attachment shock*. Training PowerPoint.

Corrigan, F. M. (2021, August). *Deep brain reorienting (DBR): Healing of emotional shock, attachment wound-ing, and other traumatic experiences*. Training PowerPoint.

Corrigan, F. M., & Christie-Sands, J. (2020). An innate brainstem self-other system involving ori-enting, affective responding, and polyvalent relational seeking: Some clinical implications for a "deep brain reorienting" trauma psychotherapy approach. *Medical Hypotheses, 136*, 109502. https://doi.org/10.1016/j.mehy.2019.109502

Ecker, B., Ticic, R., & Hulley, L. (2012). *Unlocking the emotional brain: Eliminating symptoms at their roots using memory reconsolidation*. Routledge.

Fisher, J. (2017). *Healing the fragmented selves of trauma: Overcoming internal self-alienation*. Routledge.

Fosha, D. (2000). *The transforming power of affect: A model for accelerated change*. Basic Behavioral Science.

Janet, P. (1935). Réalisation et interprétation. *Annales Médico-Psychologiques, 93*, 329–366. Reprinted in *Bulletin de Psychologie, 1994, 47*, 122–142.

Kearney, B. E., Corrigan, F. M., Frewen, P. A., Nevill, S., Harricharan, S. A., Andrew, K., Jetly, R., McKinnon, M. C., & Lanius, R. A. (2023). A randomized controlled trial of deep brain reorient-ing: A neuroscientifically guided treatment for post-traumatic stress disorder. *European Journal of Psychotraumatology, 14*(2), 1–17, 2240791.

Levine, P. (2008). *Healing trauma: A pioneering program for restoring the wisdom of your body*. Sounds True.

Ogden, P., Minton, K., & Pain, C. (2006). *Trauma and the body: A sensorimotor approach to psychotherapy.* Norton.

Panksepp, J., & Biven, L. (2012). *The archaeology of mind: Neuroevolutionary origins of human emotions.* Norton.

Schmidt, S. J. (2009). *The developmental needs meeting strategy: An ego-state therapy for healing adults with childhood trauma and attachment wounds.* DNMS Institute.

Schore, A. N. (2001). The effects of relational trauma on right brain development, affect regulation, and infant mental health. *Infant Mental Health Journal, 22,* 201–269.

Schwarz, L., Corrigan, F., Hull, A., & Raju, R. (2017). *The comprehensive resource model: Effective therapeutic techniques for the healing of complex trauma.* Routledge.

van der Hart, O. (2021). Trauma-related dissociation: An analysis of two conflicting models. *European Journal of Trauma and Dissociation, 5,* 100210. https://doi.org/10.1016/j.ejtd.2021.100210

van der Hart, O., & Piedfort-Marin, O. (2023). Amnesia and hypermnesia as a paradigm of non-realization in trauma-related dissociation: Pierre Janet's case of Irène. *European Journal of Trauma and Dissociation, 7*(4), 100357.

18. Somatic Ego State Therapy With Traumatized Children

Berrueta-Clement, J. R., Schweinhart, L. J., Barnett, W. S., Epstein, A. E., & Weikart, D. P. (1984). *Changed lives: The effects of the Perry Preschool program on youths through age 19.* Monographs of the High/Scope Educational Research Foundation, No. 8. High/Scope Press.

Cuddy, A. (2011, April 6). Boost power through body language. *Harvard Business Review.* https://hbr.org/2011/04/boost-power-through-body-langu.html

Duarte, A. (2022). *Five phases* [online training]. AléDuarte Trainings. https://www.aleduarte.com/

Hartman, W. (2023). *An introduction to ego state therapy.* Carl Auer.

Herzog, M. (2018). *Lily, Ben and Omid: Three children embark on a journey to find their "safe place."* Top Support GmbH.

Herzog, M. (2022). Lily, Ben and Omid in English. [Video]. YouTube. https://youtu.be/NozyGLOb5_s

Kline, M. (2012). *Trauma through a child's eyes: Awakening the ordinary miracle of healing* [Seminar]. Zurich.

Levine, P. (2010). *In an unspoken voice: How the body releases trauma and restores goodness.* North Atlantic.

Levine, P., & Kline, M. (2008). *Trauma-proofing your kids: A parents' guide for instilling confidence, joy and resilience.* North Atlantic.

Lynch, T. (2020). Online Workshop. Ressoucen-Therapie-Zentrum Deutschland. https://ressourcen-therapie-zentrum-deutschland.de

Phillips, M. (2019). *Somatic Ego State Therapy, Advanced 2* [Training]. Zurich.

Porges, S. W. (1995). Orienting in a defensive world: Mammalian modifications of our evolutionary heritage. A Polyvagal Theory. *Psychophysiology, 32*(4), 301–318.

Porges, S. W. (2009). The polyvagal theory: New insights into adaptive reactions of the autonomic nervous system. *Cleveland Clinic Journal of Medicine, 76*(2), 86–89.

Porges, S. W. (2022). Polyvagal theory: A science of safety. *Frontiers in Integrative Neuroscience, 16.* https://doi.org/10.3389/fnint.2022.871227

19. The Relational Intelligence Model of Psychotherapy

Bowlby, J. (1969). *Attachment and loss.* Basic Books.

Brown, D. P., & Elliott, D. S. (2016). *Attachment disturbances in adults.* Norton.

Dana, D. (2018). *The polyvagal theory in therapy.* Norton.

Kozlowska, K., Walker, P., McLean, L., & Carrive, P. (2015). Fear and the defense cascade: Clinical implications and management. *Harvard Review of Psychiatry, 23*(4), 263–287. https://doi.org/10.1097/HRP.0000000000000065

MacLean, D. (1990). *The triune brain in evolution: Role in paleocerebral functions.* Plenum.

Porges, S. W. (2011). *The polyvagal theory: Neurophysiological foundations of emotions, attachment, communication, and self-regulation.* Norton.

Schwartz, R. C. (Ed.). (1995). *Internal family systems therapy.* Guilford.

van der Hart, O., Nijenhuis, E. R. S., & Steele, K. (2006). *The haunted self: Structural dissociation and the treatment of chronic traumatization.* Norton.

van der Kolk, B. (2014). *The body keeps the score.* Penguin.

20. Sensorimotor Psychotherapy

Ardi, Z., Golland, Y., Shafir, R., Sheppes, G., & Levit-Binnun, N. (2021). The effects of mindfulness-based stress reduction on the association between autonomic interoceptive signals and emotion regulation selection. *Psychosomatic Medicine, 83*, 852–862. https://doi.org/10.1097/PSY.0000000000000994

Bowlby, J. (1988). *A secure base: Parent-child attachment and healthy human development.* Basic Books.

Buckley, T., Punkanen, M., & Ogden, P. (2018). The role of the body in fostering resilience: A sensorimotor psychotherapy perspective. *Body, Movement and Dance in Psychotherapy, 13*, 225–233. https://doi.org/10.1080/17432979.2018.1467344

Classen, C., Hughes, L., Clark, C., Hill Mohammed, B., Woods, P., & Beckett, B. (2020). A pilot RCT of a body-oriented group therapy for complex trauma survivors: An adaptation of sensorimotor psychotherapy. *Journal of Trauma and Dissociation, 22*, 52–68. https://doi.org/10.1080/15299732.2020.1760173

Cohen, B. (1993). *Sensing, feeling and action.* Contact.

de Waal, F. (2019). *Mama's last hug: Animal emotions and what they teach us about ourselves.* Norton.

Farb, N., Daubenmier, J., Price, C. J., Gard, T., Kerr, C., Dunn, B. D., Klein, A. C., Paulus, M. P., & Mehling, W. E. (2015). Interoception, contemplative practice, and health. *Frontiers in Psychology, 6*, 763. https://doi.org/10.3389/fpsyg.2015.00763

Frank, R., & La Barre, F. (2010). *The first year and the rest of your life: Movement, development, and psychotherapeutic change.* Routledge.

Gene-Cos, N., Fisher, J., Ogden, P., & Cantrel, A. (2016). Sensorimotor psychotherapy group therapy in the treatment of complex PTSD. *Annals of Psychiatry and Mental Health, 4*, 1080. https://doi.org/10.47739/2374-0124/1080

Kearney, B. E., & Lanius, R. A. (2022). The brain-body disconnect: A somatic sensory basis for trauma-related disorders. *Frontiers in Neuroscience, 16*, 1015749. https://doi.org/10.3389/fnins.2022.1015749

Kurtz, R. (1990). *Body-centered psychotherapy: The Hakomi method.* LifeRhythm.

Langmuir, J. I., Kirsh, S. G., & Classen, C. C. (2012). A pilot study of body-oriented group psychotherapy: Adapting sensorimotor psychotherapy for the group treatment of trauma. *Psychological Trauma: Theory, Research, Practice, and Policy, 4*, 214–220. https://doi.org/10.1037/a0025588

Main, M., & Hesse, E. (1990). Parents' unresolved traumatic experiences are related to infant disorganized attachment status: Is frightened and/or frightening parental behavior the linking mechanism? In M. T. Greenberg, D. Cicchetti, & E. M. Cummings (Eds.), *Attachment in the preschool years: Theory, research and intervention* (pp. 161–182). University of Chicago Press.

Maté, G., & Maté, D. (2022). *The myth of normal.* Vermilion.

Ogden, P. (2018). Play, creativity and movement vocabulary. In T. Marks-Tarlow, D. J. Siegel, & M. Solomon (Eds.), *Play and creativity in psychotherapy* (pp. 92–110). Norton.

Ogden, P. (2021a). The different impact of trauma and relational stress on physiology, posture, and movement: Implications for treatment. *European Journal of Trauma and Dissociation, 5*(4), 100172. https://doi.org/10.1016/j.ejtd.2020.100172

Ogden, P. (2021b). *Pocket guide to sensorimotor psychotherapy in context.* Norton.

Ogden, P., & Fisher, J. (2015). *Sensorimotor psychotherapy: Interventions for trauma and attachment.* Norton.

Ogden, P., Minton, K., & Pain, C. (2006). *Trauma and the body: A sensorimotor approach to psychotherapy.* Norton.

Porges, S. W. (2018). Polyvagal theory: A primer. In S. W. Porges & D. Dana (Eds.), *Clinical applications of the polyvagal theory: The emergence of polyvagal-informed therapies* (pp. 50–69). Norton.

Schore, A. (2003). *Affect regulation and the repair of the self.* Norton.

Sensorimotor Psychotherapy Institute. (2023, November 7). *About.* https://sensorimotorpsychotherapy.org/about/#mission

van de Kamp, M. M., Scheffers, M., Hatzmann, J., Emck, C., Cuijpers, P., & Beek, P. J. (2019). Body- and movement-oriented interventions for posttraumatic stress disorder: A systematic review and meta-analysis. *Journal of Traumatic Stress, 32*, 967–976. https://doi.org/10.1002/JTS.22465

van der Kolk, B. A. (2015). *The body keeps the score: Brain, mind and body in the treatment of trauma.* Viking.

21. Being Together to Face the Trauma

Bromberg, P. (2011). *The Shadow of the Tsunami: And the Growth of the Relational Mind.* Routledge.

Chaiklin, S., & Schmais, D. (1986). The Chace approach to dance therapy. In P. Lewis (Ed.), *Theoretical approaches to dance/movement therapy* (Vol. 1, pp. 17–36). Kendall/Hunt.

Dana, D. (2020). *Polyvagal exercises for safety and connection: 50 client-centered practices.* Norton.

Downing, G. (1996). *Körper und Wort in der Psychotherapie.* Leitlinien für die Praxis.

Gallese, V. (2005). Embodied simulation: From neurons to phenomenal experience. *Phenomenology and the Cognitive Sciences, 4,* 23–48.

Gallese, V. (2017). Mirroring, a liberated embodied simulation and experience. In H. Hirsch, A. Pace, G. Bernegger, & V. Gallese (Eds.), *MirrorImages: Reflections in Art and Medicine* (pp. 27–37). Verlag für modern Kunst.

Geller, S. M., & Porges, S. W. (2014). Therapeutic presence: Neurophysiological mechanisms mediating feeling safe in therapeutic relationships. *Journal of Psychotherapy Integration, 24*(3), 178–192.

Gianino, A., & Tronick, E. Z. (1998). The mutual regulation model: The infant's self and interactive regulation, coping, and defensive capacities. In T. Field, P. McCabe, & N. Schneiderman (Eds.), *Stress and coping* (pp. 47–68). Erlbaum.

Grassmann, H., & Pohlenz-Michel, C. (2008). *The reorganization of the somatic memory system.* Iasi.

Hopper, E. K., Grossman, F. K., Spinazzola, J., & Zucker, M. (2019). *Treating adult survivors of childhood emotional abuse and neglect.* Guilford.

Stupiggia, M. (2013). From hopeless solitude to the sense of being-with. *International Body Psychotherapy Journal, 11*(1), 25–40.

22. Humanual Polyvagal Smile

Coghill, G. E. (1929). *Anatomy and the problem of behavior.* Macmillan.

Dewey, J. (1978). Preoccupation with the disconnected. In W. Barlow (Ed.), *More talk of Alexander* (p. 105). Camelot Press. (Original work published 1928)

Jones, F. P. (1997). *Freedom to change.* Mouritz. Originally published as *Body awareness in action: A study of the Alexander technique.* Schocken, 1976.

Levine, P. (1997). *Waking the Tiger.* North Atlantic Books.

Levine, P. (2010). *In an unspoken voice.* North Atlantic Books.

Magnus, R. (1926). Some results of studies in the physiology of posture. *Lancet, 208,* 531–536; 585–588.

Maté, G., & Maté, D. (2022). *The myth of normal.* Avery.

Porges, S., & Howard, A. (2023). How to cultivate a state of safety. Trauma Super Conference [Online conference]. https://www.consciouslife.com/

Roberts, T. D. M. (1967). *Neurophysiology of postural mechanisms.* Plenum.

Sherrington, C. (1961). *The integrative action of the nervous system.* Yale University Press.

Stough, C. (1996). *Breathing: The source of life* [DVD video]. Stough Institute.

Stough, C., with Stough, R. (1970). *Dr. Breath: The story of breathing coordination.* William Morrow.

Tinbergen, N. (1974). Ethology and stress disease. *Science, 185,* 20–27.

Wikipedia. (2023, July 7). Ground reaction force. https://en.wikipedia.org/wiki/Ground_reaction _force

23. SIMPLE Listening

Becker, R. E. (1997a). Be still and know. In R. Brooks (Ed.), *Life in motion* (pp. 24–38). Stillness Press. (Original work published 1965)

Becker, R. E. (1997b). Using the aliveness. In R. Brooks (Ed.), *Life in motion* (pp. 16–18). Stillness Press. (Original work published 1986)

Brough, N., Lindenmeyer, A., Thistlethwaite, J., Lewith, G., & Stewart-Brown, S. (2015). *Perspectives on the effects and mechanisms of craniosacral therapy: A qualitative study of users' views. European Journal of Integrative Medicine, 7,* 172–183.

Brough, N., Stewart-Brown, S., Parsons, H., & Perera, C. (2021). Development and validation of a PROM to capture holistic outcomes in traditional, complementary and integrative medicine—the Warwick Holistic Health Questionnaire (WHHQ-18). *European Journal of Integrative Medicine, 47,* 101375.

Corbett, L. (2014). Silence, presence, and witness in psychotherapy. *Jungian Odyssey 2013, 6.*

Damasio, A. (2000). *The feeling of what happens: Body, emotion and the making of consciousness.* Random House.

Dana, D. (2018). *The polyvagal theory in therapy: Engaging the rhythm of regulation.* Norton.

Feldman Barrett, L. (2020). *Seven and a half lessons about the brain.* Picador.

Gendlin, E. T. (1997). *Experiencing and the creation of meaning: A philosophical and psychological approach to the subjective.* Northwestern University Press.

Jung, C. G. (1967). Commentary on "The secret of the golden flower." In R. F. C. Hull (Trans.), *Alchemical studies* (Vol. 13, pp. 1–56). Princeton University Press. (Original work published 1929)

Kalsched, D. (2013). *Trauma and the soul: A psycho-spiritual approach to human development and its interruption.* Routledge.

Lau, D. C. (1963). *Tao te ching: Original text translation with introduction.* Penguin.

Levine, P. A. (2010). *In an unspoken voice: How the body releases trauma and restores goodness.* North Atlantic Books.

Maté, G. (2003). *When the body says no: The cost of hidden stress.* Vintage.

Porges, S. W. (1995). Orienting in a defensive world: Mammalian modifications of our evolutionary heritage. Polyvagal theory. *Psychophysiology, 32,* 301–318. https://doi.org/10.1111/j.1469-8986 .1995.tb01213.x

Porges, S. W. (2011). *The polyvagal theory.* Norton.

Porges, S. W. (2022). Polyvagal theory: A science of safety. *Frontiers in Integrative Neuroscience, 16.* https://doi.org/10.3389/fnint.2022.871227

Siegel, D. J. (2012). *The developing mind: How relationships and the brain interact to shape who we are.* Guilford.

Sills, F. (2001). *Craniosacral biodynamics* (Vol. 1). North Atlantic.

Slingerland, E. (2015). Wu-wei—doing less and wanting more. *Psychologist, 28*(11), 882–885.

Sumner, G., & Haines, S. (2010). *Cranial intelligence.* Singing Dragon.

Sutherland, W. G., & Wales, A. L. (1990). *Teachings in the science of osteopathy.* Sutherland Cranial Teaching Foundation. (Original work published 1949)

van der Kolk, B. (2014). *The body keeps the score.* Penguin.

Watts, A. (2000). *What is tao?* New World Library.

24. Supporting Safety With Movement

Chen, W. G., Schloesser, D., Arensdorf, A. M., Simmons, J. M., Cui, C., Valentino, R., Gnadt, J. W., Nielsen, L., Hillaire-Clarke, C. S., Spruance, V., Horowitz, T. S., Vallejo, Y. F., & Langevin, H. M. (2021). The emerging science of interoception: Sensing, integrating, interpreting, and regulating signals within the self. *Trends in Neurosciences, 44*(1), 3–16. https://doi.org/10.1016/j.tins.2020.10.007

Cottingham, J. T., Porges, S. W., & Lyon, T. (1988). Effects of soft tissue mobilization (Rolfing pelvic lift) on parasympathetic tone in two age groups. *Physical Therapy, 68*(3), 352–356. https://doi.org/10.1093/ptj/68.3.352

Cottingham, J. T., Porges, S. W., & Richmond, K. (1988). Shifts in pelvic inclination angle and parasympathetic tone produced by Rolfing soft tissue manipulation. *Physical Therapy, 68*(9), 1364–1370. https://doi.org/10.1093/ptj/68.9.1364

Eneberg-Boldon, K., Schaack, B., & Joyce, K. (2020). Pain neuroscience education as the foundation of interdisciplinary pain treatment. *Physical Medicine and Rehabilitation Clinics of North America, 31*(4), 541–551. https://doi.org/10.1016/j.pmr.2020.07.004

Farb, N., Daubenmier, J., Price, C. J., Gard, T., Kerr, C., Dunn, B. D., Klein, A. C., Paulus, M. P., & Mehling, W. E. (2015). Interoception, contemplative practice, and health. *Frontiers in Psychology, 6,* 763. https://doi.org/10.3389/fpsyg.2015.00763

Gaiswinkler, L., & Unterrainer, H. F. (2016). The relationship between yoga involvement, mindfulness and psychological well-being. *Complementary Therapies in Medicine, 26,* 123–127. https://doi.org/10.1016/j.ctim.2016.03.011

Haase, L., Stewart, J. L., Youssef, B., May, A. C., Isakovic, S., Simmons, A. N., Johnson, D. C., Potterat, E. G., & Paulus, M. P. (2016). When the brain does not adequately feel the body:

Links between low resilience and interoception. *Biological .Psychology*, *113*, 37–45. https://doi.org/10.1016/j.biopsycho.2015.11.004

Ivtzan, I., & Jegatheeswaran, S. (2015). The yoga boom in Western society: Practitioners' spiritual vs. physical intentions and their impact on psychological wellbeing. *Journal of Yoga and Physical Therapy*, *5*(3). https://doi.org/10.4172/2157-7595.1000204

Ivtzan, I., & Papantoniou, A. (2014). Yoga meets positive psychology: Examining the integration of hedonic (gratitude) and eudaimonic (meaning) wellbeing in relation to the extent of yoga practice. *Journal of Bodywork and Movement Therapies*, *18*(2), 183–189. https://doi.org/10.1016/j.jbmt.2013.11.005

King, R., Robinson, V., Ryan, C. G., & Martin, D. J. (2016). An exploration of the extent and nature of reconceptualisation of pain following pain neurophysiology education: A qualitative study of experiences of people with chronic musculoskeletal pain. *Patient Education and Counseling*, *99*(8), 1389–1393. https://doi.org/10.1016/j.pec.2016.03.008

Miller, B. S. (Trans.). (2004). *The Bhagavad-Gita: Krishna's counsel in time of war*. Bantam.

Moseley, G. L., & Butler, D. S. (2015). Fifteen years of explaining pain: The past, present, and future. *Journal of Pain*, *16*(9), 807–813. https://doi.org/10.1016/j.jpain.2015.05.005

Patanjali. (1996). *Yoga: Discipline of freedom* (B. S. Miller, Trans.). University of California Press.

Payne, P., & Crane-Godreau, M. A. (2013). Meditative movement for depression and anxiety. *Frontiers in Psychiatry*, *4*, 71. https://doi.org/10.3389/fpsyt.2013.00071

Payne, P., & Crane-Godreau, M. A. (2015). The preparatory set: A novel approach to understanding stress, trauma, and the bodymind therapies. *Frontiers in Human Neuroscience*, *9*. https://doi.org/10.3389/fnhum.2015.00178

Porges, S. W. (2021). *Polyvagal safety: Attachment, communication, self-regulation*. Norton.

Robinson, V., King, R., Ryan, C. G., & Martin, D. J. (2016). A qualitative exploration of people's experiences of pain neurophysiological education for chronic pain: The importance of relevance for the individual. *Manual Therapy*, *22*, 56–61. https://doi.org/10.1016/j.math.2015.10.001

Russell, T. A., & Arcuri, S. M. (2015). A neurophysiological and neuropsychological consideration of mindful movement: Clinical and research implications. *Frontiers in Human Neuroscience*, *9*. https://doi.org/10.3389/fnhum.2015.00282

Schmalzl, L., Powers, C., & Henje Blom, E. (2015). Neurophysiological and neurocognitive mechanisms underlying the effects of yoga-based practices: Towards a comprehensive theoretical framework. *Frontiers in Human Neuroscience*, *9*, 235. https://doi.org/10.3389/fnhum.2015.00235

Schmalzl, L., Powers, C., Zanesco, A. P., Yetz, N., Groessl, E. J., & Saron, C. D. (2018). The effect of movement-focused and breath-focused yoga practice on stress parameters and sustained attention: A randomized controlled pilot study. *Consciousness and Cognition*, *65*, 109–125. https://doi.org/10.1016/j.concog.2018.07.012

Shafir, T. (2016). Using movement to regulate emotion: Neurophysiological findings and their application in psychotherapy. *Frontiers in Psychology*, *7*, 1451. https://doi.org/10.3389/fpsyg.2016.01451

Shafir, T., Tsachor, R. P., & Welch, K. B. (2015). Emotion regulation through movement: Unique sets of movement characteristics are associated with and enhance basic emotions. *Frontiers in Psychology*, *6*, 2030. https://doi.org/10.3389/fpsyg.2015.02030

Siddall, B., Ram, A., Jones, M. D., Booth, J., Perriman, D., & Summers, S. J. (2022). Short-term impact of combining pain neuroscience education with exercise for chronic musculoskeletal pain: A systematic review and meta-analysis. *Pain*, *163*(1), e20–e30. https://doi.org/10.1097/j.pain.0000000000002308

Smith, J. A., Greer, T., Sheets, T., & Watson, S. (2011). Is there more to yoga than exercise? *Alternative Therapies in Health and Medicine*, *17*(3), 22–29.

Sullivan, M. B., Erb, M., Schmalzl, L., Moonaz, S., Noggle Taylor, J., & Porges, S. W. (2018). Yoga therapy and polyvagal theory: The convergence of traditional wisdom and contemporary neuroscience for self-regulation and resilience. *Frontiers in Human Neuroscience*, *12*, 67. https://doi.org/10.3389/fnhum.2018.00067

Sullivan, M., & Hyland Robertson, L. C. (2020). *Understanding yoga therapy: Applied philosophy and science for health and well-being*. Routledge.

Sullivan, M. B., Moonaz, S., Weber, K., Taylor, J. N., & Schmalzl, L. (2018). Toward an explanatory framework for yoga therapy informed by philosophical and ethical perspectives. *Alternative Therapies in Health and Medicine*, *24*(1), 38–47.

Svatmarama. (2012). *The hatha yoga pradipika* (B. D. Akers, Trans.). YogaVidya.com.

Tsachor, R. P., & Shafir, T. (2017). A somatic movement approach to fostering emotional resiliency through Laban movement analysis. *Frontiers in Human Neuroscience*, *11*, 410. https://doi.org/10.3389/fnhum.2017.00410

Watson, J. A., Ryan, C. G., Cooper, L., Ellington, D., Whittle, R., Lavender, M., Dixon, J., Atkinson, G., Cooper, K., & Martin, D. J. (2019). Pain neuroscience education for adults with chronic musculoskeletal pain: A mixed-methods systematic review and meta-analysis. *Journal of Pain*, *20*(10), 1140.e1–1140.e22. https://doi.org/10.1016/j.jpain.2019.02.011

Weng, H. Y., Feldman, J. L., Leggio, L., Napadow, V., Park, J., & Price, C. J. (2021). Interventions and manipulations of interoception. *Trends in Neurosciences*, *44*(1), 52–62. https://doi.org/10.1016/j.tins.2020.09.010

Wijma, A. J., Speksnijder, C. M., Crom-Ottens, A. F., Knulst-Verlaan, J. M. C., Keizer, D., Nijs, J., & van Wilgen, C. P. (2018). What is important in transdisciplinary pain neuroscience education? A qualitative study. *Disability and Rehabilitation*, *40*(18), 2181–2191. https://doi.org/10.1080/09638288.2017.1327990

Wood, L., & Hendrick, P. A. (2019). A systematic review and meta-analysis of pain neuroscience education for chronic low back pain: Short- and long-term outcomes of pain and disability. *European Journal of Pain*, *23*(2), 234–249. https://doi.org/10.1002/ejp.1314

26. Perinatal Mortality and Grief

Baldwin, D. (2013). Primitive mechanisms of trauma response: An evolutionary perspective on trauma-related disorders. *Neuroscience and Biobehavioral Reviews*, *37*, 1549–1566.

Bauman, Z. (2006). *Liquid modernity*. Wiley.

Bernardi, C. (2004). *Il teatro sociale: L'arte tra disagio e cura*. Carocci.

Davis, M., & Astrachan, D. (1978). Conditioned fear and startle magnitude: Effects of different footshock or backshock intensities used in training. *Journal of Experimental Psychology: Animal Behavior Processes*, *4*, 95–103.

Downing, G. (1995). *Körper und Wort in der Psychotherapie: Leitlinien für die Praxis*. Kösel.

Fenstermacher, K., & Hupcey, J. E. (2013). Perinatal bereavement: A principle-based concept analysis. *Journal of Advanced Nursing*, *69*(11), 2389–2400.

Fondazione Confalonieri Ragonese. (2023, February 17). *Gestione della morte endouterina fetale (MEF). Prendersi cura della natimortalità*.

Geller, S. & Porges, S. (2014). Therapeutic presence: Neurophysiological mechanisms mediating feeling safe in therapeutic relationships. *Journal of Psychotherapy Integration*, *24*(3), 178–192.

Istituto Superiore della Sanità. (2020, December). *Rapporti ISTISAN 20/29: Implementazione e validazione del sistema di Sorveglianza Perinatale di Italian Obstetric Surveillance System (SPItOSS)*.

Krosch, D. J., & Shakespeare-Finch, J. (2017). Grief, traumatic stress, and posttraumatic growth in women who have experienced pregnancy loss. *Psychological Trauma: Theory, Research, Practice, and Policy, 9*(4), 425.

Layne, L. L. (2003). *Motherhood lost: A feminist account of pregnancy loss in America*. Routledge.

Liss, J. (2004). *L'ascolto profondo: Manuale per le relazioni d'aiuto*. La Meridiana.

Liss, J., & Stupiggia, M. (2000). *La terapia biosistemica: Un approccio originale al trattamento psico-corporeo della sofferenza emotiva*. FrancoAngeli.

Moules, N. J., Simonson, K., Prins, M., Angus, P., & Bell, J. M. (2004). Making room for grief: Walking backwards and living forward. *Nursing Inquiry, 11*(2), 99–107.

Sozzi, M. (2014). *Reinventare la morte: Introduzione alla tanatologia*. Gius. Laterza e Figli Spa.

Stroebe, M. S. (2001). Bereavement research and theory: Retrospective and prospective. *American Behavioral Scientist, 44*(5), 854–865.

Stupiggia, M. (2007). *Il corpo violato*. La Meridiana.

van der Kolk, B. (2015). *The body keeps the score: Mind, brain and body in the transformation of trauma*. Penguin.

Walter, T. (1999). *On bereavement: The culture of grief*. McGraw-Hill Education.

Zhang, W.-N., Murphy, C., & Feldon, J. (2004). Behavioural and cardiovascular responses during latent inhibition of conditioned fear: Measurement by telemetry and conditioned freezing. *Behavioural Brain Research, 154*, 199–209.

27. Ritual Practice, Addiction, Obsessive-Compulsive Behavior, and Routine

Alexander, B. K., & Smyth, M. (2022). Challenging global dislocation through local community and ritual. In J. Gordon-Lennox (Ed.), *Coping ritual in fearful times: An unexplored resource for healing trauma* (pp. 151–162). Springer Nature.

Dissanayake, E. (2017). The art of ritual and the ritual of art. In J. Gordon-Lennox (Ed.), *Emerging ritual in secular societies: A transdisciplinary conversation* (pp. 22–39). Jessica Kingsley.

Gordon-Lennox, J. (2016). *Crafting secular ritual: A practical guide*. Jessica Kingsley.

Gordon-Lennox, J. (2017). Introduction: The rhyme and reason of ritualmaking. In J. Gordon-Lennox (Ed.), *Emerging ritual in secular societies: A transdisciplinary conversation* (pp. 11–15; 70–85). Jessica Kingsley.

Gordon-Lennox, J. (2019). *Crafting meaningful wedding rituals: A practical guide*. Jessica Kingsley.

Gordon-Lennox, J. (2020). *Crafting meaningful funeral rituals: A practical guide*. Jessica Kingsley.

Gordon-Lennox, J. (2022). Introduction: "Dead land dead water." In J. Gordon-Lennox (Ed.), *Coping rituals in fearful times: An unexplored resource for healing trauma* (pp. 1–22; 191–210). Springer Nature.

Hinds, A. L., Woody, E. Z., Van Ameringen, M., Schmidt, L. A., & Szechtman, H. (2012). When too much is not enough: Obsessive-compulsive disorder as a pathology of stopping, rather than starting. *PLoS One, 7*(1), e30586. https://doi.org/10.1371/journal.pone.0030586

Knottnerus, J. D. (1997). The theory of structural ritualization. *Advances in Group Processes, 14*.

Knottnerus, J. D. (2016). *Ritual as a missing link: Sociology, structural ritualization theory and research*. Routledge.

Knottnerus, J. D. (2022). Foreword. In J. Gordon-Lennox (Ed.), *Coping rituals in fearful times: An unexplored resource for healing trauma* (pp. vii–xiii). Springer Nature.

Knottnerus, J. D. (2023a). *Polar expeditions: Discovering rituals of success within hazardous endeavors.* Routledge.

Knottnerus, J. D. (2023b). Ritual dynamics, theory, and research: Summary and update, structural ritualization theory (SRT) [Unpublished manuscript]. Department of Sociology, Oklahoma State University.

Maté, G., & Maté, D. (2022). *The myth of normal: Trauma, illness and healing in a toxic culture.* Penguin.

McGinnis, J. (2010). *Avicenna.* Oxford.

Nilsson Stutz, L., & Stutz, A. J. (2022). Deeply human: Archaeological traces of rituals for coping with death, adversity, and trauma. In J. Gordon-Lennox (Ed.), *Coping rituals in fearful times: An unexplored resource for healing trauma* (pp. 23–42). Springer Nature.

Porges, S. W. (2011). *The polyvagal theory: Neurophysiological foundations of emotions, attachment, communication, and self-regulation.* Norton Series on Interpersonal Neurobiology. Norton.

Porges, S. W. (2017). *The pocket guide to polyvagal theory: The transformative power of feeling safe.* Norton.

Porges, S. W. (2022a). Ancient rituals, contemplative practices, and vagal pathways. In J. Gordon-Lennox (Ed.), *Coping rituals in fearful times: An unexplored resource for healing trauma.* Springer Nature.

Porges, S. W. (2022b). Polyvagal theory: A science of safety. *Frontiers in Integrative Neuroscience, 16,* 871227. https://doi.org/10.3389/fnint.2022.871227

Porges, S. W., & Porges, S. (2023). *Our polyvagal world: How safety and trauma change us.* Norton.

Scaer, R. C. (2014). *The body bears the burden: Trauma, dissociation, and disease.* Routledge. (Original work published 2001)

Selye, H. (1984). *The stress of life.* McGraw Hill. (Original work published 1956)

28. Transcending Sexual Trauma Through Yoga

Breathe Network. (2023). Alternative therapies for survivors of sexual assault survey. Google Docs. https://drive.google.com/file/d/1_zu8J4BxYwux3n2-zIT8NmQ8tIKSHduf/view?usp=sharing

Brown, B. (2010, June). *The power of vulnerability* [Video]. TED Conferences. https://www.ted.com/talks/brene_brown_the_power_of_vulnerability/transcript?language=en

Cahill, A. J. (2001). *Rethinking rape.* Cornell University Press.

Centers for Disease Control and Prevention. (n.d.). *About the CDC-Kaiser ACE study.* United States Department of Health & Human Services. https://www.cdc.gov/violenceprevention/aces/about.html

Davidson, M. M. (2019). *Exploring the efficacy of trauma-informed yoga for survivors of sexual assault on college campuses.* Unpublished manuscript.

Einolf, C., & Boeder Harris, M. (2015). *Alternative therapies for survivors of sexual assault survey.* The Breathe Network.

Kain, K. L., & Terrell, S. J. (2018). *Nurturing resilience: Helping clients move forward from developmental trauma—an integrative somatic approach.* North Atlantic.

Levine, P. A. (2012). *In an unspoken voice: How the body releases trauma and restores goodness.* North Atlantic.

Ndefo, N., Murphy, D., Kelley, F., Schaffer, J., hayes, s., Molina-Marshall, S., Holzmann, M., Sapien, V., Howard, M., Carter, B., Gunn, A., Edison, N., Johnson, K., munson, m., Poitra, S., Barrett, M., Pauls, R., Rivera, I., Azad, A., Johnson, E., Smith, K., Yang, P., Lee, T., Mourning, R., Patterson, J., Busby, K., Benjamin, B., Siy, E., Collier, E., Gold, P., Hopper, J., Young, S., Bryant, C., Khoudari, L., & Yamasaki, Z. (n.d.). *Holding a healing space: A holistic training in supporting sexual trauma survivors.* The Breathe Network. https://www.thebreathenetwork.org/holding-healing-space/

Ogden, P., Minton, K., & Pain, C. (2006). *Trauma and the body: A sensorimotor approach to psychotherapy.* Norton.

Yamasaki, Z. (2022). *Trauma-informed yoga for survivors of sexual assault: Practices for healing and teaching with compassion.* Norton.

29. Turning Competition Into Coregulation

Eichenholz, A. (2023, September 11). Novak Djokovic is redefining what is possible: Serbian reflects on claiming his 24th major title. *ATP Tour.* https://www.atptour.com/en/news/djokovic-us-open-2023-final-reaction

30. The Free Voice

Feuerstein, U. (2000). *Stimmig sein: Die Selbstregulation der Stimme in Gesang und Stimmtherapie.* Junfermann.
Jacoby, P. (1991). Evolution und Psychosomatik der Stimmfunktion. In W. Rohmert (Ed.), *Grundzüge des funktionalen Stimmtrainings.* O. Schmidt.
Porges, S. W. (2021). *Polyvagal safety: Attachment, communication, self-regulation.* Norton.

31. Continuum Movement

Barnstaple, R., Protzak, J., DeSouza, J. F., & Gramann, K. (2021). Mobile brain/body imaging in dance: A dynamic transdisciplinary field for applied research. *European Journal of Neuroscience, 54*(12), 8355–8363.
Beaulieu, J., & Perez-Martinez, D. (2018). Sound healing, theory, and practice. In A. Bakhru (Ed.), *Nutrition and integrative medicine* (pp. 449–469). CRC Press.
Bertalanffy, L. V. (1968). *General system theory: Foundations, development, applications.* G. Braziller.
Bohm, D. (1980). *Wholeness and the implicate order.* Routledge.
Brown, R., & Gerbarg, P. (2005). Sudarshan Kriya yogic breathing in the treatment of stress, anxiety, and depression: Part I. Neurophysiologic model. *Journal of Alternative and Complementary Medicine, 11*(1), 189–201.
Brown, R. P., & Gerbarg, P. L. (2009). Yoga breathing, meditation, and longevity. *Annals of the New York Academy of Sciences, 1172*(1), 54–62.
Chaplin, D. D. (2010). Overview of the immune response. *Journal of Allergy and Clinical Immunology, 125*(2, Suppl. 2), S3–S23. https://doi.org/10.1016/j.jaci.2009.12.980
Conrad, E. (2007). *Life on land: The story of Continuum.* North Atlantic.
Continuum Movement. (2020). Emilie's legacy series Pt 1: Don Hanlon Johnson—uncontaminated creative juices. YouTube. https://www.youtube.com/watch?v=SU8AkbUzNRI
Continuum Movement. (2023). Essential elements of Continuum. https://continuummovement.com/essential-elements-of-continuum/
Damerla, V. R., Goldstein, B., Wolf, D., Madhavan, K., & Patterson, N. (2018). Novice meditators of an easily learnable audible mantram sound self-induce an increase in vagal tone during short-term practice: A preliminary study. *Integrative Medicine: A Clinician's Journal, 17*(5), 20.
Denver, J. W., Reed, S. F., & Porges, S. W. (2007). Methodological issues in the quantification of respiratory sinus arrhythmia. *Biological Psychology, 74*(2), 286–294.
Doussard-Roosevelt, J., & Porges, S. (1999). *The role of neurobehavioral organization in stress responses: A polyvagal model.* Erlbaum.

Fontanesi, C. (2020). *Rehabilitative movement: Approaches and dance interventions in Parkinson's disease.* City University of New York.

Fontanesi, C., & DeSouza, J. (2021). Beauty that moves: Dance for Parkinson's effects on affect, self-efficacy, gait symmetry, and dual task performance. *Frontiers in Psychology, 11,* 3896.

Heatherton, T., & Wagner, D. (2011). Cognitive neuroscience of self-regulation failure. *Trends in Cognitive Sciences, 15*(3), 132–139. https://doi.org/10.1016/j.tics.2010.12.005

Hunt, V. (1996). *Infinite mind: Science of the human vibrations of consciousness.* Malibu.

Inbaraj, G., Rao, R. M., Ram, A., Bayari, S. K., Belur, S., Prathyusha, P. V., … & Udupa, K. (2022). Immediate effects of OM chanting on heart rate variability measures compared between experienced and inexperienced yoga practitioners. *International Journal of Yoga, 15*(1), 52.

Kerna, N. A., Chawla, S., Carsrud, N. D. V., Holets, H. M., Brown, S. M., Flores, J. V., … & Oghenetega, E. A. (2022). Sound therapy: Vibratory frequencies of cells in healthy and disease states. *EC Clinical and Medical Case Reports, 5,* 112–123.

Kshtriya, S., Barnstaple, R., Rabinovich, D. B., & DeSouza, J. F. (2015). Dance and aging: A critical review of findings in neuroscience. *American Journal of Dance Therapy, 37,* 81–112.

Levine, P. (2012). *In an unspoken voice: How the body releases trauma and restores goodness.* Random House.

Lewis, G. F., Furman, S. A., McCool, M. F., & Porges, S. W. (2012). Statistical strategies to quantify respiratory sinus arrhythmia: Are commonly used metrics equivalent? *Biological Psychology, 89*(2), 349–364.

Marshall, J. S., Warrington, R., Watson, W., & Kim, H. L. (2018). An introduction to immunology and immunopathology. *Allergy, Asthma and Clinical Immunology, 14*(Suppl. 2), 49. https://doi.org/10.1186/s13223-018-0278-1

Neukirch, N., Reid, S., & Shires, A. (2019). Yoga for PTSD and the role of interoceptive awareness: A preliminary mixed-methods case series study. *European Journal of Trauma and Dissociation, 3*(1), 7–15.

Ogden, P., Minton, K., & Pain, C. (2006). *Trauma and the body: A sensorimotor approach to psychotherapy.* Norton.

Payne, P., Levine, P. A., & Crane-Godreau, M. A. (2015). Somatic experiencing: Using interoception and proprioception as core elements of trauma therapy. *Frontiers in Psychology, 6,* 93.

Porges, S. (2001). The polyvagal theory: Phylogenetic substrates of a social nervous system. *International Journal of Psychophysiology, 42*(2), 123–146.

Porges, S. (2005). The role of social engagement in attachment and bonding. In C. S. Carter, L. Ahnert, K. E. Grossmann, S. B. Hardy, M. E. Lamb, S. W. Porges, & N. Sachser (Eds.), *Attachment and bonding: A new synthesis,* 33–54. MIT Press.

Porges, S. (2011). *The polyvagal theory: Neurophysiological foundations of emotions, attachment, communication, and self-regulation.* Norton.

Porges, S. W. (2004). Neuroception: A subconscious system for detecting threats and safety. *Zero to Three, 24*(5), 19–24.

Porges, S. W. (2021). Cardiac vagal tone: A neurophysiological mechanism that evolved in mammals to dampen threat reactions and promote sociality. *World Psychiatry, 20*(2), 296.

Price, C. J., & Hooven, C. (2018). Interoceptive awareness skills for emotion regulation: Theory and approach of mindful awareness in body-oriented therapy (MABT). *Frontiers in Psychology, 9,* 798.

Reich, W. (1973). *The function of the orgasm.* Farrar, Straus and Giroux.

Reinhardt, K. M., Zerubavel, N., Young, A. S., Gallo, M., Ramakrishnan, N., Henry, A., & Zucker, N. L. (2020). A multi-method assessment of interoception among sexual trauma survivors. *Physiology and Behavior, 226,* 113108.

Selvaraj, N., Shivplara, N. B., Bhatia, M., Santhosh, J., Deepak, K. K., & Anand, S. (2008). Heart rate dynamics during shambhavi mahamudra—a practice of Isha yoga. *Journal of Complementary and Integrative Medicine, 5*(1). https://doi.org/10.2202/1553-3840.1137

Siegel, D. (2003). *Healing trauma: Mind, body, and brain.* Norton.

Simard, S. (2022). *Finding the mother tree.* Vintage.

Simard, S., Beiler, K., Bingham, M., Deslippe, J., Philip, L., & Teste, F. (2012). Mycorrhizal networks: Mechanisms, ecology and modelling. *Fungal Biology Reviews, 26,* 39–60. https://doi.org/10.1016/j.fbr.2012.01.001

Slepian, M. L., & Ambady, N. (2012). Fluid movement and creativity. *Journal of Experimental Psychology: General, 141*(4), 625.

University of Southampton. (2015, December 18). Is evolution more intelligent than we thought? *ScienceDaily.* https://www.sciencedaily.com/releases/2015/12/151218085616.htm

van der Kolk, B. (2002). Posttraumatic therapy in the age of neuroscience. *Psychoanalytic Dialogues, 12*(3), 381–392.

van der Kolk, B. (2006). Clinical implications of neuroscience research in PTSD. *Annals of the New York Academy of Sciences, 1071,* 277–293.

van der Kolk, B. (2014). *The body keeps the score: Mind and body in the healing of trauma.* Penguin.

Whitehead, A. N. (1929). *Process and reality.* Macmillan.

Wiens, S. (2005). Interoception in emotional experience. *Current Opinion in Neurology, 18,* 442–447.

Zaccaro, A., Piarulli, A., Laurino, M., Garbella, E., Menicucci, D., Neri, B., & Gemignani, A. (2018). How breath-control can change your life: A systematic review on psycho-physiological correlates of slow breathing. *Frontiers in Human Neuroscience, 12,* 353. https://doi.org/10.3389/fnhum.2018.00353

32. The Eros of Relational Aliveness and Continuum Inquiry

Buhner, S. (2004). *Secret teachings of plants.* Bear and Company.

Conrad, E. (2007). *Life on land.* North Atlantic.

Gendlin, E. (1978). *Focusing.* Bantam.

Keltner, D. (2023). *Awe: The new science of everyday wonder and how it can transform your life.* Penguin.

O'Donohue, J. (2004). *Beauty.* HarperCollins.

Schrei, J. (Host). (2023, January 9). Universe, adorned: Ornament in culture, cosmos, and consciousness. *The Emerald Podcast.* https://podcasts.apple.com/ro/podcast/universe-adorned-ornament-in-culture-cosmos-and/id1465445746?i=1000593323205

Schwenk, T. (1965). *Sensitive chaos.* Sophia Books.

Spangler, D. (2009). *Crafting relationship.* Lorian.

St John, D. (2022). *Healing the wounds of childhood and culture.* Archway.

Weber, A. (2017). *Matter and desire.* Chelsea Green. (Originally published in German in 2014 as *Lebendigkeit: Eine erotische Ökologie* by Kösel Verlag)

Weller, F. (2023, September 23). At the heart of all our sorrows. *Science and Nonduality.* https://www.scienceandnonduality.com/event/at-the-heart-of-all-our-sorrows/

Index

In this index, f denotes figure, n denotes note, and t denotes table.